MW01110333

ANDERSON'S
Law School Publications

ADMINISTRATIVE LAW: CASES AND MATERIALS
by Daniel J. Gifford

APPELLATE ADVOCACY: PRINCIPLES AND PRACTICE
Cases and Materials
by Ursula Bentele and Eve Cary

A CAPITAL PUNISHMENT ANTHOLOGY
by Victor L. Streib

CASES AND PROBLEMS IN CRIMINAL LAW
by Myron Moskovitz

THE CITATION WORKBOOK
by Maria L. Ciampi, Rivka Widerman and Vicki Lutz

COMMERCIAL TRANSACTIONS: PROBLEMS AND MATERIALS
Vol. 1: Secured Transactions Under the Uniform Commercial Code
Vol. 2: Sales Under the Uniform Commercial Code and the Convention on
International Sale of Goods
Vol. 3: Negotiable Instruments Under the Uniform Commercial Code
and the United Nations Convention on International
Bills of Exchange and International Promissory Notes
by Louis F. Del Duca, Egon Guttman and Alphonse M. Squillante

A CONSTITUTIONAL LAW ANTHOLOGY
by Michael J. Glennon

CONTRACTS
Contemporary Cases, Comments, and Problems
by Michael L. Closen, Richard M. Perlmutter and Jeffrey D. Wittenberg

A CONTRACTS ANTHOLOGY
by Peter Linzer

A CRIMINAL LAW ANTHOLOGY
by Arnold H. Loewy

CRIMINAL LAW: CASES AND MATERIALS
by Arnold H. Loewy

EFFECTIVE INTERVIEWING
by Fred E. Jandt

ENDING IT: DISPUTE RESOLUTION IN AMERICA
Descriptions, Examples, Cases and Questions
by Susan M. Leeson and Bryan M. Johnston

ENVIRONMENTAL LAW
Vol. 1: Environmental Decisionmaking and NEPA
Vol. 2: Water Pollution
Vol. 3: Air Pollution
Vol. 4: Hazardous Wastes
by Jackson B. Battle, Mark Squillace and Maxine Lipeles

FEDERAL INCOME TAXATION OF PARTNERSHIPS
AND OTHER PASS-THRU ENTITIES
by Howard E. Abrams

FEDERAL RULES OF EVIDENCE
Rules, Legislative History, Commentary and Authority
by Glen Weissenberger

INTERNATIONAL HUMAN RIGHTS: LAW, POLICY AND PROCESS
Problems and Materials
by Frank Newman and David Weissbrodt

Continued

INTRODUCTION TO THE STUDY OF LAW: CASES AND MATERIALS
by John Makdisi

JUSTICE AND THE LEGAL SYSTEM
A Coursebook
by Anthony D'Amato and Arthur J. Jacobson

THE LAW OF MODERN PAYMENT SYSTEMS AND NOTES
by Fred H. Miller and Alvin C. Harrell

PATIENTS, PSYCHIATRISTS AND LAWYERS
Law and the Mental Health System
by Raymond L. Spring, Roy B. Lacoursiere, M.D., and Glen Weissenberger

PROBLEMS AND SIMULATIONS IN EVIDENCE
by Thomas F. Guernsey

A PROPERTY ANTHOLOGY
by Richard H. Chused

THE REGULATION OF BANKING
Cases and Materials on Depository Institutions and Their Regulators
by Michael P. Malloy

A SECTION 1983 CIVIL RIGHTS ANTHOLOGY
by Sheldon H. Nahmod

SPORTS LAW: CASES AND MATERIALS
by Raymond L. Yasser, James R. McCurdy and C. Peter Goplerud

A TORTS ANTHOLOGY
by Lawrence C. Levine, Julie A. Davies and Ted Kionka

TRIAL PRACTICE
Text by Lawrence A. Dubin and Thomas F. Guernsey
Problems and Case Files with *Video* Presentation
by Edward R. Stein and Lawrence A. Dubin

Negotiable Instruments Under the Uniform Commercial Code and the United Nations Convention on International Bills of Exchange and International Promissory Notes

COMMERCIAL TRANSACTIONS

VOLUME ONE
Secured Transactions Under the Uniform Commercial Code

VOLUME TWO
Sales Under the Uniform Commercial Code
and the Convention on International Sale of Goods

VOLUME THREE
Negotiable Instruments Under the Uniform Commercial Code and the
United Nations Convention on International Bills of Exchange and
International Promissory Notes

Problems and Materials On

Negotiable Instruments Under the Uniform Commercial Code and the United Nations Convention on International Bills of Exchange and International Promissory Notes

LOUIS F. DEL DUCA

Associate Dean and Professor of Law
The Dickinson School of Law

EGON GUTTMAN

Louis P. Levitt Scholar,
Professor of Law
American University
Washington College of Law

ALPHONSE M. SQUILLANTE

Gustavus M. Wald
Professor of Contract Law
University of Cincinnati
College of Law

COMMERCIAL TRANSACTIONS VOLUME THREE

Anderson Publishing Co./Cincinnati, Ohio

3 Del Duca, Guttman & Squillante, Commercial Transactions: Problems & Materials on Negotiable Instruments Under the Uniform Commercial Code and the United Nations Convention on International Bills of Exchange and International Promissory Notes

Library of Congress Cataloging-in-Publication Data

Del Duca, Louis F.
    Problems and materials on negotiable instruments under the Uniform
commercial code and the United Nations Convention on International Bills of Exchange and
International Promissory Notes /
Louis F. Del Duca, Egon Guttman, Alphonse M. Squillante.
     p.   cm.—(Commerical transactions ; v. 3)
    Includes index.
    ISBN 0-87084-150-5 (set). — ISBN 0-87084-153-X (v. 3)
    1. Negotiable Instruments—United States—States. I. Guttman,
Egon. II. Squillante, Alphonse M., 1932-   . III. Title.
IV. Title: Negotiable Instruments under the Uniform commercial code
and the United Nations Convention on International Bills of Exchange and International
Promissory Notes. V. Series: Del
Duca, Louis F. Commercial transactions ; v. 3.
KF957.Z95D45 1993
346.73'096—dc20
[347.30696]
                                        93-4774
                                           CIP

Contents

See the following pages for a detailed analysis of this volume.

Detailed Analysis of this Volume

Tables of Authorities

CASES

UNITED NATIONS DOCUMENTS

United Nations Commission on International Trade Law (UNCITRAL)

United Nations Convention on Contracts for the International Sale of Goods [CISG]

United Nations Convention on International Bills of Exchange and International Promissory Notes [CIBN]

STATUTES

Miscellaneous Code Sections

REGULATIONS

Federal Trade Commission Rules

Magnuson-Moss Warranty Regulations 16 C.F.R. Parts 700-703

Securities and Exchange Commission Rules

Preface

To students steeped in the common law, the concepts of privity and proximity are perfectly understandable. A difficulty is experienced, however, when the purely mercantile concept of negotiability is in issue. The fact that as a result of the negotiability of an instrument, a thief who has no legal right or claim to the instrument or to the rights and interests that it represents can confer rights to a transferee that could in the circumstances defeat a claim of the person from whom it was stolen causes difficulties of comprehension. In some instances this is achieved by the "reification" of an obligation, for example by promissory notes embodying an obligation to pay, and in other instances by the symbolizing of goods into a document of title such as a warehouse receipt or a bill of lading. In our development of mercantile law we have strayed from the need to have a paper instrument and apply electronic data interchange, to effectuate book entry transfers. This is illustrated by the uncertificated investment securities and by the use of payment devices involved in an electronic transfer, such as debit cards.

There also are attempts to unify rules of law by means of legislation enacted/or to be enacted in all jurisdictions of the United States, laws that have been considered in international forums as well. The Negotiable Instrument Law and the Uniform Commercial Code Article 3, which replaced it, have been enacted in all U.S. jurisdictions as has U.C.C. Article 4: Bank Collection Code. Now these provisions have been revised to take account of technical as well as business developments, and an Article 4A is proposed to deal with wholesale fund transfers. So far over 20 jurisdictions have enacted these revisions. By the end of 1993 most, if not all, U.S. jurisdictions will have enacted these Revised Articles of the U.C.C.. Thus, in this approach to the issues raised by the concept of negotiability and the rules surrounding its application, we must examine not only statutory provisions, but the economic and technical developments involving the use of negotiable instruments. Courts have attempted to formulate approaches and interpretations that would support the use of such instruments in our modern domestic as well as global economies. We must inform ourselves, therefore, of rules governing negotiability that apply to international transactions. As a result, we made reference not only to the Uniform Commercial Code, but also to developments in relation to the United Nations Convention on International Bills of Exchange and International Promissory Notes, the International Chamber of Commerce - Uniform Custom and Practices governing letters of credit and to communication systems involved in both domestic and global electronic data interchanges which facilitate the transfer of funds.

We wish to thank colleagues who have read the manuscript and students who have made useful suggestions. Especially, Professor Guttman wishes to thank Ms. Jane Gollop-

Gomez, Esq., for her review of Chapter VIII and his research assistants Anthony S. Cabrera and Lisa Neubaumer who will be graduating in 1993.

The book has been written for a three credit semester course. Chapter I is an historical development which we leave to the Professor to expand or restrict. We generally spend one class period on this, but use the section on Construction when dealing with the issues raised in Chapter II and subsequent chapters. If only two credits are allocated to Negotiable Instruments, Chapter X may be omitted provided the issues regarding letter of credit can be discussed in connection with a Sales course.

Louis F. Del Duca
Egon Guttman
Alphonse M. Squillante
January 1993

I INTRODUCTION

The central feature of this casebook is the Uniform Commercial Code, Article 3—Commercial Paper/Negotiable Instruments and Article 4—Bank Deposits and Collections. We will study these Articles and the impact other laws have on the concept of negotiability by taking a practical approach. This is merchants' law, which reflects commercial concepts. Primarily we will be considering the recent revision of these Articles of the U.C.C. which are in the process of being enacted by state legislatures.[1]

The Antipathy to Legal Tender

Physical insecurity has been with us from time immemorial. Whether it is Robin Hood and his Merry Men lying in wait for rich merchants in Nottingham's Sherwood Forest, or the threat of a mugging in a modern urban setting, there is an inherent insecurity in carrying money on one's body. Yet the law permits a seller to demand payment in legal tender/cash provided a buyer is given "any extension of time reasonably necessary to procure it." U.C.C. § 2-511. Legal tender are coins and federal reserve notes,[2] the minting and printing of which is now a federal monopoly[3] protected by the criminal law.[4]

The currency of coins originally reflected the market value of the gold or silver represented thereby.[5] It was this currency that supported a monetary theory of value[6] and

[1] As of Sept. 30, 1991, 10 states have enacted these revisions.

[2] United States coins and currency (including Federal reserve notes and circulating notes of Federal reserve banks and national banks) are legal tender for all debts, public charges, taxes, and dues. Foreign gold or silver coins are not legal tender for debts. 31 U.S.C. § 5103.

[3] 31 U.S.C. §§ 5111 (coins), 5114, 5115 (currency notes).

[4] 18 U.S.C. §§ 331 (coining), 471 (counterfeiting).

[5] The distinguishing marks on early coins served a dual purpose of guaranteeing weight and fineness and covering most of the surface to make clipping (cutting off the edges of the coin) more difficult. Geva, *From Commodity to Currency in Ancient History—On Commerce, Tyranny, and the Modern Law of Money*, 25 OSGOODE HALL L.J. 115, 124-26, 130-32 (1987). Today, defacement of these distinguishing marks is punishable under 18 U.S.C. §§ 331, 332.

[6] Throughout history, gold, silver and other precious metals have served as coinage material. Geva, *From Commodity to Currency in Ancient History—On Commerce, Tyranny, and the Modern Law of Money*, 25 OSGOODE HALL L.J. 115, *Passim* (1987). Paper notes representing a promise to pay a certain value in precious metal were issued by goldsmiths in return for metal deposited with them. *Id.* at 145. In 1879, the United States officially adopted a gold standard, whereby United States notes represented a promise by the government to pay the indicated

even now is reflected in foreign exchange rates, albeit it is now based on the credit standing of the issuing country. This currency, allowing transfer without being able to trace the transferor, was helpful in periods of political unrest,[7] but it also allowed secrecy to unacceptable transactions. Not only is currency the life blood of the "underground economy", whereby goods and services are exchanged for cash and the profits from such sales or services are not being reported to evade payment of taxes, but also it is the preferred form of payment for illegal activities. Since currency inhibits the tracing of transferors and transferees, the Tax Equity and Fiscal Responsibility Act of 1982 (TEFRA) attempts to inhibit the issuance of bearer securities. Bearer securities enable a holder by mere possession to assert rights to the obligation embodied in the instrument. This Act provides that an issuer of such securities cannot deduct interest payments as a business expense and a holder cannot claim capital gain or loss deduction treatment on a sale of such registration-required obligations.[8] Further, the Bank Secrecy Act of 1982,[9] attempting to trace currency used in the underground economy or in connection with illegal activities such as the trafficking in illegal drugs, requires that a person, agent or bailee knowingly transporting into or out of the United States[10] currency or other monetary instruments to the value of $10,000[11] make disclosure to the U.S. Dept. of the Treasury to this effect.[12] To prevent money laundering (i.e. the introduction of illegally obtained cash into a legitimate stream of commerce), regulations were promulgated requiring a financial institution to file a report of each deposit, withdrawal, exchange of currency or other payment or transfer by, through, or to such financial institution which involves currency of more than $10,000.[13] Multiple transactions with the same person taking place on any one day are treated as one transaction.[14] Failure to report would place the financial institution not only in violation of the Bank Secrecy

---

amount in precious metal. The U.S. retained the gold standard until 1933. (J. Con. Res. June 5, 1933, 31 U.S.C. § 463, Gold Reserve Act of 1934, 31 U.S.C. § 443. Dam, *From the Gold Clause Cases to the Gold Commission: A Half Century of American Monetary Law*, 50 U. Chi. L. Rev. 504, 506 (1983). Thereafter, United States Currency was supported by a silver standard until abolished in favor of support by all of the assets of the United States. An Act to Authorize Adjustments in the Amount of Outstanding Silver Certificates and for Other Purposes, 81 Stat. 77 § 2 (June 24, 1967).

[7] See as to bearer securities, i.e. investment certificates recognizing the bearer as the party entitled to the property rights and profits or interest payments due to holders of such bearer securities, Guttman, *The Transfer of Shares in a Commercial Corporation - A Comparative Study*, 5 B. C. Ind. & Com. L. Rev. 491, 502–03 (1964).

[8] TEFRA § 309, 26 U.S.C. § 6049. Note, as of mid-1986, the Treasury ceased issuing new securities in certificated form. All new issues are uncertificated and recorded by book entry. Treasury bills have been this way since 1978. Treasury News, Feb. 22, 1985 at B-24.

[9] 31 U.S.C. §§ 5311–5322.

[10] 31 U.S.C. § 5316(a)(1).

[11] 31 U.S.C. § 5312(3). The definition of monetary instruments includes not only U.S. coins and currency, but also travellers' checks, bearer negotiable instruments and bearer securities. *See also* 31 C.F.R. § 103.11(j), (k).

[12] 31 U.S.C. § 5316(b). *See also* 31 C.F.R. §§ 103.23, 103.26(b).

[13] U.C.C. §§ 5313, 5314, 5315. *See also* 31 C.F.R. §§ 103.22, 103.24–103.27.

[14] Note the offense of "smurfing." 18 U.S.C. § 1956; 31 U.S.C. § 5324(3). "Smurfing" is the practice of placing just under $10,000 into an account or numerous accounts over a period of time so as to prevent triggering reporting requirements. Welling, *Smurfs, Money Laundering, and the Federal Criminal Law - The Crime of Structuring Transactions*, 41 Fla. L. Rev. 287 (1989).

Act[15] but could also make the financial institution liable as an aider and abettor of the underlying offense that gave rise to these moneys.[16] Although merchants are not subject to these reporting requirements, they are subject to the Money Laundering Control Act,[17] which makes it a crime for a merchant to knowingly participate in a financial transaction involving the proceeds of an unlawful activity.[18]

The effect of these laws is to limit the use of currency in large sum transactions and to force the use of bank drafts, order paper and other methods for the transfer of funds, such as electronic data interchanges using verified messaging.[19]

Article 3—Commercial Paper: An Updating of Well-Tried Concepts
by Egon Guttman[20]

Article 3 of the Uniform Commercial Code[21] is a continuum of commercial concepts. It is a development that can be traced directly to the genius of Lord Holt[22] and that of Lord Mansfield[23] when they incorporated the Law Merchant into the common law. What had delayed the recognition of negotiability by the common law was not only the preoccupation of the courts with matters of real property, but also the intense personal relationship surrounding choses in action resulting in their inalienability in the common law.[24] Debt was so personal a relationship that it often resulted in imprisonment of the debtor[25] and an action for debt could be defeated by compurgation.[26] Assumpsit was only slowly replacing

---

[15] 31 U.S.C. §§ 5322, 5324. *See also* 18 U.S.C. § 1956.

[16] 18 U.S.C. § 2 provides:
Whoever commits an offense against the United States or aids, abets, counsels, commands, induces or procures its commission, is punishable as a principal.

[17] 18 U.S.C. § 1956.

[18] *See also* 18 U.S.C. § 2. *See generally,* Villa, *A Critical View of Bank Secrecy Act Enforcement and the Money Laundering Statutes*, 37 CATH. U. L. REV. 489 (Winter 1988) (for a discussion of the difficulties inherent in enforcement of the act) and *note* Clark, *Beware of Columbians Bearing Gifts: What Attorneys Should Know About Currency Transaction Reporting Requirements*, 49 ALA. L. REV. 350 (1988).

[19] *Note,* Electronic Funds Transfer Act, 15 U.S.C. § 1693 et seq., U.C.C.-Article 4A (wholesale wire transfers), Fedwire (operated by the Federal Reserve system), CHIPS (Clearinghouse Interbank Payment System operated by a consortium of New York banks). On the retail side note the use of credit cards in addition to electronic fund transfers by means of "debit cards."

[20] Reprinted with permission from 11 How. L.J. 49 (1964) and revised by the author. Cited with approval in *Hardy v. Gissendaner*, 508 F.2d 1207 (5th Cir. 1975). Note: footnotes have been renumbered.

[21] Hereinafter referred to as U.C.C.

[22] Lord Holt, Chief Justice Court of Kings Bench, 1689–1710.

[23] Lord Mansfield, Chief Justice Court of Kings Bench, 1756–1788.

[24] AMES, THE INALIENABILITY OF CHOSES IN ACTION, 3 SELECT ESSAYS IN ANGLO-AMERICAN LEGAL HISTORY 586 (1932); Holdsworth, *The Origin and History of Negotiable Instruments*, II, 31 L.Q. REV. 173 (1915); MILNES J. HOLDEN, THE HISTORY OF NEGOTIABLE INSTRUMENTS IN ENGLISH LAW (University of London, Athlone Press 1955).

[25] Imprisonment for debt was not abolished in England until 1869 (32 & 33 Vict. c.62).

[26] Compurgation or wager of law consisted of an oath denying the existence of a debt, followed by eleven others swearing an oath that they believed in the truth of the "alleged debtor's" oath. The fear of perjury damning the soul was considered sufficient deterrence.

the action for debt by reason of its attraction in substituting a jury for a wager of law.[27] Merchants could not be left without remedies and the Law Merchant had to develop its own procedure. If the common law was to enlarge its sphere of influence and the common law courts their revenue, some method would have to be found to satisfy the needs of the growing mercantile class. It is this work which Lord Holt and Lord Mansfield initiated.

The direct ancestor of the draft (modern bill of exchange), a tripartite instrument can be recognized in the early contract of cambium whereby a money exchanger would change money from one currency to another so as to enable a merchant to settle his accounts.[28] It was but a short step for a merchant to direct that payments in the foreign currency be made direct to the foreign merchant-creditor. A method thus developed whereby the exchanger's receipt called upon another exchanger to pay to the person named therein or his "nominee" a sum equal to the currency indicated. The person named could be the original depositor or his creditor in the foreign country, the nominee having the status of an agent of the depositor.[29] Although the Jewish Exchequer[30] gave early recognition to the assignment of debts,[31] common law recognition of bills of exchange was slow.

In Europe, the use of the bill of exchange as evidencing a debt[32] and thus in the development of banking antedated the Jewish Exchange. It can be traced back to an early Church interpretation to protect the Florentines and the Lombards from the prohibition against the practice of usury.[33] These Italian merchants first acted as money changers and later loaned their own money; it was here that the clash with the prohibition against usury first occurred. While Jewish law requires "risk participation" before interest can be charged,[34] no such restriction was imposed by the Church's interpretation. The fact that the Church did not consider the ban on usury to apply to Jews and a narrow interpretation of the biblical prohibition against usury[35] as not applying to loans made

---

[27] See MAITLAND, THE FORMS OF ACTION AT COMMON LAW, LECTURE VI (Cambridge University Press 1948).

[28] See R. DE ROOVER, MONEY, BANKING AND CREDIT IN MEDIEVAL BRUGES (1948).

[29] Holdsworth, *The Origin and Early History of Negotiable Instruments, I*, 31 L.Q. REV. 12 (1915). Note, this approach did not permit negotiability. "The maker could, when asked for payment, deduct from the amount due on the instrument any just claim that he had against the original owner." J.M. OGDEN, THE LAW OF NEGOTIABLE INSTRUMENTS 9 (1909).

[30] The Jewish Exchequer existed from 1198 to 1290, when Jews were expelled from England. See RIGGS, INTRODUCTION: SELECT PLEAS, STARRS AND RECORDS OF THE JEWISH EXCHEQUER 15 (Seldon Society 1901); *see also*, Beutel, *The Development of Negotiable Instruments in Early English Law*, 51 HARV. L. REV. 813 (1938).

[31] 15 Seldon Society 65 (1901) sets out an instrument litigated upon in the Jewish Exchequer in 1272.

[32] MARIUS, PRACTICAL ADVICE CONCERNING BILLS OF EXCHANGE (1651).

[33] Medieval bills were bought and sold at a price determined by a fluctuating rate of exchange and not discounted. Thus, the interest was concealed in the exchange rate. Trading in that fashion was permitted by the Church and not considered a loan. It was also justified as being for the benefit of the common weal, monasteries participated in making such advances. *Supra* n.28.

[34] This basically called for a partnership relationship in which the borrower/active partner had to be compensated for his labor before profits (or losses) were shared. Rabbinical responsa developed the "Heter Iska." This involved a document, the "Shtar Iska," that recited the receipt of funds and of payment for the services to be rendered. The "working partner" guaranteed the investment and financial profit and agreed that losses would be shared. See ZIPPERSTEIN, BUSINESS ETHICS IN JEWISH LAW (Ktav Publishing House, Inc. 1983).

[35] *Leviticus* 25:35-37. "If your brother is poor and his means fail with you, then you shall uphold him. He

to gentiles,[36] led to gentile princes in need of funds granting to Jews the right to live within their realm in exchange for operating a money-lending business (pawn bank). Many of these agreements (condotte) specifically limited the amount of interest that could be charged. In many instances, specific provisions were inserted stipulating that for the first year the loan would be interest free. Similar licenses were granted to the Lombards by various princes of Europe.[37]

In England, the goldsmiths, with their established international network developed through the guild system, took over the functions of the Lombards. Civil strife, however, led to the deposit of wealth into the Tower of London and away from the goldsmiths. In 1640, Charles I confiscated such deposits and a return to deposits with the goldsmiths followed. The activities of the goldsmiths developed into private banking.

The essential change from bailment to money lending and thence to banking, was brought about by a change from a bailor-bailee relationship to that of creditor-debtor, in which the depositor became a creditor. The banker/debtor then could use assets of the "depositor," entering into further creditor-debtor relationships by means of "other peoples' money."

Although the practice of merchants using bills of exchange was recognized in England, Lord Holt was not prepared to expand the law too rapidly. He complained that merchants would not abide by existing laws but were trying to introduce an order note insisting on its validity and thereby

> Lombard Street attempted in these matters of bills of exchange to give laws to West-minster Hall. That the continuing to declare upon these notes upon the custom of merchants proceeded from obstinacy and opinionativeness, since he had always expressed his opinion against them, since there was so easy a method, as to declare upon a general indebitatus assumpsit for money lent.[38]

Shortly after Lord Holt gave this dictum, however, Parliament made promissory notes negotiable.[39] During the time Lord Mansfield was Chief Justice of the Kings Bench, Lombard Street again called upon Westminster Hall to assume its proper position, a position which

---

shall live with you just as does the stranger, and the resident alien. Do not take interest from him nor increase, but fear your God. Let your brother live with you. Do not lend him money on interest, or give him food on interest."

See also Exodus 22:24. This prohibition appears to apply to accrued interest.

[36] *Deuteronomy* 23:20-21. "You shall not deduct interest from loans to your countryman, whether in money or food or anything else that can be deducted as interest. You may deduct interest from loans to foreigners, but not from loans to your countryman." This prohibition appears to go to a deduction of interest at the time the loan is made.

[37] *See* R. DE ROOVER, MONEY, BANKING AND CREDIT IN MEDIEVAL BRUGES, ch. 6 (1948). Also note the Church was not loath to grant a dispensation to licensed usurers. *See* J. Laenen, *Usuriers et Lombards dans le Brabant au XVe siècle* BULLETIN DE L'ACADÉMIE ROYALE D'ARCHÉLOGIE DE BELGIQUE, 123-44 (1904).

[38] Clerke v. Martin, 2 Ld. Raymond 758, 92 Eng. Rep. 6 (1702). *See also* Lord Holt in Buller v. Crips, 6 Mod. Rep. 29, 87 Eng. Rep. 793 (1704) calling notes "an invention of goldsmiths in Lombard street who had a mind to make a law to bind all those who deal with them."

[39] An Act for giving like remedy upon promissory notes as is now used upon bills of exchange and for the better payment of inland bills of exchange, 3 & 4 Anne c.9 (1704-05).

had been filled by the earlier mercantile courts when they applied the lex mercatoria to disputes between merchants.

The common law courts responded. Lord Mansfield would sit with special jurymen at Guild Hall to try commercial cases, and was

> on terms of the most familiar intercourse with them, not only conversing freely with them in Court, but inviting them to dine with him. From them he learned the usage of the trade, and in return he took great pains in explaining to them the principles of jurisprudence by which they were to be guided. Several of these gentlemen survived when I began to attend Guild Hall as a student, and were designated and honored as Lord Mansfield's jurymen. One in particular I remember, Mr. Edward Vaux, who always wore a cocked hat, and had almost as much authority as the Lord Chief Justice.[40]

The circle seems to have been completed. It was a merchant who had written the first English treatise on mercantile law[41] and now it was the merchants once more who were calling upon the law to help and assist, rather than to hinder or delay. This was a realization of the commercial law as the handmaiden of commerce, with the duty to facilitate the steady and safe development of rules governing trade. Thus when it was felt that the time had come to codify the law regarding negotiable instruments which had become swamped in numerous decisions[42] and statutory enactments,[43] this law was realized to be a growing body which was not to be stunted by any statute.[44] The Bills of Exchange Act 1882,[45] drafted by Judge Chalmer and adopted throughout the British Empire, did not prevent the development of new negotiable instruments. It enabled the custom of merchants to continue to confer negotiability upon instruments not within the purview of the Act.[46]

* * * * *

Modern development in the United States commenced with the creation of the National Conference of Commissioners on Uniform State Laws (NCCUSL).[47] One of the first acts

---

[40] Campbell, Lives of the Lord Chief Justice, Vol. V. Bk. II. 407 (1846).

[41] Gerard Malynes, Consuetudo vel Lex Mercatoria (1622).

[42] There were approximately 2,500 English cases by 1882.

[43] Approximately 17 statutory enactments had some bearing on negotiable instruments by 1882.

[44] Goodwin v. Robarts, L.R. 10 Ex. 76 (1875).

[45] 45 & 46 Vic. c.61 (1882).

[46] Edelstein v. Schuler & Co., 2 K.B. 144 (1902). *Compare* U.C.C. § 9–206(1). Until the recent adoption of revised U.C.C.-Article 3, a more restricted view prevailed in the U.S.A. "Any writing to be a negotiable instrument *within* this Article must . . ." comply with certain formal requirements. U.C.C. § 3-104(1)(emphasis added). The revision of this section in 1991 allows checks, including cashier's checks or teller's checks and money orders [U.C.C. § 3-104(f)] to be negotiable although they do not indicate that they are payable to bearer or to order. Conversely, where a writing other than a check carries a conspicuous notice that it is not negotiable, albeit all formal requirements of a negotiable instrument have been satisfied, the promise or order will not be negotiable. Since checks are processed by banks in mass even a conspicuous statement that attempts to make such instrument non-negotiable will be of no effect. [U.C.C. § 3-104(d)]

[47] For a history of the Uniform Law Commissioners, see two articles by Beutel which are essential reading for the history of negotiable instruments in the United States. *The Development of State Statutes on Negotiable Paper Prior to the Negotiable Instruments Law*, 40 Colum. L. Rev. 836 (1940); *Colonial Sources of the Negotiable Instruments Law of the United States*, 34 U. Ill. L. Rev. 137 (1940).

of this Conference was to direct its Committee on Commercial Law to prepare a draft statute based upon the English Bills of Exchange Act. The draft prepared by Mr. John J. Crawford, was subsequently accepted by the Commissioners[48] and was enacted throughout the United States.[49] Unfortunately, the Uniform Negotiable Instrument Law[50] suffered from some severe drawbacks in its interpretation. Though intended as a new start, courts continued to look back to previous common law cases. Though intended to be uniformly interpreted, courts blindly went their own way, often ignoring authoritative interpretations in neighboring states. But as a whole, it was a useful and mature piece of legislation that solved more problems than it created.[51]

A similar problem has now arisen with respect to the U.C.C. Not being a code in the civil law sense but a statute in the common law tradition, uniformity has not been attained.[52] Divergent enactments and different interpretations of uniform provisions have caused problems. Further, technological developments and the realization that the U.C.C. does not give adequate protection to consumers has led to federal intervention. Finally, the globalization of commercial transactions have shown the need for the internationalization of this area of private law.[53]

The Sponsoring Organizations of the Code[54] have recognized that at some time it would be desirable, if not necessary, to develop some form of organization or mechanism that could follow the Code to observe how it works in actual operation; to provide an agency to which comments, suggestions and criticisms could be directed; and to recommend changes or amendments if at anytime this should prove to be necessary.

Consequently, in 1962 the Sponsoring Organizations organized a Permanent Editorial Board (PEB). The PEB is continuously engaged in reviewing the working of the U.C.C. and considers variations in specific provisions enacted by states.[55] By commenting on such variations, it is intended to maintain uniformity insofar as such is possible and desirable.

---

[48] 5 U.L.A. (1896).

[49] The first state to enact the Uniform Negotiable Instruments Law was Connecticut in 1897 (Laws of 1897 ch. 612) and the last state, Georgia, in 1924 (Laws of 1924, page 126). With the enactment of the N.I.L. in the Canal Zone in 1934 (title 3, c.z.c. 1934, chs. 66–69) all territories of the U.S.A. also had enacted the N.I.L.

[50] Hereinafter referred to as N.I.L.

[51] Not a small part of the blame can be laid to the lack of prior consultation with the profession before the Commissioners adopted the draft. This led to the famous Ames-Brewster controversy, 14 HARV. L. REV. 241 (1900–1901); 10 YALE L.J. 84 (1900–01); 14 HARV. L. REV. 422 (1900–01); 15 HARV. L. REV. 26 (1901–02); 16 HARV. L. REV. 255 (1902–03) which further contributed not only to divergence in interpretation but also to divergence of wording in the various enactments of a statute intended to be a "uniform act."

[52] Loomis Bros. Corp. v. Queen, 46 Del. 79 (1958)(The code is intended to be a uniform code not only uniformly adopted, but also uniformly interpreted).

[53] *See* U.N. Convention on International Bills of Exchange and International Promissory Notes A/RES/43/165, 17 January 1989.

[54] The National Conference of Commissioners on Uniform State Laws (NCCUSL) and the American Law Institute (ALI).

[55] All states, the District of Columbia, Guam, Northern Mariana Islands, and Virgin Islands, have adopted the U.C.C. Louisiana's civil law tradition prevented the enactment of Articles 2 - Sales. An adaptation of the 1972 version of Article 9 - Secured Transactions was enacted in 1988. Of the territories, only Puerto Rico with its civil law tradition has not enacted any article of the U.C.C.

Apart from some minor amendments recommended for adoption, substantial revisions of the U.C.C. also have occurred. In addition, the American Bar Association (ABA) Section of the Business Law monitors developments and reports thereon to its members in annual surveys published in the Business Lawyer.

When it is seen that law and practice diverge, subcommittees of the ABA Uniform Commercial Code Committee undertake studies and make reports to the Section of Business Law, indicating their findings and recommendations. With the approval of the Council of the ABA, these Committees (or their Working Groups) are constituted into drafting committees.

Working together with the American Law Institute (ALI) and NCCUSL, these drafts, when approved by the NCCUSL, are recommended to state legislatures for adoption.[56] In following this approach, the NCCUSL has recently recommended the adoption of a new U.C.C. Article 4A-Fund Transfers, to cover the wholesale wire transfers between business or financial institutions.[57] The United Nations Commission on Uniform Trade Laws (UNCITRAL) completed a draft of a model law regarding the transfer of funds in an international transaction for submission to the Sixth Committee (Legal) of the U.N. General Assembly. This model law has now been approved.[58] The Model Law will provide the legal rules within which the existing international wire transfers by the Society for Worldwide Interbank Financial Telecommunication (SWIFT), which merely provides a communication link between members leaving settlement of payment to bilateral agreements, will operate. Domestically, the Clearinghouse Interbank Payment System (CHIPS), operated by a consortium of New York banks, interfaces with SWIFT and provides settlement services to its members and to non-member banks clearing through the New York Federal Reserve Bank.[59]

---

[56] Following this procedure, U.C.C. Article 9-Secured Transactions was completely revised in 1972. The revision is now law in all states, except Vermont. Recently a new U.C.C. Article 2A-Leases was adopted and is wending its way through state legislatures. A revision of U.C.C. Article 8-Investment Securities, which attempts to deal with the development of uncertificated securities evidenced only by book entry, is steadily gaining acceptance by most states (To date 48 states have enacted the revision). A working group of the ABA Sub-Committee on Investment Securities has been reorganized as a drafting committee to take into account recent technological and global developments. In addition, the National Conference of Commissioners on Uniform State Law created a drafting committee that, together with the ABA drafting committee, will be preparing amendments to U.C.C.-Article 8. These amendments are being studied by a committee of the American Law Institute (ALI). After the ALI and the NCCUSL have concurred in the proposed changes, they will be recommended to the various state legislatures for adoption. The ABA has also established a subcommittee to examine the scope of the U.C.C. and its impact on other laws. In addition the Securities and Exchange Commission has created an advisory committee to examine how far federal laws require amendment to effectuate the policies underlying the development of practices that will expedite the settlement of market trades, as well as the effects of uncertificated securities trading on bankruptcy law. *See* Securities Exchange Act § 17A(f), 15 U.S.C. § 78q-1(f).

[57] U.C.C. Article 4A-Funds Transfers is the result of a realization that one law cannot cover both transactions between business and financial institutions transferring large sums of money electronically and the collection process governing checks, credit cards and consumer electronic transfer transactions. It was the opposition of consumer groups and of New York banks to a proposed "New Uniform Payment Code" under consideration by the ABA, ALI and NCCUSL that led to dividing the approaches to these methods of payment. Article 4A deals with "wholesale fund transfers." *30* states have enacted U.C.C.-Article 4A as of *Sept. 30, 1991*.

[58] *See* United Nations Document A/47/Supp. 17 (1992).

[59] *See* Delbrueck & Co. v. Manufacturers Hanover Trust Co., 464 F. Supp. 989, 992 and n.5 (S.D.N.Y. 1979). Note also the National Automated Clearing House Association (NACHA) which regulates the member Automated Clearing House (ACH). ACH is the predominant electronic payment system for corporations and consumers in the United States of America.

Finally, we should note Fedwire, operated by the Federal Reserve System Wire Transfer Network through the New York Federal Reserve Bank. This system enables participants to access their funds in reserve or clearing accounts and thereby transfer funds to pay for obligations incurred to participants.[60]

Developments regarding other payment devices have also taken place on state and federal levels. On the federal level, Congress promulgated the Electronic Fund Transfer Act[61] dealing with retail payments by means of electronic transfers. Such instantaneous transfers can originate through automated teller machines (ATM) which may issue cash (money) on demand, or through point of sale terminals (POS), which may effectuate a transfer of money out of the account of the originator of the instruction into that of an indicated payee.[62] These instructions are originated by means of a debit card requiring a personal identification number (PIN) to trigger the transfer.[63] Being confined to wholesale fund transfers, U.C.C. Article 4A is inapplicable to transactions governed by the Electronic Funds Transfer Act.[64]

In 1987, Congress passed the Expedited Funds Availability Act[65] which is intended to speed up the check collection process and to expedite the availability of funds to depositors. The Act granted to the Federal Reserve Board (FRB) power to issue regulations relating to improvements of the check processing system[66] and generally "to regulate . . . (A) any aspect of the payment system, including the receipt, payment, collection, or clearing of checks; and (B) any related function of the payment system with respect to checks."[67] The FRB, under these powers, promulgated Regulation CC.[68] Prior FRB rules dealing with the collection process applied only to member banks and those who used the federal reserve system in the collection process.[69] State law, in U.C.C. Article 4-Bank Deposits and Collections,

---

[60] Federal Reserve Bank of New York, Wire Transfers of Funds, Operating Circular No. 8 (Revised June 29, 1988).

[61] 15 U.S.C. §§ 1693–1693r.

[62] House Subcomm. on Consumer Affairs and Coinage of the House Comm. on Banking, Fin. and Urban Affairs, 98th Cong., 1st Sess., Give Yourself Credit (Guide to Consumer Credit Laws) 69 (Comm. Print 1983).

[63] Distinguish the credit card from the debit card. A credit card interposes the issuer between the supplier of goods or services and the purchaser. By paying the supplier at a discounted rate, e.g. between 3% to 6%, the supplier is assured of payment and the purchaser incurs a debt to the issuer for the full amount due, plus interest if the payment date is not met. Any dispute regarding the underlying transaction must be diligently pursued by the purchaser against the supplier of goods or services. Albeit, in a consumer transaction the issuer of the credit card who has been informed of the dispute cannot demand payment and interest until the dispute has been resolved against the purchaser-user of the credit card. *See* Truth in Lending Act, 15 U.S.C. § 1666i. Issuers usually protect themselves against loss by retaining a compensating balance, i.e. not making prompt full payment to the supplier of goods or services.

[64] 15 U.S.C. §§ 1693 to 1693r. *See* U.C.C. § 4A-108. *See also* § 4A-107, which provides for Regulations of the Board of Governors of the Federal Reserve System and operating circulars of the Federal Reserve Banks to supersede any inconsistent provision of Article 4A. Such regulations and circulars are delegated legislation deriving their force from federal enabling statutes.

[65] 12 U.S.C. § 4001 *et seq.*

[66] 12 U.S.C. § 4008(b). Note the FRB has promulgated Regulation CC, 12 C.F.R. §§ 229.1 to 229.42.

[67] *Id.* § 4008(c).

[68] Regulation CC, 12 C.F.R. §§ 229.1 to 229.42.

[69] Predominant among these regulations is Regulation J; 12 C.F.R. § 218.1 *et seq.*

permitting party autonomy, provides that the "Federal Reserve Regulations and operating circulars, . . . have the effect of agreements . . . whether or not specifically assented to by all parties interested in the items handled."[70] Legislating the check collection process on a federal level made it clear that state law would have to be reevaluated. Once more the question arose whether this area of the law should be left to federal law, a debate that preceded the enactment of the U.C.C. by state legislatures. This time, however, a further question arose: was there anything left for states to regulate?[71]

The law relating to negotiable instruments, and specifically commercial paper, is not confined to checks. There are other payment devices, albeit checks are the most widely used form. Thus, a review of U.C.C. Article 3-Commercial Paper had to be undertaken.[72] The PEB, the ALI and the ABA, in conjunction with the NCCUSL undertook the task to review U.C.C. Articles 3 and 4. Professors Robert Jordan and William Warren of the UCLA Law School were appointed reporters, and drafts of these two Articles of the U.C.C. were extensively debated. The final product proposed for enactment by state legislatures takes account of modern technology and thus of developments in practice. They also consider courts' decisions regarding the meaning of the present formulation of these Articles and their application to modern technological developments and trade practices. A final draft of these Articles has been adopted by the NCCUSL and is wending its way through the various state legislatures.[73]

Of note with regard to technology, heavily influenced as it is by economic factors, is the practice of truncation. Truncation in the check collection process eliminates, or at least delays, the physical movement of paper evidencing the obligation to be presented to the drawee. If agreed to between banks, the Depository bank, instead of physically sending a check for collection to the bank on which the check had been written (drawn), the Drawee Bank, simply forwards a computerized message setting out the number of the account of the writer (Drawer), the number of the check, the amount of the item and the identity of the bank demanding payment (the presenting bank). The payor bank (Drawee Bank) prior to payment would not have an opportunity to examine the check to determine whether the check has been signed by its customer, (Drawer). Such opportunity would only arise when, if ever, the check is received by the Drawee bank. The development of "electronic imaging" may enable a comparison of the drawer's signature to be made and thereby obviate attempts to forge such signature. Revised U.C.C. Sections 4–110 and 4–209(b) provide the legal framework for a truncation agreement.

State law, under the U.C.C., still demands a "writing," which includes printing,

---

[70] U.C.C. § 4–103(b). This provision also applies to clearing house rules and the like.

[71] *See generally* Rubin, *Uniformity, Regulation, and the Federalization of State Law: Some Lessons from the Payment System*, 49 OHIO STATE L.J. 1251 (1989).

[72] Grant Gilmore, *Formalism and the Law of Negotiable Instruments,* 13 CREIGTON L. REV. 441, 461 (1979) (". . . Article 3 really is a museum of antiquities—a treasure house crammed full of ancient artifacts whose use and functions have long since been forgotten"). By providing rigid parameters and introducing formalism, we have fossilized the development of negotiability within Article 3, and thereby stultified commercial practice. Courts could have obviated this by noting that U.C.C. § 3–104 merely indicates that "(1) Any writing to be a negotiable instrument *within this article must*" comply with certain requirements [emphasis added].

[73] 19 states have enacted Revised U.C.C.-Article 3 and U.C.C.-Article 4 as of January 1, 1993.

typewriting or any other intentional reduction to tangible form, in connection with negotiable instruments for compliance with the Statute of Frauds and for many other means of notifications. The U.C.C. is not consistent.[74] An example of the illogical approach taken by the U.C.C. can be seen in revised Article 8-Investment Securities. Having recognized the existence of the uncertificated security, which is represented only on the "books" of the issuer of the security,[75] an instruction to transfer such security can be given "to the issuer in any form agreed upon in a *writing* signed by the issuer and an appropriate person,"[76] i.e., there could be an agreement that an instruction to transfer can be given by an electronic data interchange (EDI). The issuer's acknowledgement that the transfer has occurred, however, requires an "Initial Transaction Statement," (ITS) and that has to be in written form.[77] Similarly, as to presentment of an instrument to the drawee-bank, U.C.C. § 4–110 allows an electronic presentment and U.C.C. § 4–208 allows use of a presentment notice instead of a physical presentment of an instrument to the drawee.

Finally, we should note that negotiable instruments are used in interstate and international commercial transactions both to control the movement of goods, as well as to provide a means of payment for goods and services not dependent on the economic soundness of the contracting parties. Here the clearest form of "other people's money" (OPM) being used to provide the lubricant which makes commerce run smoothly is the letter of credit. It is the letter of credit which brings together various types of negotiable instruments: the bill of lading or the warehouse receipt symbolizing the goods; and the draft evidencing the demand for payment. The letter of credit contains the undertaking of the issuer to accept the draft on tender of the documents and thus, to make payment without regard to due performance of the underlying contractual relationship.[78] To take care of the event of failure in such underlying obligation, the stand-by letter of credit or bank guarantee developed. Once again the credit of a financially sound issuer is interposed for what may be an unknown credit standing of the parties in the contractual relationship. U.C.C. Article 5-Letters of Credit, has been under review by an ABA Task force,[79] and is now in the process of being re-drafted by a drafting committee of the NCCUSL. The effort here also will be to reconcile

---

[74] U.C.C. § 1–201(46).

[75] In many instances the "book" is a computer tape capable of being printed out when needed. Note Federal Rules of Evidence, Rules 803(6) and 1001(1)(3) as to admissibility into evidence of computer stored "writings."

[76] U.C.C. § 8–308(5)(b)(1977) (emphasis added).

[77] U.C.C. § 8–408 (1977). U.C.C. § 1–201(46). The question of EDI is the subject of a recent ABA report, *Commercial Use of Electronic Data Interchange-A Report and Model Trading Partner Agreement*, prepared by the ABA Electronic Messaging Services Task Force, 45 Bus. Law 1645 (1990). The ABA recently appointed a working committee to study and propose amendments to U.C.C.-Article 1, including § 1–201(46). *See also* Trade Electronic Data Interchange Systems [TEDIS] a report prepared for the European Community member states, Official Journal of the European Communities, L 285, 8 October 1987. Note United Nations Commission on International Trade Law (UNCITRAL) Electronic Data Interchange, Preliminary study of legal issues related to the formation of contracts by electronic means, Report of the Secretary-General, A/CN.9/333, 18 May 1990 and Report of the Working Group on Electronic Data Interchange (EDI) A/CN.9/373 9 March 1993.

[78] *See* U.C.C. §§ 5–109(1), 5–114(2)(b).

[79] The Task Force was appointed by the Chair of the ABA Uniform Commercial Code Committee, Letters of Credit Sub-Committee. The report of the Task Force, *An Examination of UCC Article 5 (Letters of Credit)* is printed in 45 Bus. Law. 1521 (1990).

developments in the domestic and global arena with provisions of state law as represented by the U.C.C.[80]

The U.C.C. never adequately tackled the problems facing non-commercial consumers.[81] The consumer movement turned to federal law which responded to these needs much more effectively. This response was accelerated by the absolute failure of the Uniform Consumer Credit Code (UCCC) to gain general acceptance.[82] Various state retail installment sales acts have attempted to fill this gap,[83] but little uniformity has been achieved. One area in particular, the use of commercial paper in connection with retail installment sales and services, was seen to cause problems which neither Article 3[84] nor Article 9[85] could resolve. The effect of a commercial paper coming into the hands of a protected holder, the holder in due course, or of a waiver of defenses where the contract granting a security interest was assigned to a third party, led to consumer/debtors having no remedy should the payee of a commercial paper or the assignor of the contract be no longer economically viable.[86] The Federal Trade Commission intervened by promulgating a rule which prevents the use of a negotiable instrument where it could result in the non-commercial consumer being deprived of the right to raise defenses to the underlying transaction.[87] Studies had shown

---

[80] The International Chamber of Commerce (ICC) Uniform Rules of Practice (UCP) #500 has application to most international transactions. The UCP will be applied in New York, Alabama, Arizona, and Missouri unless the parties indicate that the transaction shall be governed by the U.C.C. Article 5. In all other jurisdictions U.C.C. Article 5 will apply unless an express reference indicates that the UCP is to apply. With regard to Stand-by Letters of Credit and Bank Guarantees, the ICC and UNCITRAL are engaged in the task of drafting modern rules [ICC] and a uniform law [UNCITRAL].

[81] The U.C.C. has few provisions clearly oriented to the non-commercial consumer. An admission of this is contained in U.C.C. § 2–102 which specifically preserves "any statute regulating sales to consumers." *See also* §§ 2–318 and 2–719(3). Article 9 recognizes the specific problem confronting consumer debtors. *See* § 9–206(1) preserving protection given by statutes and decisions governing rights of consumers against assignees of a security interest. *See also* §§ 9–109(1), 9–204(2), 9–302(1)(d), 9–307(2), 9–318, 9–404(1), 9–505(2) and 9–507(1).

[82] Uniform Consumer Credit Code, (UCCC) 1968, 7 ULA 579, enacted in Colorado, Guam, Indiana, Oklahoma, South Carolina, Utah, Wisconsin and Wyoming. Uniform Consumer Credit Code, (UCCC) 1974, 7A ULA 1, enacted in Idaho, Iowa, Kansas and Maine.

[83] Examples of such statutes appear in: Cal. Civ. Code §§ 1810 *et seq.* (West 1985); Ill. Ann. Stat. Ch.17, §§ 5202 *et seq.* (Smith-Hurd 1981); Mass. Ann. Laws Ch.255D, §§ 11 *et seq.* (Law. Co-op.1980).

[84] See pre-revision U.C.C. §§ 3–302 and 3–305 and their effect on a consumer who would be unable to raise defenses based on the underlying transaction against a claim by the transferee of commercial paper claiming to be a holder in due course. Unico v. Owen, 50 N.J. 101, 232 A.2d 405 (1967) and Commercial Credit Corp. v. Orange County Machine Works, 34 Cal. 2d 776, 214 P.2d 819 (1950) are illustrations of courts trying to obviate the effect of that doctrine on the basis of the existence of a close inter-relationship preventing the application of § 3–302. Use was also made of the doctrine of unconscionability to protect consumers from exploitative transactions.

[85] *See* U.C.C. § 9–206.

[86] The commercial purchasers of such paper or contracts generally protected themselves by retaining "recourse" against the transferor/assignor should the obligor under these transactions fail to perform. A consumer, however, did not have the economic power to insist on protection should the obligation be negotiated or assigned to such third party.

[87] Federal Trade Commission Act §§ 5, 12; 16 C.F.R. § 433.1. This rule requires that documentation exacted in a consumer transaction be legended to indicate that a holder of such documentation would be "subject to all claims and defenses" which the debtor could assert against the transferor of the documentation. The holder, therefore, having notice cannot claim to be a holder in due course. This raises the question as to the applicability of the rules in U.C.C.-Article 3 to such documentation. Pre-revision U.C.C. § 3–805 does not answer this question.

that most businesses did not require protection from such defenses since they were either self-financing consumer transactions or, in the case of financial institutions, had the paper transferred to them subject to recourse against the transferor should a failure to pay occur. An extensive use of its powers under the Federal Trade Commission Act dealing with unfair trade practices[88] led the Commission to promulgate additional regulations governing door to door sales by providing for a seventy-two hour "cooling off" period during which the consumer can rescind such purchases;[89] prohibiting confession of judgment clauses in consumer credit transactions[90] as well as prohibiting clauses that in any form would limit the protection granted by law or regulations to a consumer regarding garnishment of wages, attachment, execution or other process on real or personal property of the consumer.[91] In addition, these regulations require full disclosure of the effect of their guarantee to a guarantor of a consumer obligation.[92] Further federal protection was attained by means of the Federal Truth in Lending Act[93] which calls for full disclosure of credit terms and protects consumers from excessive garnishment.[94] The Act also recognizes the extended use of credit cards as well as the implication of their use on consumer rights.[95] Protection from excessive "dunning" of consumers was achieved by this federal legislation, which incorporates the Federal Fair Debt Collection Practices Act.[96]

The ability to contract out from the implied warranties of quality incorporated by the U.C.C. in sales transactions,[97] precluded consumers from alleging defects in quality. Only rarely was it possible for consumers to avoid such preclusion by an assertion that the seller acted unconscionably.[98] Congressional response to this problem took the form of the Magnuson-Moss Federal Trade Commission Improvement Act.[99] This Act provides a base below which sellers and suppliers cannot go in avoiding quality warranties relating to "consumer products."[100] Of interest in these developments is the novel approach of these

---

See further Sturley, *The Legal Impact of the Federal Trade Commission's Holder in Due Course Notice on a Negotiable Instrument: How Clever are the Rascals at the FTC?*, 68 N.C. L. Rev. 955 (1990). The solution in revised U.C.C. § 3–106(d) indicates that such legend would not condition the items and U.C.C.-Article 3 will be applied by analogy, but there can be no holder in due course. *Cf.* UCCC § 3.307. Note also 16 C.F.R. § 444.1 and compare UCCC §§ 3.404 and 3.405 as to credit practices. The UCCC permits the use of a check, post dated no more than ten days. But note, under revised U.C.C. §§ 3–108, 4–401(c) and 4–403(a) a bank/drawee can disregard the fact that the check has been post-dated and can pay a post-dated check, unless the drawer/customer has placed a stop payment order with the bank.

[88] Federal Trade Commission Act §§ 5, 12.

[89] 16 C.F.R. § 429.1.

[90] 16 C.F.R. § 444.2(a)(1).

[91] 16 C.F.R. § 444.2(a)(2)–(4).

[92] 16 C.F.R. § 444.3.

[93] Consumer Credit Protection Act, Title 1, 15 U.S.C. §§ 1601 *et seq.*

[94] *Id.* Title III, 15 U.S.C. §§ 1671 *et seq.*

[95] *Id.* § 1666i.

[96] *Id.* Title VIII, 15 U.S.C. §§ 1692 *et seq.*

[97] *See, e.g.*, U.C.C. §§ 2-314, 2-315.

[98] *See* U.C.C. § 2-302.

[99] 15 U.S.C. § 2301 *et seq. See also* 16 C.F.R. §§ 700.1–703.8 for regulations promulgated by the FTC.

[100] 15 U.S.C. § 2301(1), 2311(c)(2).

federal laws and regulations. They allow state laws to continue to function without pre-emption, provided such state laws do not fall below the minimum standards set by the federal laws and regulations. The Federal Trade Commission (FTC) is given the power to examine state laws to determine whether they afford "protection to consumers greater than the requirements of" the federal law or regulation.[101]

One recent attempt to develop a "New Payments Code" out of U.C.C. Articles 3 and 4 foundered because it failed to differentiate clearly between consumer and commercial transactions. The resulting strong opposition by consumer groups ended this effort. Developments continued, however, and a new U.C.C. Article 4A - Funds Transfers is proposed for enactment by state legislatures. This Article of the U.C.C. will affect only wholesale fund transfers. It will not have a direct impact on consumers. The adoption of Article 4A of the U.C.C., as well as the enactment of the Federal Electronic Fund Transfer Act,[102] the Federal Expedited Funds Availability Act,[103] and Regulation CC[104] promulgated thereunder by the Federal Reserve Bank, made a review of Article 3 and 4 imperative. It is necessary, therefore, to study the impact these laws have on U.C.C. Articles 3, 4 and 5 and to examine the changes to these Articles under consideration by state legislatures.

Advances in technology reflected in the use of credit cards, debit cards, electronic funds transfers as well as wire transfers in domestic and international transactions, led the United Nations through its Commission on International Trade Laws to seek unifying elements among various domestic laws to facilitate the easier transfer of funds across national borders. Events in Europe have accelerated this project.[105] Once agreement is reached at the General Assembly of the United Nations and a Model Law adopted, or conventions agreed to, or a treaty signed and ratified by the U.S. Senate, these rules will preempt state laws in an international transaction.[106] Such approaches are under consideration in many areas.[107]

This internationalization of commercial law returns us to an international private law governing commercial transactions; a law that existed among merchants as a *lex et consueto*

---

[101] *Id.*

[102] 15 U.S.C. § 1693 *et seq.*

[103] 12 U.S.C. § 401 *et seq.*

[104] 12 C.F.R. § 229.1 *et seq.*

[105] See in particular what has been colloquially called "Europe '92." By that date most national trade barriers now existing among members of the European Economic Communities are expected to have been removed.

[106] But note U.N. Convention on Contracts for the International Sale of Goods (1980) which is considered a self executing treaty. No federal legislation is needed to make it apply to individual litigants. *See* U.S. Const., art. VI, cl.2.

[107] *See* (as to Bills of Exchange,) U.N. Convention on International Bills of Exchange and International Promissory Notes, Resolution adopted by the U.N. Gen. Assembly 43/165 17 Jan. 1989. *See also* International Credit Transfers - Working Paper by U.N. Commission on International Trade Law (UNCITRAL) A/CN.9/WG.IV/WP 41, 7 April 1989; Letters of Credit and Bank Guarantees, UNCITRAL Report of the Working Group on International Contract Practices A/CN.9/316 12 Dec. 1988, UNCITRAL, Report of the Working Group on International Contract Practices on the Work of its Thirteenth Session: Possible Issues of a Uniform Law on Guarantees and Stand-by Letters of Credit A/CN. 9/330, 6 February 1990, and ELECTRONIC DATA INTER-CHANGE, Preliminary Study of Legal Issues Related to the Formation of Contracts by Electronic Means, Report of the Secretary-General A/CN. 9/333, 18 May 1990. Also note TEDIS (Trade Electronic Data Interchange System) proposed by the European Communities, Official Journal of the European Communities, L285/35, 8 Oct. 1987.

of merchants prior to the development of the nation state. It also raises once more the question whether this area of the law should not be federalized under the Commerce Clause of the U.S. Constitution.[108] Such an approach would also prevent a further problem created by the Supremacy Clause[109] which has been used by the federal government to assert that it is not subject to state laws, even though such law has been enacted in each of the jurisdictions of the United States.

There are numerous decisions, however, where federal courts have applied the U.C.C. as controlling. These cases are developing a body of federal case law that impacts on the interpretation of the U.C.C. and conversely results in the application of the U.C.C. to cases purely federal in nature. This has occurred despite assertions that the federal government is not bound by state law.[110] As was stated by Judge Learned Hand in *New York, N.H. & H.R. Co. v. Reconstruction Finance Corp.*: [111]

> The purpose of the doctrine that the transactions of such corporations are not subject to state law, is that such agencies, being national in their scope and aim, shall not be forced to shape their transactions to conform to the varying laws of the places where they occur, or are to be carried out. Uniformity is thought to be essential to the convenient and speedy dispatch of operations. However, the Negotiable Instruments Law has been enacted in every state of the Union as well as in the District of Columbia; it is a source of "federal law"—however that phrase may be construed—more complete and more certain, than any other which can conceivably be drawn from those sources of "general law" to which we were accustomed to resort in the days of *Swift v. Tyson*. ... [I]t will therefore determine the rights of the respondent and the liabilities of the present petitioner, for it is New York law as well as "federal law."[112]

Since this applies equally to the U.C.C. Articles 3 and 4, there would seem to be no reason not to apply these Articles in federal cases, absent some specific congressional enactment.

These developments should be born in mind when we consider the provisions of the U.C.C. and related domestic and international laws involved in the Modern Payment Systems, especially when applying policy considerations to the application of specific provisions. The U.C.C. specifically encourages such approach in Section 1–102(1) which provides that the Code should "be liberally construed and applied to promote its underlying purpose and policies."

---

[108] The Congress of the United States has power "to regulate Commerce with foreign Nations, and among the several States." U.S. Const., art. I, § 8, cl. 3.

[109] U.S. Const., art. VI, cl. 2.

[110] *See e.g.*, United States v. Kimbell Foods, 440 U.S. 715 (1979), Clearfield Trust Co. v. United States, 318 U.S. 363, 366–367 (1943). "When the United States disburses its funds or pays its debts, it is exercising a constitutional function or power.... The authority [to do so] had its origin in the Constitution and the statutes of the United States and was in no way dependent on the laws [of any state] ... In the absence of an applicable Act of Congress it is for the federal courts to fashion the governing rule of law according to their own standards" (citations and footnotes omitted).

[111] 180 F.2d 241 (2d Cir. 1950).

[112] *Id.* at 244.

* * * * *

Since we are dealing here with a subject matter governed by statute, an understanding of how the Uniform Commercial Code, our central statute, is to be read can best be learned from Soia Menschikoff who, with her husband Karl Llewellyn, was one of the original drafters of the U.C.C.

Commercial Transactions
by Soia Mentschikoff[113]

Construction

In statutory construction we start with the language of the statute. One does not paraphrase a statute. The first job in relation to an allegedly governing section is to state the precise words on which you are relying, not your own paraphrase, however more elegant and more useful the paraphrase may appear to be. Let me repeat, you start construction with the words of the statute. You then look to its reason. These are the two fundamental steps.

The form the drafting of the Code took is basically as follows: each section or subsection contains a statement of the factual conditions which are the operative conditions on which the result stated in the rule rests. This means that in terms of applying or using the rule, the very first inquiry that you have is what, under the words of the section, are the factual conditions which will put it into operation? You then test the situation which is before you to see whether or not all of the factual conditions required by the section are present. If they are not present, obviously that rule is not the one that is going to be applicable and you then search for another section or subsection. If they are present, then you move on to a consideration of what is the legal consequence as stated in the text of the presence of the factual conditions which make the rule operative.

There is a third possibility: your factual situation almost fits the stated conditions but not quite. In this situation you turn to the reason for the rule—if it applies, you use the rule; if it does not, you do not use the rule.

All this seems like a very simple task, but you will discover that it needs precise reading of language and that you are not yet skilled in this task.

The next thing it is necessary for you to know about the construction of the Code is that no one section of it stands alone. . . . The Code was not drafted . . . as a series of amendments to prior uniform acts, nor was it drafted as a series of policy decisions based on cases of conflict in the holdings of cases which had already arisen under the prior acts. The Code was drafted on the basis of recurrent typical factual situations in commercial life and on an appraisal of the desirable rules for the regulation of those situations; so that with very few exceptions—there are some to this general proposition—proper construction of the Code does not lie in movement from the prior law to the section or sections dealing

---

[113] Reprinted with permission from Soia Mentschikoff, Commercial Transactions, Cases and Materials, 7–12 (Little, Brown & Co. 1970).

with the same problem. Such a movement does not represent the manner of its drafting and can lead to very queer and inadequate results because it leaves things out or brings in problems of construction which are nonexistent when the Code is properly approached as an independent unit affording a new start to the courts on its own policy bases.

In sum, therefore, in using and construing the Code, always start with its language and end with a consideration of whether or not your situation, as it fits or almost fits into the language, also fits with both the general policy of the Code and the reason for the particular rules you are seeking to apply . . . Turn to 1-102, which is a highly important and significant section . . . The first subsection of 1-102, reads: "This act shall be liberally construed and applied, to promote its underlying purposes and policies." [This] is, of course, the basic presupposition on which the entire Code has been drafted. Unless the Code is read in accordance with its reason, there are areas which are difficult to construe. The second subsection states in general terms what the underlying purposes and policies of the Act as a whole are.

[(2) Underlying purposes and policies of this Act are
   (a) to simplify, clarify and modernize the law governing commercial transactions;
   (b) to permit the continued expansion of commercial practices through custom, usage and agreement of the parties;
   (c) to make uniform the law among the various jurisdictions.]

In addition to these statements of the purposes and policies of the Act as a whole, the Code is so drafted that it is hoped that the purpose and policy of a particular rule tend to show on its face, so that you have not only the general statement of general underlying purposes and policies, but in the particular sections some indication of reason from the section itself . . . The factual conditions delineate in the first instance the type of situation which is envisaged as the basis for the application of the legal consequence stated in the rule—so that if you stop and say to yourself, "Why in this fact situation was this the result which was chosen?" two things happen: first, you acquire a good deal of information about the underlying factual situations with which the Code deals; and second, you start getting a sense of why the Code takes the position it does as a matter of policy in the particular section. You cannot do this unless you start with the question of what are the factual conditions for the application of this rule.

The third subsection in 1-102
   (3) The effect of provisions of this Act may be varied by agreement, except as otherwise provided in this Act and except that the obligations of good faith, diligence, reasonableness and care prescribed by this Act may not be disclaimed by agreement but the parties may by agreement determine the standards by which the performance of such obligations is to be measured if such standards are not manifestly unreasonable.

expresses the growth feature of the Code in quite general terms because it indicates that the effect of the provisions of the Act may be varied by agreement, except as otherwise provided. When you look at the definition of "agreement" in 1-201(3), you will see that it means "the bargain of the parties in fact as found in their language or by implication from other circumstances; including course of dealing or usage of trade or course of performance as provided in this Act." This is the factual agreement, a factual bargain which is made by the parties, and it always includes any relevant course of dealing, usage of trade, or course of performance. And notice that those are the things, especially usage of trade, that change as the underlying techniques and technology of the particular transaction which is involved change over time, and the result of change becomes automatically a part of the agreement within the limitations of Section 1–205.

The first thing to notice, therefore, is that the effect of provisions may be varied by agreement as defined in the Act. There are, however, certain general obligations stated in the Code, apart from particular sections, which deal with effects that may not be varied by agreement, that cannot be destroyed by agreement, even through usage of trade. These are the obligations of good faith, diligence, reasonableness, and care. But because these are general concepts whose factual content will have to be filled in over time, and because they are factual issues in part which may have to be resolved by a jury, there is a further extremely significant point for any draftsman operating under the Code, and that is the "but" clause of subsection 1–102(3): "but the parties may by agreement determine the standards by which the performance of such obligations is to be measured if such standards are not manifestly unreasonable." In other words, what it says to the draftsman is, "You may set up the standards of behavior which you think are called for in the particular situation by these general obligations, and if you don't overreach, if you don't try to take the whole pie, only take, say, two thirds to three quarters of the pie, we will enforce it." In other words, if it is not manifestly unreasonable, the court will as a matter of law—not as a matter of fact—apply those standards, and, if your client behaves in accordance with those standards and anybody attacks him, you will even be able to get a summary judgment. And this is a pearl beyond price. . .

Subsection 4 of Section 1–102 takes care of what was worried about by a great many people who were asked to go over the Code at late stages of its drafting.

> (4) The presence in certain provisions of this Act of the words "unless otherwise agreed" or words of similar import does not imply that the effect of other provisions may not be varied by agreement under subsection (3).

That is that so many sections of the Code open with the words "unless otherwise agreed." The reason for this is that in the drafting of the Sales Article, which was the first article, the drafting was done quite simply on the basis of deciding for every rule at that moment in time whether the rule was one that was subject to agreement otherwise in whole or part, and, if so, that fact was expressly stated in the rule itself. Most of the rules as you will discover are "unless otherwise agreed" types of rules. The result was that on the completion of that article, the only important thing left to say was that unless the words "unless otherwise agreed," or the like, appeared, the rule was not one that could be varied by agreement. But this looks like Social Legislation, doesn't it? So then you reverse the statement. That's subsection 3. But, having reversed the statement, since in point of fact the Code was drafted the other way, the only safe thing is to say that the general principle which is expressed in subsection 3 need not be manifested by the presence of words like "unless otherwise agreed." So that subsection 4 is a completely unnecessary section, except in terms of the drafting history of the Code. All it does is make clear to a court that the absence of these words, which in point of fact are usually not absent, is nonsignificant if the situation is one which falls within the general rule enunciated by subsection 3 of 1–102.

And then, of course, subsection 5 states the obvious, which is not so obvious apparently in some states; some states require this kind of statement.

> (5) In this Act unless the context otherwise requires
>
> > (a) words in the singular number include the plural, and in the plural include the singular;
> >
> > (b) words of the masculine gender include the feminine and the neuter, and when the sense so indicates words of the neuter gender may refer to any gender.

At one time the rules on the construction of the Code were much greater in number. One of the things said in the Code was that the Comments—the joint comments of the Conference of Commissioners and the American Law Institute—could be resorted to by the courts to ascertain the underlying reasons and policies of particular sections and the Code as a whole. That went out for two reasons, both of which are interesting. The first was that some states don't have documentation in the way of legislative history as a bill goes through the state legislature and so do not permit their courts to consult what was happening in the legislature, or the documentation that was before a legislative committee or the legislature, as part of the history of the statute for purposes of construction. This would not have been a sufficient reason in and of itself because, of course, the proposed Code language was an authorizing subsection and would simply change the practice of that state. The thing that really took the proposal out of the Code was Judge Learned Hand who, when this controversy was being explained to the Council of the American Law Institute, looked over those bushy eyebrows of his and said, "How silly can we get, and how silly can they get? It doesn't matter at all whether it's in or out; of course we'll consult them anyway"; and it was on the statement that the courts would consult them anyway, whether they were officially in or not, that the reference to the comments went out. This as it turned out was an important step because there had been criticism of the Comments and all of this criticism became irrelevant, obviously, once there was no official statement that they had to be consulted by the courts. The courts can do what they like.[114]

There was another set of express provisions which dealt with construction by analogy and expressly permitted the extension or limitation of the language of the Code depending upon the situation before the court in the particular case in the light of the reason for the rule. This went out really because it was deemed to be an unnecessary red flag. I come back to the very first presupposition on which the Code is drafted. If it is correct that the grand style of appellate judging involves looking at the situation before the court in terms of its type situation and arriving at a conclusion as to what is the best policy, then if you look at the precise language of the statute and at the situation before you and the reason for the language seems to be present in the situation, you can expand by analogy or, if the reason is absent, limit the statutory language. This is a perfectly permissible reasoning by analogy with the statutes instead of with cases; the same principle exactly. You say to yourself, "This is the reason for the rule which is enunciated here; the explicit language does not cover the situation which has arisen; should I apply the policy? Are the situations

---

[114] [Editor: In some instances the comments do not reflect changes that have been incorporated in the text and vice versa. *See, e.g.*, § 2–507. The former reference in Comment 3 to a ten day limit within which a seller can reclaim goods is not reflected in the language of the section and is now rejected.]

sufficiently similar so that the reasons that make this a good policy in the situation covered precisely by the language should carry over to the situation which is not precisely covered by the language?"

The other half of the problem, of course, arises when the situation has changed in fact but seems to be one which on its face fits the factual preconditions of the rule. Now what do you do? What courts tend to do in that situation is to misconstrue the language of the rule in order to exclude the situation. They say that it is different, that it isn't really within the factual preconditions, although on any fair reading it is, because they want to escape the consequence. What the Code did was to give specific authority to the court in that situation not to mishandle the language of the text, but to say this is a factual situation which is different in terms of its reason and therefore we will not apply the rule; we will limit the rule so that it excludes the situation. The court's opinion would then move in terms of why the factual situation before the court ought as a matter of policy and reason to be excluded even though it seems to fall within the language of the statute.

If you stop to think about it, one of the reasons that we have so many techniques on the use of precedent and about how to construe statutes is that they are necessary in order to give the court the freedom of action it needs to arrive at results which are just, and also in fair consonance with the general nature of the system, the inherent stability, so to speak, of the legal order. These things are always in tension and in flux and if courts can't do it openly, then they develop techniques by which they get it done covertly. The hope was that the Code, by giving explicit permission in the text to do it openly, would prevent that kind of mishandling of the language. That section is gone. On the other hand, if sometime you should read the Comments to 1-102, you'll find there was no change in the Comment when the text disappeared, and if, on your own study of appellate processes, you were to come to agree with Llewellyn[115] that this is what the courts do anyway, then the Comment to 1-102 on this point gives any court a chance to operate this way. Nonetheless, that is not in the text, just in the Comment.

---

[115] [Editor: Karl Llewellyn—one of the draftsmen of the U.C.C.]

II INTERACTION OF CODE PROVISIONS

In seeking to understand the terminology used in the U.C.C., we must first categorize the issue. Thus we must determine whether we are dealing with a "commercial paper" or with an "investment security"; whether we are confronted with a problem relating to the "sales contract" or to that part of such transaction that relates to payment or to a credit transaction arising out of the sales contract. This categorization is important to determine the legal rules applicable to the resolution of the issues involved.

Article 1 of the U.C.C. contains definitions which apply only where the applicable Article of the U.C.C. fails to supply a definition. To name but a few examples,[1] Section 1-201(44) defines "value," and so does Section 3-303(a); and Section 1-201(19) defines "good faith" and so does Section 3-103(a)(4). Do not be misled by apparent similarities. Some of the subtleties will be analyzed as we proceed. It suffices to point out here that whereas "value" under Section 1-201(44) includes simple contract consideration, Section 3-303(a) rejects this and requires that "the promise has been performed."[2] Thus, when dealing with an instrument evidencing an obligation to pay a sum certain on a specified date, such instrument first has to be analyzed and categorized as either a "commercial paper" or as an "investment security." Only then will it be possible to determine whether the person in possession can qualify as a "holder in due course" under Article 3-Section 3-302 or must attempt to qualify as a "bona fide purchaser" under Article 8-Section 8-302. If the instrument qualifies as a commercial paper, the value given must have passed from the purchaser. But, if the instrument qualifies as an investment security, then, since there is no definition of "value" in Article 8, a promise of future performance, i.e., consideration, would suffice to satisfy the need for value.[3]

In the absence of such cross reference to Article 1 being available, it is necessary to remember that the U.C.C. is an integrated common law statute. Thus a term used in another Article, or an interpretation given by a court in relation to a similar provision in another Article, is persuasive authority. Official Comment 1 to Section 2-105 specifically states:

"Investment securities" are expressly excluded from coverage of this Article [Article 2 - Sales]. It is not intended by this exclusion, however, to prevent the application of a

---

[1] Unless expressly stated, section references throughout are to the revised U.C.C.-Article 3 and Article 4.

[2] "Consideration" is defined in traditional terms in U.C.C. § 3-303(b). The section goes on to state, however, that: "If an instrument is issued for value as stated in subsection (a), the instrument is also issued for consideration."

[3] U.C.C. § 1-201(44). Note that U.C.C. §§ 3-416 and 4-207(a) trigger "transfer warranties" not on the receipt of "value," as described in U.C.C. § 3-303(a), but on receipt of "consideration," as defined in U.C.C. § 3-303(b).

> particular section of this Article by analogy to securities . . . when the reason of that section makes such application sensible and the situation involved is not covered by the Article of this Act dealing specifically with such securities.[4]

Similarly, Article 3 is much more detailed than Article 8 and contains answers to questions that are raised by the nature of the investment security as a negotiable instrument. It is therefore appropriate to look to Article 3 for guidance in seeking answers not given by Article 8.[5] After all, a bearer paper governed by Article 3

> could become an investment security if it is one of a series and is traded on an exchange. It does not seem that the rights of the parties in a transaction involving this instrument should be markedly different under Article 8 from what they would be under Article 3.[6]

There are, however, some important differences. For example, the endorser's presumptive secondary liability on commercial paper does not apply to an endorser of an investment security. *Compare* U.C.C. §§ 3-415 and 8-308(1). Another example would be the acquisition of the status of bona fide purchaser under Article 8. This requires a delivery of the security, i.e., "a *voluntary* transfer of possession."[7] An acquisition at a sheriff's sale or as a result of a court ordered property distribution following a divorce decree would not involve a voluntary transfer by the debtor or the party ordered to transfer such property.[8] Unlike Article 3 Section 3-302(c), Article 8 contains no provision for an acquisition at a sheriff's sale. But such acquisition would not involve a voluntary transfer, U.C.C. § 1-201(14), and thus should not the policy expressed in Section 3-302(c) apply? That is, a purchaser at a sheriff's sale is "treated as a successor in interest to the prior holder and can acquire no better rights."[9]

---

[4] U.C.C. § 2-105, Official Comment 1, refers to Agar v. Orda, 264 N.Y. 248, 190 N.E. 479 (1934). *See also* Silverman v. Alcoa Assocs., 37 A. D.2d 166, 323 N.Y.S.2d 39, 43 (1st Dep't 1971) ("We believe . . . that Article 8 is to be read in conjunction with Article 2; and where Article 8 is silent, Article 2 is applicable."); Zamore v. Whitten, 395 A.2d 435, 443 (Me. 1978) ("We should look for guidance to the provisions of the Uniform Commercial Code in determining whether the parties did enter into an enforceable contract of sale of this stock. . . . We have in mind the more liberal approaches of the Code to the formation of contracts . . . (§ 2-204) . . . (§ 2-206)"); Tipton v. Woodbury, 616 F.2d 170, 177 (5th Cir. 1980) ("[T]he conduct of the parties reveals a contract. . . . [T]he terms of the contract . . . are all present: price, quantity and a sufficient description of the stock itself. . . . [O]nly missing term was time and place of payment . . ."). *See* U.C.C. § 2-204(1),(3). In re McManus, 83 A.D.2d 553, 440 N.Y.S.2d 954, 958 (1981), *aff'd*, 55 N.Y.2d 855, 432 N.E.2d 601, 447 N.Y.S.2d 708 (1982) ("We can perceive of no sound policy reason why the provisions of Section 2-207 should not be applied to the facts of this case [a sale of securities under a "buy-sell" agreement]."). *Cf.* Gruen Indus. Inc. v. Biller, 608 F.2d 274 (7th Cir. 1979).

[5] GUTTMAN, MODERN SECURITIES TRANSFERS, ¶ 1.03[2] (3d ed. 1987 & Supplement 1992) (cited in Bankhaus Hermann Lampe KG v. Mercantile Safe Deposit & Trust Co., 466 F. Supp. 1133, 1142 (S.D.N.Y. 1979)). *See* In re Ralph A. Veon, Inc., 12 B.R. 186, 189 (Bankr. W.D. Pa. 1981).

[6] E.F. Hutton & Co. v. Manufacturers Nat'l Bank of Detroit, 259 F. Supp. 513, 517 (E.D. Mich. 1966). *See also* Abraham Lincoln Ins. Co. v. Franklin Sav. & Loan Ass'n, 302 F. Supp. 54 (E.D. Mo. 1969), *aff'd*, 434 F.2d 264 (8th Cir. 1971); Hartford Accident & Indem. Co. v. Walton & Co., 21 N.Y.2d 219, 234 N.E.2d 230, 287 N.Y.S.2d 58, *aff'd*, 22 N.Y.2d 672, 238 N.E.2d 754, 291 N.Y.S.2d 366 (1968); Mazer v. Williams Bros. Co., 461 Pa. 587, 337 A.2d 559 (1975). *But see* Stoerger v. Ivesdale Co-op Grain Co., 15 Ill. App. 3d 313, 304 N.E.2d 300 (1973).

[7] U.C.C. §§ 8-302(1)(a), 1-201(14) (emphasis added).

[8] *See* Mazer v. Williams Bros. Co., 461 Pa. 587, 337 A.2d 559 (1975); Castonguay v. Castonguay, 306 N.W.2d 143 (Minn. 1981) (court-ordered distribution of property following divorce decree is not a "voluntary transfer").

[9] U.C.C. § 3-302, Official Comment 5. *Cf.* U.C.C. § 8-301(1).

Where a court can categorize an issue so as to solve it by means of a provision of Article 8, however, the court cannot apply Article 3.[10] For example, in *Stoerger v. Ivesdale Co-op Grain Co.*, 15 Ill. App. 3d 313, 304 N.E.2d 300 (1973) the omission of the year of due date on a debt obligation categorized as an investment security, called for an authorized completion of the incomplete security or for its reformation (U.C.C. § 8-206(1)) rather than a determination that the item was a demand instrument under U.C.C. § 3-108(a)(ii). We should also note that if there is a conflict between Article 3 and Article 4 - Bank Deposits and Collections, or Article 9 - Secured Transactions, those Articles and not Article 3 will govern.[11] Courts, however, will attempt to harmonize approaches to problems that are similar in nature. The effect of federal preemption of the U.C.C. must also be recognized, in that "regulations of the Board of Governors of the Federal Reserve System and operating circulars of the Federal Reserve Banks supersede any inconsistent provisions of this Article [3] to the extent of the inconsistency."[12]

Finally we must note that the U.C.C. does not cover all areas of the law. Thus, Section 1-103 provides that:

> Unless displaced by the particular provisions of this Act, the principles of law and equity, including the law merchant and the law relative to capacity to contract, principal and agent, estoppel, fraud, misrepresentation, duress, coercion, mistake, bankruptcy, or other validating or invalidating cause shall supplement its provisions.[13]

---

[10] "This Article applies to negotiable instruments. It does not apply to money, to payment orders governed by Article 4A, or to securities governed by Article 8." U.C.C. § 3-102(a).

[11] U.C.C. § 3-102(b).

[12] U.C.C. § 3-102(c).

[13] *See* Official Comment 3 to § 1-103. The listing given in this section is merely illustrative; no listing could be exhaustive. Nor is the fact that in some sections particular circumstances have led to express reference to other fields of law intended at any time to suggest the negation of the general application of the principles of this section.

Young v. Kay
443 Pa. 335, 279 A.2d 759 (1971)*

ROBERTS, J. This appeal arises out of an action in equity in the Court of Common Plea of McKean County to quiet title to 10,000 shares of stock of the Kinzua Oil and Gas Corporation, suit having been brought by appellants Fred Young and the guardian of his wife Mercedes.

It is conceded by all that the Youngs owned the stock in question until late 1966 or early 1967,

---

* [Editor: citations in [ ] refer to Revised U.C.C. Articles 3 and 4.]

at which time Fred Young on his own behalf and on behalf of his wife Mercedes caused to be executed a certificate for the 10,000 shares registered in the name of appellee Melvin Brooks. In December of that year, Brooks sold the same stock to appellee Traner Associates and Company for the sum of $50,000.

The two issues posed by this appeal are whether the stock transfer from the Youngs to Brooks is voidable because of a confidential relationship between Brooks and Young and, if so, whether Traner Associates nevertheless holds title to the stock by virtue of the circumstances in which it acquired the stock from Brooks. Having reviewed this voluminous record, we hold that the Young-Brooks transfer is voidable and that the Youngs have a claim to the stock transfer superior to that of Traner Associates.

I. The Young-Brooks Transfer

Turning now to the facts of the present case, our reading of the record convinces us that a confidential relationship did indeed exist between Brooks and Young. Though a man of sound mind, Young was an octogenarian at the time of the disputed stock transfer. He possessed no apparent knowledge of the intricacies of the federal personal and corporate income tax laws and had no independent advice on such matters, relying instead upon the trusted advice of Brooks, his "tax consultant." Moreover, Young often signed without question tax and other financial documents prepared by Brooks. The contract for the sale of Kinzua to Brooks was motivated by tax considerations brought to Young's attention by Brooks and the consideration given by Brooks was the assumption of an alleged tax liability. In these circumstances, there can be little doubt that Brooks was in a position to take advantage of Young.

Having concluded that Brooks and Young occupied a position of confidential relationship, there remains to be decided whether the record contains evidence that the transfer was "fair, conscientious and beyond the reach of suspicion." As stated above, the Youngs purchased the Kinzua stock in 1960 for $10,000, and in 1967 Fred Young donated to the corporation a valuable oil lease and transferred all of the capital stock to Brooks. Several months later Brooks resold the stock to a third party, Traner Associates, for $50,000 plus Traner's promise to indemnify Brooks up to $60,000 for any personal tax liability accruing to Brooks as a result of any tax assessments against Kinzua. The stock transfer from Young to Brooks was motivated by considerations of tax avoidance, and Young had no independent advice on the matter. To date, *no one has ever received a tax assessment imposing personal liability of Kinzua's taxes*. It would strain credulity to characterize this set of circumstances as fair and beyond the reach of suspicion, and we therefore hold the Young-Brooks transfer voidable.

We must next consider whether Traner Asso-

ciates has a claim to the Kinzua stock superior to that of Young.

II. The Brooks-Traner Associates Transfer

A series of meetings was held at a local motel in Bradford. Little is known of what transpired there, but, in any event, on or about December 15, 1967, Brooks and Traner Associates entered into a written contract for the sale of the Kinzua stock. In attendance at the execution of the agreement were Brooks, Kaye, Tudesco, and appellee Anthony Chambers, a local attorney representing Traner Associates. Under the terms of the contract, Traner Associates was to pay Brooks $50,000 over a period of four years and to indemnify Brooks up to $60,000 for any tax liability against Kinzua for which Brooks might be personally responsible.

The legal norms applicable to the resolution of competing claims to interests in securities are contained in Article 8 of the Uniform Commercial Code, Act of April 6, 1953, PL 3, Section 8-101 *et seq.* . . . Section 8-301 codifies the common law general rule that a purchaser of securities acquires only the rights of his transferor but adds the qualification that "[a] bona fide purchaser in addition to acquiring the rights of a purchaser also acquires the security free of any adverse claim." Thus, Traner Associates can establish clear title to the Kinzua stock free of Young's adverse claim *only* if it qualifies as a "bona fide purchaser."

The status of a "bona fide purchaser" is defined in Section 8-302 as: "a purchaser for value in good faith and without notice of any adverse claim who takes delivery of a security in bearer form or of one in registered form issued to him or endorsed to him in blank." Traner Associates clearly purchased the Kinzua stock for value and took delivery of the same. The record is largely silent, however, as to whether or not it purchased in good faith and without notice of Young's adverse claim. Thus arises the crucial question: in a silent record case, does the adverse claimant bear the burden of proving that the holder of the security is not a bona fide purchaser, or, to the contrary, must the holder affirmatively demonstrate that he is a bona fide purchaser? We believe the burden of proof rests upon the holder in such a situation.

Article 3 of the Uniform Commercial Code deals with negotiable instrument, and Section 3-307(3) [U.C.C. § 3-308(b)] of the Article provides:

(3) After it is shown that a defense exists a person claiming the rights of a holder in due course has the burden of establishing that he or some person under whom he claims is in all respects a holder in due course.

Under Section 3-307(3), if the adverse claimant of a negotiable instrument proves that he only transferred voidable title, the holder of the instrument must prove that he or the person under whom he claims is a holder in due course. This rule reflects the prior law. *See* Section 59 of the Uniform Negotiable Instruments Law (now repealed); *Brubaker v. Berks County*, 381 Pa. 157, 112 A.2d 620 (1955); *Bank of America v. Rocco*, 241 F.2d 455 (3d Cir. 1957).

Returning to Article 8 of the Code dealing with investment securities, we find that Section 8-105 as originally drafted and adopted by the Legislature of the Commonwealth provided that:

"(1) Securities governed by the Article are negotiable instruments.

(2) In any action on a security the rules relating to proof of signatures and to burden of proof after signature are admitted or established, *shall be the same as in actions on commercial paper* (Section 3-307)." (Emphasis added.)

Thus, the Code as originally drafted and adopted was quite clear: just as a holder of negotiable instrument must prove that he holds in due course once a defect in his title is shown to exist, so too did a holder of a security have to demonstrate affirmatively his status as a bona fide purchaser once a defect in his title was shown. Section 8-105, however, was amended and reenacted by the Act of October 2, 1959, P.L. 1023, Section 8, effective January 1, 1960, and Traner Associates argues that the former rule pertaining to burden of proof is no longer applicable.

As is readily apparent, the new and present version of Section 8-105 no longer makes any express reference to the burden of proof rules contained in Section 3-307, and subsection (d) speaks only of the "plaintiff" having the burden of demonstrating that a defect or defense is ineffective against him. Accordingly, Traner Associates argues that since it is a "defendant" in the instant action, Section 8-105 is inapplicable and it does not have the burden of proving that it is a bona

fide purchaser. This argument is defective in two respects.

In the first place, we do not believe that the Commissioners intended such a drastic change in the law by mere omission and implication. That no such change was intended is confirmed by a comparison of the text of the official comment to the original version of Section 8-105 with the text of the official comment accompanying the amended Section 8-105[3] The original comment ended by declaring that "by subsection (2) of this section the particular rules stated in Section 3-307 for the negotiable instruments governed by Article 3 are made applicable also to securities." The present comment to amended Section 8-105 contains the practically identical language that "by subsection (2) of this section the particular rules states in Section 3-307 for the negotiable instruments governed by Article 3 are adapted to securities." In these circumstances we do not believe that amended Section 8-105 changes the law relating to burden of proof.

Moreover, even if we are to accept Traner Associates' interpretation of the present Section 8-105, the most that would be established would be that the Code does not presently speak to the issue of who bears the burden of proving whether or not the holder of a security is a bona fide purchaser, and in the absence of a specific statutory directive we would apply our general common law rule of evidence that

[i]f the existence or non-existence of a fact can be demonstrated by one party, the burden of proof may be placed on that party who can discharge it most easily. *Barrett v. Otis Elevator Co.*, 431 Pa. 446, 452 246 A.2d 668, 672 (1968) (citing Wigmore).

It is manifest that in the vast majority of cases it will be much easier for the holder of a security to prove that he is a bona fide purchaser than for an adverse claimant to prove otherwise. For this reason, even if Section 8-105 were interpreted to

---

[3] It is settled in this Commonwealth that the official comments of a commission drafting legislation may be given weight in the construction of a statute. *See* Tarlo's Estate, 315 Pa. 321, 172 A. 139 (1934) (construing Intestate Act of 1917); Miles's Estate, 272 Pa. 329, 116 A. 300 (1922). *See also* Statutory Construction Act, Act of May 28, 1937, P.L. 1019, art. IV, Section 51, 46 P.S. Section 551 (reference to legislative history).

be inapplicable to this burden of proof issue, we would nevertheless place that burden upon the one claiming the status of bona fide purchaser.

As Traner Associates has not affirmatively demonstrated that it purchased the Kinzua stock in good faith and without notice of Young's adverse claim, Traner cannot be deemed a bona fide purchaser and title to the stock must revert to the Youngs.***

NOTE

Where a bearer item appears to have all the hallmarks of an investment security but is one of a kind and not "one of a class or series or by its terms divisible into a class or series of shares, participation, interests or obligations," [U.C.C. § 8-102(1)(a)(iii)], U.C.C.-Article 3 and not U.C.C.-Article 8 will apply to determine its negotiability. *Jones v. United Sav. & Loan Ass'n*, 515 S.W.2d 869, 873 (Mo. Ct. App. 1974) ("Article 8 is directed to multiple transactions in which a group of promises, all for the same amount and all due at the same time, are made to multiple parties... [i.e. the certificates must be] issued in a class or series").

A. Herein of Accord and Satisfaction Article 3, Article 1 (Section 1-207) and Common Law

County Fire Door Corporation v. Wooding Company
202 Conn. 277, 520 A.2d 1028 (1987)*

PETERS, Chief Justice.

The principal issue in this appeal is whether the Uniform Commercial Code modifies the common law of accord and satisfaction so that a creditor can now effectively reserve his rights against a debtor while cashing a check that the debtor has explicitly tendered in full satisfaction of an unliquidated debt .... The trial court's articulation and the exhibits at trial establish the following facts. On November 17, 1981, the defendant ordered a number of metal doors and door frames from the plaintiff. The plaintiff undertook responsibility for delivery of the goods to the worksite. Alleging that the plaintiff's delay in delivery of the doors and frames had caused additional installation expenses, the defendant back charged the plaintiff an amount of $2,180. The defendant informed the plaintiff that, on the basis of this back charge, and other payments and cred-

its not at issue, the remaining balance due the plaintiff was $416.88. The plaintiff responded by denying the validity of this back charge. According to the plaintiff, the balance due on its account was $2,618.88. The defendant immediately replied, in writing, that it would stand by its position on the validity of the back charge and the accuracy of its calculation of the amount owed to the plaintiff.

The defendant thereafter, on January 10, 1983, sent the plaintiff the check that is at the heart of the present controversy. The check was in the amount of $416.88. It bore two legends. On its face was the notation:

"Final Payment
Upjohn Project
Purchase Order #3302 dated 11/17/81."

On the reverse side, the check stated: "By its endorsement, the payee accepts this check in full satisfaction of all claims against the C.F. Wooding Co. arising out of or relating to the Upjohn Project under Purchase order #3302, dated 11/17/81." The plaintiff did not advise the defendant directly

---

* [Editor note: citations in [ ] refer to Revised U.C.C. Articles 3 and 4.]

that it planned to cash this check under protest. Instead, the plaintiff crossed out the conditional language on the reverse side of the check and added the following: "This check is accepted under protest and with full reservation of rights to collect the unpaid balance for which this check is offered in settlement." The plaintiff then indorsed and deposited the check in its account.

The defendant made no further payments to the plaintiff and the plaintiff brought the present action to recover the remaining amount to which it claimed it was entitled. The trial court rendered judgment for the plaintiff on two grounds. The court agreed with the plaintiff that the enactment of [U.C.C.] 1-207 had deprived debtors generally of the power unilaterally to enforce the terms of a conditional tender of a check to their creditors.... First, the defendant claims that the plaintiff's action of cashing this check constituted an acceptance of its offer, including its terms of settlement, despite the plaintiff's reliance on § 1-207 for authority to substitute words of protest for words of satisfaction. Second, the defendant claims that the amount that it tendered the plaintiff constituted a valid offer of an accord and satisfaction because the underlying debt was unliquidated in amount. We agree with both of the defendant's claims. We will, however, take them up in reverse order, because we would not reach the statutory issue if the defendant had failed to establish its common law defense to the plaintiff's cause of action.

I

When there is a good faith dispute about the existence of a debt or about the amount that is owed, the common law authorizes the debtor and the creditor to negotiate a contract of accord to settle the outstanding claim. Such a contract is often initiated by the debtor, who offers an accord by tendering a check as "payment in full" or "in full satisfaction." If the creditor knowingly cashes such a check, or otherwise exercises full dominion over it, the creditor is deemed to have assented to the offer of accord. Upon acceptance of the offer of accord, the creditor's receipt of the promised payment discharges the underlying debt and bars any further claim relating thereto, if the contract of accord is supported by consideration.[2]

---

[2] It may well be that an accord is enforceable, even

* * *

A contract of accord and satisfaction is sufficiently supported by consideration if it settles a monetary claim that is unliquidated in amount....

Where it is admitted that one of two specific sums is due, but there is a dispute as to which is the proper amount, the demand is regarded as unliquidated, within the meaning of that term as applied to the subject of accord and satisfaction.... Where the claim is unliquidated any sum, given and received in settlement of the dispute, is a sufficient consideration.[3]

Application of these settled principles to the facts of this case establishes, as the defendant maintains, that the parties entered into a valid contract of accord and satisfaction. The defendant offered in good faith to settle an unliquidated debt by tendering, in full satisfaction, the payment of an amount less than that demanded by the plaintiff.[4] Under the common law, the plaintiff could not simultaneously cash such a check and disown the condition on which it had been tendered. *Kelly v. Kowalsky*, 186 Conn. 618, 442 A.2d 1355 (1982) and authorities therein cited. Having received the promised payment, the plaintiff discharged the defendant from any further obligation on this account, unless the enactment of § 1-207 of the Uniform Commercial Code has changed this result.

---

in the absence of consideration, if it is supported by a debtor's reasonable and foreseeable reliance on a promise by a creditor to forgive the remainder of an outstanding debt. *See* D'Ulisse-Cupo v. Board of Directors, 202 Conn. 206, 218, 520 A.2d 217 (1987); Finley v. Aetna Life & Casualty Co., 202 Conn. 190, 205, 520 A.2d 208 (1987); 2 RESTATEMENT (SECOND), CONTRACTS (1981) § 281, Comment d and § 290.

[3] "It would be too technical a use of the doctrine of consideration to release a well-counselled debtor who tenders a nominal amount beyond his admitted debt but to trap one less sophisticated who is induced to pay the undisputed amount in return for his creditor's illusory promise to forgive the rest." Kilander v. Blickle Co., 280 Or. 425, 429, 571 P.2d 503 (1977).

[4] When the parties in this case asked the trial court for an articulation of its rulings in favor of the plaintiff, the plaintiff sought a finding that the defendant's tender had been in bad faith. The trial court made no such finding.

The principal dispute between the parties is what meaning to ascribe to § 1-207 when it states that

> "[a] party who with explicit reservation of rights . . . assents to performance in a manner . . . offered by the other party does not thereby prejudice the rights reserved. Such words as 'without prejudice,' 'under protest' or the like are sufficient."

The plaintiff contends, as the trial court concluded, that this section gave the plaintiff the authority to cash the defendant's check "under protest" while reserving the right to pursue the remainder of its underlying claim against the defendant at a later time. The defendant maintains that the statutory reference to "performance" contemplates something other than the part payment of an unliquidated debt. We noted in *Kelly v. Kowalsky, supra*, 186 Conn. at 622 and n.3, 442 A.2d 1355, that there was considerable disagreement in the cases and the scholarly commentaries about the scope of the transactions governed by § 1-207, but did not then undertake to resolve this disagreement. We now decide that § 1-207 does not displace the common law of accord and satisfaction and that the trial court erred in so concluding.

Because § 1-207 is part of the Uniform Commercial Code, it is important to reconcile its provisions with those found in other articles of the code. *See Barco Auto Leasing Corp. v. House*, 202 Conn. 106, 115, 520 A.2d 162 (1987); *Galvin v. Freedom of Information Comm'n*, 201 Conn. 448, 456, 518 A.2d 64 (1986); Grosse & Goggin, *Accord and Satisfaction and the 1-207 Dilemma*, 89 Com. L. J. 537, 544 (1984). Two likely candidates for such a reconciliation are the provisions of article 3, dealing generally with the law of negotiable instruments, including checks; . . . ; and the provisions of Article 2, dealing generally with contracts for the sale of goods. . . .

Article 3 provides little support for reading § 1-207 to permit a creditor unilaterally to change the terms of a check tendered in full satisfaction of an unliquidated debt. As the parties have noted, § 3-112(1)(f) [U.C.C. § 3-311] preserves the negotiability of a check that includes "a term . . . providing that the payee by indorsing or cashing it acknowledges full satisfaction of an

obligation of the drawer."[5] There is no such validation, anywhere in article 3, for a term on a check that negates a condition that a drawer has incorporated in a negotiable instrument. On the contrary, § 3-407 takes a dim view of the unauthorized alteration of an instrument. Under § 3-407(1) "*[a]ny* alteration of an instrument is material which changes the contract of *any* party thereto in any respect. . . ." [U.C.C. § 3-407(a)(i)] (Emphasis added). The effect of the material alteration of a completed instrument is either to discharge the liability, on the instrument, of "any party whose contract is thereby changed," or to continue the enforceability of the instrument "according to its original tenor." § 3-407(2), (3). [§3-407(b), 3-407(c)] According to this section, the plaintiff's conduct in substituting words of protest for words of satisfaction would have put the plaintiff at risk of discharging the defendant entirely, if such conduct were deemed to have been fraudulent. § 3-407(2)(a) [§ 3-407(b)]. Even without a finding of fraud, however, the most for which the plaintiff could hope, under Article 3, was to enforce the instrument "in full satisfaction," because that was "its original tenor." This result is supported by § 3-802(1)(b) [§ 3-310(b), (c)], which provides that, presumptively, the taking of a negotiable instrument suspends the underlying obligation "until the instrument is due," and that "discharge of the underlying obligor on the instrument also discharges him on the obligation." Under § 3-603(1) [§ 3-602(a)], a drawer is discharged from liability on an instrument "to the extent of his payment or satisfaction."

The impact of these various Article 3 rules is clear. Because the check tendered by the defendant was only enforceable "according to its original tenor," the plaintiff, by receiving "payment or satisfaction," discharged the defendant not only on the instrument but also on the underlying obligation. *See* J. White & R. Summers, *Uniform Commercial Code* (2d ed. 1980) 603–04 n.57. To read § 1-207 to validate the plaintiff's conduct in this case would, therefore, fly in the face of the relevant provisions of article 3, which signal the

---

[5] A check is a draft drawn on a bank and payable on demand. § 3-104(2)(b). [Editor: *see now* U.C.C. § 3-104(f) (1991).]

continued vitality of the common law principles of accord and satisfaction.[9]

Although § 1-207 does not fit easily within the principles of article 3 that govern checks, the section has a close and harmonious connection with article 2. Article 2 regulates ongoing conduct relating to performance of contracts for the sale of goods. That article recurrently draws inferences from acquiescence in, or objection to, the performance tendered by one of the contracting parties. A course of performance "accepted or acquiesced in without objection" is relevant to a determination of the meaning of a contract sale. § 2-208(1). Between merchants, proposals for additional terms will be added to a contract of sale unless there is a timely "notification of objection." § 2-207(2)(c); *see* W. Grosse & E. Goggin, *supra*, 551. A buyer who is confronted by a defective tender of goods must make a seasonable objection or lose his right of rejection. §§ 2-602(1), 2-605, 2-606(1), 2-607(2); *Plateq Corporation v. Machlett Laboratories, Inc.*, 189 Conn. 433, 441–42, 456 A.2d 786 (1983); *Bead Chain Mfg. Co. v. Saxton Products, Inc.*, 183 Conn. 266, 270–72, 439 A.2d 314 (1981). In an installment sale, a party aggrieved by non-conformity or default that substantially impairs the value of

the contract as a whole will nonetheless have reinstated the contract "if he accepts a nonconforming installment without seasonably notifying of cancellation. . . ." § 2-612(3). A contract whose performance has become impracticable requires the buyer, after notification by the seller, to offer reasonable alternatives for the modification or the termination of the affected contract; the buyer's failure to respond, within a reasonable period of time, causes the sales contract to lapse. § 2-616(1), (2). In these and other related circumstances, article 2 urges the contracting parties to engage in a continuing dialogue about what will constitute acceptable performance of their sales contract. *See generally* J. White & R. Summers, *supra*, §§ 3–1 through 3–9. It is entirely consistent with this article 2 policy to provide, as does § 1-207, a statutory methodology for the effective communication of objections. *See* McDonnell, *Purposive Interpretation of the Uniform Commercial Code: Some Implications for Jurisprudence*, 126 U. Pa. L. Rev. 795, 828 (1978).

From the vantage point of article 2, it is apparent that § 1-207 contemplates a reservation of rights about some aspect of a possibly nonconforming tender of goods or services or payment in a situation where the aggrieved party may prefer not to terminate the underlying contract as a whole. *See, e.g., Cherwell-Ralli, Inc. v. Rytman Grain Co.*, 180 Conn. 714, 718, 433 A.2d 984 (1980); Grosse & Goggin, *supra*, 551; Rosenthal, *Discord and Satisfaction: Section 1-207 of the Uniform Commercial Code*, 78 Column. L. Rev. 48, 63 (1978). Indeed, the official comment to § 1-207 itself explains that the section supports ongoing contractual relations by providing "machinery for the continuation of performance along the lines contemplated by the contract despite a pending dispute." *See* Hawkland, *The Effect of U.C.C. § 1-207 on the Doctrine of Accord and Satisfaction by Conditional Check*, 74 Com. L.J. 329, 331 (1969). It is significant, furthermore, that the text of § 1-207 recurrently refers to "performance," for "performance" is a central aspect of the sales transaction governed by Article 2. By contrast, Article 3 instruments, which promise or order the payment of money, are not characteristically described as being performed by anyone. The contracts encapsulated in various forms of negotiable instruments instead envisage conduct of negotiation or transfer, indorsement or guaranty, payment or acceptance,

---

[9] An earlier version of the Uniform Commercial Code, prior to its enactment in this state, contained a provision, § 3-802(3), that would have permitted a check tendered in full satisfaction of an obligation to discharge an underlying obligation even when that obligation was undisputed and liquidated. Section 3-802(3) reads as follows:

> Where a check or similar payment instrument provides that it is in full satisfaction of an obligation the payee discharges the underlying obligation by obtaining payment of the instrument unless he establishes that the original obligor has taken unconscionable advantage in the circumstances.

It was deleted in 1952 "on the ground that it would work hardship and was open to abuse." Uniform Commercial Code, 1952 Official Draft (Sup. No. 1) p.25. None of the legislative history surrounding this section indicates that the draftsmen of Article 3 contemplated that § 1-207 would affect § 3-802(3). This conclusion is further buttressed by the fact that these two sections were never cross-referenced in the relevant Official Comments. *See* Rosenthal, *Discord and Dissatisfaction: Section 1-207 of the "Uniform Commercial Code*, 78 COLUM. L. REV. 48, 58–61 (1978).

and honor or dishonor. *See, e.g.* §§ 3-201, 3-413, 3-414, 3-416, 3-418; *see generally* J. White & R. Summers, *supra*, §§ 13-6 through 13-10, 13-12. We conclude, therefore, that, in circumstances like the present, when performance of a sales contract has come to an end, § 1-207 was not intended to empower a seller, as payee of a negotiable instrument, to alter that instrument by adding words of protest to a check tendered by a buyer on condition that it be accepted in full satisfaction of an unliquidated debt.

Our conclusion is supported by the emerging majority of cases in other jurisdictions. While the case law was divided five years ago, when we postponed resolution of the controversy about the meaning of § 1-207; *Kelly v. Kowalsky*, *supra*, 186 Conn. at 621-22, 442 A.2d 1355; it is now the view of the substantial majority of courts that

have addressed the issue that § 1-207 does not overrule the common law of accord and satisfaction. . . . The majority finds support as well in much of the recent scholarly commentary. . . .

Both under prevailing common law principles, and under the Uniform Commercial Code, the parties in this case negotiated a contract of accord whose satisfaction discharged the defendant from any further monetary obligation to the plaintiff. The plaintiff might have avoided this result by returning the defendant's check uncashed, but could not simultaneously disregard the condition on which the check was tendered and deposit its proceeds in the plaintiff's bank account.

There is error, the judgment is set aside and the case is remanded with direction to render judgment for the defendant.

In this opinion the other Justices concurred.

NOTE

U.C.C. Section 1-207 was amended in 1991. The section now provides that it does not apply to an accord and satisfaction. [U.C.C. § 1-207(2)]. This conclusion was reached specifically because of the unfairness felt to result from the approach of some courts to the effect of Section 1-207. These courts have held that an endorsement and deposit of a check bearing an indication that it is sent in final payment of a disputed amount due to the payee would amount to an accord and satisfaction. An endorsement indicating a reservation of rights, however, would counter the purpose of the check as an accord, i.e. an offer to create a new contract. The sender was left in limbo, unable to determine whether or not his offer has been accepted.

By requiring the existence of an accord and satisfaction to be determined in accordance with established common law principles, (U.C.C. § 1-103) as modified by U.C.C. Section 3-311, the dilemma of the good faith debtor in tendering a check in settlement of a disputed amount was resolved. Section 1-207(2) continues the common law approach. Courts will have to analyze the facts to determine whether an accord and satisfaction has occurred. Is the sending of a check in a lower amount an attempt to trick a creditor into accepting less than his due, or is the drawer merely "master of his offer" calling for acceptance and a resulting accord and satisfaction? Common law requires that an offer of an accord be made in "good faith." Thus, the amount allegedly due must not have been a liquidated sum, but one that was subject to a bona fide dispute. The accord is thus a bona fide offer to novate the existing relationship, and the satisfaction is an acceptance of this offer. *Stultz Electric Works v. Marine Hydraulic Engineering Co.*, 484 A.2d 1008 (Me. 1984). An indication that there is a reservation regarding the amount tendered clearly negates an acceptance or an *agreement* to modify the contractual relationship (*cf.* U.C.C. § 2-209). Thus, to hold automatically that by an endorsement and deposit of a check an accord and satisfaction had occurred would leave the creditor "at the mercy of the debtor facing the dilemma of either accepting the lesser amount in full settlement or returning the check and gambling his chances of collecting anything." *Inger Interiors v. Peralta*, 30 Ohio App. 3d 94, 98, 506 N.E.2d 1199, 1202–03 (1986); *AFC Interiors v. Dicello*, 46 Ohio St. 3d 1, 544 N.E.2d 869 (1989).

Underlying the common law approach is the existence of agreement. This involves an awareness of the nature of the tender as an accord. In *John Grier Constr. Co. v. Jones Welding & Repair, Inc.*, 238 Va. 270, 383 S.E.2d 719 (1989) the payee who deposited the check in his account had failed to notice that the check carried a notation "these monies reflect payment in full on the Carillon project." The court held not only that Section 1-207 had not displaced the common law of accord and satisfaction in the majority of jurisdictions, but also that there was no *accord* and thus there was no *satisfaction*, i.e., *acceptance*, of the check in full settlement.

U.C.C. Section 3-311(a) reenacts "the common law rule with some minor variations to reflect modern business conditions. . . . [It] is based on a belief that the common law rule produces a fair result and that informal dispute resolution by full satisfaction checks should be encouraged" (Comment 3 to § 3-311). Continuing the need for an accord to be made in "good faith," (U.C.C. § 3-103(a)(4)) the Section demands that the instrument or an accompanying written notice must state conspicuously (U.C.C. § 1-201(10)) that the instrument is tendered in full satisfaction of a claim that is unliquidated and is subject to a bona fide dispute.

Where the creditor is an organization (U.C.C. § 1-201(28)) it can protect itself against an accidental accord and satisfaction by delegating the determination whether to accept an accord to specific officers. A failure to do so, which could arise when checks are processed automatically without any examination, could result in an accord and satisfaction being implied from the facts. Sections 3-311(c) and 3-311(d) provide that if it can be shown that "an agent of the claimant having direct responsibility with respect to the disputed obligation knew that the instrument was tendered in full satisfaction of the claim, or received the instrument and any accompanying written communication," the creditor will be bound. (U.C.C. § 3-311(c), (d); *cf.* § 1-201(27)). The section goes on to require that the claimant indicate to debtors where, or to whom, a notice that a payment is tendered as an accord must be directed. This will obviate an accidental accord and satisfaction. Where the debtor is informed that the claim has been assigned to a bank or finance company, the notice must be sent to the assignee as "agent of the claimant." (U.C.C. § 3-311, Comment 8).

Should the creditor have received an instrument and deposited it or tendered it for acceptance without knowing (U.C.C. § 1-201(25)) that the debtor intended to offer an accord in satisfaction of the disputed claim, a tender of repayment made within ninety days will prevent the discharge of the debtor. (U.C.C. § 3-311(c)(2),(d)).

U.C.C. Section 3-311 is designed to favor neither an individual nor a business organization. Any one of them may be the claimant or the debtor. Where an economic disparity exists between the debtor and the claimant, however, a question of "good faith" or of "unconscionability" could arise. Examples would include an insurance company tendering a check in an amount clearly disproportionate to an alleged injury suffered but stating that it is tendered in full and final settlement of a claim to a claimant in economic need and thus unable to make a free determination whether to accept the offer. Another example would be where a seller tenders an instrument in an insignificant amount to settle a warranty claim. In these instances the question arises whether the accord is made in "observance of reasonable commercial standards of fair dealing." (U.C.C. § 3-103(a)(4)). A question of unconscionability also may arise. To provide a clear answer to this type of problem specific consumer legislation may be needed. Existing legislation and Federal Trade Commission rules do not deal with negotiable instruments received by a consumer *from* a commercial entity. (*See* Uniform Consumer Credit Code § 3.307; Federal Trade Commission Rule 433.1). This raises the further question whether an instrument should ever be used for reaching an extraneous agreement?

B.   Herein of "Good Faith" and "Ordinary Care"

Watseka First National Bank v. Ruda
135 Ill. 2d 140, 552 N.E.2d 775 (1990)

[This was an action based on a claim by payee bank to accelerate payment of notes given in connection with the bank funding certain farming operations by Ken Ward. The defendant, Ruda, had given an unlimited personal guarantee that the notes would be paid. These notes contained the following language: "If the holder deems itself insecure then at its option, without demand or notice of any kind, it may declare this note to be immediately due."

A severe drought greatly affected the crops, and as a result, Ken Ward realized yields far below that which he projected. In October of that year, a meeting was held between Ken Ward, Frank Ruda, and officers and attorneys of Watseka Bank. The parties apparently agreed that, because the proceeds from the sale of Ken Ward's crops would not be sufficient to satisfy his indebtedness to the banks, Frank Ruda would have to sell some of his farmland and apply the proceeds to the various notes. Subsequently, the bank accelerated the notes and demanded payment. The defendants raised the issue whether in accelerating the debt, the bank acted in good faith. The court recited U.C.C. § 1-208]

RYAN, J. . . . This Code section specifically permits the use of insecurity clauses, but allows creditors to exercise them only if they do so in good faith. There has been considerable debate, however, concerning what the term "good faith" means and whether it is properly measured subjectively or objectively.

The term "good faith" appears repeatedly in the U.C.C. [Section] § 1-203 states that every contract or duty within the scope of the Code has an obligation of good faith. (Ill. Rev. Stat. 1987, ch. 26 par. 1-203.) Other Code sections, such as § 1-208, and several within articles 2 and 3, specifically identify the obligation of the parties to act in good faith. Just what the term means, however, remains somewhat of a mystery. Its meaning, moreover, may change, depending upon the context in which it is used.

The concept of "good faith," under the Code, has been the subject of continued debate among the commentators. One has argued that the term "good faith" has no independent meaning, and can only be determined by excluding that which can be identified as "bad faith." (Summers, *"Good Faith" in General Contract Law and the Sales Provisions of the Uniform Commercial Code*, 54 Va. L. Rev. 195 (1968)). Another author criticizes this approach and concludes that, in order to learn what "good faith" means, "we need to consider the purposes that the concept serves in legal discourse." (Patterson, *Wittgenstein and the Code: A Theory Of Good Faith Performance and Enforcement Under Article Nine*, 137 U. Pa. L. Rev. 335, 371 (1988)). Another commentator traces the origin of the term as it became codified in the Code and identifies a distinction between "good faith purchase" and "good faith performance." (Farnsworth, *Good Faith Performance and Commercial Reasonableness Under the Uniform*

Commercial Code, 30 U. Chi. L. Rev. 666 (1963)).

In the article by Professor Patterson cited above, it is suggested that "good faith," as used in article 1 of the Code, implies a subjective standard, whereas that term, as used in article 2, implies an objective standard. Section 1-201(19) defines good faith as follows: "'Good faith' means honesty in fact in the conduct or transaction concerned." Whereas § 2-103(1) defines good faith as follows: "'Good Faith' in the case of a merchant means honesty in fact and the observance of reasonable commercial standards of fair dealing in the trade." The 1950 draft of the Code did not contain a separate standard of good faith for merchants. In that draft, the good faith definition in article 1, in addition to the honesty in fact definition it now contains, also included the reasonable commercial standards provisions now found in article 2. From this difference in language and the history of the development of the Code, commentators have concluded that, as used in article 1, good faith is to be determined by a subjective test, whereas in article 2 that term implies an objective test. (137 U. Pa. L. Rev. at 380–81). As it presently appears in the Code, § 1-208, which provides that a party may accelerate only if he, in "good faith," believes the prospect of payment or performance is impaired, is governed by the definition of "good faith" as defined in article 1. "[H]onesty in fact in the conduct or transaction concerned," as noted, the

definition in article 1, makes no mention of the commercial reasonableness standard. (Ill. Rev. Stat. ch. 26, par. 1-201(19)). We construe this to mean that § 1-208 permits a creditor to accelerate a debt pursuant to an insecurity clause if that creditor has an honest belief, based on whatever information it has, that the ability of the debtor to repay the debt has in some way become impaired.

This test, which at least one court has termed "the pure heart and empty head" test, appears potentially draconian "because of the great latitude it gives the creditor and the onerous burden of proof it imposes on the debtor." (*Black v. Peoples Bank & Trust Co.*, 437 So.2d 26, 29 (Miss. 1983)). [37 U.C.C. Rep. Serv. 641]. While the debtor's burden of proof may be difficult because the debtor must delve into the creditor's state of mind, the burden is not impossible. That is, the debtor may successfully establish lack of good faith by proving that the creditor did not have possession of the information that the creditor contends caused the acceleration. (Comment, *Standards For Insecurity Acceleration Under Section 1-208 Of The Uniform Commercial Code: A Proposal For Reform*, 13 U. Mich. J.L. Ref. 623, 642 (1980)). Similarly, the debtor can establish that the creditor had possession of the information that it asserts caused it to accelerate at the time the loan was made and, as such, the creditor cannot honestly feel less secure than it did when the loan was made.

NOTE

Every contract or duty within this Act imposes an obligation of good faith in its performance or enforcement. [U.C.C. § 1-203].[14]

In addition to this general statement, numerous sections of the U.C.C. make specific the requirement of "good faith" as a predicate to rights, duties and defenses. U.C.C. Section 1-201(19) defines "good faith" as "honesty in fact in the conduct or transaction concerned." This subjective approach attempts to inquire only into the state of mind and belief of a party—but not the reasonableness of such state of mind or belief (the so-called "pure heart and empty head" rule). Yet, how can a subjective state of mind be determined other than through some objective indicia?

---

[14] Compare Restatement of Contracts (Second) Section 205, which provides: "Every contract imposes upon each party a duty of good faith and fair dealing in its performance and enforcement." It is generally agreed that this obligation cannot be disclaimed. Such disclaimer would be contrary to public policy. *See also* U.C.C. § 4-103(a).

Every act, therefore, has to be examined relative to the agreement of the parties. This introduces an objective test. The problem remains, however, in that further objective indicia are needed to answer whether a required subjective state of mind existed or was absent.

Section 2-103 (1)(b), dealing with a sale of goods[15] provides that where the good faith of a merchant is in issue, it "means honesty in fact and the observance of *reasonable commercial standards of fair dealing in the trade*." (emphasis added). This restriction to "reasonable commercial standards of fair dealing in the trade" is a logical step from the definition of a merchant as "a person who deals in goods of the kind or otherwise by his occupation holds himself out as having knowledge or skill peculiar to the practices or goods involved in the transaction or to whom such knowledge or skill may be attributed." (Section 2-104(a)). It is a restriction, however, in that it introduces a specific objective standard only applicable to a *merchant*.

Recent amendments of the Uniform Commercial Code expanded the definition of good faith by requiring not only honesty in fact but also *"the observance of reasonable commercial standards of fair dealing."*[16] Although this adds some element of objectivity to the determination of the subjective state of mind of a party, the inclusion of *commercial standards* is a matter of concern. Even though courts have the power to decide that a commercial standard is not reasonable, it is not clear whether a court could decide that the commercial standard, though reasonable when applied to one steeped in the knowledge or practice of commerce, ought not to be imposed in the circumstance because the target of the inquiry is not involved in commerce. If such determination is made and the reasonable commercial standard is held inapplicable, what standard should be applied to give effect to the objective indicia of the subjective state of mind? Deletion of the term "Commercial" has been recommended by an ABA Task Force appointed to review Article 1.

This calls for an analysis of all objective indicia relevant to the agreement to determine whether good faith exists or has been negated. In such analysis, it must be kept in mind that a party may act stupidly or even negligently and still be acting in good faith, provided such party acted honestly. Secondly, the converse of "good faith" is "bad faith," a concept involving deliberation or scienter, including recklessness and not caring whether the action or non-action is wrongful.[17]

Under the conventional approach to "good faith," the existence of "suspicious circumstances" does not negate good faith.[18] But, "there is no inherent inconsistency between a subjective standard of good faith and a reasonable inquiry into the actual known circumstances surrounding [the transaction] . . . if a party fails to make an inquiry for the

---

[15] *See also,* U.C.C.-Article 2A Leases § 2A-103(3).

[16] *See* U.C.C. §§ 3-103(a)(4), 4-104(c), 4A-105(a)(6).

[17] "Bad faith is not mere carelessness. It is nothing less than guilty knowledge or willful ignorance . . . [the purchaser] is not bound at his peril to be upon the alert for circumstances which might possibly excite the suspicion of wary vigilance." Matthysse v. Securities Processing Servs., Inc., 358 F. Supp. 1009, 1021–22 (S.D.N.Y. 1977); *but see* Ernst & Ernst v. Hochfelder, 425 U.S. 185 n.12 (1976) ("In certain areas of the law recklessness is considered to be a form of intentional conduct for purposes of imposing liability for some act."). *See also* Derry v. Peek, 14 App. Cas. 337 (H.L. 1889).

[18] The U.C.C. purports to reject Gill v. Cubitt, 3 B & C 466, 10 Eng. Rep. 215 (1824).

purpose of remaining ignorant of facts which he fears would disclose a defect in the transaction, he may be found to have acted in bad faith."[19] The test appears to be whether there was actual knowledge of some fact which would have led a reasonable person to walk away from the transaction.[20]

Introducing an objective standard of "fair dealing" does not signal a change in the approach taken by many courts to the issue of good faith. When dealing with professionals, courts in applying U.C.C. Section 1-203 have adopted a broad approach. By adding, either through Section 1-103 or independent thereof, a common law concept of decency, fairness, fair dealing or reasonableness in performance or enforcement, they applied an objective standard.[21]

U.C.C. Section 1-203 has been construed to "superimpose a general requirement of fundamental integrity in commercial transactions regulated by the U.C.C." *Skeel v. Universal CIT Credit Corp.*, 355 F.2d 846, 851 (3d Cir. 1964); *Preston v. U.S.*, 696 F.2d 528 (7th Cir. 1982). The section thus would require an analysis of "the question of fairness and reasonableness independently of the Code." *Zapatha v. Dairy Mart, Inc.*, 381 Mass. 284, 408 N.E.2d 1370, n.16 (1980). As a result, courts have tended to imply a "warranty of good faith and fair dealing" much broader than the subjective test of inquiry into "honesty in fact." *E.F. Hutton & Co., Inc. v. City National Bank*, 37 U.C.C. Rep. Serv. (Callaghan) 823, 835 (Cal. App. 1983); *Best v. United States Nat'l Bank*, 78 Or. App. 1, 714 P.2d 1049, 1054 (1986) (excessive charge widely exceeding bank's cost can constitute a breach of the bank's implied covenant of good faith and fair dealing). The present approach, where the relationship of a bank to its customer is involved, appears additionally to generate a possible fiduciary obligation in the bank. *K.M.C., Inc. v. Irving Trust Co.*, 757 F.2d 752, 760 (6th Cir. 1985) (bank cannot terminate financing without notice to borrower). But note *Copesky v. The Superior Court of San Diego County*, 229 Cal. App. 3d 678, 280 Cal. Rptr. 338 (1991) (rejecting that banks act as fiduciaries in relation to a commercial checking account.)

As a result, such objective test does not change the approach of the law but calls for an analysis of factual situations. A consistent failure by a person engaged in commerce to abide by reasonable commercial standards defining ordinary care could be held to show that there was evidence of "bad faith." Thus, "bad faith may [still] be evidenced by a consistent failure by banks to monitor and investigate a series of irregular transactions."[22]

It is in relation to the non-commercial person that the objective indicia are likely to lead to an application of the general mores and public policy in a determination based on the facts involved in the transaction. There is at present a gap in the existing definitions of good faith that only a case by case analysis can fill.

---

[19] Funding Consultants, Inc. v. Aetna Cas. & Sur. Co., ___ Conn. Supp. ___ , 477 A.2d 1163, (1982). Hollywood Nat'l Bank. v. I.B.M., 38 Cal. App. 2d 607, 614, 113 Cal. Rptr. 494, 498 ("the protection afforded the bona fide purchaser . . . does not yet permit persons seeking such status to refuse to see what is before their eyes.").

[20] Chemical Bank of Rochester v. Haskell, 51 N.Y.2d 85, 411 N.E.2d 1339 (1980); Bankers Trust Co. of Western New York v. Crawford, 781 F.2d 39 (3d Cir. 1986); Banco Di Roma v. Merchants Banks, 459 N.Y.S.2d 592 (N.Y. App. Div. 1983).

[21] *See* Note, *Tort Remedies for Breach of Contract: The Expansion of Tortious Breach of the Implied Covenant of Good Faith and Fair Dealing Into the Commercial Realm*, 86 COLUM. L. REV. 377 (1986).

[22] Kraftsman Container Corp. v. United Counties Trust Co., 404 A.2d 1288 (N.Y. 1979).

The analysis here is closely related to attempts by French jurists to define the concept of *abus de droit*. Josserand[23] argues that the exercise of a right must be governed by its conformity with the social purpose of the rule of law which creates the right. Law is for the benefit of the community and not for the advantage of the individual and there is an abuse of rights whenever a right is exercised in a manner contrary to the social interest.[24]

The approach here outlined just falls short of a need to determine whether an action was unconscionable.[25] Unconscionability, or overreaching, involves an action so egregious as to offend the social conscience of society.[26] An absence of good faith does not indicate an effect as far reaching. Thus, an unconscionable act involves scienter, while a failure to prove the existence of good faith does not require a determination that a party acted unconscionably. If it can be shown that a party has acted unconscionably, however, it is clear that there was a lack of good faith.

A number of sections of the Code impose not only a requirement of good faith, but also compliance with a duty of care measured by the "reasonable commercial standards" of the actor's business.[27] In relation to revised Articles 3 and 4, this has been replaced by calling for the exercise of "ordinary care."[28]

"Ordinary care" in the case of a person engaged in business means observance of reasonable commercial standards, prevailing in the area in which the person is located, with respect to the business in which the person is engaged. In the case of a bank that takes an instrument for processing for collection or payment by automated means, reasonable commercial standards do not require the bank to examine the instrument if the failure to examine does not violate the bank's prescribed procedures and the bank's procedures do not vary unreasonably from general banking usage not disapproved by this Article or Article 4. [U.C.C. § 3-103(a)(7)].

Article 4 - Bank Deposits and Collection governs persons "engaged in the business of banking, including a savings bank, savings and loan associations, credit union, or trust company" [U.C.C. § 4-105(1)][29] and imposes a general duty of ordinary care. Although prohibiting any disclaimer of responsibility for lack of good faith or failure to exercise

---

[23] De l'esprit des droits et de leur relativité (2° ed. Paris 1939) N° 292.

[24] In this country, this controversy was recently highlighted by the decision of Judge Easterbrook in Kham & Nate Shoes No.2, Inc. v. First Bank of Whiting, 908 F.2d 1351 (7th Cir. 1990) and an article by Professor Patterson, *A Fable from the Seventh Circuit: Frank Easterbrook on Good Faith*, 76 IOWA L. REV. 1 (1991).

[25] *Cf.* U.C.C. § 2-302(1).

[26] See Williams v. Walker-Thomas Furniture Co., 350 F.2d 445 (D.C. Cir.1965).

[27] For example:
U.C.C. § 5-109(1) (issuer of a letter of credit—"observance of any general banking usage").
U.C.C. § 7-404 (bailee—"reasonable commercial standards").
U.C.C. § 8-318 (agent or bailee—"observance of reasonable commercial standards if he is in the business of buying selling or otherwise dealing with securities").
U.C.C. § 9-318(2) (modification of assigned security agreement—made "in accordance with reasonable commercial standards").

[28] For example: U.C.C. § 3-406(a), compare prior U.C.C. § 3-406(1).

[29] *See also* U.C.C. § 4A-105(a).

ordinary care, the article allows the parties by agreement to determine "the standards by which the bank's responsibility is to be measured if those standards are not manifestly unreasonable."[30]

Whether a commercial standard governing "fair dealing" or relating to "ordinary care" is reasonable, will depend on the context. The standards are in each case directed to different aspects of commercial conduct and thus require an analysis of the facts. This resolution rejects the approach of some courts that a failure to sight check an item would amount to negligence as a matter of law.[31] In light of automation and truncation,[32] such an approach is inconsistent with technological developments that benefit both the customer as well as the drawee bank.[33]

---

[30] U.C.C. § 4-103(a).

[31] *See* Medford Irrigation District v. Western Bank, 676 P.2d 329 (Or. App. 1984). The bank argued that its failure to examine the check and to discover the forged signature of its customer-drawer was due to its computerized system automatically paying *all* checks below $5000-a practice generally accepted in the banking community. The court in rejecting this argument found the bank negligent as a matter of law in failing to exercise ordinary care. The court went on to hold that a practice not to examine *any* checks below $5,000 did not reflect a "reasonable commercial standard."

[32] Truncation takes various forms. In partial truncation the drawee bank does not return paid items to the drawer; in many instances the drawee bank will even pay an item before having the item physically exhibited to it. U.C.C. § 4-110. In total truncation the item does not leave a depository institution and presentment is made electronically by Electronic Data Interchange (EDI). *See* U.C.C. §§ 3-501(b)(2), 4-110, 4-406(b).

[33] In addition to the cost savings, note the effects of the Expedited Funds Availability Act, 12 U.S.C. §§ 4001–4010 and Regulation CC, 12 C.F.R. §§ 229.1-229.42 (1991).

K.M.C. Co., Inc. v. Irving Trust Company
757 F.2d 752 (6th Cir. 1985)

CORNELIA G. KENNEDY, Circuit Judge.

Irving Trust Company (Irving) appeals from a judgment entered against it in this diversity action for breach of a financing agreement. K.M.C. is a Tennessee corporation headquartered in Knoxville and engaged in the wholesale and retail grocery business. In 1979, Irving and K.M.C. entered into a financing agreement, whereby Irving held a security interest in all of K.M.C.'s accounts receivable and inventory and provided K.M.C. a line of credit to a maximum of $3.0 million, increased one year to $3.5 million at a lower rate of interest, subject to a formula based on a percentage of the value of the inventory plus eligible receivables. On March 1, 1982, Irving refused to advance $800,000 requested by K.M.C. This amount would have increased the loan balance to just under the $3.5 million limit. K.M.C. contends that Irving's refusal without prior notice to advance the requested funds breached a duty of good faith performance implied in the agreement and ultimately resulted in the collapse of the company as a viable business entity. Irving's defense is that on March 1, 1982, K.M.C. was already collapsing, and that Irving's decision not to advance funds was made in good faith and in the reasonable exercise of its discretion under the agreement.

Trial was conducted by a Magistrate on consent of the parties pursuant to 28 U.S.C. § 636(c). Although the financing agreement contained a jury trial waiver clause, the Magistrate ordered a jury trial over defendant's objection. He based his decision upon the statement on plaintiff's president Leonard Butler, that Butler was told by a representative of Irving prior to signing the agreement that absent fraud, which was not present in the instant case, the waiver provision would not be enforced. The jury found Irving liable for breach of contract and fixed damages at

$7,500,000 plus pre-judgment interest. Defendant's motions to dismiss and for a directed verdict and post-trial motions for judgment n.o.v., a new trial or a remittitur were denied.

Irving has raised several issues on appeal. . . . Third, it argues that it did not in fact breach the financing agreement with K.M.C., and that the jury's verdict is not supportable in law and is contrary to the weight of the evidence. Finally, it asserts that the Magistrate erred in admitting incompetent expert testimony on the question of damages.

* * *

III. Liability

Irving contends that the Magistrate erred in instructing the jury with respect to its obligations under the financing agreement, that K.M.C. failed to sustain its burden of showing that Irving acted in bad faith and that the jury's verdict was against the weight of the evidence. We conclude that the jury instructions were not in error and that the jury's verdict was supported by substantial evidence.

A. Instructions

The essence of the Magistrate's instruction to the jury was that there is implied in every contract an obligation of good faith; that this obligation may have imposed on Irving a duty to give notice to K.M.C. before refusing to advance funds under the agreement up to the $3.5 million limit; and that such notice would be required if necessary to the proper execution of the contract, unless Irving's decision to refuse to advance funds without prior notice was made in good faith and in the reasonable exercise of its discretion. Irving contends that the instruction with respect to notice gave undue emphasis to K.M.C.'s theory of the case and was an erroneous explanation of its contractual obligations, in that the decision whether to advance funds under the financing agreement was solely within the bank's prerogative. It reasons further that an implied requirement that the bank provide a period of notice before discontinuing financing up to the maximum credit limit would be inconsistent with the provision in the agreement that all monies loaned are repayable on demand.

As part of the procedure established for the operation of the financing agreement, the parties agreed in a supplementary letter that all receipts

of K.M.C. would be deposited into a "blocked account" to which Irving would have sole access. Consequently, unless K.M.C. obtained alternative financing, a refusal by Irving to advance funds would leave K.M.C. without operating capital until it had payed down its loan. The record clearly established that a medium-sized company in the wholesale grocery business, such as K.M.C., could not operate without outside financing. Thus, the literal interpretation of the financing agreement urged upon us by Irving, as supplemented by the "blocked account" mechanism, would leave K.M.C.'s continued existence entirely at the whim or mercy of Irving, absent an obligation of good faith performance. Logically, at such time as Irving might wish to curtail financing K.M.C., as was its right under the agreement, this obligation to act in good faith would require a period of notice to K.M.C. to allow it a reasonable opportunity to seek alternate financing, absent valid business reasons precluding Irving from doing so. Hence, we find that the Magistrate's instructions were an accurate statement of the applicable law. *See Wells v. Alexandre*, 130 N.Y. 642, 29 N.E. 142, 143 (1891) ("[I]f a notice was requisite to its proper execution, a covenant to give such notice will be inferred, for any other construction would make the contract unreasonable, and place one of the parties entirely at the mercy of the other." (citation omitted)); *cf.* U.C.C. § 2-309 comment 8 ("[T]he application of principles of good faith and sound commercial practice normally call for such notification of the termination of a going contract relationship as will give the other party reasonable time to seek a substitute arrangement.").

Irving cites *Grandin Industries, Inc. v. Florida National Bank*, 267 So.2d 26 (Dist. Ct. App. Fla. 1972), and *Midlantic National Bank v. Commonwealth General Ltd.*, 386 So.2d 31 (Dist. Ct. App. Fla. 1980), for the proposition that it had no legal obligation to advance funds under the financing agreement. These cases are distinguishable on a number of grounds. First, in neither case did the Florida court consider the possibility of a good faith limitation on the bank's discretion. Nor is it clear that the exercise of absolute discretion under the agreements in question conferred on the banks the same power over the continued existence of the debtors as in the instant case. Second, in neither case had there been a consistent and uninterrupted course of dealing between the parties over an extended period of time as in the instant case. It does not appear that the agreement in *Grandin* established any specific line of credit or eligibility formula, or that the ongoing financing of a high volume, capital intensive business was contemplated. *Midlantic* involved a line of credit secured by personal certificates of deposit, for which there was no written agreement and which was merely supplementary to numerous loans already outstanding from the bank to the debtor. Finally, we note that the Irving-K.M.C. agreement is governed by New York law. To the extent that our decision may be inconsistent with *Grandin* and *Midlantic,* we find them not to be controlling.

Nor are we persuaded by Irving's reasoning with respect to the effect of the demand provision in the agreement. We agree with the Magistrate that just as Irving's discretion whether or not to advance funds is limited by an obligation of good faith performance, so too would be its power to demand repayment. The demand provision is a kind of acceleration clause, upon which the Uniform Commercial Code and the courts have imposed limitations of reasonableness and fairness. *See* U.C.C. § 1-208; *Brown v. AVEMCO Investment Corp.*, 603 F.2d 1367, 1375–80 (9th Cir. 1979). The Magistrate did not err in refusing the requested charge on the demand provision.

Irving did not object to the good faith portion of the Magistrate's instruction. Nevertheless, on appeal it suggests for the first time that before liability can be imposed, the proof must establish not only abuse of discretion but also bad faith, which it defines as synonymous with dishonesty. Even if such an argument were timely at this stage in the proceedings, which it is not, none of the cases cited by Irving are on point. In *Awrey v. Progressive Casualty Insurance Co.*, 728 F.2d 352 (6th Cir. 1984), and *Gordon v. Nationwide Mutual Insurance Co.*, 30 N.Y.S.2d 601 (1972), the courts held that showing of actual bad faith would be necessary in the limited situation in which an insured sought to impose liability of an insurer in excess of policy limits. In fact, in *Gordon* the court specifically restates the familiar principle that "in every contract 'there exists an implied covenant of good faith and fair dealing' (*Kirke La Shelle Co. v. Armstrong Co.*, 263 N.Y. 79, 87, 188 N.E. 163, 167)." 30 N.Y.2d at 437, 334 N.Y.S.2d at 608. Irving also relies upon *Winner Corp. v. H.A. Caesar & Co.*, 511 F.2d 1010 (6th Cir. 1975), a bankruptcy appeal involving an agreement under which Caesar purchased Winner's accounts receivable and was allowed to retain a reserve to protect itself against claims, returns and allowances. Although *Winner* bears a closer resemblance to the instant case than *Awrey* and *Gordon*, we do not understand the court's opinion, that the reserve could not be invaded by Winner unless there was present bad faith as well as an abuse of discretion, to have been intended as a general statement of law. We conclude that the abuse of discretion standard under which the issue of liability was decided in the trial below was the correct one to apply in this instance.

B. Sufficiency of the Evidence

In diversity cases we look to the law of the state whose substantive law governs the action in determining whether there is sufficient evidence to support the jury's verdict. *Arms v. State Farm & Casualty Co.*, 731 F.2d 1245, 1248–49 & n.2 (6th Cir. 1984), *Gold v. National Savings Bank of the City of Albany*, 641 F.2d 430, 434 & n.3 (6th Cir.), *cert. denied*, 454 U.S. 826, 102 S. Ct. 116, 70 L.Ed. 2d 100 (1981). Under New York law, we may not set aside the jury's verdict unless the evidence so preponderates in favor of Irving that it is clear that the jury did not reach its conclusion on a fair interpretation of the evidence, or a contrary conclusion is the only reasonable one inferable from the proven facts. *Billiar v. Minnesota Mining & Manufacturing Co.*, 623 F.2d 240, 247–48 (2d Cir. 1980).

Irving contends that the sole factor determinative of whether it acted in good faith is whether it, through its loan officer Sarokin, *believed* that there existed valid reasons for not advancing funds to K.M.C. on March 1, 1982. It quotes *Blaine v. G.M.A.C.*, 82 Misc. 2d 653, 655, 370 N.Y.S.2d 323, 327 (1975), for the proposition that under applicable New York law, it is the bank's "actual mental state" that is decisive. The Magistrate observed that there was competent evidence that a personality conflict had developed between Sarokin and Butler of K.M.C. He suggested that the jury may have concluded that Sarokin abused his discretion in refusing without notice to advance funds despite knowing that he was fully secured because of his disapproval of Butler's management philosophy.

Were the outcome of this case solely dependent upon Sarokin's subjective state of mind, we might feel constrained, despite the conclusions of the

Magistrate above, to hold that the evidence was insufficient to support the verdict.[11] However, to a certain extent the conduct of Irving must be measured by objective standards. While it is not necessary that Sarokin have been correct in his understanding of the facts and circumstances pertinent to his decision not to advance funds for this court to find that he made a valid business judgment in doing so, there must at least be some objective basis upon which a reasonable loan officer in the exercise of his discretion would have acted in that manner.[12]

The court in *Blaine* did state that

[t]he test as to the *good faith* of the creditor in accelerating under an insecurity clause is a matter of the creditor's actual mental state and this is not negatived by showing there was no basis for the creditor's belief, *Sheppard Federal Credit Union v. Palmer* [408 F.2d 1369 (5th Cir. 1969)], supra, and it is immaterial whether the information upon which the creditor based his determination was in fact not true or the creditor was negligent in not examining to determine whether it was true. *VanHorn v. Van de Wol, Inc.*, 6 Wash.App.2d 959, 497 P.2d 252 (1972).

370 N.Y.S.2d at 327 (emphasis added). However, this definition followed the court's statement that "[t]he criterion for permissible acceleration . . . has the *dual* elements of (1) *whether a reasonable man would have accelerated the debt under the circumstances*, and (2) whether the creditor acted in good faith." *Id.* (emphasis added) (citation omitted). There is ample evidence in the record to support a jury finding that no reasonable loan officer in the same situation would have refused

to advance funds to K.M.C. without notice as Sarokin did on March 1, 1982.

James Kuharski was executive vice president and manager of secured lending activities for Irving, and two levels above Sarokin in Irving's management hierarchy. Kuharski acknowledged that Irving owed its clients a duty of good faith, that it was not a policy of Irving to terminate financing without notice, and that if Sarokin believed that Irving was adequately secured he would not have been acting in accordance with that duty of good faith to have refused without notice to advance funds to K.M.C.

William Calloway was president of the Park National Bank in Knoxville, which was the depository bank for K.M.C.'s "blocked account" and a 20% participant with Irving in the financing agreement. He also acknowledged that he believed that there is a duty of good faith from a banker to his client that would require a period of notice prior to termination of financing if a loan was well secured. He testified further that on March 1, he believed that the loan to K.M.C. was fully secured as to both interest and principal, and *that any reasonable banker looking at the loan would agree that it was fully secured.*

Gerald Connolly was an attorney in Milwaukee, Wisconsin, one of whose clients was a large wholesaler named Gateway Foods. In response to a call from Butler on March 1, Gateway's president requested that Connolly assist K.M.C. in any way he could. Connolly testified that pursuant to that request he called Sarokin, who acknowledged in their conversation that Irving was adequately secured and that terminating financing would destroy K.M.C., and that Sarokin ultimately agreed to advance the funds requested by K.M.C., in part to give Connolly the opportunity to come to Knoxville and evaluate K.M.C. for the purpose of acquisition by Gateway Foods. Connolly testified that he called Irving the next day enroute to Knoxville and was told by a subordinate that Sarokin had changed his mind about advancing funds, and that in a telephone conversation that night Sarokin stated that he had changed his mind and decided to "proceed with his game plan."

In fact, counsel for Irving conceded in his summation to the jury that the bank was adequately secured on March 1, 1982. He argued, however, that what is important is not the amount of security, but the capacity of the debtor to pay back the loan. The jury was entitled to find that a

---

[11] We do not understand the Magistrate to have relied upon this point alone. Rather, as we read his opinion, the alleged personality conflict between Butler and Sarokin was cited as just one of several relevant factors that may have persuaded the jury.

[12] While the appellee suggests in its brief that the Magistrate charged the jury on a wholly subjective standard, we do not read the charge that way. The jury was charged "that what is important *in connection with the requirement of good faith* is the actual mental state of the officers and agents of Irving Trust." The definition of an arbitrary and capricious decision that followed, as one "having no rational basis," is consonant with our analysis.

reasonable notice period would not change the ability of K.M.C. to pay the loan. The nature of the security was such that the loan would rapidly be payed down on demand. Irving's quarterly audits and other memoranda regarding K.M.C. consistently stated that the strength of its position was in the inventory, which was readily marketable. As late as two months before the events in question, the quarterly audit had concluded that even in the event of a liquidation of the company no loss would be sustained by Irving.

Generally, there was ample evidence in the record from which the jury could have concluded that March 1 simply was not that unusual a day in the history of the relationship between Irving and K.M.C. Such factors as payables and receivables, cited by Sarokin as the basis for his conclusion that K.M.C. was in a state of financial collapse, were closely monitored by Irving. Moreover, three days later, on March 4, Sarokin agreed to advance $700,000 to K.M.C., increasing its outstanding balance to $3.3 million. While the evidence was in conflict whether K.M.C.'s overall financial condition was deteriorating or improving, there is ample evidence belying Irving's characterization that on March 1, Sarokin was faced with a sudden crisis of unprecedented proportions. On this basis alone, the jury could have found that Irving did not fulfill its obligation of good faith performance to K.M.C. when it cut off financing without prior notice.

Irving also argues that it was entitled to a directed verdict on the ground that Sarokin reasonably believed that even if he advanced the $800,000 requested on March 1, K.M.C.'s checks to its suppliers would bounce in significant number and amount and K.M.C. would fold anyway. The events of March 1 were triggered by K.M.C.'s request the previous Friday for an extension of its line of credit to $4 million. Sarokin testified that he believed that K.M.C. would have required this extension, in addition to its request for $800,000 up to its $3.5 million line, to cover all of its outstanding checks. The evidence was substantially in conflict on whether with the $800,000 all of K.M.C.'s checks would have been honored when presented. The jury, by its verdict, resolved this fact issue in favor of K.M.C. In awarding damages to K.M.C. it found that Irving's breach caused K.M.C.'s injury. Irving does not object that the jury was improperly charged on causation. It necessarily follows from the jury's award

of damages to the plaintiff that it found that checks would not have bounced. There was ample evidence in the record from which the jury could have so found. However, the question of whether checks in fact would have bounced is distinct from the question of whether Sarokin reasonably could have believed that they would bounce. On the record before us we do not think that the jury could find that Sarokin could not reasonably have held such a belief. Therefore, the question that we must address is whether such a belief in itself would constitute a valid business reason for Irving to refuse to advance the funds requested by K.M.C. without prior notice. We hold, on the particular facts before us, that it would not.

Whether or not the $800,000 requested would have been sufficient to cover all of K.M.C.'s outstanding checks, Sarokin's abrupt refusal to advance funds to K.M.C. on March 1 amounted to a unilateral decision on his part to wind up the company. If Sarokin had agreed to advance the $800,000 but no more, and checks still had bounced, we would have a different case. But, given that Sarokin knew or should have known that the bank was adequately secured, and that if adequately secured it was Irving's policy that some period of notice would be due before financing was denied, Sarokin's action could only be justified if in some way he reasonably believed that it was necessary to protect the bank's interests. There was ample evidence—in particular, the conclusion of Irving's auditors that no losses would be sustained by the bank in the event of liquidation, and Sarokin's decision on March 4 to advance almost the full amount requested just three days earlier, despite the fact the K.M.C. was in much worse condition because of the intervening damage to its credit standing—from which the jury could have concluded that Sarokin had no such reason in mind and hence that his action was arbitrary and capricious.

Finally, Irving contends that even if a period of notice were required, it would be unreasonable to impose upon it an obligation to continue financing K.M.C. for the length of time that would have been necessary to arrange alternative financing or a sale of the company. If Irving had given K.M.C. 30 days, 7 days, even 48 hours notice, we would be facing a different case.[13] However, no notice was given. Until Sarokin told Butler on the phone the afternoon of March 1 that the $800,000 requested would not be advanced, not even Calloway of the Park Bank or Lipson,

---

[13] If during that period a tentative commitment was made with respect to a sale or alternative financing, since either of those once completed would result in the immediate repayment of Irving's loan, it might well be that it would be arbitrary and capricious for Irving to terminate financing at the expiration of the notice period if that period was insufficient to permit completion of the contemplated transaction.

who had been sent down to Knoxville by Sarokin the previous Friday to gather information, both of whom lunched with Butler immediately before the call to New York, had any inkling that Sarokin might act as he did. Based upon the reasoning above, whether alternative financing could have been found or a sale arranged is pertinent to causation rather than whether Sarokin acted reasonably and in good faith, and there was ample evidence in the record from which the jury could find that either would have been impossible.

* * *

The judgment is affirmed.

Copesky v. The Superior Court of San Diego County
229 Cal. App. 3d 678, 280 Cal. Rptr. 338 (1991)

PROCEEDINGS for writ of mandate to review a ruling of the Superior Court of San Diego County.

FROEHLICH, J.

This petition seeks review of the sustaining without leave to amend of a demurrer to one cause of action of petitioner's complaint. The cause so terminated was entitled, and is properly characterized as, "Breach of the Implied Covenant of Good Faith and Fair Dealing." By means of this cause of action the petitioner sought to recover tort damages because of the real party in interest bank's wrongful cashing of checks drawn without proper signature. The allegations of the complaint were obviously drawn so as to bring the action within the rationale of this court's decision in *Commercial Cotton Co. v. United California Bank*, 163 Cal.App.3d 511 (1985) (hereinafter *Commercial Cotton*). In argument before the superior court, counsel for petitioner contended the case was controlled by *Commercial Cotton*, and indeed that his case was "a mirror image of *Commercial Cotton*."

The trial court responded "*Commercial Cotton* is flat out wrong. . . . I don't think our appellate court is going to uphold the decision they took in *Commercial Cotton* back in 1985. I don't think they would do that in this case." The principal category of argument in the petitioner's brief is entitled "The sole issue is whether *Commercial Cotton* remains viable." While this pithy characterization of the issue is perhaps more abbre-

viated than would become an appellate court, it accurately goes right to the point. . . .

1. Factual and Procedural Background

Petitioner is an individual doing business as Torrey Pines Chiropractic Clinic. Petitioner maintained an ordinary commercial checking account with real party in interest bank. Checks from the account were authorized upon the signature only of petitioner or his wife. Over a period of some 18 months, from March 1987 through September 1988, a number of checks with forged signatures were presented to the bank; all checks were in denominations under $1,000. The forgeries were accomplished by petitioner's bookkeeper, using his signature stamp. Petitioner's failure to discover the forgeries over the period of 18 months was the result of the absence of his wife from the business for that period of time, the wife being the person who customarily supervised the bookkeeper's activities. The total of improperly withdrawn funds was $32,913.

The bank was negligent in cashing the checks by failing to require identification from the bookkeeper when the checks were presented, and also by accepting checks executed with a signature stamp rather than manual signature. Petitioner alleged that the checks constituted obvious forgeries which the bank reasonably should have noted. When petitioner reported the forgeries to the bank it refused to redeposit the lost funds, asserting a one-year statute of limitations on petitioner's claim as well as the contention that the bank had not been negligent in failing to discover the forgeries. Each of these defenses, petitioner contends, was without merit and constituted "stonewalling."

In addition to stating causes of action for breach of the contractual terms of the deposit agreement and for negligence, petitioner stated a "textbook" cause of action for "breach of the implied covenant of good faith and fair dealing."[2] The principal allegations of this cause of action are as follows:

Petitioner and the bank, in entering upon the contract were in inherently unequal bargaining positions and the bank dictated the terms of the contract;

Petitioner's motivation for entering into the agreement was strictly nonprofit and was to secure "peace of mind, security and protection of . . . funds;"

Ordinary contract damages would be inadequate;

Petitioner was particularly vulnerable because his funds were placed at the disposal of the bank, and a "special quasi-fiduciary relationship existed between [petitioner] and [bank]" which resulted in a duty of good faith and fair dealing;

This duty was breached when the bank refused to recredit the account but instead interposed "stonewalling" defenses without any reasonable belief in their validity;

This intentionally tortious action on the bank's part warrants the imposition of punitive damages.

A general demurrer was interposed only as to the "breach of the implied covenant" cause of action. As noted above, the demurrer was sus-

tained without leave to amend, the court concluding that as a matter of law the bank-depositor contractual status revealed by the pleadings could not give rise to a relationship between the parties sufficient to support the tort cause of action for breach of the implied covenant.

2. Revisitation of *Commercial Cotton*

Since everyone involved in this case (the court below and all counsel) agree that its disposition depends upon the continued viability of the rule in *Commercial Cotton*, we are perhaps well advised at the outset to summarize that case. *Commercial Cotton* was decided by a unanimous panel of this court in 1985. As asserted by counsel for petitioner, the facts of *Commercial Cotton* bear considerable similarity to the facts of this case. The plaintiff, a commercial enterprise, maintained an ordinary checking account with defendant bank. Some of the plaintiff's blank checks were lost, and the loss was reported to the bank. Later one of the checks was presented to the bank with forged signatures, and paid. When the loss was discovered some time later by the depositor, demand for repayment was made. The bank refused to cover the loss, relying upon the defense of the one-year statute of limitations as well as a claim of comparative negligence. (*Id.* at p. 514).

Unlike our case, *Commercial Cotton* went to trial, and the presentation to the appellate court was by way of ordinary appeal from a jury verdict in favor of the plaintiff. The portion of the appeal of interest to us is that which dealt with the breach of the covenant of good faith and fair dealing. The trial court permitted this claim to be presented to the jury, and the jury awarded $100,000 in punitive damages based thereon.

In its review of the factual background of the case, our court was particularly impressed with the shallow nature of the defenses asserted by the bank. Some eleven days before the final letter of denial from the bank's general counsel, the Supreme Court in *Sun 'N Sand, Inc. v. United California Bank*, 21 Cal.3d 671, 699 (1978), had specifically ruled that the three-year statute of limitations, rather than the one-year statute, was applicable for a claim such as that of *Commercial Cotton*.

Our court found it "inexplicable that [the bank's] general counsel could have been unaware of the Supreme Court's holding affecting the bank

---

[2] As can be seen from our review of *Wallis v. Superior Court*, 160 Cal.App.3d 1109 (1984), footnote 7, the pleading tracks the several "factors" identified in *Wallis* which give rise to the "special relationship" affording relief in tort for breach of the implied covenant of good faith and fair dealing. As such, the pleading is an excellent example of a statement of conclusions of law rather than allegations of fact, and no doubt would have been subject to a special demurrer. (*See* 4 Witkin, Cal. Procedure (3d ed. 1985). Pleading, § 332, pp. 381–383.) However, the attack on the complaint was by way of general demurrer, and both we and the trial judge therefore have passed over the rather obvious attempt to fit the individual facts of this case into a convenient mold of existing case precedent.

for which he was general counsel at the time he wrote the . . . letter." (*Commercial Cotton*, 163 Cal.App.3d at 515). Our court also found the contention of contributory negligence on the part of the depositor to be spurious, since whatever negligence was involved in failing promptly to note the forged check when it was returned to the depositor had no causal relationship to its original negligent cashing. It is fair to say, therefore, that our court regarded the bank's refusal to reimburse its depositor and its continued assertions of spurious defenses, right through a jury trial and to appeal, as an example of the most egregious of "stonewalling" tactics. Although not mentioned in the opinion, the fact that the dispute involved a mere $4,000 adds practical argument to the conclusion that the bank's position was completely unreasonable.

In its discussion of the tort of breach of the covenant of good faith and fair dealing, the *Commercial Cotton* court acknowledged the contention that the tort existed, outside the insurance context, only as to parties in a "special relationship." It cited *Egan v. Mutual of Omaha Ins. Co.*, 24 Cal.3d 809, 820 (1979) [169 Cal.Rptr. 691, 620 P.2d 141] (hereinafter *Egan*) for the proposition that this relationship (at least in the insurance context) is characterized by "elements of public interest, adhesion, and fiduciary responsibility." (*Commercial Cotton*, 163 Cal.App.3d at 516). It was noted that in the then very recent *Seaman's Direct Buying Service, Inc. v. Standard Oil Co.*, 36 Cal.3d 752 (1984) (hereinafter *Seaman's*), the Supreme Court had found it unnecessary to determine how far, if at all, the doctrine should extend to ordinary commercial contracts.

The court then ventured into what the Supreme Court had identified as uncharted seas, and found that the assertion by the bank of spurious defenses to the claim was an "unjustifiable, stonewalling effort to prevent an innocent depositor from recovering money," and constituted evidence adequate to support a jury finding of tortious breach of the covenant. (*Commercial Cotton*, 163 Cal.App.3d at 516).

The court reached the conclusion that the tort in question, originating in insurance relationships, could be applied in a banking context because "banking and insurance have much in common, both being highly regulated industries performing vital public services substantially affecting the

public welfare." (*Commercial Cotton*, 163 Cal.App.3d at 516). The court then went on to publish the famous quote, much discussed and disputed thereafter, that "The relationship of bank to depositor is at least quasi-fiduciary."[3] This statement rounded out the three findings posited in the *Egan* formula for imposition of the special duty: (1) elements of public interest, (2) adhesion contractual relationship, and (3) fiduciary responsibility.

Our digest of the rule of *Commercial Cotton* might be stated as follows: The ordinary relationship between commercial bank and its depositor is such as to impose upon the bank a duty, derived from the obligation of good faith and fair dealing implied in all contracts, to refrain from intentional breaches of contract and from interjection of spurious and bad faith defenses to contract claims, which duty if breached will give rise to an action in tort with attendant entitlement to punitive damages.

---

[3] The complete statement of the court is set forth as follows: "Analogizing to the factors set out in *Egan* we agree with [plaintiff's] contention that banking and insurance have much in common, both being highly regulated industries performing vital public services substantially affecting the public welfare. A depositor in a noninterest-bearing checking account, except for state or federal regulatory oversight, is totally dependent on the banking institution to which it entrusts deposited funds and depends on the bank's honesty and expertise to protect them. While banks do provide services for the depositor by way of monitoring deposits and withdrawals, they do so for the very commercial purpose of making money by using the deposited funds. The depositor allows the bank to use those funds in exchange for the convenience of not having to conduct transactions in cash and the con-comitant security in having the bank safeguard them. The relationship of bank to depositor is at least quasi-fiduciary, and depositors reasonably expect a bank not to claim nonexistent legal defenses to avoid reimbursement when the bank negligently disburses the entrusted funds. Here, [defendant bank's] counsel claimed defenses are spurious, and the jury found experienced legal counsel interposing them in an unjustifiable, stonewalling effort to prevent an innocent depositor from recovering money entrusted to and lost through the bank's own negligence, is a breach of the bank's covenant of good faith and fair dealing with its depositor. Viewing the evidence in a light most favorable to the verdict, we hold it is overwhelmingly supported by the evidence." (163 Cal.App.3d at p. 516.)

3. Evolution of the Tort of Breach of the
Obligation of Good Faith and Fair Dealing
(a) Early Development in Insurance and
Wrongful Termination Cases

In order to weigh the current value of the rule
of *Commercial Cotton* we are required to review
the history and evolution of the tort therein
described. We do so briefly, recognizing that this
is a field several times previously plowed by other
jurists and by academics (some of which are cited
hereunder) and hence neither merits nor requires
extended comment here.

The existence of implied covenants of good
faith and fair dealing in all contracts has long
been the law. As stated in *Universal Sales Corp.
v. Cal. etc. Mfg. Co.*, 20 Cal.2d 751, 771 (1942):
"In every contract there is an implied covenant
that neither party shall do anything which will
have the effect of destroying or injuring the right
of the other party to receive the fruits of the
contract, which means that in every contract there
exists an implied covenant of good faith and fair
dealing."

Reliance upon the covenant to support damages in excess of ordinary contract damages first
arose in the insurance context. Initially supporting
damages in excess of policy limits for wrongful
refusal to settle a claim (*Comunale v. Traders &
General Ins. Co.*, 50 Cal.2d 654 (1958) [328 P.2d
198, 68 A.L.R.2d 883]; *Crisci v. Security Ins. Co.*,
66 Cal.2d 425 (1967) [58 Cal.Rptr. 13, 426 P.2d
173]), the concept was later expanded to embrace
general tort damages for bad faith refusal to pay
a claim (*Gruenberg v. Aetna Ins. Co.*, 9 Cal.3d
566, 575 (1973) [108 Cal.Rptr. 480, 510 P.2d
1032]). The rationale for imposing tort liability in
the insurance context was explained and justified
in *Egan*. Emphasized were the nonprofit objectives of the insured in seeking protection and
peace of mind (24 Cal.3d at 819), that insurance
companies provided vital services quasi-public in
nature (*id.* at 820) and that the insurance relationship had a fiduciary quality (*id.*).[4]

The other arena in which recovery in tort for
breach of the covenant of good faith and fair
dealing was sanctioned, pre-*Seaman's*, was that
of employment termination. *Cleary v. American
Airlines, Inc.*, 111 Cal.App.3d 443 (1980) [168
Cal.Rptr. 722] is a clear statement of the proposition that an implied covenant of continued
employment can be found in certain otherwise
undefined employment circumstances, and that a
breach of this covenant by a discharge without
cause can give rise to tort damages. (*Id.* at pp.
454–456) [The Court discussed whether, and
under what circumstances, a breach of the implied
covenant of good faith and fair dealing in a commercial contract may give rise to an action in
tort.] ...

Interpretation of the evident direction of the
law on "bad faith" can best be seen by the reaction of the several Courts of Appeal. Our court
in *Commercial Cotton* was one of the first to
suggest expansion—into the field of commercial
banking. Definitive direction analyzing the concept of the "special relationship" was provided
in *Wallis v. Superior Court* (1984) 160 Cal.App.3d
1109 (hereinafter *Wallis*). Since the case arose from
the peremptory termination by an employer of
previously agreed-upon termination benefits, the
case could be considered as part of the wrongful
termination line of cases. The court's identification of factors leading to a determination of "special relationship" was not at all limited by
employment concepts, however. The "similar
characteristics" which would signal the existence
of a "special relationship" could be found in
almost any "special" kind of commercial contractual relationship.[7]

Rather than rushing to expand the tort, however, most courts followed the *Seaman's* admonition to "proced with caution." (*Seaman's* at
p. 769.)

---

[4] For a discussion of the background of commercial
bad faith cases see Putz & Klippen, *Commercial Bad
Faith: Attorney Fees — Not Tort Liability — Is the
Remedy for "Stonewalling"* (1987) 21 U.S.F. L.Rev. 419,
429 et seq.; see also the extended historical review of
the tort by Justice Croskey in *Careau & Co. v. Security
Pacific Business Credit, Inc.*, 222 Cal.App.3d 1371, 1392
et seq. (1990) [272 Cal.Rptr. 387].

[7] The *Wallis* court stated that the "similar characteristics" which must be present to permit tort liability
were (1) inherently unequal bargaining positions; (2)
nonprofit motivation, i.e., objective of securing peace
of mind, security; (3) inadequacy of ordinary contract
damages; (4) special vulnerability of one party to harm
as a result of breach of trust of the other; and (5)
awareness by the other of this special vulnerability. (*Wallis* at p. 1118.)

* * *

[The court then reviewed a decision of the California Supreme Court, *Foley v. Interactive Data Corp.*, 47 Cal.3d 654, 254 Cal. Rptr. 211 (1988) in which the court concluded that there was insufficient basis for extending the special tort relief available in insurance cases to the employment field but went on to state "No doubt there are other relationships with similar characteristics and deserving similar legal treatment." *Foley* at p. 687. Editor] . . .

The *Foley* decision did not reference commercial banking activities nor did it cite *Commercial Cotton*. We are most satisfied, however, that if the *Foley* court were to apply the same reasoning to the commercial banking business which it applied to employment contracts it would conclude that, in the usual case, the "special relationship" found in insurance cases and evaluated by the *Wallis* standards would be lacking.

Post-*Foley* Court of Appeal decisions would appear to agree with this conclusion. Our own court, in an opinion written by the same justice who authored *Commercial Cotton*, in *Mitsui Manufacturers Bank v. Superior Court*, 212 Cal.App.3d 726, 729 (1989) [260 Cal.Rptr. 793], stated: "We reject real parties' argument that the tort doctrine which has been extended only to situations where there are unique fiduciary-like relationships between the parties, should encompass normal commercial banking transactions." In an extended and scholarly opinion the court in *Careau & Co. v. Security Pacific Business Credit, Inc.*, 222 Cal.App.3d 1371 found no "special relationship" to exist in the bank-borrower situation. (*See also Lee v. Bank of America*, 218 Cal.App.3d 914 (1990) [267 Cal.Rptr. 287]).

The most directly applicable current authority is *Price v. Wells Fargo Bank*, 213 Cal.App.3d 465 (1989) [261 Cal.Rptr. 735] (hereinafter *Price*). In that case an action was brought against the bank by a commercial borrower, who complained that the bank's refusal to extend the terms of loans caused forced liquidation of assets and financial loss. One of the principal causes of action (dismissed on summary judgment by the trial court) was an action in tort for breach of the implied covenant, brought specifically in reliance upon the authority of *Commercial Cotton*. The court rejected the decision and reasoning of *Commercial Cotton*, declined seriously to attempt application

of the *Wallis* factors to the case, and held rather simply that no contractual implication can be made in a bank's lending contract which precludes it from foreclosing in accordance with the terms of the contract. Referring to *Foley*, the *Price* court stated that "The impact of the *Foley* decision cannot be assessed with certainty [but] [t]he decision surely precludes the sort of loose extension of tort recovery, based on 'quasi-fiduciary' relationship, sanctioned in [*Commercial Cotton*]. . . . " (*Price*, 213 Cal.App.3d at 478).

Coming finally to the facts of our case: We must conclude that the application of the *Wallis* five points do not indicate a "special relationship," and hence an action in tort by the depositor cannot be stated for simple breach of the deposit contract.[12] Looking to the *Wallis* criteria, we believe that a commercial entity and a bank are not ordinarily in inherently unequal bargaining positions. There is nothing in these pleadings, nor is there any aspect of common banking transactions, which suggests to us that banks in general are, or this bank in particular was, in a superior bargaining position. Banks in our society are commonly most competitive. That the bank offers a standard product certainly cannot make its bargaining position "unequal."

Referring to the second *Wallis* criterion, the motivation for entering into the contract, we can conceive of very few contracts which are more profit-oriented than the commercial bank account of a chiropractor. Obviously one chooses a bank in which to deposit his money in part because of the apparent security of the institution; this does not mean, however, that the motivation for the transaction is "peace of mind" in the sense that such motivation inheres in an insurance contract.[13]

---

[12] We of course are not saying that a bank may not under special circumstances undertake obligations which bring it into a "special relationship" with a customer. Many banks affirmatively offer trust and other specifically fiduciary services, and as such are in a position to do great harm if the trust agreement is broken in bad faith. We refer in our text, *supra*, simply to the ordinary bank-depositor relationship (and presumably, although it would be dictum, also to the ordinary bank-borrower relationship).

[13] We follow, here, the line of reasoning developed in *Foley* at pages 692–693. The employment relation was distinguished from the insurance relation by noting the

The third *Wallis* factor relates to damages. It is true that damages to be recovered for suing a bank for cashing a forged check may be inadequate. This is not because of anything special about banks or commercial deposits, however. The problem with suing banks is the same problem that besets the typical judicial remedy for all commercial breaches. Unless one has included an attorney fee clause in the contract, recovery of the fees and practical costs of litigation is not possible. No one, therefore, involved in commercial litigation these days can be made completely whole. *Wallis* was not talking about this defect in our jurisprudential system—it had to do instead with the peculiar loss associated with denial of payment of insurance proceeds or, as in *Wallis*, the peremptory interruption of monthly termination payments to an aged retired employee.

The fourth and fifth *Wallis* criteria identify special vulnerability of one party of which the other party is aware. One can posit unusual banking arrangements whereby minors or other dependent people specifically inform the bank of their complete dependence upon the liquidity of their bank account, in which case these criteria might be satisfied. The ordinary bank checking account is not, however, of this nature. We note in this case that the account was so fluid its owners did not notice the theft of some $32,000 for over a period of 18 months. Anyone who has lost money because of breach of a commercial obligation is going to consider himself damaged, and the continuing state of loss causes such person to experience a certain feeling of vulnerability. As with the damage issue, however, this is a problem common to all commercial transactions, not different in the typical bank-depositor transaction,

and certainly not the sort of vulnerability envisaged by the *Wallis* criteria.

We should refer also to the specific factors cited in *Commercial Cotton* as promotive of treating the banking industry the same as the insurance industry in terms of the implied covenant tort applicability. The *Commercial Cotton* court did not utilize the *Wallis* factors, but instead relied upon those factors stated in *Egan* and *Seaman's*: public interest, adhesion, and fiduciary responsibility. We have discounted, above, the concept that the deposit contract is an adhesion contract. We have serious doubts that the status of banking as an industry important to the public welfare should have an effect upon the issue before us. As noted in Comment, *Fiduciary Controversy: Injection of Fiduciary Principles Into the Bank-Depositor and Bank-Borrower Relationship*, 20 Loyola L.A. L.Rev. at 816–817, "The concept of 'affected with the public interest' can be applied to common carriers, theaters, restaurants, inns/motels, food retailers, garbage collectors, doctors and landlords. The list is virtually endless. Therefore, it would be absurd to single out banks as having a "special relationship" with its customers merely because banking is 'affected with the public interest.'" (Fns. omitted.)

Of most concern, however, is the statement made in *Commercial Cotton*, 163 Cal.App.3d at 516 that "[t]he relationship of bank to [its] depositor is at least quasi-fiduciary." This statement is severely criticized in *Price* at page 476, and its assertion countered by the citation of well-established authority for the proposition that the relationship between a bank and its depositor is not a fiduciary relationship, but that of debtor-creditor. (*Morse v. Crocker National Bank*, 142 Cal.App.3d 228, 232 (1983) [190 Cal.Rptr. 839]; *Downey v. Humphreys*, 102 Cal.App.2d 323, 332 (1951) [227 P.2d 484], and a case contemporaneous with *Commercial Cotton*: *Lawrence v. Bank of America*, 163 Cal.App.3d 431 (1985) [209 Cal.Rptr. 541].) We note that the statement in *Commercial Cotton* was made without benefit of citation of authority. Presuming that the court was aware of *Morse v. Crocker National Bank*, *Downey v. Humphreys*, and other authorities which had established the bank-depositor relationship as merely debtor-creditor, and that the *Commercial Cotton* court did not purport to classify the relationship actually as "fiduciary," we are led to a search for what might have been meant by the phrase "quasi-

---

unique economic dilemma faced by the insured whose insurer refuses in bad faith to pay policy benefits. The insured has lost the very benefit for which he contracted, and is not in a position to seek alternative relief from competitors. The employee, however, has not bargained for any similar type of "protection," and the breach of the employment contract causes damages essentially similar to those resulting from breaches of other kinds of contractual agreements — such as the refusal to honor a contract for the supply of goods vital to a small dealer's business. We conclude that the breach of a banker's agreement with its depositor similarly results in damage typical to all commercial contracts.

fiduciary." In Garner, *A Dictionary of Modern Legal Usage* (1987) page 457, "quasi" is defined as "seeming or seemingly; in the nature of; nearly," and its use demeaned by a quote from 1 *Corbin on Contracts* (1963 ed.) section 19, pages 45–46 that "the term *quasi* is introduced as a weasel word that sucks all the meaning of the word that follows it." (Italics in original.)

We conclude both from the manner of use and the omission of any citation that when the court in *Commercial Cotton* used "quasi-fiduciary" it intended *not* to question prior authority establishing that banks in ordinary deposit relationships are not fiduciaries, but sought only a shorthand phrase to describe attributes in the relationship which are similar to *some* of the attributes of a true fiduciary relationship. The court was, simply, grappling with the criteria described in *Egan* and *Seaman's* (elements of public interest, adhesion and fiduciary responsibility) for establishing "special relationship," and noting that some contractual features of a banking relationship establish elements of reliance and trust which "seem like" or are "in the nature of" (to refer to our dictionary definition) obligations resulting from a true fiduciary relationship.[14]

---

[14] We have had occasion in other circumstances to examine the loose characterization of relationships as fiduciary, quasi-fiduciary or fiduciary like, and have concluded such are both unhelpful and fraught with analytic pitfalls. Thus, we noted in Love v. Fire Ins. Exchange, 221 Cal.App.3d 1136, 1148–1149 (1990) [271 Cal.Rptr. 246], that particular contractual obligations, specifically undertaken in contracts such as those executed by insurance companies, can impose certain duties resembling the duties which burden true fiduciaries. This resemblance does not, however, make the insurance company a true fiduciary with all of its attendant obligations. While a bank's role as deposit keeper may resemble an insurer in some aspects, the bank is in no sense a true fiduciary. It deals at arm's length and in commercial independence with its depositor. It is not obligated to put the interests of the depositor above its own, and is not required to disregard the interest of its shareholders when evaluating claims made upon it by depositors. Just as it was imprudent in *Love, supra,* to simply label an insurer a "quasi-fiduciary" (since such a characterization carries the analytic danger that such

In light of the reasoning of *Foley*, we are convinced *Commercial Cotton*'s characterization of a bank-depositor relationship as quasi-fiduciary is now inappropriate. While some aspects of that relationship may resemble aspects of the insurer-insured relationship, there are equally marked differences between those relationships. Since appending the quasi-fiduciary label to the ordinary bank-depositor relationship runs counter to both pre- and post-*Commercial Cotton* authority, and such a label provides no analytical framework against which to evaluate (after *Foley*) the propriety of extending tort remedies for contractual breaches, we no longer approve the denomination of the ordinary bank-depositor relationship as quasi-fiduciary in character.

Conclusion and Disposition

It is thus our conclusion that banks, in general and in this case, are not fiduciaries for their depositors; and that the bank-depositor relationship is not a "special relationship" under the *Wallis* test, or any other test, such as to give rise to tort damages when an implied contractual covenant of good faith is broken. We are therefore forced to acknowledge that our decision in *Commercial Cotton*, while in its time seemingly in harmony with the direction of the Supreme Court, turned out, after *Foley*, to be misdirected. We acknowledge the accuracy of *Price, and Careau & Co. v. Security Pacific Business Credit, Inc.*, 222 Cal.App.3d 1371 (1990), in their characterization of the ordinary bank-customer relationship as *not* a special relationship giving rise to tort remedies when the bank unreasonably, and even in bad faith, denies liability on a contract or interposes spurious defenses. The third cause of action in this case, therefore, was defective and the trial court was correct in sustaining the general demurrer to it. The petition is denied. Real party in interest is entitled to costs. (*Union Trust Co. v. Superior Court*, 13 Cal.2d 541, 543 (1939) [90 P.2d 582].)

---

labeling could lead to "import[ing] uncritically the entire cargo of fiduciary obligations into the port of insurance law" (ibid.), so too we perceive equivalent dangers attend an automatic extension of "quasi-fiduciary" status to ordinary bank-depositor relationships.

NOTE
A.B.A. U.C.C. Article 1 Review Task Force

An A.B.A. Task Force reviewing the definitions appearing in U.C.C. Article 1 discussed the following conceptualization:

"Good faith" means honesty in fact and the observance of reasonable commercial standards of fair dealing in the conduct or transaction concerned. "Fair Dealing" is concerned with fairness of an act or omission to act rather than the care taken with respect to such conduct. Whether a party has acted in good faith is for the court to decide. In determining whether there has been good faith in the performance of a contract or duty within this Act (§ 1-203), the court shall determine whether the act or omission concerned is in accordance with the reasonable expectations of the parties under their agreement (§ 1-201(3)), as supplemented or qualified by any course of performance under the agreement.

The Task Force also concluded that the requirement for "observance of reasonable commercial standards of fair dealing" is not intended to create a separate cause of action for breach of a "duty" of good faith. Any development of such action would be left to the common law. *See, Copesky v. Superior Court of San Diego*, 229 Cal. App. 3d 678, 280 Cal. Rptr. 338 (1991). At a meeting of the Task Force in April 1993 it was decided to recommend that the term "commercial" be eliminated from the definition in line one. This would facilitate the court determining as a fact whether in non-commercial cases there has been an "observance of reasonable standards of fair dealing."

Finally we must note that when the Code was originally drafted, the concept of comparative negligence had not been fully adopted at common law nor had this concept received much statutory recognition.[34] As a result, negligence of a claimant often blocked recovery.[35] Recognizing that such result would be inequitable the Code now provides for a comparative negligence approach. Thus, if there was a failure to exercise ordinary care by the claimant, such failure would not preclude an action but if the claimant's failure to exercise ordinary care substantially contributed to the loss, the recovery will be apportioned. The loss will be allocated between the two parties on a basis of comparative causation.[36]

---

[34] The concept of comparative negligence has its origin in maritime law. It was incorporated into the common law by various court decisions, as well as by specific statutory enactments. For a history of comparative negligence up to 1950, *see* Turk, *Comparative Negligence on the March*, 28 CHI.-KENT L. REV. 189–245. Developments in the U.S.A. are dealt with by Turk, *id.*, 304–346 (1950). *See also* Powell, *Comparative Negligence*, 41 CAL. L. REV. 1 (1953).

[35] *See, e.g.*, former U.C.C. §§ 3-406, 4-406(3).

[36] *See, e.g.*, U.C.C. §§ 3-404(d), 3-405(b), 3-406(b), (c), 4-406(e).

Federal Insurance Company v. NCNB National Bank of North Carolina
958 F.2d 1544 (11th Cir. 1992)*

FRIEDMAN, Senior Circuit Judge:
This diversity damage suit grew out of a scheme by which a corporate employee embezzled

---

* [Editor: citations in [ ] refer to Revised U.C.C. Articles 3 and 4.]

substantial amounts from her employer by obtaining payment of corporate checks that had not been properly signed, and converting the proceeds. After the embezzlement was discovered, and the banks denied liability for the payments, the employer's insurance company paid the losses. The insurance company as the subrogee and assignee of the employer then brought this suit against the banks. The district court held that the banks were negligent in paying the checks, but that because the employer also was negligent, it was responsible for 50 percent of its losses. Both the insurance company and the banks have appealed. We uphold the district court's determination that the banks are liable, but reverse the 50 percent reduction in the damages.

I.

A. In late 1985 and early 1986, Computer Products, Inc. (Computer), a Florida corporation, opened two accounts with NCNB National Bank of North Carolina (NC Bank), for one of its operating units. Computer's corporate resolutions authorizing these accounts, submitted on forms that NC Bank furnished, provided that checks for up to $500.00 required one signature by hand or facsimile, that checks between $500.00 and $10,000.00 required one hand and one facsimile signature, and that checks of more than $10,000.00 required "two signatures by hand." The resolutions stated that they "shall remain in full force and effect until written notice of their amendment or rescission shall have been received by [NC Bank]."

Computer also submitted to the bank a signature card for each account listing the persons (and showing their signatures) authorized to sign checks on the account. Elizabeth Johnson, the comptroller of the unit for which these accounts were opened, had substantial responsibility with respect to the preparation, approval, and issuance of checks drawn on several Computer accounts, and supervised these two. She was one of the Computer personnel authorized to sign checks on the two accounts.

The first forty-six checks for more than $10,000.00 drawn on these accounts contained the required two handwritten signatures. In early 1986, a check for more than $60,000.00 for a legitimate corporate expenditure, but containing one hand and one facsimile signature, was presented to NC Bank for payment. A clerk at the bank, Kimberly Clayton, telephoned Computer about the check. She spoke to Elizabeth Johnson, who instructed her to pay the check and told her to expect to pay, in the future, many more checks exceeding $10,000.00 that would have one hand and one facsimile signature.

Clayton testified that she based her decision to pay that check, and all subsequent checks, solely on what Johnson told her on the telephone that day. The record shows no other contact between Computer and NC Bank regarding authorization to pay checks lacking the required signatures. NC Bank subsequently paid numerous checks for more than $10,000.00 drawn on the two accounts, even though they had one hand and one facsimile signature.

At about the same time, Elizabeth Johnson began to implement a plan to embezzle funds from her employer. Before the scheme was discovered, Johnson submitted nine checks, each for more than $10,000.00, the proceeds of which she converted. During the intervening three weeks she also drew a number of checks for valid corporate purposes. All the checks had one hand and one facsimile signature. NC Bank paid the checks as they were presented, apparently in reliance on the prior telephone conversation between Johnson and Clayton.

Five of the checks for more than $10,000.00 with only one handwritten signature were payable to "NCNB." Those checks were presented to NCNB National Bank of Florida (Fla. Bank), which exchanged them for its own cashier's checks payable to various individuals, including two payable to Elizabeth Johnson's husband (whose last name was not Johnson).

By the time Computer received its bank statements from NC Bank listing the fraudulent checks, all but one of them had already been paid. The remaining invalid check was paid a few days after Computer received the statements.

B. When the embezzlement was discovered, NC Bank refused to restore to Computer's account the amount it had paid on the fraudulent checks. The appellant Federal Insurance Company (Federal), a New Jersey company which insured Computer against such losses, paid Computer for the losses.

Federal then filed the present suit in the United States District Court for the Southern District of Florida against NC Bank and Fla. Bank. Suing as the assignee and subrogee of Computer, Federal sought damages for the amounts it had paid Computer to cover Computer's losses on seven of the fraudulent checks. Federal asserted that NC Bank had breached its contract with its depositor Computer and negligently had paid the checks that had only one hand signature, and that Fla. Bank negligently had exchanged the checks with only one hand signature for its own cashier's checks without properly inquiring into the propriety of the exchange.

After a bench trial, the district court held that the banks had been negligent in paying and exchanging the checks. The court found that NC Bank "disregarded the provisions of the corporate resolution and signature card requiring two hand-written signatures on all checks in excess of $10,000," and that Fla. Bank "failed to properly inquire where the proceeds of five corporate checks payable to NCNB should be distributed and breached its duty of inquiry." The court further found that Computer "was negligent in failing to employ reasonable auditing procedures and in failing to check procedures for disbursements, including signature requirements" and "also ignored its own corporate resolution and signature requirements." The court found that the banks and Computer "are equally guilty of the same amount of negligence," and that Computer and "the issuing bank are equally responsible for the embezzlement by Elizabeth Johnson."

In its conclusions of law, the court stated that "all of Plaintiff's claims should fall except for negligence," and that "on the issue of negligence, Plaintiff and Defendants bear equal responsibility and Defendants should pay 50% of all damages incurred." . . .

III.

A. The district court correctly held that NC Bank was negligent in paying the fraudulent checks for more than $10,000.00 that had one hand and one facsimile signature. The bank's duty not to pay those checks was created and defined by the contractual arrangements that the bank and Computer entered into when the accounts were opened.

The resolution of Computer's board of directors designated the NC Bank for the opening of an account, imposed the two-hand-signature requirement for checks of more than $10,000.00, and authorized the bank "to pay all instruments signed in accordance with the foregoing resolution." The clear implication was that the bank was not authorized to pay any check not signed in accordance with the resolution. "[T]he relationship between a bank and its depositing customer is contractual." *MJZ Corp. v. Gulfstream First Bank & Trust*, 420 So.2d 396, 397 (Fla.Dist.Ct.App.1981) (citing *McCrory Stores*

Corp. v. Tunnicliffe, 104 Fla. 683, 140 So. 806 (1932)). Section 4-401 of the Uniform Commercial Code (UCC) similarly contemplates that a bank will pay only in accordance with its contractual obligations to its customers. It provides: "As against its customer, a bank may charge against his account any item which is otherwise properly payable. . . . " A check bearing an unauthorized signature is not properly payable. *See Medford Irrigation Dist. v. Western Bank*, 66 Ore. App. 589, 676 P.2d 329, 333 (1984).

When NC Bank paid the seven fraudulent checks involved in this case that had only one hand signature, it acted negligently because it violated the contractual undertaking upon which the account had been opened that checks for more than $10,000.00 would not be paid unless they had two hand signatures. The corporate resolutions authorizing the accounts provided the resolutions would remain effective until the bank received "written notice" of their amendment or rescission. The bank had not received such written notice prior to paying the seven checks.

The oral notice the bank received from Elizabeth Johnson that it should pay the first such check and others similarly signed that it would receive did not justify the bank in departing from the terms upon which the bank opened the account and agreed to handle it. NC Bank's payment of the seven checks for more than $10,000.00 that had only one hand signature was negligent because it breached the bank's duty to Computer, based upon the corporate resolutions pursuant to which Computer had opened and the bank had accepted the accounts, not to pay checks that were not signed as the resolutions directed.

NC Bank argues, however, that it was authorized to pay the checks because (1) Johnson had actual authority to waive the two-hand-signature requirement by virtue of being one of the Computer officials authorized to sign checks or (2) had apparent authority to do so, or (3) Computer ratified the payment of the checks, or (4) there was a course of dealing between Computer and NC Bank that authorized the bank to deviate from the two-hand-signature requirement.

There is no indication that Johnson had any authority, either actual or apparent, to permit the bank to deviate from the two-hand-signature condition in the corporate resolutions. The resolution stated that they would remain effective until the bank received written notice of their amendment or rescission. As the district court found, "[b]etween the date NCNB North Carolina received the CPI corporate resolution for the RTP division account and the time it was advised of the embezzlement by Elizabeth Johnson there were no written agreements entered into between NCNB North Carolina and CPI altering, revising, or modifying the [two handwritten signature requirement]." The fact that Elizabeth Johnson was authorized to sign checks did not clothe her with authority to permit deviation from the conditions upon which the board of directors authorized the accounts to be operated.

Nor is there anything in the record to show that Computer ratified the payment of the fraudulent checks with only one paid signature or engaged in a course of dealing with NC Bank that permitted the bank to deviate from its contractual obligations. The first forty-six checks for more than $10,000.00 conformed to the corporate resolutions. Immediately upon learning of the bank's payment of non-conforming checks, Computer sought to stop it. Immediately upon learning of the fraudulent checks, Computer and NC Bank cooperated in investigating the matter. When Computer discovered that there were several outstanding checks for more than $10,000.00 with only one hand signature that were for legitimate purposes, it instructed NC Bank to pay them. This practical step to avoid unnecessary work and problems does not even suggest any ratification by Computer of the NC Bank's payment of the fraudulent checks or constitute a course of dealing between Computer and NC Bank authorizing such payment.

The fact, upon which NC Bank relies, that Computer may have issued a series of checks for more than $10,000.00 with one hand and one facsimile signature drawn on its account with another bank, cannot establish the propriety of NC Bank's payment of such checks. The relationship between a depositor and a particular bank controls only the dealings between those two entities, and cannot implicitly authorize the same relationship between the depositor and another bank.

B. We also agree with the district court that Fla. Bank was negligent in issuing its cashier's checks in exchange for checks for more than $10,000.00 containing only one hand signature and payable to NCNB, without inquiring about the propriety of such exchange.

A bank that receives a check payable to it, where the drawer is not indebted to it, has a duty, before paying the check, to inquire whether the drawer's agent is authorized to negotiate the check, since the bank is authorized to pay the check only in accordance with the drawer's directions. *See, e.g., Kaiser-Georgetown Comm. Health Plan, Inc. v. Bankers Trust Co. of Albany*, 110 Misc.2d 320, 442 N.Y.S.2d 48 (N.Y.Sup.Ct. 1981). In the present case, the checks that Fla. Bank exchanged for cashier's checks were payable to "NCNB." Fla. Bank has some affiliation with NC Bank: its name is "NCNB National Bank of Florida"; NC Bank designated an employee of Fla. Bank as account officer for all accounts that Computer maintained with NC Bank; and NC Bank conducted its dealings with Computer through Fla. Bank. This connection with NC Bank probably was sufficient to invoke the foregoing rule. If not, then Fla. Bank's duty of inquiry before exchanging checks payable to another bank was even stronger.

Contrary to its contention, Fla. Bank cannot justifiably claim that it relied upon the apparent authority of the Computer employee who exchanged the checks to take that action. Fla. Bank states that the employee, a Computer bookkeeper, was well known to Fla. Bank, had conducted banking business with it for Computer for a couple of years, and previously had exchanged Computer checks for Fla. Bank cashier's checks. The Fla. Bank employee who exchanged the checks testified (1) that she believed the person who made the exchange was a "runner" for Computer, but did not know that person's position; (2) that she made no inquiry whether the person exchanging the checks had authority to do so; (3) that when she was requested to exchange Computer checks payable to NCNB for cashier's checks payable to other parties, she did not attempt to confirm that request with someone at Computer; and (4) that the only information she had concerning the authority of the person exchanging the checks was what that person told her. This was insufficient to establish that the Computer bookkeeper who exchanged the checks in these unusual transactions had apparent authority to do so. *See Smith v. American Auto. Ins. Co.*, 498 So.2d 448, 449 (Fla.Dist.Ct.App.1986).

Fla. Bank next contends that the agreement under which Computer opened and maintained its accounts with NC Bank negated any duty by Fla. Bank to inquire before exchanging the checks. It relies upon the following provision in the corporate resolutions:

FURTHER RESOLVED, that NCNB NATIONAL BANK OF NORTH CAROLINA be and it hereby is authorized to honor, receive, certify, or pay all instruments signed in accordance with the foregoing resolution even though drawn or endorsed to the order of any officer or employee signing the name or tendered by him for cashing, or in payment of the individual obligation of such officer or employee, or for deposit to his personal account, and said bank shall not be required or be under any obligation to inquire as to the circumstances of the issuance or use of any instrument signed in accordance with the foregoing resolution, or the application or disposition of such instrument or the proceeds thereof.

This provision relieved NC Bank of its duty of inquiry only with respect to checks "signed in accordance with the foregoing resolution." The checks that Fla. Bank exchanged were not signed in accordance with the resolution, since, although for more than $10,000.00, they had only one hand signature. Moreover, this provision relieved only NC Bank, not Fla. Bank, of a duty to inquire. Indeed, it is difficult to understand how Fla. Bank can rely upon a provision in an agreement between Computer and a different bank.

Finally, Fla. Bank contends that even if it may have had a common law duty of inquiry, that duty was terminated when Fla. adopted the U.C.C. It relies upon [U.C.C. §§ 3–404, 3–405], which makes certain check endorsements effective and relieves from liability a bank that negotiates an instrument with a forged or unauthorized endorsement.

Fla. Bank has pointed to nothing, however, that even suggests, let alone shows, that in adopting this provision of the U.C.C. Florida intended to terminate a bank's established common law duty to make inquiry before paying checks to it from a party not indebted to it. Although we have found no Florida case deciding the question, other courts have indicated that the adoption of the U.C.C. did not abolish a bank's common law duty of inquiry. *See, e.g., Bullitt County Bank v. Publishers Printing Co.*, 684 S.W.2d 289, 292 (Ky.Ct.App.1984); *Kaiser-Georgetown Comm. Health Plan, Inc. v. Bankers Trust Co. of Albany*,

110 Misc.2d 320, 442 N.Y.S.2d 48 (1981); *Bank of Southern Maryland v. Robertson's Crab House, Inc.*, 39 Md.App. 707, 389 A.2d 388, 393 (1978); *Transamerica Ins. Co. v. United States Nat'l Bank*, 276 Ore. 945, 558 P.2d 328, 333 (1976). There is no reason to believe that the Florida courts would conclude any differently.

IV.

Federal contends that the district court erred in reducing its award against NC Bank by fifty percent based on Computer's own negligence. It does not challenge the fifty percent reduction in the award against Fla. Bank.

The precise rationale of the district court ruling is unclear. All the court stated is that Computer "and the issuing bank are equally responsible for the embezzlement by Elizabeth Johnson" and that Computer and the banks "bear equal responsibility and Defendants should pay 50% of all damages incurred." In supporting the district court's ruling, NC Bank argues that since the district court rejected all but the negligence claims of Computer, the court properly applied Florida law, which provides for allocation of damages in a negligence case, based upon comparative negligence. Presumably, this was the basis of the district court's awarding Federal only fifty percent of the $171,295.00 damages the court found Computer had incurred from NC Bank's "improper payment of" the seven checks.

Federal counters that the provisions of the U.C.C. that Florida has adopted determine a bank's liability to its depositor for improper payment of the depositor's checks, and that under those provisions, if the bank acted negligently, the depositor's own negligence is irrelevant and cannot reduce the amount of the depositor's damages.

We agree with Federal....

Since NC Bank acted negligently in paying the seven checks that had only one hand signature, necessarily the bank acted with "lack of ordinary care . . . in paying the item[s]" and failed to act in accordance with "reasonable commercial standards."

Although the Florida courts apparently have not decided the question, other state courts have interpreted these provisions of the U.C.C. as making the bank wholly and strictly liable when both it and the customer have been negligent....

See . . . the following statement by the New York Court of Appeals in *Putnam Rolling Ladder*

Co. v. Manufacturers Hanover Trust Co., 76 N.Y.2d 340, 546 N.E.2d 904 at 908, 547 N.Y.S.2d 611 at 615, in which the court awarded the plaintiff its full damages where the trial court found that the customer and the bank each had been 50 percent negligent and had apportioned the damages accordingly:

> The importation of comparative negligence into the U.C.C.—which was drafted before widespread acceptance of comparative fault—is not without its advocates (noted in, 1 White & Summers, op. cit., Sec. 16–7, n. 6, at 809), but has generally been rejected by both courts and commentators (id). We agree. As one court stated in addressing this issue, "the balancing of rights under the U.C.C. represents the ultimate distillation of a painstaking process of evolution, pursuant to which the risk of loss in commercial matters has been attempted to be adjusted in a fair and equitable manner." . . . It is not for the courts to unsettle the U.C.C.'s carefully drawn balance by introducing comparative fault principles taken from tort law.
>
> Moreover, the U.C.C. serves an important objective not shared by the law of torts (see, by analogy, *Board of Educ. v. Sargent, Webster, Crenshaw & Folley*, 71 N.Y.2d 21, 29, [523 N.Y.S.2d 475, 517 N.E.2d 1360]). Unlike tort law, the U.C.C. has the objective of promoting certainty and predictability in commercial transactions. By prospectively establishing rules of liability that are generally based not on actual fault but on allocating responsibility to the party best able to prevent the loss by the exercise of care, the U.C.C. not only guides commercial behavior but also increases certainty in the marketplace and efficiency in dispute resolution. These ends would not be furthered by the introduction of the sort of fact inquiries necessitated by comparative negligence.

Once again, there is no reason to believe that the Florida courts would disagree with this well established line of authority. As the commentary to Fla.Stat. § 674.406 states:

> Subsection (3). Under the shifting burden of proof provided in this subsection, even though the bank shows negligence on the part of the customer, it cannot escape liability if the customer succeeds in establishing that the bank was also negligent. In other words, where both are negligent, the bank bears the loss—a neat twist to the contributory negligence rule.

Although many of the foregoing cases involved unsuccessful attempts by a negligent bank to avoid any liability to a depositor because of the latter's contributory negligence, the principle those cases established is equally applicable to NC Bank's attempt to limit its liability by applying state comparative negligence principles. Indeed, those principles are inapplicable under the U.C.C.

We therefore conclude that under Florida law no reduction in the damages Computer suffered as a result of NC Bank's negligent payment of the seven checks would be appropriate to reflect Computer's own negligence.

V.

The judgment of the district court is affirmed with respect to the damage award against Florida Bank. It is vacated with respect to the damage award against NC Bank and the case is remanded to that court for entry of a judgment for Federal against NC Bank for the full amount of the damages Computer suffered as a result of NC Bank's negligent payment of the seven checks.

NOTE

Florida has adopted Revised U.C.C. Articles 3 and 4 effective January 1, 1993. Thus, consider this case in light of U.C.C. § 4–406(e).

C.   Herein of Payment

Usually, performance and payment for performance are concurrent events. Any agreed upon delay would change the transaction into a credit relationship; whether it is that payment is postponed or that performance is in the future. The U.C.C. recognizes this by providing that "unless otherwise agreed," tender of payment and tender of goods are concurrent conditions; thus payment is due when goods are tendered or delivered.[37] No problem arises in a situation where payment is in cash. Payment by an electronic transfer into the account of the payee, is instantaneous and can be analogized to a transfer of legal tender.[38] But though tender of payment can be by any means or in any manner current in the ordinary course of business,[39] "payment by check is conditional and is defeated as between the parties by dishonor of the check on due presentment." U.C.C. § 2–511(3). Until presentment and dishonor, however, the underlying obligation to pay is suspended.[40] Thus, until the check is honored following presentment for payment, the money is still in the account of the drawer/maker of the check.

---

[37] *See* U.C.C. §§ 2-511, 2-310(a).

[38] *See* U.C.C. § 4A-104(1) and note federal Electronic Fund Transfer Act 15 U.S.C. § 1693e(a) and Regulations 12 C.F.R. § 205.10 only allowing stop payment orders on pre-authorized transfer instructions.

[39] *See* U.C.C. § 2-511(2). If a demand is made that payment be by legal tender, an extension of time "reasonably necessary to procure it" must be granted.

[40] *See* U.C.C. § 3-310(b).

Ward v. Federal Kemper Insurance Company

62 Md. App. 351, 489 A.2d 91 (1985)*

ADKINS, Judge.

The issue posed to us by appellant, Aaron Ward, is whether appellee, Federal Kemper Insurance Company, properly canceled an insurance policy for nonpayment of a premium. The question is whether Ward owed the premium at the time of cancellation. The answer to this seemingly-simple question is complicated by a problem in the law of negotiable instruments: in whose hands are the funds represented by a check that the drawer (Federal Kemper) has mailed to the payee (Ward) but that is never paid by the drawee bank because never negotiated by the payee? The facts are undisputed.

On May 19, 1981, Federal Kemper issued an automobile liability policy to Ward and his then wife (hereinafter "Ward"). Ward paid the premium in full. By its terms, the policy was to expire on November 17, 1981. On August 4, because of a change of vehicles owned by Ward, Federal Kemper sent him a check (payable to him) in the amount of $12.00, and drawn on The Citizens

National Bank of Decatur, Illinois. This represented a refund of overpaid premium. Ward received the check but never negotiated it.

Soon after sending the check, Federal Kemper discovered that the proper refund should have been $4.50, rather than $12.00. On August 18, it billed Ward for the difference of $7.50. Ward did not recall receiving the bill. In any event Ward never paid the $7.50, and pursuant to provisions of the policy, Federal Kemper mailed Ward a notice of cancellation effective October 11.[1] On November 15 Ward was involved in an accident while driving the insured vehicle. The accident resulted in personal injury and property damage to him, his vehicle, and to the persons and properties of others involved in the accident. Federal Kemper declined to provide coverage.

Ward sued the insurance company in the Circuit Court for Baltimore City, seeking a declar-

---

[1] It is not clear that Ward ever actually received the bill or the cancellation notice. These were mailed to his address as shown on Federal Kemper's records. At some point, however, Ward, because of domestic difficulties, had changed his address. Although the policy required him to notify Federal Kemper of such a change of address, Ward did not notify the insurer.

* [Editor note: citations in [ ] refer to Revised U.C.C. Articles 3 and 4.]

atory judgment as to coverage. There were cross-motions for summary judgment. Because he believed that summary judgment is inappropriate in a declaratory judgment action, the hearing judge treated the proceedings as a hearing on the merits. No one objected. The judge concluded that "at the time the bill was sent... in the amount of $7.50, that amount was not due Kemper." He thought that "until the negotiable instrument is negotiated and paid by the drawee back [bank] Kemper has suffered no debit." Nevertheless he went on to opine:

I... conclude that Kemper proceeded properly on an assumption that its bill was being ignored in moving for cancellation. As a matter of fact, the negotiable instrument which it had issued to Mr. Ward was still outstanding and perfectly valid on its face for a period of six months by its very terms.

...I conclude from the stipulated facts that cancellation was proper on October 11, 1981. That being so, there was no insurance coverage... by Kemper... at the time of the accident on November 15....

He granted judgment in favor of Federal Kemper.

...[W]e agree that an insurer may not cancel a policy for nonpayment of premium unless the premium is in fact due.

...To put this self-evident point more directly:

Where the propriety of the cancellation of a policy depends upon the nonpayment of a premium it necessarily follows that there is no effective cancellation when in fact the premium has been paid. For if a premium has been paid, the insurer cannot cancel for nonpayment of such premium [citations omitted].

M. Rhodes, *Couch Cyclopedia of Insurance Law* § 67:74 (Rev. 2d Ed. 1983).

...The parties agree that the real issue is who had the $7.50 premium due balance that was included in the unnegotiated $12.00 check. If this money was Ward's by virtue of his possession of the check and his ability to negotiate it, then Ward owed Federal Kemper the $7.50 and the cancellation was proper. If, on the other hand, the $7.50 was still under Federal Kemper's control, because the check had not been negotiated when the policy was canceled, the cancellation was improper. To resolve this question we must turn to the Uniform Commercial Code...

Ward points out § 3-409(1) of the Commercial Law Article of the U.C.C. [§ 3-408] which provides that:

A check or draft does not of itself operate as an assignment of any funds in the hands of the drawee available for its payment, and the drawee is not liable on the instrument until he accepts it.

Because of this rule, he argues, his mere possession of the $12.00 check did not have the effect of transferring the $12.00 to him. Federal Kemper could have stopped payment or, for that matter, closed its account at the drawee bank prior to presentment of the check. In either of these events, he would have had nothing more than a claim against Federal Kemper of the $4.50 in fact due him; the $7.50 overpayment would at all times have remained under the insurer's control, as it in fact did. He cites *Malloy v. Smith*, 265 Md. 460, 290 A.2d 486 (1972), in which the Court of Appeals, by way of dictum, observed that a personal check cannot be the subject of a gift *causa mortis*. Referring to § 3-409(1) [§ 3-408] the Court explained:

The point is, of course, that when the donor uses his own check to make the gift, there is no assignment of funds because he does not relinquish control of the sum which the check represents. A consequence of this is that a valid delivery alone will not complete the gift. To perfect the gift the check must be presented by the donee and accepted by the drawee, because the donor could stop payment, withdraw from his account the very funds which the check represents, or die before payment is made, any one of which would revoke the gift.

265 Md. at 463, 290 A.2d 486.

Federal Kemper counters that by virtue of § 3-413 [§§ 3-412, 3-413(a), 3-414(b), (e)] the drawer of a check "engages that he will pay the instrument according to its tenor..." and further "engages that upon dishonor [as through a stop payment order] and any necessary notice of dishonor or protest he will pay the amount of the draft to the holder...." According to Federal Kemper, a stop payment order may be effective to prevent payment of a check by the drawee, but that does not affect the drawer's liability to a holder in due course. Section 3-305. [§§ 3-305(b), 3-306].

Had Ward negotiated the $12.00 to a holder in due course, thereby receiving value for it, Federal Kemper would have been liable to the holder in due course despite any stop payment order. *First National Bank of Trinity, Texas v. McKay*, 521 S.W.2d 661 (Tex. Civ. App. 1975). When Federal Kemper billed Ward for the $7.50 and when it issued the cancellation notice, it had no way of knowing whether a holder in due course had entered the picture. Thus, the argument continues, by issuing the check to Ward, Federal Kemper obligated itself to pay $12.00. And since that obligation was $7.50 more than its actual premium refund debt to Ward, Ward was obligated to pay Federal Kemper the difference. Therefore, Ward owed Federal Kemper a premium of $7.50, a sum that has never been paid.

We think Federal Kemper misapprehends the nature of a check and the relationships of the parties to it. A check is a draft or bill of exchange—an order by a drawer (Federal Kemper) to a drawee (Citizens National Bank of Decatur) to pay money to a payee (Ward). Section 3-104; B. Clark, *The Law of Bank Deposits, Collections and Credit Cards* Par.1.1[1](Rev. Ed. 1981) (hereinafter "Clark"). As between drawer, the relationship is one of creditor and debtor. The drawer does not "own" the funds it has on deposit with the drawee. Its balance on the drawee's books represents a debt owed the drawer by the drawee. The funds are "owned" by the drawee. *Id.* par. 2.1.

When the drawer draws a check on the drawee and delivers the check to the payee, the check ordinarily is regarded as only a conditional payment of the underlying obligation. *Merriman v. Sandeen*, 267 N.W.2d 714, 717 (Minn. 1978); H. Bailey, *Brady on Bank Checks* §§ 1.8, 4.5 (5th ed. 1979 & 1984 Cum. Supp.) (hereinafter "Bailey"). *See also Moore v. Travelers Indemnity Ins. Co.*, 408 A.2d 298 (Del. Super. 1979). The conditions are that the check be presented and honored. Until those conditions are met, no one is directly liable on the check itself. Clark, par. 1.3. The underlying obligation represented by the check is similarly suspended until those conditions are met. § 3-802(1)(b) [§ 3-310(b)]. If they are not met (if, for example, the check is dishonored) an "action may be maintained either on the check [check] or the obligation." *Id.* [§ 3-310(b)(3)].

The point is that the drawer is only secondarily liable on the check when he issues it. *Stewart v. Citizens and Southern Natl. Bank*, 138 Ga. App. 209, 225 S.E.2d 761 (1976); Clark, par. 1.3; §§ 3-122(3) and 3-413(2).* As Ward correctly asserts, the delivery of Federal Kemper's check did not operate as an assignment to him of any funds in the hands of the drawee; § 3-409(1) [§ 3-408]; Clark, par. 3.1[1]. Ward, when he received the check, acquired no proprietary interest in the fund on deposit. Bailey § 4.1.[5]

The $12.00 check involved in this case was, of course, never dishonored. Thus, Federal Kemper never became liable directly on the check, nor was its underlying obligation (to refund $4.50 to Ward) ever actually discharged. The check was never presented to the drawee and, therefore, never paid, so the funds it represented were never transferred to Ward. In point of fact, those funds remained (and so far as we know, still remain) in the Citizens National Bank of Decatur, subject to Federal Kemper's control. Under these circumstances, we do not think that Ward owed any premium to Federal Kemper.

It is perfectly true that when Federal Kemper billed Ward, and when it sent the cancellation notice, there might have been a holder in due course lurking in the wings. That is a business risk Federal Kemper took when it proceeded as it did. The policies underlying the protections given a holder in due course, Lawrence & Minan, *The Effect of Abrogating the Holder in Due Course Doctrine on the Commercialization of Innovative Consumer Products*, 64 B.U.L. Rev. 325, 327–330 (1984), do not affect the underlying relationships between Ward and Federal Kemper, especially when, as here, there was no holder in due course. When Federal Kemper attempted to cancel the

---

* Editor: *see now* U.C.C. § 3-414(b) and Comment 2 (1991). The requirement of notice of dishonor has been eliminated. The liability of the drawer of an unaccepted draft is treated as primary liability.

[5] In *Hoffman Chevrolet, Inc. v. Washington County Nat'l Savings Bank*, 297 Md. 691, 701, 467 A.2d 758 (1983), the Court of Appeals held that a check is "property" for purposes of attachment law. That holding, however, was based on the view that a check is a chose in action—evidence of a potential claim—not on the theory that the holder of the check had any proprietary interest in the fund in the drawee's hands.

policy the entire premium was in its bank account; Ward owed it nothing at that time.

Accordingly, we hold that the Circuit Court for Baltimore City correctly concluded that "at the date the [premium due] bill was sent in the amount of $7.50 on August 18, 1981, it was not due." That being so, Federal Kemper could not lawfully have canceled Ward's policy for nonpayment of that premium. Ward is entitled to a declaratory judgment to the effect that his Federal Kemper policy was in full force and effect when the accident occurred. *See Jennings v. Government Employees Ins. Co.*, 302 Md. 352, 488 A.2d 166 (1985).

Query: Should Kemper have been advised to argue U.C.C. § 3-310(b)(1)? What effect would that have had?

NOTE

1. Where a certified check, cashier's check or teller's check is taken for an obligation, the obligation is discharged as if cash had been paid. Should such check be for a sum less than the amount allegedly owed, the discharge would be limited by the face amount of the check [U.C.C. § 3-310(a)] unless an accord and satisfaction can be asserted [U.C.C. § 3-311(a)]. The limitation on the extent of the discharge of the underlying obligation counters a presumption inherent in U.C.C. § 3-303(b) that there was consideration to discharge the obligation. Where the certified check or the cashier's check or the teller's check is endorsed, the endorser's secondary obligation on the instrument continues [U.C.C. § 3-415].[41] Additionally, transfer warranties will continue to apply [U.C.C. § 3-416].

2. What is the effect of payment by check? Does it turn a cash transaction into a credit transaction? The importance of this issue is reflected in U.C.C. §§ 2-507(2) and 2-702(2). U.C.C. § 2-507(2) provides:

> where payment is due and demanded on the delivery to the buyer of goods or documents of title, his right as against the seller to retain or dispose of them is conditional upon his making the payment due.

U.C.C. § 2-702(2) states:

> (2) Where the seller discovers that the buyer has received goods on credit while insolvent he may reclaim the goods upon demand made within ten days after the receipt, but if misrepresentation of solvency has been made to the particular seller in writing within three months before delivery the ten day limitation does not apply. Except as provided in this subsection the seller may not base a right to reclaim goods on the buyer's fraudulent or innocent misrepresentation of solvency or of intent to pay.

The section goes on to provide [U.C.C. § 2-702(3)] that the seller's right to reclaim the goods is subject to the rights of a buyer in ordinary course [U.C.C. § 1-201(9)] or other good faith purchaser under U.C.C. § 2-403. The matter is complicated additionally by the Bankruptcy Code, 11 U.S.C. § 546(c) which permits a written reclamation to be made within ten days of goods being received by an insolvent debtor, irrespective of the sale being a cash sale or a credit sale. We must note, however, that not every insolvency will result

---

[41] *But note* U.C.C. § 3-415(b). The endorser may contract out of this secondary liability by endorsing "without recourse."

in a bankruptcy. Compare U.C.C. § 1-201(23) with Bankruptcy Code, 11 U.S.C. §§ 101(13), 303 (involuntary cases) which illustrates the need for court intervention to grant a petition of bankruptcy. Should the existence of an insolvent buyer influence the decision when the check given in payment is later dishonored? U.C.C. § 2-403(1)(b).

In the Matter of Helms Veneer Corporation, Debtor in Possession
287 F. Supp. 840 (W.D. Va. 1968)

DALTON, Chief Judge.

We address ourselves to the first claim of petitioner, namely that the transactions between the reclamation claimants (hereinafter claimants) and the debtor were credit transactions.... The record shows that ... logs were released to the debtor without receiving a check, contrary to the usual custom. Although repeated demands were made, neither party received any evidence of payment from the debtor. Mr. Wagner, of Valley Log Company, testified that he released logs to the debtor upon the promise of a check in a few days. Demands for payment over a period covering several months did not produce a payment or any evidence thereof. Mr. McKinney, of McKinney and McKinney, Inc., testified that he was not present when the logs were taken by the debtor, but that he would not have released the logs without receiving a check, had he been present. He further testified that he demanded a check and received a promise that he would receive the check in a few days. Over 15 days passed before Mr. McKinney demanded his logs be returned to him. Upon demand for return, the debtor informed him that the logs belonged under a lien to James Talcott, Inc. According to the testimony, Mr. McKinney then communicated with James Talcott, Inc. and received a promise that payment would be forthcoming within three weeks.

This court believes that the transactions involving the claims of McKinney and McKinney, Inc. and The Valley Log Company constituted credit transactions. An extension of credit no matter how brief establishes an antecedent debt under the Bankruptcy Act.... A cash sale, in law, is not necessarily a conditional or an unconditional sale. Although the delivery and payment are usually thought of as being concurrent, absolute simultaneity is not requisite, if the title is not meant to pass until the payment is actually made, ... even though bankruptcy proceedings intervene. *In*

the Matter of Mort Co., 208 F. Supp. 309 (E. D. Pa. 1962). However, by the claimants' own testimony, the logs were either voluntarily released or allowed to remain in the possession of the debtor upon receiving promises of payment in the future. There does not have to be a willing extension of credit to create an antecedent debt which would, if paid, create a voidable preference under the provisions of the Bankruptcy Act. *Engelkes v. Farmers Co-operative Co.*, 194 F. Supp. 319 (N.D. Iowa 1961).

> "Delay in making a promised payment, transfer of property, or the giving of security, in connection with a transaction which was intended by the parties to be current and upon present consideration, may result in ultimate performance being regarded as with respect to past credit and on account of antecedent indebtedness." 4 *Remington on Bankruptcy* § 1661.2 (1957)....

The testimony by Mr. Butler, of Valley Log Co., clearly shows that he released his logs on a promise of payment in the future. Mr. McKinney of McKinney and McKinney, Inc., testified "We kept asking for a check to be sent to us and they promised it would be sent on the 10th." The United States Supreme Court, in *National City Bank v. Hotchkiss*, 231 U.S. 50, at 58, 34 S. Ct. 20, at 21, 58 L. Ed. 115 (1913), in holding that a bank who had loaned money at 10 o'clock in the morning and received payment of the loan at 3 o'clock, the borrowers entering bankruptcy at 4 o'clock the same day, had received an illegal preference, said,

> "The consent to become a general creditor for an hour, that was imported, even if not intended to have that effect, by the liberty allowed to the firm, broke the continuity and established the loan as part of the assets."

The claimant's right to reclaim goods sold on

credit to an insolvent buyer, as here presented, is governed by § 2-702 of the [Virginia] Uniform Commercial Code. We do not agree with the referee that, except for bankruptcy, these particular claimant-sellers could have reclaimed the logs. The seller's right to reclaim goods sold on credit to an insolvent buyer is limited by the second provision of § 2-702, of the Uniform Commercial Code, "Where the seller discovers that the buyer has received goods on credit while insolvent he may reclaim the goods upon demand made within ten days after the receipt * * *." The Official Comment states that the discovery of the buyer's insolvency and demand within a ten day period of receipt are conditions of the right to reclaim the goods.... The testimony is clear that no demand was made for a return of the goods within a ten day period of their delivery, but rather that demands were made for payment. The record does not reveal any evidence of the buyer's insolvency at the time of the receipt of the goods or within a ten day period thereafter. Because the record does not disclose even the minimum conditions required in order for credit sellers to reclaim the goods, but rather the contrary, the claims cannot stand as priority claims. It is, therefore, ordered that the specific orders of the referee allowing the claims of McKinney and McKinney, Inc. and Valley Log Co. as priority claims are reversed.

The claim involving Van's Wood Products, Inc. is different. Mr. VanDevender, of Van's Wood Products, Inc., testified that he released three loads of logs on February 27, 1968 worth $5,084 to the debtor in return for a check in the amount of $4,000 and a promise of future payment of the remaining $1,084. The check was timely presented to the bank for payment and subsequently returned because of insufficient funds. Sometime after March 12, 1968 with the assurance of debtor's agent that funds were available, the check was again submitted to the bank and again returned for the same reason. The claimant then demanded the return of his goods.

The referee ordered that the Van's Wood Products, Inc. receive $4,000 as a priority claim with the remaining amount to be treated as a general claim.

Petitioner contends that the acceptance of a check in less than the full amount constituted a part payment on an open account. We do not agree. The acceptance of a check does not change

a cash sale into a credit transaction. If the intention of the parties was to accomplish a cash transaction, which is the custom of the trade, then an acceptance of a check in place of actual cash does not change the transaction. *Engstrom v. Wiley*, 191 F.2d 684 (9th Cir. 1951). The Uniform Commercial Code recognizes payment by check as a commercially normal and proper method of payment. Uniform Commercial Code § 2-511. The record before this court reveals nothing, except for a statement by petitioner's lawyer in the cross-examination, to indicate that the parties meant to deviate from the normal cash basis that is the custom of the trade. The customs and habits, plus the intention of the parties are governing factors in determining whether there has been a cash transaction. *Engstrom v. Wiley*, 191 F.2d 684 (9th Cir. 1951). We find no convincing evidence that the parties ever intended anything but a cash transaction. Petitioner offered no affirmative evidence either by testimony or documents to show otherwise. We therefore adopt the referee's findings and the inferences therefrom as being substantiated by the record and not clearly erroneous....

Accepting the referee's finding of a cash sale, we perceive another problem that must be answered. What are the rights of a seller in a cash transaction, upon the dishonor of a check taken as payment for goods delivered to the buyer? The court, in *In the Matter of Mort Co.*, 208 F. Supp. 309 (E.D. Pa. 1962) was confronted with this problem. The facts of that case were that a seller had delivered goods to the buyer and received simultaneously a check as payment. Past transactions between the parties had been on a C.O.D. basis. The check was immediately deposited by the seller, but was never paid because the buyer had filed for bankruptcy three days after receipt of the goods. The facts state that there was enough money on deposit to have paid the check. The seller within a ten day period filed a petition for reclamation for money received by the trustee in bankruptcy for the goods delivered and sold pursuant to an agreement between the parties. The court, in allowing the seller to prevail over the trustee in bankruptcy, interpreted Sections 2-507(2) and 2-511 of the Uniform Commercial Code (hereafter U.C.C.), which sections correspond to the same numerical sections in the Virginia U.C.C. In interpreting § 2-507(2), the court determined that the seller in a cash transaction, who accepted a check which the bank refused to pay because of the intervening of bankruptcy proceedings, had the right to reclaim the goods sold and that nothing in the Bankruptcy Act changed this. The court further stated,

"* * * if the seller has a right to reclaim the goods he stands in a position superior to any creditor." *In the Matter of Mort Co., supra,* at 310. Noting that the Official Comment to § 2-511 recognized the acceptance of a check as a commercially normal and proper method of payment, the court said:

> The check was not postdated. Moreover the buyer was seemingly solvent as far as this sale was concerned since there was enough money in the bank to cover the check. A businessman in financial difficulty must be able to carry on cash transactions or go out of business altogether. Unless we are to return to primitive commercial methods, such a businessman should be able to use a check for payment. This is certainly the proper rule when the check is not postdated and when, if the payee presents the check immediately to the bank on which it was drawn, he will be paid. *In the Matter of Mort Co., supra,* at 311.

In the present case we note two factors which we think distinguishes it from the *Mort* case, *supra.* First, the check received in payment for a cash transaction was dishonored twice, not because bankruptcy intervened, but because the debtor had insufficient funds on deposit to cover the check. Secondly, and more important, the time period involved in the present case, as revealed by the testimony of the claimant, covered a period in excess of ten days before demand was made for return of the goods. We agree with the reasoning in the *Mort* case, *supra,* that § 2-507 gives the seller a right to reclaim his goods where a check, subsequently dishonored, has been accepted for payment in a cash transaction. However the right to reclaim is limited. The Official Comment to § 2-507 of the U.C.C. reads:

> 3. Subsection (2) deals with the effect of a conditional delivery by the seller and in such a situation makes the buyer's "right as against the seller" conditional upon payment. These words are used as words of

limitation to conform with the policy set forth in the bona-fide purchase sections of this article. Should the seller after making such a conditional delivery fail to follow up his rights, the condition is waived. The provision of this article for a ten day limit within which the seller may reclaim goods delivered on credit to an insolvent buyer is also applicable here.

The Official Comment to § 2-511(3) reads:

> 6. Where the instrument offered by the buyer is not a payment but a credit instrument such as a note or a check postdated by even one day, the seller's acceptance of the instrument insofar as third parties are concerned, amounts to a delivery on credit and his remedies are set forth in the section on buyer's insolvency. As between the buyer and seller, however, the matter turns on the present subsection and the section on conditional delivery and subsequent dishonor of the instrument gives the seller rights on it as well as for breach of the contract for sale.

We interpret § 2-507 and § 2-511 of the Virginia U.C.C. as giving the seller a right to reclaim his goods from the buyer where a cash transaction has occurred, and a check, taken in payment by the seller, was dishonored. However, the right to reclaim is limited to a ten day period from the delivery of the goods as provided by § 2-507 by virtue of its cross reference to § 2-702. If the right to reclaim has not been exercised within that specified time period, the right is waived. The seller's remedy is then on the instrument as well as for breach of contract. This, as we interpret it, reduces the seller's rights to those of a general creditor. It is clear from the testimony of Mr. VanDevender that a period in excess of ten days had passed before he demanded return of the logs. Therefore, we are constrained to hold that any rights that were annexed to the original cash transaction have been reduced to those of a general creditor by the provisions of the above cited statutes. We, therefore, reverse the order of the referee allowing the claim of Van's Wood Products, Inc. as a priority claim to be paid in full.

Burk v. Emmick

637 F.2d 1172 (8th Cir. 1980)

. . . Some courts have decided that a cash seller's reclamation right is subject to the ten-day limitation provision covering credit sale transactions involving insolvent buyers under section 2-702, but those decisions are factually dissimilar.[5] The courts that have imposed the ten-day limitation have concerned the respective rights of a good faith purchaser or trustee in bankruptcy and an unpaid seller.[6] But here, a good faith purchaser is not involved. Nor are we faced with the conflicting interests of an unpaid seller and a trustee in bankruptcy representing the interests of a bankrupt's creditors.[*] Rather, the conflict is between the unpaid cash seller and the breaching buyer, and the question is whether the seller may reclaim and recover a deficiency judgment from that buyer. . . .

Our holding is quite limited. We determine that as between the seller and the buyer, where a cash seller reclaims goods sold to a breaching buyer, the only limitation imposed upon the seller's right is a reasonableness requirement. Since we determine that the buyer was not prejudiced by the seller's delay in reclaiming the cattle, we find the seller's reclamation was not unreasonable.

---

[5] The Code does not expressly require that § 2-702's ten-day limitation be applied to cash sale transactions not involving insolvent buyers. J. White & R. Summers, *Uniform Commercial Code* § 3-6 at 115 (2d ed. 1980). Several factors militate against grafting § 2-702's limitation to cash sale transactions: (1) § 2-702 by its terms applies only to credit sales. (2) The seller's reclamation right is not dependent upon Comment 3 to § 2-507. The right to reclaim is inherent in the language of the statute. *See* Dugan, *Cash Sale Sellers Under Articles 2 and 9 of the Uniform Commercial Code*, 8 U.C.C. L.J. 330, 345–349 (1976); Mann & Phillips, *The Cash Seller Under the Uniform Commercial Code*, 20 B.C. L. REV. 370, 383 & n.68 (1979). The limitation, at best, is only suggested by the Comment; the Comments to the Code cannot impose restrictions unwarranted by the statutory language. *See* Thompson v. United States, 408 F.2d 1075, 1084 n.15 (8th Cir. 1969); Dugan, *supra* at 341–342. (3) The legislative history of § 2-507 indicates that this section was intended to reflect the common law of cash sale transactions; the common law tradition includes the seller's right to reclamation. *See generally* Mann & Phillips, *supra* at 376–380, 383–384, & nn. 46–50 (1979).

[6] *But see* Szabo v. Vinton Motors, Inc., 630 F.2d 1, (1st Cir., 1980). . . . *Szabo* concerned an appeal taken by the trustee in bankruptcy of the breaching buyer. Mr. Szabo, the trustee, argued that since the seller did not make a demand for reclamation within ten days after it sold an automobile to the buyer, it lost any special right to reclamation and stood before the court in the shoes of a general creditor. The First Circuit, moved by the trustee's argument, reversed the lower court order ruling otherwise.

The Court's reasoning was simple; it stated that §§ 2-507 and 2-511 provide the cash seller the right to reclaim. The Court then noted that Official Comment 3 to § 2-507 imposed a ten-day limitation upon the cash seller's statutory right. Szabo v. Vinton Motors, Inc., *supra*, 630 F.2d at 3–4, citing In re Samuels & Co., *supra*, and In re Helms Veneer Corp., *supra*.

We reject this reasoning. In our view, it would tend to coerce the cash seller who reasonably expects the buyer to tender payment at delivery to go through the cautious motions of a credit seller dealing with an economically unstable buyer. This we are not prepared to do.

[*] [Editor's Note: In bankruptcy, whether delivery was in a cash sale or a credit transaction, a demand for reclamation made by the seller must be made in writing "before ten days after receipt of such goods by the debtor." Bankruptcy Code, 11 U.S.C. § 546(c).]

NOTE

The cross-reference to U.C.C. Section 2-702 used to appear in Comment 3 to U.C.C. Section 2-507 and was the basis for applying the ten day limit to both a cash sale or a credit sale. *See Szabo, Trustee in Bankruptcy of Bell Oldsmobile, Inc. v. Vinton Motors, Inc.*, 630 F.2d 1 (1st Cir. 1980) *but note, Burk v. Emmick*, 637 F.2d 1172, 1176 (8th Cir. 1980) ("We determine that as between the seller and the buyer, where a cash seller reclaims goods sold to a breaching buyer, the only limitation imposed upon the seller's right is a reasonableness requirement."). The reference to the ten day limit in Comment 3 to U.C.C. Section 2-507 has been deleted by the Permanent Editorial Board, P.E.B. Commentary No. 1, March 10, 1990.

> There is nothing in the language of § 2-507(2) supporting the imposition of the "ten day limit" mentioned in Comment 3 . . . There is no justification for barring the cash seller's right or remedy of reclamation before discovery of non-payment. There is no specific time limit for a cash seller to exercise the right of reclamation. The right may be exercised as long as there has not been an excessive delay causing inequitable prejudice to the buyer. Common law rules and precedents governing such circumstances are applicable.

In a bankruptcy, however, whether delivery was in a cash sale or a credit transaction, a demand for reclamation must be made by the seller in writing "before ten days after receipt of such goods by the debtor while insolvent." Bankruptcy Code, 11 U.S.C. Section 546(c).

Question: If the intention of the parties was the creation of a credit sale, is the giving of a check prior to delivery a written misrepresentation for solvency so that the ten day limitation under U.C.C. Section 2-702(2) does not apply?

D. The United Nations Convention on International Bills of Exchange and International Promissory Notes[42]

The use of negotiable instruments in international commerce has proven problematic. In attempting to use negotiable payment devices in international transactions, parties are presented with conflicting domestic laws of the legal systems impacting on the transaction. Many of these laws do not reflect the modern needs of commerce and thus are in need of modernization. It is believed that a vast majority of instruments currently in circulation internationally are not generally negotiable. In response to the need to have some uniformity for the purpose of achieving certainty, the U.N. Convention on International Bills of Exchange and International Promissory Notes, (CIBN), proposes rules governing drafts (bills of exchange) and promissory notes, while leaving checks to be regulated by domestic banking laws.

The U.N. Convention seeks to achieve this by means of uniform rules applicable to instruments used in an international transaction. The CIBN seeks to clarify what it considers to be an international transaction by requiring that the instrument must clearly indicate that it will circulate between two or more countries, one of which must be a contracting party to the CIBN.[43] The CIBN further requires that such instruments be labelled conspicuously as "international bill of exchange" or as "international promissory note".[44] This

---

[42] U.N. General Assembly Resolution 43/165, U.N. Doc. No. A/42/17 Annex 1. Reprinted 28 I.L.M. 170 (1989).

[43] CIBN Article 2.

[44] *Id.*

allows the parties to the transaction to elect the CIBN as the controlling law of the instrument. Thus, parties must "opt in" to the CIBN. To make certain that the parties intend the application of the CIBN, it is not only necessary to label the instrument as indicated, but also the text of the instrument itself must make reference to the applicability of the CIBN. Absent such express indication that the CIBN shall apply, the instrument will be subject to the usual conflict of laws rules of the forum.

The parties are able to select other rules that they decide will serve their purposes better.[45] The CIBN contains specific provisions applicable to instruments to which it is to apply. Some of these provisions may conflict with the approach taken by the U.C.C. In recognizing this possibility Comment 5 to U.C.C. Section 3-102 provides that:

> If the United States becomes a party to this Convention, the Convention will preempt state law with respect to international bills and notes governed by the Convention. Thus, an international bill of exchange or promissory note that meets the definition of instrument in Section 3-104 will not be governed by Article 3 if it is governed by the Convention.

But if the parties to the transactions do not wish to be governed by a particular provision of the CIBN it is incumbent upon them to specifically "opt out" of such provision. For the Convention to come into force, at least ten nations must ratify the CIBN. Since this may take a considerable time to achieve, there is a proposal under consideration for the North American Free Trade Association (NAFTA) members, the U.S.A., Canada, and Mexico, to enter into a protocol to bring the CIBN into operation among the members of NAFTA.[46]

---

[45] Examples are the U.C.C., the British Bills of Exchange Act (B.E.A.), the Geneva Uniform Laws on Bills of Exchange (U.L.B.), the Organization of American States (O.A.S.) Bills and Notes and Checks Convention, or any other law indicated by the conflict of laws rules of the forum state.

[46] Canada and Mexico have ratified the CIBN, and it is expected that the CIBN and this protocol will be submitted to the U.S. Senate for ratification in 1993.

III   THE CONCEPT OF NEGOTIABILITY

"Negotiability" in the legal sense means that:

1. The obligor or issuer cannot assert against a purchaser of the instrument in good faith and for value any "defense" to the holder's claim to the benefit of the obligations expressed or inherent in the instrument, except a claim that the paper is not genuine, for example, that his signature was forged or otherwise placed upon it without his authority. Specifically, the obligor cannot raise against the good faith purchaser any defect rising from the transaction financed by issuance of the instrument, as distinct from the instrument itself. *Peacock v. Rhodes*, (1781) 2 Doug. 633, 99 Eng. Rep. 402 (K.B.); U.C.C. § 3-305(a)(1)(2).

2. Similarly, a purchaser in good faith for value and without notice that the rights of any prior holder have been in any way infringed takes a negotiable instrument in all respects free of any claim by or through any prior holder. Colloquially expressed, even the thief who has no legal right or claim to the instrument or to the rights and interests that it represents can in many instances give the bona fide purchaser a "perfect title." *Miller v. Race*, 1 Burr. 452, 97 Eng. Rep. 398 (K.B. 1758); U.C.C. § 3-306.

Miller v. Race
1 Burr. 452, 97 Eng. Rep. 398 (K.B. 1758)

It was an action of trover against the defendant, upon a bank note, for the payment of twenty-one pounds ten shillings to one William Finney or bearer, on demand.

The cause came on to be tried before Lord Mansfield at the sittings in Trinity term last at Guildhall, London: and upon the trial it appeared that William Finney, being possessed of this bank note on the 11th of December 1756, sent it by the general post, under cover, directed to one Bernard Odenharty, at Chipping Norton in Oxfordshire; that on the same night the mail was robbed, and the bank note in question (amongst other notes) taken and carried away by the robber; that this bank note, on the 12th of the same December, came into the hands and possession of the plaintiff, for a full and valuable consideration, and in the usual course and way of his business, and without any notice or knowledge of this bank note being taken out of the mail.

It was admitted and agreed, that, in the common and known course of trade, bank notes are paid by and received of the holder or possessor of them, as cash; and that in the usual way of negotiating bank notes, they pass from one person to another as cash, by delivery only and without any further inquiry or evidence of title, than what arises from the possession. It appeared that Mr. Finney, having notice of this robbery, on the 13th December, applied to the Bank of England, "to stop the payment of this note:" which was ordered accordingly, upon Mr. Finney's entering into proper security "to indemnify the bank."

Some little time after this, the plaintiff applied to the bank for the payment of this note; and for that purpose delivered the note to the defendant, who is a clerk in the bank: but the defendant refused either to pay the note, or to re-deliver it to the plaintiff. Upon which this action was brought against the defendant.

The jury found a verdict for the plaintiff, and the sum of £21.10s. damages, subject nevertheless to the opinion of this Court upon this question — "Whether under the circumstances of this case, the plaintiff had a sufficient property in this bank note, to entitle him to recover in the present action?" . . .

Lord Mansfield now delivered the resolution to the Court.

After stating the case at large, he declared that at the trial, he had no sort of doubt, but this action was well brought, and would lie against the defendant in the present case; upon the general course of business, and from the consequences of trade and commerce: which would be much incommoded by a contrary determination.

It has been very ingeniously argued by Sir Richard Lloyd for the defendant. But the whole fallacy of the argument turns upon comparing bank notes to what they do not resemble, and what they ought not to be compared to, viz. to goods, or to securities, or documents for debts.

Now they are not goods, not securities, nor documents for debts, nor are so esteemed: but are treated as money, as cash, in the ordinary course and transaction of business, by the general consent of mankind; which gives them the credit and currency of money, to all intents and purposes. They are as much money, as guineas themselves are; or any other current coin, that is used in common payments, as money or cash.

They pass by a will, which bequeaths all the testator's money or cash; and are never considered as securities for money, but as money itself. Upon Ld. Ailesbury's will, £900 in bank-notes was considered as cash. On payment of them, whenever a receipt is required, the receipts are always given as for money; not as for securities or notes.

So on bankruptcies, they cannot be followed as identical and distinguishable from money: but are always considered as money or cash.

It is a pity that reporters sometimes catch at quaint expressions that may happen to be dropped at the Bar or Bench; and mistake their meaning. It has been quaintly said, "that the reason why money can not be followed is, because it has no ear-mark:" but this is not true. The true reason is, upon account of the currency of it: it can not be recovered after it has passed in currency. So, in case of money stolen, the true owner can not recover it, after it has been paid away fairly and honestly upon a valuable and bona fide consideration: but before money has passed in currency, an action may be brought for the money itself. There was a case in 1 G. 1, at the sittings, *Thomas v. Whip*, before Ld. Macclesfield: which was an action upon assumpsit, by an administrator against the defendant, for money had and received to his use. The defendant was nurse to the intestate during his sickness; and, being alone, conveyed away the money. And Ld. Macclesfield held that the action lay. Now this must be esteemed a finding at least.

Apply this to the case of a bank-note. An action may lie against the finder, it is true; (and it is not at all denied) but not after it has been paid away in currency. And this point has been determined, even in the infancy of bank-notes; for 1 Salk. 126, M. 10 W.3, at Nisi Prius, is in point. And Ld. Ch. J. Holt there says that it is "by reason of the course of trade; which creates a property in the assignee or bearer." (And "the bearer" is a more proper expression than assignee.)

Here, an inn-keeper took it, bona fide, in his business from a person who made an appearance of a gentleman. Here is no pretence of suspicion of collusion with the robber: for this matter was strictly inquired and examined into at the trial; and is so stated in the case, "that he took it for a full and valuable consideration, in the usual course of business." Indeed if there had been any collusion, or any circumstances of unfair dealing, the case had been much otherwise. If it had been a note for £1000. it might have been suspicious: but this was a small note for £21. 10s. only: and money given in exchange for it.

Another case cited was a loose note in 1 Ld.Raym. 738, ruled by Ld. Ch. J. Holt at Guildhall, in 1698; which proves nothing for the defendant's side of the question: but it is exactly agreeable to what is laid down by my Ld. Ch. J. Holt, in the case I have just mentioned. The action did not lie against the assignee of the bank-bill; because he had it for valuable consideration.

In that case, he had it from the person who found it: but the action did not lie against him, because he took it in the course of currency; and therefore it could not be followed in his hands. It never shall be followed into the hands of a person who bona fide took it in the course of currency, and in the way of his business.

The case of *Ford v. Hopkins*, was also cited: which was in Hil. 12 W. 3, coram Holt Ch. J. at Nisi Prius, at Guildhall; and was an action of trover for million-lottery tickets. But this must be a very incorrect report of that case: it is impossible that it can be a true representation of what Ld. Ch. J. Holt said. It represents him as speaking of bank-notes, Exchequer-notes, and million lottery tickets, as like to each other. Now no two things can be more unlike to each other than a lottery-ticket, and a bank-note. Lottery tickets are identical and specific: specific actions lie for them. They may prove extremely unequal in value: one may be a prize; another, a blank. Land is not more specific than lottery-tickets are. It is there said, "that the delivery of plaintiff's tickets to the defendant, as that case was, was no change of property." And most clearly it was no change of the property; so far, the case is right. But it is here urged as a proof "that the true owner may follow a stolen bank-note, into what hands soever it shall come."

Now the whole of that case turns upon the throwing in banknotes, as being like to lottery-tickets.

But Ld. Ch. J. Holt could never say "that an action would lie against the person who, for a valuable consideration, had received a bank-note which had been stolen or lost, and bona fide paid to him:" even though the action was brought by the true owner: because he had determined otherwise, but two years before; and because bank-notes are not like lottery-tickets, but money.

The person who took down this case, certainly misunderstood Lord Ch. J. Holt, or mistook his reasons. For this reasoning would prove, (if it was true, as the reporter represents it,) that if a man paid to a goldsmith £500. in bank-notes, the goldsmith could never pay them away.

A bank-note is constantly and universally, both at home and abroad, treated as money, as cash; and paid and received, as cash; and it is necessary, for the purposes of commerce, that their currency should be established and secured. . . .

Lord Mansfield declared that the Court were all of the same opinion, for the plaintiff; and that Mr. Just. Wilmot concurred.

Rule — That the postea be delivered to the plaintiff.

NOTE

1. In *Peacock v. Rhodes* (1781) 2 Doug. 633, 99 Eng. Rep. 402 (K.B.) Lord Mansfield applied the same principles to a bill of exchange payable to order which had been stolen (after having been indorsed in blank) and negotiated to the plaintiff who gave value for it in good faith. Lord Mansfield's judgment is instructive in that it contains a clear statement of the difference between assignability and negotiability. He said:

The holder of a bill of exchange or promissory note is not to be considered in the light of an assignee of the payee. An assignee must take the thing assigned subject to all the equity to which the original party was subject. If this rule applied to bills and promissory notes, it would stop their currency. The law is settled that a holder, coming fairly by a bill or note, has nothing to do with the transaction between the original parties. . . . I see no difference between a note indorsed blank and one payable to bearer. 2 Doug. at 636, 99 Eng. Rep. at 403.

This approach is now embodied in U.C.C. Section 3-408. "A check or other draft does not of itself operate as an assignment of funds in the hands of the drawee available for its payment, and the drawee is not liable on the instrument until the drawee accepts it."

It was only reluctantly that the common law accepted the concept of negotiability applicable to specific forms of instruments. The personal relationship underlying common law obligations left it to equity courts to develop the concept of assignment, whereby a third party would stand in the shoes of someone who had originally bound himself to the performance of an obligation or to receive the benefit thereof. Assignments are subject to the rights of the other party and thereby are clearly distinguishable from negotiation.[1]

2. The concept of negotiability involves the incorporation of an incorporeal concept of obligation into a corporeal writing. This *reification* of an intangible enables the obligation to be negotiated. It results in the obligation being satisfied only when the written instrument is recovered and canceled or marked to indicate that full or partial satisfaction had occurred. U.C.C. §§ 3-501(b)(iii), 7-502(1)(d). Absent such cancellation, should an instrument come into the hands of a person who takes the instrument for value, in good faith, without notice of any defense, including the defense that the obligation has been satisfied, the obligor could be called upon once more to perform or pay damages. *E.g.*, U.C.C. §§ 3-601(b), 7-502(1)(d).

3. Professor Rodgers has shown that the concept of negotiability as the core of bills and notes transactions is a recent phenomenon. *See* James Steven Rodgers, *The Myth of Negotiability*, 31 B.C. L. Rev. 266 (1990). The need for a substitute to represent coins, however, gave the stimulus needed to develop the concept of negotiability. The question remains whether the need for currency as a basis of a monetary theory is as strong today when technical developments have provided alternate means of settling payment obligations?

The person demanding payment or goods must be in possession of the document of title or of the instrument so as to make presentment. This will enable the obligor on satisfying the obligation set forth in the paper to cancel it and prevent a document of title from coming into the hands of a bona fide purchaser for value and without notice of any claims to it, through "due negotiation," U.C.C. Section 7-501(4), or prevent an instrument being negotiated to a holder in due course, U.C.C. § 3-302. In a court action, where a claimant who can prove ownership is unable to produce the instrument but can adduce facts which indicate the impossibility of production of the instrument because it has been lost, stolen or destroyed, U.C.C. § 3-309 (b) provides a solution where the claimant offers to indemnify the obligor on the instrument. But, "[t]he court may not enter judgment in favor of the person seeking enforcement unless it finds that the person required to pay the instrument is adequately protected against loss that might occur by reason of a claim by another person to enforce the instrument. Adequate protection may be provided by any reasonable means." U.C.C. § 3-309(b).

Adequate protection is a flexible concept and will relate to the degree of certainty about the facts alleged. For example, whether the instrument was in bearer form or an unendorsed order instrument. See also U.C.C. Section 3-312 which deals with a claim to a lost, destroyed or stolen cashier's check, teller check, or certified check. That section allows a bank not to honor such check subsequent to the claim having become enforceable even were it to be presented by a person who is a holder in due course. The claim under

---

[1] At common law, contractual rights could only be "assigned" by novation. Equity allowed the assignee to sue in his own name—at common law the assignor had to be joined as a party. *See* Maitland, *Equity*, Lecture XI (1913).

this section must be by a person having "the right to receive the amount of . . . [such instrument alleged to have been] lost, destroyed or stolen." U.C.C. § 3-312 (a)(b). The claimant, who must make a written "declaration of loss," is under a duty, however, to refund any monies received from the bank, or to pay such sums directly to a holder in due course of the instrument who subsequently may appear.

Until production of the instrument or satisfaction of Section 3-309 a claimant not in possession of the instrument has no standing to sue on the instrument. *Investment Serv. Co. v. Martin Bros. Container & Timber Prod. Corp.*, 255 Or. 192, 465 P.2d 868 (1970). This case seems to take the requirement for possession too far, since the claimant held the note at the time of the trial though not when the pleadings were filed. Thus, there was no fear that subsequent to payment and cancellation of the instrument by the obligor/issuer a holder in due course of the instrument could appear. As a procedural matter, however, possession seems a requirement of standing to sue. *Locks v. North Towne Nat'l Bank of Rockford*, 115 Ill. App. 3d 729, 451 N.E.2d 19 (1983). *See also* Chapter VII pp. 255–257, *infra*. A further exception to this rule applies to a presenter who has been paid by mistake and had to repay the payor. Such person will be able to sue a drawer or endorser to recover from them though the instrument will have been surrendered to the maker, drawer, or bank. U.C.C. §§ 3-301(iii), 3-309, 3-418(d).

A.   Goods

The common law's approach to property rights, expressed in the maxim *nemo dat qui non habet*, that one cannot transfer a larger right than one has, had its first inroads by the acceptance of the concept of voidable title, i.e. a valid title to rights in goods until such title was revoked. The problem arose where a transferee, whose title could be avoided, prior to such avoidance sold the goods to a bona fide purchaser for value and without notice of the inherent defect existing in the title of his seller. Holding that this category of purchaser could defeat the rights of the original transferor was "a response to the need to protect the security of the marketplace. Persons *relying* upon merchants' possession of goods, including lenders taking goods as security, had to be assured that they had good title, free of the claims of owners who had delivered the goods to the merchants. In commercial situations, this goal was achieved by applying the voidable title doctrine, thereby shifting the distribution risks to these owners."[2] It must be recognized that the concept of "voidable title" presumes the existence of a valid title until such is avoided. The race is between a party able to avoid the title of the transferor and a good faith purchaser for value without notice.

The U.C.C. developed this concept further by eliminating the restrictions the common law had placed on this concept. For example, in recognition of modern methods of communication there is no need for the parties to be "face to face" for a transferor to be

---

[2] Rapson, *A "Home Run" Application of Established Principles of Statutory Construction: U.C.C. Analogies*, 5 Cardozo L. Rev. 441, 446 (1984).

deceived as to the identity of the purchaser thus leading to voidability of the transaction.[3] U.C.C. Article 3 in Section 3-404(a) clarifies this by providing specifically that the inducement to issue an instrument to an imposter can be "by use of the mails or otherwise."[4] The U.C.C. in relation to the power in a person having a voidable title to goods to transfer good title provides in Section 2-403:

(1) A purchaser of goods acquires all title which his transferor had or had power to transfer except that a purchaser of a limited interest acquires rights only to the extent of the interest purchased. A person with voidable title has power to transfer a good title to a good faith purchaser for value. When goods have been delivered under a transaction of purchase the purchaser has such power even though
(a) the transferor was deceived as to the identity of the purchaser, or
(b) the delivery was in exchange for a check which is later dishonored, or
(c) it was agreed that the transaction was to be a "cash sale," or
(d) the delivery was procured through fraud punishable as larcenous under the criminal law

---

[3] Phelps v. McQuade, 220 N.Y. 232, 115 N.E. 441 (1917), and compare Rogers v. Dutton, 182 Mass. 187, 65 N.E. 66 (1902) where there was a representation of agency to induce transfer to a purported "principal." With regard to instruments, however, U.C.C. -Article 3, § 3-404(a) rejects the conclusion in *Rogers v. Dutton.*

[4] Philadelphia Title Ins. Co. v. Fidelity - Philadelphia Trust Co., 419 Pa. 78, 212 A.2d 222 (1965) (fraudulent representation of identity made to lawyer and real estate agent, who then informed title company clerk that they had seen the documents signed by the "mortgagor." The clerk signed as witness, though he was not present when the signature was appended, and then notarized the deeds. Held: Bank that cashed the check and obtained payment from the drawee was entitled to retain these funds). Cf. Cundy v. Lindsay [1878] 3 A.C. 459 (H.L.) (Court held no contract in this common law case; mistake as to identity of other contracting party. Letter received thought to emanate from W. Blenkiron & Son was sent by imposter, A. Blenkarn, of same street address).

Jernigan v. Ham
691 S.W.2d 553 (Tenn. Ct. App. 1985)

HIGHERS, J. This case involves the applicability of U.C.C. § 2-401 and § 2-403.

The plaintiff, a resident of Shelby County, offered his 1954 Ford Jubilee tractor for sale in the front yard of his home. In December 1982, he was contacted by an individual named John Rickman who expressed an interest in purchasing the tractor. Rickman inspected the tractor on or about December 22, 1982, and informed the plaintiff that he would discuss the matter with his brother and that he would notify the plaintiff if they wished to purchase the tractor. He later called the plaintiff and offered to purchase the tractor and blade for $2,250.00.

When Rickman returned and loaded the tractor and grader blade onto his trailer, he gave the plaintiff a check. The plaintiff stated that he did not want a check, but that he required cash. They agreed, however, that since the tractor was already loaded, Rickman could take it and return with the cash the next day at which time the plaintiff would give him a bill of sale.

On the following day, December 23, 1982, Rickman took the tractor and blade to Memphis Ford Tractor, Inc., and through William Ham sold the equipment for $1,500.00. When Ham bought the tractor and blade from Rickman, he did not ask for a bill of sale. Ham testified that it is not customary to demand a bill of sale because "it's very doubtful that people could go back and dig up a bill of sale that they've had for years and years." Rickman told Ham that the tractor had been used at a deer camp. Ham testified that although the tractor was clean, most sellers clean their equipment before bringing it to sell. Ham also noticed that Rickman's truck had Arkansas license plates, but Ham stated that he often bought tractors from individuals from Arkansas and Mississippi. Ham had no prior or subsequent dealings with Rickman.

When Rickman failed to return with cash, the plaintiff began to search for Rickman and the tractor. He located the tractor on the lot of the Memphis Ford Tractor, Inc., on the evening of December 23, 1982. On the next day, the plaintiff contacted Ham about the tractor and demanded possession, but Ham refused to relinquish the tractor.

The plaintiff filed suit in the General Sessions Court, and judgment was rendered in his favor for the return of the tractor or for $2,250.00. On appeal to the Circuit Court, this judgment was reversed and the action dismissed. In the meantime, the defendant sold the tractor in the regular course of business for $2,300.00 and the blade for approximately $150.00. Rickman never paid the check to the plaintiff, and he was subsequently convicted of larceny by trick and passing bad checks. [The Court recited U.C.C. § 2-403(1)].

The plaintiff contends that the foregoing provision does not apply because there is either a bailment or there is a theft in this case. We cannot agree that the facts of this case constitute a bailment. Bailment is the delivery of personalty to another for a particular purpose or on mere deposit of an express or implied contract that after the purpose has been fulfilled, the property should be returned to the person who delivered it. *Rhodes v. Pioneer Parking Lot, Inc.*, 501 S.W.2d 569 (Tenn. 1973). There is no indication in the record that the plaintiff and Rickman contracted for anything other than a sale. The plaintiff intended to relinquish possession on a permanent rather than on a temporary basis.

The plaintiff correctly argues that an innocent purchaser of stolen goods may be liable to the rightful owner of the proceeds of their subsequent sale. *See Duncan v. State Farm Fire & Casualty Company*, 587 S.W.2d 375 (Tenn. 1979). On the other hand, however, U.C.C. § 2-403(1) empowers a purchaser with a voidable title to confer good title upon a good faith purchaser for value where the goods were procured through fraud punishable as larcenous under the criminal law. The distinction between *theft* and *fraud* in this context is found in the statutory definitions of "delivery"

and "purchase." Delivery concerns a voluntary transfer of possession, U.C.C. § 1-201(14), and purchase refers to a voluntary transaction creating an interest in property. U.C.C. § 1-201(32). In the present case, the plaintiff voluntarily relinquished possession to Rickman. As one commentator has pointed out, "[a] thief who wrongfully takes goods is not a purchaser ... but a swindler who fraudulently induces the victim to voluntarily deliver them is a purchaser ... " 2 W. Hawkland, *Uniform Commercial Code Series*, § 2-403-03, 606-07 (1982).

The plaintiff takes the position that larceny by trick is not fraud within the meaning of the statute. We find this argument to be without merit. The Official Comments to 2-403 state:

subsection (1) provides specifically for the protection of the good faith purchaser for value in a number of specific situations which have been troublesome under prior law ...

The principle is extended in subsection (3) to fit with the abolition of the old law of 'cash sale' by subsection (1)(c). It is also free from any technicalities depending on the extended law of larceny; such extension of the concept of theft to include trick, particular types of fraud, and the like is for the purpose of helping conviction of the offender; it has no proper application to the longstanding policy of civil protection of buyers from persons guilty of such trick or fraud.

Larceny by trick is defined as theft by fraud or deception. Since the property was voluntarily delivered, we have determined that it was not procured by theft in the ordinary sense of the term and, further, that larceny by trick does not fall into the category of ordinary theft.

It is also stressed by the plaintiff that he and Rickman agreed that title to the tractor would be withheld until the plaintiff receives cash. From this proposition, the plaintiff argues the § 2-403 does not apply because title did not pass. This argument essentially postulates the cash sale doctrine which this section of the code expressly overruled. It has been stated that "subsection (c) repudiates the technical cash sale doctrine, and makes it clear that the delivery to a purchaser gives him voidable title to the goods, even though there was an express or implied agreement that the title should not pass until the transferor received the price in cash." 2 W. Hawkland, *Uni-*

form Commercial Code Series, § 2-403-03, 605 (1982).

Even if the plaintiff were correct in arguing that his reservation of title until payment would preclude the application of § 2-403, it is provided in § 2-401 that such a reservation is "limited in effect to a reservation of a security interest." If the plaintiff retained only a security interest, he would have no action against the person who ultimately purchased the tractor from defendant because that person, as a buyer in the ordinary course, takes free of a perfected or unperfected security interest pursuant to U.C.C. § 9-307.

The plaintiff further argues, however, that even if this case is governed by the Uniform Commercial Code, the defendant is not protected by § 2-403 because he was not a good faith purchaser. It is alleged that Ham had reasonable notice that Rickman did not have legal possession of the tractor. In support of this contention, the plaintiff cites *Liles Bros. & Son v. Wright*, 638 S.W.2d 383 (Tenn. 1982), and he points out that Rickman's pickup truck had an out-of-state license, that Rickman offered no indicia of ownership, and that although Rickman said the tractor had been used at a deer camp, the tractor was clean and freshly painted. The plaintiff also avers that the defendant lacked good faith because he did not write down the serial number of the tractor, he paid $1,500.00 for the tractor and blade but sold the tractor for $2,300.00 and valued the blade at $150.00, and he advertised in a newspaper that cash would be paid for used Ford tractors.

In *Liles Bros. & Son v. Wright, supra,* the plaintiff sold a new backhoe to one Magnum who then sold it to the defendant. When the check which Magnum gave to the plaintiff was returned for insufficient funds, the plaintiff sought to recover the backhoe from the defendant. The court held that the defendant was not a bona fide purchaser because he had ample knowledge of the true value of similar backhoes, the bill of sale offered by Magnum as evidence of title was written on a blank purchase order, there were no warranty papers which were standard with new equipment, Magnum told defendant that he could supply him with any make of machinery, and the defendant knew that many backhoes had been stolen. We do not believe the facts in the case sub judice are comparable to those which existed in *Liles.* In the instant case, Ham gave wholesale price for a nearly thirty-year-old tractor. In *Liles,* Magnum asked the wholesale price for a new piece of equipment. The difference in the condition of the equipment makes these situations obviously distinguishable.

Further, in *Liles,* Magnum offered a bill of sale written on a blank purchase order. In the case at bar, Rickman presented no indicia of title, but this fact alone does not indicate that defendant acted without good faith. Ham testified that it is not customary to ask for title to a used piece of equipment because it is usually unavailable. In lieu of indicia of title, Ham testified that "you usually try to ask a few questions, and just sort of size up the situation." Based upon the record, the evidence does not preponderate against the finding of the trial court that Ham acted in good faith.

Since the defendant was a good faith purchaser, the *Liles* case is inapplicable to the facts here, and U.C.C. § 2-403 controls to bar recovery by the plaintiff.

The judgment of the trial court is accordingly affirmed, and costs are adjudged against the plaintiff.

NOTE

The protection of the security of the marketplace argument is carried further by Section 2-403(2) and (3). These subsections provide that an "entrusting of possession of goods to a merchant who deals in goods of that kind," enables the merchant to sell "to a buyer in ordinary course of business," U.C.C. § 1-201(9), and thereby convey to such buyer all those rights that the entruster possessed. The buyer must not only be in good faith, but also the sale must occur in the ordinary course of business of the seller.[5]

---

[5] A sale by a pawnbroker is not a sale in ordinary course of business nor could a pawnbroker taking collateral claim to be a *"buyer* in ordinary course of business." § 1-201(9). The pawnbroker and a person acquiring goods from a pawnbroker, however, could qualify as a "purchaser." § 1-201(32), (33).

Barth v. Protetch

5 U.C.C. Rep. Serv. 2d (Callaghan) 1350 (N.Y. Sup. Ct. 1987)

CIPARICK, J. Third-party plaintiff Chemical Bank moves pursuant to CPLR 3212 for summary judgment in favor of Chemical and against plaintiffs, upon the ground that there are no triable issues of fact and that there is no merit to the cause of action asserted in the complaint against Chemical.

The case involves a painting by the late Alfred Jensen entitled "First Count in the Great Platonic Year." The plaintiffs allege that they jointly owned the painting which they bought in 1972 when they were married. Plaintiffs contend that each paid one-half of the purchase price and upon their divorce continued to jointly own the painting, agreeing not to sell it except upon mutual consent. It is alleged that plaintiffs agreed to rotate possession of the painting approximately every two years. In the two years after the divorce, plaintiff Harvey Quaytman kept the painting in his loft.

Plaintiffs assert that in September 1982 defendant Max Protetch, a gallery owner and art dealer, telephoned Quaytman and said he was interested in seeing the painting. It is asserted that the parties had earlier discussed the possibility of Protetch appraising the painting. Plaintiff states that Protetch arranged to have the painting picked up and brought to his gallery where he agreed he would appraise the painting for Quaytman. Plaintiff Quaytman contends that at no time did he authorize Protetch to sell the painting. However, early in October Protetch wrote Quaytman and informed him that he had sold the painting and would pay plaintiff $5,000 when he received payment. Plaintiff alleges that he informed Protetch that he had no authority to sell the painting and demanded that Protetch get the painting back. It is asserted that Protetch failed to return the painting and refused to tell plaintiff the identity of the purchaser. An action was commenced by the plaintiffs against Protetch on November 9, 1982.

Plaintiffs assert that on November 30, 1982, Protetch's counsel told plaintiffs' counsel that the painting had been sold to Vesti Fine Arts Corp. in Boston, but asked plaintiffs not to contact Vesti because Protetch was trying to recover the painting from Vesti. The painting was not returned and it is alleged that on December 8, 1982 plaintiffs' counsel contacted Vesti and attempted unsuccess-fully to speak to its owner, third-party defendant Wayne Anderson. A copy of the complaint was sent to defendants on December 9, 1982.

Plaintiffs assert that in January 1983, there were discussions and correspondences between plaintiffs' counsel and counsel for Vesti and Anderson. The latter advised plaintiffs' counsel that the painting has been acquired for a bank, but refused to identify the bank.

It is asserted that Protetch billed Vesti $7,500 on or about October 5, 1982, and Anderson billed Chemical Bank the same amount on or about November 15, 1982. It is asserted that Chemical Bank did not pay Anderson until on or about February 10, 1983 and Anderson and Vesti never paid Protetch, but instead continued to hold the $7,500 received from Chemical Bank.

It is alleged that Vesti advised Chemical Bank of the dispute between plaintiffs and Protetch, and asked Chemical if it was willing to return the painting but Vesti was advised by Chemical that Mr. Callander liked the painting and wanted to keep it in his office.

Plaintiffs assert that in April 1983 plaintiff Frances Barth learned independently that Chemical Bank was a client of Anderson. It is asserted that Chemical's art director refused to speak to Ms. Barth, saying Anderson had told her not to discuss the matter with Barth. Third party plaintiff Chemical Bank alleges that it has a statutory defense which compels dismissal of the complaint as to Chemical Bank.

U.C.C. § 2-403(2) provides that:

> Any entrusting of possession of goods to a merchant who deals in goods of that kind gives him power to transfer all right of the entruster to a buyer in ordinary course of business.

Chemical Bank argues that "where an owner delivers goods to a dealer for repair, appraisal, or for any purpose, and the dealer in turn sells the goods to a buyer in the ordinary course of business, the buyer gets all ownership rights of the owner, even if the dealer had no right to sell the goods" (Chemical's Memorandum of Law, pg.67). Chemical asserts that 1) Quaytman, who owned and was entitled to possession of the painting under his agreement with his ex-wife, satisfied the entrustment requirement simply by delivering the painting to Protetch; 2) Protetch clearly is a "merchant" within the meaning of U.C.C. § 2-403 since he is an art dealer; 3) since Vesti bought the painting from Protetch, a merchant, without knowledge of any adverse claims, Vesti qualified as a buyer in the ordinary course of business. Accordingly, Vesti's ownership claim was superior to that of plaintiffs; 4) Chemical as Vesti's transferee also acquired title superior to that of plaintiffs since "a purchaser of goods acquires all title which his transferor had or had power to transfer." U.C.C. § 2-403(1) (Chemical's Memorandum of Law, pg.12).

Plaintiffs argue that for several reasons Chemical Bank did not obtain title under U.C.C. § 2-403(2): 1) Quaytman was only one of two joint owners, with no power to sell the painting; 2) there is a dispute between Chemical and Vesti as to whether Vesti acted as principal or as agent for Chemical, and therefore whether Chemical or Vesti is the buyer; 3) Chemical or Vesti as the case may be is not a "buyer in the ordinary course of business" because Protetch has not been paid and no value has been given; and 4) the evasions and concealment practiced by Vesti and by Chemical at the very least create an issue of whether Vesti or Chemical, as the case may be, was a "buyer in the ordinary course of business."

Defendants Vesti Fine Arts Corp. and Wayne Anderson assert in support of the motion that whether Vesti acted as principal or agent is of no consequence to the instant motion. Additionally, Vesti stands ready, willing and able to deposit the $7,500 held by it in escrow pending the resolution of this matter.

Defendant Protetch asserts in opposition to Chemical's motion that if Vesti and Anderson are agents of and acting on behalf of Chemical, then Chemical cannot be a buyer in the ordinary course of business because it has not paid for the goods it claims to have bought.

Chemical asserts that a cash payment is not necessary in order for this court to hold that a buyer has given value. Moreover, plaintiff Barth's conduct was such that she has forfeited her right to claim an interest in the property and she is estopped from raising the joint tenancy as a defense to a transferee who takes without knowledge of her hidden interest in the property. Finally, defendant alleges that defendant's purported attempts at concealment allegedly took place after the purchase and thus are irrelevant to a determination of whether Chemical acted in good faith.

To grant summary judgment it must clearly appear that there are no material or triable issues of fact presented (*See, Sillman v. Twentieth Century Fox Film Corp.*, 3 N.Y.2d 395). Viewing the facts in a light most favorable to plaintiffs, it would appear that the plaintiffs held the painting as joint tenants agreeing that neither could sell the painting without the other's consent. Therefore, third-party plaintiff Chemical Bank cannot be said to have acquired title to the painting pursuant to U.C.C. § 2-403(2), since the statute only empowers a merchant to transfer all of the rights of the entruster. In this instance, plaintiff Quaytman only possessed a one-half interest in the property and he did not have the authority to transfer plaintiff Barth's interest (*See McLear v. Balmax*, 194 A.D. 827). Nor can the defendants rely on the theory of equitable estoppel as against plaintiff Barth since she never gave plaintiff Quaytman or defendants Protetch or Vesti authority to transfer her interest in the painting (*See Porter v. Wertz*, 53 N.Y.2d 697). Thus, a defense of statutory estoppel under U.C.C. § 2-403 cannot be maintained by third-party plaintiff Chemical Bank.

Additionally there are clear factual issues as to whether the painting was acquired by Chemical Bank in the ordinary course of business pursuant to U.C.C. § 2-403(2).

Accordingly, the motion for summary judgment by third-party plaintiff is denied.

The foregoing constitutes the order of the court.

NOTE

1. If the action of Mr. Quaytman could be considered as causing a termination of the joint ownership, converting the interest into a right in common, would the decision of the court be the same?

2. The problem of automobile theft has resulted in enactment of statutes like the *Uniform Motor Vehicle Certificate of Title and Anti-Theft Act*, 11 U.L.A. § 421 (1974). Reconcile this statute with U.C.C. § 2-403(2), (3). Note U.C.C. § 1-201(9).

Dugdale of Nebraska, Inc. v. First State Bank

227 Neb. 729, 420 N.W.2d 273 (1988)

WHITE, J. This is an appeal by the plaintiff, Dugdale of Nebraska, Inc. (Dugdale), from a decision of the district court for Dawson county. Dugdale brought an action seeking a declaratory judgment as to its ownership rights to a 1985 Ford LTD Crown Victoria. Dugdale claimed ownership rights by virtue of having paid good and valuable consideration to Vannier Ford, Inc., and having taken possession of the vehicle from Vannier Ford. The defendant, First State Bank, cross-petitioned, claiming ownership of the vehicle by virtue of its possession of the manufacturer's certificate of origin and, subsequently, possession of the certificate of title to the vehicle. The cross-petition also sought declaratory relief. The case was tried upon stipulated facts.

Roger Swenson is the vice president in charge of operations and manager of the beef processing plant owned by Dugdale, located in Norfolk, Nebraska. In the 9 years prior to this lawsuit, Swenson purchased nearly 100 vehicles for Dugdale from Vannier Ford. On one previous occasion Vannier Ford had been a few days late in delivering a certificate of origin for a vehicle purchased by Swenson.

On March 11, 1985, Dugdale purchased from Vannier Ford a 1985 Ford LTD Crown Victoria. Dugdale traded a 1984 vehicle and paid $2,890 cash for the car. The car was one of six cars purchased that year to be used by Dugdale's cattle buyers.

On the day that the vehicle was delivered, Swenson was informed by Don Vannier, president of Vannier Ford, that the title papers to the vehicle had not yet been received. Thereafter, Swenson made numerous inquiries regarding the title papers. Each time he was told that the certificate of origin either had not yet arrived or was lost, and various promises to deliver the papers were made. Swenson received no answer from Vannier Ford's business number in his final attempt to attain the certificate of origin. Shortly thereafter, approximately 2 months after taking delivery of the vehicle, First State Bank contacted Swenson and made demand for possession of the vehicle. Approximately 5 days before selling the vehicle to Dugdale, Vannier Ford pledged the 1985 Ford LTD Crown Victoria to First State Bank as collateral for an $11,636.51 loan. Vannier Ford deliv-ered the manufacturer's certificate of origin to the bank pursuant to the loan. The car was also subject to a previous security agreement with the bank. Vannier Ford defaulted on the loan, and the bank applied for and received a certificate of title, pursuant to Neb. Rev. Stat. § 60-111 (Reissue 1984).

It is apparent from these facts that Vannier Ford perpetrated fraud against both parties to this lawsuit. Vannier Ford falsely represented clear title in the sale to Dugdale and at the same time defrauded the bank by selling collateral pledged for a loan.

The district court found that the plaintiff, Dugdale, never acquired proper and legal title to the vehicle and, as such, could not claim ownership under Nebraska law. The court relied upon Neb. Rev. Stat. § 60-105 (Reissue 1984), which states in relevant part as follows:

> No person ... acquiring a motor vehicle ... shall acquire any right, title, claim, or interest in or to such motor vehicle ... until he shall have had delivered to him physical possession of such motor vehicle ... and a certificate of title or a manufacturer's or importer's certificate. ... No court in any case at law or in equity shall recognize the right, title, claim, or interest of any person in or to any motor vehicle ... unless there is compliance with this section.

The court further found that ownership of the vehicle is vested in the defendant, First State Bank.

Since all of the facts were submitted by stipulation, we review this case as if trying it originally in order to determine whether the facts warranted the judgment. *State Farm Mut. Auto. Ins. Co. v. Budd*, 185 Neb. 343, 175 N.W.2d 621 (1970).

The appellant presents six assignments of error, which can be summarized as follows: (1) Dugdale should have been free of the bank's security interest, since it was a buyer in the ordinary course of business, and § 60-105 should not have been applied to defeat that status on these facts; and (2) the bank failed to comply with Neb. U.C.C. § 9-403 (Cum. Supp. 1986) (security agreements) and § 60-111 (repossession) and therefore had no security interest or ownership interest in the vehicle.

In 1939 the Nebraska Legislature passed into Law the Certificate of Title Act. See Neb. Rev. Stat. §§ 60-101 et seq. (Reissue 1984). The act is very similar to the certificate of title act in Ohio and was adopted to protect vehicle owners, lien holders, and the public against fraud. *Securities Credit Corp. v. Pindell*, 153 Neb. 298, 44 N.W.2d 501 (1950). We have said that the certificate of title act is the exclusive means of transferring title, and a purchaser who takes possession of a motor vehicle without receiving a certificate of title acquires no ownership of the vehicle. *Boren v. State Farm Mut. Auto. Ins. Co.*, 225 Neb. 503, 406 N.W.2d 640 (1987)... None of these cases except *Boren* involved a claimant who was a buyer in the ordinary course of business, as defined by Neb. U.C.C. § 1-201(9) (Reissue 1980). Although the claimant in *Boren* was apparently a buyer in the ordinary course, that case did not involve an ownership dispute between a purchaser and a dealer's financier. As such, this is a case of first impression in Nebraska.

Within the limitations set forth in Neb. U.C.C. § 2-102 (Reissue 1980), the provisions of Neb. U.C.C. art. 2 (Reissue 1980) governing sales are applicable to the sale of a motor vehicle. *See* § 2-105(1). Section 2-312 provides that a seller warrants that he will convey good title free from any security interest or lien or encumbrance of which the buyer has no actual knowledge. This warranty, which arises as a matter of law, can only be modified or excluded by specific language or by circumstances which put the buyer on notice that the seller's claim to title is limited or non-existent. *See* § 2-312(2). In the contract between Vannier Ford and Dugdale there is no language which excludes or modifies the warranty of title, nor were the circumstances such that Dugdale had reason to know that Vannier Ford did not claim title. In fact, just the opposite is true. At the time of the contract for sale Vannier Ford represented, and continued to represent, to Dugdale that the certificate of origin would be delivered.

Section 2-403 provides as follows:

> (2) Any entrusting of possession of goods to a merchant for purposes of sale who deals in goods of that kind gives him power to transfer all rights of the entruster to a buyer in ordinary course of business.

> (3) 'Entrusting' includes any delivery and any acquiescence in retention of possession regardless of any condition expressed between the parties to the delivery or acquiescence and regardless of whether the procurement of the entrusting or the possessor's disposition of the goods have [sic] been such as to be larcenous under the criminal law.

It was stipulated that Dwight Stubbs and Marion Tatum, each an officer and director of First State Bank, would have testified that no one from the bank authorized Vannier Ford to sell the vehicle. The record indicates, however, that the vehicle remained in the possession of Vannier Ford, a licensed dealer. Under § 2-403 the bank entrusted possession of the vehicle to Vannier Ford, and as such Vannier had the authority to transfer all of the bank's rights to a buyer in the ordinary course.

It was stipulated that Bill Brandt would have testified for the defendant that in his view Dugdale was not a purchaser in the ordinary course, since, as a matter of fact, it is not in the ordinary course of business to pay for a motor vehicle, accept delivery, but fail to obtain delivery of the manufacturer's certificate of origin. The phrase "buyer in the ordinary course of business" is defined in § 1-201(9) as one who purchases in good faith and without knowledge that the sale is in violation of ownership rights or security interests of a third party. The seller must be in the business of selling goods of the type purchased. The test does not require uniform sophistication among buyers and does not attempt to measure each sale transaction against an industry standard or norm. It simply requires good faith and no knowledge that the sale is in violation of the rights of a third party. In this case good faith can be inferred from Dugdale's prior dealings with Vannier Ford and also from Dugdale's continuous efforts to obtain the certificate of origin. There was no evidence that Dugdale was aware of the bank's security interest. Vannier Ford, a licensed dealer, was certainly one in the business of selling motor vehicles. We therefore find that Dugdale was a buyer in the ordinary course of business. We further find that Vannier Ford warranted clear title under § 2-312 and that under § 2-403 First State Bank is bound by that warranty.

Vannier Ford not only warranted title under § 2-312, but was obligated to deliver such title under § 60-104. Selling a vehicle without delivering to the purchaser a certificate of title constitutes a Class III misdemeanor. § 60-117(5) and (7). While § 60-104 makes it unlawful for a purchaser to *receive* a title which does not contain the proper assignment of rights, it does not make it unlawful for a purchaser to acquire a motor vehicle without obtaining the certificate of title. It is evident then, that the certificate of title act places primary emphasis on the seller's duty to deliver title.

The need to consider the Uniform Commercial Code provisions concurrently with the certificate of title act becomes obvious in light of the facts in this case. It is clear that both the title act and article 2 of the Uniform Commercial Code apply to the transaction here in question. Statutes which relate to the same subject, although enacted at different times, are in *pari materia* and should be construed together. *Northwest High School Dist. No. 82 v. Hessel*, 210 Neb. 219, 313 N.W.2d 656 (1981). The district court refused to recognize Dugdale's claim because § 60-105 requires both physical possession and a certificate of origin or title, and Dugdale failed to have the latter. Yet, the court recognized the bank's claim even though it did not have physical possession of the vehicle. The bank was just as much a "person" acquiring or attempting to acquire a motor vehicle as was Dugdale. The result under this analysis is that no court could recognize either the bank's claim or Dugdale's claim. We must presume that the Legislature did not intend such an absurd result. *State v. Sinica*, 220 Neb. 792, 372 N.W.2d 445 (1985).

Courts in numerous other jurisdictions which have enacted the Uniform Commercial Code together with certificate of title acts similar to our own have addressed the identical question presented here. The overwhelming majority of those courts hold that a good-faith purchaser should prevail.

In *Levin v. Nielsen*, 37 Ohio App. 2d 29, 306 N.E.2d 173 (1973), the Ohio appellate court construed Ohio Rev. Code Ann. § 4505.04 (Anderson 1982) (identical in all relevant respects to § 60-105) together with the Uniform Commercial Code. The plaintiff in *Levin* purchased an automobile and later brought an action against the dealer's financier to compel delivery of title. The court found that the defendant had entrusted the vehicle to the dealer, and as such the defendant was obligated to deliver title to the plaintiff. . . .

We hold that a dealer having the authority to expose vehicles for sale in the ordinary course of business, pursuant to § 2-403, binds his financier to deliver title to any vehicle so sold, whether or not the dealer remits the proceeds to his financier. A buyer in the ordinary course of business in this limited circumstance is not within the intended purview of § 60-105.

Based upon the foregoing, it is unnecessary for us to decide whether the bank had a valid security agreement or whether the bank properly attained a certificate of title to the vehicle. The decision of the district court is reversed and the cause is remanded with directions.

Question: How far is this decision influenced by the fact that here a "consumer," albeit a business consumer, is involved? Would a dealer in cars be able to assert a claim to be a buyer in ordinary course of business when buying from another dealer in cars without obtaining the certificate of title? Would that be in observance of reasonable commercial standards? *Mattek v. Malofsky*, 42 Wis. 2d 16, 165 N.W.2d 406 (1969). Does this decision not undermine the purpose of the Uniform Motor Vehicle Certificate of Title and Anti-Theft Act? *Compare Gicinto v. Credithrift of America, No. 3., Inc.*, 219 Kan. 766, 549 P.2d 870 (1976).

B. Documents of Title

Storage and shipment of goods are vital incidents in commerce. Production and consumption whether of raw materials or of finished products only rarely coincide. The hiatus may extend over a few days or even months or years. Places of production and of consumption may be far apart involving transportation which may be of a short duration or over an extended period. During these times commerce must continue.

It is standard practice for a warehouseman or a carrier to issue a receipt for goods in their possession. Such document has three aspects. First, it is a receipt describing the goods. Since goods are often packaged by the depositor/consignor, the receipt will describe the contents of the packages as "said to contain" the goods indicated by the depositor/consignor so as to protect the warehouseman or the carrier from bailee liability. Second, the document is a contract between the parties governing the terms and conditions of the bailment and/or carriage of goods. Third, where "in the regular course of business or financing [the document] is treated as adequately evidencing that the person in possession of it is entitled to receive, hold and dispose of the document and the goods it covers, [and purports] to be issued by or addressed to a bailee and purport[s] to cover goods in the bailee's possession which are either identified or are tangible portions of an identified mass," it is a document of title. [U.C.C. §§ 1-201(15), 7-104(1)].

In particular, the type of documents involved are bills of lading,[6] dock warrants, dock receipts,[7] warehouse receipts[8] or orders for the delivery of goods. But the definition leaves open the possibility of commercial development creating other documents which could qualify as documents of title. "Baggage checks" or similar tokens used merely to identify goods stored are not documents of title.

It was realized that in commerce documents of title could be used in place of the physical goods. The goods could be sold, by means of a documentary sale[9] or pledged by a transfer of the document of title as a symbol of the goods.[10] A bank can store such document in its vault but would have difficulty in taking 10,000 bushels of wheat as collateral for a loan.

A transfer by an assignment of the rights set forth in a document of title, however, would subject the assignee to claims that a third party can assert against the goods described in the document and thus would severely hamper the commercial utility of such document. It would increase the risk to a transferee and thus lower the return expected by the transferor. This problem can be obviated by making the document of title negotiable. This requires that the document comply with certain specified indicia. U.C.C. § 7-104(1) provides:

(1) A warehouse receipt, bill of lading or other document of title is negotiable
   (a) if by its terms the goods are to be delivered to bearer or to the order of a named person;
   (b) where recognized in overseas trade, if it runs to a named person or assigns.

Once again, there is a reification of rights set forth in a document. The possession of the document of title will symbolize possession of the goods. It enables control to be

---

[6] *See* U.C.C. § 1-201(6).

[7] "A dock warrant or receipt is a kind of interim certificate issued by steamship companies upon delivery of the goods at the dock, entitling a designated person to have issued to him at the company's office a bill of lading." U.C.C. § 1-201 Official Comment 15.

[8] U.C.C. § 1-201(45).

[9] U.C.C. §§ 2-503, 2-513.

[10] U.C.C. §§ 9-103(1), 9-105(1)(f), 9-304. Such items are "instruments" U.C.C. § 9-105(i). Perfection of a security interest in such instruments will be governed by U.C.C. §§ 9-304 and 9-305.

exercised over goods until payment is received and delivery of the document of title is made. It also enables payment to be refused until control has been transferred.[11] Linking this symbol of the goods to the concept of negotiability giving rights to the document free from any claims to it, makes this a very useful tool in commercial transactions. It must be noted that the negotiability is purely that of the document and that the document only symbolizes the goods. Thus, stolen goods, for which a warehouse receipt or a bill of lading has been issued by the warehouse or by the carrier, will still be stolen goods. The document will symbolize stolen goods. The mere possession of the document of title will not convey rights superior to those of the original owner from whom the goods had been stolen. In contrast, claims to the document itself can be defeated by "a holder to whom a negotiable document of title has been *duly negotiated*" (Emphasis added).[12]

In recognition of the commercial nature of negotiable documents of title, due negotiation requires a transfer "to a holder who purchases[13] it in good faith without notice of any defense against or claim to it on the part of any person and for value, *unless it is established that the negotiation is not in the regular course of business or financing* or involves receiving the document in settlement or payment of a money obligation."[14]

---

[11] U.C.C. §§ 2-503(4), 2-513(3).

[12] U.C.C. §§ 7-501(4), 7-502. Note: by transferring or negotiating a document of title for value, the transferor warrants to the immediate transferee that the document is genuine, that he has no knowledge of any facts that would impair its worth, and that the transfer or negotiation is rightful and effective not only as to the document, but also with respect to the goods represented thereby. U.C.C. § 7-507. These warranties are not given by a collecting bank. U.C.C. § 7-508.

[13] Note in U.C.C. § 1-201(32), (33) the term purchaser encompasses more than a "buyer." It "includes taking by sale, discount, negotiation, mortgage, pledge, lien, issue or reissue, gift or any other voluntary transaction creating an interest in property."

[14] U.C.C. § 7-501(4) (emphasis added). Although a pre-existing claim is value, settling an outstanding money debt by delivery of a document of title would not be in the regular course of business and thus not a transfer by "due negotiation."

Branch Banking & Trust v. Gill
293 N.C. 164, 237 S.E.2d 21 (1977)

Plaintiff, The Branch Banking & Trust Company, hereinafter called Bank, brought this action to recover of the defendants the sum of $383,900.00, the value of yellow corn allegedly represented by 13 negotiable warehouse receipts. These receipts had been pledged to Bank by Southeastern Farmers Grain Association, Inc., hereinafter called Southeastern, as collateral for loans aggregating $314,354.38. In the alternative, Bank seeks to recover the principal of this indebtedness with interest. . . .

Woodcock, in addition to being the manager of Elevator [a unit of the North Carolina State Warehouse System], was also Secretary-Treasurer

of Southeastern, the operations of which he conducted. Southeastern, now defunct, is in receivership.

Defendants Gill and Parham,* answering the complaint, alleged that Woodcock, as manager of Elevator, unlawfully and fraudulently issued the 13 receipts to Southeastern without receiving any grain therefor, and delivered them to himself as manager of Southeastern for the purpose of using

---

* [Editor: Gill and Parham were respectively the State Treasurer and the State Warehouse Superintendent.]

them as collateral for Southeastern's notes held by Bank. Defendants denied liability to Bank on the grounds that (1) the receipts were not duly negotiated to Bank by Southeastern; (2) Bank did not purchase the receipts in good faith and without notice of the defenses to them; and (3) the receipts were irregular on their face in that each purported to acknowledge receipt of 112,000 pounds of corn (equivalent to 2,000 bushels) while specifying the amount of grain at 20,000 bushels. The answers of the other defendants in substance alleged the same defenses. . . .

SHARP, Chief Justice. . . .

Our prior holding that the Bank did not take the 13 receipts through "due negotiation" is clearly correct. In pertinent part § 7-501 provides:

(1) A negotiable document of title running to the order of a named person is negotiated by his indorsement and delivery . . .

(4) A negotiable document of title is 'duly negotiated' when it is negotiated in the manner stated in this section to a holder who purchases it in good faith without notice of any defense against or claim to it on the part of any person and for value, unless it is established that the negotiation is not in the regular course of business or financing or involves receiving the document in settlement or payment of a money obligation.

Holder, as defined by § 1-201(20) "means a person who is in possession of a document of title . . . drawn, issued or indorsed to him or to his order or to bearer or in blank."

By their terms, the grain the 13 warehouse receipts purportedly represented was to be delivered to Southeastern or to its order. These receipts, therefore, were negotiable documents of title. §§ 1-201(15), 7-102(1)(e), 7-104(1)(a). These receipts, however, were not indorsed by Southeastern at the time they were delivered to the Bank. Neither Woodcock, the secretary-treasurer, nor any other officer of Southeastern ever signed the receipts. Upon Banks' request for its indorsement, Southeastern's bookkeeper, Mrs. Carlton, stamped the name "Southeastern Farmers Grain Association, Inc." on the reverse side of the receipts.

As we said in our former opinion, "[T]he affixing of the payee's (or subsequent holder's) name upon the reverse side of a negotiable document

of title by rubber stamp is a valid indorsement, if done by a person authorized to indorse for the payee and with intent thereby to indorse. *Mayers v. McRimmon*, 140 N.C. 640, 53 S.E. 447. However, the Superior Court found that Mrs. Carlton, who stamped the name of Southeastern upon the reverse side of these receipts, had neither the authority nor the intent thereby to indorse them in the name of Southeastern. The evidence supports these findings and would support no contrary finding." *Trust Co. v. Gill, State Treasurer*, 286 N.C. 342, 358, 211 S.E.2d 327, 338 (1975). Since the receipts were not properly indorsed to the Bank, they were not negotiated to it. The Bank, therefore, not having acquired the receipt through "due negotiation," did not acquire the rights provided in § 7-502.

Under § 7-506 the Bank could compel Southeastern to supply the lacking indorsement to the 13 receipts. However, the transfer "becomes a negotiation only as of the time the indorsement is supplied." Since the Bank was specifically informed of the fraud surrounding the issuance of the receipts on the evening of 7 May 1970 any subsequent indorsement by Southeastern would be ineffective to make the Bank "a holder to whom a negotiable document of title [was] duly negotiated." § 7-501(4).

Thus, because of the lack of proper negotiation, the Bank became a mere transferee of the 13 warehouse receipts. The status of such a transferee is fixed by § 7-504(1) which provides: "A transferee of a document, whether negotiable or nonnegotiable, to whom the document has been delivered but not duly negotiated, acquires the title and rights which his transferor had or had actual authority to convey." Here Southeastern, the Bank's transferor, had no title by way of the fraudulent receipts to any grain held by Elevator, and it had no rights against Elevator. Woodcock, acting for and on behalf of Southeastern, had fraudulently procured the issuance of these receipts to Southeastern without the deposit of any grain. Then, as Southeastern manager, he had pledged them to Bank in substitution of 16 previously issued receipts purportedly representing corn deposited in Elevator. However, at least six of these represented no grain at the time they were issued, and between the warehouse examiner's inspection of 10 February 1970 and May 1970, - without requiring the surrender of any receipts - Elevator had delivered to or for the account of

Southeastern nearly 113,000 bushels of grain more than Southeastern allegedly had in storage there. Thus, Elevator had no obligation to deliver any grain to Southeastern, and it did not become obligated to Bank merely because Southeastern transferred the receipts.

The foregoing discussion analyzes the Bank's rights and Elevator's liabilities under § 7-502 and § 7-504. The primary purpose of these two sections is to determine the priority of competing claims to valid documents and goods *actually* stored in a warehouse and to determine the issuer's liability for a misdelivery of goods *actually received* by it. Generally, a holder of negotiable warehouse receipts acquired through "due negotiation" will receive paramount title not only to the documents but also to the goods represented by them, the purpose of U.C.C., Art. 7, Part 5, being to facilitate the negotiability and integrity of negotiable receipts.[1]

---

[1] A few examples will more fully explain the manner in which these sections are intended to work.

(1) An owner of goods (O) stores them in a warehouse, taking from the warehouseman negotiable receipts in bearer form. A thief (T) steals the bearer receipts and sells them to a holder who takes them through due negotiation. The holder acquires title to the receipts and to the goods represented by them and defeats O's claim to them. (7-502(2)). If the purchaser for some reason did not acquire the receipts through due negotiation, or if the receipts were nonnegotiable, O would prevail against him. Similarly, assume O stores goods in a warehouse taking in return negotiable receipts made to a named person's order. Thereafter T steals them and transfers them to an innocent purchaser for value, forging the necessary indorsement. As between O and the innocent purchaser, O would prevail. The innocent purchaser could not be a holder through due negotiation under 7-502 and 7-501. Therefore, under 7-504 he would have only the rights and title to the document that his transferor had. Since his transferor was a thief having no title to the document, O would prevail against the innocent party.

(2) O stores his goods with warehouseman (W) who is not a merchant selling goods of that kind. Thereafter W, contrary to O's instructions, issued negotiable warehouse receipts which are ultimately duly negotiated to third-party (P). As between P and O, P would have title to the goods represented by the receipts. (7-502, 7-503.) If P

In situations where there are actual goods, and there are conflicting claims either to them or to the documents, §§ 7-502, 7-503, and 7-504 determine the priority of these claims. In the present case, since the 13 receipts represented no grain in storage at the time of their issuance and no grain was subsequently acquired by the warehouseman, no question of who has paramount title to goods arises. The sole question is under what circumstances and to whom is an *issuer* liable for the issuance of warehouse receipts when it has not received the goods which the receipts purportedly cover? § 7-203 covers this situation. It provides in pertinent part:

> A party to or purchaser for value in good faith of a document of title other than a bill of lading relying in either case upon the description therein of the goods may recover from the issuer damages caused by the non-receipt or misdescription of the goods, except to the extent that . . . the party or purchaser otherwise had notice.

In the trial below, and in all their briefs submitted to this court, the parties, overlooking § 7-203, have proceeded on the theory that §§ 7-502 and 7-504 govern this case. Furthermore, we did not consider this section in our first opinion.

The purpose of § 7-203 is to protect specified parties to or purchasers of warehouse receipts by imposing liability upon the warehouseman when

---

did not take by due negotiation he would have only the rights and title of his transferor and would not prevail against O. (7-504).

(3) Warehouseman (W) fraudulently issues negotiable receipts not covering goods actually in storage to third-party (P), who takes through due negotiation. Thereafter W acquires goods purportedly covered by the receipt. As against P, W is estopped from denying that he did not have title when the receipts were issued. 7-502(1)(c) and Comment thereto.

(4) Assume that a thief (T) steals goods from their owner (O) and stores them in a warehouse, taking negotiable receipts in return. T then negotiates the receipts to a purchaser (P) who takes through due negotiation. As between O and P, O has the superior right to the goods in the warehouse even through P took through due negotiation. 7-503. *See generally* J. White and R. Summers, *Uniform Commercial Code*, 684-87 (1972).

either he or his agent fraudulently or mistakenly issues receipts (negotiable or nonnegotiable) for misdescribed or nonexistent goods. This section, coupled with the definition of issuer (§ 7-102(1)(g)), clearly places upon the warehouseman the risk that his agent may fraudulently or mistakenly issue improper receipts. The theory of the law is that the warehouseman, being in the best position to prevent the issuance of mistaken or fraudulent receipts, should be obligated to do so; that such receipts are a risk and cost of the business enterprise which the issuer is best able to absorb. *See* J. White and R. Summers, *Uniform Commercial Code*, 690 (1972).

In the Comment to § 7-203 it is said: "The issuer is liable on documents issued by an agent, contrary to instructions of his principal, without receiving goods. No disclaimer of the latter liability is permitted." Issuer is defined by § 7-102 as "a bailee who issues a document.... Issuer includes any person for whom an agent or employee purports to act in issuing a document if the agent or employee has real or apparent authority to issue documents, notwithstanding that the issuer received no goods or that the goods were misdescribed or that in any other respect the agent or employee violated his instructions." Under these provisions Elevator would clearly be liable to the Bank on the 13 fraudulent receipts issued by its agent Woodcock *provided* the Bank could carry its burden of affirmatively proving that it came within the protection of § 7-203.

Since § 7-203 governs Bank's right to recover, under § 1-103, the doctrine of agency and ratification discussed in our first opinion are "displaced."

We now consider whether the Bank qualifies for this protection. At the outset of our discussion we note that § 7-203 contains no requirement that the purchaser take negotiable documents through "due negotiation" before he can recover from the issuer. (Compare this section with the analogous U.C.C. provision covering bills of lading, which provides protection to "a consignee of a nonnegotiable bill who has given value in good faith or a holder to whom a negotiable bill has been duly negotiated relying in either case upon the description...." § 7-301(1).) Of course, had the Bank met all the requirements of due negotiation it also would have met the requirements of § 7-203.

To be entitled to recover under § 7-203 a claimant has the burden of proving that he (1) is a party to or *purchaser of a document of title other* than a bill of lading; (2) *gave value* for the document; (3) took the document in *good faith*; (4) *relied* to his detriment upon the description of the goods in the document; and (5) took *without notice* that the goods were misdescribed or were never received by the issuer. Many of these terms are defined in Article 1 of the U.C.C. (§ 1-201), and those definitions are also made applicable to Article 7, § 7-102(4).

Under § 1-201(33) and § 1-201(32) Bank acquired the 13 negotiable warehouse receipts by purchase. Further, when Bank surrendered to Southeastern its old notes and the 16 receipts securing them, taking in return the new notes secured by the 13 receipts, it gave "value." Under § 1-201(44) a person, inter alia, gives "value" for rights if he acquires them "(b) as security for or in total or partial satisfaction of a pre-existing claim.... or (d) generally in return for any consideration sufficient to support a simple contract." It now remains to determine whether Bank, at the time it relinquished the 16 old receipts in return for the 13 receipts, was acting (1) without notice that no goods had been received by the issuer for the 13 receipts, (2) in good faith, and (3) in reliance upon the descriptions in the receipts.

The trial court, after making detailed findings as to facts known to Bank at the time it accepted the 13 receipts, found and concluded the ultimate fact that "the plaintiff Bank did not receive warehouse receipts numbered 974 through 986 in good faith without notice of claims and defenses." This finding, although stated in the negative in order to use the precise language of § 7-501(4), is equivalent to a positive finding that Bank took the 13 receipts with notice that they were spurious. On the same findings the judge also concluded that plaintiff did not come into court with "clean hands." This finding likewise is equivalent in import and meaning to a finding that Bank did not take the 13 receipts in good faith. *Trust Co. v. Gill, State Treasurer*, 286 N.C. 342, 364, 211 S.E.2d 327, 342, 27 Am. Jur.2d *Equity* § 137 (1966); 30 C.J.S. *Equity* § 93 (1965). Upon these findings he held that plaintiff had no cause of action either at law or in equity based on the 13 receipts against either the State Warehouse Superintendent or against the State Treasurer as custodian of the State Indemnity and Guaranty Fund. We must, therefore, determine whether these findings are supported by competent evidence.

Upon our reconsideration of this case we have concluded (1) that the record evidence fully supports the trial judges' findings that Bank did not take the receipts in good faith and without notice that they had been fraudulently issued and (2) that his findings compel his conclusions of law.

"'Good faith' means honesty *in fact* in the conduct or transaction concerned." 1-201(19). The absence of evidence that Bank's agents had themselves verified Elevator's shortage of grain or had eyewitness knowledge that the 13 receipts were fraudulently issued does not necessarily mean they did not *in fact* know, and it did not preclude a finding by the judge that Bank did not acquire the receipts in good faith and without notice of claims and defenses.

Under § 1-201(25) a person, or corporation §§ 1-201(30), (28), (27), has "notice" of a fact not only when he has actual knowledge of it, but also when "from all the facts and circumstances known to him at the time in question he has reason to know that it exists."

Good faith ("honesty in fact") and "notice," although not synonymous, are inherently intertwined. Therefore, the relation between the two cannot be ignored. "The same facts which call a party's 'good faith' into question may also give him 'notice of a defense.'" J. White and R. Summers, *Uniform Commercial Code* § 14-6 at 471 (1972)....

It overtaxes credulity to accept plaintiff's contention that experienced bankers could have lacked notice of Woodcock's fraud. Measured by any acceptable standard of banking or business judgment, the reasons which Woodcock gave Bank on the morning of May 6th for wanting to obtain the 16 old receipts were so improbable that,

under all the circumstances, its officers, "must have known" there was a shortage of grain at the Elevator.... Bank's conduct engenders the strong inference that it willfully failed to seek actual knowledge as to why Southeastern wanted to substitute notes and receipts because of the well-founded belief that an inquiry would disclose that the new receipts represented no grain in Elevator....

Albeit "good faith" is literally defined as "honesty in fact in the conduct or transaction concerned," § 1-201(19), the Uniform Commercial Code §§ 7-203 and 1-201(25) does not permit parties to intentionally keep themselves in ignorance of facts which, if known, would defeat their rights in a negotiable document of title. *See Winter & Hirsch, Inc. v. Passarelli*, 122 Ill. App. 2d 372, 259 N.E.2d 312 [7 U.C.C. Rep. 1210] (1970). Nor will it allow Bank to recover losses which it received through its participation in Woodcock's fraudulent efforts to cover up Elevator's grain shortages.

The judgment of the trial court is therefore affirmed as to all defendants and our former decision as reported in 286 N.C. 342, 211 S.E.2d 327 (1975) is withdrawn.

Affirmed.

Justice LAKE dissenting ... [The majority] asserts that our original opinion impairs the commercial usefulness of warehouse receipts by exposing the holder to the risks of equities in favor of others....

How could the commercial usefulness of warehouse receipts be impaired by a decision permitting a transferee thereof to enforce such a receipt against the warehouseman? It is the present majority opinion, not our former decision which impairs the commercial usefulness of warehouse receipts....

NOTE

1. In case fungible goods are stored in a warehouse, the issuance of warehouse receipts for goods not actually received creates an over-issue. The remedy against the warehouse itself is clear. The holders of these warehouse receipts, however, will share in the fungible bulk *pari-passu*, i.e., in accordance with the proportion the goods actually in the warehouse bear to the quantity of goods described in the outstanding warehouse receipts.

2. With regard to bills of lading U.C.C. Section 7-301(1) provides:

A consignee of a non-negotiable bill who has given value in good faith or a holder to whom a negotiable bill has been duly negotiated relying in either case upon the description therein of the goods, or upon the date therein shown, may recover from the issuer damages caused by the misdating of the bill or the non-receipt or misdescription of the goods, except to the extent that the document indicates that the issuer does not know whether any part or all of the goods in fact were received or conform to the description, as where the description is in terms of marks or labels or kind, quantity, or condition or the receipt or description is qualified by "contents or condition of contents or packages unknown," "said to contain," "shipper's weight, load and count" or the like, if such indication be true.

These methods of limiting liability in the warehouseman/carrier/bailee are especially important where packaged goods are stored or consigned. Unless the packages are opened it will not be possible for the bailee to determine that they actually contain the goods described. Doing this may have a deleterious effect on the goods or their value in the market. Thus the bailee will indicate on receipt of 100 casks of whiskey, that they are "said to contain" whiskey. Or where the consignor has loaded a wagon with chicken, that the wagon contains "1000 chicken, shippers load and count."[15] Failure of the casks to contain whiskey or of the wagon to contain the indicated number of chicken then would not implicate the bailee, but would allow recourse against the depositor/consignor/bailor.

For both negotiable warehouse receipts and negotiable bills of lading, U.C.C. Sections 7-501, 7-502 provide:

WAREHOUSE RECEIPTS AND BILLS OF LADING: NEGOTIATION AND TRANSFER

§ 7-501.   Form of Negotiation and Requirements of "Due Negotiation."

(1) A negotiable document of title running to the order of a named person is negotiated by his indorsement and delivery. After his indorsement in blank or to bearer any person can negotiate it by delivery alone.

(2) (a) A negotiable document of title is also negotiated by delivery alone when by its original terms it runs to bearer.

(b) When a document running to the order of a named person is delivered to him the effect is the same as if the document had been negotiated.

(3) Negotiation of a negotiable document of title after it has been indorsed to a specified person requires indorsement by the special indorsee as well as delivery.

(4) A negotiable document of title is "duly negotiated" when it is negotiated in the manner stated in this section to a holder who purchases it in good faith without notice of any defense against or claim to it on the part of any person and for value, unless it is established that the negotiation is not in the regular course of business or financing or involves receiving the document in settlement or payment of a money obligation.

(5) Indorsement of a non-negotiable document neither makes it negotiable nor adds to the transferee's rights.

(6) The naming in a negotiable bill of a person to be notified of the arrival of the goods

---

[15] This is necessary since often railroad wagons are left on a "spur" at a factory site to be loaded by the consignor. The railroad company will then send a shunting engine to pick-up the wagon when preparing a train to deliver loaded goods.

does not limit the negotiability of the bill nor constitute notice to a purchaser thereof of any interest of such person in the goods.

§ 7-502. Rights Acquired by Due Negotiation.

(1) Subject to the following section and to the provisions of Section 7-205 on fungible goods, a holder to whom a negotiable document of title has been duly negotiated acquires thereby:

(a) title to the document;

(b) title to the goods;

(c) all rights accruing under the law of agency or estoppel, including rights to goods delivered to the bailee after the document was issued; and

(d) the direct obligation of the issuer to hold or deliver the goods according to the terms of the document free of any defense or claim by him except those arising under the terms of the document or under this Article. In the case of a delivery order the bailee's obligation accrues only upon acceptance and the obligation acquired by the holder is that the issuer and any indorser will procure the acceptance of the bailee.

(2) Subject to the following section, title and rights so acquired are not defeated by any stoppage of the goods represented by the document or by surrender of such goods by the bailee, and are not impaired even though the negotiation or any prior negotiation constitute a breach of duty or even though any person has been deprived of possession of the document by misrepresentation, fraud, accident, mistake, duress, loss, theft or conversion, or even though a previous sale or other transfer of the goods or document has been made to a third person.

* * *

Inter-state transportation of goods triggers application of the federal Bills of Lading Act (The Pomerene Act).[16] That Act also distinguishes between negotiable and non-negotiable bills of lading. In the case of a non-negotiable bill of lading, contrary to state law, the carrier is able to assert non-receipt of goods where the holder of the bill of lading cannot prove reliance on the recitation in the document.[17] With regard to negotiable bills of lading an approach is adopted similar to that of U.C.C. in §§ 7-301(1), 7-502.[18] International transportation of goods may be subject also to various international conventions and agreements most of which deal with limitation of a carrier's liability.[19] There is also a development under consideration for a central computerized system which will enable transfers of bills of lading by Electronic Data Interchange (EDI). The problems of "negotiability" in undoc-

---

[16] 49 U.S.C. §§ 81-124.

[17] Chesapeake & Ohio Ry. Co. v. State Nat'l Bank of Maysville, 280 Ky. 444, 133 S.W.2d 511 (1939).

[18] 49 U.S.C. § 102. *But see* Industria Nacional Del Papel, CA. v. M/V Albert F., 730 F.2d 622 (11th Cir. 1984) *cert. denied*, 469 U.S. 1037 (1984). See also as to ocean bills of lading the *Carriage of Goods by Sea Act.* 46 U.S.C. §§ 1300-15 incorporating the federal *Bills of Lading Act. See id.* § 1303(4).

[19] *E.g.* Hague Rules relating to Bills of Lading, 1921; Convention for the Unification of Rules relating to certain Bills of Lading (Brussels) 1924; Visby Rules, 1967; and Hamburg Rules, 1978, U.N. Conference on Carriage of Goods by Sea A/Conf. 89/14 at 148.

umented bills of lading have not yet been fully analyzed and remain to be considered at a future time.[20]

C. Investment Securities

The concept of investment securities encompasses both equity and debt securities. U.C.C.-Article 8 Investment Securities codified the law as it has developed in the twentieth century. With regard to debt securities, the rigid formalism of the now repealed Negotiable Instrument Law endangered the corporate and municipal bond market. The Kentucky court in *Pulaski County v. Ben Hur Life Association of Crawfordville* concluded that the bonds in issue did not comply with the strictures placed on negotiable instruments by the NIL and, having conditional payment clauses, were not negotiable. Fortunately, a pragmatic approach to economic reality, based on a recognition that bonds and debentures are not payment devices used in current transactions, led the court to reverse itself.[21] The signal was noted, however, and thus, when the Uniform Commercial Code was under consideration, it was agreed that the negotiability of bonds and debentures had to be assured. By expressly indicating that an investment security is not a payment device, an instrument which qualifies as an investment security,[22] was expressly excluded from U.C.C.-Article 3[23] and stated to be negotiable.[24]

Equity securities had a more checkered career. Originally being based on membership, negotiability was not an issue. Even today transfers of membership rights require recognition by the issuer, be it a corporation or a limited partnership. Such recognition takes the form of entry on the records of the issuer.[25] The share certificate is thus merely "a muniment of title which is evidence of the ownership of the stock."[26] Market forces led to the fusion of the intangible rights embodied in share participation, i.e. shareholders rights, with the documentary evidence of its existence, the share certificate.

---

[20] *See* Coffey, *Multimodulism and the American Carrier*, 64 Tul. L. Rev. 569, 589 (1989) ("The negotiable bill probably will long be with us. On the flip side of the same coin, the paperless bill probably will not come into widespread use for virtually the same reason. With some notable exceptions, shippers, consignees, and their bankers simply do not want and will not accept such a system.").

[21] Pulaski County v. Ben Hur Life Association of Crawfordsville, reargued 286 Ky. 119, 149 S.W.2d 738 (1941).

[22] In this Article, unless the context otherwise requires:
(a) A "Certificated security" is a share, participation, or other interest in property of or an enterprise of the issuer or an obligation of the issuer which is
(i) represented by an instrument issued in bearer or registered form;
(ii) of a type commonly dealt in on securities exchanges or markets or commonly recognized in any area in which it is issued or dealt in as a medium for investment; and
(iii) either one of a class or series or by its terms divisible into a class or series of shares, participations, interest, or obligations. [U.C.C. § 8-102(1)].

[23] U.C.C. § 3-102(a).

[24] Id. § 8-105.

[25] Id. § 8-207.

[26] Estate of Bridges v. Mosebrook, 662 S.W.2d 116, 120 (Tex. Ct. App. 1983). The first step toward the negotiability of equity securities was taken by the Uniform Stock Transfer Act, 6 U.L.A. (1922) (superseded).

Transfer of the certificate whether evidencing a debt or an equity participation results in the transferee acquiring the right to be registered on the records of the issuer, with the transferor being under a duty to assist the transferee, who has given value,[27] in attaining registration.[28]

On the part of the issuer, the duty to register the transfer arises upon a demand for registration by the transferee presenting the certificate duly endorsed with the signature of the transferor [registered owner] confirmed by a signature guarantor.[29] The issuer can not raise any claims it may have had against the transferor unless such were conspicuously noted on the certificate.[30] An adverse claim[31] by any other person to the security or to rights represented thereby also will be ineffective, where the security has come into the hands of a bona fide purchaser for value without notice of such claims.[32]

In the organized markets, securities subject to adverse claims are not accepted. Provisions exist for "reclamation rights,"[33] which allow a transferee to reject such securities and to return them to the securities professional, broker, dealer or financial intermediary,[34] that has attempted to perform its obligation under a contract of sale by delivering securities subject to an adverse claim.[35]

The organized market is unable to cope with the blizzard of certificates created on a normal trading day, when, on the New York Stock Exchange alone, over 200 million shares may be traded on a normal day. Thus, market participants immobilized securities in securities depositories and transferred securities by book entry on the records of the securities depository. This has been taken one step further now by the introduction of "uncertificated" securities. The issue of uncertificated equity securities is now authorized in a majority of jurisdictions, especially in those jurisdictions that base their corporation statute on the revised Model Business Corporation Act.[36]

The transfer of the "uncertificated security," whether debt or equity, is subject to U.C.C.-Article 8 as revised in 1977.[37] That revision provides that a "transferee" for value

---

[27] U.C.C. § 1-201(44).

[28] Id. § 8-316.

[29] Id. §§ 8-401(1)(a),(b), 8-402(1),(2), 8-312(1).

[30] Id. § 8-204. Although lack of genuineness can be raised, a defect going to the validity of a security can not be raised where the security is in the hands of a bona fide purchaser for value and without notice of the particular defect. *See* id. § 8-202.

[31] Id. § 8-302(2).

[32] Id. § 8-302(1).

[33] NYSE Rule 267, AMEX (Div. Sec.) Rule SR-112, NASD Unif. Practice Code § 53.

[34] U.C.C. § 8-313(4).

[35] Insurance Co. of N. Am. v. United States, 561 F. Supp. 106 (E.D. Pa. 1983) (stolen securities returned to selling broker and replacement bonds purchased in open market, cost of which selling broker covered).

[36] Rev. M.B.C.A. § 6.25. With respect to uncertificated debt securities note Ad Hoc Committee on Uncertificated Debt Securities, *First Report of the Committee on Uncertificated Securities, System Credit Risks and Sample Uncertificated Debt Indenture*, 46 Bus. Law. 909 (1991).

[37] Revised Article 8 is in force in forty-nine jurisdictions. Note U.S. Government securities are now issued only in uncertificated form and their transfer is effected by book-entry. *See* 31 C.F.R. §§ 306.115–306.122, subpart O-Book Entry Procedure.

and without notice of any adverse claims who is registered on the books of the issuer by receiving an initial transaction statement without such initial transaction statement containing a notation of an adverse claim, is a bona fide purchaser unaffected by any restriction on transfer or adverse claims that might exist. In effect, the revision created a "negotiable non-instrument," showing that law cannot lose contact with the realities of the marketplace. This approach is carried farther by the proposed revision of U.C.C. Article 8 presently under consideration by the National Conference of Commissioners on Uniform State Laws.

The effect of federal securities law on the issuance and transfer of investment securities cannot be ignored. Securities markets are regulated and so are participants in these markets.[38] Thus:

> It is clear that U.C.C. Article 8 can no longer be looked upon as standing alone. Federal security laws have to be integrated into state law to enable the two to co-operate, co-ordinate and reach solutions that are acceptable to the market place. This does not necessarily herald the federalization of U.C.C. Article 8. It does mean, however, that the Securities and Exchange Commission and that bank regulators must bear U.C.C. Article 8 in mind when proposing regulations. It also means that those engaged in drafting revisions of U.C.C. Article 8 must consider the approaches to and solutions adopted by the SEC, and by other federal and state regulators of banks and broker-dealers. Since few states have really tackled these issues on a regulatory basis, it will be for the U.C.C. Article 8 to provide a uniform approach, indicating how best to serve the investor and the security industry.[39]

---

[38] For example, see 17 C.F.R. §§ 240.17 Ad-1 to 240.17 Ad-15 regulating transfer agents.

[39] Guttman, *Transfer of Securities: State and Federal Interaction*, 12 CARDOZO L. REV. 437, 468–469 (1990). *See also*, Guttman, *Federal and State Influences on New Developments in Investment Securities Law*, 24 UCC L. J. 307 (1992).

IV NEGOTIABLE INSTRUMENTS

In defining negotiable instruments,[1] the U.C.C. in Article 3 considers the use of such instruments as payment devices-substitutes for cash. Thus, Article 3 is expressly stated not to apply to money,[2] wholesale payment orders used mainly in interbank transactions[3] or investment securities.[4] Except for a check, which need not contain an order to pay,[5] the Article applies to "an unconditional promise or order to pay a fixed amount of money with or without interest or other charges described in the promise or order,"[6] provided that

(1) at the time of issue it is payable to bearer or to order; and
(2) it is payable on demand or at a definite time; and
(3) it does not state any undertaking or instruction other than to pay the amount indicated.

This leaves the possibility that other negotiable documents exist or might develop outside the framework of Article 3. Examples of such negotiable documents are documents of title symbolizing goods[7] and investment securities in certificated form.[8] On the other hand, party autonomy is recognized in that Section 3-104(d) provides that "[a] promise or order other than a check is not an [negotiable] instrument if, at the time it is issued or first comes into possession of a holder, it contains a conspicuous statement, however expressed, to the effect that the promise or order is not negotiable or is not an instrument governed by this Article." Once again we note that checks are excluded. The reason for such exclusion is based on the needs of the banking industry involved in the check collection process. Automation prevents examination of each check to determine whether it carries such notation.[9]

Article 3 applies specifically to promissory notes,[10] certificates of deposit,[11] drafts,[12]

---

[1] U.C.C. § 3-101.

[2] U.C.C. § 1-201(24).

[3] U.C.C.-Article 4A - Funds Transfer, *see infra* Chapter VIII at B2 "Wholesale" Fund Transfer.

[4] U.C.C.-Article 8 § 8-102(1)(c), U.C.C. § 3-102(a).

[5] U.C.C. § 3-104(c), (f).

[6] U.C.C. § 3-104(a).

[7] U.C.C.-Article 7, § 7-104(1).

[8] U.C.C.-Article 8, § 8-105(1).

[9] *See* U.C.C. Article 4, Federal Expedited Funds Availability Act, 12 U.S.C. §§ 4001-4010 and Regulation CC, 12 C.F.R. §§ 229.1 to 299.42.

[10] U.C.C. § 3-104(e).

[11] U.C.C. § 3-104(j).

[12] U.C.C. § 3-104(e).

and checks,[13] including cashier's checks,[14] teller's checks[15] and traveller's checks.[16] Other payment devices, such as credit cards[17] and debit cards[18] developed outside the U.C.C. and do not give rise to a negotiable instrument.[19]

A promissory note is a two party instrument having a maker who states in the note that the maker promises to pay either (1) to the bearer or (2) to the order of a specified person, the payee, a sum certain in money,[20] at a specified time or at indicated times over a specified period. It is a promise to pay and not merely evidence of the existence of a debt such as an I.O.U. A promissory note is used mainly in connection with a credit transaction such as a mortgage, a lease, or a secured transaction.[21] Between merchants, delivery of goods on "open credit" creating "accounts receivable" has lessened the use of promissory notes, while recently enacted consumer protection legislation has severely restricted the use of negotiable promissory notes in consumer credit transactions.[22] Notes are used, however, in connection with real estate mortgages and in connection with loans unconnected to a consumer financing transaction and, occasionally, in connection with commercial sales of goods; an example is the banker's "collateral note." The frequency of such transactions requires a continuing knowledge of this form of payment device.

A certificate of deposit is an acknowledgment by a *bank* that it has received a sum of money and engages that it will repay it. The certificate of deposit, thus, is a note of a bank.[23]

A draft is a three party instrument. The drawer (maker) calls upon a drawee, a debtor or a person with whom a credit relationship has been established, to pay to the order of a named payee or to the bearer of the instrument, an indicated sum at a specified time or over an indicated period at specified intervals. A check is a draft, other than a documentary draft, drawn on a bank and payable on demand. U.C.C. § 3-104(f)(i).[24] A documentary draft is a draft drawn on a bank which is to be presented together with specified documents before the drawee bank can be expected to undertake the obligation embodied in the draft.[25] Revised U.C.C.-Article 3 rejects the distinction between ordinary

---

[13] U.C.C. § 3-104(f).

[14] U.C.C. § 3-104(g).

[15] U.C.C. § 3-104(h).

[16] U.C.C. § 3-104(i).

[17] *See,* Truth in Lending (Fair Credit Billing) Act, 15 U.S.C. §§ 1666 *et seq.* and Regs. Z, 12 C.F.R. §§ 226.1 to 226.30.

[18] Electronic Fund Transfer Act, 15 U.S.C. §§ 1693 *et seq.* and Regs. E, 12 C.F.R. §§ 205.1 *et seq.*

[19] Article 3 refers to "negotiable instrument," simply as "instrument." § 3-104(b). We will follow this approach, unless the context requires otherwise.

[20] U.C.C. §§ 3-104(a), 1-201(24), 3-107.

[21] *See* U.C.C. § 9-102(1)(a), a secured transaction governed by U.C.C. Article 9-Secured Transactions is "any transaction . . . which is intended to create a security interest in personal property or fixtures including goods, documents, instruments, general intangibles, chattel paper or accounts."

[22] *See supra* Chapter I n.87 and see *infra* text at notes 47, 48.

[23] *See* U.C.C. § 3-104(j).

[24] The U.C.C. does not require that the item be called a "check." A "money order" will be treated as a check if it is drawn on a bank. Thus, a draft drawn on an insurance company or on a money market fund investment, though payable *through* a bank is not a check. U.C.C. § 4-106.

[25] U.C.C. § 4-104 (a)(6). An example arises in connection with a letter of credit which indicates that the bank will accept and pay a draft drawn on the bank, if such draft is accompanied by indicated documents, e.g. a negotiable document of title.

checks, cashier's checks, and teller's checks treating them all as checks. A cashier's check is drawn by a bank on itself or on another branch of the same bank,[26] while a teller's check is drawn by a bank on another bank or payable at or through another bank.[27] An instrument which falls within the definition of both a "note" and "draft" allows the person entitled to enforce it to treat it as either.[28]

Finally we should note the traveller's check. This is an instrument, generally designated as such, issued by a bank or other commercial entity, such as American Express Company. The traveller's check is payable on demand and requires the counter signature of the person whose specimen signature appears on the instrument.[29] If it is payable *at* a bank, it will be treated the same as a check drawn on the named bank.[30] But if it is payable *through* a bank, such bank will be treated as a collecting bank requiring presentment by the named bank to the identified drawer. The item will be a draft and treated as such.[31]

In recent years, commercial entities other than banks have issued "commercial paper" to cover seasonal needs. Though not qualifying as "certificates of deposit" within Article 3, the question arises whether such instruments are "notes" or would be classified as "certificated investment securities" which have negotiability under U.C.C. Article 8.[32] Section 8-102(1)(c) specifies that "a writing that is a certificated security is governed by this Article [8] and not by Article 3, even though it also meets the requirements of that Article."[33]

The only type of instrument that would raise this issue would be a certificate of deposit issued by a bank, or a note issued by another commercial entity but denominated a certificate

---

[26] U.C.C. § 3-104(g). Note U.C.C. § 4-107, a branch or separate office of a bank is treated as a separate bank.

[27] U.C.C. §§ 3-104(h), 4-106. These items are usually issued by credit unions.

[28] U.C.C. § 3-104(e). A Teller's check does not raise this issue since it has all the elements of a tripartite instrument. A cashier's check, however, has only two parties since the drawer and the drawee are actually the same. Some courts have concluded that "the issuance of the cashier's check constitutes an acceptance by the issuing bank." Kaufman v. Chase Manhattan Bank, N.A., 370 F. Supp. 276 (S.D.N.Y. 1973), while other courts have held that a cashier's check is a promissory note of which the bank is the maker. Laurel Bank & Trust Co. v. City Nat'l Bank of Connecticut, 33 Conn. Supp. 641, 365 A.2d 1222 (1976). Although the primary issues in this connection arise in conjunction with attempts to place a stop payment order on such instrument, Dziurak v. Chase Manhattan Bank, N.A., 58 A.D.2d 103, 396 N.Y.S.2d 414 (App. Div. 1977) and note U.C.C. § 4-403, there are other issues that may require a resolution consonant with a determination whether to treat such instrument as a promissory note or as a draft. U.C.C. § 3-414 (a) clarifies this issue in that it excludes cashier's checks and other drafts drawn on the drawer when discussing the obligations of a drawer, U.C.C. § 3-414(b). The liability of the issuer of such an instrument is set forth in U.C.C. § 3-412. It is the same as that of an issuer of a note.

[29] This will not make the instrument subject to a condition so as to prevent it from being negotiable. U.C.C. § 3-106(c).

[30] U.C.C. § 4-106(b). Note Alternative B to this section.

[31] U.C.C. § 4-106(a).

[32] *See* U.C.C. §§ 8-102(1)(a), 8-105. A further question may arise whether such instruments qualify as "securities" under federal or state securities laws. See Securities Act of 1933, 15 U.S.C. §§ 77b(1), 77c(a)(3); Securities Exchange Act of 1934, 15 U.S.C. § 78c(10); Uniform Securities Act § 402(a)(10),7B ULA 600 (1985). *See* further, Reves v. Ernst & Young, 494 U.S. 56, 110 S. Ct. 945 (1990).

[33] Where there is no provision in U.C.C.-Article 8, courts have referred to U.C.C.-Article 3, and applied its provision by analogy. Bankhaus Hermann Lampe KG v. Mercantile Safe Deposit & Trust Co., 466 F. Supp. 1133, 1142 (S.D.N.Y. 1979).

of deposit, payable to "bearer," not subject to any precondition to payment, and being one of a class or series, or divisible into a series of obligations.[34] The distinction between such commercial paper and certificated securities is clearly drawn in terms of economic functions. Commercial paper ordinarily is issued to finance the manufacturing or marketing of goods or the rendering of services in relation to a specific transaction or series of transactions. Securities, on the other hand, are issued to finance the enterprise as such, providing capital without which the business could not function successfully.[35]

The sheer volume of negotiable instruments handled daily by banks and other financial institutions requires that there be simplicity and some uniformity. Most checks are now handled by automation and thus, to maintain the steady flow of such paper through the bank collection system, uniformity is required by banks in their contracts with their customers.[36]

For a writing to qualify as a negotiable instrument within Article 3, it must comply with the requisites set forth in Section 3-104(a). A failure to comply with these requisites means that U.C.C. Article 3 will not grant such item negotiability. If the instrument does not contain a preclusion to transfers but, while not indicating that it is payable "to order" or "to bearer," it is otherwise in compliance with Section 3-104(a), the instrument is termed a "mercantile specialty." Courts may apply Article 3 to such paper by analogy, but the benefit negotiability conveys will not attach to such document; there can be no holder in due course.[37] Since checks are preprinted and since the majority of checks are deposited into the account of the payee with a depository bank for collection and do not circulate as payment devices, the requirement that checks must be payable to bearer or to order has been eliminated.[38] Once deposited into the depository bank, such items stay within the bank collection system until paid by the drawee bank or dishonored. An accidental omission of these "words of negotiability" should not affect the negotiability of checks, as opposed to other commercial paper.[39]

Banks are involved in the collection process applicable to checks, drafts, notes, commercial paper, and mercantile specialties. Banks may also be involved in documentary sales

---

[34] There is a market for such paper. Thus the requirement of U.C.C. § 8-102(1)(a)(ii) will be satisfied. Article 8 requires such paper, however, to be issued to "bearer" or "registered" to the owner, while the formal requisites for negotiability of Article 3 require the paper to be issued to "bearer" or to "order." Where these "magic words of negotiability" have not been used, Article 3 can be applied only by analogy. The status of holder in due course, however, cannot be attained with regard to such instruments.

[35] *See* GUTTMAN, MODERN SECURITIES TRANSFERS, Chapter 1 ¶¶ 1.01-1.03 (1987 & Cum. Supp. 1992).

[36] Counter checks, which used to be available in stores and banks, have disappeared. Automation requires checks to be encoded with Magnetic Ink Character Recognition (MICR) symbols to make them machine readable. The absence of a contractual agreement requiring the use of checks supplied by a drawee/bank is amusingly illustrated by A.P. HERBERT, THE UNCOMMON LAW, 112-17 (1936) in the fictional case of Board of Inland Revenue v. Haddock. A disgruntled farmer undertook to pay his taxes by writing a check on the belly of a bull and presenting the bull to the Bank of England demanding that the "check" be stamped "paid."

[37] U.C.C. § 3-302 and note § 3-106(d). If the item indicates the preservation of defenses under a provision of statute law or administrative regulation, such item will not be considered to have been conditioned. But there can be no holder in due course of such an item.

[38] A problem had been created by credit unions which issued payment orders solely to a named individual.

[39] U.C.C. § 3-104(c).

and in the collection of payment for investment securities that are debt securities.[40] This involvement will trigger the application of U.C.C. Article 4—Bank Deposits and Collection. That Article resolves any conflict that might arise with regard to the applicability of other articles of the U.C.C. by providing that

> To the extent that items within this Article are also within Articles 3 and 8, they are subject to those Articles. If there is conflict, this Article governs Article 3 but Article 8 governs this Article. [U.C.C. § 4-102(a)]

Additionally U.C.C. §§ 3-102(c) and 4-103(b) provide that regulations of the Board of Governors of the Federal Reserve System and operating circulars of the Federal Reserve Bank promulgated pursuant to such regulations supersede any inconsistent provisions of U.C.C. Articles 3 and 4. Further, in recognition of the United Nations' Convention on International Bills of Exchange and International Promissory Notes, Official Comment 5 to U.C.C. § 3-102 provides:

> If the United States becomes a party to this Convention, the Convention will preempt state law with respect to international bills and notes governed by the Convention. Thus, an international bill of exchange or promissory note that meets the definition of instrument in Section 3-104 will not be governed by Article 3 if it is governed by the Convention.

A.   Formal Requisites for Negotiability

To qualify as a negotiable instrument under the Uniform Commercial Code, the instrument must contain on issue

> an unconditional promise or order to pay a fixed amount of money, with or without interest or other charges described in the promise or order

It is further required that it:

(1) is payable to bearer or to order at the time it is issued or first comes into possession of a holder;

(2) is payable on demand or at the definite time; and

(3) does not state any other undertaking or instruction by the person promising or ordering payment to do any act in addition to the payment of money, but the promise or order may contain (i) an undertaking or power to give, maintain, or protect collateral to secure payment, (ii) an authorization or power to the holder to confess judgment or realize on or dispose of collateral, or (iii) a waiver of the benefit of any law intended for the advantage or protection of an obligor. [U.C.C. § 3-104(a).]

1. *Writing:* Although U.C.C. Section 3-104(a) does not expressly refer to the need for a writing, it is clear that such is contemplated. The need for a writing is seen from the demand that certain specific matters must or must not be *stated* to allow the instrument

---

[40] It is here that the use of documentary drafts will arise. U.C.C. § 4-104(f).

to be negotiable. The need for a writing appears to be purely historical, but it does assist in having an audit trail for business purposes. The writing is the reification of the obligation or of the order which would then enable the paper to be transferred by physical delivery; one aspect of the process of negotiation. U.C.C. § 3-201(a). "Writing" is a defined term and "includes printing, typewriting or any other intentional reduction to tangible form." U.C.C. § 1-201(46). Although the transmission of electronic impulses could provide an audit trail, by enabling the recipient to generate a "print-out," such approach would not permit the transfer of rights embodied in an instrument through physical delivery, i.e., as a contemporaneous payment device.[41]

2. *Signature:* The writing must be signed by the maker or drawer, i.e., issuer. U.C.C. §§ 3-105(c), 3-401(a). Any symbol can be used to execute the writing whether manual or by means of a device or machine provided it is affixed with a present intention to authenticate the instrument. U.C.C. §§ 3-401(b), 3-308, 1-201(39).

3. *Unconditional promise or order:* The promise or order of the issuer must be unconditional.[42] There can be no express conditions,[43] albeit there are always implied conditions. For example, there is an implied condition in a note that the maker is not in bankruptcy when the note is due. The insolvency of the issuer represents an economic risk, but solvency is not a legal precondition to the validity of an instrument. All essential terms must be ascertainable from the face of the instrument. A mere reference to another writing does not introduce an express condition. Thus, for example, a reference that the instrument is collateralized with a mortgage will not condition the instrument even though the mortgage itself is subject to conditions.[44] It is thus possible for the instrument to indicate the existence of such mortgage or of the transaction which gave rise to the instrument,[45] and may include an obligation to maintain and secure such collateral. U.C.C. § 3-104(a)(3)(i). Insofar as the instrument reflects the existence of collateral to the obligation in the instrument, it will improve the economic value of the instrument and will entitle the holder of the instrument to a transfer of the collateral. What would destroy negotiability would be an incorporation by reference of such other documentation or a statement making the instrument "subject to or governed by another writing." U.C.C. §§ 3-106(a)(ii), (iii). This would be the effect

---

[41] The concept of a "writing" requires review to take account of technological developments. *Cf. The Commercial Use of Electronic Data Interchange—A Report and Model Trading Partner Agreement, Prepared by the ABA Electronic Messaging Services Task Force,* 45 Bus. Law. 1645 (1990). One proposal at present under consideration is to define writing other than for negotiable instrument purposes as
an intentionally created symbolic representation of information in objectively observable form, or susceptible to reduction to objectively observable form, with potential to last indefinitely [*See* Task Force on ABA Review of U.C.C. Article 1.]

[42] Note an endorser can condition his endorsement without the instrument ceasing to be negotiable. A person taking the instrument for value or for collection can disregard this condition. The rights and liabilities of such person will not be affected whether or not the condition has been fulfilled. U.C.C. § 3-206(b).

[43] U.C.C. § 3-106(a)(i).

[44] U.C.C. § 3-106(b).

[45] A contemporaneously executed document, even though the instrument indicates that it was issued "as per" such document, would not destroy negotiability. Such separate agreement will be binding between the immediate parties but not upon a holder in due course. U.C.C. § 3-117.

even though such other document or agreement is itself free of any conditions.[46] One such incorporation by reference is due to protection granted by state and federal statutes to consumers.[47] Consumer protection statutes attempt to prevent a negotiation of an instrument to a holder in due course who would be able to assert rights against the consumer and would be immune to defenses the consumer may have on the underlying transaction that gave rise to the instrument. As a result, such statutes, and the regulations promulgated thereunder, require that any paper generated by a consumer transaction be legended.[48] Such legend will have the effect of indicating that the rights of the holder or transferee of the paper are subject to claims the issuer could assert against the original payee. U.C.C. § 3-106(d) provides that U.C.C.-Article 3 will apply to such paper, but there can be no holder in due course of such paper.

The total credit of the maker or drawer need not back the instrument. If the instrument is payable only out of a particular fund, it will nonetheless be negotiable. U.C.C. § 3-106(b)(ii). There would appear to be no cogent reason why the general credit of a legal entity must support negotiability. This requirement goes to credit value rather than legal requirement. Market forces will determine whether to accept instruments limiting payment in this fashion.[49]

4. *Fixed amount of money:* The instrument must call for payment of a fixed amount of money. U.C.C. § 3-104(a). Money means U.S. currency or the currency of a foreign country.[50] Unless the instrument specifies that it be paid in a foreign currency, it can be satisfied by payment of an equivalent amount in dollars calculated by using the current bank rate of exchange in the place and on the day on which the instrument is payable.[51] Since these instruments are payment devices, they cannot be cluttered up with any other promise, order, obligation or power except an undertaking waiving the benefit of a defense and allowing the holder to confess judgment and realize on or dispose of collateral, should the instrument be overdue.[52]

---

[46] U.S. v. Farrington, 172 F. Supp. 793 (D. Mass. 1953).

[47] Note: U.C.C. § 3-102(c) also provides that the Article is superseded by any inconsistent regulations of the Board of Governors of the Federal Reserve System and operating circulars of the Federal Reserve Bank.

[48] *See* Federal Trade Commission (FTC) Rule 433.1, 16 C.F.R. § 433.1; *see also* Uniform Consumer Credit Code § 3.307.

[49] U.C.C. § 3-106. Official Comment 1. This attempts to change prior law which had recognized that where an instrument is issued by a government of governmental unit, public policy and enabling statutes would prohibit the instrument to be charged to an account for a purpose not approved by the legislative body. It is doubtful whether a change will have been achieved by the Revised U.C.C. -Article 3 with regard to "government" issued instruments.

[50] U.C.C. § 1-201(24). Note: "Money" also includes "a monetary unit of account established by an intergovernmental organization or by agreement between two or more nations," such as a "Europe Currency Unit (ECU)."

[51] U.C.C. § 3-107. Note that a bank that gave credit in dollars as the equivalent of the value of an item payable in a foreign currency, can charge back should the item be dishonored. The charge back or refund, however, will be calculated in relation to the exchange rate prevailing on the date the charge back or refund is notified to the customer. U.C.C. § 4-214(f).

[52] U.C.C. § 3-104(a)(3)(ii), (iii).

Although a negotiable instrument may be issued at a discount, or with a requirement that calls for interest to be paid while the instrument is current or after it becomes due,[53] or even subject to cost of collection including attorney's fee,[54] certainty must exist at the time the instrument is issued. Mathematical certainty may militate against business considerations favoring interest rate changes not only to induce payment when due, but also to take into account changing economic circumstances calling for fluctuating interest rates. U.C.C. Section 3-112(b), therefore, provides that a variable interest rate will not prevent negotiability. The amount or rate of interest may be stated to require a reference to information not contained in the instrument. For example, interest at two points above the prime rate of banks is published routinely in *The Wall Street Journal*.[55] Merely indicating that the instrument is payable "with interest" will not achieve this purpose. The instrument then will be deemed to contain an ambiguity and held to call for interest "at the judgment rate in effect at the place of payment of the instrument and at the time interest first accrues." U.C.C. § 3-112(b).

---

[53] This may raise a question whether such clause calls for a penalty but will not detract from negotiability. A question of "usury" may also arise to be resolved in accordance with applicable state law, especially a State Loan Shark Statute. This in turn may raise an issue whether the transaction for which the instrument was issued gives rise to the defense of illegality; a defense that can be raised even against a holder in due course. U.C.C. § 3-305(a)(1)(ii).

[54] U.C.C. § 3-104(a)(3). Such an instrument is often referred to as a "cognovit note" or "cognovit draft." The constitutional validity of cognovit notes was attacked as a violation of the due process clause, since the note authorized the holder to appoint an attorney to confess judgment on behalf of the party primarily liable on the note. Such party would then be obligated to pay not only the amount due on the instrument but also attorney's fee, generally assessed at 15% of the face amount of the note. The Supreme Court in Swarb v. Lennox, 405 U.S. 191 (1972) held such note, signed by a consumer, not to be unconstitutional on its face. *See also* D. H. Overmyer Co., Inc., of Ohio v. Frick Co., 405 U.S. 174 (1972) where this ruling was applied to a note issued by a corporate entity. But note, in a consumer transaction, since the principal residence of the consumer could be securing the credit, Reg. Z, 12 C.F.R. §§ 226.1 to 226.26 under the Consumer Credit Protection Act (Truth in Lending Act) 15 U.S.C. §§ 1601 to 1667e will apply, demanding full disclosure.

[55] In international transactions it is not unusual to refer to the interest rate at the London Interbank Offered Rates (LIBOR). What will not be permitted is to allow the payee to determine the interest rate, e.g. in accordance with a payee bank's own prime rate. *See* 12 C.F.R. §§ 33(e), 34.7. *Cf. Convention on International Bills of Exchange and International Promissory Notes, (CIBN), Article 8(b).*

Taylor v. Roeder
234 Va. 99, 360 S.E.2d 191 (1987)*

RUSSELL, J. The dispositive question in this case is whether a note providing for a variable rate of interest, not ascertainable from the face of the note, is a negotiable instrument. We conclude that it is not.

---

* [Editor: citations in [ ] refer to Revised Articles 3 and 4.]

The facts are undisputed. VMC Mortgage Company (VMC) was a mortgage lender in Northern Virginia. In the conduct of its business, it borrowed funds from investors, pledging as security the notes secured by deeds of trust which it had obtained from its borrowers. . . .

Olde Towne Investment Corporation of Virginia, Inc., on September 11, 1979, borrowed $18,000 from VMC, evidenced by a 60-day note secured by a deed of trust on land in Fairfax County. The note provided for interest at "[t]hree percent (3.00%) over Chase Manhattan Prime to be adjusted monthly." The note provided for renewal "at the same rate of interest at the option of the makers up to a maximum of six (6) months in sixty (60) day increments with the payment of an additional fee of [t]wo (2) points." The note was renewed and extended to November 11, 1980, by a written extension agreement signed by Olde Towne and by VMC.

In May 1981, Frederick R. Taylor, Jr., as trustee for himself and other parties, entered into a contract to buy from Olde Towne the land in Fairfax County securing the $18,000 loan. Taylor's title examination revealed the VMC deed of trust. He requested the payoff figures from VMC and forwarded to VMC the funds VMC said were due. He never received the canceled Olde Towne note, and the deed of trust was not released. . . .

Cecil Pruitt, Jr., was a trustee of a tax-exempt employees pension fund. He invested some of the pension fund's assets with VMC, receiving as collateral pledges of certain secured notes that VMC held. [T]he Olde Towne note was pledged and delivered to him on September 12, 1980. No notice was given to the makers, or to Taylor, that the notes had been transferred, and all payment on . . . notes were made to and accepted by VMC.

VMC received and deposited in its account sufficient funds to pay both notes in full, but never informed Pruitt of the payments and made no request of him for return of the original notes. In February 1982, VMC defaulted on its obligation to Pruitt for which both notes had been pledged as collateral. In May 1982, VMC filed a bankruptcy petition in federal court.

Learning that the properties securing both notes had been sold, Pruitt demanded payment from the respective original makers as well as the new owners of the properties, contending that he was a holder in due course. The makers and new owners took the position that they had paid the notes in full. Pruitt caused William F. Roeder, Jr., to qualify as substituted trustee under both deeds of trust and directed him to foreclose them. Taylor and the Pruitts filed separate bills of complaint against Roeder, trustee, seeking to enjoin the foreclosure sales. The chancellor entered a temporary injunction to preserve the status quo and heard the consolidated cases *ore tenus*. By letter opinion incorporated into a final decree entered February 3, 1984, the chancellor found for the defendant and dissolved the injunctions. We granted the complainants an appeal. The parties have agreed on the record that foreclosure will be withheld while the case is pending in this Court.

Under the general law of contracts, if an obligor has received no notice that his debt has been assigned and is in fact unaware of the assignment, he may, with impunity, pay his original creditor and thus extinguish the obligation. His payment will be a complete defense against the claim of an assignee who failed to give him notice of the assignment. *Evans v. Joyner,* 1295 Va. 85, 88, 77 S.E.2d 420, 422 (1953).

Under the law of negotiable instruments, continued in effect under the Uniform Commercial Code, the rule is different: the makers are bound by their contract to make payment to the holder. . . . Further, a holder in due course takes the instrument free from the maker's defense that he had made payment to the original payee, if he lacks notice of the payment and has not dealt with the maker. Code § 3-305 [§ 3-305(a)(1), (b)]. Thus, the question whether the notes in this case were negotiable is crucial.

Code § 3-104(1) [§ 3-104(a)] provides, in pertinent part:

> Any writing to be a negotiable instrument within this title must
>
> . . .
>
> (b) contain an unconditional promise or order to pay a sum certain sum in money. . . .

The meaning of "sum certain" is clarified by Code § 3-106 [§ 3-104(a)]:

> (1) The sum payable is a sum certain even though it is to be paid
>   (a) with stated interest or by stated installments; or
>   (b) with stated different rates of interest before and after default or a specified date; or
>   (c) with a stated discount or addition if paid before or after the date fixed for payments; or
>   (d) with exchange or less exchange, whether at a fixed rate or at the current rate; or
>   (e) with costs of collection or an attorney's fee or both upon default.

(2) Nothing in this section shall validate any term which is otherwise illegal.

Official Comment 1, which follows, states in part:

It is sufficient [to establish negotiability] that at any time of payment the holder is able to determine the amount then payable *from the instrument itself* with any necessary computation. . . . The computation must be one which can be made *from the instrument itself without reference to any outside source,* and this section does not make negotiable a note payable with interest 'at the current rate.' (Emphasis added.)

Code § 3-107 [§§ 3-107, 1-201(24)] provides an explicit exception to the "four corners" rule laid down above by providing for the negotiability of instruments payable in foreign currency.

We conclude that the drafters of the Uniform Commercial Code adopted criteria of negotiability intended to exclude an instrument which requires reference to any source outside the instrument itself in order to ascertain the amount due, subject only to the exceptions specifically provided for by the U.C.C. . . .

The appellee points to the Official Comment to Code § 3-104. Comment 1 states that by providing criteria for negotiability "within this Article," . . . "leaves open the possibility that some writings may be made negotiable by other statutes or by judicial decision." The Comment continues: "The same is true as to any new type of paper which commercial practice may develop in the future." The appellee urges us to create, by judicial decision, just such an exception in favor of variable-interest notes.

Appellants concede that variable-interest loans have become a familiar device in the mortgage lending industry. Their popularity arose when lending institutions, committed to long-term loans at fixed rates of interest to their borrowers, were in turn required to borrow short-term funds at high rates during periods of rapid inflation. Variable rates protected lenders when rates rose and benefitted borrowers when rates declined. They suffer, however, from the disadvantage that the amount required to satisfy the debt cannot be ascertained without reference to an extrinsic source—in this case the varying prime rate charged by the Chase Manhattan Bank. Although that rate may readily be ascertained from pub-

lished sources, it cannot be found within the "four corners" of the note. . . .

The U.C.C. introduced a degree of clarity into the law of commercial transactions which permits it to be applied by laymen daily to countless transactions without resort to judicial interpretation. The relative predictability of results made possible by that clarity constitutes the overriding benefit arising from its adoption. In our view, that factor makes it imperative that when change is thought desirable, the change should be made by statutory amendment, not through litigation and judicial interpretation.* Accordingly, we decline the appellee's invitation to create an exception, by judicial interpretation, in favor of instruments providing for a variable rate of interest not ascertainable from the instrument itself.

In an alternative argument, the appellee contends that even if the notes are not negotiable, they are nevertheless "symbolic instruments" which ought to be paid according to their express terms. Those terms include the maker's promises to pay "to VMC Mortgage Company *or order,*" and in the event of default, to make accelerated payment "at the option of the *holder.*" The emphasized language, appellee contends, makes clear that the makers undertook an obligation to pay any party who held the notes as a result of a transfer from VMC. Assuming the abstract correctness of that argument, it does not follow that the makers undertook the further obligation of making a monthly canvass of all inhabitants of the earth in order to ascertain who the holder might be. In the absence of notice to the makers that their debt had been assigned, they were entitled to the protection of the rule in

---

* In 1981 the legislature of Tennessee amended its version of U.C.C. § 3-106 to provide that variable-interest notes will be negotiable. Tenn. Code Ann. § (47-3-106) (1)(f) and (g).

[Editor: (1) Note also N.Y. Consolidated Laws U.C.C. § 3-106(2) (McKinney 1988).

(2) For the purposes of subsection one of this section "a stated rate of interest" shall also include a rate of interest that cannot be calculated by looking only to the instrument but which is readily ascertainable by a reference in the instrument to a published statute, regulation, rule of court, generally accepted commercial or financial index, compendium of interest rates, or announced rate of a named financial institution.]

Evans v. Joyner in making good-faith payment to the original payee of these non-negotiable notes.

Accordingly, we will reverse the decree and remand the cause to the trial court for entry of a permanent injunction against foreclosure. Reversed and remanded.

COMPTON, J., dissenting. The majority views the Uniform Commercial Code as inflexible, requiring legislative action to adapt to changing commercial practices. This overlooks a basic purpose of the Code, flexibility and adaptability of construction to meet developing commercial usage.

According to Code § 1-102(1), the U.C.C. "shall be liberally construed and applied to promote its underlying purposes and policies." One of such underlying purposes and policies is "to permit the continued expansion of commercial practices through custom, usage and agreement of the parties." § 1-102(2)(b). Comment 1 to this section sets out clearly the intention of the drafters:

> This Act is drawn to provide flexibility so that, since it is intended to be a semipermanent piece of legislation, it will provide its own machinery for expansion of commercial practices. *It is intended to make it possible for the law embodied in this Act to be developed by the courts in light of unforeseen and new circumstances and practices.* However, the proper construction of the Act requires that its interpretation and application be limited to its reason. (Emphasis added).

The majority's rigid interpretation defeats the purpose of the Code. Nowhere in the U.C.C. is "sum certain" defined. This absence must be interpreted in light of the expectation that commercial law continue to evolve. The § 3-106 exceptions could not have been intended as the exclusive list of "safe harbors," as the drafters anticipated "unforeseen" changes in commercial practices. Instead, those exceptions represented, at the time of drafting, recognized conditions of payment which did not impair negotiability in the judgment of business men. To limit exceptions to those existing at that time would frustrate the "continued expansion of commercial practices" by freezing the Code in time and requiring additional legislation whenever "unforeseen and new circumstances and practices" evolve, regardless of "custom, usage, and agreement of the parties."

The rule requiring certainty in commercial paper was a rule of commerce before it was a rule of law. It requires commercial, not mathematical, certainty. An uncertainty which does not impair the function of negotiable instruments in the judgment of business men ought not to be regarded by the courts. . . . The whole question is, do [the provisions] render the instruments so uncertain as to destroy their fitness to pass current in the business world? *Cudahy Packing Co. v. State National Bank of St. Louis,* 134 F. 538, 542, 545 (8th Cir. 1904).

Instruments providing that loan interest may be adjusted over the life of the loan routinely pass with increasing frequency in this state and many others as negotiable instruments. This Court should recognize this custom and usage, as the commercial market has, and hold these instruments to be negotiable.

The majority focuses on the requirement found in Comment 1 to § 3-106 that a negotiable instrument be self-contained, understood without reference to an outside source. Our cases have interpreted this to mean that reference to terms in another agreement which materially affect the instrument renders it nonnegotiable. *See, e.g., McLean Bank v. Nelson, Adm'r,* 232 Va. 420, 350 S.E.2d 651 (1986) (where note was accepted "pursuant" to a separate agreement, reference considered surplusage and the note negotiable); *Salomonsky v. Kelly,* 232 Va. 261, 349 S.E.2d 358 (1986) (where principal sum payable "as set forth" in a separate agreement, all the essential terms did not appear on the face of the instrument and the note was nonnegotiable).

The commercial market requires a self-contained instrument for negotiability so that a stranger to the original transaction will be fully apprised of its terms and will not be disadvantaged by terms not ascertainable from the instrument itself. For example, interest payable at the "current rate" leaves a holder subject to claims that the current rate was established by one bank rather than another and would disadvantage a stranger to the original transaction.

The rate which is stated in the notes in this case, however, does not similarly disadvantage a stranger to the original agreement. Anyone coming into possession could immediately ascertain the terms of the notes; interest payable at three percent above the prime rate established by the Chase Manhattan Bank of New York City. This is a third-party objective standard which is recognized as such by the commercial market. The rate can be determined by a telephone call to the bank or from published lists obtained on request. . . .

Accordingly, I believe these notes are negotiable under the Code and I would affirm the decision below.

Tanenbaum v. Agri-Capital, Inc.

885 F.2d 464 (8th Cir. 1989)*

III. Whether The Court Erred In Failing To Direct A Verdict And Issue A Binding Instruction On The Issue Of Whether The Promissory Note Given For The Security Was A Negotiable Instrument.

Tanenbaum contends that First National does not have the status of a holder in due course, and, therefore, First National is subject to defenses available to Tanenbaum against Savine, the original payee of the note. Tanenbaum bases his argument on the following language in the note which states that interest

* * * shall accrue on the unpaid balance of this note (the Note) from time to time outstanding from the date hereof, at a rate per annum equal to the lesser of (i) 2½ per cent per annum above the London InterBank Offered Rate (LIBOR) or (ii) the highest rate of interest permitted under applicable law until the entire principal balance of this note is paid in full.

Tanenbaum argues that the note is non-

---

* [Editor: citations in [ ] refer to Revised Articles 3 and 4.]

negotiable because it is impossible for a prospective purchaser to compute from the face of the note the amount that is then payable. The prospective purchaser would necessarily refer to an outside source to determine whether the LIBOR rate or the highest rate allowed by law applies at any specific time.

A negotiable instrument must "* * * contain an unconditional promise or order to pay a sum certain in money * * *." § 3-104 [§ 3-104(a)]. First National contends that the above language of the note meets the Eighth Circuit's criteria for "certainty." The test for "certainty" as it concerns the amount payable under an instrument for it to constitute negotiability is not mathematical certainty, but commercial certainty. *Cudahy Packing Co. v. State National Bank of St. Louis, Mo.,* 134 F. 538, 542 (8th Cir. 1904).

We agree with First National's suggestion that generally accepted commercial practices would be severely and adversely affected should we find that reference to standard published indices would render an instrument non-negotiable. The district court was correct in refusing to direct a verdict and issue an instruction that the note was non-negotiable, and this issue is denied.

NOTE

U.C.C. § 3-112(b) now resolves this dispute by advancing commercial need in an economy ever in a state of instability. The "fixed amount of money" requirement of U.C.C. Section 3-104(a) applies only to the principal and not to the interest charged on the principle debt embodied in the instrument. An ambiguity is resolved by the last sentence of U.C.C. Section 3-112(b).

If an instrument provides for interest but the amount of interest payable cannot be ascertained from the description, interest is payable at the judgment rate in effect at the place of payment of the instrument and at the time interest first accrues.

* * *

5. *Does not state any other undertaking or instruction or to do any act in addition to the payment of money:* Additional acts by the maker or drawer called for in the instrument will make it non-negotiable.[56] This does not prevent the instrument from containing an obligation to set up a sinking fund to meet the payment when due; nor would an obligation to maintain or protect or to supply additional collateral destroy the negotiability of the instrument. U.C.C. § 3-104(a)(3).[57]

6. *Payable on demand or at a definite time:* There is need for certainty as to the time of maturity. U.C.C. § 3-104(a)(2). Absence of a time when an obligation matures would create an investment in equity rather than debt and would make such instrument of no use as a payment device. Uncertainty as to time caused by calling for the occurrence of an event also creates a condition; the event may never occur. The instrument would not be negotiable even if the event is bound to happen, as would be a note due on the death of a named person. In these "post obit" notes the maker usually borrows in anticipation of a benefit expected on the death of the named person. A clause permitting acceleration of the stated time of maturity on the occurrence of a specified event, however, will not destroy negotiability. U.C.C. § 3-108(b). For example, a promissory note due ninety-nine years from date but subject to acceleration upon an indicated event such as the death of a person, would be negotiable.

In commercial situations acceleration clauses are often included in promissory notes issued in connection with secured transactions. Makers/debtors want a fixed maturity date to plan for the performance of their obligation. Holders/Creditors want prompt payment, but also wish to hedge against any insecurity that a default may occur. The solution is a fixed date with an acceleration clause on the occurrence of specified events.[58] Of note here is U.C.C. § 1-208 which provides that an acceleration clause permitting the holder of an instrument to accelerate payment "at will" or "when he deems himself insecure" or which uses words of similar import, permits the acceleration only where there is a good faith belief that the prospect of payment is impaired. The burden of establishing an absence of good faith is on the obligor on the instrument.

---

[56] U.C.C. § 3-104(a)(3). This restriction does not apply to an endorser who not only may be secondarily liable U.C.C. § 3-415(a) or act as a surety U.C.C. § 3-419 but may also guarantee collection. U.C.C. § 3-419(d).

[57] Failure to comply with such requirement set forth in the instrument may be sufficient to be a breach or to create an insecurity and may trigger an acceleration clause advancing the due date. U.C.C. § 1-208.

[58] Rights regarding the collateral need not be set forth on the instrument. To alert a holder to these rights, the commercial paper may refer to the existence of such collateral agreement without thereby conditioning the paper. For example, "this note is secured by a security interest in collateral described in a security agreement dated April 1, 1990 between the payee and the maker of this note. Rights and obligations with respect to the collateral are stated in the security agreement." Such collateral agreements may also contain provisions that accelerate the due date of the note or that permit the prepayment of the note followed by a release of the collateral. *See* U.C.C. §§ 3-108(b), 3-104(a)(3)(i), 3-106(b)(i).

Watseka First National Bank v. Ruda
135 Ill. 2d 140, 552 N.E.2d 775 (1990)

RYAN, J. . . . This lawsuit involves two promissory notes, both dated May 2, 1983. These notes evidenced Ward's indebtedness to Watseka Bank arising out of the bank's funding of Ward's farming operations. The first was termed a "renewal of capital note" that renewed loans, the proceeds of which Ward used to purchase farm equipment. The note in the amount of $125,000 was due March 27, 1984. The second was termed an "on call line of credit" that was to be used for operating expenses. It was in the amount of $121,000, $45,704.34 of which was a carryover from the preceding year, and was also to mature March 27, 1984. Both notes were secured by Ward's "farm machinery, equipment, feed, [and] crops on hand and growing," more particularly described in an accompanying security agreement. The notes were signed by Ken L. Ward alone. These notes were also accompanied by personal, unlimited guarantees signed by Frank Ruda, Virginia Ward and Patti Ward. . . .

In April of 1983, Frank Ruda submitted then current financial statements reflecting a net worth of over $2 million. According to the bank's memoranda, it suspected that this figure was overstated but felt that the Rudas' net worth was approximately $1½ million. Based on the Rudas' net worth, and despite previous cash-flow problems with both Frank Ruda and Ken Ward, the Bank restructured and extended Ward's debt, culminating in the notes that are the subject of this lawsuit. These notes contained the following language: "If the holder deems itself insecure then at its option, without demand or notice of any kind, it may declare this note to be immediately due."

The ensuing summer of 1983, unfortunately, was not a kind one for Illinois farmers. A severe drought greatly affected the crops, and as a result, Ken Ward realized yields far below that which he projected. In October of that year, a meeting was held between Ken Ward, Frank Ruda, officers and attorneys of Watseka Bank and representatives of Iroquois First State Bank. The parties apparently agreed that, because the proceeds from the sale of Ken Ward's crops would not be sufficient to satisfy his indebtedness to the banks, Frank Ruda would have to sell some of his farmland and apply the proceeds to the various notes. Attorneys for Watseka Bank prepared lease terminations for the land Ward was renting from Ruda to facilitate the sale of that property. Ward soon began to sell the personal property that served as security for the debt and applied the proceeds to the debt. . . .

Watseka Bank alleged that Ward was liable as debtor under the promissory notes, and alleged that the Rudas and Patti Ward were liable pursuant to the unlimited guarantees that they signed in 1981. The defendants set forth several affirmative defenses with their answer, including want of consideration and fraud in inducing the Rudas to sign the unlimited guarantees for the Ward indebtedness, failure by the bank to provide adequate notice of the sale of collateral pursuant to § 9-504(3) of the Uniform Commercial Code (Ill. Rev. Stat. 1987, ch. 26, par. 9-504(3)) (U.C.C. or Code), and breach of a fiduciary duty. The issue of plaintiff's failure to act in good faith in accelerating the debt appears to have first been raised in defendant's opening statement. Any procedural error that might have arisen from this method of raising this issue is inconsequential, however, because no objection appears in the record, counsel later argued the merits of the defense and the judge ruled on it. *Truchon v. City of Streator,* 70 Ill. App. 3d 89, 94 (1979).

The trial judge ruled in favor of the plaintiffs as to all matters, except for the defendants' allegation regarding plaintiff's failure to accelerate in good faith. The trial judge, nevertheless, awarded to plaintiff judgment on the notes, but ordered counsel to recalculate the amount owing on the notes because the court determined that the bank inappropriately applied the proceeds from the sale of the collateral to the indebtedness before the maturity date stated on the notes.

The judge's specific finding was that Watseka Bank "had no basis for accelerating the maturity date on the notes," but he refused to discharge the Rudas' liability as sureties because, at the time of trial, the stated maturity date on the notes had come and gone. It is not clear what standard the judge used for either of these decisions and the attorneys' memoranda of points and authorities shed little light on the question.

On appeal, the Rudas argued that the bank

failed to act in good faith pursuant to § 1-208 of the Code (Ill. Rev. Stat. 1987, ch. 26, par. 1-208), and that the bank failed to provide proper notice of the sales of the collateral pursuant to § 9-504 of the Code (Ill. Rev. Stat. 1987, ch. 26, par. 9-504). Addressing only the first issue, the appellate court concluded that "the trial court's failure to find an absence of good faith in the acceleration of the due date of Ward's debt was contrary to the manifest weight of the evidence." (175 Ill. App. 3d 753, 757 [7 U.C.C. Rep. Serv. 2d 638, 641].) The appellate court also concluded that the bank's improper acceleration of the debt materially altered the Rudas' principal obligation, thereby releasing them from that obligation. While it is also unclear whether the appellate court properly characterized the trial judge's findings, neither court, in our view, articulated the proper standard that should be applied to the facts in this case.

In this appeal Watseka Bank argues that the appellate court (1) incorrectly termed the test under § 1-208 as objective, (2) erred, in any event, in finding a lack of good faith, (3) erred in finding that the bank's acceleration of the notes served to release the Rudas from their guarantee liability, and (4) failed to properly find that the language of the Rudas' guarantees indicated a waiver of any defense based on wrongful acceleration. Because we find in favor of Watseka Bank as to the first two issues, we need not address the final two. We will discuss the Rudas' contention on cross-appeal later in this opinion.

The insecurity clauses, which provided the basis for the bank's acceleration of these notes, are specifically addressed in the Uniform Commercial Code (U.C.C.). Section 1-208 states as follows:

> A term providing that one party or his successor in interest may accelerate payment or performance or require collateral or additional collateral 'at will' or 'when he deems himself insecure' or in words of similar import shall be construed to mean that he shall have power to do so only if he in good faith believes that the prospect of payment or performance is impaired. The burden of establishing lack of good faith is on the party against whom the power has been exercised. (Ill. Rev. Stat. 1987, ch. 26, par. 1-208.)

This Code section specifically permits the use

of insecurity clauses, but allows creditors to exercise them only if they do so in good faith. There has been considerable debate, however, concerning what the term "good faith" means and whether it is properly measured subjectively or objectively.

The severity of recognizing the subjective test contemplated by § 1-208 while at the same time placing the burden of proof on the debtor to establish the creditor's subjective lack of good faith, as that section also requires, is tempered by other Code sections. For instance, § 1-103 allows courts to supplement the U.C.C. with common law principles and equity where the Code does not specifically displace them. (Ill. Rev. Stat. 1987, ch. 26, par. 1-103.) Additionally, the general obligation of good faith found in § 1-203 is "further implemented by [s]ection 1-205 on course of dealing and usage of trade." (Ill. Ann. Stat., ch. 26, par. 1-203, Uniform Commercial Code Comment, at 58–59 (Smith-Hurd 1963)). While these provisions do not go as far as measuring a creditor's actions by a "reasonable accelerator" standard, they do insure that a creditor will not be permitted to accelerate in a manner that is contrary to an established course of performance or course of dealing between the parties, in violation of the clear intention of the parties, or in a manner that is inconsistent with the express practices of the industry.

An obligation to act in a commercially reasonable manner, however, is clearly not a part of § 1-208. As noted, while this requirement may have appeared in early drafts of article 1, it ultimately made its way only into article 2 of the U.C.C. (30 U. Chi. L. Rev. at 673).* We must conclude that the drafters did so purposely, finding perhaps that inclusion of the "commercially reasonable" standard for acceleration would detrimentally affect the cost and availability of credit, and that this outweighed any potential for abuse that the provision posed.

The question of whether a particular creditor has in fact acted in good faith provides the focus

---

* [Editor: Section 3-103(a)(4) now provides: "Good Faith" means honesty in fact and the observance of reasonable commercial standards of fair dealing.

An ABA committee reviewing U.C.C.-Article 1 - General Provision recommends the adoption of this approach to the U.C.C. in general.]

of litigation involving § 1-208. Most courts that have addressed the issue have determined that the test of good faith is subjectively measured. These courts have determined that a creditor acts properly in exercising an insecurity clause so long as it does so honestly, irrespective of whether it acts reasonably. *Quest v. Barnett Bank,* 397 So.2d 1020 (Fla. App. 1981); *Builders Transport, Inc. v. Hall,* 183 Ga. App. 812, 360 S.E.2d 60 (1987); *Ginn v. Citizens & Southern National Bank,* 145 Ga. App. 175, 243 S.E.2d 528 (1978); *Farmers Co-op Elevator, Inc. v. State Bank,* 236 N.W.2d 674 (Iowa 1975); *Van Bibber v. Norris,* 275 Ind. 555, 419 N.E.2d 115 (1981) (apparently applying a subjective test); *Karner v. Willis,* 238 Kan. 246, 710 P.2d 21 (1985); *Fort Knox National Bank v. Gustafson,* 385 S.W.2d 196 (Ky. 1964); *Rigby Corp. v. Boatmen's Bank & Trust Co.,* 713 S.W.2d 517 (Mo. App. 1986); *Salsbery v. Ford Motor Credit Co.,* 54 Or. App. 522, 635 P.2d 669 (1981); *Van Horn v. Van De Wol, Inc.,* 6 Wash. App. 959, 497 P.2d 252 (1972).

Several other courts, however, have chosen to impart an objective element into the test of whether a creditor has acted in good faith in accelerating a debt. In *Kupka v. Morey,* 541 P.2d 740, 747 (Alaska 1975), the Alaska Supreme Court held that, in order to enforce an insecurity clause, "the party invoking the clause must reasonably and in good faith believe that the prospect of payment or performance has somehow been impaired." In support of this conclusion, the court looked to article 2, and cited *Sheppard Federal Credit Union v. Palmer,* 408 F.2d 1369 (5th Cir. 1969). The Sheppard court came to the following conclusion:

> In his excellent treatise on security interests, Professor Gilmore indicates that the language of U.C.C. § 1-208 means in substance that '[t]he creditor has the right to accelerate if, under all the circumstances, a reasonable man, motivated by good faith, would have done so.' (408 F.2d at 1371 n.2, quoting 2 G. Gilmore, *Security Interests in Personal Property,* § 43.4, at 1197 (1965)).

We must disagree with the professor's conclusion on this question. There appears to have been some debate as to whether the standard of commercial reasonableness would become part of § 1-208. Professor Gilmore might even have been a proponent of such a standard when the Code was being drafted. The absence of such a standard

in § 1-208, however, is conspicuous. We are not able to insert such a provision where the drafters chose to leave it out.

A Colorado court, in *Richards Engineers, Inc. v. Spanel,* 745 P.2d 1031 (Colo. App. 1987), also concluded that the proper test under § 1-208 is whether a reasonable person, under the same circumstances, would have accelerated. It also relied upon Professor Gilmore's treatise as well as § 1-201 of the U.C.C., which states that the definitions, including the definition of "good faith," apply only if the context in which they are used does not require otherwise. (*Richards,* 745 P.2d at 1032). We are not convinced, as was this Colorado appellate court, that the context of an insecurity clause mandates that we abandon the definition provided in article 1, which is also the definition to which § 1-208 is specifically cross-referenced in the Uniform Commercial Code Comment. (*See* Ill. Ann. Stat., ch. 26, par. 1-208, Uniform Commercial Code Comment, at 80–81 (Smith-Hurd 1963)). This Colorado appellate court also expressed concern for the "inequity of a purely subjective standard." (*Richards,* 745 P.2d at 1033). Equity, however, although a legitimate concern in this area, is something that must be decided on a case by case basis and cannot appropriately provide the basis for adopting a general rule of law that is contrary to the clear meaning of the statute.

The defendants cite an Indiana appellate court case. (*Universal C.I.T. Credit Corp. v. Shepler,* 164 Ind. App. 516, 329 N.E.2d 620 (1975)). In *Universal,* the court concluded that "to be in good faith the creditor must make a diligent and honest effort to discover from all available sources that the security is greatly impaired." (*Universal,* 164 Ind. App. at 521, 329 N.E.2d at 623.) While this might be the best rule, it is simply not the rule that the Code drafters adopted. The *Universal* court also stated that adoption of the subjective test would render § 1-208 meaningless. We disagree. While the burden on the debtor is great, it is not insurmountable. Because of the safety nets provided by §§ 1-103 (applicability of principles of equity) and 1-203 (general requirement of good faith in performance and enforcement of contract or duty which is broader than good-faith requirement of § 1-208), courts have the opportunity to refuse to enforce accelerations that are purely arbitrary or baseless. We also note that the persuasive value of *Universal* is suspect considering the Indiana Supreme Court opinion in *Van Bibber v. Norris,* 275 Ind. 555, 566, 419 N.E.2d 115, 122 (1981), which stated the following:

> We note, however, that the absence of a similar burden of observing 'reasonable commercial standards' on a secured party reflects the Code drafters' recognition that sales transactions are more amenable to establishment of 'reasonable commercial standards' than are the relations between secured parties and debtors.

The Mississippi Supreme Court, citing *Universal,* Professor Gilmore's treatise and its own pre-Code law, also concluded that a creditor's belief that the prospect of payment has been impaired must be reasonable. (*Black v. Peoples Bank & Trust Co.,* 437 So.2d 26, 29 (Miss. 1983). The Supreme Court of Oklahoma came to the same conclusion, citing Professor Gilmore's treatise in a footnote. *Mitchell v. Ford Motor Credit Co.,* 688 P.2d 42, 45 n.5 (Okla. 1984).

The author of a well-known general treatise on the U.C.C. has criticized this line of cases. (1 R. Anderson, *Uniform Commercial Code* § 1-208:47 (3d ed. 1981)). This author states that the confusion stems from the fact that there is a pseudo objective element to which courts look when determining the credibility of the creditor's assertion that it felt that the security had become impaired:

> As a practical matter, it can be expected that there is a theoretical breaking point and that the trier of fact will reach the conclusion that the non-merchant did not honestly believe when the circumstances are such that the trier does not think that any reasonable person could have possibly believed as the non-merchant claims to have believed. (1. R. Anderson, Uniform Commercial Code § 1-208: 47, at 463 (3d ed. 1981)).

Indeed, the question of whether a witness is credible is always an issue to be determined by the trier of fact. The proper inquiry, however, is whether the secured party acted honestly, not whether the secured party acted reasonably.

A popular U.C.C. hornbook, however, concludes differently, stating as follows: Since 1-208 requires only that the secured party act in 'good faith' ('honesty in fact'), the Code standard seems to lie somewhere between a strict objective test (reasonable prudent man) and a thoroughly subjective one (whim). The drafts-

men apparently intended an objective standard. (J. White & R. Summers, *Hornbook on the Uniform Commercial Code* § 25-3, at 1192 (3d ed. 1988)).

These authors also conclude, interestingly, through analyzing several of the cases in the area, that it makes little difference which test prevails because the question whether the creditor acted in good faith in accelerating a debt is answered in the same way regardless of whether the test is termed subjective or objective.

We conclude that a purely objective test of reasonableness was not intended to be applied to the question of whether a secured party has a good-faith belief that the prospect of payment or performance has become impaired. We likewise conclude that a moderating influence brought to bear on § 1-208 by §§ 1-103 and 1-203, and the incorporation into the definition of good faith of the honesty in fact in the conduct or transaction concept of § 1-201(19), prevents an arbitrary or capricious exercise of the power to accelerate the maturity of an instrument. Although we adhere generally to the belief that § 1-208 incorporates a subjective rather than an objective test, we find that because of the effect of the other sections mentioned, the test is not purely subjective. A certain amount of objectivity is involved in ascertaining the honesty in fact concept of good faith. This requirement insists that the desire to accelerate be based on more than the mere whim of the obligee.

Officers of Watseka Bank stated, at trial, that the reason it accelerated these notes was because it became obvious that Ward would have an insufficient cash flow, due to the small yields caused by the drought, to pay the installments on the operating loan and the capital debt. Ward's inability to meet his obligation is, apparently, not in dispute. While Watseka Bank might have had knowledge of Ward's historically poor cash flow, and the interests of Iroquois First State Bank and Robert Taylor, when it made the loan, it did not know that there would be a drought, with the resulting decreases in yields of the crops. Additionally, the Rudas, who were the guarantors, refused to cooperate after the meeting with the bank officials in October 1983. They did not take steps to liquidate farmland to raise funds to apply to the debt, as was discussed at that meeting. The Rudas also affirmatively avoided all contact with the bank. Although the Rudas' net worth may well have been sufficient to liquidate the obligation, from the Rudas' lack of cooperation there was reason for the bank to honestly believe that their farmland would not voluntarily be sold so that their obligation could be paid at maturity. The Rudas did not offer any evidence that the bank did not possess this information when it decided to accelerate the debt, or that the bank had this information when it chose to make the loans. In fact, the evidence is to the contrary. As such, the bank must prevail under the subjective test articulated here.

We are cognizant of the fact that the rule set forth in this case, that a creditor acts in good faith when exercising an acceleration clause so long as it acts honestly, irrespective of whether the "reasonable creditor" would have accelerated under the same circumstances, has a potential for abuse. We assume, however, that the Code drafters were also aware of this potential when they excluded from § 1-208 the duty to act in a commercially reasonable manner. While several courts in other jurisdictions have found unique ways to incorporate an objective element into the test of good faith (*see Baline v. G.M.A.C.,* 82 Misc. 2d 653, 370 N.Y.S.2d 323 (1975) (two-tiered test)), we choose rather to follow the majority of jurisdictions that apply the statute as it is written.

In light of this debate, there is no question that the Code drafters could have done a better job composing § 1-208. In fact, the entire concept of good faith as it appears in the U.C.C. is in need of clarification. The fact that courts and commentators have strikingly divergent views of what the term "good faith" means in § 1-208, and in other parts of the Code, is "antithetical to the idea of a *uniform* commercial code." [Emphasis in original.] (13 U. Mich. J.L. Ref. at 644.) Inconsistency and lack of clarity may unfortunately be the inevitable consequence of a statute that was

subject to extreme lobbying efforts and was the result of political compromise. Reform, however, will have to come from the legislature, not this court.

Because there is no evidence in the record in this case that Watseka Bank did not actually possess the information it claims caused it to accelerate, or that Watseka Bank actually possessed the information it asserts caused it to accelerate at the time it made the loans, the inevitable conclusion is that the Rudas have failed to establish a lack of good faith. As such, we must reverse the appellate court as to this issue. The findings of the circuit court are unclear, however, and, in any event, it must determine the proper judgment amount in light of this opinion. We therefore remand this cause to the circuit for further proceedings consistent with this opinion.

Defendants argue on cross-appeal that they were entitled to notice of the sale of the collateral pursuant to § 9-504(3) of the Code (Ill. Rev. Stat. 1987, ch. 26, par. 9-504(3)). This section requires that the secured party provide notice to the debtor, which includes a guarantor (*Commercial Discount Corp. v. Bayer,* 57 Ill. App. 3d 295, 299 (1978)), of the details of the disposition of the collateral. We concur with the logic of the appellate court in *Midwest Bank & Trust Co. v. Roderick,* 132 Ill. App. 3d 463, 468 (1985) which held that the notice provision in § 9-504 pertains only to disposition that the *secured party* effects. We hold, in the present case, that the trial court's conclusion that the debtor, Ken Ward, sold the property himself, not the bank, is not contrary to the manifest weight of the evidence.

For the reasons stated, the judgment of the appellate court is reversed, the judgment of the circuit court is affirmed in part and reversed in part, and the cause is remanded to the circuit court of Iroquois County. Appellate court reversed; circuit court affirmed in part and reversed in part; cause remanded.

Question: Is it rational that "good faith, when applied to the issue of acceleration of a negotiable instrument [U.C.C. §§ 1-208, 3-108(b)(ii)] be given a different test under U.C.C. Article 1 [§ 1-208] than would be the case where this issue arises in connection with a determination of the status of a holder in due course [U.C.C. §§ 3-302(a), 3-103(a)(4)]? U.C.C. Article 1 Section § 1-201 introduces a catalogue of general definitions by providing:

> "Subject to additional definitions contained in the subsequent Articles of this Act which are applicable to specific Articles or Parts thereof, and unless the context otherwise requires, in this Act:" . . .

NOTE

A demand instrument is due immediately. An example is a check. The check can be presented to the drawee bank immediately. Any other demand instrument that has been outstanding for an unreasonably long time (U.C.C. § 1-204) considering the circumstances in the light of the nature of the instrument and usage of trade, will be deemed overdue. U.C.C. § 3-304(a)(3). Thus, a promissory note, made payable on demand as opposed to one payable on a fixed date in the future, is treated by mercantile custom as a sixty day note subject to acceleration at will. U.C.C. § 1-205. In the case of checks U.C.C. § 3-304(a)(2) sets a ninety day period from its date. Thereafter the check will be considered overdue.[59] These commercial usages are important since anyone taking an instrument that is "stale," will have taken an overdue instrument and thus, would be unable to qualify as a holder in due course. U.C.C. § 3-302(a)(2)(iii). There is no valid commercial reason why a commercial payment system geared to the free flow of credit should protect a dilatory holder of an instrument.[60] This approach is continued further by the U.C.C. in that, unless otherwise agreed, an endorser's secondary liability on an instrument terminates after thirty days [U.C.C. § 3-415(e)] and such discharge on the instrument will also discharge the endorser/obligor from its obligation on the transaction giving rise to the endorsement of the instrument. U.C.C. § 3-310(b)(3).

The converse of acceleration is an extension. An extension clause will not necessarily violate the requirement that the instrument be "payable at a definite time." U.C.C. § 3-108(b)(ii), (iv). The holder of a note carrying a high interest rate may well want to extend the note if he believes that the maker will be able to pay on the new due date. The maker/debtor may desire to provide for an extension in the event he were to be in need of further time to meet the obligation in the note. Thus the parties may grant each other an option to extend the due date or a provision may be inserted in the note, providing for an automatic extension.

A continuous extension not only would make the promise illusory but also would trigger federal and state securities laws.[61] Such instrument would not be a payment device but an investment. An extension clause must be set out in the instrument and must indicate

---

[59] But note U.C.C. § 4-404:
A bank is under no obligation to a customer having a checking account to pay a check, other than a certified check, which is presented more than six months after its date, but it may charge its customer's account for a payment made thereafter in good faith.
The obligation of the issuer of the instrument, however, continues until the expiry of the statute of limitation. U.C.C. § 3-118. But note, U.C.C. § 3-414(f) allowing a drawer to transfer her loss due to the drawee bank suspending payment should the check not have been deposited for collection more than thirty days after issue.

[60] Note the Competitive Equality Banking Act, 31 U.S.C. § 3328, which provides a one year period during which a check issued by the U.S. Government must be negotiated to a financial institution for presentment for payment or it will become *void*. 31 C.F.R. §§ 240.3, 240.4, (effective Oct. 1, 1989) provide that government checks must bear an inscription "void after one year." These sections go on to provide that on the expiration of the one year period such checks will be canceled, (31 C.F.R. § 245.5 provides for the reissuance of checks). Claims for missing checks must be initiated within one year from the date the check was issued. 31 C.F.R. § 245.3 (effective Oct. 1, 1989). The Financial Management Service Bureau of the U.S. Treasury believes that 9.5 million checks worth some $5 billion have been uncashed for at least one year.

[61] *See* 15 U.S.C. § 77b(1), 15 U.S.C. § 78c (a)(10), Uniform Securities Act §§ 402(a)(10), 7B ULA 600 (1985).

an outside date by which time the instrument will have to be paid. This provision is important also so that indorsers and other sureties would be aware of the length of time they are obligated. A failure to indicate an extension clause would release sureties to the extent the indorser or other sureties can prove that the extension caused a loss to them with respect to their right of recourse.[62] An instrument's due date cannot be extended over the objections of a party bound by the instrument. To prevent an extension being imposed, a party to the instrument can tender payment when the instrument is due and thereby obviate having to pay interest which would otherwise accrue. U.C.C. § 3-603(c).

7. Prepayment of notes. Banks and other lending institutions claim that prepayment is depriving them of investment opportunities.[63] Deposits in a bank do not multiply. Only by using such deposits, i.e., making loans, will these funds generate profits. This is especially important to lending institutions whose depositors are demanding interest on their deposited funds. Prepayment of loans increase not only administrative costs, but also generate expenses by requiring these moneys to be placed anew to earn profits. Financial institutions often impose a prepayment "penalty." This approach developed especially in connection with car loans, where a rule of seventy-eight is often applied. To determine the liability of the obligor in a one year loan, under the "rule of seventy-eight," the sum total of twelve months is taken. This gives the number seventy-eight. A prepayment during the first month would require that 12/78 of the annual interest be paid together with the principal outstanding. Prepayment during the second month calls for $12 + 11 = 23/78$ of the annual interest to be added to the principal, and so on. A provision in the instrument providing for prepayment will not negate negotiability. U.C.C. § 3-108(b)(i).

8. Ambiguities. Where an instrument has a date, that date is presumed to be correct.[64] A postdated or antedated instrument would not lose negotiability. U.C.C. § 3-113(a). An undated instrument is deemed dated as of the date of issue, or, absent a proper issue, as of the date it first came into the possession of the holder. U.C.C. § 3-113. A bank need not concern itself with examining whether a check is postdated. Such check can be paid on presentment. Automated collection and presentment procedures have made it no longer cost effective for banks to check on the date of checks. To prevent postdated checks being paid prior to the due date, a bank customer will have to place a stop payment order with the drawee bank. U.C.C. §§ 4-401(c), 4-403.

A complication arises where the instrument is payable at a specified number of days after date, for example, "pay thirty days after date," and none is supplied. Such an instrument is an incomplete instrument. Generally, once completed as authorized, an incomplete instrument will be fully negotiable and binding on the issuer. U.C.C. § 3-115. An incomplete instrument is a signed writing the content of which shows that the signer intended that it be completed by the addition of words or numbers. U.C.C. § 3-115(a). An incomplete

---

[62] U.C.C. § 3-605(c).

[63] Such argument is not always valid, for example, should interest rates increase. Also, a maker may have reasons for paying off a debt other than a desire to refinance at a lower interest rate.

[64] Every January many persons will date checks wrongly. This may cause problems as the check will be presumed to be stale.

instrument may be enforceable, however, without any written attempt to complete the instrument. As we have seen, the U.C.C. may itself provide a missing date. On the other hand, the incompletion may give rise merely to an ambiguity. Here the U.C.C. may provide a solution to resolve the ambiguity. Thus, an instrument stating that it is payable "with interest" but failing to indicate the rate of interest, will be payable "at the judgment rate in effect at the place of payment of the instrument and at the time interest first accrues." U.C.C. § 3-112.

Where an instrument needs to be completed to comply with the requirements of U.C.C. § 3-104, for example, because it fails to state the amount due thereon, an unauthorized completion will be considered an alteration. U.C.C. §§ 3-115(b), (c), 3-407(a). If fraudulently made such alteration will discharge an obligor on the instrument. Where such fraudulently altered instrument is paid by a payor bank, or by a drawee or is presented by a holder in due course, however, these parties can enforce the incomplete instrument as completed, and a fraudulently altered instrument according to its original tenor. U.C.C. § 3-407(c).

If the completion or alteration is not fraudulent, the parties liable thereon are not discharged but remain liable on the instrument as completed or, where the instrument has been altered, in accordance with the original tenor of the instrument. U.C.C. § 3-407(b), (c). Of note here is that a person who by her negligence "substantially contributes to an alteration of an instrument . . . is precluded from asserting the alteration or [lack of authority] against a person who, in good faith pays the instrument or takes it for value or for collection." U.C.C. § 3-406.[65]

Another form of ambiguity that the U.C.C. attempts to reconcile is caused by contradictory terms. In such situation, the typewritten terms prevail over printed terms and handwritten terms over both. Also, words will prevail over numbers. U.C.C. § 3-114. The U.C.C. here solves the ambiguity on the basis of the presumption that an amendment is intended and that by writing out numbers, more care has been taken to make sure the right term has been used.

B. Formalism and Practice

Whereas the draft and a check are simplified instruments facially complying with the formal requisites, the promissory note is more often a complicated document requiring careful drafting to assure negotiability. The largest volume of negotiable instruments handled by banks are checks followed closely by drafts issued in a commercial setting. The volume of paper involved has forced banks to resort to automation and computerization of their activities. Thus banks have suggested that many of the formal requisites are outdated in a computerized world. Banks have argued that the volume of paper to be handled causes them to ignore such "trivialities" as dates on checks when such instruments are subjected to automated processing. But neither do machines read signatures and the amount of a check still has to be manually encoded on the check to make it machine readable. Courts

---

[65] A person asserting the preclusion must have exercised ordinary care, or the loss will be apportioned according to a standard of comparative negligence. U.C.C. § 3-406(b).

have been unprepared to go along with arguments advanced by banks. The Revised U.C.C. Articles 3 and 4, however, accept some of these arguments by specific provisions permitting computerized trading practices. A glance at the types of instruments involved is worthwhile for us to familiarize ourselves with the subject matter of this book.

PROMISSORY NOTE
(including a cognovit clause and providing for variable rate of interest)
Sellersville, New York

$50,000.00   Date _____

FOR VALUE RECEIVED, the undersigned jointly and severally promise to pay to the order of Vendor Inc. at 2222 Main St., Sellersville, New York, the principal amount of Fifty Thousand Dollars ($50,000.00) plus interest in the following manner. [During the year in which the execution of this Note shall take place, interest only at the rate of Ten Per Cent (10%) per annum in monthly installments of $416.50 each, the first monthly installment due and payable on the last day of the month following the date of execution of this Note. During the following five years, the principal amount of this Note together with accrued interest on the unpaid balance of this Note at the rate of Ten Per Cent (10%) per annum, shall be due and payable in twenty (20) quarter-annual installments of Three Thousand Two Hundred Seven Dollars and Fifty Cents ($3,207.50) each, commencing for the first of such installments on or before _____ , 199 ___ and terminating with the last installment on or before _____ , 199 ___ .] [The principal amount of Fifty Thousand Dollars ($50,000.00) shall be repaid in twenty-five (25) monthly payments of two thousand dollars ($2,000.00) each month plus interest on the sum outstanding on the first day of each month determined by adding four percent (4%) of the sum outstanding to the prime rate charged by New York banks and published in the Wall Street Journal on the first Monday of the preceding month.] The undersigned shall also be liable for any and all taxes on intangibles that may be assessed by reason of the holding of this Note. Maker may prepay any entire installment owing without penalty as to principal or interest [and may repay the entire principal amount outstanding by tendering the sum together with interest assessed in accordance with the rule of 78 based on the rate set forth herein].

Upon the occurrence as to any maker, indorser or guarantor of any of the following events, this Note and all other obligations, direct or contingent, of such maker, indorser or guarantor hereof shall become due and payable thirty (30) days after written notice of default: Making of any misrepresentation to the payee for the purpose of obtaining credit or an extension of credit; calling of a meeting of creditors; appointment of a committee of creditors, assignment for the benefit of creditors; voluntary or involuntary application for, or appointment of, a receiver; filing of a voluntary or involuntary petition under any of the provisions of the bankruptcy laws or amendments thereto; issuance of a Writ of Attachment for distraint, or of a notice of tax lien; entry of judgment against any of them or against the property of any of them; failure to pay, withhold, collect or remit any tax or tax deficiency when assessed or due; dissolution; suspension or liquidation of usual business; default in payment; failure to perform any obligation of this Note; or any other action which would cause the Holder hereof in good faith to deem himself insecure. It is expressly agreed that any default may be cured by the defaulting party during said thirty (30) day interim period after written notice without breach of this Note. But, in the case of default due to nonpayment of an installment when due, such cure shall require the payment of a late charge of one and one half percent of the amount due on that installment.

The undersigned does hereby authorize any Attorney at Law to appear in any Court of Record in the State of New York, or in any other State of the United States or in any United States Court, at any time after this Note has become due and payable as herein before provided, and waive the issuing and service of process and confess a judgment against it in favor of any holder of this Note, for the amount then appearing due thereon, together with costs of suit and reasonable attorney's fees, (of at least fifteen percent (15%) of the unpaid balance if not prohibited by law) and thereupon to release all errors and waive all rights of appeal and stay of execution.

This Note is secured by a Security Agreement of even date herewith, which is delivered herewith as collateral security for the payment of this and any other liability of the undersigned, and any one or ones of them, to the holder hereof, whether absolute or contingent, now existing, of which may heretofore, therewith or hereafter be contracted or incurred.

The undersigned jointly and severally waive presentment for payment, demand, protest, notice of protest and dishonor and nonpayment of this Note and consent in advance to release of the collateral and any valid extensions hereof.

_____   _____ (SEAL)
Witness   Victor Vendee

_____   _____ (SEAL)
Witness   Virginia Vendee

Attest: Vendee Corporation
_____   By_____

TIME DRAFTS

[1]

$ 5,000.00   January 15   19 93

Thirty days after sight   *Pay to the*

*Order of*____Seller & Co._____

Five Thousand and 00/100 - *Dollars*

Value Received and charge same to account of

*To*____Buyer & Co._____

*Address*___1 Church Street_____   SELLER & CO.

_____Buyersville, Cal._____   *S. L. Sela*
                                                      pm.

NO PROTEST Take this off before Presenting

[B2882]

809/00 (12-64)

This time draft requires two presentments. One for acceptance and the second thirty days later for payment.

[2]

$ 5,000.00   January 15   19 93

Three months from above date   *Pay to the*

*Order of*____Seller & Co._____

Five Thousand and 00/100 - *Dollars*

Value Received and charge same to account of

*To*____Buyer & Co._____

*Address*___1 Church Street_____   SELLER & CO.

_____Buyersville, Cal._____   *S. L. Sela*
                                                      pm.

NO PROTEST Take this off before Presenting

[B2882]

809/00 (12-64)

This time draft is due three months after January 15, 1993. On that date it needs to be presented for acceptance *and* payment. If the due date is some considerable time hence, it would be advisable to present this draft for acceptance before it is due, to ascertain whether it will be paid on the date indicated.

Magnetic Ink Character Recognition Numbers:

"50233" is the amount of the check in pennies (typed by depository bank)

"2721" is the check number

"34 5678 4" is the account number of the drawer

"05500 2341" are the routing numbers, indicating how the check is to be routed for presentment to the drawee bank:

05 indicates the Federal Reserve District in which the Drawee bank is situated. The third digit 5 directs the item to the Federal Bank within that district that serves the drawee bank. The use of the fourth digit is not clear. With some banks it identifies the processing center or is used for internal reference. Then follows the American Bankers Association (ABA) Institution Identifier, a number given to the drawee bank, 0234. Finally, the 1 is an algorithm to check the validity of the MICR.

"65-234/550" is not machine readable but enables manual handling if the MICR symbols are unreadable. For example, when a check is certified, the account of the customer will be debited. To prevent automation which would result in the account being debited a second time, the MICR line is mutilated requiring manual handling of the item.

C. Parties to Negotiable Instruments

U.C.C. § 3-401 provides:

> (a) A person is not liable on an instrument unless (i) the person signed the instrument, or (ii) the person is represented by an agent or representative who signed the instrument and the signature is binding on the represented person under Section 3-402.
> (b) A signature may be made (i) manually or by means of a device or machine, and (ii) by the use of any name, including a trade or assumed name, or by a word, mark, or symbol executed or adopted by a person with present intention to authenticate a writing.

We must determine, therefore, whether the party we wish to hold liable on the instrument executed or adopted any mark or symbol on the instrument with a present intention to be bound thereby.[66] This mark or symbol could be a manual signature, a facsimile signature or a stamp and can be made or affixed by the party to be charged or by an agent on its behalf.

Prior to the revision of U.C.C. Article 3, courts reached varying conclusions on the issue whether a representative failing to sign with an indication of representation would be held personally liable, i.e. the unnamed principal issue. This problem was compounded in the case of an undisclosed principal. Should not these issues be left to agency law? See the guidelines set out in U.C.C. § 3-402.

---

[66] *Cf.* U.C.C. § 1-201(32). The name of the drawee bank imprinted on a check is not a signature. There is no "present intention to authenticate" the check thereby so as to bind the bank. It merely indicates who is the drawee.

Valley National Bank v. Cook
136 Ariz. 232, 665 P.2d 576 (1983).*

CORCORAN, JUDGE

The issue raised in this appeal is whether an individual who signs a check without indicating her representative capacity is personally liable on the obligation evidenced by the check when the check has the name of the corporate principal printed on it. We adopt the minority rule and hold that the individual is not personally liable. J. White & R. Summers, *Handbook of the Law Under the Uniform Commercial Code* § 13-4 (2d ed. 1980).

On October 21, 1977, appellee J.M. Cook (Cook), the treasurer of Arizona Auto Auction and R.V. Center, Inc., (Arizona Auto Auction, Inc.) issued three corporate checks to Central

Motors Company. Central Motors deposited these checks in its corporate account which was held by appellant Valley National Bank, Sunnymead, a California corporation (Bank). The Bank then sent each of these checks for payment to Arizona Auto Auction, Inc.'s drawee bank, First National Bank of Arizona. However, a stop payment order had been put on these checks and the First National Bank dishonored each of the checks. The checks were returned to the Bank, and the account of Central Motors was charged back for the amount of the checks which totaled $9,795. The bank was unable to recover this amount from Central Motors. The Bank demanded payment from Arizona Auto Auction, Inc., but the demand was not honored. On March 27, 1978, the Bank commenced suit against Arizona Auto Auction, Inc., and J.M. Cook and her spouse.

---

* [Editor: citations in [ ] refer to Revised U.C.C. Articles 3 and 4.]

The case was tried to the court on August 1, 1979. After trial, the court found that the Bank was a holder in due course and that the Arizona Auto Auction, Inc., was obligated as drawer for the face amount of the checks, $9,795. However, the judgment provided that Cook was not personally liable on the checks and awarded her attorney fees as a prevailing party against the Bank. Arizona Auto Auction, Inc., does not appeal from the judgment against it. However, the Bank appeals from that portion of the judgment which is in favor of Cook and her husband as to liability and the award of attorney's fees.

The question of whether Cook signed in her individual or representative capacity is governed by section 3-403 of the Uniform Commercial Code (U.C.C.) as adopted in this state. [I]t provides:

(1) A signature may be made by an agent or other representative, and his authority to make it may be established as in other cases of representation. No particular form of appointment is necessary to establish such authority.

(2) An authorized representative who signs his own name to an instrument:

(a) Is personally obligated if the instrument neither names the person represented nor shows that the representative signed in a representative capacity;

(b) Except as otherwise established between the immediate parties, is personally obligated if the instrument names the person represented but does not show that the representative signed in a representative capacity, or if the instrument does not name the person represented but does show that the representative signed in a representative capacity.

(3) Except as otherwise established the name of an organization preceded or followed by the name and office of an authorized individual is a signature made in representative capacity.*

The Bank argues that this section conclusively established Cook's personal liability on the checks. We do not agree. Admittedly, the checks fail to specifically show the office held by Cook. However, we do not find that this fact conclusively establishes liability since U.C.C. § 3-403(2)(b) [§ 3-402(b)(2)] imposes personal liability on an agent who signed his or her own name to an instrument only "if the instrument . . . does not show that the representative signed in a representative capacity." Thus, we must look to the entire instrument for evidence of the capacity of the signer. *Southeastern Financial Corp. v. Smith,* 397 F. Supp. 649 (N.D. Ala. 1975), *rev'd on other grounds* 542 F.2d 278 (5th Cir. 1976); *Pollin v. Mindy Mfg. Co., Inc.,* 211 Pa. Super. 87, 236 A.2d 542 (1967).

The checks are in evidence and are boldly imprinted at the top "Arizona Auto Auction, Inc." and also "Arizona Auto Auction, Inc." is imprinted above a signature line appearing at the lower righthand corner. Under the imprinted name of the corporate defendant appears the signature of appellee Cook without any designation of office or capacity on each of the checks before us on appeal. Appellee Cook did not endorse the checks on the back. The record does not reflect appellee Cook made any personal guaranty of these checks or any other corporate obligation. By way of example, we reproduce one of these checks:

---

* [Editor: see now U.C.C. § 3-402.]

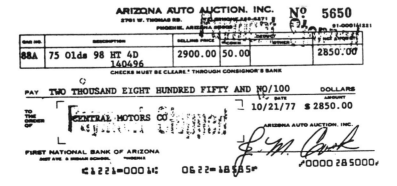

The Superior Court of Pennsylvania was confronted with a similar situation in *Pollin v. Mindy Mfg. Co., Inc., supra.* There the court denied recovery by a third party endorsee against one who affixed his signature to a payroll check directly beneath the printed corporate name without indicating his representative capacity. In *Pollin* the checks were boldly imprinted at the top with the corporate name, address, and appropriate check number. The printed name of the drawee bank appeared in the lower lefthand corner of the instrument and the corporate name was imprinted in the lower righthand corner. Directly beneath the corporate name were two blank lines. The defendant-appellant had signed the top line without any designating of office or capacity. Pointing out that the code imposes liability on the individual only when the instrument controverts any showing of representative capacity, the court considered the instrument in its entirety. The court in *Pollin* held that disclosure on the face of the instrument that the checks were payable from a special payroll account of the corporation over which the appellant had no control as an individual negated any contention that appellant intended to make the instrument his own order to pay money to the payee.

The difference in outcome in the *Pollin* case and the cases cited by the Bank in which corporate agents were held liable for failing to show a corporate title reflects the *Pollin* court's emphasis on *business expectations,* an emphasis which is proper and entirely consistent with the spirit of U.C.C. § 3-403 [§ 3-402]. J. White & R. Summers, *Handbook of the Law Under the Uniform Commercial Code* § 13-4 at 494-95 (2d ed. 1980). In determining what these expectations might be, it is important to draw a distinction between a check and a note:

> The payee of a corporate check with the corporate name imprinted on its face probably expects less from the individual drawer than the payee of a corporate note may, where both the corporate name and the maker's name may be either handwritten or typewritten. Further, it is common for creditors to demand the individual promise of officers on corporate promissory notes, specially in the case of small corporations. Thus, we think a court should be more reluctant to find an agent personally liable who has signed a corporate check than

in the case of a similar indorsement of a corporate note. This does not mean that the drawer of a corporate check will never be personally liable; indeed more than a few have been stuck. Rather, we hope that courts will be more conscious of differences in business practices with respect to different types of instruments when they evaluate the extrinsic evidence presented by the parties.

Id. at 495; *see e.g., St. Croix Engineering Corp. v. McLay,* 304 N.W.2d 912 (Minn. 1981), and *Pollin, supra.* Thus, while it may be common for creditors of small corporations to demand that corporate officers personally obligate themselves on corporate notes, it would be most unusual to demand the individual obligation of an officer on corporate checks.

The fact that common business expectations may not be consistent with a strict reading of U.C.C. § 3-403(2), as that section relates to corporate checks, as opposed to notes, is exemplified by the record before us. Regarding the checks, a branch manager employed by the Bank, testified during trial as follows:

> Q: Would it be fair to say that when a bank receives an instrument that designates at the top a name of a corporation designated by Inc., that it would deal with that item at all times as a corporate instrument?
>
> A: That is correct.
>
> Q: And in the custom and usage of banking practices that would be considered a corporate instrument, would it not?
>
> A: Yes.
>
> Q: And you receiving those instruments assumed, did you not, that Mrs. Cook was writing that instrument as a representative of the corporation, did you not?
>
> A: I would assume that she would have the authority to sign on that account.
>
> Q: And having that authority, you presume that she was writing that for and on behalf of the corporation; is that not correct?
>
> A: I would assume so, to pay these funds.
>
> Q: You didn't expect Mrs. Cook to individually pay these funds out of her pocket, did you? You expected the corporation to do it, did you not?
>
> A: I expected these funds to come from the

account number coded at the bottom of this particular check.

Q: And as far as you know, that account number was the account of the Arizona Auto Auction, Incorporated, is that not correct?

A: That is correct.

Q: You were not misled by the fact that she wrote on the instrument "J.M. Cook" were you?

A: No.

This testimony is consistent with the common business and banking expectation that where a corporate name is printed on a check any accompanying signatures relating to the corporate drawer will be the signatures of officers authorized by the bylaws or corporate resolutions to sign the instrument in a representative capacity without regard to whether there is a specific reference to the representative capacity. This is especially clear where, as here, the check is drawn against a corporate checking account.

In this case the checks clearly show the name of the corporation in two places and the money was payable from the account of Arizona Auto Auction, Inc., over which Cook as an individual had no control. *Considering the instruments as a whole, we conclude under these circumstances that they sufficiently disclose that Cook signed them in a representative and not an individual capacity.*

Our conclusion is further supported by the actions of the Bank which accepted the checks as that of the corporate defendant, Arizona Auto Auction, Inc. In its complaint it so avers. As the court in *Pollin* stated:

> On that basis it proceeded against the corporate defendant and secured a judgment. That judgment was predicated on a proper execution of the instrument by that defendant which required the signature of its representative. Therefore it accepted appellant's signature as that representative. In fact, in his complaint against appellant he avers the checks were those of the corporation.

Having secured a judgment on that basis against the corporate defendant, we are at a loss to see how he may now contend that appellant's signature was on his individual behalf and not in a representative capacity. It must be one or the other. It cannot be both.
211 Pa. Super. at 93, 236 A.2d at 545; *Viajes Iberia, S.A. v. Dougherty,* 87 S.D. 591, 596, 212 N.W.2d 656, 658 (1973).

NOTE

1. U.C.C. Section 3-402(c) now adopts this approach with regard to a check drawn on an account of a principal whose identity is disclosed on the instrument. The identity of the principal may be determined not only from a name imprinted on the instrument but also from the account number imprinted on checks with MICR numbers.

2. With respect to an undisclosed principal, prior law held that an action *on the instrument* could be brought neither by nor against such undisclosed principal, whatever action on the underlying obligation may be possible. *Ness v. Greater Arizona Realty, Inc.,* 21 Ariz. App. 231, 517 P.2d 1278 (1974). U.C.C. § 3-402(a) rejects this approach and adopts the rules of the law of agency to determine the rights and liabilities of the undisclosed principal on an instrument.

3. An agent for an undisclosed principal will be "liable *on the instrument* to a holder in due course that took the instrument without notice that the representative was not to be liable on the instrument." U.C.C. 3-402(b)(2)(ii) (emphasis added). Where the instrument is not in the hands of a holder in due course, the representative can avoid liability by showing that the original parties to the instrument did not intend the signer to be liable on the instrument, i.e. they accepted the representative status of the signer.

4. What is the effect of the signature: "X as agent," without the principal being named?

5. U.C.C. Sections 3-308(a), (b) indicate that signatures of living signers are presumed to be genuine, admitted, and effective. This presumption can be rebutted by a specific denial in the pleadings, for example by an assertion of forgery or that the signature was appended without authority. A simple denial is not enough. Some evidence must be adduced. The evidence need not be such as would require a directed verdict, but it must be such as would support a finding in favour of the defendant. U.C.C. 1-201(31). Where such denial is asserted, the burden of establishing the validity of the signature is on the person claiming rights by virtue of the signature.[67] Once the validity of a signature is admitted or established, the production of the instrument entitles the holder to recover on it unless it is possible to sustain a defense to the obligation embodied in the instrument.[68]

1. Maker and Drawer

Whereas a maker's obligation on a promissory note or on a draft drawn on itself, such as a cashier's check, is a primary obligation,[69] the obligation of the drawer of a draft or of a check is secondary.[70] The drawer calls upon the drawee to pay and engages that if the drawee fails to honor the draft when presented[71] and the drawer is given notice of such dishonor[72] the drawer will pay the amount of the draft to a person entitled to enforce the instrument.[73] Unless the instrument is a check, a drawer can repudiate this secondary liability by "drawing without recourse."[74] Once a draft has been accepted by a bank, the drawer is discharged.[75] But if the drawee is not a bank, the secondary liability of the drawer continues even though the draft has been accepted but not yet paid.[76]

2. Drawee-Acceptor

A drawee is the person to whom the draft is addressed. The drawee is called upon to pay the amount due on the draft. As such, the drawee is not a party to the instrument

---

[67] U.C.C. § 3-308(a).

[68] U.C.C. § 3-308(b).

[69] U.C.C. § 3-412.

[70] U.C.C. § 3-414.

[71] U.C.C. § 3-501.

[72] Where the draft is payable outside the United States "protest" may also be required. Basically, protest is the perpetuation of evidence that a draft has been presented and dishonored. Protest obviates the need for proof of such presentment and dishonor in subsequent litigation. U.C.C. § 3-505(b).

[73] U.C.C. § 3-301 defines a "person entitled to enforce an instrument" as a person in possession of the instrument, whether as owner or otherwise, or a person entitled to possession where the instrument has been lost, stolen or destroyed. U.C.C. § 3-309. *See also* U.C.C. § 3-418(d).

[74] U.C.C. § 3-414(e). This is a rare situation. Such paper appears to have no economic value until the drawee accepts. The Convention on International Bills of Exchange and International Promissory Notes (CIBN) prohibits a maker from issuing a note "without recourse," CIBN Article 39. A drawer's attempt to issue a draft "without recourse," or otherwise to limit liability for payment will be unsuccessful unless there is a person liable on the instrument, e.g. an acceptor, CIBN Article 38.

[75] U.C.C. § 3-414(c).

[76] U.C.C. § 3-414(d).

until the drawee accepts this obligation by signing the draft.[77] Failure by the drawee to accept may give rise to the drawee being liable to the drawer to whom a duty to accept may be owed. It does not entitle anyone, however, to sue the drawee on the instrument.[78] A draft or check does not operate as an assignment of funds in the hands of the drawee.[79] Thus, the draft directing payment to the payee will not create a legal liability in the drawee/debtor to the payee until the draft is accepted.[80] An acceptance that attempts to vary the obligation expressed in the draft can be treated by the holder as a dishonor.[81] U.C.C. § 3-413(a)(ii) provides that an acceptance varying a draft can be enforced against the drawee, but only to the extent of the draft as varied. Since this may not satisfy the obligation for which the draft has been issued, a person entitled to enforce the instrument may treat the draft as dishonored. A holder may assent to the variation, however, in which case the obligation of the drawer or of an endorser, who does not expressly agree to the variation, is discharged. U.C.C. § 3-410(c).

Acceptance of a check by a drawee/bank without a concurrent payment of the check is called "certification."[82] On acceptance the drawee becomes primarily liable to pay the instrument.[83] An acceptor should indicate the amount of the draft in its acceptance to protect against the demands of a holder in due course who took the draft without notice that, after it had been accepted, the amount of the draft was raised.[84]

Since the drawer is only secondarily liable on the instrument and the drawee is not liable on such instrument until acceptance, there only exists a secondary liability on a draft prior to acceptance.[85]

In recent years we have seen the development of a "Banker's Acceptance." This is a draft that has been accepted by a bank and thus has the primary obligation of the bank

---

[77] U.C.C. §§ 3-409, 3-413(a). There is no need for the drawee to spell out the acceptance. A simple signature will suffice to indicate acceptance.

[78] U.C.C. §§ 3-408, 3-409(a).

[79] Note that a liability of the drawee may arise outside the instrument on the basis of a contract, the commission of a tort or, where the expectation of acceptance is based on a letter of credit issued by or confirmed by the drawee, on the obligation expressed in the letter of credit or in some other representation. See further U.C.C. § 1-103.

[80] U.C.C. § 3-408.

[81] U.C.C. § 3-410(a), (b).

[82] U.C.C. § 3-409(d). A drawee/bank is under no obligation to certify a check. A refusal to certify is not a dishonor. U.C.C. § 3-409(d). A refusal to pay would be a dishonor, since a check is a demand instrument. A bank cannot be forced to have an instrument in circulation on which the bank remains liable until some later date when the instrument is again presented for payment.

[83] U.C.C. § 3-413(a). An acceptance by a non-bank drawee does not release the drawer from its secondary liability. U.C.C. § 3-414(d). The rules relating to incomplete instruments apply to a certification of such instrument. U.C.C. §§ 3-115, 3-407.

[84] U.C.C. § 3-413(b). See also § 3-406. Cf. Brower v. Franklin National Bank, 311 F.Supp. 675 (SDNY 1970) (decided under former U.C.C. § 3-406). If the bank uses an imprint to indicate the amount for which the bank is certifying the instrument it should not be possible for such instrument to fall into the hands of a holder in due course since there would be evidence of irregularity. See U.C.C. § 3-302 (a)(1). A failure to do so may result in liability. U.C.C. § 3-413(b).

[85] U.C.C. §§ 3-414(b), (c) (drawer), 3-415(a), (c) (endorsers if any exist).

to support its credit worth. Banker's acceptances have been used as investments. Their value in connection with a documentary sale, however, must not be underestimated. Parties to a sale's transaction may agree to a documentary sale. The buyer's bank may obligate itself to accept a time draft on presentment of documents by the seller. The bank on acceptance of this documentary draft will receive negotiable documents of title representing the goods and thus would be collateralized with regard to the buyer's debt to the bank. In the meantime, the seller will have a negotiable instrument, the banker's acceptance, that can be discounted to give the seller present funds to finance other transactions.

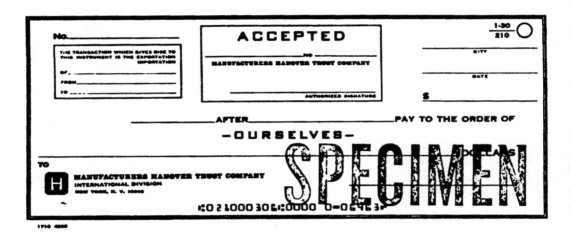

3.   Payee Endorser-Endorsee

Negotiation of a bearer instrument merely requires a transfer of possession, but in order for an instrument payable to an identified person, e.g. an order instrument, to be negotiated, a transfer of possession *and* an endorsement by the holder is required.[86] A transferee becomes a holder by virtue of a negotiation. But there can be no negotiation when taking an instrument from the issuer. Nonetheless, a person to whom a bearer instrument has been issued or who is the "identified person . . . in possession" of an order instrument issued to her, will qualify as a holder. U.C.C. § 1-201 (20). Where the instrument, such as a check, is promptly deposited into a bank, the payee normally will be called upon to

---

[86] U.C.C. § 3-201. The endorsement must be on the instrument or on an "allonge," which is a paper affixed to the instrument so as to become a part thereof. U.C.C. § 3-204(a). A purported indorsement pinned or clipped to an instrument is not sufficient. The indorsement must be on a paper so firmly affixed to the instrument as to become an extension or part of it. In accordance with what is perceived to be the Law Merchant on this issue, U.C.C. § 1-103, several jurisdictions have held that an indorsement by allonge is permitted only where there is no longer room on the instrument itself due to previous indorsements. *See* Pribus v. Bush, 118 Cal. App. 1003, 173 Cal. Rptr. 747 (1981). The view adopted by Official Comment 1 to U.C.C. § 3-204, however, is that this "rule of convenience" is not confined to an actual impossibility to indorse on the instrument itself, but that an allonge can be used at any time.

endorse the item so that it can be negotiated while it moves through the collection process.[87] Should there be more than one payee or endorser an ambiguity arises. U.C.C. Section 3-110(d) resolves this ambiguity by providing that an instrument payable to more than one person in the alternative can be negotiated, discharged or enforced by anyone of them who is in possession of the instrument. Otherwise, all of the parties named must endorse to negotiate the instrument. The obligor on the instrument will have to make certain that payment is received by the persons entitled to enforce the instrument, i.e. the payee or the endorsee or a transferee from such person.[88] Thus, any discharge of or enforcement of the instrument calls for all persons entitled to enforce the instrument to participate.

A further ambiguity may arise whether the instrument is payable in the alternative or not in the alternative, for example.

"Pay to the order of Arthur Payee and/or Joan Payee."

U.C.C. Section 3-110(d) resolves this ambiguity by providing that the obligor on the instrument can treat it as being payable in the alternative and an endorsement by either of them will suffice.[89]

An endorsement can be a "blank endorsement" which will convert the instrument into bearer paper,[90] or a "special endorsement" which specifies the person to whom or to whose order the instrument is payable and requires that person's endorsement to enable further negotiation of the instrument.[91] A special endorsement can convert a bearer instrument into an order instrument requiring endorsement and transfer for negotiation.[92]

To effect a negotiation and not a mere transfer, an endorsement must purport to convey the entire instrument or any unpaid residue thereof. In the absence of such an intent the signature and delivery will only effect a partial assignment and the transferee will not become a holder and thus cannot attain the status of a holder in due course.[93]

An attempt to condition an endorsement, for example,

"Pay to the order of X, if the goods sent are received in good order"

will not affect the negotiability of the instrument. The condition will not affect a drawee

---

[87] See Regulation J of the Federal Reserve Banks, 12 C.F.R. § 210.5, which imposes a duty on collecting banks to warrant good title to the item or that such bank has authority to obtain payment on behalf of someone having good title. This is evidenced by legending the item "Prior Endorsements Guaranteed," (PEG). Note, U.C.C. § 4-205(1) providing that, a depository bank that has taken an instrument for collection becomes a holder whether or not it supplies a missing endorsement of its customer.

[88] U.C.C. § 3-301.

[89] The CIBN would appear to reject this solution, *see* CIBN Article 10.

[90] U.C.C. § 3-205(b). An endorsement in blank specifies no particular endorsee and may consist of a mere signature.

[91] U.C.C. § 3-205(a).

[92] Where the blank endorsement consists of a mere signature, a holder, by adding words identifying the person to whom the instrument is to be paid would convert the blank endorsement into a special endorsement. U.C.C. § 3-205(c).

[93] U.C.C. § 3-203(d). All Am. Fin. Co. v. Pugh Shows, Inc., 30 Ohio St. 3d 130, 507 N.E.2d 1134 (1987).

or a person taking the instrument for value or for collection.[94] Nor will further negotiation of an instrument be prevented by an endorsement limiting payment to a particular person, e.g., "Pay only to X."[95] An indication that the proceeds are to be applied to the use or benefit of a particular person will not bind a drawee or a person taking the instrument for collection, but may give notice of a breach of fiduciary duty if, for example, payment is made into a fiduciary's personal account.[96]

In all of these instances, further transfer or negotiation cannot be prevented. Any dispute will have to be resolved between the endorser and endorsee. Subsequent holders may ignore such restrictions. It is possible, however, to restrict negotiation to keep the item within the bank collection process for presentment to the drawee bank. This can be done by indicating in the endorsement that it is "for deposit" or "for collection."[97] After a bank endorses a check, it must remain in the bank collection system until the check is returned to the depositor or the check is specially endorsed to a non-bank.[98] The check must be presented by a bank to the drawee, and the drawee bank will be entitled to pay the presenting bank without having to ascertain that the amount due will be deposited into the right account. The basic obligation designated in a restrictive endorsement such as "for deposit only," or "for collection," rests on the depository bank. Neither a drawee bank nor a bank in the chain of collection need assure itself that the funds actually reach the account indicated.[99] The duty is on the depository bank to place the funds collected into the account of the depositor.[100] Where the item is collected and presented outside the bank collection system, the drawee or maker must pay in accordance with the restrictive endorsement to avoid liability. For example, an endorsement "Pay John Smith," requires the non-bank drawee or maker to pay only to the John Smith indicated.[101]

A way to increase the economic value of an instrument is by an endorsement, "collection guaranteed." This form of endorsement gives rise to liability in the guarantor only when the instrument after being presented when due was not honored. A person entitled to enforce the instrument (1) must have reduced his claim against the issuer or acceptor to judgment, execution being returned unsatisfied; or (2) must show that the issuer or acceptor is insolvent or in insolvency proceedings; or (3) must show that it is otherwise apparent

---

[94] U.C.C. § 3-206(b). Any failure to fulfill the condition is actionable only between the endorser and the endorsee and would be based on the underlying obligation that gave rise to the transfer of the instrument.

[95] U.C.C. § 3-206(a).

[96] U.C.C. §§ 3-206(d), 3-307.

[97] U.C.C. § 3-206(c). U.C.C. §§ 4-201(b), 3-206(c). Only a bank can release such instrument to an entity that is not a bank. This will require a special endorsement naming the transferee. U.C.C. §§ 4-201(b)(2), 3-205(a). *See also* Regulation CC, 12 C.F.R. § 229.35(c), promulgated under the Expedited Funds Availability Act, 12 U.S.C. § 4001 et seq.

[98] *See also* Regulation CC, 12 C.F.R. § 229.35(c). Note Appendix D appears to inhibit the use of any restrictive endorsement such as "pay any bank or banker."

[99] U.C.C. § 3-206(c)(4).

[100] U.C.C. § 3-206(c), (2), (3).

[101] U.C.C. § 3-206(c)(1).

that it is useless to proceed against the issuer or acceptor, for example, they cannot be served with process.[102]

Question: Would an endorsement "collection guaranteed" have any value where it is appended to a draft which a drawee has refused to accept? *See* U.C.C. §§ 3-415(a), (b), 3-412, 3-413(a), 3-414, and 3-419(d). What is the effect of an endorsement "payment guaranteed"? *See* U.C.C. §§ 3-415(a), (c), 3-419(a), (c).

4. Transferor-Transferee

As we have seen, every issuance or negotiation of an instrument involves a transfer of possession for the purpose of giving rights on the instrument to the transferee.[103] If the transfer was in the course of a negotiation, the transferee will qualify as a "holder"[104] and could even qualify as a "holder in due course."[105] Negotiation requires a transfer of possession whether voluntary or involuntary by a person other than the issuer.[106] Where the transfer is by the issuer of the instrument to the payee, there will not be a negotiation, but the payee will be a holder. U.C.C. § 1-201(20). An issuer's transfer of an instrument to a remitter for negotiation by the remitter to a payee,[107] will be an issuance of the instrument. The remitter, however, will not thereby become a holder. The instrument is neither a bearer instrument, nor is the remitter "the identified person" on the instrument. The named payee to whom the remitter transfers the instrument, however, will be a holder.[108] We can see, therefore, that being the owner of an instrument does not necessarily mean being a holder. Ownership rights are determined by property law.[109] Unless the instrument is payable to bearer, transfer alone will not suffice to make the transferee a holder. In addition to a transfer, an order instrument requires an endorsement by the payee to enable the transferee to qualify as a holder.[110] A transferee who has not attained the status of a "holder" cannot qualify to the status of "holder in due course." Such transferee, however, is not completely without recourse.

Every transfer, whether or not it qualifies as a negotiation, vests in the transferee such rights as the transferor had in the instrument.[111] If the transfer of an order paper is for

---

[102] U.C.C. § 3-419(d); Floor v. Melvin, 5 Ill. App. 3d 463, 283 N.E.2d 303 (1972) (guarantee "against loss" is a "collection guarantee" not a "payment guarantee").

[103] U.C.C. §§ 3-105(a), 3-203(a).

[104] U.C.C. § 3-201(a).

[105] U.C.C. § 3-302(a).

[106] U.C.C. § 3-201(a). Note: being a holder does not mean necessarily being the owner of an instrument.

[107] A remitter is a person who purchases an instrument from an issuer generally to negotiate the instrument to a person to whom the remitter is indebted, for example the purchase of a cashier's check or teller's check payable to the purchaser's creditor. U.C.C. § 3-103(11).

[108] U.C.C. § 3-201(b).

[109] *See* Official Comment 1 to U.C.C. § 3-203.

[110] U.C.C. § 3-201(b).

[111] U.C.C. § 3-203(b).

value,[112] the transferee has the right to have the unqualified endorsement of the transferor so as to enable the transferee to qualify as a "holder."[113] It is not possible, however, for a transferee who had been a party to any fraud or illegality affecting the instrument to improve his position by taking from a "holder in due course."[114] It must be realized that the "umbrella provision" embodied in U.C.C. § 3-203(b) does not convey the *status* of a holder in due course. It merely enables a transferee, whose transferor was a holder in due course, to claim the *rights* of a holder in due course. As a result, a transfer by such person to a subsequent transferee will not convey the rights of a holder in due course on such subsequent transferee.[115] Such subsequent transferee will have to qualify herself as a holder in due course by complying with the requirements of Section 3-302(1) of the U.C.C.

The basic reason for this umbrella provision is to enable a holder in due course, confronted with the insolvency of parties to the instrument, to recover some of the losses by transferring the instrument, usually at a discount, to a transferee better able to assume the risk and able to await the outcome of the liquidation of the insolvent parties' estates. This is of especial value to a transferor, holder in due course, claiming a security interest in an instrument. The transferee of such instrument from such holder may qualify to the rights of a holder in due course, but will only be able to claim an interest limited to that held by the transferor.[116]

Where the transfer is for consideration, the transferor warrants to the transferee, and where the transfer is by endorsement and delivery to any subsequent transferee who takes the instrument in good faith, (1) that he is a person entitled to enforce the instrument, U.C.C. § 3-301; and (2) that all signatures on the instrument are authentic and authorized;[117] and (3) that the instrument has not been altered; and (4) no party to the instrument has a defense or claim in recoupment against him;[118] and (5) that the transferor has no knowledge of insolvency proceedings having been instituted with respect to a maker or acceptor or, where the draft has not yet been accepted, against the drawer.[119] These warranties cannot be disclaimed with respect to checks.[120]

---

[112] U.C.C. § 3-303.

[113] U.C.C. § 3-203(c). The transferee will not qualify as a holder until such time as the endorsement is obtained and only at that time could the transferee qualify as a holder in due course. There is no relation back to the time the instrument was first received or when value was given for the instrument.

[114] U.C.C. § 3-203(b).

[115] Smather v. Smather, 34 N.C. App. 724, 239 S.E.2d 637 (1977) (Widow found note among deceased husband's assets. The note was payable to father of the deceased and had apparently come into the possession of the deceased husband without endorsement by the father. Thus deceased husband never acquired the status of a holder in due course whatever the status of the deceased's father. Widow could not claim to have the rights of a holder in due course for she did not take from a holder in due course.)

[116] U.C.C. §§ 3-204(c), 3-302(e).

[117] *Cf.* CIBN Article 45. But, under the CIBN only the first taker from the forger gives this warranty CIBN Articles 25 and 26 and thus would be liable for breach. All subsequent transferees will have taken through a "valid transfer," CIBN Article 15 and thus would not be in breach of CIBN Article 45.

[118] U.C.C. § 3-303(b).

[119] U.C.C. § 3-416(a).

[120] U.C.C. § 3-416(c).

Breach of these warranties does not give rise to secondary liability on the instrument. The transferee who took the instrument in good faith will have a cause of action for damages for breach of warranty to the extent of loss suffered, but limited to the amount of the instrument plus expenses and interest.[121]

---

[121] U.C.C. § 3-416(b).

Hayner v. Fox

182 Ill. App. 3d 989, 542 N.E.2d 1134 (1989)*

JUSTICE BUCKLEY delivered the opinion of the court. CAMPBELL and O'CONNOR, JJ., concur.

Connecticut National Bank (Connecticut) and the Bank of Ravenswood (Ravenswood) brought this third-party action, arising from a judgment entered against them for accepting and paying a draft with forged indorsements, against Lash, Warner & Associates (Lash, Warner), a copayee and subsequent indorser of the forged instrument. The circuit court, on cross-summary judgment motions, entered judgment in favor of Connecticut/Ravenswood in the amount of $32,534. Lash, Warner appeals from these orders, contending that the circuit court erred in finding that it had created statutory warranties of good title and authenticity of prior indorsements pursuant to the Uniform Commercial Code (the Code) § 3-417(1)(a), (2)(a), (2)(b). [§§ 3-417(a)(1), 3-416(a)(1), (2)].

We reverse and remand this case to the circuit court with instructions to enter summary judgment in favor of Lash, Warner. This controversy arose from a $32,534 insurance check issued to six payees in settlement of a fire damage claim for real estate. The sequence of the payee indorsements occurred as follows. The check was first indorsed by Pioneer Bank & Trust Company, which was the land trustee, and First Federal Savings & Loan to the order of Donald Hayner and Andrew Van Styn, the contract sellers. The contract purchaser, Theresa Fox, in possession of the check with the signatures of the two banks and Hayner and Van Styn appearing on the check, then gave the check to Lash, Warner, the public

adjustor who negotiated settlement. Lash, Warner indorsed the check in exchange for Fox' check for $4,706.25 as payment for its services as adjustor. The final payee indorsement was made by Fox when she presented the check for payment to Ravenswood, which, in turn, forwarded the check to Connecticut for final payment.

Hayner and Van Styn then brought an action against Fox, Pioneer Bank & Trust Company, Ravenswood, and Connecticut alleging that their indorsements had been forged and that Ravenswood and Connecticut had converted the check. Judgment was entered in favor of Hayner and Van Styn in the full amount of the check. Connecticut/Ravenswood[1] then filed this third-party complaint now on appeal against Lash, Warner, alleging that Lash, Warner had breached its warranties under the Code. Lash, Warner denied in its answer that it breached any warranties to Connecticut/Ravenswood, but it admitted in response to discovery that at the time it indorsed the check, Hayner's and Van Styn's indorsements appeared on the check. Lash, Warner also admitted that it had indorsed the check and returned it to Fox in exchange for payment for its services in the amount of $4,706.25.

The facts of this case being undisputed, we determine whether Lash, Warner created, as a matter of law, statutory warranties under the Code.

The Code's warranty provisions in issue here are § 3-417(1)'s warranty of good title and § 3-417(2)'s warranties of good title and that all prior signatures are genuine or authorized. [§§ 3-

---

* [Editor: citations in [ ] refer to Revised U.C.C. Articles 3 and 4.]

[1] The $32,534 judgment was paid by Ravenswood, which had admitted its liability to Connecticut on its presentment warranty. [Editor: *see* U.C.C. § 4-208.]

417(a)(1), 3-416(a)(1)(2)] The precise question presented for our review is whether these warranties are triggered where a payee indorses a check in exchange for a copayee's payment for services rendered, such indorsement being made after the forged signature of another payee but before all necessary signatures appear on the check. As the parties have conceded in oral argument that no Illinois cases have addressed the effect of these warranties on this factual scenario and as we have not found any cases from other jurisdictions addressing this situation, we look to the language of the Code and the drafters' intent to reach our determination of this question.

The "presentment" warranty in section 3-417(1)(a) provides:

"Any person who obtains payment or acceptance and any prior transferor warrants to a person who in good faith pays or accepts that (a) he has a good title to the instrument or is authorized to obtain payment or acceptance on behalf of one who has a good title." (Ill. Rev. Stat. 1987, ch. 26, par. 3-417(1)(a)).

Under this provision, a person who gives his signature in exchange for payment under § 3-417(1) [§ 3-417(a)] warrants that "he has a good title to the instrument." In the absence of a Code definition for the term "good title," evidence of the drafters' intent as to this term, or the parties' citation to any authority to the contrary, we rely on the plain meaning of the above phrase in concluding that § 3-417(1) [§ 3-417(a)(1)] applies to one who presents an instrument as one who purports to have and to transfer title of the instrument by his indorsement. Lash, Warner could not have been purporting to have title to the check at the time it indorsed the check because a payee's signature was missing at the time.[2] Thus, we hold that Lash, Warner's indorsement did not create the Section 3-417(1) presentment warranty of good title.

Turning to the "transfer" warranties, Section

---

[2] 6 R. Anderson, Uniform Commercial Code § 3-417:27 (3d ed. 1984) supports our conclusion in stating that "it can be readily concluded that 'good title' requires all indorsements necessary to plaintiff's chain of title be genuine and authorized." We may infer from this comment that the necessary indorsements must exist and the warranty does not come into play where a necessary indorsement is missing. Accord First National Bank v. Nunn, 628 P.2d 1110, 1115 (Mont. 1981).

3-417(2)(a), and (2)(b) provide, in relevant part: [§ 3-416(a)(1)(2)]

"Any person who transfers an instrument and receives consideration warrants to his transferee and if the transfer is by indorsement to any subsequent holder who takes the instrument in good faith that

(a) he has a good title to the instrument * * *

(b) all signatures are genuine or authorized."

Lash, Warner contends that the events concluding in its signature did not trigger the "transfer" warranties because there was no "transfer of an instrument." It argues instead that its signature was merely a relinquishment of its rights in the instrument or an authorization to a copayee to negotiate the check. Connecticut/Ravenswood, on the other hand, argues that Lash, Warner transferred the check when it gave up all rights it had in the instrument. The Code does not define "transfer of an instrument," nor do the drafters elucidate on the usage of the phrase. The parties, though, rely on different sections of the Code as indicating the drafters' intent in this regard. We find none of these sections to be of much assistance. [see now § 3-203(a) and note § 3-204(a)].

Lash, Warner cites Section 3-116(b), [§ 3-110(d)] which states, in part, that "an instrument payable to the order of two or more persons * * * may be negotiated * * * only by all of them." This section, however, was intended by the drafters not to define the warranty liability under Section 3-417, but to clarify the distinction between an instrument payable to payees in the alternative and payable jointly as it relates to the negotiability of the instrument. Ill. Ann. Stat., ch. 26, par. 3-116, Uniform Commercial Code Comment, at 72 (Smith-Hurd 1963).

Connecticut/Ravenswood cites Section 3-201, providing that a "[transfer] of an instrument vests in the transferee such rights as the transferor has therein" [§ 3-203(b)] and this section's explicatory comment that the section "applies to any transfer, whether by a holder or not. Any person who transfers an instrument transfers whatever rights he has in it. The transferee acquires those rights even though they do not amount to 'title.'" While this section explains the effect of a transfer, it sheds no light on when there is a "transfer of an instrument." The Uniform Commercial Code Comment to the section on negotiation, Section 3-202, [§§ 3-201, 3-202] so illustrates. In stating that negotiation is merely a special form of transfer, which importance lies entirely in the fact that it makes a transferee a holder, it states that "any negotiation carries a transfer of rights as provided in * * * Section 3-201." Ill. Ann. Stat., ch. 26, par. 3-201, Uniform Commercial Code Comment 1, at 101 (Smith-Hurd 1963) [§ 3-203(b)].

Connecticut/Ravenswood further cites Section 3-118(e), [§ 3-116(a)] which provides: "[unless] the instrument otherwise specifies two or more persons who sign as maker, acceptor or drawer or indorser and as part of the same transaction are jointly and severally liable even though the instrument contains such words as 'I promise to pay.'"[3] We find no merit to Connecticut/Ravenswood's contention that this section provides for several liability against each of the payee indorsers in the instant case even though each individual indorser is not conveying the entire instrument.

As its title explains, Section 3-118 is intended to clarify ambiguous terms and rules of construction. The drafters clearly intended that this section clarify the contract liability of an indorser or coindorsers to pay if an instrument is dishonored, not define the warranty liability of indorsers. The Uniform Commercial Code Comment to Section 3-118(e) states that this joint and several liability rule "applies only where such parties sign as part of the same transaction; successive indorsers are, of course, liable severally but not jointly." [Comment 2 to § 3-116 and note §§ 3-116(b), 3-419(e)] The comment's latter sentence demonstrates that Section 3-118(e) does not address the successive indorsement situation and the warranty liability of such indorsers. The "same transaction" language obviously refers to the contract liability of coindorsers, rather than the warranty liability of successive indorsers. Moreover, as Lash, Warner urges, construing the section to apply to Section 3-417 [§§ 3-416, 3-417] would be illogical because it would suggest that if a check is issued to multiple payees, the first payee to indorse could be liable for subsequent forgeries of other payees.

Before revealing the outcome of our search for other provisions in the Code, we need to expound on the parties' dispute in this case. Connecticut/Ravenswood argues that Lash, Warner confuses the concept of transfer with negotiation when it contends that its signature constituted merely a relinquishment of its rights as opposed to a transfer of an instrument. We understand this argument to be that the distinction between transfer and negotiation is that a transfer is the relinquishment of any interest in an instrument, whereas a negotiation conveys an entire instrument.

In our judgment, the Code provision relating to negotiation and the Uniform Commercial Code Comment suggest that the distinction between transfer and negotiation is not the quantum of the interest in the instrument that a person is purporting to convey but what rights the recipient acquires. The two reveal the correlation between the terms "transfer" and "negotiation." Uniform Commercial Code Comment 1 to Section 3-202 states:

"Negotiation is merely a special form of transfer, the importance of which lies entirely in the fact that it makes the transferee a holder * * *." (Ill. Ann. Stat., ch. 26, par. 3-202, Uniform Commercial Code Comment 1, at 101 (Smith-Hurd 1963)). [Official Comment 1 to § 3-201]

Section 3-202(3) provides:

"An indorsement is effective for negotiation only when it conveys the entire instrument * * *. If it purports to be of less it operates only as a partial assignment." [§ 3-203(d)]

The Code comment demonstrates that a negotiation and transfer are not separate and distinct concepts; their dissimilarity lies only in what the recipient acquires. A negotiation confers upon the recipient the status of a holder,[4] whereas the recip-

---

[3] Lash, Warner argues that Connecticut/Ravenswood is procedurally barred from relying on section 3-118(e) [3-116(a)] on appeal because it sued Lash, Warner for breach of warranty under Section 3-417(2)(b) [Editor: *see* now § 3-416(a)(2)] and it did not argue the "joint liability theory" under Section 3-118(e) in its motion for summary judgment or in its response to Lash, Warner's motion for summary judgment. Connecticut/Ravenswood correctly points out, however, that its reliance on Section 3-118(e) is not reliance on a new theory or substantive right; rather, the section is definitional. As the section's title explains, it is intended to clarify "Ambiguous Terms and Rules of Construction." [Editor: Section 3-116 deals with the specific ambiguity surrounding joint and several liability. *See also* Section 3-110(d).].

---

[4] Status of holder of a negotiable instrument is a prerequisite to qualifying as a holder in due course, which allows a person to take the instrument free from personal defenses.

ient of a transfer may or may not acquire this status. Because the distinction in these two terms does not lie in the quantum of the instrument to be conveyed and because § 3-202(3) [§ 3-203(d)] provides that to negotiate an instrument, an indorsement must convey the entire instrument, it follows that one must convey the entire instrument to "transfer an instrument." The drafters' use of the words "partial assignment" in [the section] instead of "transfer" to describe the effect of a conveyance of less than the entire instrument further supports this conclusion.

As a separate ground for holding that the "transfer" warranties are inapplicable to the instant case, we do not believe that the drafters could have intended the warranty provisions to apply to persons in the position of Lash, Warner. It is contrary to reasonable commercial expectations that in a multiple-payee situation, a payee could not give up his personal interest, however limited, to other copayees without warranting the title to the document or the genuineness of the signatures of other copayees who have previously signed the instrument. Contrary to Connecticut/Ravenswood's argument that the drafters contemplated this situation and provided the protection of "without recourse" to such copayees, an indorser who signs "without recourse" disclaims his contract liability;...indorser makes all of the other § 3-417 warranties. See *Wolfram v. Halloway,* 46 Ill. App. 3d 1045, 1048, 361 N.E.2d 587, 589 (1977).

Accordingly, we find that Lash, Warner is not liable under the Code's warranty provisions because it did not "transfer an instrument" under § 3-417(2) [§ 3-416] or purport to convey good title under § 3-417(1)(a). [§ 3-417(a)(1)] Thus, we reverse the trial court's summary judgment order in favor of Connecticut/Ravenswood and remand this case to the circuit court with directions to enter summary judgment in favor of Lash, Warner.

Reversed and remanded with directions.

NOTE

1. Why was there no negotiation? *See* U.C.C. §§ 3-201, 3-110(d).

2. Do you agree that all that occurrred was merely a partial assignment? U.C.C. § 3-203(d).

3. What is the meaning of the "signature was merely a relinquishment of its rights in the instrument or an authorization to a copayee to negotiate the check"? U.C.C. §§ 3-204, 3-116.

4. Consider this case in light of U.C.C. § 3-203(a) defining "transfer." Would this definition of "transfer" have resulted in Lash, Warner giving transfer warranties under U.C.C. § 3-416?

V HOLDER IN DUE COURSE

The legal purpose to be achieved by negotiability is to enable the holder of a negotiable instrument to claim the status of holder in due course. Having that status enables the holder to defeat all proprietary claims to the instrument (U.C.C. §§ 3-305(a)(3), 3-306) and all defenses to the obligation underlying the instrument that might be raised by a party to the instrument with whom the holder has not dealt. U.C.C. § 3-305(a)(2). To become a holder of the negotiable instrument it must have been issued or negotiated and not just transferred to the holder, U.C.C. §§ 3-201(a), 3-203(a). That is, if the item is a bearer paper there must have been a transfer of possession or, if an order paper, there must have been an endorsement and a transfer of possession. U.C.C. § 3-201(b). To be effective, the endorsement must be by a holder or by an agent on her behalf.

If there was no negotiation, the possessor of the item would be a mere transferee. A transferee would qualify as a person entitled to enforce the instrument but would only be able to assert those rights which the transferor had. U.C.C. § 3-203.[1] The holder of an instrument starts with the presumption that she is a holder in due course. Establishing an affirmative defense to the obligation that gave rise to the commercial paper by adducing evidence that is more than a mere assertion that a defense exists[2] will deny the presumption and the holder then must prove that she is a holder in due course so that such defense cannot be raised against her. U.C.C. §§ 3-308(b), 3-306.[3] U.C.C. Section 3-302(a) requires that to qualify as a holder in due course, the holder must take an instrument that does not bear apparent evidence of forgery or alteration or is not otherwise so irregular or incomplete as to call into question its authenticity: (a) for value; and (b) in good faith; and (c) without notice that it is overdue or has been dishonored or that there is an uncured default with

---

[1] See supra, Chapter IV at C4. But note an exception claimed by the Federal Deposit Insurance Corporation (FDIC). The FDIC may either liquidate a failed bank or, in its corporate capacity, arrange a purchase and assumption of the insolvent bank by another bank. The FDIC claims that whether it acts as a receiver/liquidator or in its corporate capacity, it can assert holder in due course status. See Campbell Leasing, Inc. v. FDIC, 901 F.2d 1244 (5th Cir. 1990) (non-recorded rights on books of failed bank do not affect FDIC. D'Oench, Duhme Co. v. FDIC, 315 U.S. 487 (1942)) and note FDIC v. Jenkins, 888 F.2d 1537 (11th Cir. 1989) (FDIC in its corporate capacity does not have priorities).

[2] Sadler v. Trust Co. Bank of South Georgia, N.A., 178 Ga. App. 871, 344 S.E.2d 694 (1986).

[3] Corn Exchange Bank v. Tri-State Livestock Auction Co., Inc., 368 N.W.2d 596 (S.D. 1985). Conversely the Convention on International Bills of Exchange and International Promissory Notes (CIBN) places the burden of proving absence of "protected holder" status, CIBN, Article 29 (the equivalent of holder in due course) throughout on the party that would deny the claim to this status. There is no change in the onus of proving the absence of the status by showing a prima facie defense, CIBN, Article 32.

respect to payment of another instrument of the same series; and (d) without notice that the instrument contains an unauthorized signature or has been altered, or that there is a defense against or claim to it on the part of any person.

All of these elements must be satisfied before a claim to be a holder in due course is established. For example, if at the time the instrument is taken as a holder, i.e. when negotiation has occurred, value had not been given, and subsequently notice is received that as a result of an acceleration the instrument has become overdue or has been dishonored, or that a defense against or a proprietary claim to the instrument exists on the part of any person, this notice will affect the holder and will prevent such holder from becoming a holder in due course even though subsequently value is given. Also, if a holder is no longer in possession of the instrument when giving value, for example, the holder having transferred the item or deposited it into a bank for collection prior to giving value, the giving of value will not relate back to enable the former holder to claim the status of a holder in due course.[4] Another example would be where an order paper is delivered without having been endorsed. U.C.C. Section 3-203(c) provides that where the transferee has given value, he has "the specifically enforceable right to have the unqualified indorsement of the transferor." But not until the instrument has been endorsed will the transferee become a holder. U.C.C. § 3-201(b). There is no relation back to the time of transfer. As a result, notice during the interim that the instrument has become overdue, has been dishonored, or is subject to a defense or claim will prevent the transferee becoming a holder in due course.[5] On the other hand, once the status of holder in due course has been established, a subsequent notice or even knowledge of a defense will not affect the status of holder in due course.

Further, it must be noted that although existence of good faith (U.C.C. §§ 3-103(a)(4), 3-302(a)(2)(ii)) and lack of notice of a defense to or claim to the instrument (U.C.C. § 3-302(a)(2)(iii)) are distinct requirements and must be satisfied separately, the evidence to establish notice in a holder is often relevant in determining the existence of good faith in a claimant to holder in due course status.

---

[4] First National City Bank v. Altman, 3 U.C.C. Rep. Serv. (Callaghan) 815 (N.Y. Sup. Ct. 1966).

[5] Note FDIC v. Wood, 758 F.2d 156 (6th Cir.) *cert. denied* 474 U.S. 944 (1985). The Federal Deposit Insurance Act, 12 U.S.C. §§ 1811-32, allows the takeover of an insolvent bank by the FDIC to effect a receivership leading to a purchase and assumption or a liquidation of the insolvent bank. While in possession of the assets, the FDIC has the status of a holder in due course of commercial paper under Federal common law in order to effectively perform its congressionally mandated functions. However, the FDIC must have acted in good faith and without having acquired actual knowledge of a defense prior to taking over the insolvent bank. *See also* Campbell Leasing, Inc. v. FDIC, 901 F.2d 1244 (5th Cir. 1990). The "D'Oench Doctrine" extends the status of holder in due course to a person acquiring the instrument from the FDIC. *See* D'Oench, Duhme & Co. v. FDIC, 315 U.S. 447 (1942), codified in 12 U.S.C. § 1823(e) and *compare* U.C.C. § 3-203(b).

Security Pac. Nat'l Bank v. Chess

58 Cal. App. 3d 555, 129 Cal. Rptr. 852 (1976)*

FILES, P.J. This is a consolidated action upon thirteen installment notes, each executed by one of six defendants. The sole issue tried was whether or not the plaintiff was a holder in due course. The trial court, sitting without a jury, gave judgment for plaintiff, from which defendants appeal.

The notes involved here were executed between August and November 1969 and are a part of a larger number of notes payable to Petroleum Equipment Leasing Company of Tulsa, Oklahoma (hereinafter PELCO) as a part of oil drilling ventures, in which the makers were investors. These notes were transferred by PELCO to Equipment Leasing Company of California (hereinafter ELC) who pledged them to plaintiff bank as security for loans. The loans to ELC are in default, and payments on the pledged notes stopped after February 1970.

The defendants pleaded a number of defenses, including fraud, failure of consideration, violation of federal and state securities laws, and an oral side agreement that payment was to be made only out of money derived from the production of oil and gas from wells drilled by PELCO. These defenses were based upon the alleged conduct of PELCO. Defendants did not dispute that the notes had been made and not paid. The superior court bifurcated issues and tried first the question whether plaintiff was a holder in due course.[1] After a trial on this single issue, the court made findings of fact and conclusions of law to the effect that plaintiff was a holder in due course, unaffected by any defenses which the defendants might have against PELCO and ELC. Judgment was thereafter entered in favor of plaintiff against the defendant makers for the respective unpaid balances. The issues argued on this appeal will be discussed in two categories: First whether the record established that plaintiff became a holder of the note.

I. Plaintiff as a holder.

It is defendants' contention that plaintiff can-

not be a holder in due course because it never became a holder within the meaning of § 1-201 (20), of the U.C.C. [§ 3-201]

. . .

Each of the 13 notes involved in this appeal bears on the back side an indorsement from Petroleum Equipment Leasing Co. to Equipment Leasing of California.[5]

Although the language is that of assignment and guarantee, it is nonetheless effective as an indorsement. (See § 3-202 (4), and comments 5, 6.) [See now § 3-204(a)]

The transfer of the notes by ELC to plaintiff is evidenced by a series of separate written assignments executed by ELC, assigning the described notes to plaintiff as collateral security for any indebtedness of the assignor. These instruments are not attached physically to the notes.

Only one of the 13 notes bears an indorsement using the name of Equipment Leasing Company as indorser. Eight notes show on the back side a handwritten indorsement "Richard L. Burns" or "Richard L. Burns, Pres." Burns was at the time the president of ELC and there is no question of his authority, or any reason to doubt his intention thereby to effect a transfer of the notes to plaintiff. His handwriting therefore constitutes the signature of the corporation, under the principle that a party may adopt any form or symbol as its signature for a particular transaction. (See §§ 3-

---

* [Editor: citations in [ ] refer to Revised U.C.C. Articles 3 and 4.]

[1] U.C.C. § 3-302(1) [§ 3-302(a)].

---

[5] The form of the indorsement is as follows:
ASSIGNMENT
FOR VALUE RECEIVED, the undersigned hereby assigns to EQUIPMENT LEASING OF CALIFORNIA, a corporation, its successors or assigns, all right, title and interest in and to the within note. The undersigned guarantees full performance of the note by the maker thereof and prompt payment of all sums due thereunder, together with all collection expenses. Any extension granted by the holder thereof to the maker of the note shall not in any manner release the undersigned.
PETROLEUM EQUIPMENT LEASING CO.
By _____
[Signature of individual]

401(2) [§3-401(b)] and 1-201(39); *Hilborn v. Alford,* 22 Cal. 482 (1863).

Four of the notes contain no indorsement at all except that by PELCO to ELC.

Section 3-202 states (in pertinent part):

(1) Negotiation is the transfer of an instrument in such form that the transferee becomes a holder. If the instrument is payable to order it is negotiated by delivery with any necessary indorsement; if payable to bearer it is negotiated by delivery.

(2) An indorsement must be written by or on behalf of the holder and on the instrument or on a paper so firmly affixed thereto as to become a part thereof.

[*See* now §§ 3-201, 3-204(a)]

. . .

The instruments here in question were not payable to bearer. The notes were payable to the order of PELCO, who indorsed them to "Equipment Leasing of California, a corporation, its successors or assigns." This was a special indorsement in that it specified ELC as the person to whom the notes were to be paid. The addition of the words "successors or assigns" did not operate to make the notes payable thereafter to bearer. The form of indorsement used upon these notes does not come within the statutory definition of "indorsement in blank."

Plaintiff argues that the indorsements to ELC and "its successors or assigns," combined with the separate documents by which ELC assigned to plaintiff, should be read together as making plaintiff the holder by indorsement. This argument confuses transfer with negotiation. The separate assignment is, of course, effective as evidence that the notes were transferred to plaintiff, and plaintiff became the transferee and owner, at least for security purposes.

But a transferee is not in this situation a holder. Negotiation of an order instrument depends upon indorsement, and indorsement "must be written by or on behalf of the holder and on the instrument or on a paper so firmly affixed thereto as to become a part thereof." (§ 3-202(2)) [§ 3-204(a)] The defect in plaintiff's position is that nothing was written on the four notes by or on behalf of ELC.

Plaintiff also contends that it became a holder under §§ 4-205 and 4-207.

These sections have no application to the transfer of the 13 notes from ELC to plaintiff. Sections 4-205 and 4-207 are a part of article 4 entitled "Bank Deposits and Collections." Section 4-205 applies to an item delivered to the bank for collection or for credit to the deposit account of the transferor. Even if the 13 notes were to be collected by the bank so that the proceeds could be credited against the loan, the notes themselves were not "deposited" by ELC, and the proceeds were not credited to a deposit account. Plaintiff, of course, did not make the "statement . . . on the item" which § 4-205 says is "effective as the customer's indorsement."*

Plaintiff also contends it acquired the status of a holder under the provision of U.C.C. § 3-201 [§ 3-203(b)] that "transfer of an instrument vests in the transferee such rights as the transferor has therein. . . ." Plaintiff points out that its transferor, ELC, was unquestionably a "holder. . . ." . . .

Section 3-201 [§ 3-203], like its predecessor, assures to the transferee the "rights" of his transferor—i.e., if ELC is entitled to recover on these notes, plaintiff is likewise so entitled. But that gives no help to plaintiff on this appeal. The bifurcated trial was conducted upon the assumption that defendants may have had defenses against some other parties, and the judgment here on appeal is premised upon the findings that plaintiff was a holder in due course, entitled to prevail on its own right irrespective of any defenses existing against its predecessors in interest.

Plaintiff's theory appears to be that it acquired not merely the rights of ELC, but the status of ELC as a "holder" without indorsement or negotiation of the notes. This theory cannot be reconciled with either the language of the statute or cases interpreting and applying it. Section 3-201 [§ 3-203(c)] gives the transferee the right to compel the transferor to indorse, but also provides that negotiation takes place only when the indorsement is made.

In re Home Furniture Co., 7 F.2d 399 (N.D. Cal. 1925) involved notes executed by the bankrupt, payable to the order of Chamberlain and

---

* [Editor: There is no need to have an actual endorsement affixed by the depository bank to qualify as a holder of an item deposited by a customer in a depository bank for collection. *See* U.C.C. § 4-205(1).]

assigned for value but without indorsement to Chappell. The federal court, applying California law, held that Chappell was not a holder in due course and therefore her claim was subject to any defenses which the bankrupt might have had against Chamberlain. After referring to California Civil Code § 3130 and related sections, the court said:

[I]t is seen that the Negotiable Instruments Law clearly contemplates a distinction between a 'holder' who takes by negotiation, and a 'transferee' by assignment. That distinction is, so far as we are here concerned, that the assignee without indorsement of a negotiable instrument payable to order takes it subject to equities against the assignor arising before notice of the assignment. [Citations omitted.]

In explaining its holding the *Home Furniture* court quoted from a New York case as follows:

Section 79 of the [New York] Negotiable Instruments Law provides that, where the holder of an instrument payable to his order transfers it for value without indorsing it, the transferee obtains such title as the transferor had; but for the purpose of determining whether the transferee is a holder in due course the negotiation takes effect as of the time when the indorsement is actually made. Such indorsement never having been made, plaintiff cannot be deemed to be a holder in due course, as defined by sections 2, 60, 61, 91 and 98 of the Negotiable Instruments Law (These latter sections are all part of the Uniform Negotiable Instruments Law, which is found in §§ 3082-3268 of the Civil Code of California). *Manufacturers' Com. Co. v. Blitz,* 131 App. Div. 17, 115 N.Y.S. 402 (1909).

Other cases explaining and applying the distinction between a holder and a transferee from a holder include *Northside Bldg. & Invest. Co. v. Finance Co. of America,* 119 Ga. App. 131, 166 S.E.2d 608, 611 (1969) *United Overseas Bank v. Veneers, Inc.,* 375 F. Supp. 596 (D.C. Md. 1974); *Cheshire Commercial Corporation v. Messier,* 6 Conn. Cir. 542, 278 A.2d 413, 415 (1971).

The only court decision which plaintiff cites for its interpretation of § 3-201 [§ 3-203] is *Bowling Green, Inc. v. State Street Bank and Trust Co.,* 425 F.2d 81 (1st Cir. 1970). In that case Bowling Green negotiated a government check to Bowl-

Mor, who deposited the check in State Street Bank. The bank immediately credited a portion of the check against an overdraft in Bowl-Mor's account, and shortly afterwards applied the balance in that account against debts which Bowl-Mor owed the bank. There was no evidence that Bowl-Mor had indorsed the check. The ground of the Court of Appeals decision, as stated in its opinion, is as follows:

. . . We therefore hold that a bank which takes an item for collection from a customer who was himself a holder need not establish that it took the item by negotiation in order to satisfy § 4-209 [of the Uniform Com. Code, corresponding to California Uniform Com. Code, § 4-209]. (Id. at p. 84.) [*See* now § 4-211]

In the course of its discussion the court said:

. . . The issue, however, is not whether the Bank bears the burden of proof, but whether it must establish that it took the item in question by endorsement in order to meet its burden. We think not. The evidence in this case indicates that the Bank's transferor, Bowl-Mor, was a holder. Under Mass. Gen. Laws Ann. ch. 106, § 3-201(a), transfer of an instrument vests in the transferee all the rights of the transferor. As the Official Comment to [former] § 3-201 [§ 3-203] indicates, one who is not a holder must first establish the transaction by which he acquired the instrument before enforcing it, but the Bank has met this burden here. (*Id.* at 83-84 [7 U.C.C. Rep. 638].)

To the extent that *Bowling Green* interprets and applies article 4 generally and § 4-209 [§ 4-211] in particular, it is distinguishable from the case at bench. Bowling Green involved an item taken by the bank for collection and deposited to the customer's account. Our case does not.

If the Bowling Green court intended to say that a transfer by a holder without indorsement gives the transferee the status of a holder, that statement is irreconcilable with the language of § 3-201 [§ 3-201(b)] and with the case law cited above, interpreting § 3-201 and its antecedent in the Negotiable Instruments Law. This conflict is analyzed at length in *United Overseas Bank v. Veneers, Inc., supra,* 375 F. Supp. 596, 603, where the district court declined to follow Bowling Green. Academic commentators have also pointed out that the quoted language in Bowling Green is in conflict with the law elsewhere: see Hawkland, *Depositary Banks as Holders in Due Course,* 76 Com. L. J. 124; Comment, *Bowling Green: The Bank as Holder in Due Course,* 71 Colum. L. Rev. 302, 310 (1971); Note *How Can a Bank Become a Holder and Give Value in Order to Attain Holder in Due Course Status?* 12 B.C. Ind. & Com. L. Rev. 282 (1970).

In the light of the clear statutory language and its long history of interpretation by courts and commentators alike, we cannot regard the Bowling Green language as affecting the meaning of § 3-201 [§§ 3-201(b), 3-203] of the . . . Uniform Commercial Code.

It follows from the foregoing analysis that plaintiff is a holder of nine of the thirteen notes but is not a holder of four. As to the latter group, the judgment must be reversed for a trial of the defenses which the defendants have asserted.

Marine Midland Bank, N.A. v. Price, Miller, Evans & Flowers
57 N.Y.2d 220, 441 N.E.2d 1083 (1982)*

WACHTLER, JUDGE. The question on this appeal is whether the plaintiff, Marine Midland Bank can claim the status of a holder in due course of a check which it cashed without indorsement and stamped "credited to the account of the payee herein named," although the payee, who had presented the check, had no account at the bank. By a divided court the Appellate Division held that the bank had properly supplied the missing indorsement pursuant to subdivision (1) of section 4-205 of the Uniform Commercial Code and was otherwise a holder in due course. The defendant appeals on the basis of the dissent claiming primarily that the bank could not supply the missing indorsement because the payee was not a customer of the bank within the meaning of the statute; that if the bank could supply the indorsement it did not supply a proper indorsement, and if the indorsement was effective the bank did not give value because it did not pay consistent with the indorsement.

The facts are not disputed. The defendant is a Jamestown law firm which in 1978 and 1979 represented clients in connection with construction contracts to be performed by Leo Proctor Construction Company, Inc., a Texas corporation. Pursuant to the contracts, Proctor was to construct four Pizza Hut restaurants in New York, and was to receive progress payments for completed work.

On January 3, 1979 the defendant made a progress payment on behalf of its clients by drawing and delivering two checks totaling $36,906.54. The checks were made payable to Proctor as the named payee and had been drawn by the defendant on a trust account it maintained for disbursement of client's funds at the First National Bank of Jamestown.

On January 4, 1979 a Proctor employee brought these two checks to one of the plaintiff's branch offices at Jamestown and presented them to the manager with a request that the funds represented by the checks be wire transferred to an account maintained by Proctor at the First National Bank of Bethany in Oklahoma. The checks were not indorsed by Proctor. However, an employee of the plaintiff bank stamped the reverse side of the checks "credited to the account of the payee herein named/Marine Midland Chautauqua National Bank" and then wire transferred the funds to Proctor's account at the Oklahoma bank. Proctor has never maintained an account with the plaintiff bank.

After the defendant law firm delivered the checks to Proctor it was informed by one of its clients that Proctor was in default on the construction contracts and, at the client's request, stopped payment on the checks. Thus when the checks reached First National they were stamped "Payment stopped" and were returned to the Oklahoma bank which returned them to the plaintiff.

The plaintiff made a timely demand for payment of the checks by Proctor but was informed that Proctor had filed a petition in bankruptcy. The plaintiff then made a timely demand for payment by the defendant, but the defendant refused to honor the checks. It is conceded that the plain-

---

* [Editor: Citations in [ ] refer to revised U.C.C. Articles 3 and 4.]

tiff had no knowledge of Proctor's default on the construction contracts at the time it took the checks.

It is also noted in the agreed statement of facts that the defendant had previously made six progress payments to Proctor commencing in August, 1978. These checks had been (accepted) by the plaintiff and, at Proctor's request, the funds were wire transferred to one of Proctor's accounts in another bank in Oklahoma or Texas. On five occasions the checks were indorsed by Proctor. In the other case the plaintiff had stamped the check as having been credited to Proctor's account. Every one of these checks had been honored by the defendant.

It also appears that the plaintiff had been cashing some of Proctor's payroll checks at this particular branch in Jamestown. These checks had been drawn on Proctor's account in either the Oklahoma or the Texas bank, and were presented to the plaintiff by Leo Proctor employees. On the first occasion in May of 1978 the plaintiff's branch manager had called the Texas bank and determined that Proctor's credit was good. Each check presented by Leo Proctor in person was cashed only after the plaintiff had confirmed that there were sufficient funds in the account at the drawee bank. In one instance plaintiff refused to cash the check after learning that the funds were insufficient. On another occasion, in the summer of 1978, a check presented by a Proctor employee had been returned for insufficient funds after the employee had been permitted to withdraw against the uncollected funds. This check was being held by the plaintiff's manager on January 3, 1979.

The parties agree that the defendant has a valid defense against Proctor for lack of consideration and thus against the plaintiff, as Proctor's transferee, unless the plaintiff can qualify as a holder in due course.

Under the Uniform Commercial Code five requirements must be met before a party can obtain the special protections of a holder in due course. The party must be (1) a holder (2) of a negotiable instrument (3) who took it for value (4) in good faith (5) without notice that it is overdue, has been dishonored, or is subject to a defense or claim on the part of another person (Uniform Commercial Code, § 3-302, subd. [1] [§ 3-302(a)]; see, also, White & Summers, Uniform Commercial Code [2d ed], pp. 551-552). Although at common law a depositary bank generally could not achieve

that status, the Uniform Commercial Code permits it to qualify provided it meets the five general requirements (Hawkland, Depositary Banks as Holders in Due Course, 76 Com. L.J. 124; *Marine Midland Bank-New York v. Graybar Elec. Co.,* 41 N.Y.2d 703, 395 N.Y.S.2d 403, 363 N.E.2d 1139; *Long Is. Nat. Bank v. Zawada,* 34 A.D.2d 1016, 312 N.Y.S.2d 947; U.C.C. § 3-206(3)) [§ 3-206(b), (c), (e)].

With respect to the first requirement the code provides that a holder is "a person who is in possession of * * * an instrument * * * indorsed to him or to his order or to bearer or in blank" (U.C.C. § 1-201(20) [§ 3-201]). In this case it is conceded that the bank is in possession of the check but also conceded that the bank accepted the check without indorsement. This would generally preclude a person from being a holder, and thus a holder in due course.

However, the bank contends, and a majority of the Appellate Division agreed, that subdivision (1) of section 4-205 of the U.C.C. excuses its failure to obtain Proctor's indorsement. The statute provides: "A depositary bank which has taken an item for collection may supply any indorsement of the customer which is necessary to title unless the item contains the words 'payee's indorsement required' or the like." The stated purpose of the section is "to speed up collections by eliminating any necessity to return to a non-bank depositor any items he may have failed to indorse" (U.C.C. § 4-205 Comment 1).[*] The defendant contends that this section is inapplicable here because Proctor has no account at the bank and thus could not qualify as a depositor.

It appears that this section was designed to facilitate the collection process in the relatively common situation where a person having an account at the bank deposits a check without indorsement (*see, e.g.,* Clark, *Bank Deposits, Collections and Credit Cards,* § 4.3, p. 4–26.). By its terms, however, the statute is not limited to that situation. The bank's statutory authority to supply a missing indorsement applies to any item submitted for collection by "a customer", which

---

[*] [Editor: Revised § 4-205 dispenses with need actually to append an endorsement. § 4-205(2). By warranting that the proceeds were actually credited to the account of the customer provides adequate protection to drawers, collecting banks, and non-bank drawees.]

includes not only persons "having an account with a bank" but also anyone "for whom a bank has agreed to collect items" (U.C.C. § 4-104(1)(e) [§ 4-104(a)(5)]). Thus the fact that Proctor had no account at the bank did not necessarily preclude the bank from supplying the missing indorsement.

The bank urges that Proctor became its customer when it "agreed to collect the checks for Proctor, as it had in the past." The defendant disputes this characterization of the transaction. It states:

> Had the bank been acting as Proctor's agent for collection, it would have passed the checks through the normal channels and paid Proctor once they had cleared . . . Marine, however, advanced its own funds to Proctor on the assumption that the checks would clear. It therefore was not seeking to collect the checks in Proctor's behalf, but rather in its own behalf.

It also claims that the prior transactions were of the same character.

The drafters of the Uniform Commercial Code have noted that "Historically, much time has been spent and effort expended in determining or attempting to determine whether a bank was a purchaser of an item or merely an agent for collection" (U.C.C. § 4-201 Comment 1). In order to simplify this problem subdivision (1) of section 4-201 of the Uniform Commercial Code establishes a presumption of the bank's agency status, which prevails unless "a contrary intent clearly appears." Although this section seems to provide the relevant guidelines for this case, neither of the parties have cited it or addressed themselves to the issues it presents. Nor was the section mentioned or discussed in the opinions at the Appellate Division. However, we need not decide its applicability or effect in this case, because even if it be assumed that the bank was an agent and Proctor a "customer," the bank's handling of this transaction does not entitle it to holder in due course status.

If Proctor was the plaintiff's customer then the plaintiff was entitled to supply the missing indorsement and in our view satisfied that requirement in this case. We find no merit to the defendant's contention that the "legend" the bank stamped on the reverse side of the check does not

constitute an indorsement.[2] On this point the statute expressly provides that "a statement placed on the item by the depositary bank to the effect that the item was deposited by a customer or credited to his account is effective as the customer's indorsement" (U.C.C. § 4-205(1)). Although Proctor did not in fact have an account at the bank capable of being credited that does not impair the effectiveness of the indorsement under the terms of the statute. The section is quite explicit that the statement the bank placed on the check in this case effectively serves as the customer's indorsement. And as noted earlier, being in possession of an indorsed item would qualify the bank as a holder (U.C.C. § 1-201(20)).

However, in order to qualify as a holder in due course the bank must satisfy additional conditions, including a requirement that it give value within the meaning of the Code (U.C.C. § 3-302 (1)) [§ 3-302(a)(2)(i)]. With respect to this requirement the inconsistency between the indorsement and the manner in which the checks actually were paid is significant. On this point the code is equally explicit: "Except for an intermediary bank, any transferee under an indorsement which is conditional or includes the words 'for collection', 'for deposit', 'pay any bank', or like terms * * * must pay or apply any value given by him for or on the security of the instrument consistently with the indorsement and to the extent that he does so he becomes a holder for value. In addition such transferee is a holder in due course if he otherwise complies with the requirements of Section 3-302 on what constitutes a holder in due course." (U.C.C. § 3-206(3)) [§§ 3-206(b), (c), (e)]. Thus, a bank which has made a payment inconsistent with the indorsement cannot be said to have given value for the purpose of claiming the special protections afforded a holder in due course. Furthermore, the statute does not limit the bank's obligation to pay consistent with a restrictive indorsement, to those cases where the

---

[2] The argument is based in part on the contention that the bank conceded during argument at the Appellate Division that the stamp was not actually an indorsement. The bank makes no such concession on this appeal although, as noted later, it urges that it is not required to supply an indorsement to be a holder and thus should not be bound by the restrictions contained in the indorsement.

restriction was imposed by the payee. In another context we have held that a bank is bound to observe a restrictive indorsement even when the indorsement was forged. *Underpinning & Foundation Constructors v. Chase Manhattan Bank, N.A.,* 46 N.Y.2d 459, 414 N.Y.S.2d 298, 386 N.E.2d 1319 (1979). The plaintiff's contention that subdivision (3) of section 3-206 [§§ 3-206(b), (c), (e)] does not apply to a depositary bank which has supplied a restrictive indorsement on its customer's behalf pursuant to subdivision (1) of section 4-205, finds no support in either statute. Accordingly, inasmuch as the bank did not comply with the conditions of the indorsement which it supplied, it cannot be said to have given value within the contemplation of the code and therefore was not a holder in due course based on that indorsement.

Finally the bank argues that the terms of the indorsement may be disregarded because no indorsement was required. It is urged that the indorsement requirement was meant to prevent a thief or forger from negotiating the instrument and therefore should not be considered necessary when the check has been presented by the named payee.

The code of course does not contain any such generalized dispensation from the indorsement requirement. Even with respect to depositary banks, which are given preferred treatment under subdivision (1) of section 4-205, a customer's failure to indorse an item must be cured by the bank

supplying the indorsement. Although, as the plaintiff notes, some courts have held that this represents a mere formality which should not affect the bank's status as a holder in due course (*see, e.g., Bowling Green v. State St. Bank & Trust Co,* 307 F. Supp. 648 (D.C. Ma 1969), *aff'd* 1st Cir. 425 F.2d 81) (1970), that holding has been widely criticized (*see* Clark, *Bank Deposits, Collections and Credit Cards,* § 4.3, pp. 4.26–4.27; Hawkland, *Depositary Banks As Holders In Due Course,* 76 Com. L.J., 124, 127; Note, *Bowling Green: The Bank as Holder in Due Course,* 71 Colum. L. Rev. 302; Note, *How Can A Bank Become A Holder and Give Value In Order to Attain Holder in Due Course Status?,* 12 B. C. Ind. & Com. L. Rev. 282), and has been rejected by other courts (*see, e.g., United Overseas Bank v. Veneers, Inc.,* 375 F. Supp. 596 (D.C. Md. 1975)). In our view this approach urged by the bank cannot be reconciled with the terms of the applicable statutes or with article 4's general policy of providing fixed rules, based on sound banking practices, as the best means of insuring the type of predictable results necessary to preserve the free transfer of negotiable instruments. As one commentator has aptly observed "It hardly seems unfair to penalize the bank when it fails to perform such a simple act and then seeks the unusual shelter of the holder in-due-course status" (Clark, *op. cit.,* § 4.3, p.4–29).

Accordingly, the order of the Appellate Division should be reversed, with costs, and judgment granted to the defendant....

NOTE

1. *See* now U.C.C. § 4-205(2).

2. Banks often stamp checks deposited by their customers for collection without their customer's endorsement with the legend "Prior Endorsements Guaranteed" (PEG) to indicate that they are warranting their right to collect the item. *See* Federal Reserve Board Regulation J, 12 C.F.R. § 210.5(a)(2).

3. In its revision, U.C.C. Section 4-205 recognizes that automation may result in an omission by the depository bank to affix an endorsement. Such omission will not prevent the depository bank from attaining the status of holder. *See* U.C.C. § 4-205(1). The depository bank could also attain the status of holder in due course, by giving value and otherwise satisfying the requirements of U.C.C. § 3-302(a). This results even though U.C.C. Section 4-201(a) provides that for the collection process the bank may still be considered an agent. One issue presented in *Marine Midland Bank* was whether the depository bank had given value. *Consider* U.C.C. § 3-303. Was value given? Was the action of the depository bank in conflict with its endorsement so as to deny that value had been given? *Consider* U.C.C. § 4-205(2). Was there a breach of that warranty?

4. As to restrictive endorsement, note U.C.C. § 3-206 and Regulation CC, 12 C.F.R. § 229.35(c), promulgated under the Expedited Funds Availability Act, 12 U.S.C. §§ 4001 et seq.

Koerner & Lambert v. Allstate Ins. Co.
374 So. 2d 179 (La. Ct. App. 1979)*

SAMUEL, JUDGE. Plaintiff a professional law corporation, filed two law suits, which were later consolidated, against Allstate Insurance Company and other defendants to recover the respective sums of $2,190 and $3,389, representing drafts drawn by Allstate on Deposit Guaranty National Bank, Jackson, Mississippi. Plaintiff had deposited the drafts for collection and, after collection, had disbursed the amounts to various creditors of its client, Paul H. Boucher, d/b/a Marina-Rama, and to itself for professional services rendered. Unknown to plaintiff, the signatures of two of the payees on these drafts had been unauthorized or forged, and Allstate eventually took action, as outlined below, which caused plaintiff's bank to debit its account for $5,579, the total of the two drafts. Defendants answered, denying liability.

After a trial on the merits, judgments were rendered in favor of plaintiff and against Allstate in the amount of $2,190 in one case and $3,389 in the other, together with appropriate interest. The judgments dismissed the suits as to all other defendants. Allstate has appealed.

The record shows that Burnell Robinson and George Driscoll owned boats which were damaged in separate incidents. Coincidentally, both men were insured by Allstate and each independently selected Marina-Rama to perform the necessary repairs.

The owner of Marina-Rama, Paul H. Boucher, submitted repair estimates to Allstate, which furnished two drafts to Boucher. The first, dated August 5, 1976, was in the amount of $2,190 and made payable to the order of Burnell Robinson in full payment of repairs to be done on the Robin-

son vessel. The second, dated August 11, 1976, was in the amount of $3,389 and made payable to the order of George Driscoll and Marina-Rama for repairs to be done on the Driscoll vessel.

Allstate did not notify either Robinson or Driscoll of the delivery of the drafts to Boucher, nor did it subsequently verify that the signatures on the drafts were actually those of Robinson and Driscoll. Neither Robinson nor Driscoll signed the drafts nor did either have any knowledge of their existence.

Driscoll's signature was forged on his draft, and Robinson's brother was tricked into signing Robinson's name on the other draft after being led to believe it constituted a work authorization. Boucher never repaired the vessels.

Plaintiff represented Boucher in a contemplated bankruptcy proceeding and, in an effort to avoid bankruptcy, Boucher gave the drafts to plaintiff for payment to his creditors. During the month of August, 1976, plaintiff deposited the drafts in its notarial account at the Whitney National Bank in New Orleans for collection and requested of Whitney that it notify plaintiff when the funds were collected and deposited in its account. Only after plaintiff received such notice, also during the month of August, 1976, did it actually disburse the funds in question. As above set forth, disbursement was made to Boucher's creditors and plaintiff retained some of the funds for professional services rendered.

There is no question that plaintiff was entirely free from fault in the transaction; it had no knowledge whatever that signatures on the drafts given it by its client were unauthorized or forged.

More than five months after issuance of the drafts, Robinson contacted Allstate regarding payment for the repairs to his boat. At this time Allstate first notified Robinson that the draft had been given to Boucher. On January 27, 1977,

---

* [Editor: Citations in [ ] refer to revised U.C.C. Articles 3 and 4.]

after all checks written by plaintiff had cleared, Allstate obtained a forged signature affidavit from Robinson. Later Driscoll also contacted Allstate regarding payment for repair to his boat, and he was then notified the draft had been given to Boucher. Driscoll also executed a forged signature affidavit.

Allstate presented the affidavits to Deposit Guaranty National Bank, which made demand for collection on Whitney. Pursuant to this demand, Whitney paid Guaranty National $5,579 and debited plaintiff's notarial account for that amount. These lawsuits ensued.

In holding for plaintiff, the trial judge emphasized defendant delivered the drafts only to Boucher and honored them when presented. Only after a fraud was discovered more than five months later did Allstate take any action at all and then only to recover the amounts paid as above set forth. We repeat for emphasis that Allstate failed to notify their insured the drafts in their names had been given to Boucher.

U.C.C. § 3-406 [§ 3-406] provides as follows:

Any person who by his negligence substantially contributes to a material alteration of the instrument or to the making of an unauthorized signature *is precluded* from asserting the alteration or lack of authority against a holder in due course or against a drawee or other payor who pays the instrument in good faith and in accordance with the reasonable commercial standards of the drawee's or payor's business. (Emphasis added).*

The question of negligence is one of fact for the trial court's determination. The record contains sufficient evidence for the trial judge to have concluded that Allstate was guilty of negligence by entrusting the drafts to Marina-Rama without notifying its insureds or otherwise taking some action to verify the signature of each payee on the drafts and that such negligence substantially contributed to the unauthorized and forged signatures. The record does not justify a reversal by this court of the trial judge's finding of fact in this regard.

Defendant argues that in spite of this finding of negligence, plaintiff violated the warranties of

good title, authorized signature, lack of material alteration, etc., imputed to one who obtains payment or acceptance of a negotiable instrument from one who acts in good faith.[2] We do not agree with the argument.

Louisiana law on commercial paper is the result of the legislature's adoption of portions of the Uniform Commercial Code by Act 92 of 1974.[3] It is generally regarded by scholars of the Uniform Commercial Code that the question of negligence cuts across the issue of warranty, since the wording of U.C.C. § 3-406 [§ 3-406], quoted above, clearly states that one whose negligence contributes to an unauthorized signature (here also a forgery) "is precluded from asserting the alteration or lack of authority against a holder in due course..." This statutory provision is regarded as an estoppel against the negligent party from asserting the question of warranty under U.C.C. § 3-417 [§ 3-417].[4]

For plaintiff to be a holder in due course, it must have taken the instruments (1) for value, (2) in good faith, and (3) without notice that they were overdue, dishonored, or subject to any defense or claim of any person. Plaintiff clearly took the drafts from its client in good faith and without notice of any defects. Moreover, since it received the drafts with the understanding that a part of the proceeds thereof were to be appropriated to a fee balance owed it by its client, it also took the drafts for value. We consequently conclude plaintiff was a holder in due course insofar as U.C.C. §§ 3-406 [§ 3-406] and 3-417 [§ 3-417] are concerned.

Having concluded in this case plaintiff was a holder in due course, and having adopted the trial court's conclusion that defendant was guilty of substantially contributing negligence under the above quoted U.C.C. § 3-406 [§ 3-406], it necessarily follows that Allstate is precluded or estopped from asserting the unauthorized signature and forgery against the plaintiff.

For the reasons assigned, the judgments appealed from are affirmed.

Affirmed.

---

* [Editor: Revised § 3-406 uses the term "failure to exercise ordinary care." *See* further Chapter II at B.]

[2] U.C.C. § 3-417 [§ 3-417].

[3] *See* Comment RS 10:1-101.

[4] *See* White & Summers, Uniform Commercial Code, Section 16-1 (p. 519) and Section 16-5 (p. 537).

NOTE

1. The plaintiff in *Koerner & Lambert v. Allstate Ins. Co.* claimed to be a holder in due course. We note that to be a holder, a reading of U.C.C. Sections 3-201 and 1-201(20) require a transfer of possession of an issued instrument in bearer form or a transfer of possession of an instrument endorsed by the transferor/holder if the instrument is payable to the transferor/holder. Here the endorsements of Robinson and Driscoll were forgeries, i.e. unauthorized. U.C.C. Section 3-403(a) would make such "unauthorized signatures . . . ineffective."[6] On the facts of this case neither of them would be precluded from denying the effectiveness of their purported signature. Thus, was the court correct in applying U.C.C. Section 3-406? The negligence here was that of the drawer not that of the payees. The plaintiff was not a holder, U.C.C. §§ 3-201(b), 3-403, so as to be a holder in due course. The court attempted to delimit its holding by stating: "We consequently conclude plaintiff was a holder in due course insofar as U.C.C. §§ 3-406 [§ 3-406] and 3-417 [§ 3-417] are concerned." Can one be a holder in due course as to some provisions of the U.C.C., but not as to others? U.C.C. § 3-406(a) clarifies the situation by providing that a person whose failure to exercise ordinary care "substantially contributes to an alteration of an instrument or to the making of a forged signature on an instrument is precluded from asserting the alteration or forgery against a person that, in good faith, pays the instrument or takes it for value or for collection." The plaintiff clearly acted in good faith and took the instrument for value. Thus, the plaintiff holder, though not a holder in due course, could recover from this drawer.

2. To become a "holder" there must be a negotiation, i.e. a transfer of possession whether voluntary or involuntary. U.C.C. § 3-201(a). Thus an effective negotiation includes a negotiation by a person without capacity, such as an infant, one induced by fraud, duress or mistake and even a negotiation in breach of a duty or as a part of an illegal transaction. U.C.C. § 3-202(a). So as not to support legal rights developing out of such situations, the U.C.C. provides that unless the instrument is in the hands of a holder in due course, negotiation can be rescinded. U.C.C. § 3-202(b). This requires that greater emphasis be given to the concept of transfer which must accompany a negotiation. That concept requires that a transfer involves delivering an instrument "for the purpose of giving to the person receiving delivery the right to enforce the instrument," U.C.C. § 3-203(a).

3. The concept of a holder in due course is a commercial concept. Thus, a transferee may qualify as having the rights of a holder in due course without himself becoming a holder in due course. A transfer confers on the transferee all the rights of his transferor including, where such transferor was a holder in due course, the rights of a holder in due course. To qualify as a holder in due course the acquisition can not be "(i) by legal process or by purchase in an execution, bankruptcy, or creditor's sale or similar proceeding, (ii) by purchase as a part of a bulk transaction not in ordinary course of business of the transferor,

---

[6] Note the Convention on International Bills of Exchange and International Promissory Notes (CIBN) would permit recovery for loss only from the forger and the person who took the instrument from the forger, or any one who knowing of the forgery took the instrument. CIBN Articles 25 and 26. *See* further Felsenfeld, *Forged Endorsements Under the United Nations Negotiable Instruments Convention: A Compromise Between Common and Civil Law,* 45 Bus. Law. 397 (1989).

or (iii) as the successor in interest to an estate or other organization." U.C.C. § 3-302(c). In effect, what is called for is a voluntary transfer of possession for the transferee to be able to qualify as a holder in due course. *Cf.* U.C.C. § 1-201(14). *See* further *Mazer v. Williams Bros.*, 461 Pa. 587, 337 A.2d 559 (1975) (a judicial sale does not involve a voluntary delivery by the judgment debtor).

4. Of note is that a payee can be a holder in due course, *see* Official Comment 4 to U.C.C. § 3-302. Examples are purchases made with a cashier's check or a teller's check, whether payable directly to the seller or endorsed over by a payee buyer to the seller. There would appear to be no reason why the seller could not be a holder in due course in either of these situations. In the first instance the buyer, as remitter, would negotiate the check to the seller; in the second situation there is also a negotiation, i.e. a transfer and endorsement, to the seller. The issue in both instances is: Does the payee or endorsee qualify under U.C.C. Section 3-302(a) as a holder in due course?

A. Questionable Authenticity

Where the instrument is incomplete or irregular, or where the instrument bears apparent evidence of forgery or alteration, the authenticity of the instrument is in doubt, i.e., there are indications that the instrument may not be what it purports to be. As a result, a holder of such instrument cannot qualify as a holder in due course, U.C.C. § 3-302(a)(1). A policy consideration arises here. Should a person who purchases or pays such instrument not act at their own risk? For U.C.C. Section 3-302(a)(1) to apply the indicia of forgery, alteration, or irregularity must not just be such as to raise a doubt, rather these must be such as would raise a suspicion in a reasonable person. For example, incompleteness would indicate an irregularity, though such incompleteness can be remedied by completing the instrument as authorized. It can be argued further, that such "apparent" defects give notice of a defense. They may also raise the question whether a holder aware of such irregularities can assert to have been in good faith at the time the instrument was negotiated to her. To some extent this is a return to the approach that good faith be determined in accordance with an objective standard. *Gill v. Cubitt,* 3 B. & C. 466 (KB 1824). The existence of such apparent evidence of forgery or alteration would be an element to be considered under U.C.C. Section 3-103(a)(4). This preliminary hurdle will have to be overcome before we examine the further requirements which will indicate whether the holder can qualify as a holder in due course. U.C.C. Section 3-302(a)(2). *See St. Paul Fire & Marine Ins. Co. v. State Bank of Salem,* 412 N.E.2d 103 (Ind.Ct.App.1980).

St. Paul Fire & Marine Ins. Co. v. State Bank of Salem
412 N.E.2d 103 (Ind. Ct. App. 1980)*

NEAL, J.

This action was brought by the State Bank of Salem (Bank) against the drawer of a check, Aubrey, Inc. (Aubrey), and the Bank's insurer, St. Paul Fire and Marine Insurance Company (St. Paul), under a bankers blanket bond. Following a trial to the court without intervention of a jury, judgment was entered in favor of the Bank and against Aubrey and St. Paul. Judgment was also entered in favor of St. Paul on its cross claim against Aubrey. Aubrey and St. Paul appeal the award in favor of the Bank; Aubrey appeals the judgment in favor of St. Paul on its cross claim.

We affirm in part and reverse and remand in part.

Statement of the Facts

The facts most favorable to the judgment and relevant to our consideration of this appeal are largely undisputed and reveal the following.

On November 26, 1975, Stephens, a farmer, delivered and sold 184 bushels of corn to Aubrey for $478.23. Aubrey was engaged at the time in sale and distribution of feed and grain in Louisville, Kentucky, under the name of Aubrey Feed Mills, Inc. The following day, Aubrey prepared its check payable to Stephens in payment for the corn and mailed it to Stephens. The check was prepared in the following fashion: the amount "478.23" was typewritten upon the line customarily used to express the amount of the check in numbers, abutting the printed dollar sign. On the line customarily used to express the amount in words there appeared "The sum of $100478 and 23 cts," which was imprinted in red by a check-writing machine; the line ended with the printed word "Dollars."

On December 9, 1975, Stephens appeared at the Bank's branch in Hardinsburg, Indiana, and presented the Aubrey check and two other items totalling $5,604.51 to the branch manager Charles Anderson. Stephens told Anderson that he wished to apply these funds to the amount of his indebtedness to the Bank, to withdraw $2,000.00 in cash, and to deposit the balance in his checking account. During the interval between November 27, 1975, and December 9, 1975, someone had typed on the check the figures "100" immediately before the typed figures "478.23." This was rather crudely done, and involved typing the "100" in an uneven line; the second "0" was typed directly over the printed dollar sign on the check.

Anderson questioned Stephens about the Aubrey check since Stephens's prior dealings with the Bank had not involved transactions in the amount represented by the Aubrey check. Anderson also knew that Stephens had filed a voluntary petition in bankruptcy several months prior, but had subsequently reaffirmed his obligations to the Bank. Stephens explained that he had purchased a large quantity of corn in Northern Indiana and had sold it in Kentucky at a higher price. Evidently satisfied with his explanation, Anderson stamped nine promissory notes, of which Stephens was maker, "paid" and returned them to Stephens. Anderson then directed a teller at the Bank to fill out a deposit slip for the transaction. At that time neither Anderson nor the teller noticed the typewritten modification on the check. The transaction consisted of applying the funds represented by the three items in the deposit ($106,082.74) to Stephens's debt represented by the nine promissory notes ($31,851.81), an installment payment, of which Stephens was a joint obligor, of $27,559.27,[1] accrued interest owed the Bank by Stephens in the amount of $5,265.65 and the $2,000 cash given to Stephens. The balance was credited to Stephens's account. Stephens then left the Bank.

Later that afternoon, Anderson began thinking about the transaction and examined the items in the deposit. He noticed that Aubrey's check bore signs of possible tampering and contacted Aubrey's office in Louisville to inquire about the validity of the check. An Aubrey representative told Anderson that a check in that amount was suspicious, and Anderson then "froze" the transaction. The next day, Aubrey stopped payment on the check.

---

* [Editor: citations in [ ] refer to Revised U.C.C. Articles 3 and 4.]

[1] The other obligor assumed liability on this debt and it is not a part of this lawsuit.

Thereafter, the Bank attempted to recover possession of the nine promissory notes from Stephens but was unsuccessful. Stephens subsequently left Hardinsburg and his present whereabouts are unknown.

After freezing Stephens's account, the Bank reversed the December 9, 1979 transaction by applying the $5,604.51 then on deposit in Stephens's account (said sum representing the amount of the two checks deposited on December 9, 1979 with Aubrey's check) against the $2,000 paid to Stephens in cash on December 9, 1979, and crediting the remaining $3,054.51 against the aggregate principal balance of nine promissory notes delivered to Stephens on that date. As a result, the Bank claimed a loss of $28,193.91 and made demand therefor upon Aubrey and upon St. Paul. Such demands were refused, and this action followed.

Issues - Aubrey

The issues raised by Aubrey differ from those raised by St. Paul and we shall consider them separately. We first address Aubrey's issues, which are presented for review as follows:

I. Whether the holder of a check (the Bank) can recover from the check's maker (Aubrey) who has "stopped payment" on the check where such holder is not a "holder in due course" because it not only did not take the check "for value" but took it with notice of a defense to the check on the part of the maker;

II. ....

III. Whether the obligation of a debtor (Stephens) is discharged when the creditor (the Bank) is induced by the debtor's fraud to surrender possession of the debtor's promissory notes evidencing the indebtedness;

IV. ....

We think the only issue dispositive of Aubrey's appeal is whether the trial court could rightfully have found on the evidence that the Bank was a holder in due course of the Aubrey check under the Uniform Commercial Code (U.C.C.) as adopted in Indiana.

The Bank's right to recover on the check is conditioned upon its status as a holder in due course of the check.... [U.C.C. §§ 3-305, 3-306] ...

Assuming, without presently deciding, that

Aubrey showed the existence of a defense, the burden was on the Bank to prove by a preponderance of the evidence that it was in all respects a holder in due course of the check. §3-307(3) [§ 3-308(b)].

Section 3-302(1) [§ 3-302(a)] defines a holder in due course who takes an instrument

(a) for value; and
(b) in good faith; and
(c) without notice that it is overdue or has been dishonored or of any defense against or claim to it on the part of any person.*

There is no contention on appeal, and there was none at trial, that the Bank did not take the Aubrey check in good faith, which means honesty in fact in the transaction concerned. § 1-201(19).** There is also no question that the Bank was a holder of the instrument, as it was in possession of the check endorsed by the payee Stephens in blank. See § 1-201(20) [U.C.C. §§ 3-201, 3-202].

We initially consider whether the Bank took the Aubrey check for value. The Bank contends that it gave value for the check to the extent that it (a) acquired a security interest in the instrument under §§3-303(a), [§ 3-303(a)(2)], 4-208, [§ 4-210] and 4-209, [§ 4-211]; and (b) took the check in payment of an antecedent claim under §3-303(b) [§ 3-303(a)(3)]. Aubrey contends that the Bank did not take the check for value since it immediately froze Stephens's account upon appraisal that the validity of the check was suspect and cancelled the amounts it had credited against Stephens's debt. Aubrey considers that the Bank's action in crediting Stephens's debt on the notes merely constituted a bookkeeping procedure and the Bank did not change its position by doing so, particularly since the Bank could still maintain an action against Stephens on the notes. Finally

---

* [Editor: U.C.C. § 3-302(a) also requires:

(a) Subject to subsection (c) and Section 3-106(d), "holder in due course" means the holder of an instrument if:

(1) the instrument when issued or negotiated to the holder does not bear such apparent evidence of forgery or alteration or is not otherwise so irregular or incomplete as to call into question its authenticity; and ...]

** [Editor: Revised U.C.C. § 3-103(a)(4) adds "and the observance of reasonable commercial standards of fair dealing."]

Aubrey maintains that general principles of law and equity render the U.C.C. provisions relied on by the Bank inapplicable.

We are of the opinion that the Bank took the check for value. The issue is most readily resolved by §3-303(b) [§ 3-303(a)(3)] which states in part:

A holder takes the instrument for value

. . . . .

(b) when he takes the instrument in payment of or as a security for an antecedent claim against any person whether or not the claim is due; . . . .

The statute plainly states that value is given for an instrument when the instrument is taken in payment for an antecedent debt not yet due. The statute contains no provision precluding application of the rule when fraud is exercised by the presenter of the instrument, as Aubrey would have us find.

While this section has not been construed in Indiana, an examination of authorities from other jurisdictions lends support to the Bank's position that the application of funds made available by the Aubrey check to Stephens's indebtedness and the surrender of notes constituted taking the instrument for value.

In *Citizens Bank v. National Bank of Com.,* 334 F.2d 257 (10th Cir. 1964), an Arkansas Bank accepted from its debtor, in payment of a note, a check payable to the debtor drawn on an Oklahoma bank. The bank delivered the debtor's note to him. The Arkansas bank presented the check to the Oklahoma-drawee bank, which accepted the check and issued its cashier check in payment. Later that day, the Oklahoma bank discovered that the check presented by the Arkansas bank bore a forged drawer's signature and dishonored the cashier's check. The Arkansas bank then brought an action against the Oklahoma bank on the cashier's check. The Oklahoma bank argued, as Aubrey does here, that since the Arkansas bank had recourse against its depositor, notwithstanding discharge of the debt, it could not recover from the Oklahoma drawee bank on the cashier's check. Reversing the trial court, the Court of Appeals held that the Arkansas bank was a holder in due course, stating, "Undoubtedly, credit was given for the forged check by the discharge of the pre-existing debt," 334 F.2d at 261, and recognizing the prevailing rule, "if the negotiated instru-

ment is taken in satisfaction of an antecedent debt, the taker is a holder for value and in due course." Id. . . .

Further, we believe that the Bank gave value for the check under §§4-208(1) and 4-209, [§§ 4-210(a), 4-211] in that it acquired a security interest in the check to the extent funds represented thereby were applied to Stephens's debt. Section 4-208(1)(a) [§ 4-210(a)(1)] states in part:

(1) A [collecting] bank has a security interest in an item and any accompanying documents or the proceeds of either
    (a) in case of an item deposited in an account to the extent to which credit given for the item has been withdrawn or applied; . . . .

Section 4-209 [§ 4-211] provides:

For purposes of determining its status as a holder in due course, the bank has given value to the extent that it has a security interest in an item provided that the bank otherwise complies with the requirements of §3-302 on what constitutes a holder in due course.

In *Waltham Citizens Nat'l Bank v. Flett,* 353 Mass. 696, 234 N.E.2d 739 (1968), a depositary bank allowed its depositor, at the time he deposited a check upon which payment was later stopped, to draw a check against those funds in satisfaction of a note which the bank returned to the depositor. The court found the bank to have given value for the former check, apparently considering the bank to have "applied" credit against the deposited check under §4-208(1)(a) [§ 4-210(a)(1)]. One commentary has suggested that the bank's delivery of the note to the depositor may have been determinative of the value issue. B. Clark & A. Squillante, *The Law of Bank Deposits, Collections, and Credit Cards* 85 (1970).

We find no support for Aubrey's argument that the Bank did not give value since it did not change its position vis-à-vis Stephens and made a bookkeeping entry only of the credit given Stephens. Aubrey appears to liken the transaction under review to the situation arising when a bank provisionally credits a depositor's account pending final settlement of a deposited item. It is true that the giving of provisional credit, which has not ripened into credit available for withdrawal as a matter of right, and nothing more, does not constitute the giving of value for deposited item. §4-

208(1)(a) [§ 4-210(a)(1)]; *Universal C.I.T. Credit Corp. v. Guaranty Bank and Trust Company,* 161 F. Supp. 790 (D.C. Mass. 1958). Official Comment 3 to §3-303 states that it is not necessary to give holder in due course status to one who has not actually paid value, and cites as illustration "the bank credit not drawn upon, which can be and is revoked when a claim or defense appears."*** When the credit is drawn upon, however, value is given to that extent. §4-208(1)(a) [§ 4-210(a)(1)]. Further, if the depositor's account is overdrawn at the time the check is taken, and funds represented thereby are applied to the overdrawal by way of set-off, value is given to that extent if the check is later dishonored. *Laurel Bank & Trust Co. v. City Nat'l Bank,* 33 Conn. Supp. 641, 365 A.2d 1222 (1976); see Annotation 59 A.L.R.2d 1173.

We have been directed to two cases in which appellate courts have held that value was not given. Aubrey relies on *Coconut Grove Bank v. M.R. Harrison Construction Corp.,* 226 So.2d 120 (Fla. Dist. Ct. App. 1969). In that case, the depositor deposited a check to his order in his account at the bank. The bank allowed the depositor to withdraw some funds against the check.

*** [Editor: Official Comment 1 to Revised Section 3-303 states "Subsection (a) is a restatement of former section 3-303. . . .]

Further, the depositor drew two checks payable to the bank to be applied to a loan not then due, and the bank applied that amount on its books to the depositor's loan account. The drawer of the check stopped payment thereon, and upon notice thereof, the bank reversed its bookkeeping entry and destroyed the credit given toward the debt. The bank prevailed as to the former amount, but was denied recovery on the latter. The court did not consider whether §3-303(b), [§ 3-303(a)(3)] the section stating that taking an instrument in payment for an antecedent claim is value, applied in the case. Further, the opinion does not state whether the note evidencing the debt was returned to the depositor. We do not consider this case to be controlling on the issue.

In *Marine Midland Bank-New York v. Graybar Electric Company, Inc.,* 41 N.Y.2d 703, 395 N.Y.S.2d 403, 363 N.E.2d 1139 (1977), the bank was held not to have given value for a check deposited by its depositor. The bank had provisionally set off the amount of that check against its depositor's indebtedness. The court noted that the note had not been returned to the depositor and indicated in dicta that had the note been returned a different result might have been obtained. The case, then, is clearly distinguishable.

We hold that the Bank in the instant case gave value for the Aubrey check to the extent that funds represented thereby were supplied to Stephens's note.

NOTE

1. Consider the effect of U.C.C. Section 3-302(a)(1) on the facts of the *St. Paul Fire & Marine Ins. Co.* case. Could the bank claim to be a holder in due course? Anderson "noticed that Aubrey's check bore signs of possible tampering."

2. If value was given, the extent to which a fraudulently altered instrument can be enforced against the maker or drawer by a payor bank, a drawee, or a person who took the instrument for value, in good faith, and without notice of the alteration, is to the extent of its original terms. But, if the instrument when issued was incomplete, such persons can enforce the instrument as completed. U.C.C. § 3-407(c). *See* further Chapter VII at A3.

B. Value

1. Article 3 distinguishes between consideration (U.C.C. § 3-303(b)) and value (U.C.C. § 3-303(a)) as giving rise to different rights. Whereas a failure of consideration will affect liability on the underlying obligation and thus would not be a defense to claims made by a holder in due course, an absence of value given by a claimant will prevent the attainment

of the status of holder in due course. Value requires that the obligation for which the instrument is exchanged has been executed or that a negotiable instrument or "an irrevocable commitment to a third person" has been the exchange. U.C.C. § 3-303(a)(4). Executory consideration is not value. In the event of a partial execution of consideration, e.g. a transfer of an instrument for $1,000 with a present payment of $600 and a promise to pay a further $400, value will have been given only "to the extent the promise has been performed." The holder will be entitled to recover as a holder in due course only 600/1000 of the note's face value. *O.P. Ganjo, Inc. v. Tri-Urban Realty Co., Inc.,* 108 N.J. Super. 517, 261 A.2d 722 (1969). U.C.C. §§ 3-303(a)(1), 3-302(d). To the extent that a security interest in or a lien on the instrument has been acquired other than by legal process, U.C.C. § 3-302(e) recognizes a holder becoming a holder in due course "only to an amount payable under the instrument which, at the time of enforcement of the instrument, does not exceed the amount of the unpaid obligation secured." By giving consideration, however, a transferee will receive transfer warranties enabling recourse for breach of warranty against the transferor. These warranties if given by an endorser will extend to all subsequent transferees as well. U.C.C. § 3-416.

2. The majority of instruments used in commerce are checks. Usually checks are promptly deposited in a bank for collection. Generally, the depositor will already have an account relationship with the depository bank. The bank may have made prior loans to its customer/depositor. This ongoing relationship will have to be examined to determine whether the bank is able to assert that it gave value for the instrument so as to qualify as a holder in due course.

Although a depository bank, not being the drawee bank, also is a collecting bank and thus is an agent of the depositor to collect on the instrument, it may also be its customer's creditor. Such creditor-debtor relationship to its customer may have developed out of a prior transaction, such as an existing overdraft, or because the bank allowed the customer/depositor to make a "split deposit," i.e. to deposit a check for $1,000.00 and at the same time to ask for $200.00 in cash, so that the amount to be credited to the account would be only $800.00. These situations give rise to a common-law lien, often referred to as a "banker's lien," which would be a possessory security interest in the item deposited for collection. Restatement, Security § 62; *cf.* U.C.C. § 4-210(c). A bank on taking an instrument could apply it to the outstanding debt and thereby will have given value on the basis of the antecedent debt. U.C.C. § 3-303(a)(3). In addition U.C.C. Section 4-210 provides that a collecting bank acquires a security interest in an item and its proceeds to the extent to which credit given for the item has been withdrawn or applied; or where such credit was made available for withdrawal as of right, whether or not the bank could reverse an entry of credit based on the item being dishonored; or where the bank takes the item as collateral.

Thus, a security interest in an uncollected instrument arises when a bank honors a check in anticipation of collecting on the check deposited with the bank for collection. U.C.C. Section 4-211 goes on to provide that to the extent that a bank has a security interest in an instrument it will have given value and could qualify as a holder in due course.

A bank's claim to have given value is much clearer where it asserts the right to set off a debt owed by the customer to the bank with a debt the bank owes its customer. Once a bank collects the amount due on a check, the bank is no longer an agent for collection but becomes a debtor of its customer. As a result there may now be off-setting debts, that owed by the bank to its customer and the debt owed by the customer to the depository bank. To the extent these debts are set off, the bank will have given value. To determine whether value has been given for an instrument where there is an ongoing account relationship between the customer and the bank, U.C.C. Section 4-210(b) applies the "first in first out" test. Thus credits first given are first withdrawn.

3. U.C.C. Sections 3-303(a)(4), (5) indicate that a purchaser will have given value where he gives a negotiable instrument for it or makes an irrevocable commitment to a third person. The underlying theory here is that although there is here an executory promise, such promise will not be subject to a revocation and would be enforceable in normal circumstances against the promisor. For example, the negotiable instrument could come into the hands of a holder in due course. Also, when given in return for issuing an irrevocable letter of credit value will have been given. This would be an irrevocable commitment, obliging the issuer of the instrument to honor the obligation expressed therein.

Query: Under the availability schedule set forth in the Expedited Funds Availability Act,[7] depository institutions will have to allow withdrawal of funds from a deposited check, even though such check, to the knowledge of the depository institution, has not yet been presented and honored. What are the rights of the depository bank with regard to having given value for the item? Is there a statutorily imposed commitment or is this commitment only binding when exercised? Thus U.C.C. Section 3-303(a)(5) would not be applicable but U.C.C. Section 3-303(a)(1) would apply. If the check is a "cashier's check," consider *Real Estate Auctions, Inc. v. The Nat'l Republic Bank of Chicago,* 1991 U.S. Dist. LEXIS 17625 (N.D. Ill. 1991).

C. Good Faith

U.C.C. Section 3-103(a)(4) defines "good faith" as "honesty in fact and the observance of reasonable commercial standards of fair dealing." This definition combines a subjective test "honesty in fact" with an objective reference to "observance of reasonable commercial standards of fair dealing."

As we have already noted (in Chapter III) the only means of proving a subjective state of mind would be by objective indicia. Present U.C.C.-Article 2, dealing with sales, defines "good faith" in the case of a merchant as "honesty in fact *and* the observance of reasonable commercial standards of fair dealing in the trade." (U.C.C. § 2-103(1)(b) emphasis supplied). This supplies an objective standard by which to measure the party's actions or non-actions against a standard of reasonableness of the state of mind. Is there an anomaly in holding a merchant in relation to a sale of goods transaction to a higher standard of "good faith", than would be the case in relation to the purchase of a negotiable instrument? Is it a valid or safe conclusion to measure the duties and liabilities of a bank [a merchant in financial instruments] to say that it will be relieved of any liability for negligence as long as it has acted honestly? Is that really what "good faith" under U.C.C. § 1-203 means?

---

[7] The Competitive Equality Banking Act of 1987, 12 U.S.C. §§ 4002-4003 and Regulation CC, 12 C.F.R. §§ 229.10, 229.12.

We must not forget that bad faith, not negligence, is the opposite of good faith. Thus, negligence in failing to explore facts which might give rise to notice of a defense or to a claim to an instrument, is not bad faith. One can be an incompetent business person and still be honest.

Subject to U.C.C. Section 3-302(a)(1), the existence of "suspicious circumstances" does not prevent a transferee/holder from being a holder in due course. The question is not whether a reasonable person would have made inquiries concerning the circumstances, but whether such person, including a bank that must be deemed to have sophistication, had "actual knowledge of some fact which would prevent a commercially honest individual from taking up the instruments." *Chemical Bank of Rochester v. Haskell,* 51 N.Y.2d 85, 411 N.E.2d 1339 (1980). *Bankers Trust Co. v. Crawford,* 781 F.2d 39 (3d Cir. 1986).

On the other hand, it has been said that "there is no inherent inconsistency between a subjective standard of good faith and a reasonable inquiry into the actual known circumstances surrounding a purchase of negotiable paper" and that "if a party fails to make an inquiry for the purpose of remaining ignorant of facts which he fears would disclose a defect in the transaction, he may be found to have acted in bad faith." Under that view, expert testimony on the reasonableness of the discount price paid for a note is admissible. *Funding Consultants, Inc. v. Aetna Cas. & Sur. Co.,* 187 Conn. 637, 447 A.2d 1163 (1982).

Despite the view that the existence of "suspicious circumstances" does not mean that a person, especially a bank, did not act in "good faith," courts sometimes react differently. In *Banco Di Roma v. Merchants Bank,* 459 N.Y.S.2d 592 (N.Y. App. Div. 1983), a bank which regularly permitted overdrafts in the expectation of receiving cashiers' checks issued by another bank covering such overdrafts, was denied summary judgment when the issuing bank dishonored the cashier's checks upon discovering a check kiting scheme. The court held that "the sheer volume of cashier's checks purchased by the [perpetrator] with checks drawn on the plaintiff out of funds that would have been insufficient without the latter covering cashier's checks raises a suspicion of fraud," justifying an exception to the usual rule that a bank must honor its cashier's checks.

The conventional view is supported by legislative history. *See* Farnsworth, *Good Faith Performance and Commercial Reasonableness Under the Uniform Commercial Code,* 30 U. CHI. L. REV. 666, 673–74 (1963). However, Professor Farnsworth says that the "Code uses 'good faith' in two senses, that of good faith performance as well as that of good faith purchase;" and that "both common sense and tradition favor an objective standard of good faith performance." 30 U. CHI. L. REV. at 678. Recent cases indicate the accuracy of that observation. Here, however, we are concerned with "good faith purchase," whereby a transferee seeks to attain the status of holder in due course.

For an analysis of the issue of good faith in the acquisition of investment securities, *see* Guttman, *Modern Securities Transfers,* Chapter 6 ¶ 6.06[2] (Warren, Gorham, & Lamont 1987 & Cum. Supp. 1992).

Funding Consultants, Inc. v. Aetna Casualty and Surety Company et al.

187 Conn. 637, 447 A.2d 1163 (1982)*

PETERS, Associate Justice.

In this suit on a promissory note, the dispositive issue is whether a maker of a note may introduce expert testimony to challenge the good faith of a person seeking to enforce the note as a holder in due course. The plaintiff, Funding Consultants, Inc., brought an action, initially only against the defendant Aetna Casualty and Surety Co., Inc., but ultimately also against the defendant Benjamin C. Preisner, as co-makers of a promissory note in the amount of $68,000. Aetna Casualty, in the interim, had impleaded Preisner by a third party complaint alleging that Aetna Casualty as surety was entitled to indemnification from Preisner if Aetna Casualty were held liable to Funding Consultants. See General Statutes § 52–102a; Practice Book § 117. After a trial to a jury, judgments were rendered in favor of the plaintiff against both defendants, and in favor of the third party plaintiff against the third party defendant. Only the appeal of Preisner as defendant and third party defendant is being pursued in this court.[1]

The present action is a suit on a promissory note which was given to Paul King, Jr. in connection with the 1974 sale of the Paul King, Jr. Insurance Company to the defendant Preisner. On this note, hereinafter the Preisner note, Preisner and Aetna Casualty were co-makers, although Aetna Casualty's status was that of an accommodation party for Preisner. The Preisner note was a $68,000 noninterest bearing negotiable instrument calling for four equal installments to be paid annually beginning on November 1, 1975, and ending on November 1, 1978.

King sold the Preisner note to the plaintiff Funding Consultants, Inc. on January 18, 1975, for $5,000 cash and a promissory note. This note, hereinafter the Funding note, was a $35,000 noninterest bearing negotiable instrument calling for four equal installments to be paid at bi-monthly intervals beginning on March 20, 1975, and ending on September 20, 1975.

The defendant Preisner, after formal demand, refused to make any payments on the Preisner note because, he alleged, the execution of the note had been induced by fraudulent misrepresentations about the financial condition of the Paul King, Jr. Insurance Company. The plaintiff Funding Consultants thereupon, on December 1, 1975, in reliance upon an acceleration clause contained in the Preisner note, declared the whole amount of that note to be then due and payable. This litigation ensued.[3]

At the trial, the plaintiff sought to recover on the Preisner note as a holder in due course. Only a holder in due course may enforce a negotiable

---

* [Editor: citations in [ ] refer to Revised U.C.C. Articles 3 and 4.]

[1] The defendant Aetna Casualty took a timely appeal from the judgment rendered against it, but withdrew that appeal before this case was heard for oral argument. Insofar as Preisner is appealing from the judgment against him on the substituted complaint, his status as co-defendant allows pursuit of his appeal even though Aetna Casualty has withdrawn. The extent to which Preisner is appealing from the judgment on the third party complaint is more perplexing. No separate issue has been raised in the briefs concerning Preisner's obligation to indemnify Aetna Casualty. At the trial, the parties stipulated that any judgment against Aetna Casualty would also be a judgment against Preisner. We will assume, for the purposes of this appeal, that our resolution of the issues arising pursuant to the underlying complaint will serve to resolve the appeal concerning the third party complaint.

[3] It is of passing interest to note that the record reveals that the Funding note equally fell into immediate default. On March 20, 1975, before the due date of the first instalment of the Preisner note, the plaintiff informed King that the payment schedule on the Funding note was being readjusted to coincide with the payment schedule on the Preisner note, so that "[i]f payment is not received on your note, no payments will be made by Funding Consultants, Inc." The Funding note in turn was assigned by King to five insurance companies to whom he was indebted. These insurance companies subsequently recovered a judgment on the Funding note against the plaintiff in the amount of $48,071.47. Middlesex Mutual Ins. Co. v. Funding Consultants, Inc., Superior Court, Judicial District of New Haven, Docket No. 145988. In the present litigation, in order to collect on that judgment, the five insurance companies were permitted to intervene as additional parties plaintiff.

instrument without regard to the maker's assertion of a personal defense such as fraud in the inducement. U.C.C. § 3–305(2) [§ 3–305(a)(1)(iii)]; *see* E. Peters, *A Negotiable Instruments Primer* § I, pp. 33–34 (2d Ed. 1974); White & Summers, *Uniform Commercial Code* § 14–9 (2d Ed. 1980). Evidence of the existence of a personal defense does, however, shift to the holder of the instrument the burden of proving his due course status. U.C.C. § 3–307(3) [§ 3–308(b)]; . . . *see* Peters, *op. cit.,* § J, p. 34. That burden requires the holder to prove his taking of the instrument "(a) for value; and (b) in good faith; and (c) without notice that it is overdue or has been dishonored or of any defense against or claim to it on the part of any person." U.C.C. § 3–302 [§ 3–302]; . . . *see* Peters, *loc. cit.*; White & Summers, *op. cit.*, § 14–6.

In order to establish its due course status, the plaintiff relied on the testimony of its president, Richard R. Splain. When the good faith of the plaintiff's purchase was put into issue, Splain testified that he had little knowledge about or experience in the purchase of negotiable instruments.[4] The defendant sought to counter this testimony by offering, as an expert witness, Michael Schaeffer of the Connecticut Bank & Trust Company to testify that the plaintiff had given inadequate consideration for its purchase of the Preisner note. Such testimony would furnish some evidence, according to the defendant, that Splain had testified untruthfully about the good faith of the plaintiff's purchase. The plaintiff objected to admission of the testimony as irrelevant and prejudicial. After a hearing, the trial court sustained the plaintiff's objection on the ground of prejudice.

The case was submitted to the jury with one special interrogatory. In response to that interrogatory, the jury found the plaintiff to be a holder in due course with respect to the Preisner note. The defendant's appeal has assigned the

---

[4] Since the parties have certified only part of the transcript to this court, we do not know what other evidence to prove or to disprove the plaintiff's good faith was before the jury. Although the plaintiff's default on its own negotiable promissory note would not impair its capacity to be a holder for value; *see* U.C.C. § 3–303(c) [3–303(a)(4), (5)]; its early repudiation of that note might be some indication of notice of a defense on the Preisner note.

exclusion of the expert testimony as error.[5]

The disagreement of the parties on this appeal is a narrow one. On the one hand, the defendant concedes that the standard of good faith under the Uniform Commercial Code is, as it was under the prior Negotiable Instrument Law, a subjective standard. "Good faith," as used in U.C.C. § 3–302(1)(b) [§ 3–302(a)(2)(ii)], is defined in U.C.C. § 1–201(19) as "honesty in fact in the conduct or transaction concerned." Both the language of other sections of the Code[6] and the Code's drafting history[7] incontrovertibly demonstrate that this

---

[5] In the alternative, the defendant has also assigned as error a procedural irregularity in the amendment of the jury's verdict.

[6] Compare, in Article 3, U.C.C. § 3–406, which requires a payor to pay an instrument "in good faith and in accordance with the reasonable commercial standards of the drawee's or payor's business." [Editor: note now § 3–406 imposes a standard of "ordinary care" § 3–103(a)(7)] Compare, in Article 2, U.C.C. § 2–103(1)(b), which requires a merchant to satisfy a standard of good faith which means "honesty in fact and the observance of reasonable commercial standards of fair dealing in the trade." Good faith is similarly elaborated to include not only honesty in fact but also observance of reasonable commercial standards in provisions of Articles 7 and 8 and concerning a bailee's dealings with documents of title; U.C.C. § 7–404; and an agent's dealings with investment securities. U.C.C. § 8–318. Since the recurrent insistence, in these other sections of the Uniform Commercial Code, on the additional requirement of "observance of reasonable commercial standards" cannot be disregarded as surplusage, good faith alone cannot properly be read to include such a requirement.

[7] The Uniform Commercial Code, although officially promulgated by the American Law Institute and the National Conference of Commissioners on Uniform State Laws in 1951, continued thereafter to undergo drafting revisions. In 1952, the proposed Uniform Commercial Code required in § 3–302(1)(b) that a holder in due course take a negotiable instrument "in good faith including observance of the reasonable commercial standards of any business in which the holder may be engaged." American Law Institute, Uniform Commercial Code, 1952 Official Text Edition. Four years later, the language "including . . . engaged" was deleted, with a comment that the intent of the deletion was "to make clear that the doctrine of an objective standard of good faith, exemplified by the case of Gill v. Cubitt, 3 B & C 466 (1824), is not intended to be incorporated in Article 3." American Law Institute, Uniform Commer-

standard is one that imposes no duty of due care on the holder. The test is honesty in fact rather than negligence. *See, e.g., Industrial Nat'l Bank v. Leo's Used Car Exchange, Inc.,* 362 Mass. 797, 801, 291 N.E.2d 603 (1973); *Breslin v. New Jersey Investors, Inc.,* 70 N.J. 466, 471, 361 A.2d 1 (1976); *Chemical Bank v. Haskell,* 51 N.Y.2d 85, 91–92, 411 N.E.2d 1339, 432 N.Y.S.2d 478 (1980); *Community Bank v. Ell,* 278 Or. 417, 427–28, 564 P.2d 685 (1977). On the other hand, the plaintiff does not dispute that application of this test calls for the factfinder to determine the inferences appropriately to be drawn from all of the evidence, including testimony "regarding the relationship between the plaintiff and the [transferor of the negotiable instrument], and the circumstances surrounding the purchase of this paper. . . ." *Williams & Co. v. Wiltz,* 106 Conn. 147, 152, 137 A. 759 (1927). A defendant who wishes to overcome the plaintiff's own testimony in support of its good faith perforce must introduce evidence to contradict the plaintiff's assertions of honesty in fact. *See Favors v. Yaffe,* 605 S.W.2d 342 (Tex. Civ. App. 1980).

The issue that does divide the parties, here as in the trial court, is what evidence is admissible to test the holder's subjective good faith. In order to decide whether a holder of an instrument acted in good faith, the trier of fact must determine the intent or state of mind of the party concerned. *Breslin v. New Jersey Investors, Inc., supra; Community Bank v. Ell, supra.* As in other determinations concerning intent, the trier is entitled to consider not only the testimony of the interested party but also evidence of surrounding circumstances that inferentially illuminate his honesty in fact in view of his actual knowledge. "Although mere negligence or failure to make the inquiries which a reasonably prudent person would make does not of itself amount to bad faith, if a party fails to make an inquiry for the purpose of remaining ignorant of facts which he believes or fears would disclose a defect in the transaction he may be found to have acted in bad faith." *Community Bank v. Ell, supra,* 278 Or. 428, 564 P.2d 685; *Hollywood National Bank v. I.B.M.,* 38 Cal. App. 3d 607, 614–15, 113 Cal. Rptr. 494 (1974);

Mid-Continent Nat'l Bank v. Bank of Independence, 523 S.W.2d 569, 574–75 (Mo. App. 1975); *General Investment Corp. v. Angelini,* 58 N.J. 396, 403–04, 278 A.2d 193 (1971). Similarly, if a party pays for an instrument an amount far less than its face value, such evidence is a factor that a trier may reasonably consider in weighing whether a purchase was made in good faith. The sale of an instrument at a substantial discount may in fact have alerted prospective purchaser to a possible defense to which he may not wilfully close his eyes. *See United States Fin. Co. v. Jones,* 285 Ala. 185, 229 So.2d 495, 498 (1969); *Stewart v. Thornton,* 116 Ariz. 107, 109, 568 P.2d 414 (1977); *Security Cent. Nat'l Bank v. Williams,* 52 Ohio App. 2d 175, 179, 368 N.E.2d 1264 (1976); 2 F. Hart & W. Willier, *Commercial Paper under the Uniform Commercial Code* § 11–04, pp. 11-21 through 11-22 (1982). We therefore hold that the defendant was entitled to introduce evidence in this case to show that there was such inadequacy of consideration that this factor, among others, should have been weighed by the jury in its determination of the plaintiff's good faith.[8]

Even if evidence of inadequacy of consideration is generally admissible, the question still remains whether the particular evidence offered by this defendant was sufficiently probative so that it should not have been excluded. The plaintiff had bought a $68,000 noninterest bearing note. The expert testimony was offered by the defendant to show what a commercial bank would have paid for the Preisner note and what the effective rate of return on the plaintiff's investment would have been. It is not an answer to this offer of proof that the plaintiff's president had testified

---

cial Code, 1956 Recommendations, p. 103. *See* White & Summers, *Uniform Commercial Code* § 14-6 (2d Ed. 1980). [*But see* now U.C.C. § 3-302(a)(1).]

[8] We note that other courts have critically examined allegations of good faith, especially when the holder of a promissory note seeks to enforce that note against a consumer. *See* Unico v. Owen, 50 N.J. 101, 116, 232 A.2d 405 (1967); Gilmore, *The Good Faith Purchase Idea and the Uniform Commercial Code: Confessions of a Repentant Draftsman,* 15 Ga. L. Rev. 605, 619 (1981); White & Summers, *Uniform Commercial Code* (2d Ed. 1980) § 14-8. Although the present transaction does not involve a consumer debtor, it does involve the unitary purchase of a negotiable promissory note rather than the commercial transfer of large numbers of banking items such as checks. Cf. Gilmore, *Formalism and the Law of Negotiable Instruments,* 13 Creighton L. Rev. 441 (1979).

about his inexperience with the purchase of negotiable paper and his ignorance of the practices and procedures of commercial banks. The jury might have chosen to disregard some or all of this testimony. The expert's evidence would have provided the jury with some basis for assessing the present value of both the Preisner note and the Funding note. It is not unreasonable to offer a lay jury expert assistance in the proper calculation of values that are not obvious on the face of the instruments to be compared. The proffered evidence was relevant because it would have enabled the jury to make a more accurate assessment of whether the plaintiff took the Preisner note in good faith.

The trial court's decision to exclude the expert testimony impliedly agreed with the defendant that the testimony would have been relevant since the court made its determination on the ground that the testimony was too prejudicial to be admissible. The only basis advanced by the plaintiff for the finding of prejudice is the argument that evidence about mathematical projections by a commercial bank would unfairly bring into play the objective criteria of good faith which the Uniform Commercial Code has repudiated. As we have noted above, there is no inherent inconsistency between a subjective standard of good faith and

a reasonable inquiry into the actual known circumstances surrounding a purchase of negotiable paper. The price actually paid, the present value of the instrument actually bought, are elements which may be considered in determining a holder's good faith. Although in most instances admission of expert testimony and questions of relevancy and prejudice rest within the sound discretion of the trial court; *Going v. Pagani,* 172 Conn. 29, 34-35, 372 A.2d 516 (1976); *Katsetos v. Nolan,* 170 Conn. 637, 651-52, 368 A.2d 172 (1976); in this case the court's action was clearly erroneous. Because exclusion of the expert testimony kept admissible evidence from the jury, the defendant is entitled to a new trial.

Having decided that the trial court's evidentiary ruling requires a new trial on the merits, we need not address the defendant's alternate ground of appeal. That issue concerned an alleged procedural irregularity in the formal amendment of the jury's verdict. Since such an irregularity is unlikely to recur on retrial, we need not consider its consequences.

There is error, the judgment is set aside, and the case is remanded for a new trial in accordance with this opinion.

In this opinion the other Judges concurred.

NOTE

1. Review discussion of good faith in Chapter II at B.

2. Does this case enable you to apply a test to the issue of good faith where the claimant is not a business person aware of what would be "observance of reasonable commercial standards of fair dealing"? U.C.C. § 3-103(a)(4). There is a proposal by the A.B.A. Task Force on Review of U.C.C. Article 1 to delete the term "commercial."

D.   Notice

The U.C.C. draws a distinction between "knowledge" and "notice." To "know" a fact or to have "knowledge" of a fact involves "actual knowledge," not merely an implied or imputed knowledge. A different approach is taken with regard to "notice." Knowledge will show notice, but notice can be imputed by reason of receipt of a notice or notification, U.C.C. § 1-201(26), or if "from all the facts and circumstances known to [a person] at the time in question he has reason to know that [the fact] exists." U.C.C. § 1-201(25)(c). As a result, there can be constructive notice. In the case of an organization, knowledge or notice depends on the fact having been brought "to the attention of the individual conducting [the transaction], and in any event from the time when it would have been brought to his attention if the organization had exercised due diligence." U.C.C. §§ 1-201(27), 1-201(26)(b). Thus, an organization must have a reasonable in-house procedure for communicating significant information.[8] This does not mean, however, that in an organization every individual receiving such information must pass it along. Unless to do so is part of the regular duties of the individual notified, or "unless he has reason to know of the transaction and that the transaction would be materially affected by the information," notice may not have been given to an organization. U.C.C. § 1-201(27). To be effective, notice must be received at such time and in such manner as to give a reasonable opportunity to act on it.

Notice of a defect in the instrument or of a defense to the instrument may be apparent from the instrument itself. Thus, U.C.C. Section 3-302 (a) (1) indicates that where the instrument "bears such apparent evidence of forgery or alteration or is . . . otherwise so irregular as to call into question its authenticity," the holder cannot claim the status of a holder in due course. For this section to apply, the incompleteness or irregularity or the indicia of forgery or alteration must be obvious. The question in issue under that provision is *authenticity,* i.e., an appearance that "the instrument may not be what it purports to be." Official Comment 1 to U.C.C. § 3-302. *See also supra* Chapter V at A.

U.C.C. Section 3-302(a)(2)(iii)-(vi) indicates that the holder must have taken the instrument without notice (1) that it is overdue or has been dishonored or that there is an uncured default with respect to payment of another instrument issued as part of the same series; (2) that the instrument contains an unauthorized signature or has been altered; (3) that there is extant a claim of a property or possessory right in the instrument or its proceeds, including a claim involving a right to rescind a negotiation and to recover the instrument or its proceeds [U.C.C. §§ 3-306, 3-202]; and (4) without notice that any party has a defence or claim in recoupment, i.e., that the obligation for which the instrument was transferred was not performed by the transferee as agreed.[9]

A series of examples is given by U.C.C. Sections 3-304(a), (b) and 3-307(b). As we have seen[10] in most instances the question whether an instrument is overdue will be apparent from the face of the instrument. An instrument bearing a due date is overdue if not honored by the end of the day following the due date. U.C.C. § 3-304(b)(2). A demand instrument is overdue if not honored on the day after the day on which a valid demand for payment has been made. U.C.C. § 3-304(a)(1). If no demand is made, a check becomes stale after ninety days. U.C.C. § 3-304(a)(2). With regard to other demand instruments, a factual determination has to be made whether the instrument is stale so as to deny to a holder who took such instrument a lengthy time after it was issued the status of a holder in due course. It is a failure to make a timely payment of principal, not of interest, that will result

---

[8] U.C.C. § 1-201(26), (27). Morgan Guarantee Trust Co. v. Third Nat'l Bank of Hampden County, 529 F.2d 1141 (3d Cir. 1976) (notice of theft of securities was placed into a "lost securities file" of the bank. Officer of the bank authorized a loan collateralized with stolen securities without checking the lost securities file of the existence of which he had not been made aware. Held, bank could not claim to have taken the securities without notice that they had been stolen).

[9] A claim in recoupment will reduce the amount payable on an instrument by an obligor; for example, by the amount recoverable in a counterclaim for breach of warranty.

[10] *See* Chapter IV.

in the instrument becoming overdue. Notes payable in installments illustrate these provisions. To allow the due date of a note payable in installments to be accelerated because of non-payment of interest, there has to be an express provision to that effect in the note. U.C.C. § 3-304(c). A failure to pay interest does not automatically result in the instrument becoming due. But nonpayment of an installment of principal when due will result in the instrument being overdue. Such defect can be cured, however, by a subsequent payment of the outstanding installment. U.C.C. § 3-304(b)(1).

1. Constructive Notice

A difficulty arises in connection with constructive notice. U.C.C. Section 3-302 (b) expressly rejects the idea that a public filing of a document is effective as a notice of a defense, claim in recoupment, or claim to the instrument. In *Scoloff v. Dollahite,* 779 S.W.2d 57 (Tenn. App. 1989), the State had filed a tax lien on all properties of the payee, yet the bank that took notes, of which the debtor was the payee, without being aware of the lien having been filed, was able to claim holder in due course status. Courts have not been consistent in applying the concept of constructive notice. In many cases, courts have used this concept as authority in order to reach a decision that appeared to them to be just and equitable.

Wesche v. Martin
64 Wash. App. 1, 822 P.2d 812 (1992)

WEBSTER, ACJ. Richard and Josie Zeldenrust, the appellants, bought and sold property through Oliver Martin and his real estate brokerage firm, Elliott Bay Investment Company (Elliott Bay). In the course of their business dealings with Martin, the Zeldenrusts executed one promissory note to Elliott Bay and three to Martin for deferred commissions owed him (the Zeldenrust notes). Martin executed one promissory note to Zeldenrusts for a loan (the Martin note). Martin later endorsed the Zeldenrust notes to Nancy Christopherson, the respondent. The Zeldenrusts assert that the trial court erred in finding that: (1) the parties intended the Zeldenrust notes to bear interest and Christopherson was entitled to recover interest on the notes; (2) Zeldenrusts were estopped from asserting that the notes should be interest free; (3) Christopherson's action to recover interest on the notes was not barred by the statute of limitations; and (4) Zeldenrusts were not the prevailing party. Christopherson asserts that the trial court erred in concluding that: (1) she was not a holder in due course and the Zeldenrusts

were entitled to a set-off in the amount of the Martin note, and (2) she was not the prevailing party. Both parties assert they are entitled to attorney fees on appeal. We affirm.

FACTS

Oliver Martin created Elliott Bay Investment Company in 1976 and was its president and sole shareholder. Nancy Christopherson began her employ at Elliott Bay in 1977 as a salesperson and was the designated real estate broker for Elliott Bay from 1980 until September of 1984, when Elliott Bay went out of business. In addition to these responsibilities, she acted as office manager, bookkeeper, typist, and receptionist. Since the company had no other licensed salesperson, broker, or staff employee, she was personally responsible for the bulk of the work.

In 1979, Christopherson earned Elliott Bay a $60,000 real estate commission, which was incorporated into a promissory note issued by Bryan and Mary Lou Chesledon. The Chesledon note bore interest at 15 percent per annum and required monthly payments of interest only and full payment of the balance on October 1, 1982. Since Elliott Bay was experiencing financial difficulties, the monthly interest payments were used exclusively to cover the business's operating expenses. Christopherson did not receive any salary from Elliott Bay during this period, and she and Martin orally agreed that she would receive the $60,000 deferred commission receivable from the Chesledons. Subsequently, however, Martin assigned the Chesledon note to acquire an option to purchase the Del Rey Apartment in Ballard and forfeited the note.

Beginning in 1981, Oliver Martin and his corporation engaged in a series of real estate transactions with Richard and Josie Zeldenrust. Zeldenrusts purchased and sold property through Elliott Bay and deferred payment of real estate commissions owed Martin by executing promissory notes to Martin or Elliott Bay in the amount of each commission. Each promissory note was secured by a deed of trust. Martin and the Zeldenrusts intended to form a partnership that would own and manage two apartment buildings on Capitol Hill known as the "Bellevue Avenue properties". They envisioned that Martin would purchase his partnership interest with the promissory notes in the amount of the deferred commissions. No formal partnership ever evolved, however, and the Zeldenrusts retained ownership of the Bellevue Avenue properties.

In the meantime, Martin apparently agreed to manage the Bellevue Avenue properties with the understanding that he was responsible for meeting expenses and entitled to any net profits. The operating revenues generated by the buildings did not cover the debt against the property. Martin and the Zeldenrusts agreed that Martin would make up his share of the shortfall by issuing a promissory note to the Zeldenrusts in the amount of $17,000 bearing 20 percent interest. The note was executed on November 1, 1982.

Martin endorsed four of the Zeldenrust notes to Christopherson to satisfy his debt to her. The specific terms of the four Zeldenrust notes, as initially executed, are as follows:

1. Promissory note executed on January 25, 1982, in the amount of $29,500 and bearing interest at the rate of 12 percent per annum made payable to Elliott Bay.
2. Promissory note executed on January 26, 1982, in the amount of $15,225 and bearing inter-

est at the rate of 12 percent per annum made payable to Oliver Martin.
3. Promissory note dated November 1, 1982, in the amount of $18,725 and bearing interest at the rate of 12 percent per annum made payable to Oliver Martin.
4. Promissory note dated April 15, 1984 in the amount of $16,583.26 bearing interest at the rate of 12 percent per annum and made payable to Oliver Martin.

In 1986, when the Zeldenrusts refinanced the property, they replaced the note for $15,225 and the note for $18,725. The original notes and deeds of trust were reconveyed and backdated to 1982. Richard Zeldenrust crossed out the interest provision on the replaced notes and signed his initials. He also lined-out the interest provision on the $16,583.26 note, for which no replacement note exists. Neither Josie Zeldenrust nor Martin initialed the line-outs. At some point after execution of the replacement notes, Martin endorsed and made payable to Christopherson the replacement notes, the note on which Richard Zeldenrust deleted the interest provision, and the note that had not been replaced or altered.

Discussion

Zeldenrusts challenge the trial court's finding that the parties intended interest to accrue on the original notes executed by the Zeldenrusts. They contend that the promissory notes were intended to reflect ownership interests that Martin purchased in the Bellevue Avenue properties with sales commissions earned by him. The essence of their argument is that, because the notes do not reflect loans, Martin could not have intended interest to accrue on them. Martin responds that he intended the notes to bear interest.[1]

The four Zeldenrust notes in question expressly included interest at the rate of 12 percent per annum. Although the parties intended the notes to represent ownership interests rather than loans, they never reached an agreement on what would happen with the notes if the partnership plans did not proceed. Zeldenrusts were assisted in the pur-

---

[1] Since Zeldenrusts believed interest would not accrue on the notes, and Martin believed interest would accrue, we reject Zeldenrusts' assertion that the parol evidence was "uncontroverted." We also reject Zeldenrusts' unsupported contention that the court failed to consider the parol evidence.

chase of property by deferring payment of the commissions owed to Martin. Common sense suggests that Martin would not have agreed to defer payment of the commissions without consideration either in the form of interest, or a fixed percentage ownership interest in the property, which would have allowed him to share in any profits generated by rental or sale of the property. Since Martin never acquired any title to the Bellevue Avenue properties and no formal partnership agreement was ever created, Martin had no reason to agree to defer his compensation without interest. . . . The trial court's finding that the parties intended for interest to accrue on the notes when they were initially executed is supported by substantial evidence.[2]

* * * * *

We next address Christopherson's contention that the trial court erred in holding that she did not take the Zeldenrust notes as a holder in due course. Christopherson asserts that the trial court erred as a matter of law in applying the "close connection doctrine." Under the judicially developed close connection doctrine, the purchaser of a negotiable instrument is not a holder in due course if the purchaser is too closely connected to his or her transferor. *Maynard v. England,* 13 Wn. App. 961, 970, 538 P.2d 551 (1975). The Zeldenrusts contend that the trial court's holding rests on its finding that Christopherson had notice of the Martin note, which destroyed her status as a holder in due course. Alternatively, they contend that Martin's personal endorsement on the Zeldenrust note that was made payable to Elliott Bay rather than to Martin put Christopherson on notice that the endorsement may be defective and destroyed her status as a holder in due course. We are unable to determine from the record which

standard the trial court applied in holding that Christopherson was not a holder in due course. Since the Zeldenrusts do not argue that the close connection doctrine should apply, we do not review the trial court's decision under that standard, but address instead the legal standards upon which the Zeldenrusts assert the trial court's decision rests.

The Zeldenrusts claim that Christopherson's notice of the Martin note destroyed her status as a holder in due course. As a general rule, one who is a holder in due course takes a negotiable instrument free from "all claims to it on the part of any person" and from "all defenses of any party to the instrument with whom the holder has not dealt." RCW 62A.3-305(1), (2) [§§ 3-305 (a)(1), 3-305(b)]; see also RCW 62A.3-306 [§§ 3-305(a)(2)(3), 3-306]. RCW 62A.3-302(1) [*see now* § 3-302(a)] defines a holder in due course as follows:

> "(1) A holder in due course is a holder who takes the instrument
> (a) for value; and
> (b) in good faith; and
> (c) without *notice* that it is overdue or has been dishonored or of any defense against or claim to it on the part of any person."

(Underline ours.) "Notice" is defined in RCW 62A.1-201(25) as follows:

> "A person has 'notice' of a fact when (a) he has actual knowledge of it; or
> (b) he has received a notice or notification of it; or
> (c) from all the facts and circumstances known to him at the time in question he has *reason to know* that it exists.
> A person 'knows' or has 'knowledge' of a fact when he has actual knowledge of it."

(Underline ours.) One has "reason to know" of a fact if one actually knows information from which a person exercising reasonable care under commercially recognized standards would infer that the fact in question exists or that there is a substantial chance of its existence. *Von Gohren v. Pacific Nat'l Bank,* 8 Wn. App. 245, 252, 505 P.2d 467 (1973) (relying on Restatement (Second) of Agency § 9, comment (d), at 46 (1958)); RCW 62A.1-201(25)(c). The "reason to know" standard under 62A.1-201(25)(c) is an objective standard. *Von Gohren,* at 252.

---

[2] The Zeldenrusts also challenge the trial court's finding that there [was] no consideration for removal of the applicable rates of interest. To prove that the parties agreed to delete the interest on the reissued notes, the Zeldenrusts were required to demonstrate that they provided adequate consideration, and that Martin agreed to the deletion. . . .

In view of our decision that the parties intended the Zeldenrust notes to bear interest, we need not address Zeldenrusts' argument that the trial court erred in holding that they were estopped from deleting the interest provisions.

Whether a holder has notice of "any defense or claim to" the instrument under RCW 62A.3-302(1)(c) [§ 3-302(a)(2)(iii)-(vi)] is governed by RCW 62A.3-304 [§§ 3-302(a)(1), 3-304, 3-307 (b)]. That provision specifies the circumstances under which a purchaser has notice of a claim or defense, and the facts known by the purchaser that do not by themselves give the purchaser notice of a defense or claim. A set-off or counterclaim, which is extrinsic to the action on the instrument, is not a circumstance giving rise to a claim or defense. . . We conclude as a matter of law that Christopherson's alleged notice of the Martin note is not a "defense against or claim to" the notes Martin endorsed to her, and that Christopherson cannot be denied holder-in-due-course status on this basis.[6]

Zeldenrusts also assert that Martin's personal signature on the back of the note made payable to Elliott Bay rather than to Martin without any indication of Martin's representative capacity precluded Christopherson from taking the note as a holder in due course. We first address whether Christopherson was a "holder." RCW 62A.3-202 [§ 3-201] states in relevant part:

"(1) Negotiation is the transfer of an instrument in such form that the transferee becomes a holder. If the instrument is payable to order it is negotiated by delivery with any *necessary indorsement*. . .

(2) An endorsement must be written by or on behalf of the holder . . ."

(Underline ours.) Although the Code indicates that an instrument payable to order must be endorsed to be "negotiated", it is silent on whether an endorsement containing an insufficient signature by the payee destroys the transferee's status as a holder. The Washington

---

[6] Because we conclude that Zeldenrusts' setoff on the Martin note was not a claim or defense, we reject Zeldenrusts' assertion that proof of the existence of the Martin note shifted to Christopherson the burden of proving her status as a holder in due course. RCW 62A.3-307(3) states:

After it is shown that a *defense exists* a person claiming the rights of a holder in due course has the burden of establishing that he or some person under whom he claims is in all respects a holder in due course.

(Underline ours.) [Editor: *see* now U.C.C. § 3-308(b)]

Comments to RCW 62A.3-202 state that subsection (1) "follows" Former RCW 62.01.030,[7] which was construed in the case of *Glaser v. Connell*, 47 Wn.2d 622, 289 P.2d 364 (1955). See Cosway, *Negotiable Instruments—A Comparison of Washington Law and Uniform Commercial Code Article 3*, 38 Wash. L. Rev. 719, 740 (1963). In *Glaser*, the court entertained whether the plaintiff was a holder in due course of a promissory note executed by the defendant and made payable to the order of the "Holdorf Oyster Corporation," when the president and secretary of the Holdorf Oyster Corporation endorsed the note "Pres. Dwight Holdorf" and "Sec. Opal Holdorf" and delivered it to the plaintiff. *Glaser*, at 622-23. The court held that the note was not endorsed by the corporate payee, since the name of the corporate payee was not included in the endorsement, and that the plaintiff therefore was not a "holder." *Glaser*, at 628. The court reasoned as follows:

A holder in due course of negotiable paper enjoys certain privileges and immunities which the transferee of an unendorsed order instrument does not have. A holder in due course of such paper need look no further than the instrument itself to ascertain how much, when, and from whom a sum can be demanded. On the note involved in this case, however, any party to whom it is presented would have to resort to facts extrinsic of the instrument to ascertain whether the purported endorsement of the instrument was made by the named corporate payee.

Glaser, at 628. The court specifically rejected the plaintiff's attempt to establish the validity of the corporate indorsement by relying on the Code provisions governing the personal liability of the payee, stating that those provisions were inapposite to whether the transferee was a holder. *Glaser*, at 625-27.

Following the enactment of the U.C.C. in Washington, the Court of Appeals similarly decided the case of *Fines v. Stock*, 37 Wn. App. 101, 678 P.2d 839 (1984). In *Fines*, the defendant executed three promissory notes made payable to "Stillaguamish Estates, Inc." The reverse side of each note contained a signature, "Richard T.

---

[7] Section 30 of the Uniform Negotiable Instruments Law Act.

McClain," and an endorsement to "Viking Financial Services, Inc." Viking Financial Services subsequently indorsed the notes to the plaintiffs. *Fines,* at 102–03. Relying on *Glaser,* the court held that the plaintiffs were not holders in due course. *Fines,* at 104. The court reasoned that the signatures by McClain failed to indicate that "he was an officer of or even remotely connected with the corporation," and that whether McClain had authority was irrelevant; without the proper indorsements, the notes were not "negotiated" and the transferee did not become a "holder" under RCW 62A.3-202(1) [§ 3-201]. *Fines,* at 104–05.

The *Fines* court further reasoned that, because of the facial insufficiency of the indorsement, the plaintiffs did not take without notice of any defense under RCW 62A.3-302(1)(c) [§ 3-302 (a)(2)] and RCW 62A.3-304(1)(b):

> "Each of the plaintiffs, though the record indicates they took for value, took with notice of the facial insufficiency of the original payee's indorsements. Thus, they took with notice that 'the obligation of any party is voidable . . .' RCW 62A.3-304(1)(b). Accordingly, they could not be holders in due course, in any event, because they did not take 'without notice . . . of any defense against . . . it on the part of any person.' RCW 62A.3-302(1)(c). They, therefore, acquired no rights of a holder in due course. Specifically, they did not take their respective notes free from all defenses of the maker with whom they had not dealt. RCW 62A.3-305(2)." [§ 3-305 (a)]

Fines, at 105.

In the instant case, Martin wrote the following on the back of the promissory note in the amount of $29,500 executed by the Zeldenrusts to "Elliott Bay Investment Co."

"Pay to the order of Nancy Christopherson

Oliver H. Martin"

The indorsement was insufficient because it did not indicate that Martin was signing on behalf of Elliott Bay. Therefore, the instrument was not properly "negotiated" and Christopherson was not a "holder." *Glaser,* at 628. Moreover, Christopherson took the note with notice that the obligation of the Zeldenrusts or Elliott Bay was voidable under RCW 62A.3-304(1)(b). *Fines,* at 105. Christopherson asserts that the endorsement was valid under RCW 62A.3-403(1) [§ 3-402(a)], which provides that one's authority to sign an instrument "may be established as in other cases of representation." We reject this argument. RCW 62A.3-403(1) [§ 3-402(a)] governs who is liable on a note. It does not govern whether the owner of the note is a holder in due course. *See Glaser,* at 625–27. We conclude that Christopherson was not a holder in due course.

Once it is determined that a person possessing an instrument is not a holder in due course, that person takes the instrument subject to "all defenses of any party which would be available in an action on a simple contract." RCW 62A.3-306(b) [§ 3-305(a)(2)]. There need not be any "connection between the defense or claim which the party on the instrument is attempting to assert and the flaw which . . . deprives one of holder in due course status." 1 J. White & R. Summers, Uniform Commercial Code § 14–6 at 717 (3d ed. 1988); accord *Central Wash. Bank v. Mendelson-Zeller, Inc.,* 113 Wn.2d 346, 358, 779 P.2d 697 (1989). Thus, although Christopherson's alleged notice of the Martin note could not destroy her status as a holder in due course, because a separate claim or defense did deprive her of a holder-in-due-course status, the Zeldenrusts are entitled to assert their claim on the Martin note as a set-off against the $29,500 note executed by them.

NOTE

1. Revised U.C.C. Article 3 omitted § 3-304(1)(b).

2. Consider the impact of U.C.C. § 3-302(a)(1) on this decision, but note § 3-402(a).

(a) What effect would crossing out have on the status of a holder in due course claimed by Ms. Christopherson?

(b) Would Section 3-402(a) result in the signature of Martin amounting to an endorsement by "Elliott Bay Investment Co."? U.C.C. § 3-402.

(c) Was Ms. Christopherson a "holder" though she could not qualify as a holder in due course? U.C.C. § 3-201.

2. Forgotten Notice

Where it could not be denied that notice had been received, the claim has been made that such notice has been forgotten. This forgotten notice argument does not often gain acceptance by the courts. In *Morgan Guar. Trust Co. of N.Y. v. Third Nat'l Bank of Hampden County,* 400 F. Supp. 383 (D. Mass. 1975) *aff'd,* 529 F.2d 1141 (1st Cir. 1976) the court rejected a plea of forgotten notice because the notice was filed in a "lost securities" file whose existence was not generally known to employees of the bank. The court was able to avoid having to determine the effect of a notice allegedly forgotten. Another case in which forgotten notice was raised is *First Nat'l Bank v. Fazzari,* 10 N.Y.2d 394, 223 N.Y.S.2d 483, 179 N.E.2d 493 (1961). Due to his negligence, the drawer of a check was precluded from raising the defense that he was induced to sign with neither knowledge nor reasonable opportunity to learn of the character or essential terms of what he was signing. U.C.C. § 3–305(a)(1)(iii). He informed a local bank of the duplicity practiced upon him and was assured that the instrument would not be cashed. In reliance on this statement by the cashier he left the premises of the bank. Subsequently the bank did acquire the check and claimed that it was a holder in due course. The court held that the bank had acted in good faith and had given value, but that it had knowledge and notice of the defense. The court, however, also held, that although "the time and circumstances under which a notice or notification may cease to be effective are not determined by" the U.C.C. (U.C.C. § 1–201(25)), the bank was estopped from claiming "forgotten notice."

3. Consumer Instruments: Federal and State Enactments

The most obvious form of notice is received from a notation on the instrument itself. The Federal Trade Commission (FTC) seeking to protect consumers from being met by an assertion that the holder took an instrument as a holder in due course, and thus was not subject to any defenses a consumer customer-issuer may have had against the retailer, promulgated FTC Rule 433. 16 C.F.R. §§ 433.1, 433.2. This rule requires that instruments which arise in connection with any sale or lease of goods or services to a consumer by a person engaged in the business of selling or leasing goods or services to consumers, or of lending money to be expended in this way, be legended to indicate that the instrument arose out of a consumer transaction and that defenses the consumer has against the seller of goods or services or against a lender are preserved against a holder of these instruments. 16 C.F.R. §§ 433.1, 433.2. U.C.C. Section 3-106 (d) provides that such item, though legended, qualifies as an instrument under U.C.C. § 3-104 (a), i.e., it will not be deemed to have been conditioned. The holder of such an instrument, however, will not be able to claim the status of holder in due course, although U.C.C. Article 3 will apply to such instruments. The F.T.C. Rule provides:

§ 433.1 Definitions

(a) *Person.* An individual, corporation, or any other business organization.

(b) *Consumer.* A natural person who seeks or acquires goods or services for personal, family, or household use.

(c) *Creditor.* A person who, in the ordinary course of business, lends purchase money or finances the sale of goods or services to consumers on a deferred payment basis; *Provided,* such person is not acting, for the purposes of a particular transaction, in the capacity of a credit card issuer.

(d) *Purchase money loan.* A cash advance which is received by a consumer in return for a "Finance Charge" within the meaning of the Truth in Lending Act and Regulation Z, which is applied, in whole or substantial part, to a purchase of goods or services from a seller who (1) refers consumers to the creditor or (2) is affiliated with the creditor by common control, contract, or business arrangement.

(e) *Financing a sale.* Extending credit to a consumer in connection with a "Credit Sale" within the meaning of the Truth in Lending Act and Regulation Z.

(f) *Contract.* Any oral or written agreement, formal or informal, between a creditor and a seller, which contemplates or provides for cooperative or concerted activity in connection with the sale of goods or services to consumers or the financing thereof.

(g) *Business arrangement.* Any understanding, procedure, course of dealing, or arrangement, formal or informal, between a creditor and a seller, in connection with the sale of goods or services to consumers or the financing thereof.

(h) *Credit card issuer.* A person who extends to cardholders the right to use a credit card in connection with purchases of goods or services.

(i) *Consumer credit contract.* Any instrument which evidences or embodies a debt arising from a "Purchase Money Loan" transaction or a "financed sale" as defined in paragraphs (d) and (e).

(j) *Seller.* A person who, in the ordinary course of business, sells or leases goods or services to consumers.

§ 433.2 Preservation of consumers' claims and defenses, unfair or deceptive acts or practices

In connection with any sale or lease of goods or services to consumers, in or affecting commerce as "commerce" is defined in the Federal Trade Commission Act, it is an unfair or deceptive act or practice within the meaning of Section 5 of that Act for a seller, directly or indirectly, to:

(a) Take or receive a consumer credit contract which fails to contain the following provision in at least ten point, bold face, type:

NOTICE

ANY HOLDER OF THIS CONSUMER CREDIT CONTRACT IS SUBJECT TO ALL CLAIMS AND DEFENSES WHICH THE DEBTOR COULD ASSERT AGAINST THE SELLER OF GOODS OR SERVICES OBTAINED PURSUANT HERETO OR WITH THE PROCEEDS HEREOF. RECOVERY HEREUNDER BY THE DEBTOR SHALL NOT EXCEED AMOUNTS PAID BY THE DEBTOR HEREUNDER.

or, (b) Accept, as full or partial payment for such sale or lease, the proceeds or any purchase money loan (as purchase money loan is defined herein), unless any consumer credit contract made in connection with such purchase money loan contains the following provision in at least ten point, bold face, type:

NOTICE

ANY HOLDER OF THIS CONSUMER CREDIT CONTRACT IS SUBJECT TO ALL CLAIMS AND DEFENSES WHICH THE DEBTOR COULD ASSERT AGAINST

THE SELLER OF GOODS OR SERVICES OBTAINED WITH THE PROCEEDS HEREOF. RECOVERY HEREUNDER BY THE DEBTOR SHALL NOT EXCEED AMOUNTS PAID BY THE DEBTOR HEREUNDER.

§ 433.3 Exemption of sellers taking or receiving open end consumer credit contracts before November 1, 1977 from requirements of § 433.2(a)

(a) Any seller who has taken or received an open end consumer credit contract before November 1, 1977, shall be exempt from the requirements of 16 CFR Part 433 with respect to such contract provided the contract does not cut off consumers' claims and defenses.

* * * * *

State legislatures also have attempted to deal with this issue by prohibiting a seller, lessor, or lender of funds for the purpose of a consumer transaction to take a negotiable instrument, other than a check dated within [ten] days of its issue.[11] This is to prevent the taking of a series of post dated checks as an alternative to a promissory note payable in installments. *See,* however, U.C.C. Section 4-401(c) allowing a drawee bank to honor a post dated check before the date indicated, unless a stop payment order has been received by the bank. A Uniform Consumer Credit Code, (U.C.C.C.), proposed by the National Conference of Commissioners on Uniform State Laws, to protect consumer issuers of instruments has been adopted in only eleven jurisdictions. Variations of this type of legislation, however, have been widely enacted.

U.C.C.C. Section 3.307 [Certain Negotiable Instruments Prohibited]

With respect to a consumer credit sale or consumer lease, [except a sale or lease primarily for an agricultural purpose,] the creditor may not take a negotiable instrument other than a check dated not later than ten days after its issuance as evidence of the obligation of the consumer.

Comment

This section, together with Sections 3.403, 3.404, and 3.405, states a major tenet of this Act: that the holder in due course doctrine should be abrogated in consumer cases. Whatever beneficial effects this doctrine may have in promoting the currency of paper is greatly outweighed by the harshness of its consequences of denying consumers the right to raise valid defenses arising out of credit transactions. The first step in abolition of the doctrine is the prohibition found in this section of the use of negotiable instruments in consumer credit sales and consumer leases. The presence of the bracketed language recognizes the strong tradition of the use of negotiable instruments in agricultural transactions in some States.

Section 3.404 [Assignee Subject to Claims and Defenses]

(1) With respect to a consumer credit sale or consumer lease [, except one primarily for an agricultural purpose,] an assignee of the rights of the seller or lessor is subject to

---

[11] *Cf.* U.C.C.C. § 3.307.

all claims and defenses of the consumer against the seller or lessor arising from the sale or lease of property or services, notwithstanding that the assignee is a holder in due course of a negotiable instrument issued in violation of the provisions prohibiting certain negotiable instruments (Section 3.307).

(2) A claim or defense of a consumer specified in subsection (1) may be asserted against the assignee under this section only if the consumer has made a good faith attempt to obtain satisfaction from the seller or lessor with respect to the claim or defense and then only to the extent of the amount owing to the assignee with respect to the sale or lease of the property or services as to which the claim or defense arose at the time the assignee has notice of the claim or defense. Notice of the claim or defense may be given before the attempt specified in this subsection. Oral notice is effective unless the assignee requests written confirmation when or promptly after oral notice is given and the consumer fails to give the assignee written confirmation within the period of time, not less than 14 days, stated to the consumer when written confirmation is requested.

* * *

(4) An agreement may not limit or waive the claims or defenses of a consumer under this section.

* * *

Eachen v. Scott Housing Systems, Inc.
630 F. Supp. 162 (D. Ala. 1986)

THOMPSON, J.
MEMORANDUM OPINION
Plaintiffs Charles and Mary Eachen, two consumers, have brought this lawsuit against defendants Citicorp Acceptance Company and Scott Housing Systems, Inc., charging these defendants with breach of warranty. This cause is now before the court on Citicorp's November 20, 1985, motion for summary judgment, as amended. For reasons that follow, the motion is due to be granted in part and denied in part.

I.

The material facts of this case are undisputed. Charles and Mary Eachen purchased a Scott Showcase Mobile Home from Lawler Mobile Homes, Inc. of Phenix City, Alabama on June 10, 1983. The home was purchased on credit. In addition to a bill of sale, the Eachens and Lawler Mobile Homes signed an Alabama Mobile Home Retail Installment Contract and Security Agreement. That agreement contained the following language, as required by Federal Trade Commission (FTC) regulation, 16 C.F.R. § 433.2 (1984)

("Preservation of Consumer's Claims and Defenses"):

NOTICE: ANY HOLDER OF THIS CONSUMER CREDIT CONTRACT IS SUBJECT TO ALL CLAIMS AND DEFENSES WHICH THE DEBTOR COULD ASSERT AGAINST THE SELLER OF GOODS OR SERVICES OBTAINED PURSUANT HERETO OR WITH PROCEEDS HEREOF. RECOVERY HEREUNDER BY THE DEBTOR IS LIMITED TO AMOUNTS PAID BY THE DEBTOR HEREUNDER.

On the day of sale, Lawler Mobile Homes assigned the agreement to Citicorp.

The Eachens became dissatisfied with the mobile home because it allegedly contained serious defects in material and workmanship. Both Lawler Mobile Homes and Scott Housing, the manufacturer of the home, attempted to remedy the alleged defects, but the Eachens remained dissatisfied. Sometime before September 1985, Lawler filed for bankruptcy, thereby automatically barring any legal proceeding against it. 11 U.S.C.A. § 362.

On September 18, the Eachens filed suit in the Circuit Court of Lee County, Alabama against Citicorp and Scott Housing for breach of warranty. Citicorp then removed the Eachens' lawsuit to this court pursuant to the court's diversity and removal jurisdiction. 28 U.S.C.A. §§ 1332, 1441.

II.

Summary judgment is appropriate only if "there is no genuine issue as to any material fact and . . . the moving party is entitled to judgment as a matter of law." Fed.R.Civ.P. 56(c). Citicorp argues that, on the above undisputed facts, it is entitled to summary judgment as a matter of law against the Eachens on their warranty claim. Citicorp proffers two legal theories in support of its argument.

A. Citicorp's First Theory

Citicorp's first theory is that it is entitled to full summary judgment because, as assignee of the seller, it can be liable under Alabama law for the Eachens' claim only as a matter of *defense to or set-off against* a claim by the assignee. Since Citicorp has instituted no legal proceedings against the Eachens to collect unpaid funds, it continues, the Eachens are barred from maintaining this lawsuit. Citicorp rests this argument on the final phrase in a provision of the Alabama Consumer Finance Law:

> With respect to a consumer credit sale or consumer lease, an assignee of the rights of the seller or lessor is subject to all claims and defenses of the buyer or lessee against the seller or lessor arising out of the sale or lease, notwithstanding an agreement to the contrary, but the assignee's liability under this section may not exceed the amount owing to the assignee at the time the claim or defense is asserted against the assignee. *Rights of the buyer or lessee under this section can only be asserted as a matter of defense to or set-off against a claim by the assignee.*

1975 Alabama Code § 5-19-8 (emphasis added).

Citicorp's first theory lacks merit because the Eachens premise their lawsuit not on Alabama law but rather on the 1975 FTC regulation reported at 16 C.F.R. § 433.2 (1984) ("Preservation of Consumer's Claims and Defenses"). This federal regulation makes it "an unfair or deceptive act or practice" under the Federal Trade Commission Act, 15 U.S.C.A. § 41, *et seq.,* for a seller, directly or indirectly, to take or receive a consumer credit contract which fails to contain the provision regarding claims and defenses set forth in the consumer contract issued to the Eachens.

This regulation was specifically intended, according to the FTC, to provide that "a consumer can . . . maintain an *affirmative action* against a creditor who has received payments for a return of monies paid on account." 40 Fed. Reg. 53524 (1975) (emphasis added). The FTC expressly rejected amendments to the regulation that would limit the consumer to a "defense" or "setoff." The FTC stated,

> Many industry representatives suggested that the rule be amended so that the consumer may assert his rights only as a matter of defense or setoff against a claim by the assignee or holder. Industry representatives argued that such a limitation would prevent the financer from becoming a guarantor and that any limitation in the extent of a third party's liability was desirable. The practical and policy considerations which militate against such a limitation on affirmative actions by consumers are far more persuasive.

40 Fed. Reg. 53526 (1975) (footnotes omitted). The FTC observed, among other things, that if the consumer is limited to a purely defensive position the assignee-creditor may elect not to sue for the balance due when the consumer's defenses seem to have merit and the seller is judgment proof. The FTC observed that

> The most persuasive reason for not limiting a consumer to a wholly defensive position is the situation referred to in Professor Guttman's testimony. A consumer may stop payment after unsuccessfully attempting resolution of a complaint with the seller, or he may have finally discovered that the seller has moved, gone out of business or reincorporated as a different entity. During this period the consumer may have been making payments to the financer in good faith, notwithstanding the prior existence of defenses against the seller.
>
> If the consumer stops payment, he may be sued for the balance due by the third party financer. The financer may, however, elect not to bring suit, especially if he knows that he would be unable to implead the seller and he

knows the consumer's defenses may be meritorious. Under such circumstances the financer may elect to not sue in the hopes that the threat of an unfavorable credit report may move the consumer to pay.

40 Fed. Reg. 53527 (1975). Indeed, assuming that the Eachens can prevail on their warranty claim—an assumption which this court must make on Citicorp's motion for summary judgment—it appears that the objectionable scenario described by the FTC could very well be applicable here unless the regulation is enforced.

Citicorp argues, nonetheless, that the limitation in Alabama's section 5-19-8 should be engrafted onto the FTC regulation. It supports this argument by citing the following isolated language from an introductory paragraph to certain FTC Enforcement Guidelines issued in 1976:

> The manner and procedure by which a buyer may assert claims and defenses is governed by the terms of the contract and by applicable state law.

41 Fed. Reg. 34594 (1976). Citicorp's argument is meritless.

First, Citicorp has lifted this language out of 1976 Enforcement Guidelines addressing the regulation's definition of a "purchase money loan." Allowing affirmative actions by consumers against assignee-creditors was not addressed in these Guidelines. Therefore, it is apparent that the Guidelines and the language in them were not intended as an authoritative statement on the extent to which consumers could bring actions against assignee-creditors under the regulation.

But more importantly, it is apparent that when the quoted language from the Guidelines is read in conjunction with the history and purposes of the FTC regulation, the language is intended to mean that one must look to state law and the terms of the contract to determine the "manner and procedure" by which a consumer may affirmatively maintain an action against a creditor. For example, as noted by the FTC, an affirmative action against a creditor "will only be available where a seller's breach is so substantial that a court is persuaded that rescission and restitution are justified. The most typical example of such a case would involve non-delivery, where delivery was scheduled after the date payments to a creditor commenced." 40 Fed. Reg. 53524 (1975). The FTC staff has also observed that

Where a local jurisdiction has a two-year statute of limitations on contract claims, such claims and defenses would be extinguished after two years. Where a local jurisdiction imposes a rule analogous to laches or equitable estoppel, consumer claims and defenses would continue to be subject to such a limitation, and the consumer would have a duty to notify the potential defendant of his contention within a reasonable time.

41 Fed. Reg. 20024 (1976).

Moreover, to adopt Citicorp's understanding of the quoted language would mean that the FTC had authorized individual states to rescind the 1975 regulation to the extent the regulation specifically authorized consumers to bring affirmative actions against assignee-creditors. This drastic result is not supported by the regulation either on its face or by its history. The regulation neither expressly nor impliedly provides that states are authorized to rescind the 1975 regulation, in whole or in part; nor does a searching review of the history of the regulation uncover anything that would indicate such authorization, either expressly or impliedly.

The Eachens have requested that the court declare section 5-19-8 unconstitutional because it conflicts with the FTC regulation. The court declines this invitation for two reasons. First, there is no conflict because, as the court has demonstrated above, section 5-19-8's limitation on affirmative actions by consumers should not be engrafted on the FTC regulation and the section is therefore not applicable to the claim presented here. Second, there is no conflict because, by its own language, section 5-19-8's limitation is applicable only to consumer claims brought under that section. The section states that "[r]ights of the buyer or lessee *under this section* can only be asserted as a matter of defense to or set-off against a claim by the assignee" (emphasis added). Here, the Eachens are not relying on section 5-19-8.

The Eachens may therefore assert their warranty claim against Citicorp under the FTC regulation, irrespective of whether Citicorp has filed a lawsuit against the Eachens.

B. Citicorp's Second Theory

Citicorp's second theory is that it is entitled to partial summary judgment prohibiting the Eachens from recovering on their warranty claim more than they have paid under the contract to

Citicorp. The Eachens concede this theory. The contract expressly provides that recovery by the debtor against an assignee-creditor is limited to amounts paid by the debtor.

The court will therefore grant partial summary judgment to Citicorp prohibiting the Eachens from recovery from Citicorp more than they have paid to Citicorp under the contract.

An appropriate order will be entered.

NOTE

Although FTC Rule 433.2 applies and cannot be affected by state law, existing state law may grant additional remedies.

De La Fuente v. Home Savings Ass'n.

669 S.W.2d 137 (Tex. Ct. App. 1984)

KENNEDY, Justice.

This is an appeal from a suit on a note brought by appellee, Home Savings, against appellants, Pedro and Paula de la Fuente. The transaction underlying the note was the sale of materials and services for the installation of aluminum siding for the de la Fuente's home. We reverse and render judgment for appellants.

Trial was to the court, and findings of fact and conclusions of law were filed. The court's findings of fact are summarized as follows. In late April or early May of 1978, Roberto Gonzales, a representative of Aluminum Industries, Inc., visited the de la Fuente home to sell them aluminum siding. As a result, on May 3, 1978, the de la Fuentes executed, in their residence, a number of documents, including a contract and promissory note for improvements to their home. The contract granted a first lien on appellants' home. The total contract amount was $9,138.24 with 96 monthly installments of $95.19 and an annual percentage rate of 12%. The contract included a trust deed to Aluminum Industries which granted a first lien on the de la Fuente's residence. Aluminum Industries, Inc. is no longer in existence.

Appellants, by their fourth, sixth and seventh points of error, complain of violations of Texas Consumer Credit Code, TEX.REV.CIV.STAT. ANN. art. 5069, et seq. (Vernon 1971).

By their fourth point of error, appellants assert that the trial court erred in concluding that the lien taken in the transaction was not unlawful and, therefore, there was no violation of the Texas Consumer Credit Code. The version of art. 5069–6.05 of the Texas Consumer Credit Code in effect on May 3, 1978 read:

Art. 6.95 Prohibited Provisions

No retail installment contract . . . shall:

(7) Provide for or grant a first lien upon real estate to secure such obligation, except, (a) such lien as is created by law upon the recording of an abstract of judgment or (b) such lien as is provided for or granted by a contract or series of contracts for the sale or construction and sale of a structure to be used as a residence so long as the time price differential does not exceed an annual percentage rate of 10 percent. Act of May 4, 1977; ch. 104, section 1, 1977 Tex.Gen.Laws, Local and Spec. 212 *amended* by Act of May 8, 1981, ch. 111, section 18, 1981 Tex.Gen.Laws, Local and Spec. 284. See TEX.REV.CIV.STAT.ANN. art. 5069–6.05 (Vernon Supp. 1984).

The trial court, in the findings of fact, found that the contract for Labor and Materials and Trust Deed granted a first lien on appellants' residence. We agree. See *Jim Walter Homes v. Chapa*, 614 S.W.2d 838 (Tex.Civ.App.—Corpus Christi 1981, writ ref'd n.r.e.). The contract and trust Deed clearly grant a lien, and both the credit report filled out by Robert Gonzales, the salesman, and the undisputed testimony of Pedro de la Fuente show that there was no lien on the appellants' home at the time of the transaction. However, even if we did not agree with this finding, it was not challenged and is binding upon the appellate court . . . . The retail installment contract signed by the de la Fuentes is in violation of the Texas Consumer Credit Code, art. 5069–6.05 in that the contract provided for a first lien on the de la Fuente's home. . . .

Appellee asserts that, even if the contract is in violation of the Credit Code, appellee is not liable because of its status as a holder in due course under TEX.BUS. & COM.CODE ANN. section 3.302 (Vernon 1968). The trial court found in its conclusions of law both that the appellee, as an assignee of the contract, is derivatively liable for all claims against the contract and that appellee is not liable to appellants on the counterclaim because of its status as a holder in due course of appellants' note. We agree that an obligor may assert against the assignee the defenses he could have asserted against the assignor. . . . However, we disagree that appellee was entitled to the protection of a holder in due course of a negotiable instrument, because (1) the holder in due course doctrine has been abolished in consumer credit transactions by FTC regulation; and, (2) the appellee did not conform to the notice requirements of the Texas Credit Code so as to cut off the rights of action and defenses of the buyer. The note in question contained a notice in bold face type which reads in part:

NOTICE

ANY HOLDER OF THIS CONSUMER CREDIT CONTRACT IS SUBJECT TO ALL CLAIMS AND DEFENSES WHICH THE DEBTOR COULD ASSERT AGAINST THE SELLER OF GOODS OR SERVICES OBTAINED PURSUANT HERETO OR WITH THE PROCEEDS HEREOF. . . .

This FTC Rule, subjecting the holder of the note to the claims and defenses of the debtor, is in direct conflict with the doctrine of the holder in due course. The Federal Courts have stated, without so holding, that the effect of this FTC Rule is to abolish the holder in due course doctrine. *Federal Trade Commission v. Winters National Bank & Trust Co.,* 601 F.2d 395, 397 (6th cir. 1979). . . .

The FTC, in its Statement of Basis and Purposes specifically named the holder in due course doctrine as the evil addressed by 16 C.F.R. section 433.2 "[A] consumer's duty to pay for goods and services must not be separated from a seller's duty to perform as promised . . . " 40 Fed. Reg. 53,506, 53,523 (November 18, 1975). The FTC intended the Rule to compel creditors to either absorb the cost of the seller's misconduct or return them to sellers. 40 F.R. at 53,523. The FTC "reach[ed] a determination that it constitutes an unfair and

deceptive practice to use contractual boiler plate to separate a buyer's duty to pay from a seller's duty to perform." 40 F.R. at 53,524. The effect of this Rule is to "give the courts the authority to examine the equities in an underlying sale, and it will prevent sellers from foreclosing judicial review of their conduct. Seller and creditors will be responsible for seller misconduct." 40 F.R. at 53,524 (emphasis added). It was clearly the intention of the FTC Rule to have the holder of the paper bear the losses occasioned by the actions of the seller; therefore, the benefits of the holder in due course doctrine under TEX.BUS. & COM.CODE ANN. SECTION 3.302 are not available when the notice required by the FTC in 16 C.F.R. section 433.2 is placed on a consumer credit contract.

In addition, the holder of a note subject to the Credit Code has an independent duty to ensure that the retail installment contract conforms to the statutory requirements of the Credit Code. Art. 5069-6.97 of the Credit Code provides in part:

No right of action or defense of a buyer arising out of a retail installment transaction which would be cut off by negotiation, shall be cut off by negotiation of the retail installment contract or retail charge agreement to any third party unless such holder acquires the contract relying in good faith upon a certificate of completion of certificate of satisfaction, if required by the provisions of Article 6.06; and *such holder gives notice of the negotiation to the buyer* as provided in this Article, and within thirty days of the mailing of such notice receives no written notice from the buyer of any facts giving rise to any claim or defense of the buyer. (Emphasis added)

See TEX.REV.CIV.STAT.ANN. art. 5069.8.01 (Vernon Supp. 1984); *Horn v. Nationwide Financial Corp.,* 574 S.W.2d 218 (Tex.Civ. App.—San Antonio 1978, writ ref'd n.r.e.) (interpreting art. 5069-7.97 (b) to impose this duty).

We find that appellee is liable under the Texas Consumer Credit Code as a "person who violates this Subtitle . . . by (ii) committing any act or practice prohibited by this Subtitle. . . ." TEX.REV. CIV.STAT.ANN. art. 5069-8.01(b) (Vernon Supp. 1984). Appellee is therefore liable to appellant under art. 5069-8.01(b) for an amount equal to twice the time price differential or interest contracted for, charged, or received but not to exceed

$4,000 in a transaction in which the amount financed is in excess of $5,000 and reasonable attorney's fees fixed by the court. Appellants' fourth point of error is sustained. . . .

Appellants, by their fifth point of error, complain of a violation of the Home Solicitation Sales Act in that the obligation was assigned within five days of its execution. The trial court found that this transaction met all the requirements of and is governed by the Home Solicitation Sales Act. TEX.REV.CIV.STAT.ANN. art. 5069–13.01 et seq. (Vernon Supp. 1984). The Home Solicitation Sales Act provides:

Violations

(a) It shall constitute a deceptive trade practice and a violation of this Act for any merchant to: . . .

(6) negotiate, transfer, sell, or assign any note or other evidence of indebtedness to a finance company or other third party prior to midnight of the fifth business day following the day the contract was signed or the goods or services were purchased; . . .

(b) Any sale or contract entered into in a home solicitation transaction in violation of this Act as set out in Subsection (a) of this section is void and unenforceable.

(c) Any merchant who violates a provision of this Act is liable to the consumer for any actual damages suffered by the consumer as a result of the violation, attorneys' fees reasonable in relation to the amount of work done, and court costs. TEX.REV.CIV.STAT.ANN. art. 5069–13.03 (Vernon Supp. 1983).

Plaintiff's original petition and plaintiff's first amended original petition both contained the following provisions:

[The Court quoted from the petition alleging facts showing violations of the Home Solicitation Sales Act] . . .

[A] violation of the Home Solicitation Sales Act was admitted on the face of appellee's petition. At no time did appellees move to amend. We find, therefore, that there was a violation of the Home Solicitation Sales Act in that the note was assigned to a third party on the same day that it was executed. The contract is void and unenforceable. TEX.REV.CIV.STAT.ANN. art. 5069–13.03(b) (Vernon Supp. 1984). Under the Home Solicitation

Sales Act, it is not necessary to find that Roberto Gonzales was an agent or employee of Aluminum Industries, Inc. in order to find that the contract is void and unenforceable by any assignee. Appellants' fifth point of error is sustained.

Appellants, by their first, second and third points of error, complain of the amount of the judgment against them.

We hold that the trial court erred in finding that appellants were in default in the amount of $5,800, the original amount of the contract, since it is undisputed that appellants made a payment of $1,142.28.

Appellants' first point of error is sustained.

Because of our disposition of the other points of error, we need not address appellant's points of error numbers two and three.

Appellee, in its brief, raises the issue of the amount of attorney's fees to be awarded appellants. The trial court found that appellants had incurred attorney's fees in the amount of $3,500. Appellees contend that attorney's fees should not be awarded because appellants did not show the hours devoted to each particular cause of action or defense. *Bray v. Curtis,* 544 S.W.2d 816 (Tex.Civ.App.—Corpus Christi 1976, writ ref'd n.r.e.). However, more recent cases have applied the rule that, where recovery is had on each cause of action or where the causes of action are so intertwined as to be more or less inseparable, the total amount of attorney's fees may be awarded, if the attorney's fees are authorized by the causes upon which recovery is had. . . .

Appellants' defense to appellee's action was the assertion of various violations of statutes. This was also the substance of their cross-claims. In their cross-claims, appellants alleged ten causes of action: . . . We hold that because recovery was had on a substantial number of appellants' causes of action and because the causes of action are more or less inseparable, all requiring proof of the same facts, that the total amount of attorney's fees can be awarded.

It is, therefore, necessary to determine if attorney's fees are awarded under the relevant statutes. The Home Solicitation Sales Act provides: "Any merchant who violates a provision of this Act is liable to the consumer for . . . attorney's fees . . ." TEX.REV.CIV.STAT.ANN. art. 5069–13.03(c) (Vernon Supp. 1984). "Merchant" is defined as "a party to a consumer transaction other than a consumer." TEX.REV.CIV.STAT.ANN. art. 5069–

13.01(4) (Vernon Supp. 1984). A party to the contract is the one who has the right to bring an action to enforce the contract. . . .

Alternatively, as a matter of policy, we would hold appellee liable for attorney's fees under the Home Solicitation Sales Act. First, the trial court, in its findings of fact, found that forms for both the retail installment contract and the contract for labor and trust deed were provided to Aluminum Industries by Home Savings Association. Second, the contract was promptly assigned to Home Savings' wholly owned subsidiary. We find that this assignment is the very evil which the statute was intended to prevent. The Home Solicitation Sales Act "was designed to protect residential occupants from high pressure door-to-door salesmen and to allow a 'cooling off' period in which a contract thus negotiated might be rescinded." . . . Assignees of home solicitation contracts must be held responsible for the acts of their assignors; otherwise, we are faced with the prospect of unscrupulous salesmen pressuring consumers into contracts, assigning the benefit of the contract for cash, and disappearing. The assignee would be able to collect without risk, when the assignor could not do so.

Both as a matter of statutory interpretation and a matter of policy, we find that appellee is responsible for reasonable attorney's fees under the Home Solicitation Sales Act.

As noted above, we also find that appellee is responsible for reasonable attorney's fees under the Consumer Credit Code, TEX.REV.CIV.STAT. ANN. art. 5069–8.01(a) and (b) (Vernon Supp. 1984).

Appellee raises by cross point that the trial court erred in not finding that appellee was a member of a Federal Home Loan Bank and, as such, that it may avail itself of the protections given by 15 U.S.C.A. section 57a (f)(3). Appellee did not point out what these protections might be, and upon examination of the cited statutory provision, we cannot ascertain what they are.

Appellee's cross point is overruled.

We REVERSE the judgment of the trial court and RENDER judgment that appellee take nothing and that the contract, the subject of this suit, is null and void and that appellants recover against appellee, Home Savings, in the amount of $4,000 plus attorney's fees of $3,500 as found by the trial court. Costs are adjudged against appellee.

NOTE

1. The FTC Rule limits recovery by the debtor to the "amounts paid" on the item, while U.C.C.C. Sections 3.404 (2) and 3.405(2) limit recovery "to the extent of the amount owing to the assignee [lender] . . . at the time the assignee [lender] has notice of the claim or defense." Although the better view is that a debtor can sue as well as defend, a debtor cannot recover triple damages from an assignee where such are provided in a state consumer protection legislation. *See Home Sav. Assoc. v. Guerra,* 720 S.W.2d 636 (Tex. 1986). Such damages, being a civil penalty, are recoverable only from the supplier of goods and services, or from the lender participating openly in the extension of credit for such consumer transaction or deemed to be a participant in a "body dragging" situation. *See* U.C.C. § 3.405(1). Note also that attorney's fees are recoverable under state statutes but not under the FTC Rule.

2. FTC Rule 433 does not declare that issuance of an instrument not bearing the required legend "nullifies the obligation of the obligor." It merely provides that such failure is a violation of Section 5 of the Federal Trade Commission Act, under which the FTC can seek redress in a civil suit to compensate the consumer. 15 U.S.C. § 57b(a)(1). The FTC Rule indicates that compliance with its provision is notice of a defense entitling the issuer/consumer to recover damages limited to the amount already paid. Thus, what would be the effect if an instrument that does not bear the required legend is being negotiated to a holder in due course? It would appear that U.C.C. Section 3–305(a)(1)(ii) does not apply to give the maker or drawer a defense.

3. State consumer protection statutes vary. The Texas statutes discussed in *De La*

Fuente v. Home Savings Ass'n 669 S.W. 2d 137 (Tex. Ct. App. 1984) illustrate the various approaches taken by State Retail Sales Installment Acts. The Texas Consumer Credit Code though requiring notice to the maker does not indicate that the instrument would be void. The fact that civil penalties can be imposed for a violation of the statute is not enough to destroy the existence of a negotiable instrument. The Texas Home Solicitation Sales Act specifically provides that a violation of the statute makes "the contract . . . void and unenforceable." Although we have here an avoidance of an obligation underlying the issuance of a negotiable instrument, this would have no effect on the rights of a holder in due course. None of these provisions make the instrument void or declare the underlying transaction to be an illegal one. U.C.C. § 3–305(a)(1)(ii). But the Uniform Consumer Credit Code (U.C.C.C.) Section 3.404 provides that an assignee of a consumer credit sales or of a consumer lease, though qualifying as a holder in due course of a negotiable instrument issued in violation of U.C.C.C. Section 3.307, could be met with the claims and defenses the issuer of the instrument has against the seller or lessor.

4. Close Relationship Doctrine

Courts have used the close relationship doctrine to protect consumers from the predatory activities of sellers and lenders and thereby to prevent a finance company claiming to be a holder in due course. See *Unico v. Owen,* 50 N.J. 101, 232 A.2d 405 (1967). This doctrine is not confined to consumer transactions and has support in commercial relationships as well. It is not generally accepted, however. *See, e.g., Slaughter v. Jefferson Federal Savings & Loan Ass'n,* 538 F.2d 397 (D.C. Cir. 1977) ("in other words, if the lenders are to be charged with notice and bad faith that charge must rest, not upon any intimate connection or relationship between the lenders and Monarch, but upon other specific facts known to them").

Commercial Credit Corp. v. Orange County Machine Works
34 Cal. 2d 776, 214 P.2d 819 (1950)

[Extracted from *Unico v. Owen,* 50 N.J. 101, 232 A.2d 405, 413–414 (1967)]
. . . Machine Works was in the market for a press. Ermac Company knew of one which could be purchased from General American Precooling Corporation for $5,000, and offered to sell it to Machine Works for $5,500. Commercial Credit was consulted by Ermac, and agreed to finance the transaction by taking an assignment of the contract of sale between Ermac and Machine Works. For a substantial period before this time, Ermac had obtained similar financing from Commercial Credit and had some blank forms supplied to it by the latter. By a contract written on one of these forms, which was entitled "Industrial Conditional Sales Contract," Ermac agreed to sell and Machine Works bound itself to purchase the press.

The terms of the contract were very much like those in the case now before us. The purchase price was to be paid in 12 equal monthly installments, "evidenced by my note of even date to your order." As to the note, the contract said:

> Said note is a negotiable instrument, separate and apart from this contract, even though at the time of execution it may be temporarily attached hereto by perforation or otherwise.

It provided also, as in our case:

> This contract may be assigned and/or said note may be negotiated without notice to me and when assigned and/or negotiated shall be free

from any defense, counterclaim or cross complaint by me.

The note originally was the latter part of the printed form of contract, but could be detached from it at a dotted or perforated line.

Machine Works made the required down payment to Ermac, which in turn under its contract with Commercial assigned the contract and endorsed the note to the latter. Commercial then gave its check to Ermac for $4,261. Ermac sent its check to Precooling Corporation, which refused to deliver the press to Machine Works when the check was dishonored. Commercial sued Machine Works as a holder in due course of its note to Ermac. Machine Works contended Commercial was not entitled to the status of such a holder because the sales contract and attached note should be construed as constituting a single document. Machine Works contended also that the finance company was a party to the original transaction rather than a subsequent purchaser, that it took subject to all equities and defenses existing in its favor against Ermac, and that the claimed negotiability of the note was destroyed when it and the conditional sales agreement were transferred together as one instrument.

The Supreme Court of California said the fact that the contract and note were physically attached at the time of transfer to Commercial would not alone defeat negotiability. But the court pointed out that Commercial advanced money to Ermac (with which it had dealt previously and whose "credit had been checked and financial integrity demonstrated"), with the understanding that the agreement and note would be assigned and endorsed to it immediately; and that "[i]n a very real sense, the finance company was a moving force in the transaction from its very inception, and acted as a party to it." In deciding against Commercial, the court said:

> When a finance company actively participates in a transaction of this type from its inception, counseling and aiding the future vendor-payee, it cannot be regarded as a holder in due course of the note given in the transaction and the defense of failure of consideration may properly be maintained. Machine Works never obtained the press for which it bargained and, as against Commercial, there is no more obligation upon it to pay the note than there is to pay the installments specified in the contract. . . .[10]

[10] 214 P.2d 819, 822 (Cal. 1950). *See also* Kaw Valley State Bank & Trust Co. v. Riddle, 219 Kan. 550, 549 P.2d 927 (1976).

NOTE

An examination of the cases accepting the "close relationship doctrine" shows that courts have not been precise in stating whether they applied this approach to show an absence of good faith, the presence of notice, or simply oneness of the parties. As a result, most cases that have rejected this approach have done so on the basis that a close relationship is not evidence of a lack of good faith. *See Bankers Trust Co. v. Crawford*, 781 F.2d 39, 43 (3d Cir. 1986). Other courts have restricted its application to consumer credit transactions where the claimant to holder in due course status exercised control by (i) insisting on the use of documents drafted by the claimant; (ii) approval of the lender's procedures; and (iii) an independent determination by the claimant of the debtor's ability to pay. The policy of the courts in consumer transactions was iterated in *Mutual Fin. Co. v. Martin,* 63 So.2d 649 at 653 (Fla. 1953).

> We think the buyer—Mr. and Mrs. General Public—should have some protection somewhere along the line. We believe the finance company is better able to bear the risk of the dealer's insolvency than the buyer and in a far better position to protect his interests against unscrupulous and insolvent dealers.

To avoid being subject to the restrictions imposed by various state legislatures and by courts applying the close relationship doctrine, retailers and finance companies entered into informal arrangements whereby the potential customer would be referred to a finance company to raise a loan with which to pay for the consumer item. This approach, known as "body dragging", enabled the seller to get instant cash, i.e. the seller would take the proceeds of the loan and would then not have to discount an instrument with a finance company. The lender finance company, in turn, would claim that not having sold goods to the consumer it is not liable for any breach relating to the performance of the contract. Both, the Uniform Consumer Credit Code and the Federal Trade Commission Rule, attempt to deal with this issue. While the FTC Rule[12] merely indicates that a purchase money loan arises from a referral to the lender and also can be spelled out from an affiliation "by common control, contract, or business arrangement," i.e., "[any] understanding, procedure, course of dealing, or arrangement, formal or informal, between a creditor and a seller, in connection with the sale of goods or services to consumers or the financing thereof," the U.C.C.C. gives specific instances which help to flesh out the generalities in the FTC Rule.

Section 3.405 [Lender Subject to Claims and Defenses Arising From Sales and Leases]

(1) A lender, except the issuer of a lender credit card, who, with respect to a particular transaction, makes a consumer loan to enable a consumer to buy or lease from a particular seller or lessor property or services [, except primarily for an agricultural purpose,] is subject to all claims and defenses of the consumer against the seller or lessor arising from that sale or lease of the property or services if:

(a) the lender knows that the seller or lessor arranged for the extension of credit by the lender for a commission, brokerage, or referral fee;

(b) the lender is a person related to the seller or lessor, unless the relationship is remote or is not a factor in the transaction;

(c) the seller or lessor guarantees the loan or otherwise assumes the risk of loss by the lender upon the loan;

(d) the lender directly supplies the seller or lessor with the contract document used by the consumer to evidence the loan, and the seller or lessor has knowledge of the credit terms and participates in preparation of the document;

(e) the loan is conditioned upon the consumer's purchase or lease of the property or services from the particular seller or lessor, but the lender's payment of proceeds of the loan to the seller or lessor does not in itself establish that the loan was so conditioned; or

(f) the lender, before he makes the consumer loan, has knowledge or, from his course of dealing with the particular seller or lessor or his records, notice of substantial complaints by other buyers or lessees of the particular seller's or lessor's failure or refusal to perform his contracts with them and of the particular seller's or lessor's failure to remedy his defaults within a reasonable time after notice to him of the complaints.

(2) A claim or defense of a consumer specified in subsection (1) may be asserted against the lender under this section only if the consumer has made a good faith attempt

---

[12] 16 C.F.R. §§ 433.1(d), (g).

to obtain satisfaction from the seller or lessor with respect to the claim or defense and then only to the extent of the amount owing to the lender with respect to the sale or lease of the property or services as to which the claim or defense arose at the time the lender has notice of the claim or defense. Notice of the claim or defense may be given before the attempt specified in this subsection. Oral notice is effective unless the lender requests written confirmation when or promptly after oral notice is given and the consumer fails to give the lender written confirmation within the period of time, not less than 14 days, stated to the consumer when written confirmation is requested.

* * *

(4) An agreement may not limit or waive the claims or defenses of a consumer under this section.

* * *

The close relationship doctrine is equally applicable, however, to commercial transactions, where it would be more difficult to establish bad faith or an overreaching to the level of unconscionability. *Cf. Unico v. Owen,* 50 N.J. 101, 232 A.2d 405 (1967). The provisions of Federal Trade Commission Rule 433[13] have lessened the need of the application of this doctrine to consumer transactions. Its continuation as evidence of constructive notice, however, is undiminished. *See St. James v. Diversified Commercial Finance Corp.,* 714 P.2d 179 (Nev. 1986), an action involving recovery based on a commercial loan. "We can discern no reason to limit the doctrine to consumer transactions; we therefore adopt the close connection doctrine with respect to all transactions where the buyer can demonstrate a close connection between the seller and the lender." (*Id.* at 181).

* * *

5. Fiduciary Relationship

To prevent a holder claiming to be a holder in due course U.C.C. Section 3-307(b) requires "knowledge" of the fiduciary status, U.C.C. § 1-201(25), before notice can arise that a fiduciary has acted in breach of his duty. This approach reflects the requirements of the Uniform Fiduciary Act (UFA) Sections 4 and 6, which indicate that there is no duty to investigate whether a breach of fiduciary duty has occurred. As a result, absent bad faith, the existence of certain factors (such as that the fiduciary is the payee or an endorsee, or is the drawer or an endorser) does not of itself convey knowledge of a breach of fiduciary duty. *See Hartford Accident & Indemnity Co. v. American Express Co.,* 74 N.Y.2d 153, 544 N.Y.S.2d 573, 542 N.E.2d 1090 (1989). Some examples to clarify when notice of a lack of authority in a fiduciary will be imputed to a person taking an instrument from a fiduciary are set forth in U.C.C. § 3-307.

§ 3-307. NOTICE OF BREACH OF FIDUCIARY DUTY.

(a) In this section:

(1) "Fiduciary" means an agent, trustee, partner, corporate officer or director, or other representative owing a fiduciary duty with respect to an instrument.

---

[13] 16 C.F.R. §§ 433.1, *et seq.*

(2) "Represented person" means the principal beneficiary, partnership, corporation, or other person to whom the duty stated in paragraph (1) is owed.

(b) If (i) an instrument is taken from a fiduciary for payment or collection or for value, (ii) the taker has knowledge of the fiduciary status of the fiduciary, and (iii) the represented person makes a claim to the instrument or its proceeds on the basis that the transaction of the fiduciary is a breach of fiduciary duty, the following rules apply:

(1) Notice of breach of fiduciary duty by the fiduciary is notice of the claim of the represented person.

(2) In the case of an instrument payable to the represented person or the fiduciary as such, the taker has notice of the breach of fiduciary duty if the instrument is (i) taken in payment of or as security for a debt known by the taker to be the personal debt of the fiduciary, (ii) taken in a transaction known by the taker to be for the personal benefit of the fiduciary, or (iii) deposited to an account other than an account of the fiduciary, as such, or an account of the represented person.

(3) If an instrument is issued by the represented person or the fiduciary as such, and made payable to the fiduciary personally, the taker does not have notice of the breach of fiduciary duty unless the taker knows of the breach of fiduciary duty.

(4) If the instrument is issued by the represented person or the fiduciary as such, to the taker as payee, the taker has notice of the breach of fiduciary if the instrument is (i) taken in payment of or as security for a debt known by the taker to be the personal debt of the fiduciary, (ii) taken in a transaction known by the taker to be for the personal benefit of the fiduciary, or (iii) deposited to an account other than an account of the fiduciary, as such or an account of the represented person.

Smith v. Olympic Bank
103 Wash. 2d 418, 693 P.2d 92 (1985)*

DORE, J. We hold that, where a bank allows a check that is made payable to a guardian to be deposited in a guardian's personal account instead of a guardianship account, the bank is not a holder in due course under the Uniform Commercial Code because it has notice that the guardian is breaching his fiduciary duty.

FACTS

Charles Alcombrack was appointed guardian for his son Chad Stephen Alcombrack who was then 7 years old and the beneficiary of his grandfather's life insurance policy. The insurance company issued a check for $30,588.39 made payable to "Charles Alcombrack, Guardian of the Estate

of Chad Stephen Alcombrack a Minor." The attorney for the son's estate directed the father to take the check, along with the letters of guardianship issued to the father, to the bank and open up a guardianship savings and checking account. The father, however, did not follow the attorney's instructions. Instead, he took the check, without the letters of guardianship, to the bank and opened a personal checking and a personal savings account. The following was printed on the back of the check:

"By endorsement of this check the payee acknowledges receipt of the amount thereof in full settlement of all claims resulting from the death of Roy Alcombrack, certificate holder under Group Life Policy No. 9,745,632.

"/s/ Charles Alcombrack
Guardian of the Estate of Chad Stephen Alcombrack, a minor"

---

* [Editor: citations in [ ] refer to Revised U.C.C. Articles 3 and 4.]

. . . Despite the above written notice that the check was payable to the father in his guardianship capacity, the bank allowed the father to place the entire amount in newly opened personal accounts. On the same day that the father opened his accounts, the attorney for the guardian called a trust officer from Olympic Bank and inquired as to the fees the bank charged for maintaining guardianship accounts. Responding to the attorney's questions, the trust officer wrote the attorney, specifically mentioning the "Estate of Chad Alcombrack."[1] . . .

The father, and later his new wife,[2] used all but $320.60 of the trust money for their own personal benefit. Bank records disclosed how the estate money was withdrawn: five withdrawals were made to cash or into the father's checking account (total—approximately $16,000); one withdrawal paid off an unsecured personal loan made by the bank to the father (approximately $3,000); seven debits to the account were made by the bank exercising its right of offset to make payments on or pay off personal loans by the bank to the father (total—approximately $12,500).

After the depletion of the son's estate, J. David Smith was appointed successor guardian. He received a judgment against the father and instituted this suit against the bank. The trial court granted summary judgment in favor of the bank.

---

[1] The following is the letter sent by the trust officer to the guardian's attorney:

"October 30, 1975

"Mr. Charles A. Schaaf, Attorney
"Suite 707, Hoge Building
"Seattle, Washington 98104

"Reference: Estate of Chad Alcombrack

"Dear Mr. Schaaf:
"This is a follow up to our telephone conversation of October 28, 1975. The information you requested on the performance of our common trust funds will be available in about four weeks. October 31st is the end of our fiscal year. If this is not too long for you to wait, please let me know and I will send you a copy of our annual report.

"Our fee for handling a Guardianship account is, eight tenths (8/10) of one percent (1%), minimum of $350.00 per year."

[2] The father remarried and his new wife was authorized to write checks against the checking account. She wrote a total of 79 percent of the checks drawn on the account.

The Court of Appeals reversed and remanded, holding that the trial court should determine the factual issue whether the bank was a holder in due course.

ARGUMENT

Olympic Bank claims that it is a holder in due course (HIDC) and, as such, is not subject to the claims of the petitioner.[*] In order to qualify as a HIDC, the bank must meet five requirements. It must be (1) a holder (2) of a negotiable instrument, (3) that took the instrument for value (4) in good faith and (5) without notice that it was overdue, dishonored, or of any defense or claim to it on the part of any person. RCW 62A.3-302(1)(a)-(c) [§ 3-302(a)(1)(2)]. See also J. White & R. Summers, Uniform Commercial Code § 14-2 (2d ed. 1980). We need not decide whether the bank met the first four conditions as we hold that the bank took the check with notice of an adverse claim to the instrument and, therefore, is not a holder in due course. Consequently, the bank is liable to the petitioner.[4]

A purchaser has notice of an adverse claim when "he has knowledge that a fiduciary has negotiated the instrument in payment of or as security for his own debt or in any transaction for his own benefit or otherwise in breach of duty." RCW 62A.3-304(2) [§ 3-307(b)(2)]. Thus, the issue raised by this case is whether the bank had knowledge that the guardian was breaching his fiduciary duty when it allowed him to deposit a check, made payable to him in his guardianship capacity, into his personal accounts. As to this issue, *Von Gohren v. Pacific Nat'l Bank,* 8 Wn. App. 245, 505 P.2d 467 [12 U.C.C. Rep. 133] (1973) is persuasive and controlling. In *Von Gohren,* it was held that a bank had notice that an employee was breaching her fiduciary duty when it allowed her to deposit third-party checks payable to her employer in her personal account. The bank was put on notice despite the fact that the employer had authorized the employee to draw checks against his account and also to endorse checks made payable to him and deposit such

---

[*] [Editor: U.C.C. §§ 3-305(a)(1), 3-306 set forth the rights of a holder in due course].

[4] RCW 62A.3-306 [§§ 3-305(a), 3-306] sets forth the liabilities of one who accepts a check and who is not a holder in due course. . . .

checks into his account. The court held that notice need not always consist of actual knowledge of a breach of a fiduciary duty, but can be predicated upon reasonable commercial standards. The court concluded by stating:

> "It is our view that since defendant had notice of the claim by virtue of RCW 62A.3-304(2) [§ 3-307(b)], and since it is undisputed that defendant did nothing to investigate Mrs. Martin's authority to negotiate checks payable to her employer, we must hold as a matter of law it did not act in accordance with reasonable commercial standards."

Von Gohren, at 255. The same conclusion is mandated in the present case.

Here, the bank knew it was dealing with guardianship funds. The check was payable to the father as guardian and not to him personally. The father endorsed it in his guardianship capacity. The bank received a call from the guardian's attorney inquiring about the fee the bank charged for guardianship accounts, and a trust officer for the bank replied in a letter referring to the "Estate of Chad Alcombrack."

Reasonable commercial practices dictate that when the bank knew that the funds were deposited in a personal account instead of a guardianship account, it also knew that the father was breaching his fiduciary duty. The funds lost the protection they would have received in a guardianship account when they were placed in a personal account. If the funds had been placed in a guardianship account, the bank would not have been allowed to exercise its set-off rights which amounted to approximately $12,500. *Pitzen v. Doubleday,* 5 Wn. 2d 370, 105 P.2d 726 (1940). Nor would it have been permitted to accept a check, drawn on the guardianship account, from the father in satisfaction of the father's unsecured personal loan in the amount of approximately $3,000. *Canyon Lake Bank v. New Braunfels Utils.,* 638 S.W.2d 944 (Tex.Ct.App. 1982). Nor could the father, or bank, have authorized his new wife to write checks against the guardianship account without court approval. See RCW 11.88.010; *In re Gaddis,* 12 Wn. 2d 114, 120 P.2d 849 (1942). A fiduciary has a duty to ensure that trust funds are protected.... Here, the father breached his duty.

While this is the first time, under the Uniform Commercial Code, that we have held a bank liable for allowing a guardian to deposit trust funds in a personal account, we have held a bank liable in a pre-Code case for allowing a trustee to breach his fiduciary duty. *Rensselaer Valve Co. v. National Bank of Commerce,* 129 Wash. 253, 224 P. 673 (1924). In addition, other jurisdictions have held banks liable under similar circumstances using the Code,... and without using the Code,... The policy reasons for holding a bank liable are compelling—especially in the situation presented in this case. The ward has no control of his own estate. He must rely on his guardian and on the bank for the safekeeping of his money. In order to protect the ward, the guardian and bank must be held to a high standard of care. For the guardian, this means that he must deposit guardian funds in a guardianship account. For the bank, it means that when it receives a check made payable to an individual as a guardian, it must make sure that the check is placed in a guardianship account. This will not place an undue burden on either banks or guardians and will have the beneficial effect of protecting the ward.

NOTE

U.C.C. Section 3-307 resolves a conflict that existed between courts taking the approach adopted in *Smith v. Olympic Bank, supra,* that a depository bank taking a check payable to a fiduciary, who is so described in the instrument, would be liable when the proceeds are credited to the fiduciary's personal account, and those following *In The Matter of Knox,* 64 N.Y.2d 434, 488 N.Y.S.2d 146, 477 N.E.2d 448 (1985), and *Scoloff v. Dollahite,* 779 S.W.2d 57 (Tenn. App. 1989), requiring "knowledge" that the fiduciary intended to divert the proceeds to his personal use, before the bank would be held liable. In *Scoloff* two promissory notes had been made payable to Paneling and Home Center, Inc. of which Dollahite was the president. These notes were negotiated to Community National Bank to secure a personal loan of the president. Yet, the court sought the existence of *actual* knowledge that the fiduciary was committing a breach of his obligation.   Note further, Benfield and Alces, *Bank Liability for Fiduciary Fraud,* 42 Ala. L. Rev. 475 (1991).

6. Good Faith and Notice

In analyzing the facts to determine whether the status of holder in due course had been attained by the claimant, a distinction must be made between "good faith" and notice of facts that may prevent such status. New York used to require "knowledge" rather than "notice." *Chemical Bank of Rochester v. Haskell,* 51 N.Y.2d 85, 432 N.Y.S.2d 478, 411 N.E.2d 1339 (1980). Notice of facts may be indicative of the absence of subjective "good faith." This is further emphasized by U.C.C. Section 3-103(a)(4) calling for "observance of reasonable commercial standards of fair dealing." In recent years New York and New Jersey have developed a concept of "commercial bad faith" outside the Uniform Commercial Code. This concept is based on reckless and wanton bank conduct which amounts to more than just a lapse of "wary vigilance" or a failure to investigate where there are "suspicious circumstances which might well have induced a prudent banker to investigate."

E.   Defenses to a Holder in Due Course

As we have noted, once the status of holder in due course has been attained, notice of any defense received subsequently will not affect a change of that status. The only effect of such notice is linked to a subsequent reacquisition of the instrument. U.C.C. § 3-203(b). Thus, a holder in due course takes the instrument (i) free from proprietory or possessory claims to the instrument or its proceeds, including a claim to rescind the negotiation and recover the instrument. U.C.C. §§ 3-302(b), 3-306, 3-305,[13] and (ii) free from defenses that relate to the obligation that gave rise to the issuance of the instrument. U.C.C. § 3-305(a)(2). Defenses that can be successful against a holder in due course are those that destroy the existence of the instrument and, therefore, are often referred to as "real defenses." As a result, lack of legal capacity is a defense to the extent that state law would hold the activities of a person lacking capacity to be a nullity. Thus, infancy is only a defense to the extent it would defeat liability under a simple contract. For example, an instrument that is not issued to acquire necessaries by the infant could be denied by the infant. U.C.C. § 3-305(a)(1)(i). In all other cases where a lack of capacity is asserted, the general law must nullify the capacity for the lack of capacity to be a defense against a holder in due course. U.C.C. § 3-305(a)(1)(ii).[14] Duress and illegality which under state law render the obligation of a party a nullity are clearly "real" defenses, as would be the defense of *non est factum—* "this is not my act,"[15] or discharge of the obligor from bankruptcy. U.C.C. § 3-305.

---

[13] See Miller v. Race, 1 Burr. 452, 97 Eng. Rep. 398 (K.B. 1758).

[14] Page v. Krekey, 137 N.Y. 303, 33 N.E. 311 (1893) (Page, an intoxicated illiterate was induced to sign a guarantee on a representation it was an application for a license). First Nat'l Bank v. Fazzari, 10 N.Y.2d 394, 223 N.Y.S.2d 483, 179 N.E.2d 493 (1961) (negligence of maker-drawer of check prevented raising of defense).

[15] U.C.C. § 3-305(a)(1)(iii).

1. Illegality

The illegality must relate to the issuance of the instrument, such as an issuance of an instrument in payment of a gambling debt or an issuance in payment for some meretricious service. The fact that legal gambling may be licensed will not enable a gambling debt to be recovered in a court of law. Recovery from a casino in Nevada may require recourse to the Nevada Gaming Control Board and not to a State court. The illegality can arise in connection with the purchase of gaming chips by means of a check or through an Automatic Teller Machine set up in a licensed gambling casino. [*See, Sandler v. Eighth Judicial District Court,* 96 Nev. 622, 614 P.2d 10 (1980).][16] However, an instrument issued in payment for a legitimate debt and then endorsed by the payee to settle a gambling debt or in return for an illegal activity can be enforced by a subsequent holder in due course. For example, where an employee endorses a paycheck to cover a gambling debt, and the check is then negotiated to a holder in due course, this check could be enforced by the holder in due course against both the issuer of the check and against the endorser on his endorsement contract. Although the endorser may be able to rescind the negotiation, U.C.C. § 3-202(b), this power is lost once the check has been acquired by a holder in due course or has been paid by a payor bank without knowledge of facts that are the basis for rescission or other remedy. *See also* U.C.C. § 3-306.

Where the illegality is based on usury laws, courts are not in agreement on whether to hold the instrument void or whether to enforce the instrument without the illegal interest being recoverable. Where the rate of interest is stated *separately,* courts have often simply

---

[16] I am indebted to a student for the following item from the National Law Journal, Sept. 23, 1991:

Boston — Richard Kommit of nearby Brookline has played a hunch and won.

After borrowing $8,000 on his credit card at a gaming casino in Atlantic City in 1987, Mr. Kommit argued through his attorney that the debt could not be collected because under the laws of Massachusetts and Connecticut a gambling debt is unenforceable. The Appeals Court for the commonwealth of Massachusetts agreed, ruling on Sept. 10 that "a contract to pay money knowingly lent for gambling is void." Connecticut National Bank of Hartford v. Kommit, 98-P1116.

To beat Mr. Kommit, the lender, Connecticut National Bank, would have had to convince the court that it expected the money to be used for non-gambling purposes, according to Mr. Kommit's Boston attorney, Neal M. Brown.

But the bank threw snake eyes.

The bank had to know how the loan would be used, said Mr. Brown, because the transaction was made through an automated teller machine located smack in the heart of a casino gambling pit. Moreover, the ATM dispensed only paper chips, not cash, which then had to be traded for gambling chips at a nearby cashier's window.

"The bank admitted that's what the money would be used for when it [had previously] sought summary judgment in Superior Court," Mr. Brown said. "I argued that that violated public policy: Gambling debts are against the law. Those statutes are to prevent illegal loan-sharking and related activities."

Massachusetts is hardly alone in this view, Mr. Brown said. Laws in most states, except Nevada and New Jersey, stack the deck against gambling debts, calling them uncollectable.

Mr. Brown said his client had paid about $2,500 of his debt, but was sued "when he could not pay back" the remaining $5,500.

Mr. Kommit did not, however, win on his first throw of the judicial dice. Connecticut National won at both the state district court and superior court levels.

Mr. Brown said he expects the bank to appeal.

©The New York Law Publishing Company.

deleted the indicated usurious interest rate and enforced the note without the interest provision, "the blue pencil approach."[17] The more difficult situation arises where the instrument has a final figure indicating the sum due without showing that some of this sum includes an interest charge. It is here that the question arises, should such an instrument not be treated as void *ab initio*?

2. Duress

What motivates the courts in their approach to the allegation of a defense against a holder in due course is how to preserve the free flow of instruments while giving effect to statutory provisions and other expressions of public policy. This is shown by the expanded approach to the defense of duress. Originally confined to duress experienced by the maker or drawer of an instrument, common law now extends this defense to duress exerted on members of the family of the maker or drawer. Duress includes not only physical duress but has also been held to include economic duress.[18]

3. Fraud

The most common defense raised is that the instrument was issued as a result of a "fraud that induced the obligor to sign the instrument with neither knowledge nor reasonable opportunity to learn of its character *or its essential terms*" (emphasis supplied) (U.C.C. § 3-305(a)(1)(iii)). This defense is very close to a claim that a misrepresentation) induced the maker or drawer to issue the instrument, which would be merely a fraud in the inducement, i.e. a personal defense not available against a holder in due course. U.C.C. § 3-305(a)(2). This "real" defense available against a holder in due course, however, requires that there be excusable ignorance of the contents of the writing.

---

[17] *See* Finance America Corp. v. Moyler, 494 A.2d 926 (D.C. 1985).

[18] Day v. Ray E. Friedman & Co., 395 So. 2d 54 (Ala. 1981).

Burchett v. Allied Concord Financial Corp.
74 N.M. 575, 396 P.2d 186 (1964)*

CARMODY, JUSTICE. Plaintiffs-appellees filed separate complaints to have certain notes and mortgages held by defendant-appellant cancelled and declared void. The cases were consolidated below and on this appeal, which is from the judgments voiding the instruments.

The facts, except for one small detail, are the same. It seems that a man named Kelly repre-

---

* [Editor: citations in [ ] refer to Revised U.C.C. Articles 3 and 4.]

sented himself as selling Kaiser aluminum siding for a firm named Consolidated Products of Roswell. None of the parties knew Kelly nor had they seen him before. In each case, Kelly talked to the husband and wife (appellees) at their homes, offering to install aluminum siding on each of their houses for a certain price in exchange for the appellees' allowing their houses to be used for advertising purposes as a "show house," in order to further other sales of aluminum siding. Kelly told both of the families that they would receive a $100 credit on each aluminum siding contract sold in a specific area in Clovis, and that this credit would be applied toward the contract debt, being the cost of the installation of the siding on the appellees' houses. The appellees were assured, or at least understood, that by this method they would receive the improvements for nothing.

Following the explanation by Kelly, both families agreed to the offer and were given a form of a printed contract to read. While they were reading the contract, Kelly was filling out blanks in other forms. After the appellees had read the form of the contract submitted to them, they signed, *without reading,* the form or forms filled out by Kelly, assuming them to be the same as that which they had read and further assuming that what they signed provided for the credits which Kelly assured them they would receive. Needless to say, what appellees signed were notes and mortgages on the properties to cover the cost of the aluminum siding, and contracts containing no mention of credits for advertising or other sales.

One additional fact occurred in the case of the appellees Beevers. A few days after the original signing, Kelly again approached Mr. Beevers at his home and told him that the television and newspaper authorization that he had previously executed had been destroyed and he needed another one. Mr. Beevers, again without reading what was submitted, signed the additional form. Kelly then went to Mrs. Beevers' place of employment and she also signed the same without any examination, in view of Kelly's representations and her observation that her husband had already signed the form. The instrument was the promissory note.

Within a matter of days after the contracts were signed, the aluminum siding was installed, although in neither case was the job completed to the satisfaction of appellees. Sometime later, the appellees received letters from appellant, informing them that appellant had purchased the notes and mortgages which had been issued in favor of Consolidated Products and that appellees were delinquent in their first payment. Upon the receipt of these notices, appellees discovered that mortgages had been recorded against their property and they immediately instituted these proceedings.

Suit was actually brought not only against the appellant but also against James T. Pirtle, doing business under the name of Consolidated Prod-

ucts, Shirley McVay, a notary public in Roswell, and Kelly. No service was obtained upon Kelly, and the other parties to the proceedings below did not appeal because the judgment merely voided the notes and mortgages.

In both cases, the trial court found that the notes and mortgages, although signed by the appellees, were fraudulently procured. The court also found that the appellant paid a valuable consideration for the notes and mortgages, although at a discount, and concluded as a matter of law that the appellant was a holder in due course. The findings in both of the cases are substantially the same, with the exception that the court found in the Burchett case that the Burchetts were not guilty of negligence in failing to discover the true character of the instruments signed by them. There is no comparable finding in the Beevers case.

It is of passing interest to note that there was a definite conflict in the testimony, particularly with reference to the Burchetts, as to what, if any, of the instruments were actually signed by the Burchetts. However, at the appellees' request, the documents were submitted to an expert who determined that the signatures of all parties were genuine, and the trial court accepted the expert's determination.

The trial court's decisions are grounded upon two propositions (1) that the acknowledgments on the mortgages were nullities and therefore that the mortgages were not subject to record, and (2) that fraud in their inception rendered the notes and mortgages void for all purposes.

The theory relating to the first of the above reasons would seem to be that inasmuch as the acknowledgements were invalid the instruments were not entitled to be recorded and therefore appellant, which would not have purchased the unrecorded mortgages, is in no better position than the original mortgagee. However, these conclusions by the trial court are really of no consequence, in view of its conclusion that the appellant was a holder in due course. Actually, because of the trial court's determination that appellant was a holder in due course, it makes no difference whether the instruments were entitled to record or not; thus we do not deem it necessary for decision to consider the effect of the void acknowledgments. The only real question in the case is whether, under these facts, appellees, by substantial evidence, satisfied the provisions of the statute relating to their claimed defense as against a holder in due course.

In 1961 our legislature adopted, with some variations, the Uniform Commercial Code. The provision of the code applicable to this case is § 3-305, [§ 3-305(a)(1)(iii)] which, so far as material, is as follows: . . . [the court read U.C.C. § 3-305]

Although fully realizing that the official comments appearing as part of the Uniform Commercial Code are not direct authority for the construction to be placed upon a section of the code, nevertheless they are persuasive and represent the opinion of the National Conference of Commissioners on Uniform State Laws and the American Law Institute. The purpose of the comments is to explain the provisions of the code itself, in an effort to promote uniformity of interpretation. We believe that the official comments following § 3-305(2)(c) comment 7, provide an excellent guideline for the disposition of the case before us. We quote the same in full: . . .

7. Paragraph (c) of subsection (2) is new. It follows the great majority of the decisions under the original Act in recognizing the defense of 'real' or 'essential' fraud, sometimes called fraud in the essence or fraud in the factum, as effective against a holder in due course. The common illustration is that of the maker who is tricked into signing a note in the belief that it is merely a receipt or some other document. The theory of the defense is that his signature on the instrument is ineffective because he did not intend to sign such an instrument at all. Under this provision the defense extends to an instrument signed with knowledge that it is a negotiable instrument but without knowledge of its essential terms.

The test of the defense here stated is that of excusable ignorance of the contents of the writing signed. The party must not only have been in ignorance, but must also have had no reasonable opportunity to obtain knowledge. In determining what is a reasonable opportunity all relevant factors are to be taken into account, including the age and sex of the party, his intelligence, education and business experience; his ability to read or to understand English, the representations made to him and his reason to rely on them or to have confidence in the person making them; the presence or

absence of any third person who might read or explain the instrument to him, or any other possibility of obtaining independent information; and the apparent necessity, or lack of it, for acting without delay.

Unless the misrepresentation meets this test, the defense is cut off by a holder in due course.*

We observe that the inclusion of subsection (2)(c) in § 3-305 of the Uniform Commercial Code [§ 3-305(a)(1)(iii)] was an attempt to codify or make definite the rulings of many jurisdictions on the question as to the liability to a holder in due course of a party who either had knowledge, or a reasonable opportunity to obtain the knowledge, of the essential terms of the instrument, before signing. Many courts were in the past called upon to determine this question under the Uniform Negotiable Instruments Law. Almost all of the courts that were called upon to rule on this question required a showing of freedom from negligence, in order to constitute a good defense against a bona fide holder of negotiable paper.

* * *

We believe that the test set out in Comment No. 7 above quoted is a proper one and should be adhered to by us. (By giving approval to this Comment, we do not in any sense mean to imply that we thereby are expressing general approval of all the Comments to the various sections of the Uniform Commercial Code.) Thus the only question is whether, under the facts of this case, the misrepresentations were such as to be a defense as against a holder in due course.

The facts and circumstances surrounding each particular case, both under the Negotiable Instruments Law and the Uniform Commercial Code, require an independent determination. . . .

Applying the elements of the test to the case before us, Mrs. Burchett was 47 years old and had a ninth grade education, and Mr. Burchett was approximately the same age, but his education does not appear. Mr. Burchett was foreman of the sanitation department of the city of Clovis and testified that he was familiar with some legal documents. Both the Burchetts understood English and there was no showing that they lacked ability to read. Both were able to understand the original

---

* [Editor: Official Comment 1 to U.C.C. § 3-305 is to the same effect.]

form of contract which was submitted to them. As to the Beevers, Mrs. Beevers was 38 years old and had been through the ninth grade. Mr. Beevers had approximately the same education, but his age does not appear. However, he had been working for the same firm for about nine years and knew a little something about mortgages, at least to the extent of having one upon his property. Mrs. Beevers was employed in a supermarket and it does not appear that either of the Beevers had any difficulty with the English language and they made no claim that they were unable to understand it. Neither the Beevers nor the Burchetts had ever had any prior association with Kelly and the papers were signed upon the very day that they first met him. There was no showing of any reason why they should rely upon Kelly or have confidence in him. The occurrences took place in the homes of appellees, but other than what appears to be Kelly's "chicanery," no reason was given which would warrant a reasonable person in acting as hurriedly as was done in this case. None of the appellees attempted to obtain any independent information either with respect to Kelly or Consolidated Products, nor did they seek out any other person to read or explain the instruments to them. As a matter of fact, they apparently didn't believe this was necessary because, like most people, they wanted to take advantage of "getting something for nothing." There is no dispute but that the appellees did not have actual knowledge of the nature of the instruments which they signed, at the time they signed them. Appellant urges that appellees had a reasonable opportunity to obtain such knowledge but failed to do so, were therefore negligent, and that their defense was precluded.

We recognize that the reasonable opportunity to obtain knowledge may be excused if the maker places reasonable reliance on the representations. The difficulty in the instant case is that the reliance upon the representations of a complete stranger (Kelly) was not reasonable, and all of the parties were of sufficient age, intelligence, education, and business experience to know better. In this connection, it is noted that the contracts clearly stated, on the same page which bore the signatures of the various appellees, the following:

> "No one is authorized on behalf of this company to represent this job to be 'A SAMPLE HOME OR A FREE JOB.'"

The conduct of the Beevers in signing the additional form some weeks after the initial transaction, without reading it, is a graphic showing of negligence. This, however, is merely an added element and it is obvious that all of the parties were negligent in signing the instruments without first reading them under the surrounding circumstances. See *First National Bank of Philadelphia v. Anderson,* supra, which held that the mere failure to read a contract was not sufficient to allow the maker a defense under § 3-305 of the Uniform Commercial Code. In our opinion, the appellees here are barred for the reasons hereinabove stated.

Although we have sympathy with the appellees, we cannot allow it to influence our decision. They were certainly victimized, but because of their failure to exercise ordinary care for their own protection, an innocent party cannot be made to suffer. . . .

The finding of the trial court that Burchetts were not guilty of negligence is not supported by substantial evidence and must fall. We determine under these facts as a matter of law that both the Burchetts and the Beevers had a reasonable opportunity to obtain knowledge of the character or the essential terms of the instruments which they signed, and therefore appellant as a holder in due course took the instruments free from the defenses claimed by the appellees. . . .

Other points are raised, but, in view of our determination, need not be answered.

The judgments will be reversed and the cause is remanded to the district court with directions to dismiss appellees' complaints. It is so ordered.

NOTE

1. Compare the above case with *FDIC v. Turner,* 869 F.2d 270 (6th Cir. 1989)

It has been held that just filling in blanks on an instrument is not fraud in the factum because the signer had an opportunity to obtain knowledge of the instrument's essential terms. *FDIC v. Culver,* 640 F. Supp. 725 (D.C. Kan. 1986).

However, that is not the situation in the present case. Appellant, in this instance, was unaware of essential terms of the instrument. Butcher induced Turner into signing a guaranty based on misrepresentations concerning the principal maker and the holding bank. This is not merely a case of an incomplete guaranty being fraudulently completed. Butcher erased the original bank's name and inserted the name of another bank. Turner had no opportunity to know that until it inadvertently came to his attention at a much later time.

Thus, we conclude that the District Court correctly determined that Turner was defrauded as to the guaranty's essential terms. He may declare the defense of fraud in the factum under U.C.C. § 305(2)(c) [§ 3-305(a)(1)(iii)] against the FDIC based on misrepresentations of Butcher as to the legal essence of the guaranty. Next we must decide whether Turner's method of execution and subsequent behavior constituted negligence which substantially contributed to the alteration. Section 3-406 of the U.C.C. reads: . . .

Therefore, under § 3-406, [§ 3-406] Turner will not be able to assert the defense of fraud in the factum if he negligently contributed to the alteration of the guaranty . . .

* * *

2. The test now is "failure to exercise ordinary care." U.C.C. § 3-103(a)(7). The effect also is to apportion the loss according "to the extent to which the failure of each to exercise ordinary care contributes to the loss." U.C.C. §§ 3-406(a), (b), 3-103(a)(7).

3. Note also now FTC Rule 433.2, 16 C.F.R. § 433.2, as to the taking of a negotiable instrument in a consumer transaction and FTC Rule 429.1, 16 C.F.R. § 429.1, regarding home solicitation sales.

F.   Defenses to a Party Entitled to Enforce an Instrument Who Does Not Qualify as a Holder in Due Course

The discharge of a party to the instrument is not effective against a holder in due course who is without notice of the discharge. U.C.C. § 3-601(b). Such notice may be given by the instrument itself. For example, a person reacquiring the instrument may strike out the names of endorsers who took the instrument subsequent to her original holding and prior to its reacquisition by her.[19] Thereafter, the instrument may be negotiated again and be held by a holder in due course.

We have also noted that a holder in due course takes the instrument free from any proprietary claims to it,[20] and free from any claim in recoupment.[21] As a result, a negotiation cannot be rescinded once the instrument is in the hands of a holder in due course. U.C.C. §§ 3-306, 3-202.

---

[19] See the effect of U.C.C. § 3-415 allowing recourse to a prior endorser should the instrument be dishonored.

[20] *See* Miller v. Race, 1 Burr. 452, 97 Eng. Rep. 398 (K.B. 1758).

[21] U.C.C. § 3-305(a)(3).

Conversely, each of these allegations can be raised against a person entitled to enforce the instrument, U.C.C. § 3-301, but who does not qualify as a holder in due course or who does not have the rights of a holder in due course by having the instrument transferred to him by a holder in due course.[22] When the instrument is presented by or on behalf of such person, it will be possible to raise in defense the non-issue of the instrument, a failure of a condition for its issue such as a failure of consideration, or any other defense, for example, a set off or counter-claim that can be asserted in a simple contract action. U.C.C. § 3-105(b).

In many instances the obligor on the instrument, be he an issuer or an endorser, is asked to raise as a defense a claim asserted by an endorser who is attempting to regain possession of the instrument, for example, by an endorser claiming to have rescinded the endorsement under which the holder is asserting a right to the instrument. The obligor on the instrument cannot raise this defense to his obligation on the instrument. It is a *jus tertii,* i.e., a right asserted by a third party not involved in the relationship holder-obligor. To enable such disputes to be resolved promptly and expeditiously, the claimant would have to be joined in the action brought by the holder against the obligor on the instrument. U.C.C. § 3-305(c). This will enable this issue to be asserted directly against the person entitled to enforce the instrument. The obligor, when confronted with a presentment and with the allegation of the claimant, would pay the amount due on the instrument into court and thereby allow the court to resolve the dispute between the person entitled to enforce the instrument and the claimant.

---

[22] U.C.C. § 3-203(b).

VI TRANSFER WARRANTIES, ENDORSEMENTS, AND SURETYSHIP

As we have seen, an instrument payable to bearer can be negotiated by a mere physical transfer of possession, but an instrument payable to an identified person, in addition, requires endorsement by that person to be negotiated. U.C.C. §§ 3-201(b), 3-203(a). Transfer and presentment may give rise to warranties which, if breached, will allow an action for damages. Endorsements, whether needed to effectuate a negotiation or not, give rise to secondary liability on the instrument. A drawer also may find herself held secondarily liable if the instrument, i.e., a draft or a check, is dishonored.[1]

A. Transfer

Section 3-203(b) indicates that whether or not the transfer also is a negotiation, a transfer vests in the transferee the rights of the transferor.[2] If the transfer is for consideration, the transferee not only succeeds to the rights of the transferor, but also gets the transferor's warranties.[3] These warranties are given to the immediate transferee unless there is not only a transfer but also an endorsement by the transferor, in which case the warranties extend to ultimate transferees as well. Of major importance is the warranty that the transferor is a person entitled to enforce the instrument [U.C.C. §§ 3-301, 3-416(a)(1)] and that the instrument has not been altered [U.C.C. § 3-416(a)(3)]. The other expressed warranties, that the signatures are authentic and authorized; that there are no defenses or claims to the instrument that can be asserted against the warrantor; and, that the transferor has no knowledge of insolvency proceedings having been commenced against the maker, or acceptor, flow naturally from these two warranties.[4]

Breach of these warranties gives rise to an action for damages for the loss suffered, but does not give rise to secondary liability on the instrument. The recovery of the loss suffered, however, is limited to the "amount of the instrument, plus expenses and loss of

---

[1] *See supra,* Chapter IV at C1.

[2] *See supra* Chapter IV at C4.

[3] Hayner v. Fox, 182 Ill. App. 3d 989, 542 N.E.2d 1134 (1989).

[4] U.C.C. § 3-416(a)(2), (4), (5).

interest."[5] Thus, attorney's fees may also be recoverable since they are expenses.[6] Notice of the breach must be given within thirty days after the claimant has reason to know of the breach and the identity of the warrantor.[7] A delay in giving notice of the breach of a warranty results in a discharge of the warrantor to the extent of any loss caused by the delay.[8] Where the transfer occurs within the bank collection system, the depositor who transfers the item (U.C.C. § 4-104(a)(9)), for example a check, to the depository bank and any bank in the collection chain undertakes to reimburse a transferee should the item be dishonored. It is not possible to contract out this obligation.[9] This provision is necessary to protect depository banks which, under the Federal Expedited Funds Availability Act, 12 U.S.C. §§ 4001, et seq., may have to allow withdrawals as of right before the drawee bank is able to indicate whether or not the check will be honored.

Hayner v. Fox

182 Ill.App.3d 989, 542 N.E.2d 1134 (1989)

See supra, Chapter IV at C

B.   Presentment

"Presentment" is the demand to honor an instrument made upon a maker of a note or upon a drawee of a draft by or on behalf of a person entitled to enforce an instrument. U.C.C. § 3-501(a). Such demand would be to pay the instrument that has become due. In the case of a draft whose due date is based on the date of acceptance, presentment is made to the drawee to obtain acceptance of the draft and a further presentment for payment will then have to be made to demand payment on the due date. For example, in the case of a demand draft presentment for acceptance to obtain the obligation of the drawee and payment of the instrument will be a concurrent event.[10] A time draft may fall into this category as well when the date it is due is indicated in the draft. For example:

"On *the First day of September, 1993* pay to the order of ..."

In many instances, however, a drawee may be given a period of time as an extension of credit. For example:

"Pay thirty days from sight ..."

Here there will be two presentments. The first, for acceptance, will commence the thirty days, after which the draft will become due and will have to be presented again for

---

[5] U.C.C. § 3-416(b).

[6] Official Comment 6 to U.C.C. § 3-416.

[7] U.C.C. § 3-416(d).

[8] U.C.C. § 3-416(c).

[9] U.C.C. § 4-207(b).

[10] U.C.C. § 3-408.

payment. Where the draft is payable on a date fixed, but such date is at some future time, the person entitled to enforce the draft may present it for acceptance at an earlier time, but may not demand payment prior to the date indicated in the draft. In this fashion it is possible to determine whether the drawee is prepared to honor the draft when due at a time when the drawer and prior endorsers may still be available to be held liable on their secondary liability.[11]

Presentment can be made by any commercially reasonable means, including an oral demand, in writing or by electronic communication.[12] Unless otherwise instructed, a collecting bank may present an item not payable by, through, or at a bank by sending the drawee a written notice that the bank is holding the item and calling upon the drawee to come to the bank to accept or to pay the item.[13] This method of sending a presentment notice is often used where the payee/drawer uses a bank to collect payment on tender of documents involved in a sales transaction, i.e. collection on a documentary draft.[14] As we have seen, these documents are usually a negotiable bill of lading or warehouse receipt symbolizing the goods.[15] The seller may be loath to part with such negotiable indicia of ownership representing the goods unless the seller receives payment, or acceptance, concurrent with the negotiation of such documents.[16] Where the drawee is a bank, agreements among banks and clearing house rules may provide for presentment of an item by transmission of an image or of information describing the item.[17]

The maker or the drawee is entitled to have the instrument exhibited, however, to examine it for validity and to determine that all necessary endorsements are present on the instrument. U.C.C. § 3-501(b)(2). Where there are co-makers of a note or more than one drawee indicated on the instrument, presentment suffices if made to any one of the co-makers or drawees. U.C.C. § 3-501(b)(1).

U.C.C. Section 3-601(a) indicates that the obligation of a party to the instrument is discharged only to the extent payment is made to a person entitled to enforce the instrument. A presenter of an instrument for acceptance or for payment, therefore, warrants that he is a person entitled to enforce the instrument or is an agent of a person so entitled. U.C.C. § 3-501(a).[18] By warranting to be a person entitled to enforce an instrument payable to an identified person, the presenter in effect warrants the authenticity of any endorsement through which such claim is asserted. U.C.C. §§ 3-301(b), 3-417(a)(1), 3-403, 3-201. A

---

[11] U.C.C. §§ 3-502(b)(4), 4-212(b), 3-414. In the case of a due date having been established for payment or acceptance, the instrument will be dishonored if not paid or accepted by the end of the next business day. U.C.C. § 3-501(b)(4).

[12] U.C.C. § 3-501(b)(1).

[13] U.C.C. § 4-212(a).

[14] U.C.C. § 4-104(a)(6).

[15] *See supra,* Chapter III at B, Documents of Title.

[16] U.C.C. § 4-204(b)(3) prohibits a direct presentment of a documentary draft to a non-bank drawee.

[17] U.C.C. § 4-110(a). These agreements may also provide for check retention and other forms of truncation of the process of presentment.

[18] Such warranty is also given by a claimant making a demand on the drawer or on a prior endorser, or transferor when alleging that a dishonor of the instrument had occurred. U.C.C. § 3-501(d).

presenter does not warrant the authenticity of the maker's own signature, nor does he warrant the signature of the drawer to the drawee. In both cases, these signatures should be known to the person to whom presentment is made. A warranty to the drawee that *there is no knowledge* that the signature of the drawer is unauthorized protects the innocent presenter against liability for forgeries too difficult for an endorsee to detect. The presenter does warrant, however, that a draft has not been materially altered—a fact that a drawee may not be able to detect from the instrument, but for which a presenter-endorsee will have recourse against his transferor-endorser. U.C.C. § 3-416(a)(3).

Presentment warranties cannot be disclaimed with regard to checks which are presented within the bank collection system. Notice of a breach of warranty must be given within thirty days after the claimant has reason to know of the breach and the identity of the warrantor.[19] A delay in giving such notice will release a warrantor to the extent any loss was caused by the delay. This provision makes it clear that the presentment warranties are given not only by the actual presenter, but also by any transferor in the collection chain. Such prior transferors' warranties are limited, however, to the facts existing at the time of their respective transfer,[20] i.e., these transferors would not be liable for any warranty breached by a subsequent transferor.

A breach of warranty gives rise to an action for damages. Thus, damage must have been suffered. For example, where the drawee has paid an altered draft and claims to have suffered a loss by being unable to charge the drawer's account. The presenter could meet the allegation by the drawee that the breach of warranty had caused a loss to the drawee, by asserting that the drawer is precluded from raising an alteration or an unauthorized endorsement against the drawee. For example, where the drawer had failed to exercise ordinary care,[21] and such failure substantially contributed to the loss suffered by the drawee, the drawer would be precluded from objecting to the account being charged.[22] As a result, the drawee could charge the drawer's account and would not have suffered a loss.[23]

Where an instrument has been dishonored, the instrument may be presented to the drawer or to a prior endorser, calling on these parties to honor their secondary liability. On paying the instrument in good faith, these secondarily liable parties will receive a warranty from the presenter that she is a person entitled to enforce the instrument or is authorized to obtain payment on behalf of a person entitled to enforce the instrument. U.C.C. § 3-417(d)(1). This warranty cannot be disclaimed where the instrument is a check. Notice of the breach must be given to the warrantor within thirty days of the drawer or endorser having reason to know that the warranty has been breached. Failure to give timely notice will discharge the warrantor from liability to the extent of any loss caused by the delay. U.C.C. § 3-417(e). Damages for breach of this warranty is limited to an amount equal to the amount paid plus expenses and loss of interest resulting from the breach. U.C.C. § 3-417(d).

---

[19] U.C.C. § 3-417(e), (f).

[20] U.C.C. §§ 3-417(a), 4-208(a).

[21] U.C.C. § 3-103(a)(7).

[22] U.C.C. §§ 3-404, 3-405, 3-406.

[23] U.C.C. §§ 3-417(c), 4-401(a).

The drawer should herself be able to discern any alteration or that her signature was not authorized. There is no warranty, therefore, that there is no alteration nor is there a warranty as to the authenticity of the drawer's signatures. With regard to prior endorsers, these have warranted an absence of alteration when they transferred the instrument, they would notice a subsequent alteration where such has occurred. U.C.C. § 3-416(a)(3). They will also have warranted all signatures on the instrument to be authentic and authorized.[24] Thus, the only warranty made by the claimant is that of being a person entitled to enforce the instrument. He would do this by showing he is claiming to be a holder or a transferee from a person entitled to enforce the instrument. U.C.C. § 3-203.

C. The Endorsement Contract

U.C.C. § 3-204(a)(iii) provides that unless the instrument clearly indicates that a signature is made in some other capacity it is an endorsement. Every endorsement gives rise to an endorsement contract. That contract indicates that (1) should the instrument be presented for acceptance or for payment and dishonored, and (2) should notice of the presentment and dishonor be given to the endorser, the endorser will pay the instrument according to its tenor at the time the endorsement was affixed.[25] The holder's obligation to make presentment and to give notice of dishonor or to pass on such notice to a prior holder/endorser that presentment has been made and the instrument has been dishonored, predicates any right of recourse on an endorsement contract.[26] Presentment and notice of dishonor can be waived. U.C.C. § 3-504(a)(iv), (b). Waiver of presentment waives notice of dishonor as well. It is generally presumed that a waiver embodied in the instrument governs all parties secondarily liable. But if not so embodied, it only binds those parties to whose signature the waiver relates. In effect, the endorsement contract is akin to a surety obligation in relation to the instrument endorsed. Where the instrument passes through various hands, it will bear a number of endorsements. Endorsers are liable to one another in the order in which they endorsed.[27] Dating the endorsement is desirable since it will assist in determining the duration of liability of an endorser of a check. U.C.C. Section 3-415(e) provides that an endorser of a check is discharged from secondary liability if thirty days

---

[24] Compare the Convention on International Bills of Exchange and International Promissory Notes (CIBN) Articles 45, 25 and 26 which provides that a person suffering loss as a result of an unauthorized signature on the instrument has recourse only against the forger and the person taking directly from the forger. Under the CIBN the burden is on a transferee to assure himself that the transfer to him by his transferor is proper.

[25] U.C.C. § 3-415(a). An international instrument may also require "protest," to be enforceable in a foreign court. Protest is the perpetuation of evidence by certification of a notary or other court official that presentment has been made and the instrument was dishonored. It may also indicate that notice of dishonor was given. Waiver of "protest," also waives presentment and notice of dishonor. U.C.C. § 3-505(b). Under the U.N. Convention on International Bills of Exchange and International Promissory Notes (CIBN), protest of the instrument must be expressly called for by the instrument. A declaration of dishonor suffices. *See* Articles 60–63.

[26] U.C.C. § 3-415(c).

[27] This is presumed to be the order in which their signature appears on the instrument. *See* Official Comment 2 to U.C.C. § 3-116.

have elapsed and the check has not been presented for payment or has not been given to a depository bank for collection.

Problem

ABC Corp. supplied goods to Alma Corp. on credit. Payment was to be extended over twelve months. Since ABC Corp. owed an equivalent sum to Beta Corp., ABC Corp. drew on Alma Corp. and indicated that Alma Corp. was to pay Beta Corp. the amount due.

"To Alma Corporation Pay to the order of Beta Corp. on September 1, 1993, or earlier if payee deems itself insecure, the sum of $ x dollars.

Signed ABC Corp.
Abe See, President"

Beta Corp. considering money in hand, even if less than the face value of the draft, to be worth more than the full amount, transferred the draft to Finance Corp. after endorsing the draft.

"Pay to the order of Finance Corp.
Beta Corp.
by Harold Beta, President"

On delivery of the draft to Finance Corp., Beta Corp. received the face amount of the draft less 6% discount. Assume it is March 1993. Finance Corp. has now heard a rumor that Alma Corp. has ceased paying its debts as they became due and was desperately seeking to secure lines of credit from other financial institutions. Can Finance Corp. proceed against

(a) Alma Corp.

(b) Beta Corp.

(c) ABC Corp.

Work through the following sections of the U.C.C. in the following order. Note that these provisions are subject to agreement of the parties, clearing house rules, and the like. [This reservation applies especially where banks are involved, in which case U.C.C. Article 4, Federal Reserve Regulations and Circulars, and Clearing House Rules would also be applicable.]

Acceptance - Acceleration: U.C.C. §§ 1-208, 3-103(a)(4), 3-413.

Transfer Warranties: U.C.C. § 3-416.

Endorsement Liability: U.C.C. § 3-415.

Presentment: §§ 3-501(a), 3-504(a), 3-501(b).

Dishonor: §§ 3-502, 3-501(b)(3).

Evidence of Dishonor or of Protest: §§ 3-505(a), 3-505(b).

Notice of Dishonor: §§ 3-503, 3-504(b), (c), 1-201(25), (26), (27).

Waiver of Presentment, Protest, Notice of Dishonor: § 3-504(a)(iv), (b).

Effect of Failure to Make a Presentment or to Give a Notice of Dishonor to an Endorser: §§ 3-503(a), 3-415(c), 3-415(e) (check).

With regard to the drawer, note: §§ 3-414(d), 3-414(f) (check)

The economic value of an instrument is clearly increased by a transferor's endorsement unless the endorsement is "without recourse."[28] An endorsement "without recourse" will allow a transferee to attain the status of a holder without the endorser/transferor engaging himself in a secondary liability on the instrument. The transferor, however, will have given transfer warranties, if she received consideration for the transfer.[29] It is possible, of course, also to contract out of transfer warranties by specifically stating that the transfer is also "without warranties."

There is no need for an endorser to be in the chain of negotiation. The liability of an endorser is independent of the endorser also being a transferor. Thus, unless an instrument clearly indicates that a signature is made in some other capacity, the signature will be deemed an endorsement.[30]

Since corporations and other incorporeal entities affix their signatures through agents who authenticate the signatures of entities by signing their name, a question arises whether the intention of the signer was merely to authenticate, or whether the signer intended to add their credit to that of the entity whose signature they were authenticating. Section 3-402 provides that agency law be applied. Thus, if it is shown that the unnamed or undisclosed principal would be liable for the undertaking as expressed in the instrument, the fact that such person is not disclosed or fully disclosed in the instrument will not preclude liability on the instrument. The agent, however, remains liable and can only defend against a holder, who is not a holder in due course, by showing "that the original parties did not intend the representative to be liable on the instrument."[31]

Valley National Bank v. Cook
136 Ariz. 232, 665 P.2d 576 (1983)
See supra, Chapter IV at C

D. Accommodation Party[32]

In a credit transaction, it may well be that the creditor would desire the additional liability of a person other than the obligor on the instrument. Such additional liability could

---

[28] U.C.C. § 3-415(b). Note also Federal Trade Commission Rule 443.3, 16 C.F.R. § 443.3, which attempts to protect a natural person proposing to co-sign a consumer obligation. The Rule makes it a deceptive act or practice "for a lender or retail installment seller, directly or indirectly, to misrepresent the nature or extent of cosigner liability," or "directly or indirectly to obligate a cosigner unless the cosigner is informed prior to becoming obligated" of the extent of liability assumed by becoming a cosigner.

[29] U.C.C. §§ 3-303(b), 3-416.

[30] U.C.C. § 3-204(a). By practice, a signature in the lower right hand corner of an instrument will be deemed to indicate an intent to sign as a maker of a note or as a drawer of a draft. *See* Official Comment to U.C.C. § 3-204. On the other hand, a counter-signature on a traveller's check does not effectuate an endorsement. *See* Official Comment 2 to U.C.C. § 3-106. A signature on the back of an instrument, however, is generally considered to be an endorsement.

[31] U.C.C. § 3-402(b)(2).

[32] *See* Neil B. Cohen, *Surety Principles in the New Article 3: Clarification and Substantive Changes,* 42 Ala. L. Rev. 595 (1991).

be assumed by an endorsement expressly indicating that the purpose is to act as surety for a party to the instrument, i.e. as an accommodation party.[33] An example would be "payment guaranteed." Where an endorsement is not in the chain of negotiation, it is an "anomalous endorsement"—it will be considered to be an endorsement by an accommodation party.[34] An accommodation party, however, may sign the instrument in any position, for example, as a maker, drawer, acceptor, or endorser.[35] A problem may arise here whether the signature, without indicating the status of accommodation party, results in the assumption of a liability other than that of a surety for the party accommodated; e.g. as a co-maker. Parol evidence will be admitted to show the status of the signer as an accommodation party. Such evidence cannot be used, however, to support a claim to a discharge based on such accommodation status against a holder in due course, who, on taking the instrument, had no notice of the accommodation status. U.C.C. § 3-605(h).[36]

The party to be accommodated must be named in the instrument. In a dispute between these parties parol evidence will be admitted to show who is the party accommodated and who is the accommodation party. An accommodation party cannot derive a direct benefit from the obligation for which the instrument was issued or negotiated.[37] An accommodation party may be compensated for assuming this obligation. The obligation of the accommodation party, however, is not predicated on a receipt of consideration by the accommodation party. The consideration that is the basis of the obligation of the principal supports the obligation of the surety. Further, the obligation of the accommodation party is enforceable notwithstanding any requirements of a statute of frauds. U.C.C. § 3-419(b). In commercial terms, an accommodation exists.

> [I]f an instrument is issued for value given for the benefit of a party to the instrument ("accommodated party") and another party to the instrument ("accommodation party") signs the instrument for the purpose of incurring liability on the instrument without being a direct beneficiary of the value given for the instrument, the instrument is signed by the accommodation party "for accommodation." U.C.C. § 3-419(a).

The circumstances surrounding the signing of the instrument may indicate the existence of an accommodation by disclosing the intent of the signer. For example, when considering whether a signature was appended as a party issuer or as an accommodation party: (1) was there participation in the negotiations leading to the loan; (2) what was the purpose for which credit was extended as represented by the instrument; and (3) was the signature

---

[33] U.C.C. § 3-419(a).

[34] U.C.C. § 3-419(c). J. & B. Schoenfeld, Fur Merchants, Inc. v. Kilbourne & Donohue, Inc., 704 F. Supp. 466 (S.D.N.Y. 1989). *But note,* Weather-Rite, Inc. v. Southdale Pro-Bowl, Inc., 301 Minn. 346, 222 N.W.2d 789 (1974).

[35] U.C.C. §§ 3-105(c), 3-103(a)(3), (5); Official Comment to U.C.C. § 3-204.

[36] Weather-Rite, Inc. v. Southdale Pro-Bowl, Inc., 301 Minn. 346, 222 N.W.2d 789 (1974).

[37] First Nat'l Bank of North Idaho, N.A. v. Burgess, 118 Idaho 627, 798 P.2d 472 (1990); Burke v. Burke, 891 Ill. App. 3d 803, 412 N.E.2d 204 (1980). An indirect benefit arises where a shareholder signs for the accommodation of his corporation. Though the obligation for which the instrument was given benefits the corporation, and thus indirectly the shareholder, the shareholder can claim the status of an accomodation party.

necessary to secure the loan. *Rahal v. Tweed,* 411 S.E.2d 461 (W.Va. 1991).

The obligation of an accommodation party arises when the party accommodated fails to honor its obligation and notice of the dishonor is given to the accommodation party/surety.[38] An accommodation party can waive notice of dishonor.[39] Expecting a pending dishonor, the accommodation party under suretyship law could call on the party accommodated to perform so as to be exonerated from its obligation.[40] This, however, is a rare occurrence. After honoring the obligation of the party accommodated, the accommodation party can (1) subrogate to the person entitled to enforce the instrument and proceed against the party accommodated; or (2) sue such party for reimbursement. U.C.C. § 3-419(e). When subrogating, the accommodation party will have all the rights of the party to whom she would be subrogating. As such U.C.C. Section 3-416(b) and Section 3-417(e) would give a right to recover expenses including attorney fees. *Mobley v. Harmon,* 304 Ark. 500, 803 S.W.2d 900 (1991), illustrates that the action of the accommodation party to be reimbursed, however, is based on the rights of the accommodation party as such. Thus, the party accommodated will not be able to assert a release by the person entitled to enforce the instrument so as to avoid its liability to the accommodation party. The court rejected the argument that by releasing the debtor, there was no right which the accommodation party could assert.

Typically, the surety/accommodation party, in defense, will allege that the person entitled to enforce the instrument has changed the obligation or has impaired the collateral which secured it. U.C.C. Section 3-605(b) specifically provides that not only an undertaking not to sue, but also a discharge of a party to the instrument will not discharge the obligation of an endorser or accommodation party having rights against the party discharged. The rights of the accommodation party against the party accommodated are preserved. U.C.C. § 3-604(b). The accommodation party, however, will be able to raise all other defenses available to the party accommodated. Where the person entitled to enforce the instrument extends the due date of the instrument without such extension being agreed to by an endorser or accommodation party, or agrees to any other type of modification of the obligation, or commits an act that impairs the value of collateral, the obligation of the endorser or accommodation party is discharged in so far as such action causes a loss to the accommodation party or to the endorser.[41] U.C.C. § 3-605. The burden of proving impairment and loss is on the party claiming a discharge.

---

[38] U.C.C. § 3-503(a).

[39] U.C.C. § 3-504(a)(iv).

[40] U.C.C. § 1-103. Warren v. Washington Trust Bank, 19 Wash. App. 348, 575 P.2d 1077 (1978), *modified,* 92 Wash. 2d 318, 598 P.2d 701 (1979).

[41] Note: where the face of the instrument provides for an extension, all parties are deemed to have assented to such extension should it be granted by the person entitled to enforce the instrument.

Langeveld v. L.R.Z.H. Corp.

74 N.J. 45, 376 A.2d 931 (1977)*

The opinion of the court was delivered by MOUNTAIN, J.

This case presents an important question of commercial law requiring the interpretation of N.J.S.A. 12A:3-606 [3-605(b)(c)(e)], a section of the Uniform Commercial Code which we have not hitherto been called upon to consider.

In the trial court, summary judgment in the amount of $57,500, together with interest, was entered against defendant Higgins,[1] 130 N.J. Super. 486, 327 A.2d 683 (Ch. Div. 1974). The Appellate Division affirmed, substantially for the reasons expressed by the court below. 137 N.J. Super. 557, 350 A.2d 76 (App. Div. 1975). We granted defendant's petition for certification. 70 N.J. 511, 361 A.2d 526 (1976).

On March 10, 1972, defendant, L.R.Z.H. Corporation, made and delivered to plaintiff, Langeveld, its promissory note in the sum of $57,500. The indebtedness evidenced by the note was secured by a mortgage in like amount on land in Montvale in Bergen County owned by the defendant corporation. This mortgage was junior in lien to a first mortgage in the sum of $825,000 held by the Howard Savings Institution and to a second mortgage in the approximate amount of $58,000 held by the persons named Castellane. The latter mortgage covered only a portion of the whole tract upon which The Howard Savings and Langeveld mortgages were liens. By an instrument of guaranty set forth at the foot of the note, defendant, together with certain other persons not here involved, undertook to become individually obligated for the payment of the debt. The note matured February 15, 1973 and was not paid.

It was then for the first time discovered, apparently by defendant, that the Langeveld mortgage had never been recorded. Upon this being brought to plaintiff's attention, the instrument was forthwith recorded on March 1, 1973. It then developed that between the execution and delivery of the

Langeveld mortgage on March 10, 1972 and the recording of the instrument on March 1, 1973, the following lien claims had become a matter of record:

1. Mortgage by L.R.Z.H. Corporation to James E. Hanson and Company in the amount of $100,000.

2. Mechanic's Notices of Intention filed by Reed Electric Corporation in the total sum of $111,825.48.

3. Mechanic's Notice of Intention filed by Samuel Braen and Company in the sum of $12,804.56.

On March 8, 1973 plaintiff instituted this suit on the guaranty. In defense of the claim thus asserted against him, defendant pointed out that there existed here the tripartite arrangement typical of a suretyship relationship.[2] L.R.Z.H. Corporation was principal debtor. Plaintiff was its creditor; defendant stood in the position of a guarantor or surety. He further called attention to the fact that plaintiff, as such creditor, held the mortgage from L.R.Z.H. Corporation as collateral security for the corporate obligation and that it owed a duty to him, as surety for the same debt, to protect this security and allow nothing to occur to impair its value and worth that reasonable effort and foresight on plaintiff's part could prevent or avoid. Failure to record the mortgage for about a year, predictably followed by the intervention of recorded liens in substantial amounts, constituted, he argued, a failure on plaintiff's part to fulfill this duty. Accordingly, concluded defendant, he should be released from all liability on his guaranty. Particular attention was drawn to a section of the Uniform Commercial Code, which in pertinent part reads,

Impairment of Recourse or of Collateral

[The court quoted Pre-Revision
U.C.C. § 3-603(1)(b)]

Doctrines and rules taken from the common

---

* [Editor: citations in [ ] refer to Revised U.C.C. Articles 3 and 4.]

[1] The term "defendant" as used hereafter in the opinion will, unless otherwise indicated, refer to defendant Higgins.

[2] Suretyship is invariably a tripartite relationship in which the obligation of the surety is intended to supplement an obligation of the principal (also described as the debtor or obligor) owed to the creditor (also described as the obligee). [Clark, *Suretyship in the Uniform Commercial Code,* 46 TEX. L. REV. 453 (1968)].

law of suretyship have been incorporated within various provisions of the Uniform Commercial Code. It has been said that "[s]ection 3-606 [§ 3-605] is probably the most important provision in the Code to the surety." Clark, *Suretyship in the Uniform Commercial Code, supra,* 46 Tex. L. Rev. at 457. "Perhaps the most significant provision of the U.C.C. affecting suretyship is section 3-606." [§ 3-605] Note, *Suretyship in Article 3 of the Uniform Commercial Code,* 17 West. Reserve L. Rev. 318 (1965).

It is a well-recognized principle of the law of suretyship that a release of collateral held by a creditor, or its impairment by improper action or inaction on his part, will extinguish the obligation of the surety, at least to the extent of the value of the security released or impaired. This rule has come to be accepted as the law of our State. . . . The section of the Uniform Commercial Code we are considering is essentially a restatement of this rule, as the courts that have examined it have consistently held. . . .

The doctrine is an equitable one, designed to protect the surety's right of subrogation. Upon paying the debt, the surety is, as a matter of law, subrogated to all the creditor's rights against the principal debtor and is entitled to all benefits derivable from any security of the principal debtor that may be in the creditor's hands. The rule forbidding impairment of collateral has as its chief aim the protection of these potential benefits made available through subrogation.

Defendant has made out a prima facie case to support his contention that he comes within the favor of the rule. Relating his contentions to the language of the act clearly demonstrates that this is so. Thus we see that plaintiff is the "holder" of collateral, as the word is used in the statute. Defendant is a "party to the instrument"[3] in his capacity as guarantor. A failure to record a mortgage held as collateral security—absent waiver, estoppel or the like—seems clearly to be an

instance of unjustifiable impairment. Common law authorities so held, almost without exception. . . . The mortgage is "collateral for the instrument" (note) "given by [a] person (L.R.Z.H. Corporation) against whom he (Higgins) has a right of resource."

Plaintiff essentially disputes defendant's position on two grounds. He urges, first, that the guaranty is unconditional in form and that this being so, the alleged impairment of collateral in no way affects the obligation to which the guaranty gives rise. In the second place he contends that there has in fact been no impairment of collateral, or at least none that has caused defendant to suffer loss.

The form of guaranty appears below.[4] The provisions dispensing with presentment, notice of dishonor and protest add nothing not already provided by the Code. . . . The language assuring

---

[3] Since the guaranty is appended at the foot of the note, we are not called upon to decide whether any different result might ensure were the guaranty to take the form of a separate document. Supporting the view that the result should be the same, see Murray, *Secured Transactions—Defenses of Impairment and Improper Care of Collateral,* 79 Com. L. J. 265, 267 (1974) (collecting authorities).

---

[4] To induce the said JOHN P. LANGEVELD to accept the above note, the undersigned hereby guaranty performance of all obligations of the obligors under the note and under the mortgage securing the indebtedness described in the note. The said undersigned guarantors agree to be principally liable on the indebtedness jointly and severally and further agree to their obligation jointly and severally without the necessity of presentment, demand or notice of dishonor.

The undersigned guarantors agree to pay the tenor of this instrument notwithstanding that L.R.Z.H. CORPORATION may effectuate an assignment for the benefit of creditors, be declared a bankrupt, be discharged from Bankruptcy, or otherwise be excused, except by payment, of the debt.

/s/ Joseph A. Higgins, Sr.   L.S.
JOSEPH A. HIGGINS, SR.

/s/ Albin H. Rothe   L.S.
ALBIN H. ROTHE

/s/ Louis J. Zoghby   L.S.
LOUIS J. ZOGHBY

In addition to the guaranty itself, the following paragraph of the note should be considered.

The undersigned and all other parties who at any time may be liable hereon in any capacity, jointly and severally waive presentment, demand for payment, protest and notice of protest of this note, and authorize the holder hereof, without notice to grant extensions in the time of payment and reductions in the rate of interest on any moneys owing on this note.

continued liability on the part of the guarantor in the event of the obligor's insolvency was likewise superfluous. Such liability would continue in the face of this eventuality whether explicitly so stated or not.

The only expression which may be said at all to support plaintiff's contention is found in the words, "[t]he said undersigned guarantors agree to be *principally* liable on the indebtedness. . . ." (emphasis added). Plaintiff argues that this language justified him in treating Higgins as if he were in every sense a principal. This contention must be carefully examined. To accept plaintiff's argument literally would be to deprive defendant of all right of recourse against the true principal, or at the very least render the right of recourse of uncertain value by permitting the impairment of collateral. This result should be permitted only where the instrument of guaranty specifically frees the creditor from liability for such impairment.

If the destruction or impairment of such a right [subrogation to unimpaired collateral] is to be waived by a guarantor, it should only be by the most unequivocal language in the guaranty agreement. The right does not originate in contract, and it cannot lightly be destroyed by contract. [*D. W. Jaquays & Co. v. First Security Bank,* 101 Ariz. 301, 419 P.2d 85, 89 (1966)]

Here there has been no unequivocal waiver. We think the wording of this guaranty may fairly be equated with language purporting to make a person in defendant's position an "unconditional guarantor." Such language is normally held to permit the creditor to move against the guarantor without first proceeding either against the principal debtor or the collateral. It is not customarily interpreted as providing a creditor with any further rights. As one commentator has put it,

> It is one thing to say that a creditor need not pursue the collateral as a condition precedent to pursuing the guarantor of payment and quite another to say that because of this condition precedent the creditor can by misfeasance or nonfeasance prevent the guarantor of payment from ever recovering from the collateral. [Murray, *Secured Transactions— Defenses of Impairment and Improper Care of Collateral, supra* 79 Com. L. J. at 278]

Recent case law expressly sustains the position that terms of absolute or unconditional guaranty should be so limited. *See Behlen Mfg. Co. v. First National Bank of Englewood,* 472 P.2d 703 (Colo. App. 1970) (payment "absolutely and unconditionally" guaranteed); . . .

The point to be made and emphasized is that absent express agreement, waiver or renunciation, a surety's right of subrogation to *unimpaired* collateral will be protected. We do not find this right to have been waived or relinquished by anything contained in this guaranty.

Plaintiff's second contention is that the collateral has not as a matter of fact been impaired, or at least not to an extent that it has caused defendant any loss.

On March 9 and 20, 1973, James E. Hanson and Company and The Howard Savings Institution commenced separate actions to foreclose their respective mortgages. On July 3, 1973 an order was entered consolidating the two foreclosure suits. On August 26, 1974, at sheriff's sale, Higgins, acting through a corporation, purchased the property for $1,080,000. By this time the amounts due on The Howard Savings and Castellane mortgages had substantially increased. The sum received at sheriff's sale was sufficient only to satisfy the amount due on the first mortgage and to apply about $20,000 in reduction of the second. The trial judge took the position that the amount received at sheriff's sale represented the fair market value of the premises. Since it was insufficient to satisfy the two mortgages admittedly senior to plaintiff's mortgage, this demonstrated that plaintiff's mortgage was without value. Therefore, although he found that plaintiff's failure to record his mortgage was "unjustifiable," the trial judge concluded that this had not harmed Higgins because the Langeveld mortgage had now been shown to be valueless. Accordingly, plaintiff's motion for summary judgment was granted. We find this disposition of the case to have been error.

In the first place, and most importantly, the factual situation and the respective rights and obligations of the parties should have been assessed and determined not at the time of the sheriff's sale, in August, 1974, but rather at the time the obligation matured, in February, 1973. It was then that defendant was entitled to exercise his rights as surety. Had he paid plaintiff the amount then due—$57,500, together with interest at the rate of 10% from October 15, 1970—he would have stood in plaintiff's shoes as holder of the note and mortgage. Had the mortgage originally been promptly recorded, as it should have been, there would then have been available to him a variety of options, the relative merits of which we are in no position to evaluate at this time and on this record. For instance, as holder of a junior lien (the Langeveld mortgage) he would have had a right to redeem either or both The Howard Savings and Castellane mortgages. Osborne, *Law of Mortgages,* 628–29. He could have foreclosed any mortgage acquired. Other possibilities suggest themselves. The point is that defendant appears to have been deprived of the opportunity effectively to exploit his right of subrogation to unimpaired collateral by the failure of plaintiff to record the mortgage given him by L.R.Z.H. Corporation.

The Hanson mortgage as well as various mechanics' notices of intention had intervened before the Langeveld mortgage was recorded. Although the Hanson mortgage is said to contain a clause subordinating it to the lien of the Langeveld mortgage, Hanson has nevertheless filed various contentious pleadings apparently attacking the alleged priority of plaintiff's lien. Reed Electric Company claims to have been junior in lien only to The Howard Savings Institution and complains that the relative priority of its claim has *never* been adjudicated. These points of contention and others as well should have been resolved at trial. The facts so found should have then been assayed to determine their effect, if any, with respect to the alleged impairment of collateral. The case was in no way ripe for the entry of summary judgment.

The parties express sharply differing views as to the extent to which an impairment of collateral should be held to discharge one secondarily liable. Defendant suggests that the Code has adopted the rule, sometimes referred to as that of *strictissimi juris,* that a surety is completely discharged by any impairment of collateral, whether or not he has sustained loss or prejudice. Plaintiff, on the other hand, contends that the surety should only be released from liability to the extent that actual, calculable monetary loss can be shown to have occurred.

We think the statute should be read as adopting a rule somewhere between these extremes. If the impairment of collateral can be measured in monetary terms, then the calculated amount of the impairment will ordinarily measure the extent of the surety's discharge. But there are factual situations—this may or may not be one of them—where a surety may be able to establish that he has sustained prejudice, but be unable to measure the extent of the prejudice in terms of monetary loss. Where such a situation is presented the surety will normally be completely discharged.

To recapitulate briefly, at the plenary hearing which must follow our order of remand, the Chancery Division judge will determine from all of the evidence presented, to what extent, if at all, plaintiff's failure seasonably to record his mortgage impaired the collateral given by L.R.Z.H. Corporation to plaintiff as security for the indebtedness. The effect of the impairment upon one secondarily liable may or may not be translatable into dollars. There may be clear prejudice without precisely calculable loss. This will normally result in the discharge of the surety. To the extent that such impairment is found, defendant, Higgins will stand discharged of his obligation as guarantor.

The judgment of the Appellate Division is reversed and the case is remanded to the Chancery Division for further proceedings not inconsistent with what has been said above.

NOTE

1. In *Langeveld v. L.R.Z.H. Corporation,* the court adopted the principle that the obligation of the guarantor was discharged or released only to the extent that he has been disadvantaged by the creditor's failure to adequately protect the collateral. "If the impairment of collateral can be measured in monetary terms, then the calculated amount of the impairment will ordinarily measure the extent of the surety's discharge. However, there are factual situations—this may or may not be one of them—where a surety may be able to establish that he has sustained prejudice, but be unable to measure its extent in terms of monetary loss. Where such a situation is presented the surety will normally be completely discharged." 74 N.J. 45, 376 A.2d 931, 937.

Consider this dictum in light of U.C.C. § 3-605(e), (f), (g).

Problem

The holder of an instrument secured by collateral had failed to claim the collateral in a foreclosure proceeding brought by other creditors. The holder claimed "that it would have been futile had he continued to pursue his claim in a time-consuming and expensive proceedings," since there were claims having priority that would have exhausted the value of the collateral. The collateral has now been sold and the proceeds distributed. The note is due and has been dishonored. Holder has brought an action against the accommodation party. Discuss. *Katsoufris v. Adamo,* 216 N.J. Super 84, 522 A.2d 1046 (1987). ("We agree that it was not incumbent upon plaintiff to pursue his first mortgage claim in the foreclosure proceeding if, as the record to some extent suggests, there was no reasonable likelihood of obtaining partial or total satisfaction of the debt owed by ANK, the principal obligor, by taking such a course.")

2. John A. Spanogle: *The U.N. Convention on International Bills of Exchange and Notes (CIBN): A Primer for Attorneys and International Bankers,* 25 U.C.C. L.J. 99, 121–122 (1992):

Liability of the Guarantor

CIBN Articles 46–48 set forth the liability of guarantors under the Convention. In most common law countries, including the United States, the "guarantor" undertakes risks relating to the creditworthiness of his principal, but is not necessarily deprived of defenses concerning the authority of his principal to sign or the authenticity of his signature. In other words, this "guarantor" is entitled to the actual signature of his principal or an authorized agent. The guarantor, therefore, has a number of defenses available, even against a holder in due course.

Civil law countries, such as those that subscribe to the Uniform Law on Bills of Exchange and Promissory Notes,[42] employ the concept of an *aval*. The "avaliste" has fewer defenses against a holder than does the analogous common law "guarantor." Accordingly, the civil law holder is in a stronger position to enforce his rights on the instrument against an avaliste than is the common law holder to enforce the rights against a guarantor. This comes in part from the fact that the avaliste undertakes not only creditworthiness risks, but also risks related to authority to sign and the authenticity of the principal's signature. This is true even if the avaliste signs before the principal signs and reflects the difference between the civil law and the U.C.C. in their treatment of forged signatures.

CIBN Article 47 strikes a compromise between these two systems by allowing the parties to choose which type of guarantee to provide. Either type can be chosen simply by indicating the words *"aval"* or *"guarantor."* Thus, the parties can deliberately choose how they wish to allocate risks between the guarantor and holders by expressly using either of these designations. The more difficult problem arises when the guarantor is an anomalous indorser, and uses

---

[42] 143 League of Nations Treaty Series 257 (1933–34).

neither term. In that situation, CIBN Articles 47(4)(d) and 47(4)(e) assign the liability of an "avaliste" to the anomalous signature if it is made by a "bank or financial institution" and assigns the liability of a "guarantor" to the anomalous signature if it is made by anyone else. The rationale was that banks should identify their status clearly, especially on an international instrument. While the actual operation of this dual system is likely to be complicated, given international differences in the definition of a financial institution and varying perceptions of how the new formulation will operate, the provisions will facilitate the circulation of these instruments, especially in forfeiting transactions.

3. As between sureties or accommodation parties, contribution can be called for by any surety who paid more than her aliquot part of the debt. U.C.C. § 3-419(e).

Fithian v. Jamar
286 Md. 161, 410 A.2d 569 (1979)*

COLE, JUDGE.

The dispute in this case involves the rights and liabilities of co-makers of a note in a suit among themselves, where none of the disputants is a holder of the note. We granted certiorari to consider two questions, which simply stated are:

1. Whether a co-maker of a note was also an accommodation maker of the note and thus not liable to the party accommodated;

2. Whether the agreement of one co-maker to assume another co-maker's obligation on a note constitutes a defense to the latter when sued for contribution by the former.

In 1967 Walter Fithian (Walter) and Richard Jamar (Richard), who were employed as printers at Baltimore Business Forms, decided to form a partnership to carry on their own printing business. They applied to the People's Bank of Chestertown, Maryland (Bank) for an $11,000 business loan to enable them to purchase some equipment. The Bank agreed to lend the money to Walter and Richard only if Walter's wife, Connie, Richard's wife, Janet, and Walter's parents, Walter William (Bill) and Mildred Fithian would co-sign the note. The Executive Vice-President of the Bank explained that the additional signatures were required to make the Bank more secure. The note, which authorized confession of judgment in the

event of default, was signed on its face in the bottom righthand corner by these six parties. The monies loaned were deposited in Walter and Richard's business checking account and were used to purchase printing equipment.

By 1969, Walter and Richard were encountering business problems. They spoke with Frank Hogans (Hogans) and Gerald Bos (Bos) (who were interested in joining the business) about forming a corporation to be called J-F Printing Co., Inc. and refinancing the note so that it (the note) could become a corporate rather than an individual obligation. The business continued to falter and on March 23, 1972, Walter, Richard, Hogans and Bos met and entered into a written agreement in their individual capacities whereby Richard was to take over management and ownership of the business in exchange for his assumption of liability for the company's outstanding obligations, one of which was the note in question in this case. The agreement also provided that should Richard default in the performance of those obligations, Walter, Hogans, and Bos would have the right to terminate the agreement and resume ownership of the business.

Pursuant to the agreement Richard assumed control of the business but was unable to make any further payments on the note. Consequently, the Executive Vice-President of the Bank requested that Bill and Mildred Fithian pay the note in full. They did and the Bank assigned the note to them for whatever disposition they might

---

* [Editor: citations in [ ] refer to Revised U.C.C. Articles 3 and 4.]

choose. Bill demanded that Richard indemnify him for the total amount Bill paid on the note.

Receiving no satisfaction from Richard, Bill and Mildred sought judicial relief. On November 10, 1976, a confessed judgment against Richard and Janet of $8,953.95, the balance on the note paid by Bill and Mildred, with interest from January 18, 1974, court costs, and attorney's fees of $472.70, was entered in the Circuit Court for Kent county. Richard and Janet filed a motion to vacate the judgment, which the circuit court granted and ordered a hearing on the merits. Prior to trial, Richard and Janet filed a third party claim against Walter and Connie averring that as co-makers of the note, Walter and Connie were liable to Richard and Janet for any judgment that Bill and Mildred might recover against Richard and Janet. Walter and Connie counterclaimed contending that the agreement barred Richard's recovery.

The matter was brought to trial on August 25, 1977 before the circuit court, sitting without a jury. The court found that the J-F Printing Company, Inc. was never a de jure corporation and that those who attempted to act under that name were merely acting in their individual capacities; that the March 23, 1972 agreement was not material to the determination of the case; that Bill and Mildred were accommodation makers for Richard, Janet, Walter and Connie and were entitled to collect from any one of the four.

Final judgment was entered on September 6, 1977 for Bill and Mildred against Richard and Janet in the amount of $8,953.95, the principal sum due, plus $2,288.95, representing interest from January 18, 1974 to August 25, 1977. The court denied Bill and Mildred's claim for collection fees specified in the note and also entered a judgment for Richard and Janet on Walter and Connie's counterclaim. In the third party claim of Richard and Janet against Walter and Connie, judgment was entered for Richard and Janet in the amount of $5,621.45, fifty percent of the total judgment. The costs of the case were to be divided equally between Richard and Janet and Walter and Connie.

Bill and Mildred Fithian filed a timely appeal to the Court of Special Appeals, complaining of the circuit court's adverse ruling as to the collection fees. Walter and Connie took their own appeal, challenging the lower court's findings concerning both Connie's status in relation to the note and the materiality of the March, 1972 agreement.

These appeals were consolidated for oral argument in that court.

In an unreported per curiam decision filed on April 7, 1978, *Fithian v. Jamar,* No. 946, Sept. Term, 1977, the Court of Special Appeals affirmed the circuit in part and reversed in part. The Court of Special Appeals reversed on the issue of collection fees, ruling that there was a "valid and enforceable contract right of Bill and Mildred to the payment of collection costs. . . ."; the Court of Special Appeals affirmed the circuit court's finding that Connie Fithian was a co-maker of the note, and not an accommodation party. The Court of Special Appeals also affirmed the trial court's finding that the March, 1972 agreement was not material to the case because it was "a private agreement between only two (2) of the six (6) makers of the note."

Walter and Connie (appellants) requested review of these rulings in this Court, and we granted their petition for certiorari on June 21, 1978 to consider the two questions presented: whether Connie Fithian was an accommodation maker of the note and thus not liable to the party accommodated; and whether the March, 1972 agreement constitutes a defense to Richard and Janet's (appellees) third party claim against Walter and Connie.

Our disposition of the questioned rulings requires us to reverse and remand. The error which occurred in the court below was caused in part by a failure to fully analyze the individual rights and obligations of Connie, Walter, Janet and Richard. Therefore, in the discussion which follows, in addition to examining the two questions presented, we will clarify the resulting rights and obligations of these parties.

RICHARD v. CONNIE

Since there is no dispute that Connie signed the note, the answer to the first question depends on her purpose in doing so. This is made clear by Maryland Code (1975), § 3-415(1) [§ 3-419(a)] of the Commercial Law Article which provides that an accommodation party is "one who signs the instrument in any capacity for the purpose of lending his name to another party to it." The undisputed evidence as presented by the Executive Vice-President of the Bank was to the effect that the wives' signatures were required before the Bank would make the loan to Walter and Richard. Such practices are common among lending institutions which recognize that

[one] with money to lend, goods to sell or services to render may have doubts about a prospective debtor's ability to pay. In such cases he is likely to demand more assurance than the debtor's bare promise of payment. The prospective creditor can reduce his risk by requiring some sort of security. One form of security is the Article 9 security interest in the debtor's goods. Another type of security takes the form of joining a third person on the debtor's obligation [J. White and R. Summers, *Uniform Commercial Code* § 13-12, at 425 (1972)].

It is readily apparent, therefore, that Connie lent her name to facilitate the loan transaction. As such she lent her name to two parties to the instrument, Richard and Walter, to enable them to receive a *joint* loan for the purchase of equipment for their printing business, thereby giving the Bank the added assurance of having another party to the obligation. Connie signed as an accommodation party as to both Walter and Richard.

Nor is there any merit in the argument advanced by Richard that Connie must be either a co-maker or an accommodation party, that she cannot be both. The actual language of § 3-415(1) [§ 3-419(b)] indicates that an accommodation party also signs in a particular capacity, as maker, acceptor or indorser of an instrument. The Official Comment 1 to § 3-415 explains that

[subsection] (1) recognizes that an accommodation party is always a surety (which includes a guarantor), and it is his only distinguishing feature. He differs from other sureties only in that his liability is on the instrument and he is a surety for another party to it. His obligation is therefore determined by the capacity in which he signs. An accommodation maker or acceptor is bound on the instrument without any resort to his principal, while an accommodation indorser may be liable only after presentment, notice of dishonor and protest. [*See* Revised U.C.C. § 3-419(b)]

Moreover, § 3-415(b) [§ 3-419(b)] refers specifically to the liability of an accommodation party "in the capacity in which he has signed." It follows, therefore, that the fact that Connie was a co-maker of the note does not preclude her from also being an accommodation party.

Section 3-415(5) [§ 3-419(e)] of the Commercial Law Article states that "[an] accommodation party is not liable to the party accommodated"; thus, Connie is not liable to Richard. Our predecessors, prior to Maryland's adoption of the Uniform Commercial Code, explained the reasons for this proposition in *Crothers v. National Bank,* 158 Md. 587, 593, 149 A. 270, 273 (1930):

Since the accommodating party lends his credit by request to the party accommodated upon the assumption that the latter will discharge the debt when due, it is an implied term of this agreement that the party accommodated cannot acquire any right of action against the accommodating party.

Richard contends, however, that Connie intended to accommodate only her husband, Walter. Even if there were evidence to this effect (and there is none), the subjective intent of a co-maker of a note is of little weight when objective facts and circumstances unambiguously demonstrate the capacity in which the note was signed.... It is clear to us that the signatures of both wives were required to effect this joint business venture and thus Connie's signature was as much an accommodation to Richard as it was to Walter. We hold that Connie was an accommodation maker and that she cannot be liable to Richard, the party accommodated. The Court of Special Appeals erroneously held to the contrary.

JANET v. CONNIE

The preceding discussion of Connie's status demonstrates that each of the four parties, Walter, Connie, Richard, and Janet, had certain rights and obligations with respect to this note which are not affected by his or her marital status. The court below erred in not fully analyzing these separate rights and obligations. It follows that our finding that Connie has no liability to Richard in no way changes any obligation she may have to Janet. Janet as well as Connie, is a co-accommodation maker on this note.

The question is therefore whether one co-accommodation maker who pays more than her proportionate share of the debt has a right of contribution against another co-accommodation maker. The Uniform Commercial Code contains no provision expressly dealing with the right of an accommodation party to contribution from another accommodation party. However, the Code does provide that the principles of the common law remain applicable "[u]nless displaced by the particular provisions" of the Code. Maryland Code (1975), § 1-103 of the Commercial Law Article.

That an accommodation maker has a right of contribution from a co-accommodation maker is a settled principle of the law. The Restatement of Security provides:

A surety who in the performance of his own obligation discharges more than his proportionate share of the principal's duty is entitled to contribution from a co-surety. [Restatement of Security § 149 (1941)].

. . .

Maryland has followed this rule. *Jackson v. Cupples,* 239 Md. 637, 212 A.2d 273 (1965). *Jackson* was decided after the effective date of the U.C.C. in Maryland, but the note in question had been executed prior to that date. The Court held that a co-surety who pays a debt has a right of contribution from his co-sureties.

This Court has not addressed this question in regard to a note controlled by the U.C.C. Our research revealed only one case which directly confronted the effect of the U.C.C. on the common law rule. The court stated that the U.C.C. does not change the rule of suretyship law permitting contribution by one surety from a co-surety. *McLochlin v. Miller,* 139 Ind. App. 443, 217 N.E.2d 50 (1966).

Accordingly Janet has a right of contribution against Connie. But this right to contribution is an inchoate claim which does not ripen into being unless and until Janet pays more than her proportionate share to Bill and Mildred. . . . Judgment can be entered on behalf of Janet against Connie, but it must be fashioned so that it may not be enforced until Janet proves she actually paid more than her proportionate share to Bill and Mildred.[1]

RICHARD v. WALTER

We now turn to the second question as to

---

[1] A surety who is called upon to pay more than his proportionate share of the debt has a right of contribution from his co-sureties in an amount not to exceed each co-surety's proportionate share of the debt. *See* Schindel v. Danzer, 161 Md. 384, 157 A. 282 (1931); 72 C.J.S. Principal and Surety § 369 (1951). Here the note was signed by four sureties (Bill, Mildred, Connie and Janet); Janet's proportionate share of indebtedness to her co-sureties is 25% of the debt.

whether the March, 1972 agreement by which Richard assumed full liability on the note constitutes a defense to Richard and Janet's third party claim that Walter and Connie reimburse them for fifty percent of the primary judgment granted to Bill and Mildred against Richard and Janet. In the circuit court Bill and Mildred Fithian, having paid the instrument to the Bank, successfully exercised their right of recourse on the note under § 3-415(5) [§ 3-419(e)] of the Commercial Law Article which provides that "[a]n accommodation party is not liable to the party accommodated, and if he pays the instrument has a right of recourse on the instrument against such party." In discussing this general principle of suretyship law Professors White and Summers explain that

[a]s between the surety and the debtor it is clear that the debtor has the primary obligation to pay the debt. Since the creditor is entitled to only one performance and the debtor receives the benefit of the transaction, the surety's obligation is undertaken with the expectation that the debtor will meet his commitment to the creditor. Thus, if the surety is made to pay his principal's debt, he has the right to recover from the principal. [J. White and R. Summers, *Uniform Commercial Code.* § 13-12, at 426 (1972) (footnote omitted)]

This Court has adhered to the principle that if an accommodation party pays the note to the holder, he has a right of recourse against the party accommodated . . . . Other courts have also adopted this viewpoint. . . .

Similarly, it is axiomatic that one joint obligor may ordinarily claim contribution from a co-obligor after having discharged their mutual obligation, . . . However, this principle is not controlling in the instant case. While the courts below ruled that Walter and Connie must reimburse Richard and Janet for one-half the judgment against them and discounted the significance of the 1972 agreement on this question, we believe that under both statutory and common law principles the 1972 agreement is material to the decision of this case and plays a substantial role in our determination of whether Walter was properly required to pay contribution to Richard. Because neither Connie nor Janet were parties to the agreement, their rights and obligations are not affected.

In the first place, § 3-601(2) [§ 3-601(a)] of the Commercial Law Article and the Official

Comments thereto specifically recognize the possibility of discharge by act or agreement of a party who is otherwise liable on an instrument. Section 3-601(2) [§ 3-601(a)] reads: "Any party is also discharged from his liability on an instrument to another party by any other act or agreement with such party which would discharge his simple contract for the payment of money."*...

Applying these principles to the present case, we believe that the 1972 agreement operated to modify the liabilities of Richard and Walter on the note between themselves.... Thus, the agreement expressed the intentions of these individuals as between themselves, and as such reflects the transfer of all of the assets and liabilities of the business to Richard in return for his promise to keep the other interested parties, Walter, Hogans and Bos, free from any responsibility for payment of any and all of the business debts, including the note in question. The only safety valve for the transferring individuals was their right upon their own decision to terminate the agreement if Richard demonstrated an inability or unwillingness to keep his promise. Richard and Janet in their briefs concede that the evidence of this agreement is "arguably material" but contend that is "not highly probative." We disagree. The language of the agreement shows that Richard specifically consented to take responsibility for the obligations of the printing business, including the $11,000 note to the Bank: ...

By this agreement, which was not terminated when Richard defaulted on payment of the loan in subsequent years, Walter and Richard agreed that Richard alone was to henceforth bear respon-

sibility for the note. Thus the document's operative effect was to discharge Walter from any obligation on the note as to Richard. Thus the trial court should have entered judgment for Walter on his counterclaim against Richard for indemnification. In other words, by the agreement, Richard gave up his right to claim contribution from his joint obligor, Walter. Therefore, the Court of Special Appeals below erred in affirming judgment for Richard against Walter.

JANET v. WALTER

That the 1972 agreement serves as a defense by Walter against Richard in no way serves to insulate Walter against Janet. Janet's status as an accommodation maker is unaffected by the agreement. As an accommodation maker, Janet has a right to look to any principal, including Walter for any amounts she actually pays. Maryland Code (1975), § 3-415 [§ 3-419(e)] of the Commercial Law Article. Janet's status as Richard's wife does not affect her status as an accommodation maker. She is entitled to judgment from either principal when she actually pays any amount of the debt.

In summary, Richard is not entitled to judgment against Walter because of the agreement. Rather, Walter is entitled to indemnification from Richard for any amount Walter is forced to pay. Richard is not entitled to judgment against Connie because an accommodation party is not liable to the party accommodated. Janet is entitled to contribution from her co-surety, Connie, the judgment being unenforceable unless and until Janet proves she actually has paid more than her proportionate share of the debt to Bill and Mildred. Similarly, Janet as a surety is entitled to judgment against Walter as a principal for any amount of the debt for which Janet proves payment.[3]

---

* [Editor: The Section now reads:

The obligation of a party to pay the instrument is discharged as stated in this Article or by an act or agreement with the party which would discharge an obligation to pay money under a simple contract. U.C.C. § 3-601(a).]

---

[3] Whether Bill and Mildred were entitled to judgment in the full amount of the debt against Janet we do not decide because Janet did not appeal from that judgment.

NOTE

1. Note footnotes 1 and 3. What can Janet recover from Connie?

2. An accommodation party may enter into a variant obligation whereby her obligation does not arise merely because of a failure by the accommodated party meeting his obligation when called upon. By indicating unambiguously that it is not payment but collection that is guaranteed, a limitation is placed on the liability of the accommodation party. The usual method of indicating this limitation is by adding the words "collection guaranteed" to her signature as an accommodation party. The effect of this limitation is that unless the party accommodated is insolvent or in an insolvency proceeding, for example, a petition in bankruptcy has been filed, or such party cannot be served with process, the person entitled to enforce the instrument cannot proceed against the accommodation party without first reducing his claim to judgment and showing that execution of judgment has been returned unsatisfied or that it is otherwise apparent that payment cannot be obtained from the party accommodated. U.C.C. § 3-419(d).

VII UNAUTHORIZED PAYMENT ORDERS

The promise, order or assumption of an obligation on an instrument all start from the premise that

> A person is not liable on an instrument unless (i) the person signed the instrument, or (ii) the person is represented by an agent or representative who signed the instrument and the signature is binding on the represented person under Section 3-402.

U.C.C. § 3-401(a).

U.C.C. Section 4-401(a) carries this farther by providing that a bank may charge the account of its customer only for "an item that is *properly* payable from the account" (emphasis added). This raises the issue of an unauthorized signature, including a forgery, on a payment order. An unauthorized signature "is ineffective except as the signature of the signer in favor of a person who in good faith pays the instrument or takes it for value." U.C.C. § 3-403(a). Unless such unauthorized signature is ratified, the signer would be liable on the instrument as an issuer, acceptor, or endorser, irrespective of any other civil or criminal liability incurred by his action.[1] It is only in the rarest cases that such liability has an economic value. The person defrauded will seek to establish the defense that due to the forgery, no liability should attach to her. Where it can be shown that the party alleging such forgery, or alleging an alteration, had substantially contributed to her loss[2] by failing to exercise ordinary care, such defense would be precluded. But we must note that the party *taking* such instrument, whose failure to take ordinary care also substantially contributed to the loss, will have to help alleviate the loss. The loss will be apportioned on the basis of comparative negligence. U.C.C. § 3-406(b). The burden of proving failure to exercise ordinary care is on the party asserting the preclusion, whether as a claimant or while defending herself against having to bear the total loss. U.C.C. § 3-406(c). Once banks are involved, and with such involvement automation, we must note that the definition of "ordinary care" in U.C.C. Section 3-103(a)(7) provides:

> In the case of a bank that takes an instrument for processing for collection or payment by automated means, reasonable commercial standards do not require the bank to examine the instrument if the failure to examine does not violate the bank's prescribed

[1] U.C.C. § 3-403(c).

[2] Note: the adjective "substantial" modifies the word "contributes," not the word "negligence." *See* Commonwealth of Pennsylvania v. Nat'l Bank & Trust Co. of Central Pennsylvania, 469 Pa. 188, 364 A.2d 1331 (1976).

procedures and the bank's procedures do not vary unreasonably from general banking usage not disapproved by this Article or Article 4.

In relation to a bank, we must note that an item that is the subject of a "stop payment order" is not an item that is properly payable so that payment of such item can be charged against the customer's account. U.C.C. Section 4-401 provides "[A]n item is properly payable if it is authorized by the customer and is in accordance with any agreement between the customer and bank." A stop payment order will have withdrawn the bank's authority to pay. It will be difficult for a bank to raise the preclusion defense against a customer where the bank has failed to honor a valid stop payment order. But the bank is given subrogation rights. Thus, where the presentment and payment was by or on behalf of a holder in due course, the bank could subrogate to the holder in due course and claim against the issuer of the item. U.C.C. § 4-407(1). Where payment was made to a holder or payee not qualifying as a holder in due course, the bank can subrogate to the rights of the holder or payee either on the instrument or on the underlying obligation, and to the issuer on the underlying obligation. As a result the bank will be made whole and the issue giving rise to the stop payment order will be resolved. U.C.C. § 4-407(2), (3).

A. Frauds—Forgery—Unauthorized Signatures—Alterations and the Preclusion Defense

1. Forgery

Commercial Credit Equipment Corp.
v.
First Alabama Bank of Montgomery, N.A.
636 F.2d 1051 (5th Cir. 1981)

FAY, Circuit Judge.

From a judgment for plaintiff-appellee, Commercial Credit Equipment Corporation (Commercial), as drawer of a forged check, against defendant-appellant, First National Bank of Montgomery (Bank), as payor of that check, ordering the Bank to remove the hold payment on Commercial's account for the amount of the check, the Bank appeals. The Bank asserts as error the trial court's rejection of its defense, based on Alabama Code § 3-406, that various acts by Commercial constituted negligence substantially contributing to the making and acceptance of the forged check, which should estop Commercial from asserting its claim against the Bank for the removal of the hold on its account. We hold that the trial court erred, as a matter of

law, in failing to find for the Bank on the basis of its defense. Accordingly, we reverse and remand with instructions to enter judgment for the Bank.

The primary figure in this case is C. Mercer Jones (Jones), a former employee of Commercial. Jones was hired on May 15, 1978 to serve as the Company's collection manager, a position all parties agree was one of trust. Jones was responsible for collecting past due accounts. His work was largely unsupervised and involved handling relatively substantial amounts of cash.[2] He was under a fidelity bond while working in that position.

---

[2] Jones routinely carried between $1,000 and $8,000 of the company's money on his person. At the time he was asked to resign he had $2,000 of company money which he had not turned in.

Jones' employment with Commercial originated when he was referred by an employment agency in early May 1978. Prior to that time he was unknown to the individuals at Commercial responsible for hiring, E. L. Norris, the assistant regional manager, and J. L. Stewart, the regional manager. Norris interviewed Jones on May 9, 1978, at which time Jones filled out a job application. After a second interview, conducted by Stewart, Jones was hired. Jones was not investigated by a credit bureau or credit reporting service, although it was Commercial's admitted standard practice to do so; he was not asked for credit references; no check was made of his creditors in Dothan, the city in which he previously had resided; and the personal references which he provided were not even contacted. The only inquiry made was to E. L. Gregory (Gregory), the manager of the Ford Motor Credit Corporation in Dothan, and Jones' former employer. The parties do not agree when Norris called Gregory, nor does either claim to recall the precise language of that conversation. We do not think either of those facts are particularly significant. What is important is that Gregory was not questioned in any way as to Jones' honesty or trustworthiness, nor was Gregory asked why Jones left his employment or if the company would rehire him. Had even such perfunctory inquiry been made, Norris would have discovered that Jones was forced to resign his position with Ford when they discovered him carrying out certain fraudulent practices against the company. Had Norris' inquiry gone further, he also would have discovered that Jones had carried out fraudulent schemes against the First Alabama Bank of Dothan. It was admitted that had Norris or Stewart possessed this information, Jones would not have been hired. Nonetheless, on May 15, 1978, Jones was hired to serve in a position of trust with Commercial.

The second significant link in this chain of events has to do with Commercial's method of operation in its Montgomery office; in particular, the manner in which it stores and supervises its checks and check writing equipment. Both the checks and a mechanical check embossing machine were stored in an unlocked metal cabinet in an unoccupied storeroom.[3] It takes little imag-

ination to guess what happened next. On June 28, 1978, some six weeks after coming to work for Commercial, Jones went into the storeroom, took check no. 134-5898, and used the embossing machine to print in the amount of $45,500. After everyone left that day, Jones, completed the stolen check by making it payable to Jones Farms and forging the signatures of Commercial's authorized agents, Norris and Stewart.

The following day Jones negotiated the forged check to the Union Bank and Trust Company of Montgomery. He received three cashiers checks: the first payable to himself for $10,359; the second payable to the First Alabama Bank of Dothan for $30,000; and the third payable to the Union Bank for $5,140.95. The Union Bank then [presented] the forged check to First Alabama Bank of Montgomery [Bank] which paid it on June 30, 1978.

Joan Hill, Commercial's clerk who had primary check writing responsibility, discovered the stolen check missing on July 5, 1978. She informed Commercial's home office in Maryland and was told to attach an explanatory notation to her daily Branch Cash Report. Though she testified such notation was made, it was never produced at trial. Both Joan Hill and Norris believed that a stop payment order was sent to the bank on the day the check was discovered missing. The bank never received that order. There are two possible explanations: the first is that Hill's and Norris' general recollection that it was sent was in fact erroneous, and the second is that the person asked to deliver the order to the Bank, none other than Jones himself, elected not to do so.

Commercial first became aware of the forgery on October 20, 1978,[4] and informed the Bank of that fact, by letter, that day. Upon acknowledging receipt of the forged check on October 31, 1978, the Bank credited Commercial's account in the amount of $45,500. On December 27, 1978, having concluded to its satisfaction that the forgery was caused by Commercial's own negligence, and upon advice of counsel, the Bank informed Commercial that it was putting a hold on Commercial's account in the amount of the potential loss. Suit was filed by Commercial to have the hold removed some eleven weeks later. From a judgment for Commercial, the Bank appeals.

As a preliminary matter we note that, since

---

[3] The check embossing machine printed the amount of the check only, it did not duplicate the authorized signatures necessary to complete the instrument.

[4] Jones was asked to resign three days later.

this Court's jurisdiction is based on diversity of citizenship, we are bound to apply the law of the jurisdiction in which the District Court hearing the case is located. *Erie Railroad Co. v. Tompkins*, 304 U.S. 64, 58 S. Ct. 817, 82 L. Ed. 1188 (1938). In this case, Alabama law is binding on us. We also note that this case was tried without a jury, strictly on stipulated facts, affidavits, and depositions. Though we are still governed by the clearly erroneous standard of review, with respect to factual findings of the District Court, Fed. Rules Civ. Proc. Rule 52(a), the appellant's burden of showing clear error is not as heavy as it would be had the District Court's determination involved the assessment of the credibility of witnesses by way of personal observation. *Marcum v. United States*, 621 F.2d 142, 145 (5th Cir. 1980).

The only issue presented on appeal is whether the trial court erroneously rejected the defense offered by the Bank, set forth in Alabama Code § 3-406. . . . The trial court ruled that the interpretation of that section was governed by *East Gadsden Bank v. First City National Bank of Gadsden,* 50 Ala. App. 576, 281 So. 2d 431 (1973). The court also held that, applying *East Gadsden,* the Bank had failed to establish either the requisite degree of negligence or the causal relationship between such negligence and the payor bank's *acceptance* of the check in question necessary to invoke the Section 3-406 defense. Though we agree with the trial court that *East Gadsden* is controlling, we disagree with its interpretation and application of that case.

In *East Gadsden,* plaintiff, payor bank, sued defendant, collecting bank, on the latter's guarantees of endorsement on a check which later was discovered to bear a forged endorsement. As one of its defenses to payment on the check, collecting bank asserted § 3-406, arguing that the negligence of the drawer of the check substantially contributed to its *making* and, therefore, liability should be placed on said drawer. The Alabama Court of Appeals held Section 3-406 inapplicable to those facts on the grounds that (1) the actions of the drawer were not negligent and (2) to the extent that negligence existed, it bore no causal relationship to the collecting bank's *acceptance** of the check.

The conduct of the drawer found to be non-negligent involved its acceptance from the forger

---

* [Editor: "taking" the check for collection.]

of a loan application which was accompanied by a buyer's order, for an automobile, bearing the forged signature of the purported seller. The court said that, while the drawer's failure to verify the order with the selling company may have been a poor practice, "[m]ere laxity in the conduct of the business affairs of the drawer is not such negligence as to preclude or estop him from recovery against the drawee bank for the amount charged against his account as a consequence of the bank's payment of a check bearing a forged endorsement." 281 So. 2d at 436.

The Alabama court also thought that, to the extent the drawer's issuance of check on a forged purchase order may have been negligent, "[s]uch act of the drawer was not the proximate cause of the acceptance of the forged endorsement." 281 So.2d at 436. By so holding, the Alabama Court of Civil Appeals interpreted the language of Alabama Code § 3-406 to mean that the drawer's negligence in *making* or contributing to the *making* of a negotiable instrument does not bar the drawer from recovering against the payor of such instrument when the drawer's negligence did not substantially contribute to the payor's *acceptance* of the instrument. Contrary to our appellant's contention, the Alabama Court did not erroneously construe the statutory language of "negligence substantially contributes . . . to the making" to mean negligence substantially contributing to the acceptance. The court simply held the fundamental principles of tort law to be applicable; that is that a negligent act does not in itself give rise to a right of recovery, unless it can be shown that such act caused the injury complained of. We think such interpretation of § 3-406 is wholly reasonable. We also think it is clear that, in *East Gadsden,* the payor bank accepted the check because of its negligence in failing to detect the forged *endorsement,* not because the drawer drafted the check initially. As drafted, the instrument was valid and negotiable. The check was drawn payable to both the automobile dealer and forger. The forger presented the instrument with a forged *endorsement* in the name of the automobile dealer.

East Gadsden establishes three criteria which must be established by a payor seeking to invoke § 3-406 as a defense against a drawer's suit to force the payor to assume liability for an altered or unauthorized instrument. They are the following: the payor must have paid the instrument in good faith and in accordance with reasonable commercial standards; the drawer must have acted negligently so as to contribute to the *making* of the alteration or unauthorized signature; and the drawer's negligent acts must be the proximate cause of the payor's *acceptance* of the instrument.[5]

In the present case it is undisputed that the Bank acted in good faith and that its normal practice of verifying the authenticity of signatures and endorsements is commercially reasonable. There is no evidence as to the processing of the specific check in question. The trial court did not deal with this point because it concluded that the Bank had failed to establish Commercial's negligence. Commercial offered no evidence to indicate that the Bank failed to follow its standard practice with respect to the negotiation of the check. Moreover, the Bank was prevented from producing direct evidence on that point as a result of Commercial's failure to notify the Bank of the forgery within a reasonable time thereafter. The Bank keeps records for ninety days of which employee verified the authenticity of signatures and endorsements on every check. After that time they are destroyed. This is a commercially reasonable practice. The check was negotiated on June 29, 1978. Commercial received it as part of its normal monthly statement on or about July 7, 1978. The Bank was not notified by Commercial of the forgery until October 20, 1978. By that time, the record that would have indicated which employee handled the check had been destroyed. We conclude that the

---

[5] Both parties make much ado about the extent to which *East Gadsden* interprets § 3-406 in a manner consistent with the interpretation the same provision has received in other jurisdictions. The Bank has provided this Court with citations from numerous jurisdictions, for the purpose of establishing that Alabama's interpretation is erroneous. We think it important to point out that such argument is meritless. Though uniformity in the interpretation and application of the Uniform Commercial Code may be desirable, it is not this Court's function to work toward such goal. The Courts of Alabama are free to construe their own law as they see fit. Had the Courts of Alabama not considered the question, the law of other jurisdictions might be instructional. Since they have done so in this case, we are bound to follow their direction. Additionally, we would point out that the interpretation given § 3-406 in *East Gadsden* is not significantly different than that adopted in many other jurisdictions. *See* Annot., 67 A.L.R. 3d 144 (1975).

Bank must be presumed to have followed its standard practice, absent evidence by Commercial to the contrary, particularly in view of the fact that Commercial's slowness in discovering the fraudulent check and giving notice prevented the presentation of the only evidence that existed. We are not willing to indulge in the presumption that the fact of negotiation established failure to follow reasonable practices. To take such a position would render § 3-406 meaningless. Though the burden would ordinarily be on the Bank to prove its adherence to its standard practice we believe the earlier recited facts warrant a somewhat different allocation of the burden in this case.

The next issue is whether Commercial committed acts of negligence that substantially contributed to the making of an unauthorized signature or the material alteration of the instrument in question. The District Court held that Commercial had not committed such negligent acts. The Bank asserts error in the District Court's failure to find negligence in Commercial's hiring of Jones and in Commercial's failure to adequately safeguard its checks and embossing equipment from being misused by him. We hold that those acts, when considered collectively, constituted clear negligence as a matter of law. Accordingly, we hold the District Court's determination to be clearly erroneous. We disagree with the trial court's characterization of the facts as being similar to the "merely lax business practices" discussed in *East Gadsden*. Commercial hired a person who would have been uncovered as a known defrauder had anything greater than a perfunctory inquiry to verify prior employment been made. Commercial admits they did not follow their own standard investigatory procedure for hiring new employees. Commercial further admits that had they had the knowledge that such investigation would doubtlessly have uncovered, Jones would never have been hired. To hire such an individual, without any meaningful inquiry, into a position in which his activities would be closely supervised, may be a lax business practice. To do the same, and place the person in a position of trust in which he is required to handle significant sums of money, and fail to provide any supervision, goes well beyond lax business practices. To compound the situation by giving the employee ready access to the company's checks and check embossing equipment is to ask for precisely the type of result that occurred. This is not to suggest that failure to keep the checks and embosser absolutely secure from all employees at all times constitutes negligence. The realities of day-to-day business operations obviously dictate otherwise. On the other hand, there must be some point at which a company's failure to monitor its employees and its financial records becomes both irresponsible and negligent. We believe the present situation goes well beyond that point. This is not like *East Gadsden,* in which the drawer was simply mislead. In this case, Commercial was an active participant in the activities that resulted in the forgery. As a direct result of Commercial's negligence, Jones was put in the position in which he had ready access to the company's checks and check embosser. It is difficult to imagine how Commercial could have more substantially contributed to the alteration of the check or the making of the forged signatures than it did, without being a party to the forgery.

The final question is whether Commercial's negligence in contributing to the making of the forged instrument was the proximate cause of the Bank's acceptance of the check. The District Court, having concluded that Commercial was not negligent, did not reach the issue. For the reasons set out below, we hold that Commercial's negligence was the proximate cause of the Bank's acceptance of the check.

Commercial contends that *East Gadsden* requires that the question of proximate cause be resolved in its favor. We disagree, because we think that case is factually distinct from the one at bar. In *East Gadsden,* the payor was presented with a valid check bearing a false endorsement. The negligence, if any, was in drafting a valid check without first authenticating the purchase order to which it was to be applied. The negligence of the drawer in no way enhanced the negotiability of the instrument nor contributed to its acceptance by the payor. Quite simply, the payor accepted the check because it failed to detect the forged *endorsement,* not because the drawer negligently issued it. In the present case, the question is not one of a forged endorsement. The instrument itself was invalid. It appeared to be valid and authentic, however, as a direct result of Commercial's negligence. Moreover, it was this apparent authenticity that substantially contributed to the Bank's negotiation of the check. Clearly, Commercial's negligence proximately caused the Bank to accept the invalid instrument.

We conclude that the Bank has proven all the elements necessary to set-up the § 3-406 defense to Commercial's suit to have the hold removed from its account. The Bank was entitled to recoup from Commercial the amount it lost when it negotiated Jones' check. Accordingly, the judgment of the District Court for Commercial is reversed and the case is remanded with instructions to enter judgment consistent with this opinion for appellant Bank.

NOTE

It is not possible to allege that a forgery has occurred where an instrument at issue[3] identifies a person to whose order the instrument is payable,[4] but the person (whether or not authorized), signing as, or in the name or on behalf of the issuer[5] (1) does not intend such person to have any interest in the instrument; or (2) clearly indicates a fictitious entity as the payee.[6] In both these circumstances, any person in possession of the instrument,

---

[3] U.C.C. § 3-105(a).

[4] U.C.C. § 3-109(b). This can be an entity other than a human, e.g. a trust, corporation, fund or even an account. *See* U.C.C. §§ 3-110(c), 1-201(28), (29), (30).

[5] U.C.C. §§ 3-105(b), 3-110(a). The actual signature can be manual or by means of an automated facsimile signature machine. U.C.C. §§ 3-110(b), 1-201(30).

[6] U.C.C. § 3-404(b). This situation must be distinguished from that where a mere misdescription of the payee had occurred, i.e. where the person is identified in the instrument by a name or other identification that is inaccurate in describing the intended person. For example:
"Pay to the Order of Miss Rita Income."
Miss Income has since married Mr. Tax and assumed her husband's name. For convenience and clarity such instrument should be endorsed by her:

Ms. Rita Income
Mrs. Rita Tax

including the wrongdoer who initiated this as a fraud on a principal or beneficiary, would be a holder and an endorsement in the name indicated on the instrument would be effective and thus would be neither a forgery nor an unauthorized signature. The signature would be effective to negotiate the instrument when it is taken by "a person who, in good faith, pays the instrument or takes it for value or for collection." U.C.C. § 3-404(b). The indorsement need not be in the same name as that on the instrument, so long as it is substantially similar. Where the instrument is deposited into a bank account by that name or one substantially similar, the fact that the instrument was not endorsed will create no problem for the depository/collecting bank.[7]

Many of these situations arise in connection with fraudulent activities of partners, fiduciaries, and employees. Employees are often given authority to issue small checks; for example, up to an amount below $5,000. A check in excess of that amount would thus not have been within the actual authority of the fraudulent employee. The employer, however, may be precluded from raising the unauthorized signature if he failed to exercise ordinary care and thereby is held to have substantially contributed to the loss. U.C.C. § 3-406.

Problem

The checks of X Corporation require the signature of the president and of the treasurer. The treasurer prepared a check payable to Joiner, Inc., a supplier of goods to X Corporation, but to whom no debt is at present owed. The treasurer signed the check and gets the president of X Corporation to sign the check. The treasurer then deposited the check in Depository Bank without endorsing the check. The deposit is into an account the treasurer had opened in the name of the Joiner Corporation. The check was honored by Drawee Bank. Treasurer withdrew the money in the account and has absconded.

(i) Can Drawee Bank debit X Corporation's account? *See* U.C.C. §§ 3-110, 3-404(b), 3-404(c), 4-205.

Note that where the taker has failed to exercise ordinary care, and that failure substantially contributed to the loss resulting from payment of the instrument, liability could be apportioned on the basis of comparative negligence. U.C.C. §§ 3-404(d), 3-103(a)(7).

(ii) Assuming Drawee Bank dishonored the check, can Depository Bank recover from X Corporation? *See* U.C.C. §§ 3-110, 3-404(b), (c), (d).

2. The Fraudulent Employee

Where an employee[8] has the responsibility of processing instruments for issuance or for deposit into a bank account, the employer may be held responsible for the fraudulent activities of such employee. These are situations in which the employer can be held responsible even though principles of the law of agency may not apply. The employer's protection lies in supervision and in fidelity bonding. The type of responsibility involved is defined by U.C.C. Section 3-405(a)(3) to mean authority

---

[7] *See* id. §§ 3-404(c) and 4-205.

[8] The term "employee" is given a wide meaning. It includes an independent contractor as well as an employee of an independent contractor. U.C.C. § 3-405(a)(1). For example, where the issuance of payroll checks is delegated to an outside firm.

(i) to sign or indorse instruments on behalf of the employer, (ii) to process instruments received by the employer for bookkeeping purposes, for deposit to an account, or for other disposition, (iii) to prepare or process instruments for issue in the name of the employer, (iv) to supply information determining the names or addresses of payees of instruments to be issued in the name of the employer, (v) to control the disposition of instruments to be issued in the name of the employer, or (vi) to act otherwise with respect to instruments in a responsible capacity. "Responsibility" does not include authority that merely allows an employee to have access to instruments or blank or incomplete instrument forms that are being stored or transported or are part of incoming or outgoing mail, or similar access.

U.C.C. Section 3-405(b) provides that the "fraudulent endorsement" appended by an employee having responsibility regarding the instrument will be effective and thus will be binding on the employer, when a demand is made by a person who, in good faith, has paid such instrument or had taken it for value or for collection. A failure by such person to have acted in accordance with the standard of ordinary care and thereby to have substantially contributed to the loss resulting from the fraud, however, may give rise to liability to the employer. Such liability will relate to the loss suffered by the employer and will be assessed in accordance with the concept of comparative negligence. Fraudulent endorsement includes a forgery of the employer's endorsement, as well as the forged endorsement of the person identified as payee on an instrument purporting to have been issued by the employer. This arises where the name of the payee or the address of the payee was supplied to the employer by the wrongdoer; for example, a payroll clerk who supplies the names and amounts due to employees by preparing checks for signature or by submitting records from which pay-checks will be prepared. U.C.C. § 3-405(a)(2). What we see here is a fusion of the preparer's intent with action by the employer. Thus, even though the name or address supplied may be that of an existing person, such as an employee who recently retired and who may be known to the employer or of an entity known as a supplier to the employer, an endorsement in that name or in a name substantially similar to the name of the person identified as the payee, will be effective. Also, a bank may accept such instrument for deposit into an account with a similar name even though the instrument is not endorsed. U.C.C. § 3-405(c). Where the facts indicate a failure to exercise ordinary care by a claimant under such instrument, the loss suffered from the fraud will be subject to alleviation on the basis of comparative negligence. U.C.C. § 3-405(b). For examples showing the extent of this section, see Comment 3 to U.C.C. Section 3-405.

Merrill Lynch, Pierce, Fenner & Smith, Incorporated
v.
Chemical Bank
57 N.Y.2d 439, 456 N.Y.S.2d 742, 442 N.E.2d 1253 (1982)*

FUCHSBERG, Judge.

This appeal requires us to explore the extent to which, if at all, immunity from liability accorded a drawee bank by section 3-405 ... of the Uniform Commercial Code may be limited by the drawee's negligence in paying checks over forged indorsements.

The section at issue, commonly referred to in commercial circles as either the "fictitious payee" or "padded payroll" rule, provides: "An indorsement by any person in the name of a named payee is effective if * * * an agent or employee of the maker or drawer has supplied him with the name of the payee intending the latter to have no such interest."

The factual context in which the case is here is undisputed. The defendant, Chemical Bank, unaware that the indorsements of the payees' name were forged, routinely paid 13 checks drawn by the plaintiff, Merrill Lynch, on its Chemical account in the aggregate sum of $115,180. The forgeries were occasioned by chicanery of a Merrill Lynch accounts payable employee who, by presenting his employer's New York check issuing department with false invoices which ostensibly represented obligations due its suppliers, caused checks to be issued to the order of these supposed creditors. The malefactor or accomplices then indorsed the names of the payees and, in face of the fact that New York addresses appeared below the payees' names, caused the checks to be deposited in California and Ohio bank accounts in names other than those to whose order they had been drawn. Seven of the checks were presented to Chemical by the Federal Reserve Bank (FRB) as collecting bank and the remainder by the depositary banks themselves. In due course, Chemical charged its Merrill Lynch account.

This suit, instituted by Merrill Lynch to recover the amount so debited, was brought on three theories. As set out in its complaint, the first was that "Chemical acted negligently and contrary to

normal and accepted banking practices, breached its duty of good faith and failed to exercise ordinary care." Particularizing, it added that Chemical should have been alerted to the irregular nature of the checks because "the purported indorsements of the corporate payees were handwritten, and in many instances illegible," were indorsed "in blank, rather than for deposit only" and bore "second indorsements of unrelated persons or entities." Reiterating the allegations of the first count, the second sounded in breach of contract and the third in conversion. In its answer, Chemical relied, among other affirmative defenses, on what, in the circumstances of this case, it took to be the exculpatory effect of section 3-405 [§§3-405(a)(2), (b)].

At the same time, Chemical, by way of a third-party summons and complaint, impleaded FRB essentially on the rationale that, if Merrill Lynch recovered, Chemical, in turn, should be made whole by FRB, which, as a collecting bank, would then have to be found in breach of its warranty of good title (Uniform Commercial Code, § 4-207). FRB countered with a motion for summary judgment, premised on the position that, under section 3-405 [§§3-404(b)(2), 3-405], "endorsement of the checks in the name of the payee thereof was sufficient and effective to transfer title to the instrument[.]" On the same ground, Chemical thereupon cross-moved for partial summary judgment dismissing Merrill Lynch's complaint.... Special Term denied both motions.

On appeal, the Appellate Division unanimously modified Special Term's order, on the law, by granting the motion directed to Chemical's third-party case against FRB. In so deciding, the court agreed that, under Section 3-405 [§§3-404(b), 3-405] of the Uniform Commercial Code, the forged indorsements were effective to transfer title to the checks. However, as to Chemical's cross motion against Merrill Lynch, the court, by a vote of 3 to 2, found that section 3-405 [§§3-404(b),

---

* [Editor: citations in [ ] refer to Revised U.C.C. Articles 3 and 4.]

3-405] was "not available to defendant to avoid liability for its own negligence" (82 A.D.2d 772, 773, 440 N.Y.S.2d 643); on this view, it affirmed, thus relegating the issue of Chemical's negligence to trial.

On the present appeal, which brings up for review Chemical's motion against Merrill Lynch only, the appellant in the main presses the point that its alleged negligence in disregarding irregularities in the indorsements may not deprive it of the benefits of section 3-405 [§§3-404(b), 3-405] of the Uniform Commercial Code and, in the alternative, that, in any event, it was not negligent because it was under no obligation to inspect the indorsements, a duty which, it insists, was the responsibility of FRB and the depositary banks alone. Echoing the dissent of Presiding Justice Murphy and Justice Silverman at the Appellate Division, Chemical also advances the pragmatic argument that a contrary reading of the statute would impose what, at least for large commercial banks, would constitute an unrealistically onerous and expensive burden of inspecting an "immense volume of checks," all the more so since these checks must be "processed and paid or alternatively, returned or dishonored by midnight of the following business day" (see *David Graubart, Inc. v. Bank Leumi Trust Co. of N.Y.,* 48 N.Y.2d 554, 557-558, 423 N.Y.S.2d 899, 399 N.E.2d 930). Merrill Lynch, on the other hand, choosing to interpret our decision in *Underpinning & Foundation Constructors v. Chase Manhattan Bank, N.A.,* 46 N.Y.2d 459, 414 N.Y.S.2d 298, 386 N.E.2d 1319 as supportive of its stance, continues to contend that section 3-405 [§§3-404(b), 3-405] of the Uniform Commercial Code will not absolve a banking institution, be it a depositary, drawee or collecting bank, from liability for its own negligence.

For the ensuing reasons, we believe that, under the circumstances of this case, Chemical's motion for partial summary judgment should have been granted.

Our analysis may well begin with the observation that section 3-405 [§§3-404(b), 3-405] bespeaks an exception to the general rule governing the responsibility of a bank to its customers. For it is basic that ordinarily a drawee bank may not debit its customer's account when it pays a check over a forged indorsement. This is because the underlying relationship between a bank and its depositor is the contractual one of debtor and creditor (*Brigham v. McCabe,* 20 N.Y.2d 525, 285 N.Y.S.2d 294, 232 N.E.2d 327), implicit in which is the understanding that the bank will pay out its customer's funds only in accordance with the latter's instructions (*Tonelli v. Chase Manhattan Bank, N.A.,* 41 N.Y.2d 667, 670, 394 N.Y.S.2d 858, 363 N.E.2d 564). Thus, absent contrary instruction or legislative exception, when a drawer issues a check in the name of a particular payee, the drawee bank is to apply funds from the drawer's account to its payment only upon receiving the payee's authorized indorsement. In this perspective, a forged indorsement, since it is an unauthorized signature (Uniform Commercial Code, § 1-201, subd. [43]), in and by itself would be "wholly inoperative" (Uniform Commercial Code, § 3-404, subd. [1] [§ 3-403(a)]).

It follows that, in the typical case in which payment is made on a check that is not properly payable (*see* Uniform Commercial Code, § 4-401, subd. [1] [§ 3-403(a)]), the payment is deemed to have been made solely from the funds of the drawee bank rather than from those of its depositor. But, when the conditions which section 3-405 contemplates prevail, the indorsement, though forged, is still effective, and the instrument then must be treated as "both a valuable instrument and a valid instruction to the drawee to honor the check and debit the drawer's account accordingly" (*Underpinning & Foundation Constructors v. Chase Manhattan Bank, N.A., supra,* at p. 465, 414 N.Y.S.2d 298, 386 N.E.2d 1319).

This departure from the general rule is explained by section 3-405's Official Comment 4, which advises, "The principle followed is that the loss should fall upon the employer as a risk of his business enterprise rather than upon the subsequent holder or drawee. The reasons are that the employer is normally in a better position to prevent such forgeries by reasonable care in the selection or supervision of his employees, or, if he is not, is at least in a better position to cover the loss by fidelity insurance; and that the cost of such insurance is properly an expense of his business rather than of the business of the holder or drawee".[*]

Since the assumptions instinct in this rationalization are hardly indisputable, it is no surprise

---

[*] [Editor: *See* Official Comment 1 to § 3-405 to the same effect.]

that the rule it supports represents a conscious choice between the traditional one, which, as we have seen, was more protective of the bank's customer, and the one in the code, which, as some commentators have bluntly acknowledged, was "a banker's provision intended to narrow the liability of banks and broaden the responsibility of their customers" (White & Summers, *Uniform Commercial Code*, § 16-8, p. 639). Thus, whatever, in the abstract, may have been the equities of the respective contentions of the competing commercial camps, there can be little doubt but that the outcome, so far as the adoption of section 3-405 of the Uniform Commercial Code is concerned, was calculated to shift the balance in favor of the bank "in situations in which the drawer's own employee has perpetrated the fraud or committed the crime giving rise to the loss" (1 Hawkland, *A Transactional Guide to the Uniform Commercial Code*, pp. 391-394).

That this represents contemporary legislative thinking is clear from the way in which the statutory scheme evolved. Long before section 3-405 of the Uniform Commercial Code came into being, subdivision 3 of section 28 of the former Negotiable Instruments Law already provided that a check is "payable to bearer * * * [w]hen it is payable to the order of a fictitious or non-existing person, and such fact was known to the person making it so payable." Carrying this language to its logical limits, one then might have thought that, because an instrument forged by an employee was to be treated as bearer paper, the fact of forgery had been rendered irrelevant to its negotiability.

Nevertheless, most courts, reluctant to read the statute this broadly, applied it only when the faithless employee made or drew the check himself, but not, as in the case before us now, when he had merely furnished the payee's name to the employer, for then the falsity presumably would not be "known to the person making it so payable" (Hawkland, *op. cit.*). This narrow interpretation apparently fell short of the drafters' intention because the reaction, first, in 1960, was to amend section 28 of the Negotiable Instruments Law to make it explicit that knowledge to the malefactor who furnished the name was sufficient (Britton, *Handbook of the Law of Bills and Notes*, § 149, pp. 433–437). And, secondly, by the adoption of section 3-405 of the Uniform Commercial Code, the bearer fiction device was

replaced by the more forthright effective indorsement concept (see Official Comment 1 to § 3-405 . . .).

The special scrutiny this legislative course demanded also highlights the fact that section 3-405's failure to delineate a standard of care, to which a bank itself must adhere if it is to advantage itself of this section, was no oversight. In contrast are sections 3-406 and 4-406 of the Uniform Commercial Code, which, along with section 3-405's "padded payroll" provision, deal with defenses which may be available to a drawee bank in forged indorsement cases.

For instance, subdivision (2) of section 4-406 [§ 4-406(d)], which otherwise precludes a customer from asserting a claim which might have been averted but for its neglect in examining "the [bank] statement and items to discover his unauthorized signature or any alteration on an item" (subd. [1] [§ 4-406(a), (c)]), makes preclusion inapropos when "the customer establishes lack of ordinary care on the part of the bank in paying the item" (subd. [3]). [see now § 4-406(e) which applies a comparative negligence approach to the loss suffered] And, similarly, section 3-406, which puts the onus for a forgery on a customer who "substantially contributes to a material alteration of the instrument or to the making of an unauthorized signature", still requires the bank to have paid the instrument "in good faith and in accordance with the reasonable commercial standards of the drawee's or payor's business".

It is fair to conclude, therefore, that, unlike cases which fall within the foregoing sections, a drawee bank's mere failure to use ordinary care in the handling of a check whose forgery has brought it within the embrace of section 3-405 (subd. [1], par. [c]) will not subject it to liability (White & Summers, *Uniform Commercial Code*, § 16-8, p. 639).[3]

---

[3] Because of the manifest advantages of uniformity in the law of bills and notes, we observe that other courts which have considered the matter have arrived at the same conclusion (*see, e.g.,* Prudential Ins. Co. of Amer. v. Marine Nat. Exch. Bank of Milwaukee, 371 F. Supp. 1002; Kraftsman Container Corp. v. United Counties Trust Co., 169 N.J.Super. 488; Fair Park Nat. Bank v. Southwestern Inv. Co., 541 S.W.2d 266 [Tex]; General Acc. Fire & Life Assur. Corp. v. Citizens Fid. Bank & Trust Co., 519 S.W.2d 817 [Ky]; Western Cas. & Sur. Co. v. Citizens Bank of Las Cruces, 33 UCC Rep 1018).

This is not to say that, if a check is "tainted in *some other way* which would put the drawee on notice, and which would make its payment unauthorized" (*Underpinning & Foundation Constructors v. Chase Manhattan Bank, N.A.,* 46 N.Y.2d 459, 466, 414 N.Y.S.2d 298, 386 N.E.2d 1319, *supra;* emphasis supplied), a drawee bank may yet not be liable. For instance, a drawee bank surely is not immunized by section 3-405 when it acts dishonestly. In short, "a basis for liability *independent* of any liability which might be created by payment over a forged instrument alone" may very well survive (*Underpinning & Foundation Constructors v. Chase Manhattan Bank, N.A., supra,* at p. 469, 414 N.Y.S.2d 298, 386 N.E.2d 1319; emphasis supplied).

In contrast, without more, in the present case, it is at once clear that the irregularities on which Merrill Lynch here focuses were part and parcel of the forgeries themselves and, as the dissenters at the Appellate Division observed, "could not possibly have alerted the bank to the fact that the checks were tainted, indeed it would have been most remarkable if the drawee bank had even noticed them". (82 A.D.2d 772, 774, 440 N.Y.S.2d 643, *supra*.)

Finally, Merrill Lynch's reliance on *Underpinning* is misplaced. The checks there, unlike the ones here, contained restrictive indorsements, e.g., "for deposit only", by which the maker explicitly limited deposit to the restrictive indorsers' accounts alone, failure to conform to which would create an independent cause for liability. Indeed in *Underpinning,* we are not called upon to resolve the liability of a drawee bank, but that of a depositary bank which, as the first to take the checks with the restrictive indorsements, could most readily have prevented the fraud (Uniform Commercial Code, § 3-206, subd. [2]; see, gen-

erally, Whalley, *Forged Instruments and the UCC's "Holder",* 6 Ind. L. Rev. 45, 50). Significantly, even there, we pointed out that the forgeries and disregard of the restrictions were distinct defects, one not justifying the other. Obviously, then, *Underpinning* and the present case are not akin.

Accordingly, the order of the Appellate Division, insofar as appealed from, should be reversed, with costs, and defendant Chemical's motion for partial summary judgment granted. The certified question should be answered in the negative.

COOKE, Chief Judge (concurring). . . .

As a general rule, a forged indorsement is wholly inoperative and ineffective to negotiate an instrument (see Uniform Commercial Code, § 3-404, subd. [1]). Consequently, the item is not properly payable and the drawer's account may not be charged (see Uniform Commercial Code, § 4-401, subd. [1]; Harbus, *The Great Pretender— A Look at the Impostor Provision of the Uniform Commercial Code,* 47 U.Cin.L.Rev. 385, 387). . . .

Section 3-405 should be recognized as the exception it is, however, and applied narrowly (White & Summers, *op. cit.*). When the indorsement is in a form that would not arouse suspicion, it would be effective to negotiate the check. If, however, the form of the impostor's or fictitious payee's indorsement is such that, under any other circumstances, it would raise a question as to the item's validity or regularity, the drawee's conduct would be scrutinized and, if found to be negligent, the drawee charged with the forged indorsement. . . .

JASEN, GABRIELLI, JONES and MEYER, JJ., concur with FUCHSBERG, J. COOKE, C.J., concurs in a separate opinion in which WACHTLER, J., concurs.

NOTE

In many instances there are double forgeries. The majority of "double forgery" cases arise in connection with employee fraud.

Problem #1

Jane, a companion to an elderly bedridden invalid, took some check forms and, after filling out the checks for various sums and payable to herself, signed them in the name of her employer. Over a period of six months she took these checks to the local supermarket, where her employer has check cashing privileges, and made purchases for herself, requesting the excess of the checks in cash. She also opened a checking account with Local Bank into which she paid some of the checks. These checks were all honored by the drawee bank. Each month the drawee bank has been sending monthly statements which were all piled up on the desk of the invalid who was too weak to reconcile the checks with the check stubs in the check book and with the monthly statements. You have been appointed "guardian" and have discovered these facts.

What are your remedies? Consider: U.C.C. §§ 3-403(a), 3-404(b), (d), 3-405(a)(3), (b), 3-406, 4-406(c), (d), (e), (f). Note also U.C.C. § 3-103(a)(7) as to meaning of ordinary care.

Problem #2

Assume that Bookkeeper, a 20-year employee of the law firm of Jones & Smith, for the past year has prepared fraudulent invoices covering services allegedly rendered by expert witnesses, investigators, and various companies allegedly selling supplies and equipment to Jones & Smith. Bookkeeper then forged checks made payable to the order of said parties and issued in the amount allegedly due to each one of them. Bookkeeper forged the named payees' indorsements on the checks and deposited them in an account which Bookkeeper had with Depositary Bank. Depositary Bank then forwarded the checks for payment to the drawee/Payor-Bank in which Jones & Smith had its account. Bookkeeper's fraudulent scheme involving fifty checks totaling $80,000 was not discovered until an outside auditor discovered the scheme on a routine inspection.[9]

Advise.

Since both the Jones & Smith drawer signature and the named Payees' indorsements were forged by Bookkeeper, we are dealing with the so-called "double-forgery" case. This type of case can be treated as a "forged drawer's signature" or a "forged indorsement" situation. Irrespective of whether this type of episode is treated as a "forged drawer's signature" or "forged indorsement" case, Payor-Bank would be liable to the drawer on the ground that the forgeries made the payment of the item improper. However, if treated as a "forged drawer's signature" case, the ultimate loss is suffered by the Payor-Bank under the rule of *Price v. Neal*.[10] On the other hand, treated as a "forged indorsement" case, the ultimate loss is suffered by Depositary Bank on its presentment warranty covering forged indorsements under U.C.C. § 4-208(a)(1). *Cf.* U.C.C. § 3-417(a)(1).

The majority of cases took the position that the forged indorsement is irrelevant because it is not the proximate cause of the loss since the named Payee of the forged check was not entitled to payment. It accordingly treats the "double forgery" case as a "forged drawer's signature" case.[11] The minority view treated the "double forgery" situation as a "forged indorsement" case, arguing that the majority treatment of such cases as "forgery of a

---

[9] Because the Payees whose names Bookkeeper had used had not rendered the services or delivered the supplies or equipment referred to in Bookkeeper's fraudulent invoices, they made no complaints of nonpayment to Jones & Smith and the fraud was therefore difficult to uncover.

[10] Price v. Neal, 3 Burr. 1354, 97 Eng. Rep. 871 (K.B. 1762).

[11] Perini Corp. v. First Nat'l Bank of Habersham County, 533 F.2d 398 (5th Cir. 1977), *re'h den.* 557 F.2d 823 (5th Cir. 1977).

drawer's signature" case ignores the fact that the fraud in many instances could have been avoided if Depositary Bank had exercised proper care and avoided negligence in taking the check.[12]

The above distinctions were of consequence in cases where the drawer was not negligent or otherwise precluded from raising the unauthorized indorsement or unauthorized drawer's signature. However, adoption of the comparative negligence attribution of liability by the revised U.C.C. in the imposter,[13] fictitious payee,[14] "faithless employee,"[15] and general accountability for negligence contributing to forged signatures or alterations of an instrument[16] situations make the classification of the Bookkeeper "double forgery" episode as a "forged indorsement" or "forged drawer's signature" case less important. This results from attribution of the loss between the payor and the drawer in each of the four situations indicated according to the extent to which each contributed to the loss.[17] In addition, U.C.C. Section 3-418(c) preserves rights of the payor against the presenting bank based on presentment warranties.[18]

3. Alterations

We noted that a signed writing, whether or not issued by the signer, the contents of which show that although incomplete at the time of signing was intended to be completed, is an "incomplete instrument."[19] Once completed as authorized, such writing will be binding on the issuer. The completion may be one necessary to satisfy the requirements of U.C.C. Section 3-104, so as to qualify the writing as a negotiable instrument; for example, where the amount has been left blank the completion now will show that the writing contains an "unconditional promise or order to pay a fixed amount of money." An unauthorized completion is treated as an alteration.[20] The burden of establishing that the completion was without authority is on the person asserting such lack of authority.[21]

An alteration is an unauthorized change in an instrument.[22] If not made fraudulently, the instrument can be enforced according to its original terms, but if made fraudulently it will discharge a party whose obligation is affected by the fraudulent alteration unless such person is precluded from asserting the alteration.[23] An exception to this rule exists. A drawee

---

[12] See McCall v. Corning, 3 La. Ann. 411 (1848); Mechanics' Natl. Bank of Worcester v. Worcester County Trust, 341 Mass. 465, 170 N.E.2d 476 at 480 (1960); Turner Graybill, *Reconsidering an Old Conundrum: The Case for Indorsement Liability on Double Forgeries.* 83 COMM L.J. 61 (1978).

[13] U.C.C. § 3-404(a)(c). *See* A4, p. 222 *infra.*

[14] U.C.C. § 3-404(b), (c).

[15] U.C.C. § 3-405.

[16] U.C.C. § 3-406.

[17] U.C.C. §§ 3-404(c), 3-405(b), 3-406(b).

[18] U.C.C. § 3-417(a)(1).

[19] U.C.C. § 3-115(a). *See supra* Chapter IV, p. 108.

[20] U.C.C. § 3-115(c).

[21] U.C.C. § 3-115(d).

[22] U.C.C. § 3-407(a).

[23] U.C.C. § 3-407(b).

paying a fraudulently altered instrument and "a person taking the [instrument] for value, in good faith and without notice of the alteration" can enforce the instrument according to its original terms. Where the alteration takes the form of an unauthorized completion of an incomplete instrument, the drawee, or a person taking the instrument in good faith, for value and without notice of the unauthorized completion can enforce the instrument as completed.[24] The U.C.C. does not require such person to qualify as a "holder in due course," but refers to "a person taking the instrument for value, in good faith and without notice of the alteration." U.C.C. § 3-407(c). There may be reasons why such person may not qualify as a holder in due course.[25] But, though not a holder in due course, a transferee or holder will be able to assert the rights embodied in the instrument as originally drawn or as completed. This is an exception to the general rule that a holder who does not qualify as a holder in due course can be met by all defenses available to the obligor on the underlying transaction or on the instrument. U.C.C. § 3-305(a)(2).[26] It is also a reconciliation of U.C.C. Section 3-406 (failure to exercise ordinary care) with U.C.C. Section 3-407 (an unauthorized change in an instrument paid by an innocent drawee or in the hands of a person who took the instrument for value in good faith and without notice of the alteration).

The assertion that there has been an alteration must be substantiated by the obligor on the instrument. This is especially important where the obligor asserts that the alteration was fraudulently made so as to discharge "a party whose obligation is affected by the alteration." U.C.C. § 3-407(b). The obligor, however, may be precluded from alleging an alteration by reason of his failure to observe due care, where such failure substantially contributed to the alteration. The drawee or a person taking the instrument must also have exercised ordinary care or the obligor will be able to assert that their failure substantially contributed to the loss and entitles the obligor to contribution to alleviate the loss suffered by him. U.C.C. §§ 3-103(a)(7), 3-406.

Where the instrument is in the hands of a person who was not a party to the alteration, such person will have recourse against his transferor on the basis of the transfer warranty that the instrument has not been altered. U.C.C. § 3-416(a)(3). Where there has been a negotiation, recourse will be based on the secondary liability embodied in the endorsement contract. U.C.C. § 3-415(a).

---

[24] U.C.C. § 3-407(c).

[25] *See* Chapter V.

[26] *See also* Convention on International Bills of Exchange and International Promissory Notes (CIBN) Article 28(d) which indicates that against a holder who is not a "protected holder," a party may raise defenses which may be raised in an action on a contract between such party and the holder. The closest analogy to a protected holder is a holder in due course. The basic difference between the approach of the CIBN and the U.C.C. is that only facts known to the holder can be raised as a defense against him under CIBN while no such knowledge of the defense is called for under the U.C.C.

Galatia Community State Bank v. Eugene Kindy
307 Ark. 467, 821 S.W.2d 765, 16 U.C.C. Rep. Serv. 2d (Callaghan) 710 (1991)*

NEWBERN, J. The appellant, Galatia [Illinois] Community State Bank, honored a check for $5,550.00 which was the amount imprinted by a check writing machine in the center underline section of the check commonly used for stating the amount in words. The imprint looks like this:

"RegistereD
No. 497345** 5550 DOL'S 00 CTS"

The impression made by the check-writing machine can be felt on the front and the back of the check, and "**5550 DOL'S 00 CTS" is imprinted in red ink. In the box on the right hand side of the check commonly used for numbers "6,550.00" appears in handwriting, but the 6 has been altered by hand so the amount reads "5550.00." Galatia Bank sued the appellee, Eugene Kindy, who was the drawer of the check after it had been dishonored. We must decide whether Galatia Bank was a holder in due course and thus entitled to recover despite the failure of consideration defense Kindy has against the payee.

The Trial Court held that, because a Galatia Bank employee changed the "6" in the handwritten portion to a "5," the bank did not take the check in "good faith" and thus was not a holder in due course. We hold Galatia Bank was a holder in due course because it was entitled to rely on the imprinted center underline section of the check, and the "alteration" which reconciled the terms was not a sufficient basis to hold that Galatia Bank acted in other than good faith.

Kindy buys and sells diesel engine parts. He agreed to buy four diesel engines from Tony Hicks who was to deliver them. The purchase price was $13,000. Kindy agreed to wire transfer $6,500 and pay the remainder by check. Kindy testified he and Hicks agreed the check would not be cashed until the motors were delivered to an address in Canada.

Kindy wired the $6,500 in late June of 1989, and concurrently wrote and mailed the check which was postdated July 6, 1989. Kindy placed two different amounts on the check because he did not want the check to be honored until Hicks delivered the engines. Kindy testified he thought if he made the check out with the two different amounts a bank would either call him to find out if it was good, or at least notify him before honoring it. He felt he could protect himself in that manner.

Hicks presented the check to the Galatia Bank on July 10, 1989. He received $800 in cash and credit to his account for $4,750. To reach the factual conclusion that a Galatia Bank employee had altered the check, the court first determined that the party filling out the accompanying deposit slip originally wrote 6550.00, crossed out that amount, changed it to 5550.00, and initialed the change. Those initials on the deposit slip were not the initials of Tony Hicks. The change was presumed to be the work of a Galatia Bank employee based on the particular steps taken in changing the slip. The court found a difference between the handwriting on the deposit slip and Hicks's endorsement on the back of the check. From this evidence, the court inferred a Galatia Bank employee filled out the deposit slip. The Court then found the handwriting on the deposit slip similar to the "5" which had been written over the "6." It was thus concluded that a Bank employee had made the alteration.

Galatia Bank sent the check through the Federal Reserve System for collection, and it was presented to First National Bank of Siloam Springs/Gentry for final payment. Kindy had previously told First National Bank to call him when the check was presented so he could determine whether Hicks had delivered the engines. First National Bank called Kindy when the check was presented, and Kindy said not to pay the check because the engines had not been delivered.

The check was returned to Galatia Bank on July 18th. Galatia Bank again presented the check to First National Bank, but the check was again returned as Kindy had placed a stop payment order. Galatia Bank sued for $4,753.64, the amount it lost as the result of Hicks drawing down the account in which the check had been deposited.

The trial court reviewed Ark. Code Ann. § 4-3-118(b) and (c) (1987) which has since been superseded by Ark. Code Ann. § 4-3-114 (Supp. 1991)

---

* [Editor: Citations in [ ] refer to Revised U.C.C. Articles 3 and 4.]

but which was in effect at the time in question in this case.[**]

In its opinion the trial court found the statute not to be helpful as the two subsections as applied in this case were contradictory.[***] That conclusion was not crucial, however, to the [trial] court's ultimate holding that the Galatia Bank acted other than in good faith and thus did not meet the requirement of Ark. Code Ann. § 4-3-302(b) (1987), now found at Ark. Code Ann. § 4-3-302(a)(2)(ii) (Supp. 1991).

Holder in due course
1. Good faith

If Galatia Bank had made a "fraudulent and material" alteration of the check without Kindy's assent, no doubt Kindy's liability on the instrument would have been discharged. Ark. Code Ann. § 4-3-407(2)(a) (1987). The new Code provision is slightly different. *See* Ark. Code Ann. § 4-3-407 (Supp. 1991). The trial court found specifically that the alteration was not done "fraudulently," and refused to hold Kindy was discharged. That finding was correct. . . . The court held, rather, that Galatia Bank was not a holder in due course because it did not take the check in "good faith."

"Good faith" is defined at Ark. Code Ann. § 4-1-201(19) (1987 and Supp. 1991) as "honesty in fact in the conduct or transaction concerned."

[**] [Editor: If an instrument contains contradictory terms, typewritten terms prevail over printed terms, handwritten terms prevail over both, and words prevail over numbers. U.C.C. § 3-114.]

[***] [Editor: The contradiction has been eliminated by Revised U.C.C. § 3-114.]

While we have referred to the "good faith" requirement found in § 4-3-302(1)(b) (1987) [3-302(a)], *Richardson v. Girner,* 282 Ark. 302, 668 S.W.2d 523 (1984), it has not, so far as we know, been the basis of a holding by this Court. Professors White and Summers write that the good faith requirement is closely related to the requirement of Ark. Code Ann. § 4-3-302(1)(c) (1987) that the holder not have "notice that it [the instrument] is overdue or has been dishonored or of any defense against or claim to it on the part of any person." 1 J. White and R. Summers, *Uniform Commercial Code* (3rd ed. 1988). The authors point out that there is a difference between the two requirements, and suggest that the good faith should be a subjective one as was intended by the drafters of the Code.

We cannot agree with the trial court's conclusion that Galatia Bank was not acting in good faith. There is neither evidence nor legitimate speculation that Galatia Bank or the employee found to have performed the alteration intended harm to any party. As will be discussed below, it was proper for Galatia Bank to accept the check as being in the amount of $5,550, and the alteration did no more than cause the instrument to recite that amount uniformly. There was no evidence before the Court to suggest that the change was done other than with "honesty in fact in the . . . transaction concerned."

Given these authorities, we conclude Galatia Bank was a holder in due course with respect to the check and should be allowed to recover against Kindy. Therefore, we reverse and remand for entry of a judgment consistent with this opinion.

Reversed and remanded.

NOTE

The situation involved an ambiguous term due to contradictions. U.C.C. Section 3-114 resolves an ambiguity where there are contradictory terms. *See also* U.C.C. Section 3-116 as to an ambiguity created by joint and several parties being named on an instrument. The court appears to have treated the imprint of the check writing machine as a "writing" or as "words" to allow the sum indicated by the check writing machine to prevail.

Problem

Drawer issued a check made payable to the Internal Revenue Service and mailed the check to its Florida office for forwarding to the Internal Revenue Service. When the manager of the Florida office received the check, he altered, without authority, the name of the payee from "Internal Revenue Service" to "Plantation Island for Internal Revenue Service." The check was then indorsed by the Plantation Homeowner's Association. A bank in Florida cashed the check, and the proceeds were paid into the account of the Plantation Island Homeowner's Association. Drawee, in turn, accepted the check and paid the face amount to the Florida bank, and debited drawer's account. Drawer alleges that the check was not "properly payable" and the account could not be charged the amount of the check.

    (i).   Was there an alteration? [§ 3-407(a)]

    (ii).   Was the alteration fraudulent? [§ 3-407(b)]

    (iii).   What about § 3-406?

    (iv).   Does §§ 3-405 or 3-404 apply?

    Consider *Biltmore Assoc., Ltd. v. Marine Midland Bank, N.A.,* 578 N.Y.S.2d 798 (App. Div. 1991).

4. The Impostor

We noted in Chapter V that even against a holder in due course an issuer can assert that she was fraudulently induced "to sign the instrument with neither knowledge nor reasonable opportunity to learn of its character or its essential terms." U.C.C. § 3-305(a)(1)(iii). *Burchett v. Allied Concord Fin. Corp.,* 74 N.M. 575, 396 P.2d 186 (1964). Fraud in the inducement to issue or sign an instrument as opposed to fraud in factum—this is not my act—is a defense to a person entitled to enforce the instrument[27] who can not qualify as a holder in due course.

Enter the imposter who represents herself as a person entitled to have a check issued to her; for example, by representing herself as an agent of a supplier of goods, or services who has come to collect the amount due therefor. Clearly there is an intention to issue the instrument and there is knowledge that what is signed is a check or other instrument. In the normal course of events, such instrument will be deposited into a bank, presented in the course of the bank collection process, and honored. The amount may then be withdrawn by the crook who absconds. Who bears the loss?

U.C.C. § 3-404(a) provides:

§ 3-404 - Imposters; Fictitious Payees.

    (a) If an imposter, by use of the mails or otherwise, induces the issuer of an instrument to issue the instrument to the impostor, or to a person acting in concert with the impostor (by impersonating the payee of the instrument or a person authorized to act for the payee), an indorsement of the instrument by any person in the name of the payee is effective as the indorsement of the payee in favor of a person who, in good faith, pays the instrument or takes it for value or for collection.

---

[27] U.C.C. § 3-301.

Philadelphia Title Ins. Co. v. Fidelity-Philadelphia Trust Co.
419 Pa. 78, 212 A.2d 222 (1965)*

COHEN, Justice.

This is an appeal in an action in assumpsit brought by plaintiff-appellant, Philadelphia Title Insurance Company, against defendant-appellee, Fidelity-Philadelphia Trust Company, to recover the sum of $15,640.82 which was charged against the Title Company's account with Fidelity in payment of a check drawn by the Title Company on Fidelity. The complaint alleged that the endorsement of one of the payees had been forged and that, therefore, Fidelity should not have paid the check. Fidelity joined the Philadelphia National Bank as an additional defendant claiming that if Fidelity were liable to plaintiff, PNB was liable over to Fidelity for having guaranteed the endorsements. PNB joined the Penn's Grove National Bank and Trust Company as a second additional defendant claiming that if PNB were liable to Fidelity, Penn's Grove was liable to PNB for having cashed the check and guaranteed the endorsements. By way of defense all of the banks asserted that none of them were liable because the issuance of the check by the Title Company was induced by an impostor and delivered by the Title Company to a confederate of the impostor thereby making the forged endorsement effective.

The case was tried before the lower court sitting without a jury. The trial judge found in favor of the Title Company. Exceptions to said finding were sustained unanimously by the court en banc and judgment was entered against the Title Company and in favor of the banks. The judgment must be affirmed.

The pertinent facts are stated by the lower court:

"Edmund Jezemski and Paula Jezemski were husband and wife, estranged and living apart. Edmund Jezemski was administrator and sole heir of his deceased mother's estate, one of the assets of which was premises 1130 North Fortieth Street, Philadelphia. Mrs. Jezemski, without her husband's knowledge, arranged for a mortgage to be placed on this real estate. This mortgage was obtained for

---

Mrs. Jezemski through John M. McAllister, a member of the Philadelphia Bar, and Anthony DiBenedetto, a real estate dealer, and was to be insured by Philadelphia Title Insurance Company, the plaintiff. Shortly before the date set for settlement at the office of the title company, Mrs. Jezemski represented to McAllister and DiBenedetto that her husband would be unable to attend the settlement. She came to McAllister's office in advance of the settlement date, accompanied by a man whom she introduced to McAllister and DiBenedetto as her husband. She and this man, in the presence of McAllister and DiBenedetto, executed a deed conveying the real estate from the estate to Edmund Jezemski and Paula Jezemski as tenants by the entireties and also executed the mortgage, bond and warrant which had been prepared. McAllister and DiBenedetto, accompanied by Mrs. Jezemski, met at the office of the title company on the date appointed for settlement, the signed deed and mortgage were produced, the mortgagee handed over the amount of the mortgage and the title company delivered its check to Mrs. Jezemski for the net proceeds of $15,640.82 made payable, as we have already mentioned, to Mr. and Mrs. Jezemski individually and Mr. Jezemski as administrator of his mother's estate."

* * *

"[The Title Company's] settlement clerk, in the absence of Edmund Jezemksi at the settlement, accepted the word of McAllister and DiBenedetto that the deed and mortgage had been signed by Jezemski; he himself, though he had not seen the signatures affixed, signed as a witness to the signatures on the mortgage; he also signed as a witness to the deed, and in his capacity as a notary public he acknowledged its execution."

* * *

"* * * Paula Jezemski, one of the payees, * * * presented [the check], with purported endorsements of all the payees, at the Penns Grove National Bank and Trust Company in

---

* [Editor: citations in [ ] refer to Revised U.C.C. Articles 3 and 4.]

Penns Grove, New Jersey, for cash. Edmund Jezemski received none of the proceeds, either individually or as administrator of the estate of Sofia Jezemski; and it is conceded that the endorsements purporting to be his were forged. The Penns Grove bank negotiated the check through the Philadelphia National Bank, and it was eventually paid by Fidelity-Philadelphia Trust Company, which charged the amount of the check against the deposit account of plaintiff.''

* * *

"There is no question that the man whom Mrs. Jezemski introduced to McAllister and DiBenedetto was not Edmund Jezemski, her husband. It was sometime later that Edmund Jezemski, when he tried to convey the real estate, discovered the existence of the mortgage. When he did so he instituted an action in equity which resulted in the setting aside of the deed and mortgage and the repayment of the fund advanced by the mortgagee.''

The parties do not dispute the proposition that as between the payor bank[1] (Fidelity-Philadelphia) and its customer[2] (Title Company), ordinarily, the former must bear the loss occasioned by the forgery of a payee's endorsement (Edmund Jezemski) upon a check drawn by its customer and paid by it. * * *

However, the banks argue that this case falls within an exception to the above rule, making the forged indorsement of Edmund Jezemski's name effective so that Fidelity-Philadelphia was entitled to charge the account of its customer, the Title Company, who was the drawer of a check. The exception asserted by the banks is found in § 3-405(1)(a) [§ 3-404(a)]. . . . The lower court found and the Title Company does not dispute that an impostor appeared before McAllister and DiBenedetto, impersonated Mr. Jezemski, and, in their presence, signed Mr. Jezemski's name to the deed, bond and mortgage; that Mrs. Jezemski was a confederate of the impostor; that the drawer, Title Company, issued the check to Mrs. Jezemski

naming her and Mr. Jezemski as payees; and that some person other than Mr. Jezemski indorsed his name on the check. In effect, the only argument made by the Title Company to prevent the applicability of Section 3-405(1)(a) [§ 3-404(a)] is that the impostor, who admittedly played a part in the swindle, *did not "by the mails or otherwise" induce the Title Company* to issue the check within the meaning of Section 3-405(1)(a) [§ 3-404(a)]. The argument must fail.

Outside the Uniform Commercial Code, the impostor doctrine has taken many forms and been based on numerous theories, see Annotation 81 A.L.R.2d 1365 (1962), all of which, when applicable, place the loss on the "innocent" duped drawer of the check rather than the "innocent" duped drawee or payor. Although one form of the doctrine had existed in Pennsylvania for at least fifty-three years before the adoption of the Commercial Code, see *Land Title and Trust Company v. Northwestern National Bank,* 196 Pa. 230, 46 A. 420 (1900), no case has been found which decided whether or not the pre-Code doctrine would have applied to the instant factual situation—when the impostor, rather than communicating directly with the drawer, brings his impersonation to bear upon the drawer through the medium of the representations of third persons upon whom the drawer relies, in part, in issuing the check. But, regardless of the pre-Code form of the impostor doctrine and its applicability to the instant factual situation, the matter must be decided by statutory construction and application of the impostor doctrine as it now appears in Section 3-405(1)(a) [3-404(a)] of the Code.

Both the words of Section 3-405(1)(a) [3-404(a)] and the official Comment thereto leave no doubt that the impostor can induce the drawer to issue him or his confederate a check within the meaning of the section even though he does not carry out his impersonation before the very eyes of the drawer. Section 3-405(1)(a) [§ 3-404(a)] says the inducement might be by "the mails or otherwise." . . .

Moreover, the Legislature's use of the word "otherwise" and the Comment, which suggests that results should not turn upon "the type of fraud which the particular impostor committed," indicates that the Legislature did not intend to limit the applicability of the section to cases where the impostor deals directly with the drawer (face-to-face, mails, telephone, etc.). Naturally, the

---

[1] ["Payor bank" means a bank that is the drawee of a draft. U.C.C. § 4-105(3).]

[2] ["Customer means a person having an account with a bank or for whom a bank has agreed to collect items, . . . U.C.C. § 3-104(a)(5).]

Legislature could not have predicted and expressly included all the ingenious schemes designed and carried out by impostors for the purpose of defrauding the makers or drawers of negotiable instruments. Something had to be left for the courts by way of statutory construction. For purposes of imposing the loss on one of two "innocent" parties, either the drawer who was defrauded or the drawee bank which paid out on a forged endorsement, we see no reason for distinguishing between the drawer who is duped by an impostor communicating directly with him through the mails and a drawer who is duped by an impostor communicating indirectly with him through third persons. Thus, both the lan-

guage of the Code and common sense dictates that the drawer must suffer the loss in both instances.

The parties have argued at length respecting the effect that should be given to the "negligence" of the Title Company's settlement clerk. . . . [T]he Code does include a separate provision, § 3-406, wherein the drawer's or maker's negligence is quite material to his right to recover. However, it is unnecessary to decide whether that section applies here to defeat Title Company's recovery since recovery is precluded by reason of the applicability of § 3-405 [§ 3-404(a)].

Judgment affirmed.

NOTE

U.C.C. Section § 3-404(a) expands the approach taken by the common law in *Phelps v. McQuade,* 220 N.Y. 232, 115 N.E. 441 (1917), which required a face-to-face confrontation with the impostor, and rejects the approach taken by the English House of Lords in *Cundy v. Lindsay* [1878] AC 459 (H.L.), which allowed an assertion of the defense of "mistake" to deny the existence of a contractual relationship where the impostor made use of the mails. But the section goes even further. In modern commerce, most impostor situations arise when the crook represents himself to be the agent of a corporation and receives an instrument payable to the corporation. Former Section 3-405(1)(a) had held that the intention being to issue the check to the corporation, i.e., the purported principal, a signature by the fraudulent person would be a forgery and thus ineffective. *Cf. Rogers v. Dutton,* 182 Mass. 187, 65 N.E. 52 (1902). The question may be asked who should bear the loss as between two equally innocent parties, where the instrument is paid, or taken for value, or for collection in good faith? U.C.C. Section 3-404(a) gives an answer precluding the issuer from raising the fraud practiced on him by asserting that the signature of the payee is a forgery. The taker, however, must comply with the requirement of "ordinary care" (§ 3-103(a)(7)) so as not to have substantially contributed to the loss resulting from payment of the instrument. If held to have substantially contributed to the loss, the taker could be called upon to contribute to the alleviation of such loss. (U.C.C. § 3-404 (d)).

The endorsement of such instrument by any person in the name of the payee is "effective" as the indorsement of the payee in favor of a person who in good faith pays the instrument or takes it for collection. U.C.C. § 3-404(a). It is sufficient to satisfy the requirement of U.C.C. Section 3-201, so as to enable the taker to have rights against the party asserting a forgery and defenses against a claim of liability for conversion based on U.C.C. Section 3-420. Further, the indorsement is effective not only if made in the name of the payee, but also if it is made in a name substantially similar to that of the payee on the instrument. In addition, where the instrument, whether endorsed or not, is deposited for collection into a bank account in a name substantially similar to that of the payee indicated on the instrument, the depository bank will be able to avoid liability for conversion, U.C.C. Section 3-420, or for breach of transfer warranties or of presentment warranties,

U.C.C. §§ 4-207, 4-208. This latter provision again shows the influence of the banking industry in gaining such exculpation. *See* D.J. Rapson, *Loss Allocation in Forgery and Fraud Cases: Significant Changes Under Revised Articles 3 and 4,* 42 Ala. L. Rev. 435 (1991); *compare* E. Rubin, *Efficiency, Equity and the Proposed Revision of Articles 3 and 4,* 42 Ala. L. Rev. 551 (1991).

B. Unauthorized Orders

Absent a preclusion to raising an unauthorized signature or an alteration, U.C.C. Sections 3-403, 3-404, 3-405, 3-406, 3-407, it is not possible to charge a maker or drawer on a forged[28] or fraudulently altered instrument. A drawee honoring, i.e., paying or accepting such instrument, will not be able to charge the account of the drawer. There would be no direction to the drawee to pay such item or, in the case of an amount altered albeit not fraudulently altered, the altered amount. The claim of the drawer to have his credit reinstated would be based on the underlying transaction, usually contract, on the basis of which the drawee undertook to pay items "properly payable." Having nonetheless paid the item, the drawee will be deemed to have done so out of its own funds and would have to recover its loss in some other manner.[29] Similarly, having accepted a forged or altered instrument, the drawee/acceptor becomes primarily liable to pay the draft "according to its terms at the time it was accepted." U.C.C. § 3-414(a). Such payment or acceptance, however, can be revoked on the ground of mistake and a claim to restitution can be asserted. Recovery will not be possible, however, where payment was made to a person who took the instrument in good faith and for value or who in good faith changed position in reliance on the payment or acceptance. U.C.C. §§ 3-418(a), (b), (c). This approach has been under attack by banks for some time, but has survived since 1762.[30]

The presenter's warranties will not help to recover a payment made on a forged instrument since the presenter merely warrants that "the warrantor has no knowledge[31] that the signature of the drawer of the draft is unauthorized." U.C.C. §§ 3-417(a)(3), 4-208(a)(3). On the other hand, a breach of warranty can be shown to have occurred where the instrument has been altered, U.C.C. §§ 3-417(a)(2), 4-208(a)(2), or where there has been a forgery of an indorsement through which the presenter claims to be a person entitled to enforce the instrument. U.C.C. §§ 3-417(a)(1), 3-301, 3-403.[32] The presenter of course can raise the

---

[28] "Forged instrument" means an instrument on which the signature of the maker or that of the drawer is forged.

[29] Note as to bank drawee, the effect of U.C.C. § 4-406(c), (d). In the case of a repeat wrongdoer, a customer may be precluded from asserting the existence of his unauthorized signature, or of an alteration against the bank drawee, due to failure to report such violation to the bank within a period not to exceed 30 days from receipt of a statement of account containing reference to the disputed item. In all other cases the customer must assert the alteration or the fraudulent signature against a drawee/payor bank within one year. U.C.C. § 4-406(f).

[30] Price v. Neal, 3 Burr. 1354, 97 Eng. Rep. 871 (K.B. 1762).

[31] This calls for actual knowledge. U.C.C. § 1-201(25).

[32] Compare the Convention on International Bills of Exchange and International Promissory Notes (CIBN) Articles 25 and 26 which confine this warranty liability to the forger, a transferee from the forger, and a party that paid the forger to discharge the obligation in the instrument.

preclusion defenses where applicable, e.g., U.C.C. Section 3-406, to enforce his claim to be entitled to enforce the instrument.

The effect of a stop payment order terminating the authority to pay the instrument, or of a notice that the drawer has died or become incompetent is to change an authorized order into an unauthorized one. Various questions arise in connection with such revoked authority and the effects of a failure to react to such revocation of authority. U.C.C. Sections 4-403, 4-405 and 4-407 provide answers to some of the issues raised.

1. Recovery by Drawee for Mistaken Payment or Acceptance

A drawee, acting under the mistaken belief that payment of a draft had not been stopped, U.C.C. Section 4-403, or that the signature of the drawer was authorized, may recover the amount of the draft from the person to whom payment was made or, in the case of acceptance, may revoke the acceptance. This power exists even though the drawee has failed to exercise ordinary care when paying or accepting the draft. U.C.C. §§ 3-418(a), 3-103(a)(7). In all other cases, where a drawee paid or accepted an instrument, for example, a bank certifying a check in the mistaken belief that there were adequate funds in the drawer's account to cover the draft, U.C.C. Section 3-418(b) allows recovery to the extent the law governing mistakes and restitution would do so. Recovery under U.C.C. Section 3-418(a) or (b) is possible even though final payment by a bank drawee/payor under U.C.C. Section 4-215 may have occurred and even though a cashier's check has been issued in payment for, or in settlement of, the instrument accepted. Although the bank that issued the cashier's check will have to honor its check when it is presented by a holder in due course, the right to seek restitution from the presenter of the check that led to the issuance of the cashier's check survives and can be asserted by the bank issuer. It was the mistake in failing to honor the stop payment order, or in believing the account of the drawer to be adequate to cover the amount of the check, that led to the issuance of the cashier's check in payment for the check presented. This is a mistake remediable by the provisions of U.C.C. Section 3-418 (a) and (b).

Demos v. Lyons
151 N.J. Super. 489, 376 A.2d 1352 (1977)*

BRODY, J.J.D.R.C.

This litigation arises out of the failure of George and Christine Demos (buyers) to go through with the purchase of the Summit Squire Restaurant—the business from Summit Squire, Inc. and the realty from Anna L. Pizzi and Raymond C. Zeltner, trading as Cranford Hall Nursing Home (sellers). Sellers contend that the terms of sale are embodied in a signed contract. Buyers characterize the writing as merely a memorandum of intent, subject to approval by their attorney who had not seen it before they signed. When the document was signed, and in accordance with its terms, buyers gave sellers' attorney Raymond T. Lyons, Jr. a $25,000 check drawn on Somerset Trust Company (the bank) to hold in escrow as a deposit. Bank paid the check even though doing so produced a $9,638.28 overdraft against buyers' account.

---

* [Editor: citations in [ ] refer to Revised U.C.C. Articles 3 and 4.]

The dispute between the buyers and sellers over disposition of the deposit must be resolved at trial. Now before the court for summary adjudication are the bank's claims against the buyers for reimbursement and against the stakeholder Lyons for return of the $9,638.28. I granted the bank partial summary judgment against the buyers for reasons given in an oral opinion. See [U.C.C. § 4-401(a)], which permits a bank to charge an overdraft against its customer's account. More troublesome is the question of whether the bank should have judgment as well against the stakeholder. Sellers resist the bank's motion and make their own against the bank, seeking to foreclose it from retrieving the $9,638.28.

It appears from the bank's evidence that the check was presented to it for payment late in the afternoon of June 2, 1976. One of the buyers, George Demos, had been in the bank that morning and advised its personnel that he was buying the Summit Squire, a substantial restaurant business in downtown Summit. He requested the bank to prepare an amortization schedule of payments to be used, he said, in connection with private financing he had arranged to complete the purchase. When the check arrived the bookkeeper's records disclosed that the buyers' account lacked $9,638.28 to cover it. It was too late in the day to learn from the bank's computer whether Demos had made a deposit to his account that morning to cover the check, and the bank was unable to reach him by telephone to determine whether he had done so. The check bore a notation "Deposit Summit Squire," which, with what they learned from Demos's appearance earlier that day, correctly led officers of the bank to conclude that it was the deposit on the buyers' purchase of the restaurant.

The bank had to decide whether to hold the check until the following day, dishonor it, or pay it. Because the check was for a large sum, the officers felt obliged by custom to advise Lyons' depositary bank that afternoon if it was going to dishonor it. So as not to embarrass their customer in this important transaction, the bank officers decided to pay the check. In fact, Demos had made no deposit to cover the check.

The bank contends that its claim is governed by *Maplewood Bank and Trust Co. v. F.I.B., Inc.,* 142 N.J. Super. 480 (App. Div. 1976), where the court, dealing with a strikingly similar set of facts, gave the bank judgment because it had paid the check by mistake. The court applied U.C.C. § 3-418, which reads in pertinent part, that "* * * payment or acceptance of any instrument is final in favor of a holder in due course, or a person who has in good faith changed his position in reliance on the payment." The issue in *Maplewood Bank* was whether the stakeholder was a holder in due course. The court held he was not and therefore the bank was entitled to restitution because it had mistakenly paid the check.

The sellers have conceded that, as was the case in *Maplewood Bank,* they were not holders in due course and did not change their position in reliance on the payment. They contend, however, that *Maplewood Bank* does not control because that court did not consider the effect of [U.C.C. § 4-215(a)], which reads in part, "An item is finally paid by a payor bank when the bank has [first] done any of the following, [(1)] paid the item in cash; [etc.] * * *." The sellers argue that this provision bars restitution absolutely because of the absence of § 3-418 language that applies the bar only to protect a holder in due course or a person who relied on the payment.

Given the asserted conflict between the chapter 3 ("Commercial Paper") section and the chapter 4 ("Bank Deposits and Collections") section, the sellers contend that the chapter 4 section should prevail in accordance with [U.C.C. § 4-102(a)], which provides in part, ["If there is a conflict this Article governs Article 3 * * *."] Their position is supported in White and Summers, *Uniform Commercial Code* (1972), 16-2 and 16-3 at 519-529.

The word "final," as used to describe a payment, embraces two distinct concepts: one, a rule of law; the other, the time payment occurs.

As a rule of law, "payment is final" refers to the common law principle that one cannot recover back money paid, simply because of a change of mind. Its rationale is repose. Establishing the finality of a payment tends to assure stability in people's affairs. However, the law may compel restitution where there are competing considerations—such as fraud, duress and mistake—favoring the payor. When these considerations are raised, the evidence must be examined and equities balanced. Under some circumstances the payor's equities are insufficient to overcome those of the payee or others who may have relied in good faith on the payment. But even where no one has relied on the payment, the policy of repose may nevertheless prevail where the payor's asserted equity is based on facts he knew before payment and freely chose to disregard. Where the payor is denied restitution because others relied in good faith on the payment, he is said to be estopped. Where no one relied upon the payment but restitution is denied because the payor voluntarily paid knowing he had reason not to, he is said to have waived his right to restitution based on that reason. See *Ross Systems v. Linden Dari-Delite, Inc.,* 35 N.J. 329, 334 (1961), and *Great American Ins. Co. v. Yellen,* 58 N.J. Super. 240, 245 (App. Div. 1959).

As a description of the time when payment occurs, "payment is final" means that commercial paper is paid at the moment the payor performs some defined act, such as delivery of cash to the payee or making a book entry. The moment when payment has thus been "finalized" often becomes important to establish priorities (e.g., between an attaching creditor of drawer and a payee) or to establish when the payor must have a prevailing equity to get back the money.

Legislation that fails to distinguish between the normative and descriptive uses of the expression "payment is final" may cause confusion. Thus, a statute stating only that payment is final upon the happening of a particular event could either be stating a rule of law intended to change the common law by denying the payor restitution regardless of the equities, or merely by pinpointing the moment when payment occurs, thereby freezing priorities and compelling the payor to account absent prevailing common law equities.

The sellers give the former construction to [4-215(a)]. * * *

The sellers' interpretation of this section must be matched against legislative intent as gleaned from the language of the statute and, if the language lacks clarity, as found in the policy objectives of the statutory scheme. *Dvorkin v. Dover Tp.,* 29 N.J. 303, 313 (1959); *N.J. Builders, Owners and Managers Ass'n v. Blair,* 60 N.J. 330, 338 (1972).

The statutory language is oriented to time of payment, not legal effect of payment. "Finally paid" suggests that act in a sequence of acts which establishes the time of payment. The word "when" can refer only to time of payment. Looking beyond the section in question, one finds in the Uniform Commercial Code other sections that expressly deal with the legal effect of payment.

For example, § 4-303 freezes priorities and § 3-418 deals with restitution. This view is expressed in New Jersey Study Comment No. 1 to § 4-213, which reads in part:

> In other words, section [4-215] does not address itself to the problem of finality of payment—meaning, when can the bank not recover back money paid out. It deals only with the question of when checks are paid for limited purposes.*

* * * This leads to the more fundamental point, that even if [§ 4-215(a)] is considered a rule of law, its silence as to common law restitution cannot be read as abolishing it. The Code expressly retains common law principles except where displaced by a particular provision. U.C.C. § 1-103 provides:

> Unless displaced by the particular provisions of this Act, the principles of law and equity, including the law merchant and the law relative to capacity to contract, principal and agent, estoppel, fraud, misrepresentation, duress, coercion, mistake, bankruptcy, or other validating or invalidating cause shall supplement its provisions.

Legislative intent to change the common law must be clearly and plainly expressed. *Fivehouse v. Passaic Valley Water Comm'n,* 127 N.J. Super. 451, 456 (App. Div. 1974). See also, *Union Beach Bd. of Ed. v. N.J. Ed. Ass'n,* 53 N.J. 29, 46 (1968); *Boileau v. De Cecco,* 125 N.J. Super. 263, 268 (App. Div. 1973). Section [4-215(a)] cannot displace common law restitution by implication from silence.

Finally, the sellers' construction of [§ 4-215(a)] would lead to an absurd result and is therefore a construction to be avoided. * * * If [§ 4-215(a)] absolutely deprived a payor bank of restitution, a payee could coerce or defraud the bank into making payment, yet be permitted to keep the money so obtained.

The court in *Maplewood Bank* read "mistake" into § 3-418 as a common law basis for restitution available to a payor bank unless, as that section provides, the payee was a holder in due course or someone relied in good faith on the payment.

---

* [Editor: Note, U.C.C. § 4-215 (b) "If provisional settlement for an item does not become final, the item is not finally paid."]

While the court in ordering restitution did not expressly consider the effect of [§ 4-215(a)], I conclude that that section does not diminish a payor bank's common law right to restitution.

Nonetheless, the result in *Maplewood Bank* is not dispositive of the result here. *Maplewood Bank* proceeded from the conclusion that the bank there paid because of an unspecified mistake of fact. From its own evidence in the case at bar, the bank here paid with full knowledge that, according to its bookkeeper, the buyers' account would thereby be substantially overdrawn. It thus assumed the risk of the buyers' credit. If computer corroboration of the account balance was necessary, then by its established procedures the bank either prematurely shut down the computer for the day or prematurely chose to pay. In either event, it assumed the risk that Demos did not cover the check and it thereby waived any claim of a mistaken belief that he had.

Restatement, Restitution, § 11(1) at 42 (1937), provides in part, "A person is not entitled to rescind a transaction with another if * * * he * * * intended to assume the risk of a mistake for which otherwise he would be entitled to rescission and consequent restitution." The court in *George J. Meyer Mfg. Co. v. Howard Brass & Copper Co.,* 246 Wis. 558, 18 N.W. 2d 468, 474 (Sup. Ct. 1945), held that restitution is denied a payor who assumed the risk of mistake. * * * The bank's "mistake" was an improvident extension of credit to its customers. This is not a mistake of fact warranting restitution.

Whether the bank is considered to have paid despite learning from its bookkeeper the insufficiency of the buyers' account, or to have paid without determining the true state of the account from its computer, it assumed the risk that the account was insufficient and thereby waived any claim for restitution based on mistake. Even

though a bank that pays an overdraft is thus denied restitution regardless of whether it checks its customer's account, there are still circumstances, presumably present in *Maplewood Bank,* where a genuine mistake entitling the bank to restitution might occur. Human error without the element of assumption of risk and waiver would be such a case. *E.g., Yonkers Nat'l Bank & Trust Co. v. Yerks & Co.,* 142 Misc. 640, 254 N.Y.S. 543 (Sup. Ct. 1931), *aff'd* 234 App. Div. 885, 254 N.Y.S. 548 (App. Div. 1931) (bookkeeper checked account of wrong customer with nearly identical name). Unanticipated computer error might be another. While opportunities for restitution to a payor bank creating an overdraft in its customer's account may be few, this is not inequitable given a bank's ability to verify its customer's account before payment and given its right to reimbursement from the customer under U.C.C. § [4-401(a)].[1]

Somerset Trust Company's motion for partial summary judgment is denied. The motion of Summit Squire, Inc., and Anna L. Pizzi and Raymond C. Zeltner trading as Cranford Hall Nursing Home is granted.

---

[1] [U.C.C. § 4-407(3)], which subrogates a payor bank to the rights of the drawer against the payee or other holder, does not apply. A payor bank may charge its customer's account for an overdraft under [U.C.C. § 4-401(a)] only if the item "is otherwise properly payable." Where a customer/drawer issued a timely stop order, a payor bank that nevertheless pays is stuck except as it may qualify for subrogation under [U.C.C. § 4-407(3)]. To qualify under that section, the bank would have had to pay "under circumstances giving a basis for objection by the drawer" (i.e., [U.C.C. § 4-401(a)] reimbursement is unavailable) and the payment would have had to be an "unjust enrichment" of the payee. Neither requisite appears in this case.

NOTE

1. *See* U.C.C. § 3-418(d) as to the effect of U.C.C. § 4-215 on this situation.

2. The situation changes, however, where payment or acceptance of the instrument was made to a person who in good faith and for value took the instrument or who, acting in good faith, changed her position in reliance on the payment or acceptance of that instrument. U.C.C. § 3-418(c).

For Example: A buyer, in expectation that a contract for the sale of goods would be performed by the seller, sent seller a check in payment for the goods. Buyer, finding the goods to be defective, placed a stop payment order on the check. Drawee bank mistakenly ignored the stop payment order and, when the seller presented the check, paid cash for the check, or issued its cashier's check in payment of the buyer's check. Bank can recover the payment or its cashier's check from the seller. But, if the seller negotiated the buyer's check and it came into the hands of a holder in due course, or of a person who in good faith took the instrument for value, recovery would not be possible when presentment was made by such holder. Neither would it be possible for the bank to recover where the recipient of the cash or of the cashier's check in good faith changed her position in reliance on such receipt of cash or of the bank's cashier's check. The bank will be confined to seek its remedy from the seller/payee named in the buyer's check. It would do so by subrogating to the rights of the buyer/drawer of the check on the underlying obligation. Additionally the possibility of a remedy existing for breach of presentment warranties must be borne in mind. (U.C.C. §§ 3-417, 4-407.) The preferable approach for the drawee lies in U.C.C. Section 3-418. That section sets forth a claim in recoupment. There would be no need to show that actual damage was suffered by reason of an alleged breach of a presentment warranty or of a provision in the underlying obligation for which the check had been issued.

Price v. Neal
3 Burr. 1354, 97 Eng. Rep. 871 (K.B. 1762)

[The drawee, Price, had paid two bills of exchange presented to him by Neal who had acquired them in good faith and for value. One of the bills of exchange had been acquired by Neal after Price had accepted it. On it being discovered that the drawer's signature had been forged (the forger was executed). Price sought to recover from Neal.]

LORD MANSFIELD

It is an action upon the case, for money had and received to the plaintiff's use. In which action, the plaintiff can not recover the money, unless it be against conscience in the defendant, to retain it: and great liberality is always allowed, in this sort of action.

But it can never be thought unconscientious in the defendant, to retain this money, when he has once received it upon a bill of exchange indorsed to him for a fair and valuable consideration, which he had bona fide paid, without the least priority or suspicion of any forgery.

Here was no fraud: no wrong. It was incumbent upon the plaintiff, to be satisfied "that the bill drawn upon him was the drawer's hand," before he accepted or paid it: but it was not incumbent upon the defendant, to inquire into it. Here was notice given by the defendant to the plaintiff of a bill drawn upon him: and he sends his servant to pay it and take it up. The other bill he actually accepts; after which acceptance, the defendant innocently and bona fide discounts it. The plaintiff lies by, for a considerable time after he has paid these bills; and then found out "that they were forged": and the forger comes to be hanged. He made no objection to them, at the time of paying them. Whatever neglect there was, was on his side. The defendant had actual encouragement from the plaintiff himself, for negotiating the second bill, from the plaintiff's having without any scruple or hesitation paid the first: and he paid the whole value, bona fide. It is a misfortune which has happened without the defendant's fault or neglect. If there was no neglect in the plaintiff, yet there is no reason to throw off the loss from one innocent man upon another innocent man: but, in this case, if there was any fault or negligence in any one, it certainly was in the plaintiff, and not in the defendant.

* * *

First National City Bank v. Altman
3 U.C.C. Rep. Serv. (Callaghan) 815 (N.Y. Sup. Ct. 1966)

TIERNEY, J. This is a motion by defendant Altman for summary judgment and a cross-motion by defendant Trade Bank and Trust Company for leave to pay the sum of $23,900.75 into court, and for related relief.

The facts are as follows:

This action was brought to recover the proceeds of two checks, in the respective sums of $22,300.80 and $23,900.75, drawn on the account of J. W. Mays, Inc., a depositor in plaintiff bank, deposited in Altman's account in the Trade Bank and Trust Company, collected by said bank, and credited to Altman's account, on the ground that the signature of the drawer had been forged and the checks were not issued or drawn by J. W. Mays, Inc. nor with its authority or consent; and that payment was made by mistake, in good faith, in reliance on the endorsements of both defendants, without notice or knowledge of any defect in the instruments or in defendants' title thereto, and in the belief that the instruments had been drawn by the depositor, J. W. Mays, Inc.

Defendant Altman interposed an answer consisting of a general denial, an affirmative defense and counterclaim that plaintiff was negligent in failing to discover the forgery before making payment and that its negligence caused him to part with merchandise of the value of the checks, and an additional affirmative defense of estoppel as a result of such negligence. The answer of the Trade Bank and Trust Company consists of a general denial.

Defendant Altman is a wholesale diamond dealer. A Mr. Nieman presented himself at Altman's place of business and introduced himself as a buyer for J. W. Mays, Inc. Nieman selected a number of unset diamonds which Altman placed inside an envelope and sealed. Altman kept the diamonds. A few days later, Nieman sent a letter, on his own stationery, confirming the sale. He also enclosed a check drawn on plaintiff bank against the account of J. W. Mays, Inc., in the sum of $22,300.80, as full payment for the diamonds. Altman deposited the check in his account. Nieman then revisited Altman's place of business and selected more diamonds. The same procedure was followed, and Nieman's letter confirming the sale arrived with a check for $23,900.75, in full payment of the second group of diamonds. Altman, immediately upon receipt, deposited each check into his account at the Trade Bank. When Nieman requested delivery of the first envelope of diamonds, Altman communicated with the Trade Bank and determined that the first check had been paid defendant bank by the drawee, prior to turning over the diamonds. He turned over the second selection of diamonds several days later, but did not first ascertain that the second check had been paid, although in fact plaintiff had made payment; that same afternoon the Trade Bank notified him that plaintiff bank had given notice that both checks had been forged and that payment had been made by mistake.

Payment or acceptance of any instrument is final in favor of "a person who has in good faith changed his position in reliance on the payment" (U.C.C. § 3-418). This legal principle was long ago enunciated in *Price v. Neal,* 3 Burr. 1354 (1762) where it was held that a drawee who pays an instrument on which the signature of the drawer is forged is bound on his acceptance and cannot recover back his payment from a holder in due course, or a person who has in good faith changed his position in reliance on the payment.

In moving for dismissal of the complaint defendant Altman contends that the doctrine of *Price v. Neal* is a bar to a recovery by plaintiff on either of the two forged checks herein.

The facts are clear that with respect to the first packet of diamonds, defendant Altman did not make delivery thereof until he had first ascertained that the check by which payment therefor had been made had been paid by plaintiff. Accordingly, defendant Altman, the payee of the check, does qualify as a person who changed his position in reliance on the drawee's payment. However, in all of the circumstances, the court is of the view that the issue of his good faith presents a triable issue of fact which precludes summary dismissal of the action based on the first check (*see Banca C.I. Trust Co. v. Clarkson,* 274 N.Y. 69). It has been held that the negligence of the purchaser, at the time he acquired title to the instrument, in not making inquiries which, if made, might reveal the fact of forgery, releases the drawee from the rule of *Price v. Neal,* and enables the drawee to recover from the purchaser the amount paid to him on the instrument (Whitney, *The Law of Modern Commercial Practices,* 2d ed. section 338, p. 504 [1965]).

Inasmuch as defendant Altman did not determine that the second check had been paid by plaintiff prior to delivery of the second packet of diamonds, said defendant is not in a position to claim the status of "a person who has . . . changed his position in reliance on the payment." Therefore, the proscription against the drawee stated in the rule of *Price v. Neal* loses its impact and all the issues relative to plaintiff's right to recover the

proceeds of the second check remain in issue.

Accordingly, the motion for summary judgment dismissing the complaint is denied.

There is no real opposition to the cross-motion by defendant Trade Bank and Trust Company to deposit the proceeds of the second check into court. Therefore, the cross-motion is granted to the extent of directing said defendant to turn over the sum of $23,900.75 to the proper authorities. Otherwise the cross-motion is denied. Any taxable costs or disbursements shall be chargeable to the unsuccessful party at the conclusion of litigation.

Settle order.

NOTE

1. Why could Altman not qualify as a holder in due course? *See* U.C.C. § 3-302(a)(2).

Did Altman *take* the instruments for value, or did he give value after the instruments had been paid and he had received the deposit?

This raises once more the issue of a "double forgery." This issue arises where not only the signature of the drawer but also that of an endorser has been forged. If payment or acceptance followed presentment by a person "who took the instrument in good faith and for value, or who in good faith changed his position in reliance on the payment or acceptance," U.C.C. § 3-418(a), (b), the drawee will not be able to allege a mistaken payment so as to recover from such person. U.C.C. Section 3-418(c), however, preserves the right of the drawee to proceed under the presentment warranties in U.C.C. Section 3-417. A payor bank is able also to subrogate under U.C.C. § 4-407, and thereby to recover its loss. Since the presenter does not warrant the authenticity of the drawer's signature, a forgery of the drawer's signature does not give rise to a breach of warranty. The presenter merely warrants that he "has no knowledge that the signature of the drawer . . . is unauthorized." U.C.C. § 3-417(a)(3).[33] The presenter does warrant, however, that the presenter is a person entitled to enforce the instrument. U.C.C. § 3-417(a)(1). If an indorsement has been forged, the presenter would be in breach of this warranty. The forgery of an endorser's signature would make the indorsement ineffective. Therefore, there would be a break in the chain of negotiation under which the presenter claims to be entitled to enforce the instrument. U.C.C. § 3-403(a)(1). The double forgery issue is thus resolved in favor of the minority view,[34] and the forgery of the endorser's signature is treated as the proximate cause of the loss suffered by drawee who is unable to recover from the drawer. U.C.C. § 3-418(c). The presenter will have recourse against his transferor on the applicable underlying obligation or on the basis of transfer warranties, U.C.C. § 3-416(a), a right to which a payor bank could subrogate. U.C.C. § 4-407.

2. The fact that a drawee or payor bank has honored an instrument containing an

---

[33] The presenter does warrant, however, that the draft has not been altered. U.C.C. § 3-417(a)(2).

[34] *See,* Turner Graybill, *Reconsidering an Old Conundrum: The Case for Indorsement Liability on Double Forgeries,* 83 COMM. L.J. 61 (1978).

unauthorized signature or an alteration will not be apparent until the issuer of the instrument discovers this and demands that his account be recredited. Such demand on a drawee must be made within three years after the cause of action accrued. U.C.C. § 3-118(g). In the case of a drawee/payor bank that sends or makes available to a customer paid items or a statement of account showing payment of items sufficient to enable the customer to reasonably identify such items, the period of limitation is one year. U.C.C. § 4-406(f). Once that time has elapsed, the customer is precluded for asserting against the bank the unauthorized signature or alteration. Consequently the bank also is precluded from recovering from a presenter for breach of warranty of presentment. U.C.C. §§ 4-406(f), 4-208(a).

3. Where the bank makes available to the customer the items and a statement of account, the customer must promptly examine the items and the statement of account and inform the bank of any unauthorized signature or alteration that the customer should reasonably have discovered from such examination. Failure to examine the items and the statement of account and to inform the bank of any unauthorized signature or alteration may preclude the customer from raising an unauthorized signature or alteration when claiming restitution from the bank. Absent an agreement, however, items are only rarely returned to the customer.[35] Thus, the customer must examine the statement of account with care. This statement need only describe the items by item number, amount and date of payment, i.e., in accordance with information gleaned primarily from the Magnetic Ink Character Recognition Numbers (MICR).

Official Comment 1 to U.C.C. Section 4-406 justifies this approach by stating:

> This policy results in less cost to the check collection system and thus to all customers of the system. It is expected that technological advances such as image processing may make it possible for banks to give customers more information in the future in a manner that is fully compatible with automation or truncation systems. At that time the Permanent Editorial Board may wish to make recommendations for an amendment revising the safe harbor requirements in the light of those advances.[36]

Under the present approach, litigation can be expected as to the factual determination whether the customer should, "based on this statement or items provided,... reasonably have discovered the unauthorized payment."[37] The 1993 Official Comments provide some guidance:

> ...[A] customer is bound to consider only 'statement or items provided' and to make reasonable discovery on that basis. If a bank elects to provide the minimum information

---

[35] Often an additional charge is made when a customer demands a return of items. Also note check retention under U.C.C. §§ 4-110(a), and 4-406(b). If items are not returned, the item or a legible photocopy of the item must be kept and made available to the customer for a period of seven years. U.C.C. § 4-406(b). Note also that the section merely requires the bank to make the statement and items available. It does not require that the items or the statement be sent to the customer.

[36] "Imaging" is making technological progress. Although cost factors in the past have impeded widespread use of the new technology, it is apparent that it is the wave of the 90s and that it will be in widespread use in the very near future. *See,* Thomas C. Baxter, Jr. & Debra W. Cook, *The Impact of Technological Developments on Payments Law,* 1993 COM. L. ANN. 301 (eds. Louis F. Del Duca & Patrick Del Duca).

[37] U.C.C. § 4-406(a); *see further* Official Comment 1 to U.C.C. § 4-406.

that 'is sufficient' under § 4-406(a), the customer has only a limited basis for the customer's duty of discovery and notification. For example, if a fraud-doer altered the check by changing the name of the payee, the customer could not normally detect the fraud unless the customer had been given the paid check or otherwise informed of the name of the payee of the altered check. In such circumstances, the customer might not be able to 'reasonably have discovered the unauthorized payment' under § 4-406(c) and therefore would not be precluded under § 4-406(d) from asserting the alteration.

A failure to give prompt notice will preclude the customer from asserting a claim against the bank should the bank be able to prove that, having acted in good faith,[38] it suffered loss by reason of such failure to give prompt notice. Reasonable promptness "depends on the nature, purpose and circumstances of" the action called for. U.C.C. § 1-204(2). It generally requires that, unless a different reasonable time has been agreed to, notice be given within fourteen days of receipt of the statement of account. Where there has been a repeated wrongful act by the same wrongdoer, the customer will be precluded from asserting an unauthorized signature or an alteration where more than thirty days have elapsed since the customer received an item or a statement of account and failed to notify the bank which, in the meantime, paid another item containing such wrongful acts prepared by the same wrongdoer. U.C.C. § 4-406(d). However, where the customer can show that the bank has failed to exercise ordinary care in paying an item[39] and that failure substantially contributed to the loss suffered by the bank, the loss is allocated between the customer precluded and the bank asserting the preclusion. The allocation will be apportioned according to the concept of comparative negligence, i.e., according to the extent to which the failure of the customer to give notice of the unauthorized signature or alteration and the failure of the bank to exercise ordinary care contributed to the loss. U.C.C. § 4-406(e).

---

[38] U.C.C. § 3-103(a)(4).

[39] U.C.C. § 3-103(a)(7).

Rhode Island Hospital Trust National Bank v. Zapata Corporation
848 F.2d 291 (1st Cir. 1988)*

BREYER, Circuit Judge.

The issue that this appeal presents is whether Zapata Corporation has shown that the system used by Rhode Island Hospital Trust National Bank for detecting forged checks—a system used by a majority of American banks—lacks the "ordinary care" that a bank must exercise under the Uniform Commercial Code § 4-406(3) (1977)

---

* [Editor: note citations in [ ] refer to Revised U.C.C. Articles 3 and 4.]

[§§ 4-406(e), 3-103(a)(7)]. The question arises out of the following district court determinations, all of which are adequately supported by the record and by Rhode Island law.

1. In early 1985, a Zapata employee stole some blank checks from Zapata. She wrote a large number of forged checks, almost all in amounts of $150 to $800 each, on Zapata's accounts at Rhode Island Hospital Trust National Bank. The Bank, from March through July 1985, received and paid them.

2. Bank statements that the Bank regularly sent Zapata first began to reflect the forged checks in early April 1985. Zapata failed to examine its statements closely until July 1985, when it found the forgeries. It immediately notified the Bank, which then stopped clearing the checks. The Bank had already processed and paid forged checks totaling $109,247.16.

3. The Bank will (and legally must) reimburse Zapata in respect to all checks it cleared before April 25, 1985 (or for at least two weeks after Zapata received the statement that reflected the forgeries). *See* U.C.C. §§ 3-401(1), 4-406(2) (1977) [§§ 3-401(a), 4-406(d)].

4. In respect to checks cleared on and after April 25, the Bank need not reimburse Zapata because Zapata failed to "exercise reasonable care and promptness to examine the [bank] statement." U.C.C. § 4-406(1) (1977) [§ 4-406(a), (c)].

The question before us is whether this last-mentioned conclusion is correct or whether Zapata can recover for the post-April 24 checks on the theory that, even if it was negligent, so was the Bank.

To understand the question, one must examine U.C.C. § 4-406. . . . Ordinarily a bank must reimburse an innocent customer for forgeries that it honors, § 3-401(1), but § 4-406 makes an important exception to the liability rule. The exception operates in respect to a series of forged checks, and it applies once a customer has had a chance to catch the forgeries by examining his bank statements and notifying the bank but has failed to do so [U.C.C. § 4-406(d)(2)].

The statute, in relevant part, reads as follows:

(1) *When a bank sends to its customer a statement of account* accompanied by items paid in good faith in support of the debit entries or holds the statement and items pursuant to a request or instructions of its customer or otherwise in a reasonable manner makes the statement and items available to the customer, *the customer must exercise reasonable care and promptness to examine the statement and items to discover his unauthorized signature or any alteration on an item and must notify the bank promptly* after discovery thereof.

(2) *If the bank establishes that the customer failed* with respect to an item *to comply with* the duties imposed on the customer by *subsection (1) the customer is precluded from asserting against the bank*.

(a) *His unauthorized signature* or any alteration on the item if the bank also establishes that it suffered a loss by reason of such failure; *and*

(b) *An unauthorized signature or alteration by the same wrongdoer on any other item paid in good faith by the bank after the* first item and *statement was available to the customer for a reasonable period not exceeding fourteen (14) calendar days* and before the bank receives notification from the customer of any such unauthorized signature or alteration. § 4-406(1)-(2) (1985) (emphasis added).[*]

The statute goes on to specify an important exception to the exception. It says:

(3) The preclusion under subsection (2) does not apply if the customer establishes lack of ordinary care on the part of the bank in paying the item(s). § 4-406(3) [§ 4-406(e)].

Zapata's specific claim, on this appeal, is that it falls within this "exception to the exception"— that the bank's treatment of the post-April 24 checks lacked "ordinary care."

Zapata says as a preliminary matter, that the district court failed to make a finding on this "ordinary care" question. We do not think that is so. The court, while considering a different, but related, issue, found that the bank's practices met "reasonable commercial standards." The word "reasonable" implies that use of those standards was not by itself negligent or lacking in ordinary care. *See Vending Chattanooga, Inc. v. American National Bank and Trust Co.,* 730 S.W.2d 624, 628 (Tenn. Sup. Ct. 1987) (equating "ordinary care" with "reasonable commercial standards" of banking industry). . . .

Whether or not the district court made an explicit finding, however, we should, and do, affirm the district court's judgment in the bank's favor. Our examination of the statute reveals that the statute places the burden of proof on Zapata. Our examination of the record reveals that Zapata failed to shoulder that burden; and, given the record, no reasonable person could find the contrary.

a. The statute places the burden of proof on Zapata. It says that strict bank liability terminates fourteen days after the customer receives the

---

[*] [Editor: this period is now thirty days.]

bank's statement unless *"the customer establishes lack of ordinary care."* § 4-406(3) (emphasis added); *see, e.g., Vending Chattanooga,* 730 S.W.2d at 628. And, the U.C.C. commentary makes clear that the statute means what it says. The commentators explain the purpose of the statutory section as follows:

> One of the most serious consequences of failure of the customer . . . [to examine his statement and notify the bank promptly of an unauthorized signature] . . . is the opportunity presented to the wrongdoer to repeat his misdeeds. Conversely, one of the best ways to keep down losses in this type of situation is for the customer to promptly examine his statement and notify the bank . . . so that the bank will be alerted to stop paying further items.

U.C.C. § 4-406 comment 3. The Commentary goes on to say:

> [E]ven if the bank succeeds in establishing that the customer has failed to exercise ordinary care, if in turn the customer succeeds in establishing that the bank failed to exercise ordinary care in paying the items[,] the preclusion rule does not apply. *This distribution of the burden of establishing between the customer and the bank provides reasonable equality of treatment and requires each person asserting the negligence to establish such negligence rather than requiring either person to establish that his entire course of conduct constituted ordinary care.*

Id. comment 4 (emphasis added).

b. The record convinces us that Zapata failed to carry its burden of establishing "lack of ordinary care" on the part of the Bank. First, the Bank described its ordinary practices as follows: The Bank examines all signatures on checks for more than $1,000. It examines signatures on checks between $100 and $1,000 (those at issue here) if it has reason to suspect a problem, e.g., if a customer has warned it of a possible forgery or if the check was drawn on an account with insufficient funds. It examines the signatures of a randomly chosen one percent of all other checks between $100 and $1,000. But, it does not examine the signatures on other checks between $100 and $1,000. Through expert testimony, the Bank also established that most other banks in the nation follow this practice and that banking industry experts recommend it.

Indeed, Trust National Bank's practices are conservative in this regard, as most banks set $2,500 or more, not $1,000, as the limit beneath which they will not examine each signature.

This testimony made out a *prima facie* case of "ordinary care." U.C.C. § 4-103(3) (1977); [§ 3-103(a)(7)] ("[a]ction or nonaction . . . consistent with . . . a general banking usage not disapproved by this [Article or] chapter, prima facie constitutes the exercise of ordinary care"); *see Vending Chattanooga,* 730 S.W.2d at 628-29 (§ 4-103(3) indicates that "ordinary care" exercised if practice accords with "reasonable commercial standards"). . . . Of course, Zapata might still try to show that the entire industry's practice is unreasonable, that it reflects lack of "ordinary care." *The T.J. Hooper,* 60 F.2d 737, 740 (2d Cir.), *cert. denied,* 287 U.S. 662, 53 S.Ct. 220 (1932). In doing so, however, "the *prima facie* rule does . . . impose on the party contesting the standards to establish that they are *unreasonable, arbitrary, or unfair."* U.C.C. § 4-103 comment 4 (emphasis added).

Second, both bank officials and industry experts pointed out that this industry practice, in general and in the particular case of the Trust National Bank, saved considerable expense, compared with the Bank's pre-1981 practice of examining each check by hand. To be specific, the change saved the Bank about $125,000 annually. Zapata accepts this testimony as accurate.

Third, both a Bank official and an industry expert testified that changing from an "individual signature examination" system to the new "bulk-filing" system led to no significant increase in the number of forgeries that went undetected. Philip Schlernitzauer, a Bank vice-president and the officer in charge of the Zapata account, testified that under the prior "individual signature examination" system, some forgeries still slipped through. The Bank's loss was about $10,000 to $15,000 per year. He also determined through a feasibility study that by implementing a "bulk-filing" system in which 99 percent of checks under $1,000 were not individually screened, the loss would remain between $10,000 and $15,000. Dr. Lipis, an executive vice-president of a large consulting firm to the financial industry, testified that among its purposes was the following:

> Well, it improves the ability to return checks back to customers more correctly, simply that

the checks do not get misplaced when they are handled; generally [it] can improve the morale within th[e] bank because . . . the signature verification is very tedious, very difficult, and not a function that is liked by anybody who does it. In addition, *it does not impact the amount of forgeries that are produced at the bank.*

Rec. App. 179 (emphasis added).

Zapata points to *no* testimony or other evidence tending to contradict these assertions. An industry-wide practice that saves money without significantly increasing the number of forged checks that the banks erroneously pay is a practice that reflects at least "ordinary care." *Cf. Vending Chattanooga,* 730 F.2d at 628-29 (weighing economic feasibility and business practice into definition of "ordinary care" or "reasonable commercial standards").

Fourth, even if one assumes, contrary to this uncontradicted evidence, that the new system meant *some* increase in the number of undetected forged checks, Zapata still could not prevail, for it presented *no* evidence tending to show any such increased loss unreasonable in light of the costs that the new practice would save. Instead, it relied simply upon the assertion that costs saved the bank are irrelevant. But, that is not so, for what is reasonable or unreasonable insofar as "ordinary care" or "due care" or "negligence" (and the like) are concerned is often a matter of costs of prevention compared with correlative risks of loss. *See Vending Chattanooga,* 730 F.2d at 628-29; *United States v. Carrol Towing Co.,* 159 F.2d 169, 173 (2d Cir. 1947) (Hand, J.) ("duty" defined by calculating probability of injury times gravity of harm to determine "burden of precaution" that is warranted). One does not, for example, coat the base of the Grand Canyon with soft plastic nets to catch those who might fall in, or build cars like armored tanks to reduce injuries in accidents even though the technology exists. . . . In arguing that the Bank provided "no care" in respect to the checks it did not examine, Zapata simply assumed the very conclusion (namely, the unreasonableness of a selective examination *system*) that it sought

to prove. Aside from this assumption, its evidentiary cupboard is bare. . . .

As Zapata contends, there are several cases that hold or imply that "ordinary care" necessarily implies individualized scrutiny of every check. But, several of those cases are old, decided in different technological circumstances and before the U.C.C. . . . The U.C.C. intends technological change to make a difference, a fact which its *prima facie* equation of "ordinary care" and "general banking usage" implies, *see* § 4-103(3) [§ 3-102(a)(7)], and which its commentators made explicit. *See* U.C.C. § 4-103 comment 1 ("[i]n view of the technical complexity of the field of bank collections, the enormous number of items handled by banks, . . . and the possibility of developing improved methods of collection to speed the process, it would be unwise to freeze present methods of operation by mandatory statutory rules"); *see also Vending Chattanooga,* 730 S.W.2d at 628 ("ordinary care" cannot "require the bank to hire such a large number of skilled handwriting experts so as to be economically not feasible, . . . [not] commercially reasonable").

We have found a few, more modern cases that arguably support Zapata's view, but they involve practices more obviously unreasonable than those presented here. *See, e.g., Hanover Insurance Cos. v. Brotherhood State Bank,* 482 F. Supp. 501 (D. Kan. 1979) (no ordinary care where *no* examination of *any size* checks, conspicuous forgeries); *Perley,* 170 Conn. at 702-03, 368 A.2d at 155 (no ordinary care where *no* authentication of endorsements of *any size* checks); *Indiana National Corp. v. Faco, Inc.,* 400 N.E.2d 202 (Ind. App. 1980) (checks *without signatures* paid, 30 check copies lost); *Medford Irrigation District, supra* (same where *no* examination of any checks under $5,000). And, in any event, we believe Rhode Island would follow the more significant body of modern case law suggesting analysis along the lines we have undertaken.

For these reasons, the judgment of the district court is

Affirmed.

NOTE

1. U.C.C. Section 1-202(3) provides that the obligation of reasonableness and care prescribed by the U.C.C. may not be disclaimed by agreement. The parties, however, may determine the standards by which the performance of such obligations are to be measured, provided such standards are not manifestly unreasonable. U.C.C. Section 3-103(a)(7) follows on this by defining "ordinary care" for the purpose of U.C.C.-Article 3 and Article 4 as calling for the application of a reasonable commercial standard; included in such standard is the use of automation. In determining whether this standard has been attained, the *Zapata* case gives an approach by referring not only to accepted banking practice but also in seeking a justification for such banking practice showing it is "commercially reasonable" by means of a cost-benefit analysis.

2. U.C.C. Section 4-406(e) provides for an allocation of loss where a customer can show that the bank has failed to exercise "ordinary care" and it is also apparent that but for such failure by the bank the customer would be precluded from raising an unauthorized signature or alteration; for example, the bank was negligent but the customer, having received the item or a statement of account, had failed to give a timely notice to the bank. The allocation of loss would be based on a comparative negligence test. Should the bank have failed to act in good faith, however, the loss would fall entirely on the bank.

Federal Insurance Company
v.
NCNB National Bank of North Carolina

958 F.2d 1544 (11th Cir. 1992)
See supra, Chapter II at B

* * *

NOTE

Florida adopted Revised U.C.C. Articles 3 and 4, effective January 1, 1993.

Would Computer Products, Inc. be precluded from recovering any of its loss by virtue of U.C.C. Section 3-405?

American Security Bank
v.
American Motorists Insurance Company*

538 A.2d 736 (D.C. 1988)

BELSON, A.J.

This appeal involves a bank's liability, under article three of the Uniform Commercial Code, for a series of checks it paid over a forged drawer's signature. Although the trial court found that the bank's customer had negligently contributed to the forgeries, it also found that the bank had not exercised reasonable commercial standards when it failed to detect the forgeries and paid the checks. The court therefore found the bank liable under

---

* [Editor: citations in [ ] refer to Revised U.C.C. Articles 3 and 4.]

[U.C.C.] §§ 3-406 and 4-406. Because the trial judge's factual finding that the bank was negligent in cashing the checks was not clearly erroneous, we affirm.

I.

The American Society for Parenteral and Enteral Nutrition, Inc. ("ASPEN") is a nonprofit membership organization. ASPEN maintained a checking account with appellant American Security Bank ("the bank"). ASPEN's executive director, Barney Sellers, was one of five persons having signing authority for the account.

At the time of the events leading up to this case, ASPEN had a total of five or six employees. In May 1982, it hired Diane McCrae to serve as office manager and as Sellers' secretary. McCrae, who was hired in part because of her experience in bookkeeping and business practices, maintained physical possession of ASPEN's checkbook and prepared checks for Sellers' signature. McCrae was also responsible for receiving and reviewing the bank statements and cancelled checks, and for delivering them to ASPEN's bookkeeper, who was to reconcile the items in the bank statement with the numbers on the checks. At some point during McCrae's employment, ASPEN hired a financial manager, who also was responsible for looking at the bank statements.

In mid-September, one of ASPEN's employees noticed a cancelled check that listed as payee a company with which the employee was unfamiliar. Unable to find an invoice that corresponded with the check, Sellers examined the check and discovered that his name on the signature line "was not [his] handwriting." An examination of prior bank statements uncovered twenty-four checks bearing similarly forged drawers' signatures. On some of the checks the payee line appeared to have been erased. The bank had paid a total of $38,016.48 from ASPEN's account for the unauthorized checks. McCrae later pled guilty to criminal charges arising from this incident.

Sellers notified the bank of the forged checks the morning after he discovered them. Several days later, ASPEN's attorney sent a letter to the bank asking it to recredit ASPEN's account for the amount it had paid on those checks. The bank refused. ASPEN filed an insurance claim with its insurer, appellee American Motorists Insurance Company ("insurer"), which paid ASPEN's claim for $38,016.48. Insurer sued the bank for reimbursement in that amount.

* * *

At trial, the bank presented as a witness Joann Bell, the manager of its account maintenance department. Bell testified to the procedures followed by the bank in filing checks presented for payment. According to Bell, checks from a particular account are given to one of six check filers, each of whom handles approximately 5,000 checks per day. The check filer verifies that the account number is correct, that the date is current, that the checks are signed, and, for checks over $20,000, that the endorsement is proper. The filer then compares the drawer's signature on the check with the signature card for the account. Bell testified that the check filer for ASPEN's account had followed these prescribed procedures, that the signatures were sufficiently similar that the filer could not have detected the forgery in the normal course of business, and that, in Bell's opinion, the filer had performed her duties satisfactorily.

The bank also presented Donald Beck, a former employee of the bank, as an expert in the area of bank operations and check processing. Beck testified that the bank's check filing procedures were the same as or similar to those at other banks, and that the individual filers' workloads met national and local banking standards. He explained that, in checking for forgeries, the check filers "are not specifically forgery experts[,]" and look only for "large dissimilarities." Beck testified further that, in his opinion, the specific procedures followed in processing ASPEN's checks were in accordance with commercially reasonable standards.

The trial court issued a written order holding the bank liable for having paid the forged checks. The court first found that ASPEN's negligent supervision of McCrae, as well as its inadequate accounting procedures, "substantially contributed" to the making of the forgeries under [U.C.C.] § 3-406. It also found that ASPEN did not exercise reasonable care and diligence in examining its bank statements and in reporting the forgeries, as required by [U.C.C.] § 4-406. The court went on to find, however, that although the bank had instituted commercially reasonable procedures, it had negligently failed to comply with those procedures, and thus "did not act in accordance with its own reasonable commercial standards." In making this finding, the court relied on its own examination of copies of the checks and signature card, as well as on the fact that the check filer had been "lightly reprimanded" for not detecting the forgeries. Despite its determination that ASPEN was negligent, therefore, the court held that the bank was liable for the full amount of the checks for which it had debited ASPEN's account. See [U.C.C.] §§ 3-406, 4-406 (3). The bank appeals from the court's finding of liability, and the insurer cross-appeals from the court's finding of negligent supervision.

II.

Generally, a person is not liable on an instrument unless it bears his or her signature. [U.C.C.] § 3-401(1) [§ 3-401(a)]. Thus, a drawee bank may not charge a drawer's account for a check bearing a signature other than that of the drawer, because the "unauthorized signature is wholly inoperative as that of the person whose name is signed. . . ." [U.C.C.] § 3-404(1) [§ 3-403(a)]. An exception to the above rule applies when the drawer "is precluded from denying" the unauthorized signature. Id. Specifically,

[a]ny person who by his negligence substantially contributes to a material alteration of the instrument or to the making of an unauthorized signature is precluded from asserting the . . . lack of authority . . . against a drawee [the bank] or other payor who pays the instrument in good faith and in accordance with the reasonable commercial standards of the drawee's or payor's business.

[U.C.C.] § 3-406. Thus, a drawer's negligence that contributes to a forgery negates the drawee bank's liability, but only if the drawee bank meets its burden of proving by a preponderance of the evidence that it complied with reasonable commercial standards when it cashed the check. *See American Machine Tool Distrib. v. Nat'l Permanent Fed. Sav.,* 464 A.2d 907, 912 (D.C. 1983).

In the instant case, the trial court found that the bank had not complied with reasonable commercial standards when it cashed the series of forged checks, and thus held it liable for having paid those checks from ASPEN's account. The trial court reasoned that, although the bank had instituted reasonable banking practices, the nature of the forgeries that it failed to detect was such that the bank could not have been exercising those practices when it cashed the checks. The court reasoned as follows:

The procedures used by the [bank] which comported with reasonable commercial banking standards included the undertaking of comparing the drawer's signature on the check which was presented for payment with the signature appearing on the authorization card. The evidence presented at trial and a review of the exhibits which were introduced into evidence disclose that none of the forged checks bore the correct spelling of the drawer's name [Barney Sellers]. The ending "s" was clearly omitted from all of the forged signatures. . . . It is hard to imagine the purpose behind having a check filer compare signatures if it is not to at least check for the correct spelling of the drawer's name. . . . This is not [a] case where the ending letter of the name was scribbled or otherwise undiscernible. In the true signature of Mr. Sellers, the ending "s" was clearly evident; in the forged signature, the ending "r" and the omission of the "s" were clearly evident. When the [bank] has imposed on itself the duty to compare signatures (a duty which is in keeping with reasonable banking procedure according to the testimony), it has the duty to see what is clearly there to be seen.

The court also relied to some extent on the check filer's testimony that she had received a mild reprimand for not detecting the forgery; however, the court's order indicates that its principal reliance was on its own examination of the documentary evidence, viz., the signature card, and this court reviews the trial court's findings in that light.

* * *

We therefore affirm the court's finding that the bank did not exercise commercially reasonable procedures when it paid the forged checks, and thus that it was foreclosed from asserting as a defense against liability that ASPEN's negligence had substantially contributed to those forgeries.

III.

The bank argues that, even if ASPEN's contribution to the forgeries did not preclude the insurer from asserting the bank's liability under [U.C.C.] § 3-406, its liability is nevertheless limited under [U.C.C.] § 4-406. That section provides in relevant part: [*See* U.C.C. §§ 4-406(a), (b), (c), (d)(2).]

* * *

Citing this provision, the bank argues that ASPEN did not exercise reasonable care and promptness in examining its bank statement, and thus that the insurer is precluded from asserting the bank's liability for those checks paid more than fourteen days after ASPEN received the first bank statement that contained checks paid over McCrae's forged signature.

We need not address the issue of ASPEN's negligence in failing earlier to examine its bank statements and to report the forgeries to the bank, however, because the trial court found that ASPEN had established the bank's lack of ordinary care under § 4-406(3). That subsection provides, "The preclusion under subsection (2) does not apply if the customer establishes lack of ordinary care on the part of the bank in paying the item(s)." [U.C.C.] § 4-406(3). We note that this provision shifts the burden imposed under § 3-406, i.e., that the bank must prove commercial reasonableness, *see American Machine, supra,* 464 A.2d at 912, to the customer, who must prove the bank's lack of reasonableness, that is, its lack of ordinary care. It is clear from the trial court's order that it applied the latter, correct standard when it found the bank negligent in honoring the forged checks. As discussed above, we cannot say that this finding was clearly erroneous. Since the trial court found that the bank did not exercise reasonable care when it paid the checks over the forged drawer's signatures, the bank cannot rely on ASPEN's lack of promptness in discovering and reporting the forgeries to limit its liability.

* * *

NOTE

Consider the effect of U.C.C. Section 4-406(e) on the decisions in *Federal Insurance Company* and *American Security Bank, N.A.*

Comment 4 to U.C.C. Section 4-406 now provides:

4. Subsection (e) replaces former subsection (3) and poses a modified comparative negligence test for determining liability. See the discussion on this point in the Comments to Sections 3-404, 3-405, and 3-406. The term "good faith" is defined in Section 3-103(a)(4) as including "observance of reasonable commercial standards of fair dealing." The connotation of this standard is fairness and not absence of negligence.

The term "ordinary care" used in subsection (e) is defined in Section 3-103(a)(7), made applicable to Article 4 by Section 4-104(c), to provide that sight examination by a payor bank is not required if its procedure is reasonable and is commonly followed by other comparable banks in the area. The case law is divided on this issue. The definition of "ordinary care" in Section 3-103 rejects those authorities that hold, in effect, that failure to use sight examination is negligence as a matter of law. The effect of the definition of "ordinary care" on Section 4-406 is only to provide that in the small percentage of cases in which a customer's failure to examine its statement or returned item has led to loss under subsection (d) a bank should not have to share that loss solely because it has adopted an automated collection or payment procedure in order to deal with the great volume of items at a lower cost to all customers.

2. Rights that can be asserted against the Drawee by the Drawer or by the Payee (Instrument was Abstracted from them and subsequently Paid by the Drawee)

(a) *Rights of Drawer*: As we have seen from U.C.C. Sections 3-403(a), 3-405, 3-407(b) and 4-406(d), unless precluded, the drawer has rights against a drawee who pays an instrument that has not been issued or is not properly payable; i.e., a creditor of a drawee has the right to have her account recredited with an amount improperly debited to it by the drawee. Under U.C.C. Sections 3-417 and 4-208, the drawee is able to recover on presentment warranties for any loss suffered by honoring an instrument bearing an alteration or an unauthorized signature of an endorser, or, under U.C.C. Section 3-418, from the person paid, where such a person did not qualify as a person entitled to enforce the instrument. In addition, we have noted that although a presenter merely warrants that he has no knowledge that the signature of the drawer is unauthorized [U.C.C. Sections 3-417(a)(3), 4-208(a)(3)], the Code allows the drawee to recover the amount of the draft from a person to whom or for whose benefit payment was made on an unauthorized signature, provided such person has not in good faith given value for the instrument or has not in good faith changed his position in reliance on the payment received. U.C.C. § 3-418(c). Can an issuer proceed directly against such presenter or recipient of the money so as to short circuit the two actions—drawer-vs.-drawee, drawee-vs.-presenter? The desirability to do so from the drawer's point of view is that unless the payee has received the instrument, the underlying obligation for which the instrument was issued is not suspended. U.C.C. § 3-310. Receipt of an instrument other than a cashier's check, teller's check or certified check does not discharge the underlying obligation, it merely suspends the obligation until dishonor, or until the obligation is discharged by honor of the instrument; for example, the check is paid or is certified by the drawee bank. The issuer's rights against the drawee are based on U.C.C. Sections 3-401(a), 3-403(a), 3-407(b), 4-401(a), but the issuer does not have any right to sue in conversion. U.C.C. § 3-420(a)(i). Can it be argued that the presentment warranties extend to the drawer of a draft?

Stone & Webster Engineering Corp. v. First National Bank & Trust Co.
345 Mass. 1, 184 N.E.2d 358 (1962)*

WILKINS, Chief Justice.

In this action of contract or tort in four counts for the same cause of action a demurrer to the declaration was sustained, and the plaintiff, described in the writ as having a usual place of business in Boston, appealed. G.L. (Ter. Ed.) c. 231, § 96. The questions argued concern the rights of the drawer against a collecting bank which "cashed" checks for an individual who had forged the payee's indorsement on the checks, which were never delivered to the payee.

In the first count, which is in contract, the plaintiff alleges that between January 1, 1960, and May 15, 1960, it was indebted at various times to Westinghouse Electric Corporation (Westinghouse) for goods and services furnished to it by Westinghouse; that in order to pay the indebt-

edness the plaintiff drew three checks within that period on its checking account in The First National Bank of Boston (First National) payable to Westinghouse in the total amount of $64,755.44; that before delivery of the checks to Westinghouse an employee of the plaintiff in possession of the checks forged the indorsement of Westinghouse and presented the checks to the defendant; that the defendant "cashed" the checks and delivered the proceeds to the plaintiff's employee who devoted the proceeds to his own use; that the defendant forwarded the checks to First National and received from First National the full amounts thereof; and that First National charged the account of the plaintiff with the full amounts of the checks and has refused to recredit the plaintiff's checking account; wherefore the defendant owes the plaintiff $64,755.44 with interest.

Count 2, also in contract, is on an account annexed for money owed, namely $64,755.44, the

* [Editor: citations in [ ] refer to Revised U.C.C. Articles 3 and 4.]

proceeds of checks of the plaintiff "cashed" by the defendant on forged indorsements between January 1, 1960, and May 15, 1960.

Counts 3 and 4 in tort are respectively for conversion of the checks and for negligence in "cashing" the checks with forged indorsements.

By order, copies of the three checks were filed in court. The checks are respectively dated at Rowe in this Commonwealth on January 5, March 8, and May 9, 1960. Their respective amounts are $36,982.86, $10,416.58, and $17,355. They are payable to the order of "Westinghouse Electric Corporation, 10 High Street, Boston." The first two checks are indorsed in typewriting, "For Deposit Only: Westinghouse Electric Corporation By: Mr. O. D. Costine, Treasury Representative" followed by an ink signature "O. D. Costine." The third check is indorsed in typewriting, "Westinghouse Electric Corporation By: [Sgd.] O. D. Costine Treasury Representative." All three checks also bear the indorsement by rubber stamp, "Pay to the order of any bank, banker or trust co. prior indorsements guaranteed . . . [date]¹ The First National Bank & Trust Co. Greenfield, Mass."

The demurrer, in so far as it has been argued, is to each count for failure to state a cause of action.

* * *

1. Count 1, the plaintiff contends, is for money had and received. We shall so regard it. "An action for money had and received lies to recover money which should not in justice be retained by the defendant, and which in equity and good conscience should be paid to the plaintiff." *Cobb v. Library Bureau,* 268 Mass. 311, 316, 167 N.E.2d 765, 767; *Adams v. First Nat'l. Bank,* 321 Mass. 693, 694, 75 N.E.2d 502; *Trafton v. Custeau,* 338 Mass. 305, 308, 155 N.E.2d 159.

The defendant has no money in its hands which belongs to the plaintiff. The latter had no right in the proceeds of its own check payable to Westinghouse. Not being a holder or an agent for a holder, it could not have presented the check to the drawee for payment. Uniform Commercial Code §§ 3-504(1) [§ 3-301]. . . . See Am. Law Inst.

---

¹ The respective dates are January 13, March 9, and May 11, 1960. Each check bears the stamped indorsement of the Federal Reserve Bank of Boston and on its face the paid stamp of The First National Bank of Boston.

Uniform Commercial Code, 1958 Official Text with comments, § 3-419, comment 2: "A negotiable instrument is the property of the holder." See also Restatement 2d: Torts, Tent. Draft No. 3, 1958, § 241A. The plaintiff contends that "First National paid or credited the proceeds of the checks to the defendant and charged the account of the plaintiff, and consequently, the plaintiff was deprived of a credit, and the defendant received funds or a credit which 'in equity and good conscience' belonged to the plaintiff."

In our opinion this argument is a non sequitur. The plaintiff as a depositor in First National was merely in a contractual relationship of creditor and debtor . . . . The amounts the defendant received from First National to cover the checks "cashed" were the bank's funds and not the plaintiff's. The Uniform Commercial Code does not purport to change the relationship. *See* §§ 1-103, 4-401 to 4-407. Section 3-409(1) [§ 3-408] provides: "A check or other draft does not of itself operate as an assignment of any funds in the hands of the drawee available for its payment, and the drawee is not liable on the instrument until he accepts it." This is the same as our prior law, which the Code repealed. . . . Whether the plaintiff was rightfully deprived of a credit is a matter between it and the drawee, First National.

If we treat the first count as seeking to base a cause of action for money had and received upon a waiver of the tort of conversion—a matter which it is not clear is argued—the result will be the same. In this aspect the question presented is whether a drawer has a right of action for conversion against a collecting bank which handles its checks in the bank collection process. Unless there be such a right, there is no tort which can be waived.

The plaintiff relies upon the Uniform Commercial Code § 3-419, [§ 3-420(a) indicates that "the law applicable to conversion of personal property applies to instruments"] which provides, "(1) An instrument is converted when . . . (c) it is paid on a forged indorsement." This, however, could not apply to the defendant, which is not a "payor bank," defined in the Code, § 4-105(b) [§ 4-105(3)], as "a bank by which an item is payable as drawn or accepted." . . .

A conversion provision of the Uniform Commercial Code which might have some bearing on this case is § 3-419(3) [§ 3-420(c)].[3] This section implicitly recognizes that, subject to defenses, including the one stated in it, a collecting bank, defined in the Code, § 4-105(d) [§ 4-105(5)], may be liable in conversion. In the case at bar the forged indorsements were "wholly inoperative" as the signatures of the payee, Code §§ 3-404(1) [§ 3-403(a) uses the term "ineffective"], 1-201(43), and equally so both as to the restrictive indorsements for deposit, see § 3-205(c) [omitted], and as to the indorsement in blank, see § 3-204(2) [§ 3-205(b)]. When the forger transferred the checks to the collecting bank, no negotiation under § 3-202(1) [§ 3-203(b)] occurred, because there was lacking the necessary indorsement of the payee. For the same reason, the collecting bank could not become a "holder" as defined in § 1-201(20), and so could not become a holder in due course under § 3-302(1) [§ 3-302(a)]. Accordingly, we assume that the collecting bank may be liable in conversion to a proper party, subject to defenses, including that in § 3-419(3) [§ 3-420(c)]. See *A. Blum Jr.'s Sons v. Whipple*, 194 Mass. 253, 255, 80 N.E. 501. But there is no explicit provision in the Code purporting to determine to whom the collecting bank may be liable, and consequently, the drawer's right to enforce such a liability must be found elsewhere. Therefore, we conclude that the case must be decided on our own law, which, on the issue we are discussing, has been left untouched by the Uniform Commercial Code in any specific section.[*]

In this Commonwealth there are two cases (decided in 1913 and 1914) the results in which embrace a ruling that there was a conversion, but in neither was the question discussed and, for aught that appears, in each the ruling seems to have been assumed without conscious appreciation of the issue here considered. *Frankline Sav.*

Bank v. International Trust Co., 215 Mass. 231, 102 N.E. 363; *Quincy Mut. Fire Ins. Co. v. International Trust Co.*, 217 Mass. 370, 140 N.E. 845. . . . The *Frankline Sav. Bank* case cannot be distinguished on the ground of the limited powers of a city treasurer. That issue was important as charging the bank with notice of the treasurer's lack of authority to indorse but, that fact established there was this further question as to whether there was a remedy in tort for conversion.

The authorities are hopelessly divided. We think that the preferable view is that there is no right of action. . . .

We state what appears to us to be the proper analysis. Had the checks been delivered to the payee Westinghouse, the defendant might have been liable for conversion to the payee. The checks, if delivered, in the hands of the payee would have been valuable property which could have been transferred for value or presented for payment; and, had a check been dishonored, the payee would have had a right of recourse against the drawer on the instrument under § 3-413(2) [§ 3-414(b)]. Here the plaintiff drawer of the checks, which were never delivered to the payee (*see Gallup v. Barton*, 313 Mass. 379, 381, 47 N.E.2d 921), had no valuable rights in them. Since, as we have seen, it did not have the right of a payee or subsequent holder to present them to the drawee for payment, the value of its rights was limited to the physical paper on which they were written, and was not measured by their payable amounts. . . .

The enactment of the Uniform Commercial Code opens the road for the adoption of what seems the preferable view. An action by the drawer against the collecting bank might have some theoretical appeal as avoiding circuity of action. . . . It would have been in the interest of speedy and complete justice had the case been tried with the action by the drawer against the drawee and with an action by the drawee against the collecting bank. . . . So one might ask: If the drawee is liable to the drawer and the collecting bank is liable to the drawee, why not let the drawer sue the collecting bank direct? We believe that the answer lies in the applicable defenses set up in the Code.[4]

The drawer can insist that the drawee recredit his account with the amount of any unauthorized

---

[3] "Subject to the provisions of this chapter concerning restrictive indorsements a representative, including a depositary or collecting bank, who has in good faith and in accordance with the reasonable commercial standards applicable to the business of such representative dealt with an instrument or its proceeds on behalf of one who was not the true owner is not liable in conversion or otherwise to the true owner beyond the amount of any proceeds remaining in his hands." *See* Code §§ 1-201(35); 4-201(1) [§ 4-201(a)].

[*] [Editor: *see* now U.C.C. § 4-406(f).]

---

[4] Cases where a payee has acquired rights in an instrument may stand on a different footing.

payment. Such was our common law. . . . This is, in effect, retained by the Code. §§ 4-401(1),[5] 4-406(4) [§§ 4-401(a), 4-406(f)]. But the drawee has defenses based upon the drawer's substantial negligence, if "contributing," or upon his duty to discover and report unauthorized signatures and alterations. §§ 3-406, 4-406. As to unauthorized indorsements, see § 4-406(4) [§ 4-406(f)].[6] Then, if the drawee has a valid defence which it waives or fails upon request to assert, the drawee may not assert against the collecting bank or other prior party presenting or transferring the check a claim which is based on the forged indorsement. § 4-406(5) [§ 4-406(f)].[7] . . . If the drawee recredits

---

[5] ["A bank may charge against the account of a customer an item that is properly payable from that account * * *."]

[6] ["Without regard to care or lack of care of either the customer or the bank a customer who does not within one year after the statement or items are made available to the customer (subsection (a)) discover and report the customer's unauthorized signature on or any alteration on the item is precluded from asserting against the bank the unauthorized signature or alteration."]

[7] ["[I]f there is a preclusion under this subsection, the payor bank may not recover for breach of warranty under Section 4-208 with respect to the unauthorized signature or alteration to which the preclusion applies."]

the drawer's account and is not precluded by § 4-406(5) [§ 4-406(f)], it may claim against the presenting bank on the relevant warranties in §§ 3-417 and 4-207 [§§ 3-417 and 4-208], and each transferee has rights against his transferor under those sections.

If the drawer's rights are limited to requiring the drawee to recredit his account, the drawee will have the defenses noted above and perhaps others; and the collecting bank or banks will have the defenses in § 4-207(4) [§ 4-208(e)][8] and § 4-406(5) [§ 4-406(f)], and perhaps others. If the drawer is allowed in the present case to sue the collecting bank, the assertion of the defenses, for all practical purposes, would be difficult. The possibilities of such a result would tend to compel resort to litigation in every case involving a forgery of commercial paper. It is a result to be avoided.

The demurrer to Count 1 was rightly sustained . . . order sustaining demurrer[s] sustained.

---

[8] ["Unless notice of a claim for breach of warranty is given to the warrantor within thirty days after the claimant has reason to know of the breach and the identity of the warrantor, the warrantor is discharged to the extent of any loss caused by the delay in giving notice of the claim."]

NOTE

In *Sun 'N Sand, Inc. v. United California Bank,* 21 Cal. 3d 671, 148 Cal. Rptr. 329, 582 P.2d 920 (1978), the court was prepared to extend the presentment warranties to the drawer and thereby to allow the telescoping of the two actions. This approach is rejected by Revised U.C.C. Section 4-208. The same effect can be achieved, however, by the drawee effecting service of a third party notice on the presenter. *Cf.* U.C.C. §§ 3-305(c), 3-306, 3-602(b). The "circuity argument" has been criticized as being exaggerated and inconsequential in the modern era of long-arm jurisdiction, negotiated settlements, and liberal rules of impleader. *See* J.J. White and R.S. Summers, *Uniform Commercial Code,* § 15-5 (1988).

Any attempt by the drawee to proceed on the basis of presentment warranties raises the issue that damages must be proximate to the breach of warranty. If the drawer is precluded from objecting to a debit being entered against his credit, the drawee will not have suffered a loss. It is this absence of damages that leads U.C.C. Section 4-406(f) to indicate that the drawee would not be able to recover on presentment warranties where the customer is precluded from proceeding against the drawee/bank. The drawee bank cannot waive its right to assert a preclusion and thereby create a cause of action based on the presentment warranties. Note, however, the drawee has rights under U.C.C. Section 3-418 based in restitution or mistake when bringing an action in recoupment against a person not qualifying as having taken the instrument in good faith and for value, or as not having changed her position in good faith reliance on the payment or acceptance of the instrument. (U.C.C. § 3-418(c)).

(b) *Rights of Payee/Endorsee*: Receipt of the instrument by the payee suspends the underlying obligation and gives rise to a proprietary interest in the instrument to the amount payable on the instrument to the claimant. U.C.C. § 3-420(b). But not until the instrument has been received by the payee will the payee be a person entitled to enforce the instrument. U.C.C. § 3-301. This proprietary interest enables the payee and any subsequent endorsee from whom the instrument has been stolen or whose signature has been forged to proceed against the drawee or anyone who took the instrument (other than a person qualifying as a holder in due course) by alleging conversion. U.C.C. § 3-420(a)(ii).

Where an instrument is given to an agent for collection, such as being placed into the bank collection system, an agent other than a depository bank is only liable in conversion up to the amount of any proceeds that are still in the agent's control. The depository bank, however, is liable for the amount of the item. The depository bank not only makes presentment warranties, U.C.C. § 4-208(a)(1), but it is also the most convenient defendant in cases involving multiple checks drawn on different banks. Further, it is in a customer-bank relationship with the depositor, a relationship that presupposes that a bank knows its customers.

Knesz v. Central Jersey Bank and Trust Co.

188 N.J. Super. 391, 457 A.2d 1162 (1982)*

PRESSLER, J.A.D.

The issue raised by this appeal, unaddressed in this State since its adoption of the Uniform Commercial Code, N.J.S.A. 12A:1-101 et seq., is whether the payee of a check whose indorsement has been forged has a cause of action in conversion against the depositary-collecting bank which has paid on the forged indorsement. We hold that N.J.S.A. 12A:3-419(3) [§ 3-420(c)], relied on by defendant bank, does not immunize it from a conversion action by the payee and hence that the Code does not deprive the payee of the common-law conversion action theretofore available to him. Accordingly, we reverse the summary judgment entered in defendant bank's favor and remand for trial.

The facts giving rise to this action are basically undisputed insofar as they implicate the viability

of plaintiff-payee's cause of action in conversion against defendant, the depositary and collecting bank. Plaintiff Steve Knesz was the nonoccupant owner of a cooperative apartment in New York City. He employed a New York attorney, Thomas G. Moringiello, who has since been disbarred, to act as his rental agent. It appears that Moringiello did not regularly transmit rental proceeds to plaintiff since the amount of the rent did not exceed the disbursements required to be made for taxes, mortgage amortization and maintenance expenses. In any event, in March 1979 Moringiello, without plaintiff's knowledge or authority, sold the apartment to Lois Gartlir. She paid the purchase price by way of five checks drawn on three different banks and totaling $32,651. Four of these checks, three drawn on Morgan Guaranty Trust Company of New York and one drawn on Bankers Trust, were payable to the order of Gartlir who, in turn, endorsed them under the legend "pay to the order of Steve Knesz." The fifth was a bank check of Citibank, N.A., payable to plain

* [Editor: citations in [ ] refer to Revised U.C.C. Articles 3 and 4.]

tiff's order. Moringiello forged plaintiff's indorsement on all five instruments. He apparently deposited three of the checks payable to Gartlir to his own account in Citibank, N.A., which ultimately repaid plaintiff.

Thus, the controversy involves only two instruments, a check drawn on Morgan Guaranty payable to Gartlir in the amount of $5,000 and the Citibank check payable to plaintiff in the amount of $16,974.24. These two checks were delivered by Moringiello to a New Jersey attorney, James E. Collins, under the following circumstances. Moringiello at the time of this transaction was representing other clients in connection with their sale of a residence in Staten Island. Collins fortuitously represented the same people in connection with their purchase of a residence in Monmouth County, New Jersey. The proceeds of the Staten Island sale were intended to be applied to the New Jersey purchase and, in accordance with this plan, Moringiello sent Collins a check drawn on his "special attorney account" in the amount of $24,000 purportedly representing the sales proceeds. Collins deposited this check into the trust account maintained by his firm, Cerrato, O'Connor, Mehr & Saker (firm) in the Central Jersey Bank and Trust Co. of Freehold (Central Jersey). Moringiello's attorney's check was returned for insufficient funds, and Collins made demand upon Moringiello for the immediate replacement of his bad check. Moringiello obliged by turning over to Collins the two checks on which he had forged Knesz's indorsement, placing his own indorsement immediately below Knesz's forged signature. He added to these another check drawn by him on his attorney's account making up the difference between Knesz's $21,974.24 and the required $24,000. Collins indorsed all three instruments and deposited them in the firm's account in Central Jersey. The collection process proceeded and was completed in due course.

Some nine months later, in January 1980, plaintiff first learned of the unauthorized sale of the apartment. He apparently chose to ratify the sale and seek recovery of the proceeds. With the gratuitous assistance of yet another bank, he finally obtained the necessary information regarding the five instruments, and in August, 1980 he executed affidavits of forgery as to each. As noted, Citibank paid him the amount of the three checks Moringiello had deposited to his account there. Central Jersey refused to pay, however, on

the two checks as to which it was both depository and collecting bank. Plaintiff consequently brought this action against the bank, which filed a third-party complaint against the firm.

Both plaintiff and the bank moved for summary judgment. Plaintiff took the position that the bank, having paid on a forged instrument, was absolutely liable to him in conversion. The bank cross-moved for summary judgment. Its theories of defense included the claims that the bank was not liable in conversion pursuant to the terms of N.J.S.A. 12A:3-419(3) [§ 3-420(c)]; that plaintiff had been negligent and hence was foreclosed from recovery by N.J.S.A. 12A:3-406, and finally, that in ratifying Moringiello's sale of the apartment, plaintiff also necessarily ratified Moringiello's disposition of the proceeds thereof. It was on the basis of N.J.S.A. 12A:3-419(3) [§ 3-420(c)] that plaintiff's motion was denied and the bank's motion granted. We agree with plaintiff that the trial judge erred in his construction of this section.

N.J.S.A. 12A:3-419(1)(c) states with unmistakable clarity that "an instrument is converted when . . . it is paid on a forged indorsement." [§ 3-420(a) provides in part "[t]he law applicable to conversion of personal property applies to instruments. . . . "] N.J.S.A. 12A:3-419(3) [§ 3-420(c)], which poses the constructional problem here, provides in full as follows:

> Subject to the provisions of this Act concerning restrictive indorsements a representative, including a depositary or collecting bank, who has in good faith and in accordance with the reasonable commercial standards applicable to the business of such representative dealt with an instrument or its proceeds on behalf of one who was not the true owner is not liable in conversion or otherwise to the true owner beyond the amount of any proceeds remaining in his hands.

Thus, the question is whether a depositary or collecting bank, when it engages in the customary business of accepting checks for cash payment or ordinary collection, is entitled to the statutory immunity from conversion liability afforded by § 3-419(3) [§ 3-420(c)].

We note preliminarily that this is a question which has generated substantial controversy among those courts and commentators who have addressed it and who apparently are unanimous in their conclusion that there is neither commercial nor practical nor rational justification for construing it as applicable to depositary and collecting banks engaging in normal check collection business. Consequently, the section has either been ignored altogether, applied reluctantly, or held inapplicable on a variety of theories. For the reasons hereafter stated we agree with those courts which have concluded that the section does not apply in this situation but we reach that conclusion on grounds somewhat different from those heretofore articulated.

Our beginning point is pre-Code common law, which virtually universally recognized the right of the payee whose indorsement was forged to recover on theories of conversion, contract or money had and received directly against the depositary-collecting bank which paid on the forged indorsement. . . .

The common law right of action by the payee against the depositary-collecting bank rests, of course, upon sound and established principles dependent upon the legal fact that neither the forger of the indorsement nor those taking through him have title to the instrument and hence that the payee or last genuine indorser remains its owner. The check owner's right of direct action against the depositary-collecting bank is also recognized as resting upon sound considerations of public policy as well. First, the loss is appropriately placed upon the depositary bank since it has dealt most immediately with the forged instrument and consequently has the best as well as the last opportunity to have avoided the loss. Second, since the depositary bank is the most immediately connected with the transaction involving the forged instrument, it is, in most situations, in the best position to raise the traditional defenses of negligence, estoppel and ratification. Finally, it is the depositary bank upon which, as a consequence of the normal operation of the collection system the loss will in any event be ultimately placed since, as a consequence of their respective indorsement warranties, each bank in the collection chain, from drawee to depositary, has a right to look to its own transferor for recovery.[1] See, e.g.,

Cooper v. Union Bank, 9 Cal.3d 371, 107 Cal. Rptr. 1, 507 P.2d 609, 616-617 (Sup.Ct.1973); . . .

If N.J.S.A. 12A:3-419(3) [§ 3-420(c)] is construed as applying to the normal and customary check collection business of a depositary and collecting bank, then by the terms of that provision its liability in "conversion or otherwise" to the payee of the check whose indorsement has been forged will be limited to those situations in which the bank has acted either in bad faith or contrary to a reasonable commercial standard, and to those situations in which it still has the proceeds of the check available to it because of the pendency of the collection process. Unless one of these liability-triggering elements is available to the payee, he will be unable to proceed directly against the depositary-collecting bank. Rather, his remedy will be against the drawer of the check or the drawee bank. The drawer will then look to the drawee and the drawee, as noted, will have the right to recover successively against its transferor, who in turn will look to its transferor until ultimately, the loss will be borne by the depositary bank. The effect of N.J.S.A. 12A:3-419(3), therefore, would be in no way to immunize the depositary bank from the consequences of its payment on a forged indorsement. It undertakes that liability by the mere act of sending the check through for collection. All that such a construction of N.J.S.A. 12A:3-419(3) would therefore accomplish would be the replacement of a single direct action by a circuity of action. If the depositary bank and the payee are in the same jurisdiction and the drawee-payor bank is in another jurisdiction as is typical, that construction of N.J.S.A. 12A:3-419(3) would also have the effect of prejudicing the recovery opportunity of the payee, who would be forced to go elsewhere to sue. Furthermore, the raising and litigating of defenses based on the payee's culpability are ordinarily most effectively accomplished by the bank closest to the transaction, and customarily this is the depositary rather than the drawee bank.[2]

---

[1] This right over has been codified by the Code, N.J.S.A. 12A:4-207 [§ 4-208(a)], which specifies the warranties undertaken by each customer or collecting bank obtaining payment or acceptance of an item. Among them is the warranty of good title. N.J.S.A. 12A:4-207(1)(a) [§ 4-208(a)(1)] and (2)(a) [§ 4-207(a)(2)].

[2] *Cf.* Western Union Tel. Co. v. Peoples Nat'l Bk., Lakewood, 169 N.J. Super. 272 (App. Div. 1979), a case dealing with the right of action of a drawer rather than a payee. There the drawer was denied the right of direct action against the depositary-payor on the ground that the proximate cause of its loss was the drawee's improper handling of its account. Despite the circuity of action thus created, the court noted that the drawee is in the best position to raise Code defenses against the drawer based upon the drawer's own negligence and failure to inspect its statements.

The question, then, is whether the framers of the Code and the New Jersey Legislature intended by enactment of § 3-419(3) [§ 3-420(c)] to abrogate a common law principle which is legally sound, commercially practical and judicially expeditious, and to replace it, not by altering the allocation of ultimate liability, but only by limiting the remedy of the wronged party in a manner which is inevitably circuitous, cumbersome, burdensome and impractical. We conclude that this was neither the legislative intention nor the legislative prescription.

...*Ervin v. Dauphin Deposit Trust Co.,* 38 Pa.D. & C.2d 473 (C.P.1964). The court in *Ervin* relied, first, on legislative history, noting that the Official Comment on this section (Comment 5 on § 3-419) does not evince an intention to abrogate the common law.... [T]he California Supreme Court in *Cooper v. Union Bank,* 107 Cal.Rptr. 1, 507 P.2d 609 ... also rejected the applicability of § 3-419(3) [§ 3-420(c)] to depositary banks acting in a check-collection function. Noting the unlikelihood that the Code's framers would have intended to so radically depart from the common law without making some comment either acknowledging or explaining that departure, the California court reasoned that for purposes of § 3-419(3), whether the depositary bank has cashed the forged check or has merely accepted it for collection, it never actually pays over the "proceeds" within the intendment of that section if it pays on a forged indorsement to one who is not entitled thereto. *Cooper* further relied on the conclusion, reinforced by its own state's study comments on the Code, that "representative," as used by § 3-419(3), was intended only to protect investment brokers, those acting as investment brokers, and other "true agents." 107 Cal.Rptr. at 10, 507 P.2d at 618.

Ervin and *Cooper* generated considerable commentator response, the consensus of which was that there was little justification, if any, for generally immunizing a depositary bank from direct liability to the owner of a check which was paid by it on a forged indorsement; that the Code apparently did not intend such a result, but that the reasoning of both *Ervin* and *Cooper* was nevertheless strained....

The judicial response to *Ervin* and *Cooper* is even more instructive. Virtually all courts which have had to address § 3-419(3), whether or not they have finally opted to apply that section to a

depositary bank which has paid on a forged check indorsement, have expressly failed to find any policy justification for such an immunity....

Other courts, however, have been willing to conclude, whether or not they accept the *Ervin-Cooper* rationales, that in view of the common law precedents and the strong public policy arguments against immunity, the immunity intent of the Code is simply too improbable to warrant judicial enforcement. They have accordingly refused to apply the section to depositary and collecting banks paying on forged indorsements. *See, e.g., Tubin v. Rabin,* 389 F. Supp. 787 (N.D.Tex.1974), aff'd 533 F.2d 255 (5th Cir. 1976); *Sherriff-Goslin Co. v. Cawood,* supra, 91 Mich.App. 204, 283 N.W.2d 691 (Ct.App.1979). Still other courts have avoided the immunity consequence by a strict construction of the exception based on failure to comply with a reasonable commercial standard. *See, e.g., Salsman v. National Community Bank of Rutherford, supra,* 102 N.J.Super. 482, 246 A.2d 162.... And, finally, despite the adoption of the Code by their states, some courts have applied the common law rule and accorded a right of direct action against the depositary-collecting bank under § 3-419(1)(c) without any reference at all to § 3-419(3)....

Here, we agree with the trial judge that the conduct of the bank was *prima facie* in accord with a reasonable commercial standard and that plaintiff made no showing which might raise a question of fact with respect thereto. We are satisfied that the bank was perfectly justified in accepting the checks with its own depositor's indorsement. While it is true that Moringiello himself was one of the prior indorsers and that the bank constructively knew that Moringiello had drawn a previous check payable to its customer on insufficient funds, we do not conclude that the bank was obligated by that circumstance to inquire into every subsequent instrument presented to it which was indorsed by Moringiello, particularly since that indorsement and all prior indorsements were effectively guaranteed to it by virtue of its customer's own and final indorsement. Having concluded that there was no question of fact impugning the bank's adherence to the required reasonable commercial standard, we are perforce constrained to address the question of the general applicability of § 3-419(3).

In concluding that that section does not apply to depositary or collecting banks engaging in customary check payment and collection activities, we are in full accord, for the reasons we have already stated, with both the judicial and commentator expressions of the public policy concerns militating against immunity. We recognize however, that our view of salutary public policy may not override or contravene the Legislature's expressed view and that if the Legislature had indeed expressly elected to abrogate the common law, we would be obliged to enforce that election. It is, however, our conviction, based both on legislative history and textual considerations, that our Legislature did not so intend. . . .

In view of this historical perspective and its focus on the broker-securities situation, the intended meaning of the Official Comment on § 3-419(3) becomes clear. That Comment . . . begins with the statement that the section "is intended to adopt the rule of decisions which has held that a representative, such as a broker or depositary bank, who deals with a negotiable instrument for his principal in good faith is not liable to the true owner for conversion or otherwise. . . . " There was never, however, as heretofore discussed, a "rule of decisions" absolving the depositary bank from liability to the owner of a check which has been paid by the bank on a forged indorsement. To the contrary, the "rule of decisions" expressly and virtually uniformly imposed that liability on depositary banks in that situation, the question of their good faith notwithstanding. In the light of the section's history, it becomes evident then that the "rule of decisions" to which the official Comment referred was, rather, a well established pre-Code common law exception to the general principle that an agent is liable in conversion in respect of property which his principal has no authority to dispose of. The exception was intended to protect an agent who acts in good faith in transferring, on his principal's account, cash or securities which by their nature require only delivery for passage of good title, typically, bearer instruments. This exception has been codified by 1 Restatement, Torts 2d, § 233(4) at 454 (1965), as follows:

The statement in Subsection (1) [general rule of agent liability] is not applicable to an agent or servant who disposes of current money, or a document negotiable by common law or by statute, pursuant to a transaction by which the transferee becomes a holder in due course of

such money or document, unless the agent or servant knows or had reason to know that his principal or master does not have authority so to dispose of it.

And see Comment e. on § 233(4), id. at 456. This exception is also recognized by 2 Restatement, Agency 2d, § 349 at 116 (1958). That section restates the general rule of agent liability for conversion of property to which the principal is not entitled to possession, but Comment g. at 119 explains that the agent is nevertheless protected when he deals in good faith with commercial paper to which title is transferable by delivery alone. . . .

[W]e find § 3-419(3) inapplicable in this situation because we conclude that a depositary bank functioning within the check collection system is not a "representative" encompassed by that section. First, as heretofore discussed, it was not, as a matter of legislative history, intended to be so encompassed. Nor is it required to be so encompassed by any textual imperatives.

The term "representative" is defined by the Code, N.J.S.A. 12:1-201(35), as "an agent, an officer of a corporation or association, or a trustee, executor or administrator of an estate, or any other person empowered to act for another." The argument for inclusion of a depositary or collecting bank within this definition customarily relies on Article 4 of the Code dealing with bank deposits and collections, and more particularly on § 4-201 [§ 4-201(a)], which provides in pertinent part that

Unless a contrary intent clearly appears and prior to the time that a settlement given by a collecting bank for an item is or becomes final . . . the bank is an agent or sub-agent of the owner of the item and any settlement given for the item is provisional.

The theory, then, is that by the act of accepting a check for collection, the bank constitutes itself an agent, hence a "representative," and hence is entitled to the benefit of § 3-419(3). Indeed, it is this statutorily-created agency status that has led one commentator at least to the conclusion that when a bank accepts a check for collection it is an agent entitled to rely on § 3-419(3), but when it cashes the check "over the counter," it is not within the agency definition of § 4-201 since it would then be a purchaser of the check and would consequently not be entitled to rely on § 3-419(3).

See Farnsworth and Leary, *"UCC Brief No. 10: Forgery and Alteration of Checks,"* 14 Prac.Law. No. 3, at 75, 79 (1968). We regard this distinction as sophistical in terms both of the text of § 4-201 and the common sense of the transaction. First, there is no practical justification from the perspective of either the payee or the bank for liability to be made to depend on the fortuity of whether the check is cashed or a credit given by the depositary bank. Moreover, typically the forged indorsement is not discovered until after final settlement when the bank's agency status in respect of that instrument has in any case already terminated. More significantly, however, this distinction is contrary to the text of § 4-201.

As we view it, the key concept of § 4-201 is acceptance by the bank of a check for collection *from the owner.* It is perfectly clear that if an instrument requires indorsement in order for its title to be transferred, title cannot have passed on the basis of a forged indorsement. Therefore, a person tendering such an instrument cannot be deemed to be its owner. As to such an instrument, consequently, the bank is not an agent for the owner when it accepts it for collection from a person who is not the owner. In this context we note that had an agency status been intended by the Code in respect of a forged check, other terminology would easily have accomplished that result, such as use of the word "customer," defined by § 4-104(e) [§ 4-104(a)(5)] to include any person for whom a bank has agreed to collect an item. It is, moreover, clear that the statutory agency presumption of § 4-201 was intended only to make uniform and to clarify the consequences of bank insolvency during the collection process. See New Jersey Study Comment 1 to N.J.S.A. 12A:4-201. It does not appear that there was any intent to transport that statutory agency presumption into the general definition of "representative" for purposes of either § 1-201(35) or § 3-419(3).

We are able to discern no basis, other than § 4-201, for concluding that a depositary bank, in accepting a forged instrument for collection, is acting as an agent. Since § 4-201 predicates agency status on acceptance from an owner, we are persuaded that, in respect of the forged instrument, the bank is not an agent, hence not a representative, and hence beyond the protection of § 3-419(3).

. . . If § 3-419(3) is understood as intended to codify the common law broker-bearer instrument exception to agent liability, the answer is obvious. Where indorsement of an instrument is not necessary for transfer of title, a *bona fide* transferee of the instrument obtains good title thereto, even if the transfer was not authorized by the prior actual owner—the true owner. It is thus only in the context of such instruments, as to which there can simultaneously be two "owners," that the concept of "true owner" as distinguished from "owner" has relevance. That concept is inapposite to forged checks since a check can only have one owner at a time.

Furthermore, by immunizing an agent dealing with bearer instruments, § 3-419(3) effectively affords real immunity from liability since ordinarily the agent would be liable only to the true owner. Extension of that immunity to a bank accepting an instrument with a forged indorsement does not similarly immunize the bank from ultimate liability since it is always in any case responsible to its transferee by reason of its statutory warranties. The immunity would, therefore, not affect liability but only the remedy of the wronged party and would deprive him of a remedy well recognized at common law with no apparent off-setting legitimate advantage to the commercial establishment. This result in our view is aberrational, was not intended, and is not dictated by any policy or provision of the Code.

The summary judgment in favor of defendant is reversed and the matter remanded to the trial court for further proceedings with respect to the Bank's defenses and for prosecution of its third-party complaint.

NOTE

1. On appeal the New Jersey Supreme Court reversed this decision. *Knesz v. Central Jersey Bank & Trust Co.,* 97 N.J. 1, 477 A.2d 806 (1986). Agreeing that the bank had acted in good faith and in accordance with commercially reasonable practice, the court held that former U.C.C. Section 3-419(3) granted immunity to a depositary bank as a "representative."

The court disagreed "with the conclusion of the court below, while acknowledging, as we must, respectable decisional and scholarly support for its result."

The controversy is now settled by U.C.C. Section 3-420(c). That section specifically excludes a depository bank when it exculpates a "representative" who has acted in good faith from liability beyond the amount of proceeds that have not been paid out.

2. Where a payee or an endorsee never received the instrument/check, and there was neither an actual nor a constructive possession of the instrument, it cannot be argued that the underlying obligation is suspended or that the payee or endorsee has a proprietory interest in the instrument so as to have standing to sue in conversion.

State of New York v. Barclays Bank of New York
76 N.Y.2d 533, 563 N.E.2d 11 (1990)

HANCOCK, Judge.

In the absence of actual or constructive possession of a check, does the named payee have a right of action against the depositary bank which has paid out the proceeds over a forged indorsement? This is the question presented in plaintiff's appeal from a dismissal of its action to recover the amounts of several checks drawn by taxpayers to the order of various State taxing authorities. The checks were never delivered to plaintiff; the taxpayers' dishonest accountant misappropriated them, and deposited them in his own account at Banker's Trust Company of Hudson Valley, N.A.[1]

The case stems from the activities of Richard Caliendo, an accountant. Caliendo prepared tax returns for various clients. To satisfy their tax liability, the clients issued checks payable to various State taxing entities, and gave them to Caliendo. Between 1977 and 1979, he forged indorsements on these checks, deposited them in his own account with defendant, and subsequently withdrew the proceeds. In November 1980—shortly after the scheme was uncovered—Caliendo died when the plane he was piloting crashed. The State never received the checks. In 1983, after learning of these events, the State commenced this action seeking to recover the aggregate face amount of the checks.

Supreme Court denied defendant's motion to dismiss the complaint and its subsequent motion

for summary judgment, concluding that the payee's possession of the checks was not essential to its action against the depository bank. On appeal, the Appellate Division reversed and dismissed the complaint. It held that requiring "delivery, either actual or constructive, [as] an indispensable prerequisite for" a conversion action under U.C.C. § 3-419(1)(c) is consistent with the view of most authorities and supported by practical considerations (*State of New York v. Barclays Bank,* 151 A.D.2d 19, 21-24, 546 N.Y.S.2d 479). We agree.[2]

II

It has long been held that a check has no valid inception until delivery.... Further, a payee must have actual or constructive possession of a negotiable instrument in order to attain the status of a holder (*see,* U.C.C. § 1-201 [20]) and to have

[1] Defendant Barclays Bank of New York, N.A. is a successor to Bankers Trust Company. Henceforth, "defendant" will refer to Barclays and Bankers Trust as one entity.

[2] Plaintiff's complaint is framed as one for money had and received. Supreme Court in denying defendant's dismissal motion under CPLR 3211(a)(7), however, treated the action as one in contract, alone, or in both contract and conversion. Although, in its brief, plaintiff now appears to view the action primarily as one for money had and received or quasi contract, it cites cases and authorities pertaining to a conversion action under U.C.C. § 3-419(1)(c), and the Appellate Division apparently viewed it as such. For purposes of resolving the legal question before us—the effect of lack of delivery of the checks—it makes no difference whether plaintiff's action is under U.C.C. § 3-419(1)(c) or under some common-law theory. The result is the same (*see,* part III, infra). We accordingly discuss the authorities as being applicable to both the statutory and common-law theories.

an interest in it. These are established principles of negotiable instruments law. . . .

Permitting a payee who has never had possession to maintain an action against the depositary bank would be inconsistent with these principles. It would have the effect of enforcing rights that do not exist. For this reason, most courts and commentators have concluded that either actual or constructive delivery to the payee is a necessary prerequisite to a conversion action . . .

Henderson v. Lincoln Rochester Trust Co., 303 N.Y. 27, 100 N.E.2d 117, on which plaintiff relies, does not support its argument in this respect. There, in concluding that the payee could maintain an action either in contract or conversion, the court did not reach the issue of nondelivery of the check. Other cases cited by plaintiff are readily distinguished. They involve situations where the plaintiff, unlike the State here, had received constructive possession of the check through delivery to the payee's agent, to a copayee, or to a coindorsee (*see, e.g., Lund's, Inc. v. Chemical Bank,* 870 F.2d 840 [2d Cir.] [delivery to coindorsees];[3] *United States v. Bankers Trust Co.,* 17 U.C.C. Rep.Serv. 136 [E.D.N.Y. 1975] [delivery to copayee]; *Burks Drywall v. Washington Bank & Trust Co.,* 110 Ill.App.3d 569, 66 Ill.Dec. 222, 442 N.E.2d 648 [1982] [delivery to copayee or agent]; *Thornton & Co. v. Gwinnett Bank & Trust Co.,* 151 Ga.App. 641, 260 S.E.2d 765 [1979] [delivery to agent]).

Plaintiff maintains, however, citing language in *Burks Drywall,* 66 Ill.Dec. at 226, 442 N.E.2d, *supra,* at 652 and *Thornton,* 260 S.E.2d, *supra,* at 767, that, based solely on its status as named payee and intended beneficiary of the checks, it has a sufficient interest to bring a conversion action under U.C.C. § 3-419(1)(c) or a common-law action for money had and received. We believe such a rule would be contrary to the underlying theory of the U.C.C. and, to the extent that the

cases cited by plaintiff suggest it, we decline to follow them. Plaintiff's contention that depositary banks could frequently avoid liability for paying over forged indorsements—if payees could not bring suit against them in the absence of delivery—is unfounded. The depositary bank could still be liable to the drawee bank. . . .

Nor are we persuaded by plaintiff's suggestion that permitting a suit . . . by a payee not-in-possession would promote judicial economy and avoid circuity of action. On the contrary, relegating such a payee to a suit against the drawer on the underlying obligation would give full effect to the U.C.C.'s loss allocation scheme by furthering the aim of placing ultimate responsibility on the party at fault through an orderly process in which each defendant in the transactional chain may interpose the defenses available to it. . . . And requiring a payee-not-in-possession to sue the drawer on the underlying claim would actually avoid circuity of action in some instances—for example, where the drawer's suit against the drawee bank is barred by valid defenses (*see,* U.C.C. §§ 3-406, 4-406) or where the drawer has an effective defense against the payee's claim. This concern has particular pertinence here where—as the Appellate Division observed (151 A.D.2d, at 20, 546 N.Y.S.2d 479)—it is contended that some of the checks were for inflated or nonexistent tax liabilities for which the drawers-taxpayers would have valid defenses against the State. In such cases, permitting a payee-not-in-possession to sue the depositary bank at the other end of the transactional chain would only produce unnecessary litigation. Accordingly, we agree with the Appellate Division that the rule requiring actual or constructive possession by a payee as a prerequisite for a suit against the depositary bank is preferable . . . and we adopt it.

III

Plaintiff contends, nevertheless, that even if possession is a prerequisite to a cause of action by a named payee against a depositary bank, it should prevail because the drawers' delivery of the checks to Caliendo constituted constructive delivery to the State. It is a general rule that putting a check in the hands of the drawer's own agent for purpose of delivery to the payee does not constitute delivery to the payee . . . ; this is so because the drawer has control of the agent and the check is revocable and ineffective until the

---

[3] Lund's involved three checks, two of which were indorsed and delivered to coindorsees of plaintiff, thus, giving plaintiff sufficient possession to maintain a conversion action with respect to those checks under U.C.C. § 3-419(1)(c). A third check indorsed solely to Lund's, Inc. was determined on remand not to have been constructively delivered to plaintiff Lund. As to that check, the action was dismissed in reliance upon the Appellate Division's decision in this case (*see,* Lund v. Chemical Bank, 1990 WL 17711 [S.D.N.Y.]).

agent delivers it. . . . Here, of course, Caliendo had no agency or other relationship with the State which might have imputed his possession of the checks to it. Indeed, the State does not contend that it knew of Caliendo's dealings with the drawers or even of the checks' existence. Thus, applying these general rules, the State's claim must fail.

Wolfin v. Security Bank, 170 App.Div. 519, 156 N.Y.S. 474, affd. 218 N.Y. 709, 113 N.E. 1068, relied on by plaintiff, is not to the contrary. There, the drawer of the check gave it to the named payee with instructions that it be indorsed and delivered to plaintiff. Unlike the case at bar—where the checks were never delivered to the payee but remained in the hands of the drawers' accountant and agent—in *Wolfin* the drawer retained no control after the check was delivered to the named payee as a fully negotiable instrument. . . .

Finally, contrary to plaintiff's contentions, it cannot recover under a theory of unjust enrichment or quasi contract. It is true that, in creating a statutory right to bring a conversion action for payment over a forged indorsement . . . at the time of the Uniform Commercial Code's enactment, the Legislature did not intend to abrogate the payee's pre-Code common-law rights to sue in assumpsit, for money had and received or unjust enrichment. . . . This does not help plaintiff, however.

The theory of an action in quasi contract "rests upon the equitable principle that a person shall not be *allowed to enrich himself unjustly at the expense of another.* . . . It is an obligation which the law creates, in the absence of any agreement, when and because the acts of the parties or others have placed in the possession of one person money, or its equivalent, under such circumstances that in equity and good conscience he ought not to retain it" (*Miller v. Schloss,* 218 N.Y. 400, 407 [emphasis added]; *see,* Restatement of Restitution § 1, at 12-15). The general rule is that "the plaintiff *must have suffered a loss* and an action not based upon loss is not restitutionary." (Restatement of Restitution 128, comment f, at 531 [emphasis added]). On this point, plaintiff's action in quasi contract, like its action for conversion . . . must fail. The checks were never actually or constructively delivered to plaintiff. It, therefore, never acquired a property interest in them and cannot be said to have suffered a loss.

The order of the Appellate Division should, accordingly, be affirmed, with costs.

NOTE

This issue is now resolved by U.C.C. Section 3-420(a)(ii): "a payee or indorsee who did not receive delivery of the instrument either directly or through delivery to an agent or a co-payee" has no cause of action for conversion.

Locks v. North Towne National Bank of Rockford
115 Ill. App. 3d 729, 451 N.E.2d 19 (1983)*

LINDBERG, J.

Plaintiff, David H. Locks, appeals from the judgment of the circuit court of Winnebago County in favor of defendant North Towne National Bank of Rockford (North Towne). Locks seeks payment by North Towne on a cashier's check which it issued and later dishonored. Because Locks has no standing to bring an action to recover on the cashier's check, we affirm.

The material facts of this case were either stip-

---

* [Editor: citations in [ ] refer to Revised U.C.C. Article 3 and 4.]

ulated or uncontradicted. Locks, an attorney, represented Patrick Newell, the purchaser in a real estate transaction. Thorsen Realtors (Thorsen) was the real estate broker for this transaction, having been retained by the seller, and was to act as escrowee for the purposes of receipt and distribution of an earnest money deposit concerning the property.

Newell had an agreement with Gail Russie, whereby Russie was to advance a portion of the $8,500 earnest money deposit that Newell was required to transmit to Thorsen pursuant to the real estate sales contract. On December 16, 1977, Russie negotiated to North Towne a check for

$4,250 drawn on the account of "Russie's Floor Maintenance & Supplies, Inc." at the DeKalb Bank. In exchange for the Russie check, North Towne issued its own cashier's check in the amount of $4,250 payable to Thorsen. Thereafter, the cashier's check found its way into the hands of Newell who personally delivered it to Thorsen. Thorsen deposited the cashier's check into its escrow account at First Security Bank of Oak Brook, a trial defendant not a party on this appeal.

Subsequently, the DeKalb Bank dishonored the Russie check used to purchase the cashier's check, and North Towne discovered a large overdraft in Russie's account with it. North Towne informed Thorsen of its decision to stop payment on the cashier's check on December 23, 1977, prior to the closing date of the real estate transaction, and dishonored the cashier's check upon presentment. Newell then raised other funds to satisfy his earnest money obligation.

As a result of a debt Newell owed to Locks for previously rendered legal services, Newell assigned all interest, legal or equitable, that he had in the cashier's check to Locks. Locks, as assignee of Newell, instituted this action to recover payment on the cashier's check. Although Thorsen was originally named as one defendant, it was dismissed by stipulation of the parties at the start of trial. After a bench trial, the circuit court entered its judgment of July 9, 1982, in favor of defendants.

On appeal, Locks raises two issues: (1) whether he has standing to sue North Towne for recovery on the dishonored cashier's check; and (2) whether North Towne improperly dishonored the cashier's check.

Locks claims standing to sue as a holder, but not as a holder in due course. Any interest he may have is derived from Newell's, as the assignment shows and the trial court found. Locks argues that Newell was the beneficial owner of the instrument and that Thorsen, the payee, acted merely as "technical holder" for Newell's benefit. Furthermore, Locks argues that Thorsen surrendered the instrument to him at trial where Locks produced it as an exhibit, this act rendering Locks the transferee of the holder with the rights that were vested in the transferor.

Section 3-301 of the Uniform Commercial Code (U.C.C.), under which Locks claims recovery from North Towne, provides that "[t]he holder

of an instrument whether or not he is the owner may * * * enforce payment in his own name."[*] . . . Thus, only the *holder* of the instrument has standing in an action under this section. A "holder" is defined as a person in possession of an instrument drawn, issued or indorsed to him or to his order or to bearer or in blank (§ 1-201(20)). Thus, proof of possession is essential for standing to enforce payment on an instrument. . . .

Locks neither alleged nor proved physical possession of the cashier's check. Each version of Locks' complaint, including the second amended complaint under which this cause was tried, alleged that *Thorsen* "holds and owns" the cashier's check, albeit for the benefit of Newell. We regard this as an admission by Locks in his pleadings and, therefore, proper evidence that Thorsen, not Newell or Locks, was the possessor of the instrument at the time the complaint was filed. . . . Locks presented no evidence at trial of his or Newell's physical possession. The cashier's check itself was introduced into evidence as a stipulated exhibit.

The thrust of Lock's argument is that he has standing as the assignee of the beneficial owner (Newell) of the instrument. He cites no authority, however, for the proposition that a beneficial owner can sue to recover on an instrument where the legal holder does not sue. To the contrary, Illinois cases prior to the adoption of the U.C.C. point to the opposite conclusion. It was held that a legal holder alone can maintain an action on instrument. . . . While a holder with no beneficial interest in an instrument could maintain a suit upon it . . . , our research uncovers no case permitting the owner of solely the beneficial interest to sue. The section of the U.C.C. authorizing enforcement of payment on an instrument by a holder does not attempt to change the law in this regard. . . . We hold that Newell's position as beneficial owner of the cashier's check, even if it were

---

[*] [Editor: Revised U.C.C. § 3-301 includes as a person entitled to enforce an instrument "(ii) a nonholder in possession of the instrument who has the rights of a holder, or (iii) a person not in possession of the instrument who is entitled to enforce the instrument pursuant to Section 3-309 or 3-418(d). A person may be a person entitled to enforce the instrument even though the person is not the owner of the instrument or is in wrongful possession of the instrument."]

established at trial, considered alone, is insufficient to confer standing upon him to enforce payment of that instrument.

We note that some jurisdictions have recognized that a principal's constructive possession through his agent's physical possession may render the principal a holder of commercial paper. (*See, e.g.,...Investment Service Co. v. Martin Bros. Container & Timber Products Corp.,* 255 Ore. 192, 465 P.2d 868 (1970), suggesting that whether constructive possession is sufficient under the U.C.C. is questionable.) One Illinois case might be read to permit constructive possession as sufficient for holder status. (*Schranz v. I. L. Grossman, Inc.,* 90 Ill. App. 3d 507, 412 N.E.2d 1378 (1980) which found delivery to the plaintiffs in the placing of the instrument in escrow where neither plaintiffs nor the previous holder could retrieve it until the happening of a certain event.) We need not address whether that concept is applicable here because Locks has not argued that theory...; nor was an agency relationship between Newell and Thorsen proved at trial. At opening argument, Locks stated that, "Thorsen was acting as agent of the seller [of the real estate Newell was purchasing]." During his testimony, Locks stated that Thorsen "was acting as broker having been retained by the seller." The depository of an escrow is a special and not a general agent, and his powers are limited to the conditions of the deposit.... Since the escrow agreement in this case or its provisions were not produced at trial, it could not be determined whether Thorsen's possession of the cashier's check after it had been dishonored and after the real estate transaction had been closed was pursuant to an agency relationship with Newell.

Since Newell was not the holder of the cashier's check, his assignment to Locks could not have given Locks standing to enforce payment on the instrument. Locks also maintains, however, that

he has standing as Thorsen's transferee. The U.C.C. provides that a transfer of an instrument vests in the transferee such rights as the transferor has. U.C.C. § 3-201 [U.C.C. § 3-203(b)] Transfer of an instrument in such form that the transferee becomes a holder is a "negotiation," and negotiation always requires delivery. U.C.C. § 3-202 [U.C.C. § 3-201]. "Delivery" with respect to an instrument means the voluntary transfer of possession. U.C.C. § 1-201(14).

Locks argues that a transfer took place at trial when the cashier's check was admitted into evidence as an exhibit stipulated to by the parties. He asserts that he produced the instrument at trial after Thorsen surrendered it to him in exchange for dismissal of Thorsen as a defendant. However, the record only shows that the instrument was introduced as a stipulated exhibit and does not reveal the reason for Thorsen's dismissal. No other evidence of a delivery to Locks is suggested. We cannot see how the introduction of the instrument as an exhibit by all parties with the non-party-holder's apparent acquiescence would constitute delivery, negotiation, or transfer to Locks.

Moreover, a plaintiff's legal interest to sue upon an instrument must be shown as of the commencement of the suit. (*Kroer v. Smith,* 318 Ill. App. 489, 48 N.E.2d 743 (1943); *Investment Service Co. v. Martin Bros. Container & Timber Products Corp.,* 255 Ore. 192, 465 P.2d 868 (1970).) Transfer at the time of trial, even if it had taken place, came too late and the complaint was never amended to reflect that now-alleged transfer.

We conclude that Locks did not have an interest in the cashier's check such as to give him standing to bring a suit to enforce it. Because of this conclusion, we need not address the issue of the propriety of North Towne's dishonoring of the instrument. Accordingly, we affirm the judgment of the circuit court of Winnebago County.

Affirmed.

NOTE

The underlying policy for requiring the claimant to be in possession of the instrument when the action is commenced, *Locks v. North Towne Nat'l Bank of Rockford,* 115 Ill. App. 3d 729, 451 N.E.2d 19 (1983), *supra,* or, at the latest when the pleading can still be amended to assert such possession, *Invest Serv. Co. v. Martin Bros. Container & Timber Prod. Corp.,* 255 Ore. 192, 465 P.2d 868 (1970); *Hanalei, BRC Inc. v. Porter,* 760 P.2d 676 (Hawaii Ct. App. 1988), is to protect the obligor from a subsequent holder in due course being able to demand payment of the instrument. U.C.C. §3-601(b). But the need for possession of the instrument at the time the action is commenced seems unnecessary, should the claimant qualify as a person entitled to enforce the instrument, (U.C.C. § 3-301), at the time the instrument has to be placed into evidence. Thereafter it would no longer be possible for the instrument to be negotiated. On payment of the judgment, if in favor of the claimant, the instrument could be legended as paid. U.C.C. § 3-602(a). This would prevent any subsequent acquirer claiming to be a holder in due course.

Problem*

Brighton, Inc. was in the real estate construction business. Norman was the corporate treasurer. The corporation maintained a checking account at Jersey Shore Bank with Norman being the authorized signatory.

Furman was a construction foreman for Brighton. Each month, over a period spanning five years, he requisitioned payment for certain suppliers with whom Brighton did business. Included were requisitions for some suppliers to whom Brighton did not owe the money covered by the requisitions. Norman then issued checks payable to these suppliers, without verifying the requisitions or requiring supporting invoices and delivered them to Furman for delivery to the payees. Many of these payees were corporations.

Furman cashed the checks at Colonial Bank, forging the indorsements of the payees and then adding his own indorsement, and pocketed the proceeds. Neither Brighton nor Furman maintained an account at Colonial Bank. Norman had no knowledge of Furman's scheme and defalcations.

During each month for the five-year period, Jersey Shore Bank sent a bank statement with cancelled checks (including those cashed by Furman) to Brighton, where they were handled by Norman who had control over the corporation's internal auditing and bank reconciliations.

The scheme went undiscovered for five years before it was discovered during the course of an independent audit. The checks totalled approximately $350,000.

Brighton then instituted suit against Colonial Bank based on its having improperly cashed checks bearing forged indorsements.

Issues

See Brighton Inc. v. Colonial First Nat. Bank, 176 N.J. Super. 101, 422 A.2d 433, 29 UCC Rep. Serv. (Callaghan) 1551 (App. Div. 1980), aff'd 86 N.J. 259, 430 A.2d 902, 31 UCC Rep. Serv. (Callaghan) 591 (1981).

1. May Brighton (the drawer) assert a claim directly against Colonial Bank (the depository bank)? *See Stone & Webster Engineering Corp. v. First National Bank & Trust Co.,* 345 Mass. 1, 184 N.E.2d 358 (1962) *supra,* page 243.

2. May the drawee bank defend on the ground that the drawer's negligence in failing (1) to properly supervise Furman, (2) to properly supervise the issuance of checks and the internal audits by not having "dual controls" and (3) to discover that the checks had been indorsed by Furman "substantially contributed" to the forged indorsements?

---

* Prepared by Donald J. Rapson, Esq.

What is meant by negligence that "substantially contributes to *** the making of a forged signature ***? Does it shorten the chain of causation or must the bank establish that Brighton's negligence directly and proximately caused the bank to accept the checks with the forged indorsements? For example, was Brighton's negligence in not discovering that Furman had indorsed the checks a proximate cause of the loss? *See* U.C.C. §§ 3-404(b), 3-405(a)(3), (b), 3-406(b), 4-406(e).

3. If the drawee bank (Jersey Shore Bank) sues the depository bank, may the depository bank use these defenses even if it were negligent, e.g. in cashing checks for Norman which were payable to corporate payees? *See* U.C.C. §§ 3-417, 4-208, 3-406.

4. Can U.C.C. §§ 3-404, 3-405 be raised by a depository bank where it cashed the checks, as differentiated from taking the checks for deposit and collection?

5. May the drawee or the depository bank defend on the ground that all or part of Brighton's claim is barred because five years have passed since the scheme was first perpetrated? *See* U.C.C. §§ 4-406(f), 3-118.

6. What if Furman perpetrated the scheme by also forging Norman's signature, so that there were "double forgeries," i.e., both the drawer's signatures and the indorsements were forged? Who bears the loss as between the payor bank and the depository bank? *See* §§ 3-418(c), 3-417, 4-208, 4-407.

Summary

Brighton cannot bring an action directly against Colonial Bank. It can only proceed against Jersey Shore Bank, the payor bank, for having paid a check that was not properly payable. [U.C.C. § 4-401(1)]. The payor bank, in turn, can recover or be indemnified by Colonial Bank for breach of warranty under U.C.C. Sections 3-417(a)(1), 4-208(a)(1) that it is "entitled to enforce the draft or authorized to obtain payment" on behalf of "a person entitled to enforce the draft." Unless Brighton is precluded under U.C.C. Sections 3-404, 3-405, 3-406, or 4-406, the warranty would have been breached because Furman was not "a person entitled to enforce the instrument" defined in U.C.C. § 3-301. If, however, Jersey Shore Bank asserts this warranty claim against Colonial Bank, the latter may defend by establishing that Brighton was precluded from asserting the claim for a credit against the drawee by reason of U.C.C. Sections 3-404(b), 3-405, 3-406, or 4-406. This is provided in U.C.C. Sections 3-418(c) and 3-417(c) which reject the argument that a payor bank may waive these defenses against a customer and enforce a warranty claim against a depositary bank. *See Girard Bank v. Mt. Holly State Bank,* 474 F. Supp. 1225 (D. N.J. 1979).

3. Rights Against the Issuer—The Lost, Stolen, or Destroyed Instrument

Where the payee never had possession of the instrument, the payee can demand payment from the maker or drawer based on the underlying obligation. Once the instrument is in the payee's possession, however, the underlying obligation is suspended. U.C.C. § 3-310(b). Where the payee received a certified check, cashier's check or teller's check the underlying obligation will be discharged. U.C.C. § 3-310(a).

Where the instrument is lost, stolen, or destroyed after the payee had possession, the underlying obligation will remain suspended to the amount payable on the instrument. The payee, therefore, will have to sue on the instrument itself and cannot sue on the underlying obligation.[40] To have standing in court a claimant must qualify as a person entitled to enforce the instrument. U.C.C. § 3-301. The claimant not in possession of the instrument, because the instrument has been lost, stolen or destroyed, may try to obtain a duplicate instrument by persuading the issuer to issue a duplicate. If such persuasion is unsuccessful, there will have to be recourse to the court. U.C.C. § 3-309. Whether or not persuasion is successful, the claimant must be prepared to give adequate assurance to the issuer that would protect the issuer against the instrument being presented by a holder in due course against whom it is no defense that a duplicate instrument has been issued or that the obligation in the instrument has been discharged. U.C.C. §§ 3-302, 3-305(a)(2), (b), 3-602.

Should there be recourse to the court, the claimant will have to prove the terms of the instrument and her right to enforce it. If such proof is made, the obligation under the instrument will have been established as if the instrument has been put into evidence by a person having standing to enforce the instrument. U.C.C. §§ 3-301, 3-308, 3-309(b). But the court cannot order payment of the instrument without making certain that the person required to pay the instrument is adequately protected against loss that might occur by reason of another person being able to assert a claim to enforce the instrument. U.C.C. § 3-309(b).

Adequate protection is a flexible concept and will relate to the degree of risk involved. For example, a lost bearer instrument or one endorsed in blank may subsequently surface in the hands of a holder in due course against whom the prior payment of the obligation embodied in the instrument would not be a defense. U.C.C. §§ 3-602, 3-305(a)(2), (b). On the other hand, an order paper would require endorsement by the payee or endorsee. If an order paper were lost or stolen without the required indorsement, it would most likely be presented with an unauthorized indorsement which is "ineffective" to bind the obligor on the instrument. U.C.C. § 3-403(a). The possessor of an instrument bearing an unauthorized indorsement would be unable to claim to be a holder in due course. This lowers the risk of the obligor on the instrument and, thereby, the extent of the "adequate protection," demanded. It is usual for the court to require as a "reasonable means" of such protection that a bond be obtained covering possible liability. U.C.C. § 3-309(b).[41]

Most cases involving a missing instrument deal with a lost, stolen or destroyed cashier's check, teller's check or certified check. To enforce an obligation on such check, the claimant must be a "person entitled to enforce" the instrument. U.C.C. § 3-301, i.e., (i) a holder, or (ii) a nonholder in possession who has the rights of a holder, or (iii) a person not in possession who is entitled to enforce an instrument that has been lost, stolen, or destroyed, or from whom a mistaken payment has been recovered under U.C.C. Section 3-418(d). A remitter, i.e., a person who takes an instrument from an issuer for transfer to the payee, would not qualify as a "holder," U.C.C. § 3-201(a); nor would the remitter qualify as a transferee, U.C.C. § 3-203(a). Similarly, a drawer who obtains certification of his check

---

[40] U.C.C. §§ 3-310(a), (b)(1), (b)(4).

[41] Some courts arbitrarily require a bond in an amount of twice the face value of the instrument claimed to have been lost, stolen or destroyed. We do not see the logic in such arbitrary requirement.

cannot qualify as a person entitled to enforce the instrument. He is an issuer. This does not change even though the drawee, by certifying/accepting the check, assumes primary liability on the check to anyone other than the drawer/issuer. Such persons, having been in direct relationship with the bank that certified the check or issued the cashier's check or teller's check could attempt to have the bank rescind the transaction resulting in the issue of the cashier's check, or teller's check or the certification of the check presented by them. A problem arises where these instruments are no longer held by such person or where the instrument has been lost, stolen or presumably destroyed. Here the attempt is to have the issuing bank or certifying bank dishonor the instrument were it to be presented for payment. Section 3-312 acts as an alternative to Section 3-309 where a demand is made by a person entitled to enforce an instrument under either of these provisions. U.C.C. § 3-312(d). But, whereas U.C.C. Section 3-309 requires a court to intervene and to order the claimant to give to the obligor on the check adequate assurance against loss, e.g., post a bond, no such intervention is necessary under U.C.C. Section 3-312 in relation to a lost, destroyed or stolen cashier's check, teller's check, or certified check.

In both instances, U.C.C. Section 3-309 and Section 3-312, the claimant must assert that the loss was not due to a transfer by the claimant nor due to a lawful seizure of the instrument/check. If the instrument was lost, stolen or destroyed, the claimant must certify that she cannot reasonably obtain possession of the instrument/check because it was destroyed or its whereabouts cannot be determined, or that the instrument/check is in the wrongful possession of an unknown person or of a person that cannot be found or of a person not amenable to service of process.[42] In making such declaration of loss the claimant is asserting a claim to the amount of the instrument/check and is warranting the truth of such assertion. If it is intended to obtain a replacement of a certified check, cashier's check or teller's check, the declaration of loss is made to the bank. A court action to enforce rights to a lost, stolen or destroyed cashier's check, teller's check or certified check may also have to be contemplated.

The declaration of loss must be received by a bank before the bank has honored the check, or has otherwise become liable on the check. U.C.C. §§ 4-302, 4-303. The declaration of loss becomes enforceable not earlier than ninety days following the date of the check or its certification by the bank. Until the declaration of loss becomes enforceable the bank may honor the check by payment to a person entitled to enforce the check. U.C.C. §§ 3-301, 3-312(b). Thereafter the bank must return any payment received for the cashier's or teller's check to the claimant, and will not be obliged to honor a certified check or the cashier's check or the teller's check were it to be presented. This dishonor will allow a person entitled to enforce the instrument to proceed against the claimant on the underlying obligation that gave rise to the certified check, the cashier's check, or the teller's check. But, where the check is subsequently presented by a holder in due course, the bank may honor the check to preserve its reputation. In such case the claimant will have to refund to the bank the amount it paid. Alternatively, should the bank dishonor the check, the claimant is obliged to pay the amount direct to the holder in due course. U.C.C. § 3-312(c).

---

[42] If the person can be found and served, the remedy would be in recoupment U.C.C. § 3-305(a)(b).

4. Stop Payment Order

A drawer dissatisfied with the payee's performance may try to stop payment made by means of a draft. There are various advantages to such approach. The payee may be in a different jurisdiction, or may be in a distant place or country. In all these instances there is a tactical advantage in having the payee come to the jurisdiction of the drawer to recover payment for performance. If payment has occurred, however, the drawer would have to bring suit to recover the payment or for damages. This may require proof of her dissatisfaction in a jurisdiction and locality different from the one where the evidence may be located. There also may be procedural problems regarding onus of proof and adduction of evidence. It may all be in vain, of course, if the instrument has been negotiated to a holder in due course. On the other hand, the stop payment order will give the drawer some "breathing room."

Where the drawee is a bank or where payment of the note is called for at a bank, U.C.C. Section 4-403 provides:

Customer's Right to Stop Payment

(a) A customer or any person authorized to draw on the account if there is more than one person may stop payment of any item drawn on the customer's account or close the account by an order to the bank describing the item or account with reasonable certainty received at a time and in a manner that affords the bank a reasonable opportunity to act on it before any action by the bank with respect to the item described in Section 4-303. If the signature of more than one person is required to draw on an account, any of these persons may stop payment or close the account.

A stop payment order, if oral, is effective for fourteen calendar days and, if in writing, lapses after six months. To renew a stop payment order a writing is required. U.C.C. § 4-403(b). The right to place a stop payment order is absolute.[43] A drawee bank cannot refuse a stop payment order that describes "the item or account with reasonable certainty and is received at a time and in a manner that affords a reasonable opportunity to act on it." Thus, the stop payment order must be received before the drawee bank accepted a draft or paid a check, or has otherwise become accountable on the item. U.C.C. §§ 4-303 (a)(1)-(4).[44]

U.C.C. Section 4-303 sets forth four events after which the bank will no longer be

---

[43] A former Comment to U.C.C. § 4-403 provided:

The position taken by this section is that stopping payment is a service which depositors expect and are entitled to receive from banks notwithstanding its difficulty, inconvenience and expense. The inevitable occasional losses through failure to stop should be borne by the banks as a cost of the business of banking.

There is no reason to assume that this expectation has changed.

[44] In the case of a check, the stop payment order must have been received before an indicated cut-off hour, U.C.C. § 4-108(a), or, if none is indicated, no later than the close of the banking day following the banking day on which the check was received. U.C.C. §§ 4-303(a)(5), 4-104(a)(3). Where a clearing house is involved the deadline for settlement under the clearing house rules will govern the time after which a stop payment order can no longer be given. U.C.C. §§ 4-303(a)(4), 4-103(b).

subject to what is referred to as "the four legals" affecting its obligations.[45] These "four legals" are: (1) knowledge, (2) notice, (3) a stop payment order, and (4) legal process, such as garnishment of the account. Each of these "four legals" could affect priorities in dealing with the account of a customer. Whether any of the "four legals" have an effect will be determined by considering the time knowledge is acquired, a notice, a stop payment order, or legal process has been received by or served upon the bank and there having been a reasonable time for the bank to act in response.

A bank may charge a fee to cover the expense of programming the computer to reject an item as to which a stop payment order has been received. Comment 3 to U.C.C. Section 4-401 indicates that "[T]his Act does not regulate fees that banks charge their customer for a notice of postdating or other services covered by the Act, but under principles of law such as unconscionability or good faith and fair dealing, courts have reviewed fees and the bank's exercise of a discretion to set fees." Courts require a contract between the bank and its customer to allow a bank to charge a fee. Courts also have examined the fee structure of a bank in relation to the purpose of the fee and the services performed to determine whether such fees were reasonable.[46]

The drawee bank can reject a stop payment order that does not describe "the item or account with reasonable certainty." U.C.C. § 4-403. But by agreement with its customer, a bank may determine "the standards by which the bank's responsibility is to be measured *if those standards are not manifestly unreasonable.*" U.C.C. § 4-103(a) (emphasis added).

---

[45] The term "four legals" has also been applied to the events set forth in U.C.C. § 4-303, i.e., (1) acceptance or certification; (2) payment in cash; (3) settlement without right of revocation under statute, clearing house rule or agreement; or (4) accountability under U.C.C. § 4-302(a) due to delay. After these events knowledge, notice, stop order, or legal process will have no effect.

[46] Perdue v. Crocker National Bank, 38 Cal.3d 913, 216 Cal. Rptr. 345, 702 P.2d 503 (1985) (check dishonored for insufficient funds. Court ordered trial to determine whether the fee structure was unconscionable). *See also* opinions of Attorney General of Michigan, 30 UCC Rep. Serv. (Callaghan) 1626 (1981); 33 UCC Rep. Serv. (Callaghan) 1445 (1981).

Parr v. Security National Bank

680 P.2d 648 (Okla. 1984)*

REYNOLDS, J.

We are called upon to decide whether Security National Bank had a reasonable opportunity to stop payment on a check when the description received is exact in all respects except for a single digit error in the check amount. This issue has not been decided by an Oklahoma court.

Parr wrote check number 949 to Champlin Oil.

She dated and mailed it September 14, 1981. The amount of the check was $972.96. On September 15, 1981, Parr ordered payment stopped by telephone. Parr gave the bank her account number, the check number, the date, the payee and the amount of the check. A 50 cent error was made in identifying the amount of the check. Parr went to the bank on September 16th or 17th and executed a written stop order dated September 15, 1981. The written stop order was also in error. Security National paid check number 949 on September 17, 1981.

---

* [Editor: citation in [ ] refer to Revised Articles 3 and 4.]

Parr brought suit against Security National seeking recovery for the amount of the check, 12% interest on that amount, reasonable attorney's fees and costs. Security National defended by showing their computers were programmed to stop payment only if the reported amount of the check were correct. They argued Parr's 50 cent error relieved them of liability. Timeliness of notice was not at issue.

Section 4-403(1) [§ 4-403(a)] of the Uniform Commercial Code, contains the applicable law on stop payment orders:

A customer may by order to his bank stop payment of any item payable for his account but the order must be received at such time and in such manner as to afford the bank a reasonable opportunity to act on it prior to any action by the bank with respect to the item described in Section 4-303.

It is appropriate to examine the purpose of this section before construing it.[1] The policy underlying § 4-403 is found in Comment 2 following the section:

The position taken by this section is that stopping payment is a service which depositors expect and are entitled to receive from banks notwithstanding its difficulty, inconvenience and expense. The inevitable occasional losses through failure to stop should be borne by the banks as a cost of the business of banking.

Security National contends that whether a stop payment order has been received "in such manner as to afford the bank a reasonable opportunity to act" should be determined after examining how the defendant bank handles stop orders. This interpretation has found favor among highly respected legal authorities, but not among the majority of courts that have addressed this issue.[3]

Both groups acknowledge § 4-403(1) [§ 4-403(a)] has not changed the common law rule that a stop payment order must identify the check with "reasonable accuracy."[4] It is from this premise that courts have determined whether the description is reasonably accurate without consideration of the defendant/bank's computer program. In *Elsie Rodriguez Fashions, Inc. v. Chase Manhattan Bank,* 23 UCC Rep. 133 (N.Y. Sup.Ct. 1978), the customer gave the bank the correct payee, check number and date but made a 10 cent error in the amount of the check. The court determined the check had been described with sufficient accuracy to allow the bank to stop payment. The opinion makes no mention of the bank's computer program. In accord with this approach on similar facts are the New York cases of *Pokras v. National Bank of North America,* 30 UCC Rep. 1089 (N.Y. App. Term. 1981), and *Thomas v. Marine Midland Tinkers National Bank,* 86 Misc.2d 284, 381 N.Y.S.2d 797 (N.Y. Civ.Ct. 1976). A different result was reached by a New York court where the customer was told by the bank the stop order would not be effective unless she provided the exact amount of the check. *Poullier v. Nacua Motors, Inc.,* 108 Misc.2d 913, 439 N.Y.S.2d 85 (N.Y. Sup.Ct. 1981). Security National does not

---

[1] U.C.C. § 1-102(1): "This Act shall be liberally construed and applied to promote its underlying purposes and policies." Comment 1 following § 1-102 states:
The Act should be construed in accordance with its underlying purposes and policies. The text of each section should be read in the light of the purpose and policy of the rule or principle in question, as also of the Act as a whole, and the application of the language should be construed narrowly or broadly, as the case may be, in conformity with the purposes and policies involved.

[3] See e.g., Sherrill v. Frank Morris Pontiac-Buick-GMC, Inc., 366 So.2d 251 (Ala. 1979); Delano v. Putnam Trust Co., 33 UCC Rep. 635 (Conn. Super. Ct. 1981); Pokras v. National Bank of North America, 30 UCC Rep. 1089 (N.Y. App. Term. 1981); Elsie Rodriguez Fashions, Inc. v. Chase Manhattan Bank, 23 UCC Rep. 133 (N.Y. Sup.Ct. 1978); Thomas v. Marine Midland Tinkers Nat'l Bank, 86 Misc.2d 284, 381 N.Y.S.2d 797 (N.Y. Civ.Ct. 1976); FJS Electronics, Inc. v. Fidelity Bank, 431 A.2d 326 (Pa. Super. Ct. 1981). But see, Midgen v. Chase Manhattan Bank, N.A., 32 UCC Rep. 937 (N.Y. Civ.Ct. 1981) (finding for customer on grounds that bank was negligent in failing to program its computer to avoid payment where reported amount of check was in error by only 2/3 of one percent of actual check amount).

[4] See notes 1 and 2, supra. See also Capital Bank v. Schuler, 421 So.2d 633, 635 (Fla.Dist.Ct.App. 1982). This is not so in states like California and Florida whose legislatures added to § 4-403(1) the requirement that the item be described "with certainty". See Cal. Com. Code § 4-403(1) (West 1964); Fla. Stat. 674.4-403(1) (1966); See also D.C. Code § 28:4-403(1) (1967). [Editor: U.C.C. § 4-403(a) now calls for "reasonable certainty."]

contend they gave notice to Parr that any discrepancy in the check amount would prevent compliance with her stop payment order.

In *Delano v. Putnam Co.,* 33 UCC Rep. 635 (Conn. Super. Ct. 1981), a single digit error in the amount of $100.00 did not prevent recovery where customer supplied bank with the correct check number, date, payee, and account number of the check. The bank's computer program required an exact match of check amount before it would stop payment. Court held bank had received sufficient information to allow it a "reasonable opportunity to act" on the stop payment order. Court stated the bank had a duty to inform its customer of the need for precision in reporting the amount before it could rely on customer's error to relieve it of liability.

The Supreme Court of Alabama denied customer's recovery in *Sherrill v. Frank Morris Pontiac-Buick-GMC, Inc.,* 366 So.2d 251 (Ala. 1979). Customer gave bank three descriptive elements of the check: check amount, payee and date. The check was not numbered. Two of the three pieces of information were incorrect. Court determined the check was not described with reasonable accuracy, therefore the bank was not afforded a "reasonable opportunity to act" on the stop payment order.

In *FJS Electronics, Inc. v. Fidelity Bank,* 431 A.2d 326 (Pa. Super.Ct. 1981), Court allowed customer to prevail even though its 50 cent error in check amount prevented bank's computer from acting on stop payment order. The bank asserted § 4-403 "should be read to require compliance with the procedures of a particular bank, regardless of what they are and regardless of whether the customer has been made aware of them." Id. at 328. Court determined that the drafter's policy stated in Comment 2 to § 4-403 precluded such an interpretation. They reasoned:

> Fidelity made a choice when it elected to employ a technique which searched for stopped checks by amount alone. It evidently found benefits to this technique which outweighed the risk that an item might be inaccurately described in a stop order. This is precisely the type of inevitable loss which was contemplated by the code drafters and addressed by the comment quoted above. The focus of § 4-403 is the service which may be expected by the customer, and a customer may expect a check to be stopped after the bank is given reasonable notice. A bank's decision to reduce operating costs by using a system which increases the risk that checks as to which there is an outstanding stop payment order will be paid invites liability when such items are paid.

We find this analysis, as well as that in *Delano,* supra, persuasive. We hold Parr described her check with reasonable accuracy, and Security National had a reasonable opportunity to act on the stop payment order.

We are aware of the burden this may place on Oklahoma banks. However, the industry has two alternatives to avoid liability if banking procedures necessitate an exact description of an item: (1) notify the customer at the time a stop order is given,[5] or (2) seek a legislative amendment to § 4-403.[6]

We recognize Parr received the benefit of having her debt paid to Champlin Oil and will recover from Security National for failure to stop payment. To avoid this possibility of unjust enrichment, § 4-407(b) [§ 4-407(2)] subrogates the payor bank [Security National] to the rights of the payee [Champlin] against the maker [Parr]. In such a suit, an award of attorney's fees and costs to Security National would be proper under 12 O.S. 1981 § 936, as Champlin would have been suing Parr on an open account if Security National had stopped payment on the check.

Trial court is REVERSED and this cause REMANDED for award of $972.96 plus reasonable attorney's fees and costs consistent with this opinion.

REVERSED AND REMANDED.

---

[5] See Delano v. Putnam Trust Co., *supra;* Poullier v. Nacua Motors, Inc., supra.

[6] See note 4, supra.

NOTE

1. What is the effect of U.C.C. Section 3-103(a)(7) on a defense that a computer cannot determine that an error had been made? Must computers be programmed to find a check even if only one item of information is erroneous? If two items in error?

2. A stop payment order that is accepted by an officer of the bank who is aware that the order does not comply with the requirement calling for a description of "the item or account with reasonable certainty," will be effective and binding on the bank. *Rimberg v. Union Trust Co. of the District of Columbia,* 12 UCC Rep.Serv. (Callaghan) 527 (D.C. Super. Ct. 1973) (Customer unsure of exact amount was told she could leave the bank after filling out a stop payment order. Held bank waived its right to have the exact amount indicated).

3. A stop payment order to a bank, or an order closing an account can be given only by a customer[47] and must be in relation to an item payable *from* the account of the customer or relating to a closing of the customer's account. Thus, a customer cannot give a stop payment order on a cashier's check nor on a teller's check. Payment of this type of instrument is not from the account of the customer, albeit that the customer allowed the bank to charge the customer's account when issuing such check. A teller's check, being a draft drawn by a bank on an account of the bank with another bank or payable at or through another bank,[48] U.C.C. § 3-104(h), could be the subject of a stop payment order. But such order will have to be given by the bank that has issued the teller's check and directed to the bank on which it was drawn. Where the customer who procured the teller's check, or the payee or the endorsee of the teller's check files a "declaration of loss" with the issuing bank and that declaration of loss becomes enforceable, the issuing bank must place a stop payment order on its teller's check to meet the claim of the filer of the effective declaration of loss to the right to receive the amount of the check. U.C.C. § 3-312(b)(3).

4. "Declaration of loss" and claim. The remitter or a payee of a cashier's check or of a teller's check and the drawer or payee of a certified check who claim the right to receive the amount due on a certified check, a cashier's check, or on a teller's check that was lost, destroyed or stolen, cannot give a stop payment order since these instruments are not payable from their account with the certifying or issuing bank. But, by presenting to the certifying bank or to the issuing bank a written declaration of loss, it may be possible to recover the cost of the check or to obtain payment thereof where the check has been lost, stolen or destroyed. These are the only three causes which would obligate the bank to comply with a claim when the declaration of loss becomes enforceable. U.C.C. § 3-312(b).

A declaration of loss must be in writing and is made under penalty of perjury. It can only be submitted to a bank in this restricted set of circumstances. The declaration of loss must state that the declarant lost possession involuntarily but not as a result of a lawful seizure of the instrument. This can be shown by alleging that the instrument has been destroyed, or that its whereabouts cannot be determined, or that the check has been taken wrongfully and cannot be recovered. The instrument must be described "with reasonable

---

[47] If the account is in the name of more than one person, any one of them can give the stop payment order or close the account. U.C.C. § 4-403(a).

[48] *See* U.C.C. § 4-106(a). An item payable through an identified bank can only be presented by that bank. While, depending on the alternative adopted by a jurisdiction, an item payable at a bank is considered either a draft drawn on that bank or treated the same as an item payable through a named bank. U.C.C. § 4-106(b).

certainty," or it will not be possible for a bank to place a stop payment order on its teller's check or to dishonor a cashier's check or a certified check.

The declaration becomes enforceable no earlier than ninety days from certification or the issuance of the cashier's or teller's check. If the check is presented for payment prior to the declaration of loss becoming enforceable, the bank may honor the instrument. Once the declaration of loss has become enforceable the "bank is not obligated to pay the check," U.C.C. Section 3-312(b)(3). The bank will then have to pay to the claimant the amount of the check or recredit its customer's account where she is the claimant who filed the declaration of loss. U.C.C. § 3-312(b)(4).

If the instrument subsequently is presented to the bank by a holder in due course, the claimant will have to reimburse the bank, where the bank paid the check, or the claimant must pay direct to the holder in due course the amount of the check where the bank has dishonored the check. U.C.C. § 3-312(c).

U.C.C. Section 3-312 does not indicate whether a claimant, being entitled to receive the amount of the check, will have to give any "assurance" to the bank that should the check be presented by a holder in due course it will be paid. The bank is protected by the exculpation in U.C.C. Section 3-312(b)(3). The bank would simply dishonor the check and indicate to the presenter the obligation of the claimant under the written declaration of loss. The requirement for a ninety day delay, after which the check would be overdue, also gives some protection that a holder would not be able to claim to be a holder in due course. U.C.C. § 3-302(a)(2)(iii). The possibility of a late presentment by a holder in due course cannot be ignored, however.

A person entitled to enforce the instrument, U.C.C. § 3-301, has a choice to proceed under either U.C.C. Section 3-309 or under U.C.C. Section 3-312. U.C.C. Section 3-312 is advantageous mainly to a remitter or a drawer who had possession of a check obligating the bank, when it was lost, stolen or destroyed. Prior to the revision of the U.C.C. Article 3 such person could only use "gentle suasion" to gain cooperation from the bank to obtain rescission of the transaction that gave rise to the issuance of the cashier's check, the teller's check, or the certification of a check. To protect the bank from the risk that such check may subsequently be presented by a holder in due course the certifying or "issuer bank" would demand assurances against loss. This often led to recourse to the court.

Bank of New York v. Welz
118 Misc. 2d 645, 460 N.Y.S.2d 867 (Sup. Ct. 1983)*

SEYMOUR SCHWARTZ, J.

Plaintiff, the Bank of New York, ("BONY") moves pursuant to CPLR 3212 for summary judgment against defendants the Greater New York

---

* [Editor: citations in [ ] refer to Revised U.C.C. Articles 3 and 4.]

Savings Bank ("GNYSB") and Robert Welz. GNYSB cross moves pursuant to CPLR 3212 for summary judgment against BONY or in the alternative for summary judgment against third-party defendant Anne Welz.

The facts are undisputed. On April 23, 1981, Anne Welz purchased a teller's check from GNYSB drawn to BONY. The check was drawn on GNYSB's account with Manufacturer's Hanover Trust ("MHT"). Anne Welz tendered $1,900 to GNYSB but through GNYSB's error she received a teller's check in the amount of $19,000. Ms. Welz delivered the teller's check to her husband, defendant Robert Welz, who on April 24 brought it to BONY to purchase shares of Dreyfus Liquid Assets. Because BONY was the named payee on the teller's check, it was not necessary for Mr. or Ms. Welz to endorse it.

On April 24 GNYSB recognized its error and issued a stop payment order to its drawee bank MHT. BONY did not send the check to MHT for collection until May 26. In the interim BONY allowed Mr. Welz to redeem his Dreyfus Liquid Assets shares purchased with the $19,000 check. Mr. Welz also received additional funds of $9,966.16 from BONY to which he was not entitled.

BONY and GNYSB argue that as between themselves, the other is liable for the loss.

BONY contends that New York does not permit a teller's check to be stopped by a drawer bank.

GNYSB contends that the loss was caused by BONY waiting more than one month before presenting the check to MHT, the drawee bank. GNYSB also contends that BONY permitted Mr. Welz to redeem his Dreyfus shares seven days after it received the check in violation of the understanding with Dreyfus permitting redemption only after fifteen days from its receipt.

If GNYSB is not entitled to stop payment, BONY's delay in presenting the check and its rapid redemption of Robert Welz's Dreyfus shares would not relieve GNYSB from liability to BONY. Therefore, the court will first address the question whether a teller's check may be stopped in these circumstances.

U.C.C. § 4-403(1) [§ 4-403(a)] provides that "[a] customer may by order to his bank stop payment of any item payable for his account. . . ." As defined in U.C.C. § 4-104(1)(e) [§ 4-104(a)(5)] " 'Customer' . . . includes a bank carrying an account with another bank." Here, GYNSB carried an account with MHT and is therefore entitled to stop payment on teller's checks.

The Code distinguishes between teller's checks (drawn by a bank on an account carried with another bank) and cashier's checks (drawn by a bank where the bank is both drawer and drawee). A cashier's check is accepted in advance by the act of issuance, *Taboada v. Bank of Babylon,* 95 Misc.2d 1000, 408 N.Y.S.2d 734, and once a check is accepted, which occurs when a bank issues a cashier's or certified check, it cannot stop payment even on its customer's order. *Id.*

While the code allows a teller's check to be stopped, New York courts nevertheless have frequently imposed liability on the drawer bank where it has stopped payment. *See e.g. Meckler v. Highland Falls Sav. & Loan Assn.,* 64 Misc.2d 407, 314 N.Y.S.2d 681; *Malphrus v. Home Sav. Bank of City of Albany,* 44 Misc. 2d 705, 524 N.Y.S.2d 705. In those cases, the courts dealt with the effect of U.C.C. § 3-802(1) [§ 3-310(a)] which provides that an "obligation is pro tanto discharged if a bank is drawer . . . and there is no recourse on the instrument against the underlying obligor." Thus, where a party accepts a check where the bank is the drawer (a teller's check), the party (the underlying obligor) giving it in payment is discharged if he does not endorse the teller's check.

The effect of U.C.C. § 3-802(1) [§ 3-310(a)] is that when Mr. Welz gave BONY the teller's check he became discharged on the underlying obligation to pay for the Dreyfus Liquid Assets. Thus, as payee, BONY's only remaining recourse is against GNYSB which stopped payment.

In *Malphrus, supra,* the court was concerned with this result and limited a bank's right to stop a teller's check to cases "where the bank issuing the teller's check is an actual party to a transaction." *Id.* at 707, 254 N.Y.S.2d 980. Here GNYSB is not a party to the Dreyfus transaction.

A teller's check may also be stopped where it is endorsed to a third party who sues on the instrument. *Fur Funtastic v. Kearns,* 104 Misc.2d 1030, 430 N.Y.S.2d 27. There the teller's check was made payable to the purchaser of the check, who endorsed it to the plaintiff as payment for services. Unlike the instant case and *Malphrus,* the teller's check in *Fur Funtastic* did not discharge the underlying obligation because the purchaser of the check, the underlying obligor, was an endorser and so there was recourse on the instrument against him, making U.C.C. § 3-802(1) [§ 3-310(a)] inapplicable.

Limiting a bank's right to stop payment on a teller's check to instances where the payee is a party to the transaction with the bank, or where the payee endorses the check to a third party is unnecessary. See Note, Personal Money Orders &

Teller's Checks: Mavericks Under the U.C.C., 67 Col.L.Rev. 524, 542. A payee such as BONY has a cause of action against the drawer (GNYSB) on the instrument even if the drawer stops payment. U.C.C. § 3-413 [§ 3-414]. Moreover, a payee who has not dealt directly with the drawer may take the instrument as a holder in due course free from all defenses of any party to the instrument with whom the holder has not dealt with certain exceptions not relevant here. *See* U.C.C. § 3-305 [§§ 3-302, 3-305(a)(1), (b), 3-306].

In other words, the code permits stop payment of a teller's check but the stop payment does not automatically preclude recovery on the instrument. Defenses may be raised by the endorser where an instrument is endorsed to a third party. Where the payee is a party to the transaction, defenses may be raised to recover on the instrument against the drawer. But where the payee is the holder in due course a stop payment does not permit defenses to be raised because such a payee has exchanged the underlying obligation for the instrument and must be protected.

GNYSB argues that BONY is not a holder in due course because of its failure to present the instrument for payment for more than a month after it was received. The argument lacks merit. U.C.C. 3-302(1)(b) [§ 3-302(a)(2)(ii)] provides that good faith requires honesty only.[**] It does not require the exercise of due care. *Industrial Nat'l Bank of R.I. v Leo's Used Car Exch., Inc.*, 362 Mass. 797, 291 N.E.2d 603 (1973).

None of the defenses available against a holder in due course (U.C.C. § 3-305) [§ 3-305(a)(1)] are applicable here. Therefore, summary judgment is granted to BONY against GNYSB. Robert Welz is discharged from his obligation to pay BONY the amount of the teller's check. BONY is granted summary judgment on default against Robert Welz in the amount of $9,966.16.

GNYSB's cross motion for summary judgment against BONY is denied. Its alternative motion for summary judgment against Anne Welz is granted on default in the amount of $17,100.

[**] [Editor: *see* now § 3-103(a)(4)].

NOTE

The mere fact that an obligation is discharged by tender of a draft issued by a bank or a check certified by a bank, U.C.C. § 3-310(a), does not mean that the issuing or the certifying bank may not have recourse against the procurer of the draft or of the certification. *See* U.C.C. § 1-103 and note § 3-417. Is it possible, however, for the issuer of the cashier's check or of the teller's check to renege on its obligation to a person entitled to enforce the draft, such as a holder in due course, because the procurer of its instrument failed to give consideration for it? Note U.C.C. § 3-412 as to the obligation of the issuer of a cashier's check; U.C.C. § 3-414 as to the obligation of the drawer of a teller's check; and U.C.C. § 3-413 which indicates the obligation of a bank that has certified a check.

Bank One, Merrillville v. Northern Trust Bank/DuPage
775 F. Supp. 266 (N.D. Ill. 1991)[*]

MEMORANDUM OPINION
AND ORDER

JAMES F. HOLDERMAN, District Judge:
Plaintiff, Bank One, Merrillville, NA ("Bank One"), brought this diversity action against defen-

---

[*] [Editor: citations in [ ] refer to Revised Article 3 and 4.]

dant, Northern Trust Bank/DuPage ("Northern"), claiming wrongful dishonor of a cashier's check. Northern asserted affirmative defenses and a counterclaim based on fraud, bad faith and misconduct. Bank One has moved, pursuant to Fed.R.Civ.P. 56, for partial summary judgment on the issue of Northern's wrongful dishonor. For the reasons stated in this opinion, Bank One's motion is granted.

FACTS

This case concerns two banks, Bank One of Merrillville, Indiana ("Bank One") and Northern Trust Bank/DuPage of Oak Brook, Illinois ("Northern"), and two of their customers, Zaragoza Motors Inc. ("Zaragoza") and Sakoff Media Enterprises, Inc. ("Sakoff"). In June 1990, Zaragoza had a checking account at Bank One, while Sakoff had one at Northern.

On or before June 7, 1990 Sakoff wrote a check for $98,581.40 ("the Sakoff check") on its account at Northern, payable to the order of Zaragoza. Zaragoza deposited the Sakoff check in its account at Bank One on June 7, 1990. Bank One sent the Sakoff check to Northern for payment. On June 13, 1990, it was returned to Bank One, as the funds in Sakoff's account were insufficient to cover the amount of the Sakoff check.

Kenneth Dykstra, a Bank One employee, telephoned Northern upon receiving the returned Sakoff check on June 13, and was told that Sakoff's account did contain sufficient funds to cover the check. On the same day, Dykstra drove to Northern's offices and exchanged the Sakoff check for a Northern cashier's check for $98,581.40. When Bank One sent the endorsed cashier's check through the Federal Reserve Bank to Northern for payment, however, Northern refused to honor the check.

The reasons for Northern's refusal to pay relate to another check ("the Zaragoza check"), drawn on Zaragoza's account at Bank One, for $103,200, which Zaragoza presumably transferred to Sakoff at about the same time that Zaragoza received the Sakoff check for $98,581.40. At some point before June 12, 1990, Sakoff deposited Zaragoza's check into Sakoff's account at Northern. Northern then sent the Zaragoza check to Bank One for collection. Bank One received the check on June 12 but, on June 13, issued notice to Northern, through the Federal Reserve Bank, that it was dishonoring the Zaragoza check, because of insufficient funds in Zaragoza's account. This notice did not reach Northern until after Dykstra had obtained the cashier's check. As a result of Bank One's rejection of the Sakoff check, the funds in Sakoff's account were insufficient to cover the Sakoff check for which Northern had issued its cashier's check.

DISCUSSION

Under Fed.R.Civ.P. 56(c), summary judgment is proper "if the pleadings, depositions, answers to interrogatories, and admissions on file, together with the affidavits, if any, show that there is no genuine issue as to any material fact and that the moving party is entitled to a judgment as a matter of law." According to Bank One, Illinois law forbids a bank from dishonoring its cashier's checks for any reason. On the basis of this understanding of the law, Bank One contends that it is entitled to summary judgment, since any arguments Northern might make and any factual issues they might raise are immaterial to the issue of wrongful dishonor.

In response, Northern asserts bad faith on the part of Bank One. Northern contends that when Dykstra drove to Northern to obtain the cashier's check, he was aware that his bank was in the process of dishonoring the Zaragoza check. According to Northern, Bank One feared that its dishonor of the Zaragoza check would result in there being insufficient funds to cover the Sakoff check. This fear allegedly prompted Dykstra to hurry to Northern in order to obtain the cashier's check before Northern received notice of Bank One's dishonor. Northern contends that bad faith such as that alleged justifies a refusal to honor a cashier's check, and that the factual issue of Bank One's bad faith precludes summary judgment.

The transaction in this case involved an official of an Indiana bank coming into Illinois and receiving a cashier's check from an Illinois bank. Plaintiff, in its brief, assumed the application of Illinois law. Defendant, while citing cases from other jurisdictions, raised no explicit protest. Because the outcome of the case hinges on the applicability of Illinois law, the court must first confirm the parties' implicit choice of law.

In a diversity case, the court must apply the conflict of law rules of the state in which it sits. *Klaxon Co. v. Stentor Electric Mfg. Co.,* 313 U.S. 487, 61 S.Ct. 1020, 85 L.Ed. 1477 (1941). This case involves a negotiable instrument, so it implicates the Illinois version of the Uniform Commercial Code ("the Code"). Ill.Rev.Stat.ch. 26 ¶ 1-101 *et seq.* The relevant choice of law provision is therefore Ill.Rev.Stat.ch. 26 ¶ 1-105, which provides that the Illinois Code applies to "transactions bearing an appropriate relation to this state." The cashier's check in this case was issued by an Illinois bank to a person in Illinois. The relation of this transaction to Illinois therefore calls for the application of Illinois law.

Although the Illinois Code does not specifically address the subject of a bank's cashier's checks, the Illinois Appellate Court interpreted the Code's application to the issue in *Able & Associates, Inc. v. Orchard Hill Farms of Illinois, Inc., Etc.,* 77 Ill.App.3d 375, 395 N.E.2d 1138, 32 Ill. Dec. 757 (1st Dist. 1979). In *Able & Associates,* the court rejected defendant Union National Bank's argument that a failure of consideration justified its refusal to honor a cashier's check. The court instead employed a line of analysis under the Code which led it to endorse "a rule which prohibits a bank from refusing to honor its cashier's checks." *Id.,* 77 Ill.App.3d at 381-82, 32 Ill.Dec. at 761, 395 N.E.2d at 1142.

Characterizing the bank's issuance of a cashier's check as acceptance of the item, the court in *Able & Associates* applied § 4-303 of the Code, which provides that a stop order on a check is ineffective after acceptance.[1] 77 Ill.App.3d at 380, 32 Ill.Dec. at 761, 395 N.E.2d at 1142. As a consequence, under Illinois law, a bank cannot refuse to pay a cashier's check which it has issued. The court in *Able & Associates* viewed its holding as compelled by policy concerns about the negotiability of cashier's checks:

> A cashier's check circulates in the commercial world as the equivalent of cash . . . to allow a bank to stop payment on such a check would . . . undermine the public confidence in the bank and its checks and thereby deprive the cashier's check of the essential incident which makes it useful.

Able & Associates, 77 Ill.App.3d at 382, 32 Ill.Dec. at 761, 395 N.E.2d at 1142, quoting *National Newark & Essex Bank v. Giordano,* 111 N.J.Super. 347, 268 A.2d 327 (1970).

The 1979 ruling in *Able & Associates* relied upon and reflected that of a 1973 Seventh Circuit decision applying Illinois law, *Munson v. American National Bank & Trust Co.,* 484 F.2d 620 (7th Cir. 1973). In *Munson,* the Seventh Circuit

ruled, as the Illinois Appellate Court later would in *Able,* that a bank could not assert failure of consideration as an excuse for the dishonor of a cashier's check. The Seventh Circuit applied Code § 4-303, and explained that, as a consequence, a bank has "no more right to countermand its cashier's checks than" it has rights "to refuse to pay cash it has already paid." *Id.* at 623-24.

In both *Able & Associates* and *Munson,* the courts, while holding that the cashier's checks must be honored, permitted the banks to raise their defenses and issues relating to the underlying transactions as part of their own affirmative claims. *Able & Associates,* 77 Ill.App.3d at 382-83, 32 Ill.Dec. at 761-62, 395 N.E.2d at 1142-43; *Munson,* 484 F.2d at 624. The defendants in both cases had to pay the cashier checks, and then seek to recover the funds from the hands of the plaintiffs just as they would as if they had paid cash.[2]

In the face of this case law which holds that a bank has no right to dishonor its cashier's checks but must instead assert its reason for non-payment as part of its own action to recover the funds, Northern essentially argues for a "bad faith" or "fraud" exception to the general principle. Northern reasons that, while Illinois courts have held that failure of consideration is no excuse for dishonoring a cashier's check, they have never ruled that the procurer's bad faith does not provide a defense. (Defendant's Memorandum at 6.)

In support of the distinction, Northern argues that "better authority for the law that governs this particular situation" appears in cases which hold that banks can refuse to honor cashier's checks obtained through fraud. (Defendant's Memorandum at 6.) Defendant then cites cases such as *Farmers & Merchants State Bank v. Western Bank,* 841 F.2d 1433 (9th Cir. 1987) and *TPO, Inc. v. Federal Deposit Insurance Corp.,* 487 F.2d

---

[1] Code § 4-303 provides, in relevant part: "(1) Any knowledge, notice or stop-order received by . . . a payor bank, whether or not effective under other rules of law to terminate, suspend, or modify a bank's right or duty to pay an item . . . comes too late to so terminate, suspend or modify such right or duty if the knowledge, notice, [or] stop-order is received . . . after the bank has . . . (a) accepted or certified the item."

[2] In Munson, the bank's counterclaim for a setoff was ripe for summary judgment, which the court granted. The plaintiff's success on the wrongful dishonor issue was therefore empty, since it simultaneously lost on the issue of liability in the underlying transaction. In Able & Associates, the court, after resolving the cashier's check issue, remanded for determination of the bank's affirmative claim regarding the underlying transaction.

131, 135-36 (3rd Cir. 1973) as authority for its argument.[3]

These cases interpret the U.C.C. in a way that enables a bank to stop payment on a cashier's check in case of fraud, and thereby support defendant's position. This court, however, could not rely on the authority cited by Northern even if it were persuasive. As stated earlier in this opinion, this diversity case must be decided according to Illinois law. The interpretation of the U.C.C. found in the cases cited by Northern, which grants a bank the power to stop payment on its cashier's checks, is, however, directly and explicitly contrary to the law articulated by Illinois courts.

As previously discussed, Illinois courts view an issued cashier's check as accepted under Code § 4-303 and as the equivalent of cash. In *Farmers & Merchants State Bank,* however, the Ninth Circuit rejected the approach taken in *Able & Associates,* concluding that § 4-303 "had no bearing on the question whether [a bank] may assert its own defenses to liability on its cashier's check," *Farmers & Merchants State Bank,* 841 F.2d at 1451. The Ninth Circuit cited the Seventh Circuit's *Munson* opinion as an opposing view. *Id.* at 1440 n. 11. Likewise, in *TPO, Inc. v. Federal Deposit Insurance Corporation,* the Third Circuit expressly spurned the § 4-303 "acceptance" mode of analyzing the issuance of cashier's checks. *TPO,* 487 F.2d at 135-136.

The Ninth Circuit, in *Farmers & Merchants State Bank,* also explicitly eschewed the notion, adopted in Illinois, that certified checks must be viewed as cash equivalents, reasoning that "nothing in the U.C.C. suggests that cashier's checks should be treated differently from other instruments subject to Articles 3 and 4." *Farmers and Merchants State Bank,* 841 F.2d at 1440. Similarly, the Third Circuit, in *TPO,* explained its view that a cashier's check "is equivalent to a negotiable promissory note of a bank . . . not the same as

cash as has been loosely asserted." *TPO,* 487 F.2d at 136.

The rejection by the non-Illinois courts of the "acceptance" and "cash equivalency" treatment of cashier's checks leads directly to their recognition of a bank's ability to stop payment in the case of fraud. Having concluded that issuance of a cashier's check is not acceptance under § 4-403 and that a cashier's check is not necessarily equivalent to cash, the courts, not applying Illinois law, were free to analyze the check as they would any other negotiable instrument, in terms of whether the plaintiff seeking payment was a holder in due course. If the plaintiff in a wrongful dishonor action is guilty of fraud, he would not be a holder in due course. Consequently, under § 3-306 [§§ 3-305(a), (c), (d), 3-306], the bank would be entitled to present all defenses which would be available on a simple contract such as lack of consideration or fraud. *Farmers & Merchants State Bank*, 841 F.2d at 1442; *TPO,* 487 F.2d at 136.

The holding and reasoning of *Able & Associates* clearly indicates that Illinois courts have adopted the § 4-303 acceptance and cash equivalency method of analyzing cashier's checks, not the holder in due course analysis exhibited in the cases cited by Northern. Indeed, the Illinois Appellate Court, in *Able & Associates,* explicitly considered and rejected the approach taken by the Third Circuit in *TPO.*[4] *Able & Associates,* 77 Ill. App. 3d at 380-82, 32 Ill. Dec. at 759-60. This court cannot accept Northern's attempt to avail itself of the defenses to dishonor provided by the Third and Ninth Circuit's interpretations of the U.C.C. because Illinois law, which applies in this case, contradicts the theory of cashier's checks

---

[3] The defendant also cites other cases to support its argument. Anderson, Clayton & Co. v. Farmers National Bank of Cordell, 624 F.2d 105 (10th Cir. 1980); Banco Di Roma v. Merchants Bank of New York, 92 A.D.2d 42, 459 N.Y.S.2d 592 (1983); Gates v. Manufacturer's Hanover Trust Co., 98 A.D.2d 829, 470 N.Y.S.2d 492 (1983). These cases either rely on the cases discussed at pp. 269–270 of the opinion or utilize the same interpretation of the U.C.C.

[4] The diverging approaches taken in the various opinions reflects a wider split of authority regarding the character of cashier's checks, between courts that take the § 4-303 approach, viewing an issued cashier's check as accepted, and those that view cashier's checks as being subject, in the same way as other negotiable instruments, to the defenses of § 3-305 and § 3-306, such as lack of consideration and fraud. *See* DaSilva v. Sanders, 600 F.Supp. 1008 (D.D.C. 1984) (discussing split of authority and citing cases); L. Lawrence, *Making Cashier's Checks and Other Bank Checks Cost Effective: A Plea for Revision of Articles 3 and 4 of the Uniform Commercial Code,* 64 MINN.L.REV. 275, 285-320 (discussing different approaches).

upon which they, and Northern, rely.

As a consequence of the application of Illinois law to the subject of cashier's checks, Northern, under § 4-303, can raise no excuse "whether or not effective under other rules of law" justifying its refusal to pay.[5] The proper context for Northern's arguments regarding Bank One's alleged bad faith is its counterclaim rather than as a defense to Bank One's action for wrongful dishonor. Unfortunately for Northern in this case, its claim concerning the underlying transaction is not yet ready for judgment.[6]

Northern therefore must honor its cashier's check and seek to recover the funds in the hands of Bank One, just as it would have to do if it had paid cash. Under Illinois law, Northern assumed the risk of having to pursue litigation to recover improperly paid funds when it issued the cashier's check. This result, which is dictated by Illinois law, serves the interest of preserving the free negotiability of cashier's checks while at the same time affording Northern the opportunity to remedy what it views as a wrong.

CONCLUSION

For the foregoing reasons, plaintiff's motion for partial summary judgment is GRANTED. The parties are urged to discuss settlement. The case is set for status on October 23, 1991 at 10 a.m.

---

[5] In addition to its arguments based on Bank One's alleged bad faith, Northern raises an argument premised on its contention that Bank One suffered no damage as a result of the cashier check's dishonor. (Defendant's Memorandum at 7-8.) This argument is grounded in principles of contract law concerning the underlying transaction. Therefore, like the bad faith arguments, it is irrelevant to the controlling principle that a bank must honor its cashier checks.

[6] As Northern has not yet paid the cashier's check, its counterclaim requests only incidental damages. Now that it must honor the check, Northern may, before the date set for the next status report in the case, amend its counterclaim to allege damages it suffers thereby.

NOTE

The court in *TPO, Inc. v. F.D.C.,* 487 F.2d 131, 135 (3rd Cir. 1973) stated "there are no third parties, or customers of the bank, or holder in due course whose rights are involved . . . Hence, the strong consideration of public policy favoring negotiability and reliability of cashier's checks are not germane." Where presentment is by an endorsee who is not a holder in due course, a Florida appeals court held that on those facts "a cashier's check loses its cash like aspects and becomes more like a negotiable instrument to which claims of other parties . . . will attach." *Barnett Bank of Jacksonville, N.A. v. Warren Finance, Inc.,* 532 So. 2d 676, 680 (Fla. Disv. Ct. App. 1988). *See* further, U.C.C. Section 3-412 as to the obligation of an issuer of a cashier's check. Can a maker stop payment on a note on which it is the primary party liable? In *Bank One* the court left open the issue of a counterclaim by Northern Trust bank. Also note, U.C.C. Section 3-418(b) may enable a claim based on the law of mistake or restitution to succeed.

What is the effect of U.C.C. § 3-310(a) on the debate regarding payment with a cashier's check, a teller's check or a certified check? Can the bank refuse to pay? Does U.C.C. Section 3-312 undermine these approaches? (Note Illinois has adopted Revised U.C.C. § 3-312).

U.C.C. Section 4-403(c) deals with the issue of a bank failing to observe a stop payment order. The customer who gave the stop payment order must establish not only that there was a failure to observe the stop payment order, but also must prove the facts and amount of loss resulting from the payment of the instrument. Merely showing that the customer's account has been debited is not enough to prove a loss. *Grego v. South Carolina*

Nat'l Bank, 283 S.C. 546, 549, 324 S.E.2d 94 (1984). Also, a bank may not raise as a defense "that the payee of the check which was the subject of a valid stop order, was justly entitled to the money." This is not a defense to a violation of U.C.C. Section 4-403, albeit that a bank can subrogate to the payee and recover against its customer under U.C.C. Section 4-407. *See Hughes v. Marine Midland Bank,* 127 Misc.2d 209, 484 N.Y.S.2d 1000, (Cir. Ct. Rochester Co. 1985). The fact that the customer failed to complain in a timely fashion after receiving her bank statement has been held not to be a bar to an action based on damages suffered as a result of the non-observance of the stop payment order. In *Begg & Daigh, Inc. v. Chemical Bank,* the court rejected the application of U.C.C. Section 4-406 as a defense and held the bank's remedy is in subrogation. *Begg & Daigh, Inc. v. Chemical Bank,* 575 N.Y.S.2d 638 (Sup. Ct. 1991) (U.C.C. § 4-406 "specifically refers to a forged or altered instrument; it is not applicable where a bank has disregarded a concededly valid stop-payment order." *Id* at 639). Honoring an item subject to a stop payment order would be a violation of the contract between a bank and its customer to honor items that are "properly payable from the account." Payment would be a breach of that obligation; not the least damage caused thereby could be a dishonor of subsequent items. Such dishonor would then be a wrongful dishonor giving rise to liability for damages suffered by the customer. U.C.C. § 4-402. This threat is especially strong where the stop payment order is given to prevent a post-dated check from being honored by the bank/drawee before its due date.

U.C.C. Section 4-403(c) states:

> The burden of establishing the fact and amount of loss resulting from the payment of an item contrary to a stop-payment order or order to close an account is on the customer. The loss from payment of an item contrary to a stop-payment order may include damages for dishonor of subsequent items under Section 4-402.[49]

Finally we must note that at common law the mental incompetency of the customer will automatically affect the authority of a bank to accept, pay or collect an item or to account for proceeds of its collection. This common law rule has been changed by the Uniform Commercial Code. U.C.C. § 4-405(a) specifically provides that "[n]either death nor incompetence of a customer revokes the authority to accept, pay, collect or account until the bank knows of the fact of death or of an adjudication of incompetence and has reasonable opportunity to act on it."

This provision conforms to § 542(c) of the Bankruptcy Code.[50] That section recognized the volume and the speed with which items are handled by banks. The section, therefore, exempts bank items from automatically becoming part of the bankrupt's estate and thus subject to an automatic stay.[51] The section provides that banks can handle such items until

---

[49] *See also* U.C.C. § 4-401(c). "If a bank charges against the account of a customer a check before the date stated in the notice of postdating, the bank is liable for damages for the loss resulting from its act. The loss may include damages for dishonor of subsequent items under Section 4-402."

[50] 11 U.S.C. § 542(c).

[51] 11 U.S.C. §§ 362, 541.

they have actual notice or actual knowledge of the bankruptcy proceedings having been commenced or that a petition in bankruptcy has been granted.[52]

In the case of death, U.C.C. Section 4-405(b) allows a bank a ten day grace period after the death of its customer. During this time a bank may pay or certify checks "unless ordered to stop payment by a person claiming an interest in the account." This rule applies, even though the bank has actual knowledge of the death. The reason for this rule is to enable holders to assert claims based on such checks without having to wait until the will is probated or letters of administration are granted. In most instances such checks are issued for legitimate payments due from the deceased. If such is not the case, a person interested in the estate can give a stop payment order. This is the only time a person who is not a customer has standing to give a stop payment order.

Before leaving this subject we must note that U.C.C. Section 4-407 allows a bank to subrogate to the rights of its customer whose stop payment order it has failed to observe. The bank can, of course, also subrogate to the rights of the person to whom payment was made. Payment may have been made to a holder in due course against whom the drawer would have had no defense even had the stop payment order been observed. If such payment was not made to a holder in due course, the bank could subrogate to the drawer to recover from such person the amount the bank had to replace in its customer's account and then subrogate to the person paid to recover the amount due to such person from the customer. *See* U.C.C. §§ 4-403(c), 4-407(2). In effect, except for its legal costs, the bank will be fully reimbursed.

---

[52] *See* Bank of Marin v. England, 385 U.S. 99 (1966), decided under the Bankruptcy Act of 1898.

VIII ALTERNATIVE PAYMENT METHODS

Negotiable instruments relating to the payment of money are either a written undertaking to pay money signed by the person undertaking to pay, i.e. a promise,[1] or "a written instruction to pay money signed by the person giving the instruction," i.e. an order.[2] In both instances there is a demand for a writing and that writing must comply with the formal requirements of U.C.C. § 3-104 to be negotiable.[3] In recent years we have seen the development of alternate payment methods in the form of credit cards, debit cards and electronic transfers of funds on a retail and on a wholesale level.

A. Credit Cards

In the case of credit cards, other than an identification card identifying a customer to whom a merchant has agreed to extend credit,[4] we have the intermediation of the credit card issuer between the purchaser and the supplier of goods or services. This triangular relationship involves three different contracts.

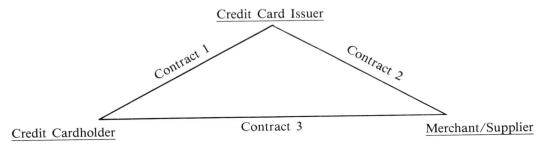

Contract 1

The issuer and the cardholder agree to the total amount of credit extended by the issuer to the cardholder.[5] They further agree to the amount of interest payable on the sums

---

[1] U.C.C. § 3-103(a)(9).

[2] U.C.C. § 3-103(a)(6).

[3] *See supra* Chapter IV.

[4] Examples of such identification cards are the Sears, Roebuck & Company or the Montgomery Ward cards. These merchants are often self-financing the debts of their customers who use these cards.

[5] Some credit cards, especially some business credit cards, do not have a dollar limit.

advanced. Generally, interest is payable only as of the due date within a predetermined billing cycle. The holder, therefore, could pay off the charges incurred without having to pay interest on the advance.[6] This contract is usually a contract of adhesion, triggered by an application for a card and its subsequent user. The requirement that there be an application for the card is the federal response to issuers sending unsolicited cards through the mail to targeted individuals. Many cards were stolen and used improperly, thereby endangering the credit standing of the intended recipient. Since 1988 the Federal Consumer Credit Protection Act, 15 U.S.C. § 1642,[7] has prohibited the sending of unsolicited credit cards.

If a credit card is stolen after it has been received by the cardholder, liability of the cardholder for unauthorized use is predicated on a failure to promptly notify the card issuer of the loss. The card issuer must not only give the cardholder adequate notice of potential liability, but also must supply him with a description of the means by which such notice must be given. In any event the cardholder cannot be held liable beyond the first fifty dollars of liability incurred in the unauthorized use of the credit card.[8]

The obligation of the credit cardholder arises from the authorized use of the credit card and is evidenced by the cardholder signing a receipt evidencing the transaction. This receipt will be forwarded by the merchant/supplier to the card issuer. It must be noted that the "credit card charge slip" is not a negotiable instrument; such charge slips do not comply with U.C.C. Section 3-104.[9] It is an authorization to the card issuer to pay the amount due to the supplier of the goods or services. It also contains a reiteration of the agreement between the cardholder and the card issuer that the cardholder will pay the amount due, and any other appropriate charges, when billed by the issuer.[10] The Consumer Credit Protection Act (Fair Credit Billings Act § 170), 15 U.S.C. § 1666i, provides that the cardholder can raise defenses on the underlying transaction against the card issuer. Notice to the card issuer of the existence of a dispute with the merchant/supplier will suspend the obligation to pay. The cardholder must make a good faith effort to pursue his remedy against the merchant/supplier.

For this provision to apply, the amount of the transaction must exceed fifty dollars and the place where the transaction occurred must have been within one hundred miles of the cardholder's billing address.[11] Should the dispute be settled against the consumer card-

---

[6] Exceptions exist, especially where the card is used to obtain a cash advance. In such case interest often would be payable as of the date the cash is received.

[7] Truth in Lending Act § 132.

[8] Consumer Credit Protection Act (Truth in Lending Act §§ 133, 135), 15 U.S.C. §§ 1643, 1645. This provision applies both to personal as well as business credit cards.

[9] Broadway National Bank v. Barton-Russell Corp., 585 N.Y.S.2d 933 (N.Y.S. Ct. 1992). At one time card issuers printed the word "draft" on the "credit card charge slip." This was done as an inducement to make payment despite the existence of a dispute between the cardholder and the merchant/supplier regarding the transaction. This misrepresentation had an *in terrorem* effect on cardholders who felt they had to pay without having the right to defend against such charges. The Consumer Credit Protection Act (Fair Credit Billing Act § 161), 15 U.S.C. § 1666, preserves the rights of the cardholder against the merchant/supplier to demand correction of billing errors. The Act also allows the cardholder to inform the card issuer of the existence of a defense to the transaction giving rise to the credit card charge and that these defenses will be raised against the card issuer. Consumer Credit Protection Act, (Fair Credit Billing Act § 170), 15 U.S.C. § 1666i.

[10] Some card issuers, to induce use of the card, give a cardholder up to 1% credit toward the amount due.

[11] Israelewitz v. Manufacturers Hanover Trust Co., 120 Misc. 2d 125, 455 N.Y.S.2d 480 (1983) (supplier in Hawaii, cardholder in New York, Mail Order).

holder, the cardholder will have to pay the amount due, plus any incidental charges, such as interest, as of the date when payment should have been made.[12]

Regulation Z, 12 C.F.R. § 226.12(c)(2)[13] prohibits an issuer from reporting the amount withheld by the cardholder "as delinquent until the dispute is settled or judgment is rendered." Nor can the issuer make further demands on the cardholder until the dispute is determined against the cardholder.[14] A card issuer who fails to comply with these requirements may be subject to the forfeiture penalty under the Consumer Credit Protection Act (Fair Credit Billing Act § 161(e)), 15 U.S.C. § 1666(e) (the forfeiture appears to be limited to an amount which "may not exceed $50").

Contract 2

The second contract is between the card issuer and a merchant, whereby the merchant agrees to accept payment from the issuer for obligations incurred by their customers using the credit card. This contract imposes on the merchant a duty to check that the card is being presented by an authorized person and that the credit limit has not been exceeded. A check to obtain authorization on the card's limit will also inform the merchant of any notice received by the issuer that the card has been lost or stolen.

This contract also will contain an agreement that the issuer will pay to the merchant the amount due on the cardholder's contract with the merchant/supplier, less a discount. The amount of the discount varies with the amount of risk of default by customers in the industry-sector involved. The merchant will have incorporated the discount in his price and will have evaluated the risk involved in a sale on credit to his customers generally. For example, the merchant/supplier may decide that receiving ninety-seven cents on the dollar from the card issuer outweighs taking the risk involved in the expectation that the customer will pay the full one dollar if credit is extended directly to the customer.[15] Thus, the credit card is also a risk shifting device from the point of view of the merchant.

The card issuer will protect itself further by providing that it is taking the assignment of the customer's obligation "with recourse." This enables the issuer to return the obligation to the merchant where the cardholder raises a defense to the underlying transaction. The Consumer Credit Protection Act (Fair Credit Billing Act § 170), 15 U.S.C. Section 1666i, provides that where the cardholder is unable to get satisfaction from the merchant, the issuer "shall be subject to all claims (other than tort claims) and defenses arising out of any transaction in which the credit card is used as a method of payment or extension of credit."

To protect itself in case the merchant/supplier is unable to reimburse the issuer on such returned items, the issuer may retain a "compensating balance" against which to charge a disputed item. For example, on a purchase to the value of $1000, the merchant may be

---

[12] In considering whether the cardholder has a remedy against the merchant/supplier, the underlying transaction must be considered to determine the type of remedy that may have been agreed upon. In *Israelewitz v. Manufacturers Hanover Trust Co.*, 120 Misc. 2d 125, 455 N.Y.S.2d 486 (1983) the contract indicated a "no refund" policy, which was considered "fair" in the circumstances. *See* Regulation Z, 12 C.F.R. § 226.12(e). Thus, the cardholder could not resist paying the issuer the amount due.

[13] Promulgated under the Consumer Credit Protection Act (Truth-in-Lending Act § 105, Fair Credit Billing Act § 162), 15 U.S.C. §§ 1604a, 1666a.

[14] Regulation Z, 12 C.F.R., §226.13(d)(1).

[15] Some merchants offer to split the discount with a customer paying cash.

entitled to $970, i.e., a discount of 3%. The issuer may retain 25% of this sum in case the cardholder raises a defense to having to pay the amount due. Should the cardholder succeed in his claim, there would be a compensating balance against which the cardholder's claim can be charged by the issuer. After a period of time during which no claims have been raised, the issuer will pay the remaining amount to the merchant.

Contract 3

This is the usual contract between a purchaser and a supplier of goods or services. Such contract will be governed by applicable U.C.C., common law and, where applicable, federal and state regulatory laws. For example, the Federal Trade Commission Regulation governing Door-to-Door Sales, 16 C.F.R. § 429.1 which permits cancellation of such transaction within three business days; or federal and state laws calling upon a merchant/supplier to comply with applicable consumer protection laws, such as the federal Magnusson-Moss Warranty Act, 15 U.S.C. §§ 2301–2312; or state Retail Installment Sales Acts.[16] Most of these statutes indicate that the rights of the consumer-debtor can be raised as defenses to a claim by an assignee of the contractual obligation incurred by the consumer.

The cardholder may seek to avoid liability beyond the fifty dollar limit imposed by law, by asserting that there was an unauthorized use of the credit card.[17] The burden of proof is on the card issuer to show that the use was authorized.[18] The question arises whether an unauthorized use requires the theft of the credit card or extends also to a use of the card by an agent whose agency has been terminated or who has exceeded the limits of his agency. Existence of actual, implied or apparent authority would indicate an authorized use. But, where the credit card issuer is informed of the termination of authority or of a limitation on authority, will the credit card issuer be able to recover from the credit cardholder the full amount charged on the credit card, or will there have been an unauthorized use limiting liability of the credit cardholder to fifty dollars? Consumer Credit Protection Act (Truth-in-Lending Act §§ 103(o), 133), 15 U.S.C. §§ 1602(o), 1643(a).

Courts have held that where "a credit cardholder authorizes another to use the card for a specific purpose, and the other person uses it for another purpose, such use is not an 'unauthorized use' within the meaning of 15 U.S.C. Section 1602(o)."[19] Courts take this position even where the issuer is informed of the credit limit authorized by the cardholder and that limit is exceeded by the person to whom the "cardholder voluntarily and knowingly allows" the use of the credit card.[20] The ability to protect oneself is in the cardholder rather than the card issuer.

---

[16] *See, e.g.,* Uniform Consumer Credit Code 7A U.L.A. §§ 1.101-6.415 (1974).

[17] Consumer Credit Protection Act (Truth-in-Lending Act § 133(a)), 15 U.S.C. § 1643(a)). Note, any unauthorized use after the cardholder communicated a loss of the credit card to the card issuer cannot be charged to the cardholder.

[18] Consumer Credit Protection Act (Truth-in-Lending Act § 133 (b)), 15 U.S.C § 1643 (b).

[19] Mastercard v. Town of Newport, 133 Wis. 2d 328, 334, 396 N.W.2d 345, 348 (1986).

[20] Martin v. American Express, Inc., 361 So. 2d 597 (Ala. Ct. App. 1978). But note Michigan Nat'l Bank v. Olson, 44 Wash. App. 898, 723 P.2d 438 (1986) (The factual issue whether bank was negligent in allowing an excess over the credit granted the cardholder prevented a summary judgment).

Towers World Airways Inc. v. PHH Aviation Systems Inc.

933 F.2d 174 (2d Cir. 1991)

NEWMAN, Circuit Judge

The Truth-in-Lending Act, 15 U.S.C. § 1643(a) (1988), places a limit of $50 on the liability of a credit cardholder for charges incurred by an "unauthorized" user. This appeal concerns the applicability of this provision to a card bearer who was given permission by the cardholder to make a limited range of purchases but who subsequently made substantial additional charges on the card. The appeal is brought by Towers World Airways, Inc. ("Towers"), a credit cardholder, and two related corporations from the June 19, 1990, judgment of the District Court for the Southern District of New York (Kevin Thomas Duffy, Judge) denying their request for a declaratory judgment to absolve them of liability for the sums charged and granting judgment for the card issuer, PHH Aviations Systems ("PHH"), on its counterclaim for the amounts charged. We conclude that the person incurring the charges was not an "unauthorized" user within the meaning of section 1643(a) and therefore affirm.

Background

In February 1988, PHH issued a credit card to Towers to purchase fuel and other aircraft-related goods and services for a corporate jet leased by Towers from PHH. World Jet Corporation, a subsidiary of United Air Fleet, was responsible for maintaining the aircraft. An officer of Towers designated Fred Jay Schley, an employee of World Jet, as the chief pilot of the leased jet and gave him permission to make purchases with the PHH credit card at least in connection with non-charter flights, which were used exclusively by Towers executives. Notwithstanding United Air Fleet's agreement to pay the cost of fuel on chartered flights, which provided service for other clients, Schley used the credit card to charge $89,025.97 to Towers in connection with such flights, prior to the cancellation of the card in August 1988.

Towers filed a complaint in state court seeking a declaratory judgment (i) absolving it of liability for any charges incurred in connection with fuel purchases for chartered flights, (ii) holding PHH responsible for knowingly permitting these purchases and consequently for breaching the credit

agreement issued in connection with the PHH credit card, and (iii) requiring an accounting and disgorgement of all improperly charged amounts. After removing to federal court, PHH moved for summary judgment on its counterclaims seeking recovery for the $89,025.97 in unpaid charges.

The District Court granted PHH's motion, denied Towers' prayer for declaratory relief, and entered judgment for the full amount in dispute. Judge Duffy held Towers liable under the terms of the credit agreement between Towers and PHH, which provided that "[the] Aircraft Operator shall be responsible for all purchases made with a Card from the date of its issuance until the Aircraft Operator reports that a card is lost, stolen, misplaced or cancelled by calling PHH." Judge Duffy further held that the Truth-in-Lending Act, which limits a cardholder's liability for "unauthorized" uses, was inapplicable to charges incurred by one to whom the cardholder has "voluntarily and knowingly allow[ed]" access for another, limited purpose.

On appeal, Towers concedes liability under its credit agreement with PHH but contends that summary judgment was improperly granted on the question of whether the Truth-in-Lending Act limits its liability to $50. The issues on appeal are whether Schley's use of the card to incur the $89,025.97 in connection with chartered flights was "unauthorized" within the meaning of the Truth-in-Lending Act and whether that question was properly decided on summary judgment.

Discussion

Congress enacted the 1970 Amendments to the Truth-in-Lending Act, 15 U.S.C. §§ 1602(j)-(o), 1642–44 (1988), in large measure to protect credit cardholders from unauthorized use perpetrated by those able to obtain possession of a card from its original owner. In addition to imposing criminal sanctions for the most egregious cases, those involving fraud, 15 U.S.C. § 1644 (1988), the amendments enacted a scheme for limiting the liability of cardholders for all charges by third parties made without "actual, implied or apparent authority" and "from which the cardholder receives no benefit." 15 U.S.C. §§ 1602(o), 1643 (1988). Where an unauthorized use has occurred, the cardholder can be held liable only up to a limit of $50 for the amount charged on the card, if certain conditions are satisfied.[1] 15 U.S.C. § 1643(a)(1)(B) (1988); *Credit Card Service Corp. v. FTC*, 161 App. D.C. 424, 495 F.2d 1004, 1006 (D.C. Cir. 1974). Except as provided in section 1643, "a cardholder incurs no liability from the unauthorized use of a credit card." 15 U.S.C. § 1643(d).

By defining "unauthorized use" as that lacking in "actual, implied, or apparent authority," Congress apparently contemplated, and courts have accepted, primary reliance on background principles of agency law in determining the liability of cardholders for charges incurred by third-party card bearers. *See, e.g., Fifth Third Bank/VISA v. Gilbert*, 17 Ohio Misc. 2d 14, 478 N.E.2d 1324, 1326 (1984); *Walker Bank & Trust Co. v. Jones*, 672 P.2d 73, 75–76 (Utah 1983), *cert. denied*, 466 U.S. 937, 104 S. Ct. 1911 (1984); see also 12 C.F.R. § 226.12 n.22 (1990). Under the parameters established by Congress, the inquiry into "unauthorized use" properly focuses on whether the user acted as the cardholder's agent in incurring the debt in dispute. A cardholder, as principal, can create express and implied authority only through manifestations to the user of consent to the particular transactions into which the user has

---

[1] 15 U.S.C. § 1643(a)(1) (1988) provides:

A cardholder shall be liable for the unauthorized use of a credit card only if —

(A) the card is an accepted credit card;

(B) the liability is not in excess of $50;

(C) the card issuer gives adequate notice to the cardholder of the potential liability;

(D) the card issuer has provided the cardholder with a description of a means by which the card issuer may be notified of loss or theft of the card, which description may be provided on the face or reverse side of the statement required by section 1637(b) of this title or on a separate notice accompanying such statement;

(E) the unauthorized use occurs before the card issuer has been notified that an unauthorized use of the credit card has occurred or may occur as the result of loss, theft, or otherwise; and

(F) the card issuer has provided a method whereby the user of such card can be identified as the person authorized to use it.

entered. *See Restatement (Second) of Agency* § 7 (1958).

In the pending case, there remains an unresolved issue of fact as to whether Steven Hoffenberg, the Towers officer who dealt with Schley, expressly or impliedly authorized Schley to purchase fuel on chartered flights. Hoffenberg's testimony that he instructed Schley to limit his use of the card to purchases "benefit[ting] . . . Towers' use of the airplane" supports the inference that Schley lacked both express and implied authority to make the disputed purchases. Whether Schley's testimony to the contrary should be credited can be resolved only by a factfinder. Accordingly, we cannot affirm the grant of summary judgment on the theory that Schley possessed express or implied authority.

A. Did the Card User Have Apparent Authority?

Unlike express or implied authority, however, apparent authority exists entirely apart from the principal's manifestations of consent to the agent. Rather, the cardholder, as principal, creates apparent authority through words or conduct that, reasonably interpreted by a third party from whom the card bearer makes purchases, indicate that the card user acts with the cardholder's consent. *See Restatement (Second) of Agency* §§ 8, 27 (1958). Though a cardholder's relinquishment of possession may create in another the appearance of authority to use the card, the statute clearly precludes a finding of apparent authority where the transfer of the card was without the cardholder's consent, as in cases involving theft, loss, or fraud. However elastic the principle of apparent authority may be in theory, the language of the 1970 Amendments demonstrates Congress's intent that the category of cases involving charges incurred as a result of *involuntary* card transfers are to be regarded as unauthorized under sections 1602(o) and 1643. The description in section 1643 of the conditions precedent to an issuer's recovery of up to $50 from the cardholder for unauthorized uses clearly assumes that cases of loss or theft fall within the definition of unauthorized uses, see 15 U.S.C. § 1643(a)(1)(D) (1988) (requiring that "the card issuer has provided the cardholder with a description of a means by which the card issuer may be notified of loss or theft of the card"); *id.* § 1643(a)(1)(E) (unauthorized use must occur before the "card issuer has been notified that an unauthorized use of the credit card has occurred or may occur as the result of loss, theft, or otherwise"), while section 1644's imposition of criminal penalties for "fraudulent use of credit cards" makes a similar assumption with respect to fraudulently induced transfers, *id.* § 1644 (1988).

Because the statute provides no guidance as to uses arising from the *voluntary* transfer of credit cards, the general principles of agency law, incorporated by reference in section 1602(o), govern disputes over whether a resulting use was unauthorized. These disputes frequently involve, as in this case, a cardholder's claim that the card bearer was given permission to use a card for only a limited purpose and that subsequent charges exceeded the consent originally given by the cardholder. Acknowledging the absence of express or implied authority for the additional charges, several state courts have adopted the analysis of the Court of Civil Appeals of Alabama in *Martin v. American Express, Inc.*, 361 So. 2d 597, 600 (Ala. Civ. App. 1978), and declined to apply the Truth-in-Lending Act to limit the cardholder's liability, reasoning that the cardholder's voluntary relinquishment of the card for one purpose gives the bearer apparent authority to make additional charges. *See Cities Service Co. v. Pailet*, 452 So. 2d 319, 321–22 (La. Ct. App. 1984); *Standard Oil Co. v. Steele*, 22 Ohio Misc. 2d 27, 489 N.E.2d 842, 843–44 (1985); *Michigan National Bank v. Olson*, 44 Wash. App. 898, 723 P.2d 438, 441 (1986); *Mastercard v. Town of Newport*, 133 Wis. 2d 328, 396 N.W.2d 345, 348 (1986).

Though we agree that a cardholder, in lending or giving his card for one purpose, acts in a way that significantly contributes to the appearance of authority, at least as perceived by the third-party merchant, to make other purchases, we need not decide whether voluntary relinquishment for one purpose creates in every case apparent authority to incur other charges. In the pending case, the appearance of authority for Schley to purchase fuel on chartered flights was established not only by Towers' consent to Schley's unrestricted access to the PHH card but by other conduct and circumstances as well.

Nothing about the PHH card or the circumstances surrounding the purchases gave fuel sellers reason to distinguish the clearly authorized fuel purchases made in connection with non-charter flights from the purchases for chartered flights. It was the industry custom to entrust credit cards used to make airplane-related purchases to the pilot of the plane. By designating Schley as the pilot and subsequently giving him the card, Towers thereby imbued him with more apparent authority than might arise from voluntary relinquishment of a credit card in other contexts. In addition, with Towers' blessing Schley had used the card, which was inscribed with the registration number of the Gulfstream jet, to purchase fuel on non-charter flights for the same plane. The only difference between these uses expressly authorized and those now claimed to be unauthorized—the identity of the passengers—was insufficient to provide notice to those who sold the fuel that Schley lacked authority for the charter flight purchases.

B. Was Apparent Authority Limited by Notice to the Card Issuer?

Towers contends that, despite its own failure to have the card cancelled, once PHH, as the card issuer, learned, either through Towers or a third party, that Schley lacked authority to make certain charges, any such transaction that Schley entered into becomes an unauthorized use even if fuel sellers reasonably perceived that Schley had apparent authority to charge fuel purchases. Whether notifying the card issuer that some uses (or users) of a card are unauthorized makes them so has divided those courts that have considered the issue. *Compare Cities Service Co.*, 452 So. 2d at 320–22 (authority terminated), *and Standard Oil Co.*, 489 N.E.2d at 844 (same), *with Martin*, 361 So.2d at 600–01 (notice to card issuer ineffective), *and Walker Bank*, 672 P.2d at 75 (same).

With respect to this claim as well, the agency principles incorporated in section 1602(o) remains Congress's chosen vehicle for establishing a card bearer's authority, and whether a cardholder can limit a card bearer's authority by notifying the card issuer must be resolved by looking first to these principles and then to other indicia of Congressional intent that might qualify the application of agency principles to credit card transactions. Under well-established principles of agency law, codified in *Restatement (Second) of Agency* § 166 (1958), notice to a third party of limitations on an agent's authority qualifies the agent's apparent authority to act on the principal's behalf. *See Warner v. Central Trust Co.*, 798 F.2d 167, 171 (6th Cir. 1986); *Cox v. Pabst Brewing Co.*, 128 F.2d 468, 472 (10th Cir. 1942); H. Reuschlein & W. Gregory, *Agency and Partnership* 164 (1979).

However, in making a purchase with a third-party credit card, where the card issuer and the selling merchant are distinct entities, a card bearer not only reaches an agreement with one third party, the merchant, but also indirectly deals with a different third party, the card issuer. Use of a third-party credit card by its bearer is made possible by arrangements, previously entered into by both the merchant and the card issuer, that simultaneously obligate the card-holder and the issuer to the merchant and the cardholder to the card issuer each time the card is used to charge purchases.[2]

The rule of agency law contained in section 166 of *the Restatement* would permit the principal to qualify the authority of an agent to make purchases from a merchant by giving the merchant notice of the limitation. The limitation would surely be effective in an ordinary three-party arrangement in which an agent charges purchases on a principal's running account with a merchant. It is more doubtful whether a principal can similarly avoid liability by notifying the merchant of limitations on an agent's authority when an agent makes purchases using a credit card. Both cardholders and merchants normally regard anyone voluntarily entrusted with a credit card as having the right to make any purchases within the card's contractually specified limits. But to whatever extent a cardholder can limit the authority of a card user by giving notice to a merchant, we do not believe he can accomplish a similar limitation by giving notice to a card issuer. In four-party arrangements of this sort, it is totally unrealistic to burden the card issuer with the obligation to convey to numerous merchants whatever limitations the cardholder has placed on the card user's authority.[3]

Finally, there is no substance to the argument that our construction of the 1970 Amendments inadequately protects cardholders against liability for charges made without their consent. Admittedly, third-party credit cards ordinarily permit the bearer to charge purchases made from a vast number of merchants, and cardholders, who typically do not know which merchants have contracted to accept the card, cannot contact each merchant to selectively revoke a card bearer's authority. However, a cardholder need not do so to prevent unauthorized use by one entrusted with the card. In many cases, the cardholder can avoid unwanted charges simply by repossessing the card. Where a card issuer permits a cardholder to cancel the card, and thereby any contractual obligation to pay, a cardholder can limit his liability even if unable to regain possession by cancelling his card. Even where the card issuer also requires return of the card prior to cancellation of the agreement, a cardholder who has tried and failed to recover a card from an "estranged spouse, a dishonest employee, or a disappeared 'friend,'" R. J. Rohner, F. H. Miller, J. H. Mancuso, *The Law of Truth-in-Lending* para. 10.03[2][a], at S10-9 (Supp. 1989), likely can prevail on the claim that the card user has stolen the card and that any subsequent charges are for that reason unauthorized. Finally, we note that by foreclosing card issuers from recovering unauthorized charges from cardholders, section 1643(a)(1) undoubtedly encourages card issuers to facilitate the cancellation of cards once a possible unauthorized use has been reported.

Because the disputed charges were not unauthorized within the meaning of 15 U.S.C. §§ 1602(o) and 1643(a)(1), PHH was entitled to recover their full value from Towers under their credit agreement.

The judgment of the District Court is affirmed.

---

[2] As compared to the other set of third parties, the selling merchants, PHH would have been aware of different facts bearing on Schley's authority, not all of which could be attributed to Towers as the principal. Towers has not questioned and we therefore need not decide whether an issuer seeking recovery for credit card charges under a theory of apparent authority must establish that it, as well as the merchant, reasonably believed the agent to have apparent authority.

[3] As framed by *the Restatement*, the notice rule is subject to certain restrictions, such as the requirement that the principal's communication of the limits on the agent's authority must be clear. But the existence of these restrictions does not necessarily mean that the notice rule itself is applicable in all contexts where those restrictions are satisfied. *See Restatement of Agency (Second)* at § 166, comment e.

NOTE

In *Walker Bank & Trust Co. v. Jones*, 672 P.2d 73 (Utah 1983) *cert. denied* 466 U.S. 937 (1984) an estranged spouse used the credit card after the credit cardholder had notified the card issuer of the termination of authority. The cardholder was unable to return the card promptly to the issuer. Further purchases were made with the card before the card could be returned. The majority of the court found for the card issuer. But note Justice Durham's powerful dissent:

Durham, J.

I dissent from the majority opinion because I believe that the federal statute and the specific cardholder agreements in question relieve the defendants of liability for the unauthorized use of their credit cards by their spouses. . . .

Thus, the pivotal issue in this case is whether the defendants' notification to the Bank was sufficient to revoke the defendants' husbands' "actual, implied, or apparent authority" to use the credit cards, thereby rendering the husbands' use unauthorized. The majority opinion responds in the negative by contending that the defendants' husbands were clothed with apparent authority because they carried credit cards imprinted with the husbands' names and bearing the husbands' signatures. The majority opinion holds that, despite notification to the Bank by the defendants that all authority has been expressly revoked, this apparent authority continues to exist until the defendants obtain the cards from their estranged husbands and return them to the Bank. I disagree with that holding for three reasons.

First, the result of the majority opinion runs counter to the purpose of § 1643 of the TILA,* which has been described as follows:

The federal credit card statute reflects a policy decision that it is preferable for the issuer to bear fraud losses arising from credit card use.

. . . [I]ssuers are in a better position to control the occurrence of these losses. They not only select the merchants who may accept the card and the holders who may use it, but also design the security systems for card distribution, user identification, and loss notification. Hence, *the statutory choice of issuer liability assures that the problem of credit card loss is the responsibility of the party most likely to take efficient steps in its resolution.* Weistart, *Consumer Protection in the Credit Card Industry: Federal Legislative Controls*, 70 Mich. L. Rev. 1475, 1509–10 (1972) (citations omitted) (emphasis added). *Cf. First National Bank of Mobile v. Roddenberry*, 701 F.2d 927 (11th Cir. 1983) (stating that, by issuing a credit card, a bank assumes the risk of nonpayment and that only the bank can decide when and if credit will be revoked). Under the present circumstances, I acknowledge that the burden or risk of liability should initially fall on the cardholder because use of the credit card by a spouse is, and remains, authorized until notice is given to the card issuer that the authority to use the credit card is revoked. However, once the cardholder notifies the card issuer of the revocation of that authority, it is clear that the card issuer is in the best position to protect itself, the cardholder and third parties. The card issuer can protect both itself and the cardholder by refusing to pay any charges on the account, and it can protect third parties by listing the credit card in the regional warning bulletins. See Weistart, supra; *Standard Oil Co. v. State Neon Co.*, 120 Ga. App. 660, 171 S.E.2d 777 (1969). The issuer need only terminate the existing account, transfer all existing charges to a new number, and issue a new card to the cardholder.

In circumstances similar to the present case, the Supreme Court of New York stated:

It is interesting to note, parenthetically, that under the provisions above quoted, defendant [cardholder] would not be liable for purchases made after notice of loss or theft of the card and if he was in fact unable to obtain the card from his estranged wife, the result was not greatly different. Indeed the plaintiff's [card

---

* [Editor: Truth-in-Lending Act.]

issuer's] situation was no worse than in the case of a loss of theft but probably considerably better since it knew the whereabouts of the card and of the holder.

Socony Mobile Oil Co. v. Greif, 10 A.D. 2d 522, 197 N.Y.S.2d 522, 523–24 (1960) (decided prior to the enactment of § 1643 of the TILA and based on the language of the particular cardholder agreement). Thus, in conformance with the purpose of § 1643 of the TILA, the better holding in this case, as a policy matter, is that, after notification to the card issuer, the cardholder should be relieved of all liability for the unauthorized use of the credit card by an estranged spouse.[21]

Second, the language of § 1643 and the law of agency require that the defendants be relieved of liability. As the majority opinion recognizes, state law determines the question of whether the defendants' husbands are clothed with "apparent authority." See, e.g., FRB Letter of July 23, 1974, No. 822, by J. Kluckman, Chief, Truth-in-Lending Section (excerpted in Consumer Credit Guide (CCH) ¶ 31,144 (Oct. 8, 1974)). Under Utah law, a husband or wife may terminate an agency created in the spouse in the same manner as any other agency. *See* U.C.A., 1953, § 30-2-8. The majority opinion holds that the defendants' husbands' use was authorized because the husbands had "apparent authority." This is apparently a reference to the relationship between the husband and third-party merchants who rely on the husband's possession of a credit card with his name and matching signature on it. It cannot refer to the existence of apparent authority vis-a-vis the Bank, because the Bank has been *expressly notified* of the revocation of all authority. I fail to see why the existence of "apparent authority" as to third-party merchants should govern the liability of a cardholder whose spouse "steals" a card in the context of marital difficulties, any more than it would govern in the case of a cardholder whose card is stolen before delivery and bears a "matching signature" forged there-on by a thief. . . .

[In] *In re Shell Oil Co.*, 95 F.T.C. 357 (1980) several cardholders petitioned the Federal Trade Commission (FTC), which is vested with authority to enforce both the Federal Trade Commission Act and the TILA, for relief from certain practices of the Shell Oil Co. which were allegedly in violation of those Acts. Shell Oil Co. issued credit cards to cardholders to enable them to purchase goods and services at Shell's service stations. Some cardholders authorized third persons to use their credit cards. In certain instances, several cardholders notified Shell Oil Co. that such previously authorized users were no longer authorized. Shell Oil Co. responded by informing the cardholders that they would remain liable for charges incurred by the third persons until the credit cards used by the third persons were returned. The FTC ordered Shell Oil Co. to forthwith cease and desist from:

> 1. Failing to limit the liability of a cardholder for use of a credit card by a third person, in those cases where such third person has been given authorization by the cardholder to use such credit card, to the amount of money, property, labor, or services obtained by use prior to notification . . . by the cardholder that such use is no longer authorized . . . [and]
>
> 2. Informing a cardholder that [the card issuer] considers the cardholder liable for use of a credit card by a third person which occurs after the cardholder notifies [the card issuer] that such use is no longer authorized.

In re Shell Oil Co., supra, at 359–60 (emphasis added). Thus, under Section 1643 as interpreted by the FTC in the *Shell Oil* case, the defendants' liability in the present case is limited to the charges incurred by their husbands prior to notification. . . .

---

[21] It is interesting to point out that the husbands' use of the defendants' credit cards in the present case may in fact violate one of our criminal statutes. *See* U.C.A., 1953, § 76-6-506.2 (regarding fraudulent use of a credit card).

Finally, the majority opinion ignores the impracticality of imposing the burden on a cardholder of obtaining a credit card from an estranged spouse in order to return it to the Bank. It is unrealistic to think that estranged spouses will be cooperative. Moreover, it is extremely unwise to arm one spouse with a weapon which permits virtually unlimited spending at the expense of the other. As is illustrated by the facts of these cases, where the whereabouts of the unauthorized spouse are unknown, the cardholder may be powerless to acquire possession of his or her card and return it to the Bank, which, according to the majority opinion, is the only way to limit liability. One result of the majority opinion will surely be to encourage the "theft" by divorcing spouses of credit cards they were authorized to use during the marriage and the liberal use of those cards at the other spouse's expense. . . .

Question

Could the cardissuer demand that if there is no return of the credit card, the credit card will have to be cancelled? The card would then be an invalid card on which further credit would not be extended.

Problem

What if the carduser was a child of the cardholder who had given the credit card to the child to pay college tuition and other college expenses to the amount of $5,000.00. The cardholder has informed the college, the college store, and the card issuer of the limit to be placed on the use of the credit card.
1. The child exceeded that amount by $1,000 by buying books and a computer?
2. The child lent the credit card to a friend who took a ski trip during the Christmas vacation with other students, spending $5,000.00.

Discuss.

B. Electronic Fund Transfers

The use of checks permits the creation of a "float," i.e., a short term credit whereby the drawer retains the amount of the check in his account until it is honored on presentment and a debit entered in his account. In the meantime the recipient of the check considers payment to have been received and by depositing the check in her account receives a provisional credit. Albeit such credit can be reversed should the check be dishonored. U.C.C. § 4-214. But after a while the amount becomes withdrawable even though actual funds may not, as yet, have been received.[22] In effect the two banks would report the amount; by the drawee as being in the account of the drawer not yet debited and by the depository bank as credited in the depositor's account. This could indicate a greater amount of money in the economy than is actually the case. On a macro level this could affect monetary policies aimed at controlling inflation, while on a micro level it gives a wrong impression of the

---

[22] *See* Federal Expedited Funds Availability Act, 12 U.S.C. § 4002.

credit worth of the parties involved. The policy to prevent this imbalance, linked with the desire of suppliers to receive prompt availability of credit, led to electronic fund transfers. On the retail level this policy is achieved by use of "debit cards" and preauthorized "pay orders."[23] On the wholesale level we have electronic presentment and fund transfers, to which the Uniform Commercial Code Articles 4 and 4A apply. Additionally, there are the contractual relationships between transferors of substantial sums of money and clearing corporations that facilitate such transfers, such as the New York Federal Reserve Bank and the New York Clearing House Association. In effectuating the transmission of payment orders, various wire transfer systems exist such as the National Federal Reserve Wire Network (Fedwire), the Clearing House Interbank Payment System (CHIPS), and the Society for Worldwide International Financial Telecommunications (SWIFT) which provide facilities for the transfer of funds. On the international level, we should also note the efforts of the United Nations Commission on International Trade Law which proposed the adoption of a Model Law of Fund Transfers. This model law was adopted by the U.N. General Assembly in 1992.[24]

1. Consumer Electronic Fund Transfers—Debit Cards and Pay Orders

Consumer electronic fund transfers must be initiated by means of an access device (debit card) or by a prearranged agreement with the financial institution (a bank) to execute a "pay order." The Electronic Fund Transfer Act, 15 U.S.C. § 1693a(6) defines an electronic transfer as "any transfer . . . which is initiated through an electronic terminal, telephonic instrument, or computer or magnetic tape."

---

[23] Retail (consumer) electronic fund transfers are governed by the Consumer Credit Protection Act (Electronic Fund Transfer Act), 15 U.S.C. §§ 1693 to 1693r.

[24] Report of the United Nations Commission on International Trade Law, 25th Sess. Gen. Assembly Doc. Supp. No. 17 (A/47/17) Annex 1 (1992).

Wachter v. Denver National Bank
751 F. Supp. 906 (D.Colo. 1990)

JIM R. CARRIGAN, District Judge

Pro se plaintiff June Elga Wachter commenced this suit seeking damages for alleged violations of the Electronic Funds Transfer Act, 15 U.S.C. § 1693 et seq. Currently pending are defendants' motions to dismiss and for summary judgment. Plaintiff has responded by opposing the motions.

The parties have briefed the issues and oral argument would not materially assist the decision process. Jurisdiction is alleged to exist pursuant to 28 U.S.C. § 1331.

This suit concerns a wire transfer of funds made by Denver National Bank ("the bank") for the plaintiff. On December 1, 1988, the plaintiff paid $153.42 in cash to the bank for a $143.42

wire transfer to California. Bank personnel initiated the transfer and the funds were received in California that same day. Plaintiff later requested confirmation from the bank that the funds had reached their intended destination. The bank provided the plaintiff a copy of the actual wire transfer, and then confirmed and orally notified her that the transfer had been received. The bank followed oral confirmation with a copy of a letter from the recipient California bank confirming that the transferred funds indeed had reached the person intended. Still dissatisfied, the plaintiff traveled to California and confirmed that the funds appropriately had been transferred.

I have read the parties' briefs and have fully

considered their arguments. Defendants move for dismissal pursuant to Federal Rule of Civil Procedure 12(b)(6).[2] A complaint is not subject to dismissal pursuant to Rule 12(b)(6) unless it appears to a certainty that no relief can be granted under any set of facts that can be proven in support of its allegations. *Jones v. Metro. Denver Sewage Disposal Dist. No. 1*, 537 F. Supp. 966, 969 (D. Colo. 1982). Plaintiff's allegations and claim for relief are based solely on alleged violations of the Electronic Funds Transfer Act ("the Act"), 15 U.S.C. § 1693 et seq. Therefore, the question whether the Act applies here to provide the plaintiff grounds for relief controls my decision.[3]

The Act's intended scope is clarified by its legislative history and by case law. The Act was designed to create rights for consumers in an era in which banking could be conducted almost exclusively through machines. S. Rep. No. 915, 95th Cong., 2d Sess. at 3, reprinted in 1978 U.S. Code Cong. & Admin. News at 9405. The absence of personal contact was seen as a disadvantage in an automated system that is much more vulnerable to fraud, embezzlement and unauthorized use than traditional payment methods. See *Kashanchi v. Texas Commerce Medical Bank, N.A.*, 703 F.2d 936, 940 (5th Cir. 1983), quoting H.R. Rep. No. 1315, 95th Cong., 2d Sess. 2 (1978). The Act was passed to alleviate this concern and "to provide a basic framework establishing the rights, liabilities, and responsibilities of participants in electronic transfer systems." 15 U.S.C. § 1963. Accordingly, liability under the act is predicated on a finding that an electronic fund transfer has occurred. *Spain v. Union Trust*, 674 F. Supp. 1496, 1498 (D. Conn. 1987).

The Act defines "electronic fund transfer," in relevant part, as:

> "any transfer of funds, other than a transaction originated by check, draft, or similar paper instrument, which is initiated through an electronic terminal, telephonic instrument,

or computer or magnetic tape so as to order, instruct, or authorize a financial institution to debit or credit an account. Such term includes, but is not limited to, point-of-sale transfers, automated teller machine transactions, direct deposits or withdrawals of funds, and transfers initiated by telephone." 15 U.S.C. § 1693a(6).

Thus, two requirements must be met to qualify a transaction as an electronic fund transfer: (1) it must be initiated through an electronic terminal, telephonic instrument, or computer or magnetic tape, and (2) it must order, instruct or authorize a financial institution to debit or credit an account.

Whether the first requirement is satisfied depends in part on who initiated the transfer, the financial institution or the consumer. *Spain*, 674 F. Supp. at 1498–1500. A bank's use of an electronic device merely to process a transaction internally does not constitute an electronic funds transfer within the Act's meaning. *Id.; see also* Federal Reserve Official Staff Commentary Q2-25, republished in 12 C.F.R. Part 205, Supp. II, at 119 (definition of "electronic terminal" does not include computer equipment used internally by bank to process transfers). Rather, the Act's focus is upon consumer-initiated or consumer-authorized transfers where electronic devices are utilized in place of face-to-face banking transactions. *Spain*, 674 F. Supp. at 1500. The presence of personal contact with bank personnel who intercede between a consumer and the electronic device used to facilitate a transaction removes that transaction from the scope of the Act. *Id.* The transfer here does not fit the definition of "electronic fund transfer." First, the transfer was not initiated through an electronic device as defined by the Act. Instead, the plaintiff initiated her wire transfer through contact with the bank's personnel. The face-to-face nature of this personal banking transaction removes it from the scope of the Act's coverage. The fact that the bank used an electronic device to process the transfer internally does not change the result. See Federal Reserve Official Staff Commentary, *supra; Spain*, 674 F. Supp. at 1499.

Second, the plaintiff's transfer did not order, instruct or authorize the bank to debit or credit an account. Because the Act was designed to protect consumers, the only reasonable interpretation would apply it only to debits or credits of the

---

[2] Defendants motion is entitled "Motion to Dismiss for Failure to State a Claim Pursuant to Rules 12(b)(5) and 56." As noted, insufficiency of service of process is not an issue. Accordingly, this motion is treated as a Rule 12(b)(6) motion.

[3] I note at the outset that there are no disputed issues of fact in this case.

consumer's accounts. *Spain*, 674 F. Supp. at 1499. Here the plaintiff paid for her wire transfer with cash. Her account at the bank, if any, was not debited, and the account at the California bank credited with the wire transfer was not the plaintiff's.

For the reasons stated, I find and conclude that the Act does not apply to the instant wire transfer.

Plaintiff's claims are based solely on alleged violations of the Act. While the plaintiff may complain about the way her transfer was handled, it appears to a certainty that no relief can be granted under any set of facts that could be proven to support her complaint's allegations. Therefore, the plaintiff has failed to state a claim upon which relief can be granted and this suit must be dismissed.

NOTE

Debit cards work similarly to credit cards. The use of the debit card is predicated on the cardholder's available credit with the debit card issuer. The debit cardholder must have sufficient funds with the card issuer or must have a line of credit with the card issuer on which she can draw when giving a "pay order." The debit card may work through an automated teller machine [ATM] at the issuing bank, which dispenses cash when the card is inserted and the machine activated by means of a personal identification number [PIN]. The ATM may also be used to effectuate an electronic transfer by instructing the bank to make payment on specifically identified bills, such as may have been received from a local utility. In effect the transfer of funds is instantaneous. When the transaction is completed, the account of the cardholder will be debited and that of the beneficiary will have been credited.

The issuing bank may also place an ATM on a merchant's premises, a point-of-sale terminal [POS]. The customer may then withdraw cash to make payment or indicate that the merchant is to receive a direct credit to his account. The cardholder's account thereby will be promptly debited.

Since not all parties use the same banking organization, clearing corporations have developed through which the credit and debit entries will be facilitated, *e.g.* Most, Cirrus, etc. Merchants will participate in these systems which may charge the cardholder for such service. Some banks have developed payment methods allowing customers to give telephonic instructions authorizing "pay orders" and even permitting customers to communicate such pay orders through a home computer linkup using a modem. Whether an ATM or POS would violate a prohibition against multi-branch banking is a question of state law.[25] States have a legitimate interest in regulating banking. State law therefore can regulate use of an ATM, even though the ATM is part of an interstate system.[26]

Congress established the National Commission on Electronic Fund Transfer to "conduct a thorough study and investigation and recommend appropriate administrative action and legislation necessary in connection with the possible development of public or private

---

[25] Independent Bankers Association of America v. Smith, 175 App. D.C. 184, 534 F.2d 921 (D.C. Cir.) *cert. denied*, 429 U.S. 862 (ATM machine is a branch bank for purpose of National Bank Act, 12 U.S.C. § 36(h)); First National Bank of Logan v. Walker Bank & Trust Co., 385 U.S. 252 (1966) (National Banks subject to state law governing branch banking).

[26] Valley Bank of Nevada v. Plus System, Inc., 914 F.2d 1186 (9th Cir. 1990) (such regulations will not per se violate the commerce clause of the U.S. Constitution).

electronic fund transfer systems."[27] The report of that Commission[28] resulted in Congress passing the Consumer Credit Protection Act (Electronic Fund Transfer Act §§ 902 to 920 [EFTA]), 15 U.S.C. §§ 1693 to 1693r, and the promulgation of Regulation E by the Federal Reserve Board.[29]

The EFTA states

> It is the purpose of this subchapter to provide a basic framework establishing the rights, liabilities, and responsibilities of participants in electronic fund transfer systems. The primary objective of this subchapter, however, is the provision of individual consumers rights.

Consumer Credit Protection Act (EFT Act § 902(b)), 15 U.S.C. § 1693(b).

"The Act establishes the basic rights, liabilities, and responsibilities of consumers who use electronic money transfer services and of financial institutions that offer these services."[30] Consumer is a defined term; it "means a natural person,"[31] thus excluding banks and business entities from the EFTA other than as the means by which the electronic fund transfer may be executed. An electronic fund transfer is "any transfer of funds, other than a transaction originated by . . . [a] a paper instrument, which is initiated through an electronic terminal, telephonic instrument, or computer or magnetic tape so as to order, instruct, or authorize a financial institution to debit or credit an account. Such term includes, but is not limited to, point-of-sale transfers, automated teller machine transactions, direct deposits or withdrawals of funds, and transfers initiated by telephone."[32]

---

[27] 12 U.S.C. § 2403(a).

[28] EFT in the United States: Policy Recommendations and the Public Interest.

[29] 12 C.F.R. §§ 205.1 to 205.14.

[30] 12 C.F.R. § 205.1(b).

[31] 15 U.S.C. § 1693a(5).

[32] EFTA § 903(6) 15 U.S.C. § 1693a(6).

Kashanchi v. Texas Commerce Medical Bank, N.A.
703 F.2d 936 (5th Cir. 1983)

Appeal from the United States District Court for the Southern District of Texas.

RANDALL, C. J.:

The plaintiff, Morvarid Paydar Kashanchi, appeals from a final judgment of the district court dismissing her complaint for lack of subject matter jurisdiction. The issue on appeal is whether the term "electronic fund transfer" as used in the Electronic Fund Transfer Act ("EFTA" or "the Act"), 15 U.S.C. § 1693 (Supp. V 1981), includes a transfer of funds from a consumer's account, initiated by a telephone conversation between someone other than the owner of the account and an employee of a financial institution, when the transfer is not made pursuant to a prearranged plan or agreement under which periodic transfers are contemplated. For the reasons set forth below, we affirm.

On or about February 9, 1981, the plaintiff and her sister, Firoyeh Paydar, were the sole owners of a savings account at Texas Commerce Medical Bank in Houston, Texas. On or about that date, $4900 was transferred from their account. The transfer was allegedly initiated by a telephone conversation between an employee of the bank and someone other than the plaintiff or her sister.

Upon receipt of a March 31, 1981, bank statement showing the $4900 withdrawal, Firoyeh Paydar sent a letter to the bank, dated April 15, 1981, notifying the bank that the withdrawal was unauthorized. After the bank refused to recredit the account with the amount of the allegedly unauthorized withdrawal, the plaintiff filed this action on December 4, 1981, alleging violations by the bank of the EFTA. The district court granted the defendant's motion to dismiss on the ground that the plaintiff's cause of action was excluded from the coverage of the Act under 15 U.S.C. § 1693a (6)(E). The plaintiff timely appealed.

This is apparently the first case in which we have been called upon to interpret any of the substantive provisions of the EFTA. We begin our inquiry with the language of the statute itself, recognizing that "absent a clearly expressed legislative intent to the contrary, the plain meaning of the language is ordinarily controlling." *Johnson v. Department of Treasury, Internal Revenue Service*, 700 F.2d 971 (5th Cir.1983); *see also United States v. Martino*, 681 F.2d 952, 954 (5th Cir.1982) (en banc).

The parties agree that the telephonic transfer that allegedly occurred in this case falls within the broad definition of "electronic fund transfers" in the Act:

> [T]he term "electronic fund transfer" means any transfer of funds, other than a transaction originated by check, draft, or similar paper instrument, which is initiated through an electronic terminal, telephonic instrument, or computer or magnetic tape so as to order, instruct, or authorize a financial institution to debit or credit an account. Such term includes, but is not limited to, point-of-sale transfers, automated teller machine transactions, direct deposits or withdrawals of funds, and transfers initiated by telephone.

15 U.S.C. § 1693a(6). Some of what Congress has given, however, it has also taken away. Excluded from the definition of an electronic fund transfer is

> any transfer of funds which is initiated by a telephone conversation between a consumer and an officer or employee of a financial institution which is not pursuant to a prearranged plan and under which periodic or recurring transfers are comtemplated.

15 U.S.C. § 1693a(6)(E). The plaintiff concedes

that the unauthorized transfer of her funds was not made "pursuant to any prearranged plan," and that it was made by an employee of the bank. The question in this case is whether the telephone conversation was between the employee and a "consumer."[1]

The Act defines a consumer as "a natural person." 15 U.S.C. § 1693a(5). If we were to apply this definition to the language in the exclusion, we would have to conclude that the withdrawal of the plaintiff's funds was excluded from the coverage of the Act since a natural person, even if the person was neither the plaintiff nor her sister, made the withdrawal. The plaintiff argues, however, that we should read the term "consumer" more narrowly in this portion of the Act; she would have us interpret the provision to exclude only transfers made by the account holder.

The plaintiff maintains that the legislative history of the Act supports her narrow reading of the exclusion. She points out that the House version of the bill used the word "holder," meaning "the individual who is recognized as the owner of the account by the financial institution where the account is held," H.R. 13007, § 903(i), 95th Cong., 2d Sess., 124 Cong.Rec. 25737 (1978), where the Senate version, eventually adopted by Congress as the EFTA, uses the word "consumer." The plaintiff would have us infer that the Senate intended the word "consumer" to be synonymous with "holder." There is no indication in the legislative history, however, that this is what the Senate intended.[2] The only criticism leveled at the

---

[1] Relying on the Federal Reserve Board's use of the conjunction "and" in its regulations implementing the EFTA, rather than the relative pronoun "which" used in the Act, the plaintiff maintains that the test for whether a particular transfer falls within the exclusion is two-pronged. The federal regulations exclude:

> Any transfer of funds and (1) is initiated by a telephone conversation between a consumer and an officer or employee of a financial institution *and* (2) is not under a telephone bill-payment or other prearranged plan or agreement in which periodic or recurring transfers are contemplated.

12 C.F.R. § 205.3(e) (1982) (emphasis added). We do not think that the difference in grammatical construction changes the nature of the exclusion.

[2] One Senate version of the bill used the words "person" and "customer" instead of

definition of consumer concerned the exclusion of corporations, particularly nonprofit corporations, from that definition. *See The Electronic Funds Transfer Consumer Protection Act, 1977: Hearing on S. 2065 Before the Subcomm. on Consumer Affairs of the Senate Comm. on Banking, Housing and Urban Affairs*, 95th Cong., 1st Sess. 37 (1977) (Statement of Linda Hudak, Legislative Director, Consumer Federation of America).

Secondly, Congress demonstrated in other sections of the EFTA that when it wanted to limit a particular provision of the Act to an account holder, rather than to all natural persons, it was perfectly capable of adding language to do so. For example, the Act defines an "unauthorized electronic fund transfer" as "an electronic fund transfer from a consumer's account initiated by a person other than the consumer without actual authority to initiate such transfer." 15 U.S.C. § 1693a(11). It is a well established principle of statutory construction that "where Congress includes particular language in one section of a statute but omits it in another section of the same Act, it is generally presumed that Congress acts intentionally and purposely in the disparate inclusion or exclusion." *United States v. Wong Kim Bo*, 472 F.2d 720, 722 (5th Cir.1972).[3] In addition,

reading "consumer" as the equivalent of "holder" would create redundancies in other portions of the Act. *See, e.g.*, 15 U.S.C. § 1693a(8).[4] "[W]ords in statutes should not be discarded as 'meaningless' and 'surplusage' when Congress specifically and expressly included them, particularly where the words are excluded in other sections of the same act." *Wong Kim Bo*, 472 F.2d at 722; *see also Meltzer v. Board of Public Instruction*, 548 F.2d 559, 578 n. 38 (5th Cir.1977), *cert. denied*, 439 U.S. 1089, 99 S.Ct. 872, 59 L.Ed.2d 56 (1979). In short, the language of the statute would seem to exclude the transfer in this case from the coverage of the Act.

Further, the legislative history of the EFTA is consistent with the plain meaning of the language in the statute and with the presumption arising from Congress's disparate inclusion and exclusion of words of limitation. The plaintiff emphasizes that Congress designed the Act to provide a comprehensive scheme of federal regulation for all electronic transfers of funds. *See* H.R.Rep. No. 1315, 95th Cong. 2d Sess. 2 (1978); *see also* E. Broadman, *Electronic Fund Transfer Act: Is the Consumer Protected?*, 13 U.S.F.L.Rev. 245 (1979). Congress undoubtedly intended the Act's coverage to be broad; the Act itself provides that its list of electronic fund transfers is not all-inclusive. 15 U.S.C. § 1693a(6). Aware that computer technology was still in a rapid, evolutionary stage of development, Congress was careful to permit coverage of electronic services not yet in existence: "The definition of 'electronic fund transfer' is intended to give the Federal Reserve Board flex-

---

"consumer." The term "person" was defined as an individual who is a citizen of the United States or an alien lawfully admitted for permanent residence, or a partnership, corporation, association, trust, or any other legal entity organized under the laws of a State of the United States. The term "customer" was defined as

any natural person who is a debit instrument patron of a debit instrument issuer who utilizes electronic fund transfer services primarily for personal, family or household purposes.

Consumer Protection Aspects of EFT Systems, 1978; Hearings on S. 2546 and S. 2470 Before the Subcomm. on Consumer Affairs of the Senate Comm. on Banking, Housing, and Urban Affairs, 95th Cong., 2d Sess. 131 (1978). The Senate did not explain, however, why it chose the word "consumer" and the broader definition of that word over the word "customer."

[3] The plaintiff reads the definition of an "unauthorized electronic fund transfer" as an indication that not every natural person is a consumer within the context of the EFTA. She emphasizes that the federal regulations state that the definitions apply "unless the context indicates otherwise." 12 C.F.R. § 205.2 (1982). While the plaintiff's interpretation of the unauthorized

---

transfer definition is not without merit, her own emphasis on the importance of the context in which the language is used undercuts her argument. In a context where Congress has expressly narrowed the class of consumer to whom a specific provision in the statute applies, the more narrow definition is controlling. Congress did not, however, narrow the class of consumers to be covered by the exclusion, as it did in the unauthorized transfer section.

[4] Section 1693a(8) provides:

the term "financial institution" means a State or National bank, a State or Federal savings and loan association, a mutual savings bank, a State or Federal credit union, or any other person who, directly or indirectly, holds an account belonging to a consumer.

15 U.S.C. § 1693a(8).

ibility in determining whether new or developing electronic services should be covered by the act and, if so, to what extent." S.Rep. No. 915, 95th Cong., 2d Sess. 9 (1978), U.S.Code Cong. & Admin.News 1978, pp. 9273, 9411; *see also* National Commission on Electronic Fund Transfers, *EFT in the United States*, 4 (Final Rep.1977).

Congressional concern about electronic systems not specifically mentioned in the Act was focused, however, on future and as yet undeveloped systems, not on systems that Congress has simply failed to discuss. For example, the report on the House version of the Act explained the need for flexibility in dealing with *future* electronic systems:

> Many aspects of electronic fund transfer systems are undergoing evolutionary changes and, thus, projections about future events necessarily involve a degree of speculation. Consequently, the appropriate approach to those new financial service concepts is, in general, to permit further development in a free market environment and, to the extent possible, in a manner consistent with the nature and purpose of existing law and regulations governing financial services.

H.R.Rep. No. 1315, *supra*, at 33. The absence of discussion about informal personal phone transfers would seem to indicate an intent not to cover these transfers, or at least an absence of congressional concern about them, in light of the extensive discussion throughout the hearings and reports of the other existing types of electronic transfers. It is highly unlikely that this silence was a result of congressional ignorance of the problem since these informal phone withdrawals presumably had been occurring since shortly after the time of Alexander Graham Bell.

The exclusion of these informal transactions was not in the House version of the EFTA, and presumably it was not in the original version of the Senate bill either, since the minority report criticized the bill's coverage of incidental telephone instructions:

> In an attempt to reach the automatic telephone payments (transfers through a touch-tone telephone and computer network routing instructions to the financial institution) the Committee has also covered incidental telephone instructions by (a) depositor to a teller to make a transfer from a savings account to cover an overdraft or pay a bill.

S.Rep. No. 915, *supra*, at 24, U.S.Code Cong. & Admin.News 1978, p. 9425. Apparently, this criticism led to the inclusion in the final version of the EFTA of the exemption which is the subject of this suit. Focusing on the Federal Reserve Board's statement that phone transfers made as an "accommodation to the consumer" are not covered by the Act, 46 Fed.Reg. 46880 (1978), and the Senate minority report's discussion of telephone instructions made by a "depositor," the plaintiff would have us conclude that only transactions made as a favor to the actual account holder were excluded from the Act.

These transfers were more probably excluded, however, not because they are made as a favor to the account holder, but because of the personal element in these transfers. On the one hand, as the plaintiff points out, all phone transfers are particularly vulnerable to fraud because there is no written memorandum of the transactions; there is no signature to be authenticated. This lack of a written record was one of the factors that motivated Congress to pass the EFTA. See H.R.Rep. No. 1315, *supra*, at 2, 4. The other factor, however, was the dependency of electronic fund transfer systems on computers and the resulting absence of any human contact with the transferor. The House report explains: "Consequently, these impersonal transactions are much more vulnerable to fraud, embezzlement, and unauthorized use than the traditional payment methods." *Id.* at 2. Senator Proxmire opened the hearings on the Senate bill with the warning that "[c]omputer systems are far from infallible, and electronic fund transfers—so totally dependent on computers—will also be error prone." *The Electronic Funds Transfer Consumer Protection Act, 1977: Hearings on S. 2065 Before the Subcomm. on Consumer Affairs of the Senate Comm. on Banking, Housing and Urban Affairs*, 95th Cong., 1st Sess. 2 (1977); *see also* 124 Cong.Rec. 25731 (1978) (statement of Rep. Annunzio, bill sponsor). As one commentator explains, telephonic communications were included in the definition of electronic fund transfers in order to extend coverage over computerized pay-by-phone systems; informal non-recurring consumer-initiated transfers were excluded, however, because they are not prone to computer error or institutional abuse since they are handled on a personal basis:

> The final exemption from the purview of the EFT Act is an exclusion for nonrecurring

transfers of funds that are initiated by an ordinary telephone conversation between a consumer and an officer or employee of the financial institution. In order to extend coverage over computerized "pay-by-phone" systems, the general definition of the term "electronic fund transfer" had to be broad enough to encompass transactions initiated through a telephone. Like automatic debiting of service charges and automatic crediting of interest, however, ordinary nonrecurring transfers informally initiated by a consumer's call to an officer or employee of his neighborhood bank or savings and loan association was not considered to pose a serious threat warranting the coverage and additional costs of the EFT Act. Such requests are handled on a personal basis, so the possibility of computer error or institutional abuse, believed to exist with respect to some other EFT systems, was deemed to be absent. Brandel & Oliff, *The Electronic Fund Transfer Act: A Primer*, 40 Ohio St.L.J. 531, 545 (1979). Telephonic transfers made between a natural person and an employee of the financial institution share this element of human contact, regardless of whether the transfer is made by the account holder or someone else.

Finally, we note that the EFTA was passed because "[e]xisting law and regulations in the consumer protection area are not applicable to some aspects of the new financial service concepts." H.R.Rep. No. 1315, *supra*, at 33. *See also* 15 U.S.C. § 1693a. The plaintiff suggests in her reply brief that she would have no adequate legal remedy for the wrong she has suffered if she were denied relief under the EFTA. While she conceded at oral argument that she might have an action under state law for conversion or breach of contract (her deposit agreement with the bank), she maintained that a person suffering a loss resulting from the abuse of one of the other electronic fund transfer systems[5] would also have such an action under state law.

The plaintiff ignores the essential difference between electronic fund transfer systems and personal transfers by phone or by check. When the bank employee allegedly agreed to withdraw funds from the plaintiff's account, he or she presumably could have asked some questions to ascertain whether the caller was one of the account holders. The failure to attempt to make a positive identification of the caller might be considered negligence or a breach of the deposit agreement under state law. When someone makes an unauthorized use of an electronic fund transfer system, however, the financial institution often has no way of knowing that the transfer is unauthorized.[6] For example, in order to make a transfer at an automatic teller machine, a person need only possess the machine card and know the correct personal identification number. The computer cannot determine whether the person who has inserted the card and typed in the magic number is authorized to use the system. What might be a withdrawal negligently permitted by the financial institution in one situation might not be a negligent action in the other.

Our analysis of both the language of the EFTA and the legislative history of the Act leads us to conclude that Congress intended to exclude from the Act's coverage any transfer of funds initiated by a phone conversation between any natural person and an officer or employee of a financial institution, which was not made pursuant to a prearranged plan and under which periodic and recurring transfers were not contemplated. Accordingly, we hold that the withdrawal of funds from the plaintiff's account is not covered by the Act even though said withdrawal allegedly was not made by either the plaintiff or her sister. The district court's dismissal of the plaintiff's action for lack of subject matter jurisdiction is AFFIRMED.

---

[5] Congress was specifically concerned with four principal types of electronic fund transfer services: (1) automated teller machines, (2) pay-by-phone systems, (3) direct deposits and automatic payments, and (4) point-of-sale transfers, S.Rep. No. 915, *supra*, at 2 U.S. Code Cong. & Admin.News 1978, p. 9404.

[6] One of the purposes of the EFTA was to determine who should bear the loss for these unauthorized transfers. S.Rep. No. 915, *supra*, at 3, 5-6. U.S.Code Cong. & Admin.News 1978, pp. 9405, 9407-9408. Limitations on the consumer's liability for unauthorized transfers are contained in 15 U.S.C. § 1693g.

NOTE

1. Why did the plaintiff bring this action under the EFT Act? *Note* 15 U.S.C. § 1693m(a)(3). In addition to damages, the EFT Act allows recovery of the costs of an action, including reasonable attorney's fees as determined by the court. Attorneys' fees are generally not recoverable in a common law action for conversion. *See Alyeska Pipeline Service v. Wilderness Society*, 421 U.S. 240 (1975).

2. The electronic fund transfer must be originated with an "accepted access device"[33] such as a debit card and personal identification number (PIN), or other type of identification that is "readable" by the electronic means of communication which is to execute the electronic fund transfer. The consumer must apply for such access device to the issuer. This access device must have been used with "actual authority", or there will have been an "unauthorized electronic fund transfer."[34] An unauthorized electronic fund transfer does not include a transfer initiated by a person whom the consumer has furnished with the access device. The authority will be terminated by the consumer informing the financial institution, the issuer of the access device, that a person is no longer authorized to use the device.[35] An unauthorized use of an access device creates a liability in the consumer of up to fifty dollars. Where the consumer fails to notify the financial institution, within two business days of discovering the loss or theft of an access device, the liability may be up to $500.00.[36] Where there is a failure to make such report within sixty days, the consumer will be liable for all unauthorized use after the sixty days, provided the financial institution can show that, but for the failure to notify them, the loss would not have occurred.[37]

---

[33] 12 C.F.R. §§ 205.2(a)(1), (2).

[34] 12 C.F.R. § 205.2(*l*).

[35] *Id.*

[36] 12 C.F.R. § 205.6(b)(1).

[37] 12 C.F.R. § 205.6(b)(2).

Joyce Russell v. First of America Bank-Michigan
File No. K87-428-CA4
1988 U.S. Dist. LEXIS 17225 (D. Mich. 1988)
September 28, 1988, Decided

RICHARD A. ENSLEN, D.J.

This matter is before the court on Defendants' Motion for Summary Judgment. For the reasons stated below, the Court will deny that motion in part and grant it in part.…

Facts

Plaintiff brings this action pursuant to the Electronic Fund Transfer Act, 15 U.S.C. § 1693a et seq., alleging that the defendants wrongfully failed to reimburse her for unauthorized withdrawals from her savings account. The facts are essentially undisputed. Mrs. Russell opened a savings account with the First of America Bank (the bank) in June, 1986. At the same time, she obtained an Automatic Teller Machine (ATM) card and a personal identification number (PIN) to enable her to access her savings account and make withdrawals from or deposits into that account using an automatic teller machine. A customer account may only be accessed through such a machine by using the PIN. Plaintiff was also given an Electronic Fund Transfer Agreement (EFT Agreement). This agreement explained, among other things, how to use the automatic teller machines, which transactions could be made using the card, the limitations on her liability for unauthorized transfers made using the card and what to do if her card was lost or stolen.[2] These disclosures are required under the Electronic Fund Transfer Act. See, 15 U.S.C. § 1693c. The bank required Mrs. Russell to sign the agreement before obtaining the card.

Mrs. Russell used the card and the automatic teller machines without incident for approximately one year. In September, 1987 she gave the card and her PIN to her oldest daughter, Dorothy, to use while Mrs. Russell was out of town. . . . Mrs. Russell wrote her PIN either on the card itself or on a piece of paper, to aid Dorothy in remembering the number. On September 28, 1987 Dorothy took the card and the PIN with her when she went to visit her doctor. . . . On the way home from the doctor's office, Dorothy left her wallet on a city bus, with the card and PIN inside it. . . . Although the wallet was later recovered, the card and PIN were not. . . . That day, Mrs. Russell returned from her trip and her daughter informed her that the card was missing. Mrs. Russell and her daughter went to the bank that evening, but it was closed. . . . Cleaning people working inside the bank gave them two telephone numbers to call to report the loss. . . . Upon returning home, Mrs. Russell phoned the numbers given to her. The first was a recording; the second was answered by a man who identified himself as an employee of the bank. This individual told Mrs. Russell that she would have to wait until the bank opened in the morning in order to report the loss of her card. . . . That evening, some individual other than Mrs. Russell or her daughter, used the card and PIN to withdraw $310 from Mrs. Russell's account. . . . This left a balance in the account of $7.42.

---

[2] Paragraph 2 of that agreement states as follows: You agree not to reveal your PIN to any person and not to write the PIN on the Card or on any item kept with the Card. Furthermore, you understand and acknowledge that the security of any account accessible through use of the Card depends upon maintaining possession of the Card and the secrecy of the assigned PIN. While Mrs. Russell contends that she did not read this agreement and that it was not explained to her, the Court finds this argument to be irrelevant to her claim. To the extent that the agreement is enforceable, it binds Mrs. Russell, regardless of whether she read it.

The next morning, September 29, 1987, Mrs. Russell went to the bank and informed them of the loss of her card. . . . The bank promptly discontinued the card's viability. Because Mrs. Russell had given her card to another person, and because she had written the PIN on the card or on a piece of paper kept with the card, the bank refused to reimburse Mrs. Russell for the amounts withdrawn from her account on September 29, 1987.

The bank argues in its motion that Mrs. Russell breached the EFT agreement by giving her card and PIN to her daughter, and by writing the PIN either on the card or on an item kept with the card. Because she breached the agreement, the bank contends that it has no duty to reimburse her for funds withdrawn from her account after the card and PIN were lost but before the loss was reported. . . .

Standard

In considering a motion for summary judgment, the narrow questions presented to this Court are whether there is "no genuine issue as to any material fact and [whether] the moving party is entitled to judgment as a matter of law." F.R.Civ.P. 56(c). The Court cannot try issues of fact on a Rule 56 motion, but is empowered only to determine whether there are issues to be tried. . . .

Discussion

Defendants' Motion for Summary Judgment. Section 1693g of the Electronic Fund Transfer Act limits a consumer's liability for unauthorized transfers from a bank account made through use of an automatic teller machine. 15 U.S.C. § 1693g(a). An unauthorized transfer is "an electronic fund transfer from a consumer's account initiated by a person other than the consumer without actual authority to initiate such transfer and from which the consumer receives no benefit." 15 U.S.C. § 1693a(11).

The term does not include any transfer "initiated by a person other than the consumer who is furnished with a card, code or other means of access to such consumer's account by such consumer, unless the consumer has notified the financial institution that transfer by such other person are no longer authorized." 15 U.S.C. § 1693a(11)(A).

Section 1693(a) provides that "In no event . . . shall the consumer's liability for an unauthorized transfer exceed the lesser of—" $50.00 or the amount of money transferred prior to the bank's receiving notice of an unauthorized transfer. 15 U.S.C. § 1693g(a). The statute further provides that reimbursement need not be made to the consumer where the consumer fails to promptly notify the bank of an unauthorized transfer. The consumer's liability for unauthorized transfers that result from the loss or theft of an ATM card may not exceed the lesser of $500.00 or the amount of money transferred from the account prior to notice, where the consumer fails to promptly notify the bank of the loss or theft.[4]

Section 1693g and the regulations promulgated by the Federal Reserve Board under that section evidence a clear congressional intent to limit consumers' liability for unauthorized transfers made with an ATM card. The statute and regulations establish a ceiling, rather than a floor, on the consumer's liability. While a state law or a contract between a financial institution and a consumer may further limit a consumer's exposure to loss from unauthorized transfers, 15 U.S.C. § 1693g(d), no consumer may be liable for losses in excess of the statutory text. 15 U.S.C. § 1693g(d) ("Except as provided in this section, a consumer incurs no liability from an unauthorized electronic fund transfer").[5]

The bank argues that its contract with Mrs. Russell makes her responsible for maintaining the secrecy of her PIN. Since she gave her card and PIN to her daughter, and since she wrote down her PIN, the bank argues that she breached the agreement and is liable for any transfers made as a result of this breach. This argument is clearly refuted both by the unequivocal language of section 1693g(e), and by the regulations promulgated

by the Federal Reserve Board pursuant to that statute. 15 U.S.C. 1693b.

Section 1693g(d) provides that "Nothing in this section imposes liability upon a consumer for an unauthorized . . . transfer in excess of his liability for such a transfer under . . . any agreement with the consumer's financial institution." Regulations promulgated under this section indicate that a consumer's liability for unauthorized transfers "shall not exceed" the liability imposed under an agreement between the consumer and the bank if "an agreement between the consumer and financial institution imposes *lesser liability*" than that imposed by the statute. 12 C.F.R. § 205.6(b)(5) (1988) (emphasis added). Thus, the statute and regulations clearly indicate that a financial institution may provide protection to its customers, in addition to that provided by federal law. Nothing in the statute indicates that the financial institution may, by agreement or otherwise, provide less protection to its customers, or increase its customers' exposure to liability for unauthorized transfers. Congress was able to write a statute allowing financial institutions to increase the protections available to consumers. Had it intended to allow financial institutions to decrease the available protections, it certainly was capable of indicating that intent in the statute. To hold that a bank's agreement with its customer could abrogate the protections provided by the statute would nullify section 1693g(e), which provides that no consumer may be subjected to liability in excess of that provided for under the statute. To the extent that the bank's Electronic Fund Transfer Agreement purports to increase a consumer's liability for unauthorized transfers, it is unenforceable.

This conclusion is further bolstered by the Federal Reserve Board's Official Interpretation of the Act. 12 C.F.R. § 205 Supp. II (1988). In a section containing questions and answers designed to interpret the Act for financial institutions, the Board noted:

Q: Consumer negligence. A consumer writes the PIN on the ATM card or on a piece of paper kept with the card—actions that may constitute negligence under state law. Do such actions affect the liability for unauthorized transfers that may be imposed upon the consumer?

A: No. The extent of the consumer's liability is determined by the promptness in reporting

---

[4] Mrs. Russell notified the bank within twenty-four hours of learning that her card and PIN were missing. The statute requires that notice of a lost or stolen card be given within two business days from the time she learns of the loss or theft. 15 U.S.C. § 1693g(a). Thus, there is no question that she complied with the statute's notice provisions.

[5] Cases decided under 15 U.S.C. § 1643, a statute providing similar protections to consumers whose credit cards have been subject to unauthorized use, further indicate congressional intent to limit customer liability in such instances to the $50.00 statutory maximum. . . .

loss or theft of an access device or unauthorized transfers appearing on a periodic statement. Negligence on the consumer's part cannot be taken into account to impose greater liability than is permissible under the act and Regulation E.

Id. at 133. This interpretation by the Federal Reserve Board staff, which is charged with the administrative enforcement of the Act, is entitled to deference from the Court, especially where it appears to be entirely consistent with the congressional intent in enacting this statute. Moreover, the interpretation indicates the board's opinion that, in circumstances directly analogous to those in the case at bar, the consumer's negligence is not grounds for exposing that individual to liability for unauthorized transfers above the statutory maximum.

Mrs. Russell promptly reported the loss or theft of her ATM card and PIN. Because she gave the bank notice within the two-day time period established by the statute, the bank was required to limit her liability for unauthorized transfers to $50.00. The fact that she may have breached the EFT Agreement by placing her PIN on or near her ATM card can have no effect on her liability. To hold otherwise would be to contravene the clear congressional intent to place a ceiling on consumers' liability for unauthorized transfers.

The bank's only other argument is that Mrs. Russell authorized the transfers from her account when she gave her ATM card and PIN to her daughter Dorothy. Section 1693a(11) of the Act indicates that transfers initiated by a person who has been given access to a consumer's account by the consumer are not to be considered "unauthorized" until the consumer gives the financial

institution notice that the third person is no longer authorized to use the account. The bank argues that "Any withdrawals from plaintiff's account through the use of the ATM card were initiated by plaintiff's daughter, who was furnished the card, together with the PIN, by plaintiff." Defendants' Brief at 7–8. Since Dorothy was given permission to use the card, the transfers are "authorized" and the Act's liability limitations do not apply. There is no support in the record for the contention that Dorothy made the transfers at issue. In her affidavit, she denies having done so, and there is no evidence to contradict that statement . . . . The only person Mrs. Russell authorized to use her account was her daughter Dorothy. . . . Again, the bank's submissions present no evidence to contradict that statement.[6]

Section 1693a(11) makes plain that, if the individual who transferred the funds at issue here was authorized to do so by Mrs. Russell, the bank would have no liability for transactions which occurred before Mrs. Russell notified the bank of the loss. However, Mrs. Russell's negligence in giving the card and PIN to her daughter, and her daughter's negligence in losing those items does not mean that the transfers were authorized by Mrs. Russell. The bank's argument would only have merit if Dorothy or some other authorized individual transferred the funds at issue. Since there is, at the very least, a dispute as to that factual issue, summary judgment is inappropriate.

---

[6] The bank bears the burden of proving that the transfer was authorized, or if unauthorized, to show that the exceptions to limited liability apply in this case. 15 U.S.C. § 1693g(c). The bank has, at least on this motion, failed to sustain that burden of proof.

NOTE

Since the use of an electronic fund transfer is practically instantaneous, it is not possible to stop payment once the pay order is given. But, where the pay order is an instruction to make periodic payments such as rental, mortgage, or installment payments, *i.e.*, a preauthorized transfer,[38] a consumer may stop payment by giving the financial institution an oral or written stop payment notice. Such notice must be received by the financial institution not later than three business days before the scheduled day on which the transfer was to occur. A written confirmation of an oral stop payment order can be

---

[38] 12 C.F.R. § 205.10(a).

demanded by the financial institution and will then have to be sent within fourteen days from the time of the demand, since oral stop payment orders cease to be binding after fourteen days.[39]

* * *

2. "Wholesale" Fund Transfers

Wholesale fund transfers involve the transfer of large amounts of money between banks or corporate giants. In the United States, Article 4A of the Uniform Commercial Code was developed to provide a legal framework for this type of transfer. U.C.C. Section 4A–104(a) defines a funds transfer as "the series of transactions, beginning with the originator's payment order, made for the purpose of making payment to the beneficiary of the order." To illustrate, Corporation A has contracted to pay Corporation B $10 million for the purchase of computer equipment. If both corporations have accounts at First National Bank, then Corporation A, as the originator of the funds transfer, will issue a payment order to the bank instructing it to credit the account of Corporation B for the amount stated above. This type of transfer, though involving an in-house electronic execution, is not a "Funds Transfer" within U.C.C. Article 4A. If both corporations do not use the same bank, a wire transfer will need to be arranged which may require the services of an intermediary bank. The resulting transaction, or series of transactions, is a "Funds Transfer" covered under U.C.C. Article 4A.[40]

To communicate the payment order, and to credit and debit the respective accounts involved in a funds transfer, a bank will need to depend on a wire transfer system. Several wire transfer systems, noted for high speed communication, efficiency, and relatively low transaction costs, exist to facilitate the transfer of funds internationally as well as domestically. In the United States, the National Federal Reserve Wire Network, or Fedwire, links Federal Reserve banks and their branches through an electronic central switch system. This system acts as a message and settlement service between depository institutions having accounts with Federal Reserve banks. As transactions are completed, the Federal Reserve credits and debits accounts of the Fedwire users involved, i.e., the transaction is settled on the books of the New York Federal Reserve Bank by off-setting debits and credits. The federal government and agencies also use Fedwire to transfer U.S. government securities between members of the Federal Reserve System.

Banks or corporations having no relation with Federal Reserve banks have available to them other wire transfer systems. CHIPS, the Clearing House Interbank Payment Systems, is the privately operated wire transfer service of the New York Clearinghouse Association. Transactions through CHIPS often involve international customers engaging in dollar transactions with domestic banks. Like Fedwire, CHIPS offers both a communications and a settlement service.[41] However, settlement through CHIPS occurs between accounts on the books of the New York Federal Reserve Bank. Then there is the National Automated

---

[39] 12 C.F.R. § 205.10(c).

[40] *Compare* the Electronic Fund Transfer Act, 15 U.S.C. §§ 1693 to 1693r.

[41] CHIPS rules have incorporated the provisions of U.C.C. Articles 4 and 4A.

Clearing House Association, (NACHA), which regulates the Automated Clearing House (ACH). ACH is the predominant electronic payment system for corporations and consumers in the United States.[42] ACH offers clearing and payment services to banks and corporations, as well as to consumers.[43]

Finally, the Society for Worldwide International Financial Telecommunications (SWIFT) provides a communications service for international funds transfers. This service, like CHIPS, is a non-government operation. Its purpose is to facilitate multicurrency transactions. SWIFT does not provide a settlement service for transactions communicated through it. As its client base expanded, SWIFT developed not only more efficient communications, but also a wider variety of services.[44]

The United Nations Commission on International Trade Law (UNCITRAL) draft Model Fund Transfer Law was adopted by the U.N. General Assembly.[45] This model law, if enacted by member states, will unify the rules governing international wholesale credit transfers.[46]

---

[43] BAUM & PERITT, ELECTRONIC CONTRACTING, PUBLISHING, AND EDI LAWS, 232 (John Wiley & Sons, Inc., 1991).

[43] On the consumer level contractual rules will be subject to the Federal Electronic Fund Transfer Act, 15 U.S.C. §§ 1693 to 1693r. *See also* U.C.C. § 4-103 which allows such clearing house rules to operate as "variation by agreement." On the wholesale level, NACHA has adopted U.C.C. Articles 4 and 4A by incorporating these provisions into its rules.

[44] For a more extensive treatment of the workings of wire transfer systems, *see* D. BAKER AND R. BRANDEL, THE LAW OF ELECTRONIC FUND TRANSFER SYSTEMS (1989).

[45] Report of the United Nations Commission on International Trade Law, 25th Sess. U.N. Gen. Assembly Doc. Supp. No. 17 (A/47/17) Annex 1 (1992).

[46] For a comparison of Article 4A and the Model Law, see Felsenfeld, *Strange Bedfellows for Electronic Funds Transfers: Proposed Article 4A of the Uniform Commercial Code and the UNCITRAL Model Law* 42 ALA. L.REV. 723 (1991).

Delbrueck & Co. v. Manufacturers Hanover Trust Company

609 F.2d 1047 (2nd Cir. 1979)

[Footnote 1 at p. 1049]

1. We reproduce in full Judge Broderick's discussion of the CHIPS system, 464 F.Supp. 989 at 992 n.5:

"The mechanics of effecting an interbank payment under the CHIPS system are as follows: When the paying or sending bank receives a telex from one of its customers instructing it to make a payment to a receiving bank, another member of the CHIPS system, for the account of one of the receiving bank's customers, the paying bank first tests and verifies the telex. Thereafter, the tested and verified telex is sent to one of the CHIPS computer terminal operators and the payment order contained in the telex is programmed into the terminal by typing into the computer the relevant information—*i.e.*, the identifying codes for the party originating the transfer, the remitting bank, the receiving bank, the party for whom the receiving bank is receiving the transfer and the amount of the transfer. This information is then transmitted to the central computer located at the Clearing House, which, based upon the identifying codes searches out all the necessary clerical information, stores the message and causes a sending form to be automatically typed at the sending bank.

Once the programming of the computer has been completed, the send form is sent to the appropriate area at the sending bank for approval. When a determination is made at the sending bank to make the payment, the form is returned to one of the computer terminal operators, reinserted in the computer and the release is depressed. At that moment, the central computer at the Clearing House causes a credit ticket to be printed automatically at the terminal of the receiving bank and a debit ticket to be printed at the terminal of the sending bank. Further, the central computer automatically makes a permanent record of the transaction and debits the Clearing House account of the sending bank and credits the Clearing House account of the receiving bank. . . .

The funds received by a receiving bank for the account of one of its customers via the receipt of a CHIPS credit message are made available to the customer and can be drawn upon by the customer in the discharge of its obligations that same day, as soon as the receiving bank is aware of the fact that the funds have been received. This running tabulation by the receiving bank is generally referred to as a 'shadow balance.'

At the end of the day, the central computer correlates all the day's transactions, nets out the debits and credits, and prints out reports showing which banks owe money and which have money due them. That information is delivered to the New York Federal Reserve Bank the next business day and adjustments are made on the appropriate books of account."

See generally Richard M. Gottlieb, *Payment, Settlement, and Finality*, in *UCC Article 4-A, A Practical Guide for Bankers and Bank Counsel* (Am. Bankers Ass'n 1991).

3. How a Funds Transfer is Initiated—The Payment Order

The originator of a fund transfer begins the process by initiating an instruction, a payment order, to her bank, the originator's bank, to pay a stated amount to a beneficiary through a designated receiving bank, the beneficiary's bank. The originator's bank receiving a customer's payment order qualifies as a receiving bank. On accepting the payment order,

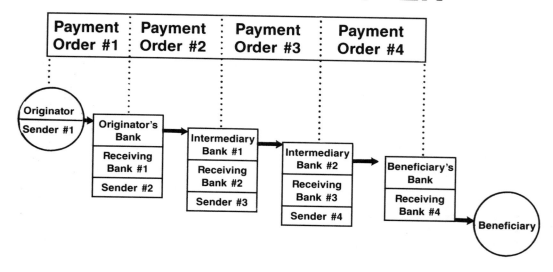

the bank will originate its own payment order (as a sender) either direct to the beneficiary's bank or, if it is not in a relationship with that bank, to an intermediary bank which will then be a receiving bank. This bank, if it accepts the payment order, will execute it by originating a payment order and sending it on. This process will continue until the payment order is received and accepted by the beneficiary's bank. The beneficiary's bank then will make payment to the beneficiary or it will credit the beneficiary's account. It can be seen, therefore, that a number of originating and receiving banks could be involved before the beneficiary's bank credits the beneficiary's account.

Each bank in this process must check the authenticity of the payment order in accordance with its agreement with the originator/sender/intermediary bank from which it has received a payment order. Such agreement generally provides some specifics including "that the authenticity of payment orders . . . will be verified pursuant to a security procedure." If a receiving bank can show that its security procedure is commercially reasonable and that, on acceptance, it acted in good faith and in compliance with its security procedure and any written instructions received from the originator/sender, it will be able to charge the originator/sender from which it received the payment order even where the payment order was not authorized.[47] Where payment orders are sent by electric data input (EDI), cryptography may be used for such verification.

U.C.C. Section 4A-103(a)(1) requires that the payment order be an unconditional order to pay a fixed or determinable amount of money to the beneficiary. It may also contain an indication to do so on a specified "due date." The originator/sender of the payment order undertakes to reimburse the receiving bank for its compliance with the payment order. There is an expectation of the existence of a corresponding credit relationship between the banks in the system. Absent such correspondent relationship, a receiving bank can insist on payment before it accepts the payment order from the sender.[48] In transmitting a payment order, an originator/sender may use one of the available communication systems, for example, Fedwire, CHIPS or SWIFT. These communication systems act as agents of the sender who will be bound to the receiving bank accepting the payment order, in accordance with a message transmitted by such communication system.[49] If an error arises in such transmission, the originator will have to seek its remedy against the communication system[50] and not against the receiving bank.[51]

Once the receiving bank accepts the payment order it cannot be rescinded. U.C.C. § 4A-211(b). The parties may, however, by rules of a fund transfer system or otherwise, agree to cancellation of an accepted payment order. A cancelled payment order cannot be

---

[47] U.C.C. § 4A-202(b). The "commercial reasonableness" of a security procedure is a question of law for the court to decide. U.C.C. § 4A-202(c).

[48] U.C.C. §§ 4A-209(b)(2), 4A-403(a)(1), (2).

[49] U.C.C. § 4A-206.

[50] Absent bad faith, consequential damages will not be recoverable. Nor is there strict liability in tort created by such error. The message transmitted is not a "product" in the physical sense. Central Coordinates, Inc. v. Morgan Guarantee Trust Co., 129 Misc. 2d 804, 494 N.Y.S.2d 602 (Special Term 1985).

[51] A recovery from the beneficiary on the underlying transaction may also be possible should the error result in an over payment.

accepted subsequently.[52] Neither the originator nor the originator's bank can rescind a payment order when intermediary banks have accepted the payment order. The originator is confined to seek her remedy from the beneficiary. It may be possible for the originator, if timely, to obtain an injunction to prevent the originator's bank from executing a payment order; or to prevent the beneficiary's bank from disbursing the funds to the beneficiary; or to prevent the beneficiary from withdrawing funds credited to his account with the beneficiary's bank. Intermediary banks cannot be enjoined. Proper cause must be shown before a court will issue an injunction. U.C.C. § 4A-503.

Where an execution date is indicated, banks should delay acceptance until that date, since the originator/sender is not obligated to reimburse the receiving bank until that date.[53] A payment by the sender prior to that date may create difficulties if the obligation to pay does not arise, or local law prevents recovery for such erroneous payment by the originator/sender.[54]

a. Obligations of the Parties

(i) *Sender (originator) and Receiving Bank*

U.C.C. Article 4A does not impose on a receiving bank a duty to accept and therefore to execute a sender's payment order. Such duty must be expressly agreed to by the parties.[55] Article 4A, however, does encourage a party to take action when a payment order is received, as failure to act may result in a bank being liable to a sender for interest earned during the lapsed time on the sums received.

A receiving bank may accept or reject a sender's payment order. Acceptance can take the form of acting on the payment order, for example when a receiving bank, other than the beneficiary's bank, executes its own payment order. For an acceptance to have occurred in this manner, the payment order sent by the receiving bank must comply with and follow the instructions of the sender's payment order.[56] The decision to accept a payment order may turn on whether, after performing an agreed-upon security procedure,[57] a bank determines that the payment order was authorized or was unauthorized, fraudulently issued, or erroneous.[58]

If a receiving bank wishes to reject the payment order, it must provide the sender with oral, written or electronic notice of rejection.[59] Notice is effective when given. It must be communicated by reasonable means or it will be effective only as of the time it was received. If a bank neither accepts (executes) or rejects, it may be liable to pay the sender interest

---

[52] U.C.C. §§ 4A-211(e), (f).

[53] U.C.C. § 4A-402(b).

[54] U.C.C. § 4A-402(d). *See also* Banque Worms v. Bankamerica Int'l, 77 N.Y. 2d 362, 568 N.Y.S.2d 541, 570 N.E.2d 189 (1991); and 928 F.2d 538 (2d Cir. 1991).

[55] U.C.C. § 4A-212.

[56] U.C.C. § 4A-302(a)(1).

[57] U.C.C. § 4A-201.

[58] U.C.C. §§ 4A-201 to 4A-205.

[59] U.C.C. § 4A-210.

on the amount of the order for the number of days that elapsed after the execution date.[60]

A sender may avoid liability on an erroneous or unauthorized payment by timely revocation of that order. To be effective, a sender's revocation request must be received at a time and in a manner that gives the receiving bank a chance to act on the revocation, i.e., before having accepted the payment order.[61] For this reason, banks are advised not to accept a payment order before an indicated execution date.

(ii) *Obligations arising out of execution*

U.C.C. Section 4A-301 provides that execution of a payment order occurs when a receiving bank, other than the beneficiary's bank, issues a payment order intended to carry out the payment order it has received.[62]

If a receiving bank decides to accept and execute a payment order, it is responsible for ensuring that funds are transferred in the correct amount, at the correct time. The sender will only be liable for the amount stated in its payment order as transmitted by the communication system. If a receiving bank has executed by issuing a wrong payment order, the sender is not obligated to pay. The burden of detecting errors however, is on the sender of a payment order.[63]

Recovery from the originator of a payment order erroneously executed in a larger amount is limited to the actual amount of the payment order received.[64] Where an erroneous execution or payment of a payment order results in payment to the wrong beneficiary, reimbursement cannot be demanded from the originator/sender.[65] In either case any recovery from the person paid will be governed by local laws regarding mistake and restitution.[66] The issue will be whether the jurisdiction applies the "discharge for value" rule.

---

[60] U.C.C. § 4A-210(4). The UNCITRAL Model Law requires a receiving bank to give notice if it intends to reject. Failure to do so, however, is an implicit acceptance, and the bank must therefore execute the payment order or face the possibility of being held liable for the customer's losses (interest, exchange-rate changes, expense of new order and attorney fees, and consequential damages if bank's failure to act was intentional). *See* Article 5(2)(a).

[61] U.C.C. § 4A-211.

[62] Communications systems, such as Western Union or SWIFT, and wire transfer systems, such as Fedwire or CHIPS, cannot execute payment orders. They are not banks. A beneficiary's bank also does not execute a payment order. It accepts a payment order by paying the beneficiary or crediting her account.

[63] *See* U.C.C. §§ 4A-303, 4A-304. The UNCITRAL Model Law places the responsibility of detecting errors on the receiving bank, which is placed under the obligation of continually checking for errors in payment orders. This approach is contrary to the quick execution encouraged by Article 4A. *See* Articles 6 and 8 of the Model Law.

[64] U.C.C. § 4A-303(a). If a lesser sum is sent or paid, recovery from the orginator/sender requires prompt correction. U.C.C. § 4A-303(b).

[65] U.C.C. § 4A-303(c).

[66] U.C.C. § 4A-303(a), (c). A customer of the originator's bank may have had her account debited by the bank for an unauthorized payment order, *see* U.C.C. § 4A-202, the customer has one year to claim reimbursement. U.C.C. § 4A-505.

Banque Worms v. BankAmerica International

77 N.Y.2d 362, 568 N.Y.S.2d 541, 570 N.E.2d 189 (1991)

ALEXANDER, Judge.

[The United States Court of Appeals for the Second Circuit certified to the N.Y. Court of Appeals the question whether New York would apply the "discharge for value" rule to a mistaken wire transfer, or the common law rule that money paid under mistake may be recovered, unless the payment caused the recipient to change position so that it would be unjust to demand restitution. The discharge for value rule provides that where a sum of money is sent to a creditor by mistake, the creditor need not return the money when he has applied it in discharge of a debt owed to him. The Court of Appeals, Alexander, J., held that the "discharge for value" rule would be applied. The Second Circuit accepted this resolution and applied it to the facts holding that Banque Worms was entitled to retain the money involved, 928 F.2d 538 (2d Cir. 1991).]

On April 10, 1989, Security Pacific International Bank (Security Pacific), a Federally chartered banking corporation with offices in New York City, mistakenly wired $1,974,267.97 on behalf of Spedley Securities (Spedley), an Australian corporation, into the account of Banque Worms, a French Bank, maintained with BankAmerica International (BankAmerica), another Federally chartered bank with New York offices. Initially intending to make payment on its debt to Banque Worms under a revolving credit agreement, Spedley instructed Security Pacific, which routinely effected wire transfers for Spedley, to electronically transfer funds from Security Pacific to Banque Worms' account at BankAmerica.

A few hours after directing this wire transfer, Spedley, by a second telex, directed Security Pacific to stop payment to Banque Worms and to make payment instead to National Westminster Bank USA (Natwest USA) for the same amount. At the time Security Pacific received the telexes, Spedley had a credit balance of only $84,500 in its account at Security Pacific, but later that morning, Security Pacific received additional funds sufficient to cover the transaction and then began to execute the transaction. However, in mis-

taken disregard of Spedley's second telex canceling the wire transfer to Banque Worms, Security Pacific transferred the funds into Banque Worms' account at BankAmerica. The funds were credited to the account after Banque Worms was notified through the Clearing House Interbank Payment System (CHIPS) that the funds had been received. That afternoon, Security Pacific executed Spedley's second payment order and transferred $1,974,267.97 to Natwest USA. Spedley's account at Security Pacific was debited twice to record both wire transfers thus producing an overdraft.

Meanwhile, at Security Pacific's request made prior to the transfer to Natwest USA, BankAmerica agreed to return the funds mistakenly transferred, provided Security Pacific furnished a United States Council on International Banking, Inc. (CIB) indemnity. The indemnity was furnished and the funds returned to Security Pacific on the following day. Banque Worms, however, refused BankAmerica's request that it consent to its account being debited to reflect the return of the funds. Consequently BankAmerica called upon Security Pacific to perform pursuant to the CIB indemnity and return the funds. Security Pacific's attempt to obtain funds from Spedley to cover this indemnity was unavailing because by that time, Spedley had entered into involuntary liquidation.

Banque Worms brought suit against BankAmerica in the United States District Court for the Southern District of New York seeking to compel BankAmerica to recredit $1,974,267.97 to Banque Worms' account. BankAmerica instituted a third-party action against Security Pacific for return of the funds, and Security Pacific counterclaimed against Banque Worms seeking a declaration that neither Banque Worms nor BankAmerica were entitled to the $1,974,267.97. Eventually, for reasons not here pertinent, Security Pacific returned the funds to BankAmerica, BankAmerica recredited Banque Worms' account and was voluntarily dismissed from the case leaving only Banque Worms and Security Pacific as the sole contestants seeking entitlement to the $1,974,267.97.

On their respective motion and cross motion for summary judgment, the District Court, applying the "discharge for value" rule, granted judgment for Banque Worms. Security Pacific appealed to the United States Court of Appeals for the Second Circuit, arguing that New York neither recognized nor applied the "discharge for value" rule in situations such as this; that the controlling rule under New York law was the "mistake of fact" rule pursuant to which, in order to be entitled to retain the mistakenly transferred funds, Banque Worms was required to demonstrate detrimental reliance. The case is before us upon a certified question from the Second Circuit (*see*, section 500.17 of the Court of Appeals Rules of Practice [22 NYCRR]) inquiring "[w]hether in this case, where a concededly mistaken wire transfer by [Security Pacific] was made to [Banque Worms], a creditor of Spedley, New York would apply the 'Discharge for Value' rule as set forth at section 14 of the Restatement of Restitution or, in the alternative, whether in this case New York would apply the rule that holds that money paid under a mistake may be recovered, unless the payment has caused such a change in the position of the receiving party that it would be unjust to require the party to refund."

For the reasons that follow, we conclude that, under the circumstances of this case, the "discharge for value" rule should be applied, thus entitling Banque Worms to retain the funds mistakenly transferred without the necessity of demonstrating detrimental reliance.

I

A

In the area of restitution, New York has long recognized the rule that "if A pays money to B upon the erroneous assumption of the former that he is indebted to the latter, an action may be maintained for its recovery. The reason for the rule is obvious. Since A was mistaken in the assumption that he was indebted to B, the latter is not entitled to retain the money acquired by the mistake of the former, even though the mistake is the result of negligence." (*Ball v. Shepard*, 202 N.Y. 247, 253, 95 N.E. 719.) This rule has been applied where the cause of action has been denominated as one for money had and received ... for unjust enrichment or restitution ... or upon a theory of quasi contract.... Where, however, the receiving party has changed its position to its detriment in reliance upon the mistake so that requiring that it refund the money paid would be

"unfair," recovery has been denied....

This rule has evolved into the "mistake of fact" doctrine, in which detrimental reliance is a requisite factor, and which provides that "money paid under a mistake of fact may be recovered back, however negligent the party paying may have been in making the mistake, unless the payment has caused such a change in the position of the other party that it would be unjust to require him to refund." (*National Bank v. National Mechanics' Banking Assn.*, 55 N.Y. 211, 213.)

The Restatement of Restitution, on the other hand, has established the "discharge for value" rule which provides that "[a] creditor of another or one having a lien on another's property who has received from a third person any benefit in discharge of the debt or lien, is under no duty to make restitution therefor, although the discharge was given by mistake of the transferor as to his interests or duties, if the transferee made no misrepresentation and did not have notice of the transferor's mistake" (Restatement of Restitution § 14 [1]).

The question as to which of these divergent rules New York will apply to electronic fund transfers divides the parties and prompts the certified question from the Second Circuit. Security Pacific argues that New York has rejected the "discharge for value" rule and has required that detrimental reliance under the "mistake of fact" rule be demonstrated in all cases other than where the mistake was induced by fraud. Banque Worms, on the other hand, invokes the "discharge for value" rule, arguing that because it is a creditor of Spedley and had no knowledge that the wire transfer was erroneous, it is entitled to keep the funds. It points out, as indicated by the official comment to section 14 (1) of the Restatement of Restitution, that the "discharge for value" rule is simply a "specific application of the underlying principle of bona fide purchase" set forth in section 13 of the Restatement (Restatement of Restitution § 14, *comment* a)....

Indeed one may find, as does Banque Worms, language in a myriad of cases that arguably lends support to the proposition that New York, long ago, embraced the "discharge for value" rule.... On the other hand, cases can also be cited where the language employed supports the contrary view—that New York not only eschews the "discharge for value" rule, as Security Pacific argues, but also embraces exclusively the detrimental reliance rule-mistake of fact doctrine . . . These cases for the most part, however, present issues involving more traditional aspects of mistake and restitution, and do not satisfactorily address the unique problems presented by electronic funds transfer technology.

While courts have attempted in wire transfer cases to employ, by analogy, the rules of the more traditional areas of law, such as contract law, the law of negotiable instruments and the special relations between banks, these areas are governed by principles codified in articles 3 and 4 of the Uniform Commercial Code. Various commentators found these efforts ineffective and inadequate to deal with the problems presented (see, Official Comment to U.C.C. § 4A–102; Revisions of UCC Article 4A Postponed Due to Federal Preemption, ABA is Told, 51 Banking Rep. 282 [BNA] [Aug. 15, 1988]). As pointed out by the Official Comment to article 4A, "attempts to define rights and obligations in funds transfers by general principles or by analogy to rights and obligations in negotiable instruments law or the law of check collection have not been satisfactory" (Official Comment to U.C.C. § 4A–102, 2A ULA [Master ed.], 1990 Supp.Pamph; see also, Revisions of UCC Article 4A Postponed Due to Federal Preemption, ABA is Told, 51 Banking Rep. 282 [BNA] [Aug. 15, 1988]). Consequently, it was concluded, as the Prefatory Note to the new article 4A of the UCC approved by the National Conference of Commissioners on Uniform State Law and the American Law Institute observes, that a new article was needed because "[t]here is no comprehensive body of law that defines the rights and obligations that arise from wire transfers." (2A ULA [Master ed.], at 143, 1990 Supp Pamph.)

B

Electronic funds transfers have become the preferred method utilized by businesses and financial institutions to effect payments and transfers of a substantial volume of funds. These transfers, commonly referred to as wholesale wire transfers,[1]

---

[1] The Official Comment to U.C.C. § 4A–102 notes that while most payments covered by article 4A are usually referred to as "wire transfers" and involve an electronic transmission, other types of transmissions such as letter, or other written communication or oral communication, are also covered, thus the broader term "funds transfer" is used in preference to the narrower term "wire transfer." (2A ULA [Master ed.], at 147, 1990 Supp.Pamph.).

differ from other payment methods in a number of significant respects, a fact which accounts in large measure for their popularity. Funds are moved faster and more efficiently than by traditional payment instruments, such as checks. The transfers are completed at a relatively low cost, which does not vary widely depending on the amount of the transfer, because the price charged reflects primarily the cost of the mechanical aspects of the funds transfer (Prefatory Note to U.C.C. art. 4A). Most transfers are completed within one day and can cost as little as $10 to carry out a multimillion dollar transaction. . . . (Prefatory Note to U.C.C. art. 4A). The popularity of wholesale wire transfers is evidenced by the fact that nearly $1 trillion in transactions occur each day, averaging $5 million per transfer and on peak days, this figure often approaches $2 trillion. . . .

Wholesale wire transfers are generally made over the two principal wire payment systems: the Federal Reserve Wire Transfer Network (Fedwire) and the CHIPS. The CHIPS network handles 95% of the international transfers made in dollars, transferring an average of $750 billion per day (see generally, Note, Liability for Lost or Stolen Funds in Cases of Name and Number Discrepancies in Wire Transfers: Analysis of the Approaches Taken in the United States and Internationally, 22 Cornell Intl.L.J. 91 [1990]). These funds are transferred through participating banks located in New York because all of the banks belonging to the CHIPS network must maintain a regulated presence in New York. As a result, this State is considered the national and international center for wholesale wire transfers.

The low cost of electronic funds transfers is an important factor in the system's popularity and this is so even though banks executing wire transfers often risk significant liability as a result of losses occasioned by mistakes and errors, the most common of which involve the payment of funds to the wrong beneficiary or in an incorrect amount (see, American Law Institute Approves UCC Article Governing Wire Transfers, 52 Banking Rep. 1150 [BNA] [June 5, 1989]). Thus, a major policy issue facing the drafters of U.C.C. article 4A was determining how the risk of loss might best be allocated, while preserving a unique price structure. In order to prevent or minimize losses, the industry had adopted and employed various security procedures designed to prevent losses[3] such as the use of codes, identifying words or numbers, call-back procedures and limits on payment amounts or beneficiaries that may be paid.

As indicated above, it was the consensus among various commentators that existing rules of law did not adequately address the problems presented by these wholesale electronic funds transfers. Thus, the National Conference of Commissioners on Uniform State Laws (NCCUSL) and the American Law Institute (ALI) undertook to develop a body of unique principles of law that would address every aspect of the electronic funds transfer process and define the rights and liabilities of all parties involved in such transfers (Prefatory Note to U.C.C. art. 4A, *op. cit.*). After extensive investigation and debate and through a number of drafts, in 1989, both the NCCUSL and the ALI approved a new article 4A of the Uniform Commercial Code (*see generally*, Ballen, Baxter, Davenport, Rougeau, and Veltri, *Commercial Paper, Bank Deposits and Collections, and Other Payment Systems*, 45 Bus.Law 2341 [Aug. 1990]). In 1990, the New York State Legislature adopted the new article 4A and incorporated it into the New York Uniform Commercial Code....[4] Although the new statute, which became effective January 1, 1991, may not be applied retroactively to resolve the issues presented by this litigation, the statute's legislative history and the history of

article 4A of the Uniform Commercial Code from which it is derived and the policy considerations addressed by this legislation, can appropriately inform our decision and serve as persuasive authority in aid of the resolution of the issue presented in this case....

II

Both the NCCUSL and ALI drafters of article 4A and the New York Legislature sought to achieve a number of important policy goals through enactment of this article. National uniformity in the treatment of electronic funds transfers is an important goal, as are speed, efficiency, certainty (i.e., to enable participants in fund transfers to have better understanding of their rights and liabilities), and finality. Establishing finality in electronic fund wire transactions was considered a singularly important policy goal (*American Law Institute Approves UCC Article Governing Wire Transfers*, 52 Banking Rep. 1150 [BNA] [June 5, 1989]). Payments made by electronic funds transfers in compliance with the provisions of article 4A are to be the equivalent of cash payments, irrevocable except to the extent provided for in article 4A ... *see also*, *Delbrueck & Co. v. Manufacturers Hanover Trust Co.*, 609 F.2d 1047, 1049–1051 [2d Cir. (1979)] [once an electronic fund transfer is completed and the funds released, the transaction is final and irrevocable under the CHIPS system]).

This concern for finality in business transactions has long been a significant policy consideration in this State. In a different but pertinent context, we observed in *Hatch v. Fourth Natl. Bank,* 147 N.Y. 184, 192, 41 N.E. 403, that "to permit in every case of the payment of a debt an inquiry as to the source from which the debtor derived the money, and a recovery if shown to have been dishonestly acquired, would disorganize all business operations and entail an amount of risk and uncertainty which no enterprise could bear."*

---

[3] The Official Comment to U.C.C. § 4A-201 as drafted by the American Law Institute and National Conference of Commissioners on Uniform State Laws states that "it is standard practice to use security procedures that are designed to assure the authenticity of the message * * * [and] to detect error in the content of messages. * * * The question of whether loss that may result from the transmission of a spurious or erroneous payment order will be borne by the receiving bank or the sender or purported sender is affected by whether a security procedure was or was not in effect and whether there was or was not compliance with the procedure." (2A ULA [Master ed.], at 156–157, 1990 Supp.Pamph.)

[4] The new article 4A will regulate funds transfers other than consumer transactions governed by the Federal Electronic Fund Transfer Act of 1978 (15 USC § 1693 *et seq.*). It will not apply to consumer transactions such as check payments or credit card payments for the Federal EFTA will continue to govern these transactions. If any part of a fund transfer is covered by the EFTA, the entire funds transfer will be excluded from article 4A.

---

* [Editor: *See*, however, the effect of the U.S. Government's power to consider funds alleged to be proceeds of illegal narcotic transactions forfeited under 21 U.S.C. § 881 et seq. and 18 U.S.C. § 981 et seq. discussed in Manufacturas International, Ltda. v. Manufacturers Hanover Trust Co., 792 F.Supp. 180 (E.D. N.Y. 1992) (forfeitures of funds transferred by electronic transfer is not a violation of wiretap laws, such funds can be demanded even from intermediary banks)].

A consequence of this concern has been the adoption of a rule which precludes recovery from a third person, who as the result of the mistake of one or both of the parties to an original transaction receives payment by one of them in good faith in the ordinary course of business and for a valuable consideration (*see, Ball v. Shepard*, 202 N.Y. 247, *supra*). This rule is grounded in "considerations of public policy and convenience for the protection and encouragement of trade and commerce by guarding the security and certainty of business transactions, since to hold otherwise would obviously introduce confusion and danger into all commercial dealings." ... We have previously held that from these considerations, "[t]he law wisely * * * adjudges that the possession of money vests the title in the holder as to third persons dealing with him and receiving it in due course of business and in good faith upon a valid consideration." (*Stephens v. Board of Educ.*, 79 N.Y. 183, 187–188.)

The "discharge for value" rule is consistent with and furthers the policy goal of finality in business transactions and may appropriately be applied in respect to electronic funds transfers. When a beneficiary receives money to which it is entitled and has no knowledge that the money was erroneously wired, the beneficiary should not have to wonder whether it may retain the funds; rather, such a beneficiary should be able to consider the transfer of funds as a final and complete transaction, not subject to revocation.

We believe such an application accords with the legislative intent and furthers the policy considerations underlying article 4-A of the New York Uniform Commercial Code. Although no provision of article 4-A calls, in express terms, for the application of the "discharge for value" rule, the statutory scheme and the language of various pertinent sections, as amplified by the Official Comments to the UCC, support our conclusion that the "discharge for value" rule should be applied in the circumstances here presented.

Subject to certain exceptions not here relevant, N.Y. U.C.C. § 4-A-209 (b) provides that a beneficiary's bank accepts a payment order when the bank pays the beneficiary by crediting the beneficiary's account and notifying the beneficiary of the right to withdraw the credit (*see*, U.C.C. § 4-A-209 [b] [1]; 4-A-405 [a] [i]). When a payment order has been accepted by the beneficiary's bank, cancellation or amendment of that payment order is not effective unless, for example, the order was

issued because of a mistake of the sender resulting in a duplicate payment order or an order that directs payment to a beneficiary not entitled to receive the funds (*see*, U.C.C. § 4-A-211 [c] [2] [i], [ii]). Where a duplicate payment order is erroneously executed or the payment order is issued to a beneficiary different from the beneficiary intended by the sender, the receiving bank in either case is entitled to recover the erroneously paid amount from the beneficiary "to the extent allowed by the law governing mistake and restitution" (*see*, U.C.C. § 4-A-303 [a], [c]).

More specifically, U.C.C. § 4-A-303(c) instructs that "[i]f a receiving bank executes the payment order of the sender by issuing a payment order to a beneficiary different from the beneficiary of the sender's order and the funds transfer is completed on the basis of that error, the sender * * * [is] not obliged to pay the payment order. The issuer of the erroneous order is entitled to recover from the beneficiary * * * to the extent allowed by the law governing mistake and restitution." The Official Comment to U.C.C. § 4A-303 from which the identical New York statute is derived, explains that although section 4A-402(c) obligates the sender to pay the transfer order to the beneficiary's bank if that bank has accepted the payment order, section 4A-303 takes precedence and "states the liability of the sender and the rights of the receiving bank in various cases of erroneous execution" (*see*, Official Comment to U.C.C. § 4A-303, comment 1, 2A ULA [Master ed.], 1990 Supp.Pamph).

Thus, as in the example discussed in comment 2, where the originator's bank mistakenly directs payment of $2,000,000 to the beneficiary's bank but payment of only $1,000,000 was directed by the originator, the originator's bank is obligated to pay the $2,000,000 if the beneficiary's bank has accepted the payment, although the originator need only pay its bank the $1,000,000 ordered. The originator's bank ordinarily would be entitled to recover the excess payment from the beneficiary. The comment points out, however, that "if Originator owed $2,000,000 to Beneficiary and Beneficiary received the extra $1,000,000 in good faith in discharge of the debt, Beneficiary may be allowed to keep it. In this case Originator's Bank has paid an obligation of Originator and under the law of restitution * * * Originator's Bank would be subrogated to Beneficiary's rights against Originator on the obligation paid by Originator's Bank" (*see, Official Comment to*

U.C.C. § 4A-303, comment 2, 2A ULA [Master ed.], 1990 Supp.Pamph).

A further example discussed in comment 3 of the Official Comment is of a duplicate payment order erroneously made, which transfers a second $1,000,000 payment to beneficiary's bank and beneficiary's bank accepts the payment. Although the originator's bank is only entitled to receive $1,000,000 from the originator, it must pay $2,000,000 to beneficiary's bank and would be relegated to a remedy the same as "that of a receiving bank that executes by issuing an order in an amount greater than the sender's order. It may recover the overpayment from Beneficiary to the extent allowed by the law governing mistake and restitution and in a proper case * * * may have subrogation rights if it is not entitled to recover from Beneficiary" (Official Comment to U.C.C. § 4A-303, comment 3, 2A ULA [Master ed.], 1990 Supp.Pamph).

Although it seems clear from these provisions of article 4A and the Official Comments that the drafters of U.C.C. article 4A contemplated that the "discharge for value" rule could appropriately be applied in respect to electronic fund transfers, Security Pacific argues that to do so would undermine the low cost structure of wholesale electronic fund transfers and impose extraordinary risks upon banks implementing these enormously large transactions. This argument is unpersuasive. Article 4A contemplates, in the first instance, that a mistake such as occurred here can be effectively held to a minimum through the utilization of "commercially reasonable" security procedures in effecting wire transfers. These security procedures are for the purpose of verifying the authenticity of the order or detecting error in the transmission or content of the payment order or other communication (*see, e.g.,* N.Y. U.C.C. § 4-A-201).

For example, under N.Y. U.C.C. § 4-A-202 (b), if a bank accepts a payment order that purports to be that of its customer after verifying its authenticity through an agreed upon security procedure, the customer is bound to pay the order even if the payment order was not authorized. The customer will be liable, however, only if the court finds that the security procedure was a "commercially reasonable" method of providing security against unauthorized payment orders (*id.*). If the bank accepts an unauthorized payment order without verifying it in compliance with a security procedure, the loss will fall on the bank.[5]

Other mechanisms for preventing loss are also provided for in the statute. A bank may avoid a loss resulting from the insolvency of a sending bank by accepting the payment order on the condition that it first receives payment from the sending bank (*see,* N.Y. U.C.C. § 4-A-209 [b] [1] [ii]; [3]; 4-A-403 [a] [1], [2]; *see also, American Law Institute Approves UCC Article Governing Wire Transfers,* 52 Banking Rep 1150 [BNA] [June 5, 1989]; Prefatory Note to UCC art. 4A [a receiving bank can always avoid this risk by accepting a payment order after the bank has received payment]). Risk of loss can also be minimized by the institution keeping track of all transactions with a particular bank so that over-all debits and credits can be netted.

Application of the "discharge for value" rule to the circumstances presented here is particularly appropriate. The undisputed facts demonstrate that Security Pacific executed Spedley's initial order directing payment to Banque Worms notwithstanding having already received a cancellation of that order. The District Court also found that the second transfer to Natwest USA was executed despite the fact that Spedley's account did not have sufficient funds to cover this second transfer. Moreover, it appears that, as a creditor of Spedley, Banque Worms was a beneficiary entitled to the funds who made no "misrepresentation and did not have notice of the transferor's mistake."

Accordingly, we conclude, in answer to the certified question, that the "discharge for value" rule as set forth at section 14 of the Restatement of Restitution, should be applied in the circumstances in this case.

---

[5] Whether or not a particular security procedure is commercially reasonable is a question of law for the court, while whether the procedure was complied with is a question of fact (*see,* Official Comment to U.C.C. § 4A-203, comment 4, 2A ULA [Master ed.], 1990 Supp.Pamph).

(iii) *Payment and Settlement Obligations*

Assuming that the payment order is authorized and error-free, the obligation of a sender, including the originator of the order, to pay or settle a payment order issued to a receiving bank arises upon the receiving bank (1) accepting the order, and (2) executing the order on the due date, or (3) on making payment on the due date.[67] Erroneous execution or acting on unauthorized payment orders, however, do not give rise to this obligation. Likewise, if the funds transfer is not completed for these or other reasons, there exists no obligation on the part of the originator to pay. If payment has been made, but the fund transfer is not completed, the sender is entitled to a refund, referred to as the "money-back guarantee," with interest earned.[68] The obligation to pay interest may be excused if a sender has failed to use care in addressing the error.[69]

---

[67] U.C.C. §§ 4A-202, 4A-209.

[68] U.C.C. § 4A-402(d), (e).

[69] The UNCITRAL Model Law does not distinguish between delayed execution and transfers that were not completed. The Model Law provides that if a bank fails to properly execute a payment order, it may be liable for interest, exchange rate changes, and consequential damages if the bank's failure to act is intentional.

Evra Corporation v. Swiss Bank Corporation

673 F.2d 951 (7th Cir. 1982)

POSNER, Circuit Judge.

The question—one of first impression—in this diversity case is the extent of a bank's liability for failure to make a transfer of funds when requested by wire to do so. The essential facts are undisputed. In 1972 Hyman-Michaels Company, a large Chicago dealer in scrap metal, entered into a two-year contract to supply steel scrap to a Brazilian corporation. Hyman-Michaels chartered a ship, the *Pandora*, to carry the scrap to Brazil. The charter was for one year, with an option to extend the charter for a second year; specified a fixed daily rate of pay for the hire of the ship during both the initial and the option period, payable semi-monthly "in advance"; and provided that if payment was not made on time the *Pandora's* owner could cancel the charter. Payment was to be made by deposit to the owner's account in the Banque de Paris et des Pays-Bas (Suisse) in Geneva, Switzerland.

The usual method by which Hyman-Michaels, in Chicago, got the payments to the Banque de Paris in Geneva was to request the Continental Illinois National Bank and Trust Company of Chicago, where it had an account, to make a wire transfer of funds. *Continental would debit Hyman-Michaels' account by the amount of the payment and then send a telex to its London office for retransmission to its correspondent bank in Geneva—Swiss Bank Corporation—asking Swiss Bank to deposit this amount in the Banque de Paris account of the Pandora's owner.* The transaction was completed by the crediting of Swiss Bank's account at Continental by the same amount.

When Hyman-Michaels chartered the *Pandora* in June 1972, market charter rates were very low, and it was these rates that were fixed in the charter for its entire term—two years if Hyman-Michaels exercised its option. Shortly after the agreement was signed, however, charter rates began to climb and by October 1972 they were much higher than they had been in June. The *Pandora's* owners were eager to get out of the charter if they could. At the end of October they thought they had found a way, for the payment that was due in the Banque de Paris on October 26 had not arrived by October 30, and on that day the *Pandora's* owner notified Hyman-Michaels that it was canceling the charter because of the breach of the payment term. Hyman-Michaels had mailed a check for the October 26 installment to the Banque de Paris rather than use the wire-transfer method of payment. It had done this in order to have the use of its money for the period that it would take the check to clear, about two weeks. But the check had not been mailed in Chicago until October 25 and of course did not reach Geneva on the twenty-sixth.

When Hyman-Michaels received notification that the charter was being canceled it immediately wired payment to the Banque de Paris, but the *Pandora*'s owner refused to accept it and insisted that the charter was indeed canceled. The matter was referred to arbitration in accordance with the charter. On December 5, 1972, the arbitration panel ruled in favor of Hyman-Michaels. The panel noted that previous arbitration panels had "shown varying degrees of latitude to Charterers;" "[i]n all cases, a pattern of obligation on Owners' part to protest, complain, or warn of intended withdrawal was expressed as an essential prerequisite to withdrawal, in spite of the clear wording of the operative clause. No such advance notice was given by Owners of M/V Pandora." One of the three members of the panel dissented; he thought the *Pandora*'s owner was entitled to cancel.

Hyman-Michaels went back to making the charter payments by wire transfer. On the morning of April 25, 1973, it telephoned Continental Bank and requested it to transfer $27,000 to the Banque de Paris account of the *Pandora*'s owner in payment for the charter hire period from April 27 to May 11, 1973. *Since the charter provided for payment "in advance," this payment arguably was due by the close of business on April 26. The requested telex went out to Continental's London office on the afternoon of April 25, which was nighttime in England.* Early the next morning a telex operator in Continental's London office dialed, as Continental's Chicago office had instructed him to do, Swiss Bank's general telex number, which rings in the bank's cable department. But that number was busy, and after trying unsuccessfully for an hour to engage it the Continental telex operator dialed another number, that of a machine in Swiss Bank's foreign exchange department which he had used in the past when the general number was engaged. We know this machine received the telexed message because it signaled the sending machine at both the beginning and end of the transmission that the telex was being received. Yet Swiss Bank failed to comply with the payment order, and no transfer of funds was made to the account of the *Pandora*'s owner in the Banque de Paris.

No one knows exactly what went wrong. One possibility is that the receiving telex machine had simply run out of paper, in which event it would not print the message although it had received it. Another is that whoever took the message out of the machine after it was printed failed to deliver it to the banking department. Unlike the machine in the cable department that the Continental telex operator had originally tried to reach, the machines in the foreign exchange department were operated by junior foreign exchange dealers rather than by professional telex operators, although Swiss Bank knew that messages intended for other departments were sometimes diverted to the telex machines in the foreign exchange department.

At 8:30 a.m. the next day, April 27, Hyman-Michaels in Chicago received a telex from the *Pandora*'s owner stating that the charter was canceled because payment for the April 27-May 11 charter period had not been made. Hyman-Michaels called over to Continental and told them to keep trying to effect payment through Swiss Bank even if the *Pandora*'s owner rejected it. This instruction was confirmed in a letter to Continental dated April 28, in which Hyman-Michaels stated: "please instruct your London branch to advise their correspondents to persist in attempting to make this payment. This should be done even in the face of a rejection on the part of Banque de Paris to receive this payment. It is paramount that in order to strengthen our position in an arbitration that these funds continue to be readily available." Hyman-Michaels did not attempt to wire the money directly to the Banque de Paris as it had done on the occasion of its previous default. Days passed while the missing telex message was hunted unsuccessfully. Finally Swiss Bank suggested to Continental that it retransmit the telex message to the machine in the cable department and this was done on May 1. The next day Swiss Bank attempted to deposit the $27,000 in the account of the *Pandora*'s owner at the Banque de Paris but the payment was refused.

Again the arbitrators were convened and rendered a decision. In it they ruled that Hyman-Michaels had been "blameless" up until the morning of April 27, when it first learned that the Banque de Paris had not received payment on April 26, but that "being faced with this situation," Hyman-Michaels had "failed to do everything in [its] power to remedy it. The action taken was immediate but did not prove to be adequate, in that [Continental] Bank and its correspondent required some 5/6 days to trace and effect the lost instruction to remit. [Hyman-Michaels] could have ordered an immediate duplicate payment— or even sent a Banker's check by hand or special messengers, so that the funds could have reached owner's Bank, not later than April 28th." By failing to do any of these things Hyman-Michaels had "created the opening" that the *Pandora*'s owner was seeking in order to be able to cancel the charter. It had "acted imprudently." The arbitration panel concluded, reluctantly but unanimously, that this time the *Pandora*'s owner was entitled to cancel the agreement. The arbitration decision was confirmed by a federal district court in New York.

Hyman-Michaels then brought this diversity action against Swiss Bank, seeking to recover its expenses in the second arbitration proceeding plus the profits that it lost because of the cancellation of the charter. The contract by which Hyman-Michaels had agreed to ship scrap steel to Brazil had been terminated by the buyer in March 1973 and Hyman-Michaels had promptly subchartered the *Pandora* at market rates, which by April 1973 were double the rates fixed in the charter. Its lost profits are based on the difference between the charter and subcharter rates.

Swiss Bank impleaded Continental Bank as a third-party defendant, asking that if it should be ordered to pay Hyman-Michaels, then Continental should be ordered to indemnify it. Continental filed a cross-claim against Hyman-Michaels seeking to shift back to Hyman-Michaels the cost of any judgment that Swiss Bank might obtain against it, on the ground that any errors by Continental were caused by Hyman-Michaels' negligence. Hyman-Michaels in turn counterclaimed against Continental, alleging that Continental had both been negligent and broken its contract with Hyman-Michaels in failing to effect payment on April 26, and was therefore liable to Hyman-Michaels along with Swiss Bank.

The case was tried to a district judge without a jury. In his decision, 522 F. Supp. 820 (N.D.Ill.1981), he first ruled that the substantive law applicable to Hyman-Michaels' claim against Swiss Bank was that of Illinois, rather than Switzerland as urged by Swiss Bank, and that Swiss Bank had been negligent and under Illinois law was liable to Hyman-Michaels for $2.1 million in damages. This figure was made up of about $16,000 in arbitration expenses and the rest in lost profits on the subcharter of the *Pandora*. The judge also ruled that Swiss Bank was not entitled to indemnification from Continental Bank, which made Continental's cross-claim moot; and lastly he dismissed Hyman-Michaels' counterclaim against Continental on the ground that Continental had not breached any duty to Hyman-Michaels. The case comes to us on Swiss Bank's appeal from the judgment in favor of Hyman-Michaels and from the dismissal of Swiss Bank's claim against Continental Bank, and on Hyman-Michaels' appeal from the dismissal of its counterclaim against Continental Bank.

Logically the first question we should address is choice of law. The parties seem agreed that if Swiss law applies, Hyman-Michaels has no claim against Swiss Bank, because under Swiss law a bank cannot be held liable to someone with whom it is not in privity of contract and there was no contract between Swiss Bank and Hyman-Michaels. Illinois does not have such a privity requirement. But this creates a conflict of laws only if Hyman-Michaels has a good claim against Swiss Bank under Illinois law; if it does not, then our result must be the same regardless of which law applies. Because we are more certain that Hyman-Michaels cannot recover against Swiss Bank under Illinois law than we are that Swiss rather than Illinois law applies to this case under Illinois choice-of-law principles (which we must apply in a diversity suit tried in Illinois, see *Klaxon Co. v. Stentor Elec. Mfg. Co.*, 313 U.S. 487, 496–97, 61 S.Ct. 1020, 1021–22, 85 L.Ed. 1477 (1941)), we shall avoid the choice-of-law question and discuss Swiss Bank's liability to Hyman-Michaels under Illinois law without deciding—for, to repeat—whether it really is Illinois law or Swiss law that governs.

When a bank fails to make a requested transfer of funds, this can cause two kinds of loss. First, the funds themselves or interest on them may be lost, and of course the fee paid for the transfer, having bought nothing, becomes a loss item. These are "direct" (sometimes called "general") damages. Hyman-Michaels is not seeking any direct damages in this case and apparently sustained none. It did not lose any part of the $27,000; although its account with Continental Bank was debited by this amount prematurely, it was not an interest-bearing account so Hyman-Michaels lost no interest; and Hyman-Michaels paid no fee either to Continental or to Swiss Bank for the aborted transfer. A second type of loss, which either the payor or the payee may suffer, is a dislocation in one's business triggered by the failure to pay. Swiss Bank's failure to transfer funds to the Banque de Paris when requested to do so by Continental Bank set off a chain reaction which resulted in an arbitration proceeding that was costly to Hyman-Michaels and in the cancellation of a highly profitable contract. It is those costs and lost profits—"consequential" or, as they are sometimes called, "special" damages—that Hyman-Michaels seeks in this lawsuit, and recovered below. It is conceded that if Hyman-Michaels was entitled to consequential damages, the district court measured them correctly. The only issue is whether it was entitled to consequential damages.

If a bank loses a check, its liability is governed by Article 4 of the Uniform Commercial Code, which precludes consequential damages unless the bank is acting in bad faith. See Ill.Rev.Stat. ch. 26, § 4-103(5) [U.C.C. § 4-103(e)]. If Article 4 applies to this transaction, Hyman-Michaels cannot recover the damages that it seeks, because Swiss Bank was not acting in bad faith. Maybe the language of Article 4 could be stretched to include electronic fund transfers, see section 4-102(2) [U.C.C. § 4-102(b)], but they were not in the contemplation of the draftsmen. For purposes of this case we shall assume, as the Second Circuit held in *Delbrueck & Co. v. Manufacturers Hanover Trust Co.*, 609 F.2d 1047, 1051 (2d Cir. 1979), that Article 4 is inapplicable, and apply common law principles instead.*

Hadley v. Baxendale, 9 Ex. 341, 156 Eng. Rep. 145 (1854), is the leading common law case on liability for consequential damages caused by failure or delay in carrying out a commercial undertaking. The engine shaft in plaintiffs' corn mill had broken and they hired the defendants, a common carrier, to transport the shaft to the manufacturer, who was to make a new one using the broken shaft as a model. The carrier failed to deliver the shaft within the time promised. With the engine shaft out of service the mill was shut down. The plaintiffs sued the defendants for the lost profits of the mill during the additional period that it was shut down because of the defendants' breach of their promise. The court held that the lost profits were not a proper item of damages, because "in the great multitude of cases of millers sending off broken shafts to third persons by a carrier under ordinary circumstances, such consequences [the stoppage of the mill and resulting

loss of profits] would not, in all probability, have occurred; and these special circumstances were here never communicated by the plaintiffs to the defendants." 9 Ex. at 356, 156 Eng. Rep. at 151.

The rule of *Hadley v. Baxendale*—that consequential damages will not be awarded unless the defendant was put on notice of the special circumstances giving rise to them—has been applied in many Illinois cases, and *Hadley* cited approvingly. See, e.g., *Underground Constr. Co. v. Sanitary Dist. of Chicago*, 367 Ill. 360, 369, 11 N.E.2d 361, 365 (1937); *Western Union Tel. Co. v. Martin*, 9 Ill.App. 587, 591–93 (1882); *Siegel v. Western Union Tel. Co.*, 312 Ill.App. 86, 92–93, 37 N.E.2d 868, 871 (1941); *Spangler v. Holthusen*, 61 Ill.App.3d 74, 80–82, 18 Ill.Dec. 840, 378 N.E.2d 304, 309–10 (1978). In *Siegel*, the plaintiff had delivered $200 to Western Union with instructions to transmit it to a friend of the plaintiff's. The money was to be bet (legally) on a horse, but this was not disclosed in the instructions. Western Union misdirected the money order and it did not reach the friend until several hours after the race had taken place. The horse that the plaintiff had intended to bet on won and would have paid $1650 on the plaintiff's $200 bet if the bet had been placed. He sued Western Union for his $1450 lost profit, but the court held that under the rule of *Hadley v. Baxendale* Western Union was not liable, because it "had no notice or knowledge of the purpose for which the money was being transmitted." 312 Ill.App. at 93, 37 N.E.2d at 871.

The present case is similar, though Swiss Bank knew more than Western Union knew in *Siegel*; it knew or should have known, from Continental Bank's previous telexes, that Hyman-Michaels was paying the Pandora Shipping Company for the hire of a motor vessel named *Pandora*. But it did not know when payment was due, what the terms of the charter were, or that they had turned out to be extremely favorable to Hyman-Michaels. And it did not know that Hyman-Michaels knew the *Pandora*'s owner would try to cancel the charter, and probably would succeed, if Hyman-Michaels was ever again late in making payment, or that despite this peril Hyman-Michaels would not try to pay until the last possible moment and in the event of a delay in transmission would not do everything in its power to minimize the consequences of the delay. Electronic funds transfers are not so unusual as to automatically place a bank on notice of extraordinary consequences if

---

* [Editor: *see* now U.C.C. Article 4A.]

such a transfer goes awry. Swiss Bank did not have enough information to infer that if it lost a $27,000 payment order it would face a liability in excess of $2 million. . . .

It is true that in both *Hadley* and *Siegel* there was a contract between the parties and here there was none. We cannot be certain that the Illinois courts would apply the principles of those cases outside of the contract area. As so often in diversity cases, there is an irreducible amount of speculation involved in attempting to predict the reaction of a state's courts to a new issue. The best we can do is to assume that the Illinois courts would look to the policies underlying cases such as *Hadley* and *Siegel* and, to the extent they found them pertinent, would apply those cases here. . . .

The district judge found that Swiss Bank had been negligent in losing Continental Bank's telex message and it can be argued that Swiss Bank should therefore be liable for a broader set of consequences than if it had only broken a contract. But *Siegel* implicitly rejects this distinction. Western Union had not merely broken its contract to deliver the plaintiff's money order; it had "negligently misdirected" the money order. "The company's negligence is conceded." 312 Ill.App. at 88, 91, 37 N.E.2d at 869, 871. Yet it was not liable for the consequences.

Siegel, we conclude, is authority for holding that Swiss Bank is not liable for the consequences of negligently failing to transfer Hyman-Michaels' funds to Banque de Paris; reason for such a holding is found in the animating principle of *Hadley v. Baxendale*, which is that the costs of the untoward consequence of a course of dealings should be borne by that party who was able to avert the consequence at least cost and failed to do so. In *Hadley* the untoward consequence was the shutting down of the mill. The carrier could have avoided it by delivering the engine shaft on time. But the mill owners, as the court noted, could have avoided it simply by having a spare shaft. 9 Ex. at 355–56, 156 Eng. Rep. at 151. Prudence required that they have a spare shaft anyway, since a replacement could not be obtained at once even if there was no undue delay in carting the broken shaft to and the replacement shaft from the manufacturer. The court refused to imply a duty on the part of the carrier to guarantee the mill owners against the consequences of their own lack of prudence, though of course if the parties had stipulated for such a guarantee the court would have

enforced it. The notice requirement of *Hadley v. Baxendale* is designed to assure that such an improbable guarantee really is intended.

This case is much the same, though it arises in a tort rather than a contract setting. Hyman-Michaels showed a lack of prudence throughout. It was imprudent for it to mail in Chicago a letter that unless received the next day in Geneva would put Hyman-Michaels in breach of a contract that was very profitable to it and that the other party to the contract had every interest in canceling. It was imprudent thereafter for Hyman-Michaels, having narrowly avoided cancellation and having (in the words of its appeal brief in this court) been "put... on notice that the payment provision of the Charter would be strictly enforced thereafter," to wait till arguably the last day before payment was due to instruct its bank to transfer the necessary funds overseas. And it was imprudent in the last degree for Hyman-Michaels, when it received notice of cancellation on the last possible day payment was due, to fail to pull out all the stops to get payment to the Banque de Paris on that day, and instead to dither while Continental and Swiss Bank wasted five days looking for the lost telex message. Judging from the obvious reluctance with which the arbitration panel finally decided to allow the *Pandora*'s owner to cancel the charter, it might have made all the difference if Hyman-Michaels had gotten payment to the Banque de Paris by April 27 or even by Monday, April 30, rather than allowed things to slide until May 2. This is not to condone the sloppy handling of incoming telex messages in Swiss Bank's foreign department. But Hyman-Michaels is a sophisticated business enterprise. It knew or should have known that even the Swiss are not infallible; that messages sometimes get lost or delayed in transit among three banks, two of them located 5000 miles apart, even when all the banks are using reasonable care; and that therefore it should take its own precautions against the consequences—best known to itself—of a mishap that might not be due to anyone's negligence.

We are not the first to remark the affinity between the rule of *Hadley v. Baxendale* and the doctrine, which is one of tort as well as contract law and is a settled part of the common law of Illinois, of avoidable consequences. See Dobbs: *Handbook on the Law of Remedies* 831 (1973); cf. *Benton v. J.A. Fay & Co.*, 64 Ill. 417 (1872). If you are hurt in an automobile accident and unreasonably fail to seek medical treatment, the injurer, even if negligent, will not be held liable for the aggravation of the injury due to your own unreasonable behavior after the accident. See, e.g., *Slater v. Chicago Transit Auth.*, 5 Ill.App.2d 181, 185, 125 N.E.2d 289, 291 (1955). If in addition you failed to fasten your seat belt, you may be barred from collecting the tort damages that would have been prevented if you had done so. See, e.g., *Mount v. McClellan*, 91 Ill.App.2d 1, 5, 234 N.E.2d 329, 331 (1968). Hyman-Michaels' behavior in steering close to the wind prior to April 27 was like not fastening one's seat belt; its failure on April 27 to wire a duplicate payment immediately after disaster struck was like refusing to seek medical attention after a serious accident. The seat-belt cases show that the doctrine of avoidable consequences applies whether the tort victim acts imprudently before or after the tort is committed. See Prosser: *Handbook of the Law of Torts* 424 (4th ed. 1971). Hyman-Michaels did both.

The rule of *Hadley v. Baxendale* links up with tort concepts in another way. The rule is sometimes stated in the form that only foreseeable damages are recoverable in a breach of contract action. E.g., Restatement (Second) of Contracts § 351 (1979). So expressed, it corresponds to the tort principle that limits liability to the foreseeable consequence of the defendant's carelessness.... The amount of care that a person ought to take is a function of the probability and magnitude of the harm that may occur if he does not take care.... If he does not know what that probability and magnitude are, he cannot determine how much care to take. That would be Swiss Bank's dilemma if it were liable for consequential damages from failing to carry out payment orders in timely fashion. To estimate the extent of its probable liability in order to know how many and how elaborate fail-safe features to install in its telex rooms or how much insurance to buy against the inevitable failures, Swiss Bank would have to collect reams of information about firms that are not even its regular customers. It had no banking relationship with Hyman-Michaels. It did not know or have reason to know how at once precious and fragile Hyman-Michaels' contract with the *Pandora*'s owner was. These were circumstances too remote from Swiss Bank's practical range of knowledge to have affected its decisions as to who should man the telex machines in the foreign

department or whether it should have more intelligent machines or should install more machines in the cable department, any more than the falling of a platform scale because a conductor jostled a passenger who was carrying fireworks was a prospect that could have influenced the amount of care taken by the Long Island Railroad. See *Palsgraf v. Long Island R.R.*, 248 N.Y. 339, 162 N.E. 99 (1928); cf. *Ney v. Yellow Cab Co.*, 2 Ill.2d 74, 80–84, 117 N.E.2d 74, 78–80 (1954).

In short, Swiss Bank was not required in the absence of a contractual undertaking to take precautions or insure against a harm that it could not measure but that was known with precision to Hyman-Michaels, which could by the exercise of common prudence have averted it completely. As Chief Judge Cardozo (the author of *Palsgraf*) remarked in discussing the application of *Hadley v. Baxendale* to the liability of telegraph companies for errors in transmission, "The sender can protect himself by insurance in one form or another if the risk of nondelivery or error appears to be too great.... The company, if it takes out insurance for itself, can do no more than guess at the loss to be avoided." *Kerr S.S. Co. v. Radio Corp. of America*, 245 N.Y. 284, 291–92, 157 N.E. 140, 142 (1927).

But *Kerr* is a case from New York, not Illinois, and Hyman-Michaels argues that two early Illinois telegraph cases compel us to rule in its favor against Swiss Bank. *Postal Tel. Cable Co. v. Lathrop*, 131 Ill. 575, 23 N.E. 583 (1890), involved the garbled transmission of two telegrams from a coffee dealer—who as the telegraph company knew was engaged in buying and selling futures contracts—to his broker. The first telegram (there is no need to discuss the second) directed the broker to buy 1000 bags of August coffee for the dealer's account. This got changed in transmission to 2000 bags, and because the price fell the dealer sustained an extra loss for which he sued the telegraph company. The court held that the company had had notice enough to make it liable for consequential damages under the rule of *Hadley v. Baxendale*. It knew it was transmitting buy and sell orders in a fluctuating market and that a garbled transmission could result in large losses. There was no suggestion that the dealer should have taken his own precautions against such mistakes. In *Providence-Washington Inc. Co. v. Western Union Tel. Co.*, 247 Ill. 84, 93 N.E. 134 (1910), a telegram from an insurance company canceling a policy was misdirected, and before it turned up there was a fire and the insurance company was liable on the policy. This was the precise risk created by delay, it was obvious on the face of the telegram, and the telegraph company was therefore liable for the insurance company's loss on the policy. Again there was no suggestion that the plaintiff had neglected any precaution. Both cases are distinguishable from the present case: the defendants had more information and the plaintiffs were not imprudent.

The legal principles that we have said are applicable to this case were not applied below. Although the district judge's opinion is not entirely clear, he apparently thought the rule of *Hadley v. Baxendale* inapplicable and the imprudence of Hyman-Michaels irrelevant. See 522 F. Supp. at 833. He did state that the damages to Hyman-Michaels were foreseeable because "a major international bank" should know that a failure to act promptly on a telexed request to transfer funds could cause substantial damage; but *Siegel*—and for that matter *Lathrop* and *Providence-Washington*— make clear that that kind of general foreseeability, which is present in virtually every case, does not justify an award of consequential damages.

We could remand for new findings based on the proper legal standard, but it is unnecessary to do so. The undisputed facts, recited in this opinion, show as a matter of law that Hyman-Michaels is not entitled to recover consequential damages from Swiss Bank.

Since Hyman-Michaels' complaint against Swiss Bank must be dismissed, Swiss Bank's third-party complaint against Continental Bank and Continental Bank's cross-claim against Hyman-Michaels are moot. . . .

On the merits, we agree with the district judge that Hyman-Michaels did not prove its case. Continental did not break any contract with Hyman-Michaels. All it undertook to do on April 25 was to transmit a telex message to Swiss Bank, and it did so. All it undertook to do on April 27, by the evidence of Hyman-Michaels' own confirming letter, was to advise its correspondent—that is, Swiss Bank—to "persist in attempting to make... payment," and it did so advise its correspondent. Nor was Continental negligent on either occasion. Its telex operator had used the machine in Swiss Bank's foreign department before, for the same purpose and without incident; he had no reason to expect a mishap. And Continental used due care in assisting Swiss Bank in the latter's vain hunt for the missing telex. The district court's findings on these issues were skimpy but the facts are clear and a remand is unnecessary.

No other issues need be decided. The judgment in favor of Hyman-Michaels against Swiss Bank is reversed with directions to enter judgment for Swiss Bank. The judgment in favor of Continental Bank on Swiss Bank's third-party complaint is vacated with instructions to dismiss that complaint as moot. The judgment dismissing Continental's cross-claim against Hyman-Michaels as moot, and the judgment in favor of Continental on Hyman-Michaels' counterclaim, are affirmed. The costs of the appeals shall be borne by Hyman-Michaels (Evra Corporation).

SO ORDERED.

NOTE

1. Under U.C.C. Article 4A, Hyman-Michaels (EVRA) is the originator of the fund transfer, U.C.C. § 4A-104(c), and Continental Illinois is the originator's bank, U.C.C. § 4A-104(d). Continental Illinois became an originator of the payment order sent to Continental (London), a receiving bank, U.C.C. § 4A-103(a)(4), which as originator sent a payment order to Swiss Bank, which as a receiving bank was to make payment into the account of the owners of the *Pandora* with Banque de Paris et des Pays-Bas (Suisse) in Geneva, the beneficiary's bank. U.C.C. § 4A-103(a)(3). All three of these banks are intermediary banks. U.C.C. § 4A-104(b).

2. Consider the liabilities of each of these banks under U.C.C. Article 4A.

(a) as to duties of receiving and executing a "payment order." *See* U.C.C. §§ 4A-212, 4A-302, 4A-103(a)(1).

(b) if the payment order was unauthorized, ineffective, or not enforceable in whole or in part. *See* U.C.C. § 4A-202, 4A-203, 4A-204.

(c) if there was a failure to properly execute a payment order. *See* U.C.C. § 4A-305.

(d) what are the rights of the originator or other senders if the fund transfer is not completed? *See* U.C.C. § 4A-402(c), (d).

3. The obligation of the communication system is not affected by U.C.C. Article 4A. Contract law would govern that relationship. But note U.C.C. § 4A-206—the system is deemed to be an agent of the sender. The prohibition against varying the liability of banks does not apply to communication systems, U.C.C. § 4A-305(f).

(iv) *Obligations of the Beneficiary's Bank*

Before the payment obligation is discharged, the beneficiary must be paid. U.C.C. Section 4A-404 describes the obligations of the beneficiary's bank, which include payment and notice to the beneficiary. Generally, the beneficiary's bank must pay the beneficiary when it accepts the payment order. If the beneficiary's bank refuses a demand for payment, the bank may be held liable for consequential damages suffered by the beneficiary. The beneficiary must notify the bank of the damage suffered. A beneficiary's right to receive payment and damages may not be altered by agreement.

U.C.C. Section 4A-405 provides that the obligation to the beneficiary is discharged when its account is credited with withdrawable funds, or the funds are otherwise made available to the beneficiary, or the credit is lawfully applied to a debt of the beneficiary to the beneficiary's bank. Payment to the beneficiary is final and cannot be conditioned.[70] The originator, the originator's bank, the beneficiary's bank and the beneficiary may expressly agree, however, to a fund transfer system rule that payment be provisional on the fund transfer system receiving the funds. If funds are not received by the system, the payment order will be nullified.[71] Aside from these exceptions, any condition attached to payment will be unenforceable.

Completion of the fund transfer occurs when the beneficiary's bank accepts the payment order, which involves payment to the beneficiary. Completion of the fund transfer will normally discharge the underlying obligation of the originator. U.C.C. § 4A-406.

Should there have been a misdescription of the beneficiary so that the beneficiary's bank is unable to identify the beneficiary from the information given, no person has the rights of a beneficiary. Such payment order cannot be accepted, even where the banks have agreed that payment orders will be accepted and executed when received. A payment order need not identify the beneficiary by name. It suffices if the payment order gives the account number of the beneficiary. A problem may arise where the name and account number given in the payment order do not match, for example, they belong to different entities. U.C.C. Section 4A-207(b)(1) provides that the beneficiary's bank can proceed on the basis of the account number and need not verify whether they both belong to the same person. If the

---

[70] U.C.C. § 4A-405(c).

[71] U.C.C. § 4A-405(d)(e).

originator/sender is a bank, it will have to pay on the payment order as executed. But if the originator is not a bank, liability will arise only if the originator was on notice that payment will be made on the basis of the account number indicated. U.C.C. § 4A-207(c). If such payment results in the wrong person being paid, the originator can recover the funds from the person having no right to be paid. U.C.C. § 4A-207(d).

IX THE BANK COLLECTION PROCESS

Banks do not act only in connection with check collection. Among the many activities in which banks are involved we find banks not only as drawers, or as drawees or as endorsees of drafts, especially documentary drafts, U.C.C. § 4–104(a)(6), but also collecting on bond coupons,[1] and collecting on bonds and debentures that have been called or are being redeemed, and participating in letter of credit transactions. As a result, U.C.C. Article 4 collectively refers to "items" when describing the subject matter of the collection process, U.C.C. § 4-104(a)(9).[2]

Since checks are also subject to federal law by virtue of the Federal Expedited Funds Availability Act (EFA Act),[3] we must consider that Act and the regulations promulgated under it by the Board of Governors of the Federal Reserve System.[4] In addition we must note that U.C.C. Article 4 specifically states that it is subject to Federal Reserve Regulations and operating circulars, clearinghouse rules, and the like, which have the effect of agreement "whether or not specifically assented to by all parties interested in items handled." U.C.C. § 4-103(a)(b).

A. Check Collection

For a considerable time, the check collection process has been a matter of custom and agreement among banks. These rules became codified first by agreement in the American

---

[1] Bond coupons payable to bearer are being phased-out by reason of the Tax Equity and Fiscal Responsibility Act of 1982, § 309, 26 U.S.C. § 6049, which inhibits the issuance of bearer coupons by denying corporate issuers the right to deduct interest payments on debt securities payable by means of such bearer coupons as a business expense.

[2] Banks also collect on credit card charge slips but U.C.C. Article 4 does not apply to this activity. *See* U.C.C. § 4-104(a)(9). This activity is governed by contract and by the Federal Consumer Credit Protection Act, 15 U.S.C. §§ 1601 to 1693r. Official Comment 8 to U.C.C. § 4-104 indicates that "the functional limitation on the meaning of this term [item] is the willingness of the banking system to handle the instrument, undertaking or instruction for collection or payment." In the light of the court's decision in Broadway National Bank v. Barton-Russell Corp., 585 N.Y.S.2d 933 (N.Y. Sup.Ct. 1992) which had held that pre-revision U.C.C. Article 4 does apply to banks when collecting on credit card charge slips, this express exclusion in the revision of U.C.C. Article 4, was a victory for banks over the claims by merchants to have U.C.C. § 4-202 apply, i.e., a duty of ordinary care imposed by statute, U.C.C. § 3-103(a)(7), as compared to a duty determined by reference to U.C.C. § 1-103, requiring reference to the common law and equity, i.e., common law negligence and fiduciary duty in equity.

[3] 12 U.S.C. §§ 4001 to 4010.

[4] *See* Greater Buffalo Press, Inc. v. Federal Reserve Bank of New York, 866 F.2d 38 (2d Cir.) *cert. denied* 490 U.S. 1107 (1989).

Bankers Association Bank Collection Code and later in the Uniform Commercial Code Article 4 by state law. Federal involvement dates back to 1913 with the enactment of the Federal Reserve Act.[5] But not all bank collection took place within the Federal Reserve System. One of the effects of the Federal Expedited Funds Availability Act [EFA Act] is that it not only confers on the Board of Governors of the Federal Reserve System the power to promulgate regulations "to carry out the provisions of this chapter;"[6] and "to improve the check processing system" by considering a number of proposals including "check truncation,"[7] "incentives to return items promptly to the depository institution of first deposit"[8] if possible by "automated process,"[9] but also gives the Federal Reserve Board the power to regulate

> (a) any aspect of the payment system, including the receipt, payment collection, or clearing of checks; and
> (b) any related function of the payment system with respect to checks.[10]

The effect of this grant of power may well lead to the federalization of the present state law relating to checks, U.C.C. Article 3, and to check collection, U.C.C. Article 4.

1. The Basic Check Collection System

Banks handle approximately 52 billion checks annually. Some of these checks are drawn on and payable to a depositor of only one bank, the "on us" check. For example, John Smith and William Jones are both residents of Maryland. Both have accounts with the Maryland National Bank (MNB). Smith owes Jones $100 and draws a check to that amount payable to Jones. On Monday before 2 p.m. Jones deposits this check into his account.[11] The bank will process the check that night and Tuesday morning the amount of $100 will have been credited to Jones' account and a debit to that amount will appear on Smith's account. Jones will have the money available as of the opening of the bank on Tuesday morning.[12]

Most checks, however, are drawn on a bank other than the depository bank. The check may be drawn on a local bank using the same clearing house facility or on a distant drawee bank requiring the check to pass through a number of processing operations before being presented finally to the drawee bank. This process can be diagramed as follows:

---

[5] Dec. 13, 1913, ch. 6, 38 Stat. 251, 12 U.S.C. §§ 221 to 226.

[6] 12 U.S.C. § 4008(a)(1).

[7] *Id.* § 4008(b)(2).

[8] *Id.* § 4008(b)(3).

[9] *Id.* § 4008(b)(4).

[10] *Id.* § 4008(c).

[11] "Banking day" means the part of the day on which a bank is open to the public for carrying out substantially all of its banking functions. U.C.C. § 4-104(a)(3). *Compare* the EFA Act § 4001(3). The term "business day" means "any day other than a Saturday, Sunday, or legal holiday." Many banks consider a deposit made after "bankers' hours" to be made on the next "banking day," a practice recognized by U.C.C. § 4-303(a)(5) allowing a "cut-off hour." *See* U.C.C. § 4-108.

[12] *See also* EFA Act 12 U.S.C. § 4002 (a)(2)(E).

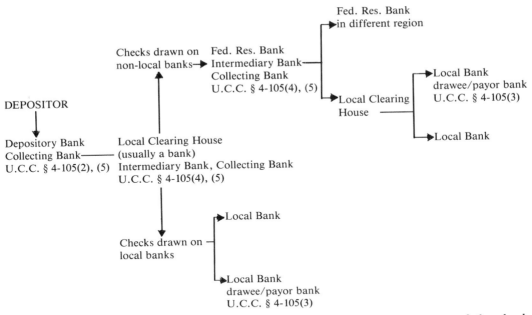

Depositor deposits check into depository bank which adds the amount of the check to the Magnetic Ink Character Recognition (MICR) symbols on the bottom line of the check and places its routing symbols on the back of the check. These MICR symbols allow machine reading of checks and enable automation of the check collection process as well as notification of dishonor and a return of a dishonored check to the depository bank.

At the Local Clearing House, an Automated Clearing House (ACH) and member of the National Automated Clearing House Association (NATCHA), the check will be automatically sorted into those that are drawn on a local bank and those that are drawn on banks in a more distant locale and that do not use the Local Clearing House. The latter checks are then forwarded to the Federal Reserve Bank serving the area in which the Local Clearing House operates, while checks drawn on banks using the same Local Clearing House will be sorted to await collection and will be presented to the banks on which they are drawn. Local bank, drawee/payor bank, will machine read the check and debit the account of drawer if there is no stop payment order on file and if there are sufficient funds in the account or a line of credit exists.[13] Otherwise it will dishonor the check and return the check to the presenting bank. On arrival at the regional Federal Reserve Banks, checks will be sorted by machine reading of the MICR symbols and sent to the various Local Clearing Houses served by the Regional Federal Reserve Bank, or forwarded to the Regional Federal Reserve Bank serving the area within which the drawee bank is operating.[14]

---

[13] Note: Many customers have "overdraft protection," a line of credit in case their account has insufficient funds to meet the amount of a check drawn on it. See further U.C.C. § 4-401(a), indicating that a bank may charge a customer's account with an item that is properly payable, even if this creates an overdraft.

[14] An IBM reader-sorter reads the microline on the check, microfilms the check and sorts them into packets for transfer at the rate of 100,000 checks per hour (1,600 per minute, 25 per second). William Davenport, *Facilitation of the Automated Processing of Checks by the 1990 Amendment to U.C.C. Articles 3 and 4*, 1993 Com. L. Ann., 169, 171 (L.F. Del Duca & P.L. Del Duca, eds., 1993).

On receipt of an item each bank in this chain will make a provisional settlement on its books by entering a credit in favor of its transferor and, when transferring the item, entering a debit against the transferee. U.C.C. §§ 4-104(a)(ii), 4-213. In return, the bank will have received transfer warranties from its transferor, U.C.C. § 4-207, and the authority to make presentment warranties to the payor/drawee, U.C.C. § 4-208.

Once a check is dishonored, the check will commence on its return journey through all these banks until it once more reaches the depository bank. Where the dishonored check is in excess of $2,500 the drawee bank must give prompt notice of dishonor. Such notice can be by any reasonable means but must be "received by the depository bank by 4 p.m. (local time) on the second business day following the banking day on which the check was presented to the" drawee bank.[15] Such notice is usually given by electronic data interchange (EDI) or by telegram. Each bank in the system has to abide by the midnight deadline, U.C.C. § 4-104(a)(10), i.e., it must execute its functions by midnight of the next banking day following the banking day on which it received the item or notice or from which the time for taking action commences to run. To allow a bank time to perform its functions, a bank can announce a time, the cut-off hour, after which items received are deemed to have been received on the next banking day. U.C.C. § 4-108.

Every bank in the collection chain must exercise ordinary care. This will require it to have taken action before the midnight deadline. The onus of proving that a longer time was reasonable is on the bank that exceeded the midnight deadline. U.C.C. § 4-202. For example, where the delay is caused by interruption of a communication or failure of computer facilities or other equipment, the bank must not only prove this had occurred, but also that the bank exercised such diligence to deal with the delay as the circumstances required. U.C.C. § 4-109(b). These time limits will be subject to clearing house rules whether or not there is assent to such rules. U.C.C. § 4-103(b).[16]

---

[15] Regulation CC, 12 C.F.R. § 229.33(a).

[16] Note: Where the item is not drawn on a payor-bank, the collecting bank may waive, modify or extend time limits for a period not exceeding two additional banking days without approval of any party involved. Such extension will not discharge drawers, indorsers or transferors from their liability, provided the extension is a good faith effort to secure payment. *See* U.C.C. § 4-109(a).

Greater Buffalo Press, Inc. v. Federal Reserve Bank of New York
866 F.2d 38 (2d Cir.), *cert. denied* 490 U.S. 1107, 104 LEd2d 1022 (1989)[*]

MESKILL, C.J.

This is an appeal from a judgment of the United States District Court for the Western District of New York, Curtin, C.J., granting the summary judgment motion of the Federal Reserve Bank of New York (Fed NY) and John T. Keane and dismissing the complaint.

[*] [Editor: citations in [ ] refer to Revised U.C.C. Articles 3 and 4.]

The suit also included as a defendant Marine Midland Bank, N.A. (Marine). Marine's own motion for dismissal was granted by the district court; plaintiffs do not appeal from this decision. The sixty-five plaintiffs alleged that they had suffered injury because of defendants' participation in the processing of checks belonging to the plaintiffs.

We affirm.

BACKGROUND

A. Federal Reserve Banks and the Process of Check Collection

Federal Reserve Banks play a major role in the nation's system of check collection. See The Comptroller General, Report to the Congress: The Federal Reserve Should Move Faster to Eliminate Subsidy of Check Clearing Operations 4 (1982) (the Federal Reserve collects over forty percent of the checks written in the United States), J. App. 935, 936; Clarke, Check-Out Time for Checks, 21 Bus. Law. 931, 932 (1966) (one-third of checks are sent to Federal Reserve Banks), J. App. 793, 795. The check collection process, or specifically Fed NY's participation in it, is at the center of this dispute. For that reason, we briefly examine some background. See generally H. Hutchinson, Money, Banking, and the United States Economy 117–27 (5th ed. 1984); Baxter and Patrikis, *The Check-Hold Revolution,* 18 U.C.C. L.J. 99, 114–17 (1985), J. App. 751, 766–69.

When payment is made by means of a check, a payor draws the check against an account at his or her bank, the payor bank. Upon receiving the check, the payee will often deposit it in his or her own bank, the depositary bank. At this point, two processes must occur. First, the check itself must be physically transported from the depositary bank to the payor bank. Second, payment must be made from the payor bank back to the depositary bank.

One option available to the depositary bank is to utilize the check clearing services of the Federal Reserve System. In order to do so, the depositary bank must send the check to the Federal Reserve Bank for its district. If the payor bank is in the same district, then the Federal Reserve Bank can present the check directly to the payor bank. If the payor bank is located in a different district, the Federal Reserve Bank receiving the check will forward it to the Federal Reserve Bank for the payor bank's district. That Federal Reserve Bank will then present the check to the payor bank.

In addition to effecting the physical delivery of the check, the Federal Reserve System also serves to facilitate payment between the payor and depositary banks. After sending a check to its Federal Reserve Bank for processing, the depositary bank will receive credit for the check in its reserves account with the Federal Reserve. This credit will be given usually within one or two days, depending on how long it is expected to take the check to reach the payor bank for payment. After the check reaches the payor bank, the Federal Reserve System uses transfers of credit through an Interdistrict Settlement Fund to achieve payment.

If there is an unexpected delay in transporting the check to the payor bank, then the credit for the check will be given by the Federal Reserve to the depositary bank before payment can be received from the payor bank. This so-called "float" in effect gives the depositary bank an interest-free advance at the expense of the Federal Reserve. Thus, delays in processing not only adversely affect Federal Reserve Banks with respect to the competitive attractiveness of their check clearing services, but also result in direct economic costs, see Baxter and Patrikis, supra at 117, J. App. at 769.

Throughout most of its history, the Federal Reserve has provided these check clearing services only to member banks, or other banks that maintained reserve accounts with the Federal Reserve. *See Jet Courier Services, Inc. v. Federal Reserve Bank of Atlanta,* 713 F.2d 1221, 1222–23 (6th Cir. 1983); *Carson v. Federal Reserve Bank of New York,* 172 N.E. 475, 478 (N.Y. 1930) (Cardozo, C.J.); 14 Fed. Reserve Bull. 80 (1928). These services were provided at no charge, apparently to promote Federal Reserve membership by compensating member banks for the costs associated with having to maintain non-interest bearing reserves with the Federal Reserve. See *Oversight on the Payments Mechanism, the Federal Reserve's Role in Providing Payments Services, and the Pricing of Those Services: Hearings Before the Senate Comm. on Banking, Housing, and Urban Affairs,* 95th Cong., 1st Sess. 120–21 (1977) (testimony of Philip E. Coldwell) (hereinafter Coldwell testimony), J. App. 944, 954–55. In 1980, however, Congress enacted the Monetary Control Act of 1980, Pub. L. 96–221 tit. I, 94 Stat. 132, 132–41. This Act provided, inter alia, that all banks in the United States would be required to maintain reserves with the Federal Reserve. Additionally, check clearing services were now to be made available to all banks, regardless of whether or not they were member banks, but all banks would henceforth have to pay for the service. See *Jet Courier Services,* 713 F.2d at 1222–23; McNeill and Rechter, *The Depository Institutions Deregulation and Monetary Control Act of 1980,* 66 Fed. Reserve Bull. 444, 444–48 (1980), J. App. 908, 908–12.

B. The Facts Leading to This Litigation

In 1977, the sixty-five plaintiffs-appellants were all supplier-creditors of Neisner Brother's, Inc. (Neisner), a retail department store chain. The dispute in this case arises from seventy-five checks drawn by Neisner, in October and November of 1977, on its account at Lincoln First Bank of Rochester (Lincoln) and made payable to the appellants. After receiving the checks, the appellants deposited them at their various depositary banks around the country. Greater Buffalo Press, for example, maintains that it deposited one check for $43,537.66 on November 21, 1977 and one check for $109,671.55 on November 23, 1977 in its account at Marine.

After receiving the checks, the various depositary banks forwarded them for collection to the defendant-appellee Fed NY, either directly or indirectly, through other Federal Reserve Banks. The district court accepted Fed NY's contentions as to the dates it received the checks.[1] The court found that Fed NY received three of the seventy-five checks between November 19–22, nine of the checks between November 24–25 and sixty-three of the checks on or after November 26.

The next step in the collection process called for Fed NY's Buffalo Branch to forward the checks to the payor bank, Lincoln, for payment. The parties are in substantial agreement as to the days the checks were finally received by Lincoln, and Fed NY concedes that there were delays due to an "unprecedented" increase in the volume of checks requiring processing, Br. of Defendants-Appellants at 12. For example, the $43,537.66 check payable to Greater Buffalo Press was received by Fed NY on either November 21 or 22,

but was not presented to Lincoln until December 5, J. App. at 566.

Neisner filed a petition for bankruptcy December 1, 1977. The district court found that Lincoln had begun to dishonor the checks of Neisner on November 29, but the appellants maintain that Lincoln only began to dishonor Neisner's checks after learning of the filing of the bankruptcy petition on the morning of December 1.[2] When the checks were presented for payment, Lincoln dishonored them. The checks were returned to Fed NY, and from there back to the appellants' depositary banks. In at least some cases, a second attempt at collection was made, but the checks were again dishonored by Lincoln.

* * *

DISCUSSION

. . . We thus examine first the "substantive law applicable in the case." . . .

A. Governing Law with Respect to Liability

1. The Legal Basis for the Cause of Action

The crux of appellants' complaint is that but for Fed NY's delays in processing their checks, the appellants would have been paid because the checks would have arrived at Lincoln in time to be honored. The appellants have cited Fed NY's assurance to the public of prompt and efficient check clearing services, contending that it was all the while sitting on a mountain of checks that continuously grew faster than Fed NY could process them. They contend that Fed NY foresaw or should have foreseen the processing delays and should have either remedied the situation or warned its customers of potential problems. Instead, the appellants contend, Fed NY sought to cover up the situation. * * *

It is obvious that the appellants cannot recover against Fed NY by simply criticizing its operations. In order to survive a summary judgment motion, the appellants had to present supporting facts and arguments showing some legal basis for liability on the part of the defendants; it was not enough simply to put forth conclusory allegations of wrongdoing. *See Miracle Mile Associates v.*

---

[1] In accepting the dates offered by Fed NY, the district court rejected plaintiffs' counsel's argument that these dates were incorrect. Plaintiffs' counsel asked for and was given permission to file a compilation of his version of the dates Fed NY received the checks, but counsel did not do so. In this appeal, the appellants now offer such a compilation, maintaining, essentially, that most of the checks were received one day earlier than Fed NY contends. Fed NY asks us not to consider this showing, arguing that it cannot properly be considered part of the record.

In view of our disposition of this case, *see infra,* this factual dispute is immaterial, and therefore it does not affect the propriety of the granting of summary judgment.

[2] These disputed facts might be relevant to issues of causation, but again, *see* n.1 *supra,* this dispute is immaterial in light of our analysis of the governing law, *see infra.*

City of Rochester, 617 F.2d 18, 21 (2d Cir. 1980); *Securities and Exchange Commission v. Research Automation Corp.*, 585 F.2d 31, 33 (2d Cir. 1978).

We agree with the district court's approach in viewing the cause of action on this record as sustainable only by reliance on the provisions of New York's Uniform Commercial Code that deal specifically with the duties of banks in collecting and processing checks. *See* U.C.C. [§§ 4–201, 4–202]. The district court found meritless the appellants' arguments as to possible alternative theories of liability. * * * We too are unable to discern from the record any other legal basis for liability on the part of Fed NY or Keane. To the extent that the facts might support some other conceivable basis for such liability, we find that the appellants' unsubstantiated conclusory allegations of wrongdoing were properly considered by the district court to have been insufficient to survive the summary judgment motion.

2. Liability Under The New York Uniform Commercial Code

The Uniform Commercial Code, Section 4–202(1) imposes certain duties on "collecting bank[s]." Three of these duties on a quick reading might seem relevant to the facts of this case. The Code provides:

[(a)] A collecting bank must [exercise] ordinary care in

[1] (a) presenting an item or sending it for presentment; . . .

[2] (b) sending notice of dishonor or non-payment or returning an item . . . to the bank's transferor . . . after learning that the item has not been paid or accepted, as the case may be; . . .

[4] (e) notifying its transferor of any loss or delay in transit within a reasonable time after discovery thereof.

U.C.C. [§ 4-202(a)]. Fed NY does not contest that, as a "collecting bank," these provisions apply to its processing of checks.

This provision imposes on Fed NY a duty of ordinary care in its presentment of checks for payment. The focus of the appellants' complaint is Fed NY's delay, after having received the checks, in presenting them to Lincoln. They base their cause of action in part on the contention that Fed NY breached its duty and that the breach caused the dishonor of their checks. If applicable

to this case, Fed NY would bear the burden of showing that it exercised ordinary care in processing the checks if the checks were not properly processed within the "midnight deadline." See U.C.C. § [4-202(b)].

Section [4-202(a)(2)] requires collecting banks to give prompt notification of the dishonor of checks. This provision has no application to this case, however. Appellants have not shown or even argued that Fed NY delayed in providing notification of Lincoln's dishonor of the checks. Rather, their alleged injury stems from the dishonor itself, not from any delay in notification of the dishonor. Cf. *Washington Petroleum and Supply Co. v. Girard Bank*, 629 F.Supp. 1224, 1226 (M.D. Pa. 1983) (allegation of injury from delayed notification of dishonor).

Section [4-202(a)(4)] requires collecting banks to give prompt notice to a transferor of any "loss or delay in transit." At oral argument, the appellants relied on this section, contending that Fed NY at the very least should have alerted the appellants to the delays in the processing of their checks, thus giving them an opportunity to arrange alternative means of processing.

The appellants have not shown, and we have serious doubt as to whether they would be able to show, how a failure to warn of the delays would be causally linked to the dishonor of the checks. A trier of fact would have to question whether the appellants, armed with notice of the processing delay but without the benefit of hindsight or advance warning of Neisner's bankruptcy petition, would have either retrieved their checks from Fed NY or arranged for alternative clearinghouse services. In our review of a grant of summary judgment, however, we do not rely on these weaknesses in the appellants' case. Rather, we simply note that the appellants have no cause of action on these facts based on section [4-202(a)(4)]. That section applies where delays were caused by "mishaps in the mails," not to delays caused by the collecting bank's own internal processing operations, the situation present in our case. See *United States Fidelity and Guaranty Co. v. Federal Reserve Bank of New York*, 590 F.Supp. 486, 494 (S.D. N.Y. 1984) (citing *Northpark National Bank v. Bankers Trust Co.*, 572 F.Supp. 524, 531 (S.D.N.Y. 1983)), aff'd, 786 F.2d 77 (2d Cir. 1986) (per curiam).

Thus, we find that the only duty created by section 4-202(a) that is relevant here is Fed NY's duty of ordinary care in the presentment of checks under section 4-202(a)(1). But, in order to recover under this section, the appellants must show more than Fed NY's breach of duty. They also must show that the duty extended to them.

Section 4-201 of the Uniform Commercial Code says: "Unless a contrary intent clearly appears and [before] the time that a settlement given by a collecting bank for an item is or becomes final ... the bank [with respect to the item] is an agent or sub-agent of the owner of the item." As the Fifth Circuit has recognized: "The agency relationship established by § [4-201] is the only basis in the Code for determining to whom the duties imposed on collecting banks [by § 4-202(a)] run. Once that agency relationship is severed, the duties are no longer owed. More simply stated, liability flows only from agency status." *Childs v. Federal Reserve Bank*, 719 F.2d 812, 814 (5th Cir. 1983) (per curiam) (emphasis added). The appellants' cause of action thus rests solely on an agency theory, and their complaint must stand or fall on their contention that Fed NY acted as their agent.

3. The Effect of Federal Regulation J

In considering the availability to the appellants of a cause of action based on the U.C.C., we have thus far considered only New York state law. As required by the Supremacy Clause, U.S. Const. art. VI, however, the state U.C.C. statutes cannot be considered in isolation but instead must be read together with applicable federal statutes and regulations. See *United States Fidelity*, 590 F.Supp. at 489 n.4, aff'd per curiam, 786 F.2d 77.

The Board of Governors of the Federal Reserve System promulgates regulations governing the operation of the Federal Reserve System. See 12 C.F.R. §§ 201–269b (1988). Pursuant to its authority under 12 U.S.C. §§ 248(i), 248(o), 342, 360 (1982) and other laws, the Board of Governors has promulgated Regulation J, concerning the collection of checks. See 12 C.F.R. § 210.1 (1988); 14 Fed. Reserve Bull. 80 (1928). The appellants have not called into question the Board of Governors' authority to promulgate regulations, nor the propriety of the promulgation of this particular regulation. ... Thus, as a properly promulgated substantive regulation, Regulation J must be given the force and effect of federal law. See *Chrysler Corp. v. Brown*, 441 U.S. 281, 295–96 (1979).

* * *

... In establishing the Federal Reserve System, Congress showed concern for the nation's costly and circuitous check processing system. Consistent with its goal of creating an equitable and efficient system of exchange, Congress provided for the Federal Reserve to serve as a national clearinghouse for checks. See H.R. Rep. No. 69, 63rd Cong., 1st Sess. 55–56 (1913); S. Rep. No. 133, 63rd Cong., 1st Sess., pt. 2, at 27 (1913). Soon after its creation, a major concern of the Federal Reserve was to implement federal policy by addressing the check collection problem. See W.P.G. Harding, The Formative Period of the Federal Reserve System 38–39, 49–60 (1925). Through their regulatory authority, the Governors of the Federal Reserve sought to establish and maintain "a direct, expeditious, and economical system of check collection and settlement of balances." See *Carson*, 172 N.E. at 478 (quoting Regulation J (series of 1924)); 14 Fed. Reserve Bull. 80; 2 Fed. Reserve Bull. 259 (1916). Regulation J was an early tool in this endeavor. See 14 Fed. Reserve Bull. 80. As noted supra, until the enactment of the Monetary Control Act of 1980, check clearing services were provided by Federal Reserve Banks free of charge to member banks in order to ease the burden of Federal Reserve membership. See Coldwell testimony at 120–21, J. App. at 954–55. As Fed NY explains: "The sender rule [of Regulation J] was a natural complement to the gratuitous service, because it effectively limited the Reserve Bank's duty to exercise ordinary care to only those institutions who were receiving the gratuitous service, thereby reducing losses as well as the overall cost of the service." Br. of Defendants-Appellees at 24.

This understanding of the policy behind Regulation J finds support in recent changes in the Federal Reserve System. It appears that the Monetary Control Act of 1980 was designed in part to improve the efficiency of the Federal Reserve System and promote competition by other banks and check clearinghouses. *See Bank Stationers Ass'n v. Board of Governors*, 704 F.2d 1233, 1236 (11th Cir. 1983); Subcomm. on Domestic Monetary Policy of the House of Representatives Comm. on Banking, Finance and Urban Affairs, 98th Cong., 2nd Sess., Report on the Role and Activities of the Federal Reserve System in the Nation's Check Clearing and Payments System 68–69 (Comm.

Print 1984), J. App. 924, 925–26; see also *Jet Courier Services*, 713 F.2d at 1227 (Congress did not intend to protect competitive positions of private collection services). Such a change would undermine an existent "protectionist" policy that supports giving the Federal Reserve Banks the competitive advantage of limited liability under Regulation J. Accordingly, the Board of Governors, in 1986, amended Regulation J and repealed the sender rule in order to permit the owner of a check or other item who is allegedly injured by a Reserve Bank's alleged failure to exercise ordinary care or act in good faith in collecting an item to bring an action against the Reserve Bank, regardless of whether that person is a "sender" as defined in Regulation J. 51 Fed.Reg. 21740 (June 16, 1986), J. App. at 557.

Nevertheless, this change in the law came too late to aid the appellants, whose complaint and supporting evidence must be governed by the law in place in November of 1977. Under that law, Fed NY and its Branch Manager Keane breached no duty to the appellants in this case.

NOTE

1. Plaintiff failed to succeed because at that time Regulation J provided that the Federal Reserve System owed a duty only to the *sender*, i.e., a bank, and not to the customer whose check was in transit to the drawee bank. This has now changed. *See* 12 C.F.R. § 210.6(a) (1992). "A Reserve Bank may be liable to the owner, to the sender, to a prior collecting bank, or to the depository bank's customer with respect to a check. . . ."

2. Banks in the collection system must exercise ordinary care [U.C.C. § 3–103(a)(7)] to meet the midnight deadline. U.C.C. Section 4-103(e) provides:

The measure of damages for failure to exercise ordinary care in handling an item is the amount of the item reduced by the amount which could not have been realized by the use of ordinary care, and where there is bad faith it includes other damages, if any, suffered by the party as a proximate consequence.[17]

NOTE
MICR FRAUD

With the development of automated check collection, facilitated by the use of MICR symbols, a new type of fraud developed. This involved the depositor changing the MICR line to delay presentment. Retention of the funds in the depositor's account while the check was "floating around" the collection system enabled the depositor to have a non-interest bearing loan until the check was presented.[18] A more egregious case involved the deposit

---

[17] The measure of damage can not be varied by agreement. U.C.C. § 4-103(a). *See also* Regulation CC, 12 C.F.R. § 229.37.

[18] See the scam perpetrated by various managers of E.F. Hutton & Co., stockbrokerage firm, described by Haight, J. in United States Fidelity & Guaranty Co. v. The Federal Reserve Bank of New York, 620 F.Supp. 361, 366 n. 8 (S.D.N.Y. 1985)

Hutton had checks printed with incorrect MICR numbers to foil its banks' computer-aided check-processing machines, thereby lengthening the time needed for processing the checks and increasing Hutton's "float," or amount of funds on deposit by checks which have not yet been collected from the payor bank. Hutton deposited the flawed checks drawn on its own accounts at various banks in its accounts at other banks. Until the checks were paid by the former banks, Hutton received payment for use of the funds by both banks at once. The longer the time required to process the check, the greater the "double" payments Hutton received. This was where the incorrect MICR numbers came in handy. *See* Bleakley, *How Hutton Scheme Worked*, N.Y. TIMES, May 17, 1985 at D4, cols.2–4.

of a check with fraudulent MICR symbols into an account and obtaining a provisional credit from the depository bank. Funds were then withdrawn when such withdrawal became possible after the expiration of the time indicated in the schedule provided by the Federal Expedited Funds Availability Act.[19] The depository bank would allow such withdrawal in the belief that, not having received a notice of dishonor, the check had been honored by the drawee/payor bank.[20] On receipt of the funds the crook would disappear. By acting expeditiously and with care it may be possible to prevent some of these scams. Agreements between banks providing for direct electronic presentment should also assist in preventing these types of fraud.[21]

---

[19] 12 U.S.C. § 4002.

[20] *See* 12 C.F.R. § 229.33(a) calling for telegraphic notice of dishonor where the check is in excess of $2,500.

[21] U.C.C. § 4-110.

Northpark National Bank v. Bankers Trust Co.

572 F. Supp. 524 (S.D.N.Y. 1983)*

WHITMAN KNAPP, D.J.

On November 7, 1979 a customer of plaintiff — a Dallas Bank — deposited with it a $62,500 check and thereby set in motion a clever fraud which would result in his bilking plaintiff out of some $60,000, and in the institution of this lawsuit to determine who should ultimately be left holding the proverbial "bag." The case is before us on defendant Federal Reserve Bank of New York's (FRBNY) motion to dismiss for failure to state a claim and on defendant Federal Reserve Bank of Chicago's (FRBC) motion to dismiss for lack of personal jurisdiction. This opinion deals only with the motion by the FRBNY; the application by the FRBC is considered in a separate opinion reported at 572 F.Supp. 520.

BACKGROUND

Two features of the modern check collection process are central to the understanding of this fraud. The first is that, notwithstanding the colloquial suggestion to the contrary, checks deposited for collection do not generally "clear." That is, provisional checks [credits] — on the customer's account at the depositary bank and on the accounts of intermediary banks involved in the collection process — become final by the mere passage of time, rather than by an advice of actual

payment. See Uniform Commercial Code (U.C.C.) § 4-213 [§ 4-215]. See also 6 Reitman Banking Law § 135.08 (1981). It being statistically unlikely that a particular check will not be paid, see U.C.C. § 4-212 comment 1,** the practicalities of the process call for giving actual notice ("down" the chain of collection) only in the event a check is not paid. Accordingly, the temporary "hold" which a depositary bank customarily

---

** [Editor: the Official Comment 1 to pre-1991 Revision of U.C.C. § 4-212 states:

Under current bank practice, in a major portion of cases banks make provisional settlement for items when they are first received and then await subsequent determination of whether the item will be finally paid. This is the principal characteristic of what are referred to in banking parlance as "cash items". Statistically, this practice of settling provisionally first and then awaiting final payment is justified because more than ninety-nine percent of such cash items are finally paid, with the result that in this great preponderance of cases it becomes unnecessary for the banks making the provisional settlements to make any further entries. In due course the provisional settlements become final simply with the lapse of time. . . .

There is no reason to suppose the reasoning for the practice to have changed.]

---

* [Editor: citations in [ ] refer to Revised U.C.C. Articles 3 and 4.]

places on the withdrawal of proceeds from a check deposited for collection is intended to give the collection chain an opportunity to notify the depositary bank, if it be necessary, that the check has not been paid. Thus, the hallmark of the "normal" completion of collection — i.e., the check having been paid — is the receipt of no notice by the depositary institution.

The second important feature is that the collection process has been, of course, automated by the use of check-sorting computers. *See Bank Leumi Trust v. Bally's Park Place*, 528 F.Supp. 349, 350–51 (S.D.N.Y. 1981). The vast amount of items processed allows no practical alternative. See 68 Annual Report, Board of Gov. of the Fed. Res. Syst. 233, table 9 (1981) (more than 16 billion checks handled in 1981); Aldom, Purdy, Schneider & Whittingham, *Automation in Banking* 13–15 (1963); U.C.C. § 4-101 comment. Along the bottom of a check's face there are so-called "MICR numbers" which identify the drawer's bank, branch, and account number. A computer "reads" these numbers and automatically routes the check to the appropriate destination for collection. The initial destination depends, therefore, entirely on the MICR routing number printed on the check.

With the foregoing in mind it is clear how a fraud of this type is accomplished. Its object is to cause a worthless check deposited for collection to take a sufficiently long detour in its progress to the drawee bank, to insure that the notice of non-payment will not arrive at the depositary bank until after the expiration of the "hold" which is placed on the availability of the proceeds from transit items. Having received no such notice before the expiration of the "hold," the depositary bank supposes the items to have been paid and allows its "proceeds" to be withdrawn. By the time notice arrives the malefactor has, of course, absconded with the spoils. The crucial detour is caused by imprinting the fraudulent check with the "wrong" MICR routing number — i.e., one that does not correspond to the bank designated on the face of the check as the drawee bank, but to a different bank, preferably one that is distant from the institution designated as the drawee bank on the face of the check. The fraudulent check in our case bore the MICR routing number of Bankers Trust Co. in New York and identified the

"Bank of Detroit" — a fictitious institution — as the drawee Bank.[4]

A brief chronology is now in order. The malefactor deposited the fake check in his account with plaintiff on November 7, 1979. Plaintiff put a 14-day "hold" — through November 20 — on the availability of the check's proceeds.[*] On the next day, November 8, the check was presented to the Republic National Bank of Dallas — plaintiff's correspondent bank for out-of-state collections — which, in turn, presented the check on November 9 directly to the FRBNY for collection, without routing the item through the "local" Federal Reserve Bank of Dallas. See 12 C.F.R. § 210.4 (1983) (allowing "direct send" to Federal Reserve Banks). The complaint goes on to allege that the check bears a stamp showing that it had been presented to Bankers Trust Co. for collection on November 13. The precise timing of events during the next few days has not yet been established. It is clear, however, that at some time after November 13, Bankers Trust determined that the check[5] was not drawn on it and returned the item to the FRBNY. The FRBNY, having now extracted the

---

[4] The fact that the "Bank of Detroit" does not exist is immaterial to this motion. As we understand the mechanics of this fraud, it would work as well if the institution identified as the drawee bank on the face of the fraudulent check were a "real" bank, or if the account on which the check is ostensibly drawn were a "real" account. It is irrelevant whether the fraudulent check is returned unpaid because the drawee "bank" does not exist, because the account on which it is drawn at a (real) drawee bank does not exist, or because the (real) account on which it is drawn at a (real) drawee bank is without funds. The outcome of this motion should not depend, in our view, on the fortuitous choice of check "style" which the malefactor has made. In this connection we observe, moreover, that defendant's penchant for referring to the fraudulent check as a "non-check" on grounds that it was not drawn "on a bank," see U.C.C. § 3-104(2)(b) [§ 3-104(f)], is of no legal moment.

[*] [Editor: the "hold" is now reduced to four days, *see* EFA Act 12 U.S.C. § 4002.]

[5] The complaint does not indicate whether the plaintiff's client was the malefactor or a victim who had dealt with one. At oral argument plaintiff's counsel advised us, however, that the (former) customer can now be found in a Pennsylvania jail, presumably on account of a less successful venture than the one which spawned this litigation.

check from the computer-directed addressing system, then forwarded the check to the FRBC on the strength of the designation "Bank of Detroit" which the check bore on its face.[6] The complaint states that the check is stamped as having been in the hands of the FRBC on November 20. Meanwhile, back in Dallas, the malefactor withdrew $9,000 from his account on November 21 and an additional $40,250 on Saturday, November 24. The precise schedule of the check's vicissitudes after November 20 is yet undetermined. It must, however, have been sent to the Detroit branch of the FRBC, which branch, in turn, established that the "Bank of Detroit" did not exist. The check must then have followed the self-same route back to the FRBC and then to the FRBNY. The complaint alleges that the FRBNY again received the check on November 29, well after the malefactor had eloped with the plundered funds, leaving — we suppose — a barren account. What happened to the check thereafter is immaterial. Suffice it to say that the Federal Reserve Bank of Dallas advised plaintiff some time in December that the check would be returned unpaid, and upon the check's return debited plaintiff's account at the Dallas Fed for the amount of the phony check.

DISCUSSION

The complaint is altogether parsimonious in describing the legal foundation of the charges against the FRBNY. As developed in its submission in opposition to the FRBNY's motion, the specific legal grounds for plaintiff's claim are that, having received the check unpaid from the FRBC on November 29, the FRBNY (a) failed timely to send notice or timely to forward the check "down" the collection chain, as required by U.C.C. § 4-212(1) [§ 4–214(a)] and, therefore, forfeited its right to charge-back under that provision; that, having received the unpaid check from Bankers Trust on November 13, the FRBNY (b) failed to send notice "down" the collection chain of the check's delay in transit, as required by U.C.C.

---

§ 4-202(1)(e); [§ 4-202(a)(4)] (c) failed timely to forward the check for presentment to the FRBC, as required by U.C.C. [§ 4-202(a)(1)]; and (d) failed to send notice of non-payment "down" the collection chain, as required by U.C.C. § 4-202(1)(b) [§ 4–202(a)(2)].

I

At the outset the parties have vigorously disputed whether the FRBNY is a "collecting bank" for purposes of U.C.C. §§ 4-212 [§ 4-214] and 4-202 because the strictures of those sections apply only to such banks. Defendant argues, see Defendant's Reply Memorandum at 1–3, that it cannot be a collecting bank because they are defined as "any bank handling the item for collection except the payor bank," U.C.C. § 4-105(d) [§ 4-105(5)] (emphasis added), and it had no authority to handle the check "for collection," as it was not drawn on a bank located in the geographic district served by the FRBNY. For the latter proposition the FRBNY refers us to 12 U.S.C. § 360 and 5 Fed.Res.Bull. 467 (1919) (Exhibit F to Defendant's Reply Memorandum). This argument is without merit. The purpose of the Federal Reserve Act of 1913, as amended — whose section 16 is the forerunner of what is now 12 U.S.C. § 360 — was to organize the Federal Reserve Bank. There is not the slightest indication that the grant of authority in § 360 was intended as a "shield" against the application of U.C.C. §§ 4-212 [§ 4-214] and 4-202 or, conversely, that the drafters of the U.C.C. intended those sections to be read in conjunction with 12 U.S.C. § 360. Section 4-105(d) [§ 4-105(5)] of the U.C.C. sets out a very practical, commonsensical definition of "collecting" bank as every bank in the collection chain except the payor bank. The FRBNY was certainly a link in that chain.

Defendant argues further that it is not a collecting bank because it was sent the check "by mistake." See Citizens State Bank v. Martin, 227 Kan. 580, 609 P.2d 670, 676 (1980) (holding that a bank receiving a check because of a encoding error is not a collecting bank). The check, however, was not sent by "mistake." It was properly addressed to the FRBNY in accordance with a MICR routing number which called for such destination. This was, of course, part of a fraudulent

---

[6] Detroit lies in the geographic district served by the FRBC. The FRBNY is permitted further to route the check to Chicago by virtue of note 3 to 12 C.F.R. § 210.6 (1979), currently codified at 12 C.F.R. § 210.6(a) (2) (1983) with minor stylistic variations. It allows a Federal Reserve Bank to route a check based on any addressing symbol, whether or not it be consistent with other symbols on the item.

scheme but it surely was not a "mistake ."[12] Last, the FRBNY argues that it should not be subjected to U.C.C. §§ 4-212 [§ 4-214] and 4-202 because "[p]laintiff should not be permitted to impose significant legal obligations on the New York Fed simply by sending it a worthless piece of paper." Defendant's Reply Memorandum at 3. This is yet another strained argument. The check is no less "valuable" than a check drawn on insufficient funds at an account with an in-district bank. The "value" of the check is of no consequence to the role which the FRBNY played in the collection process or to the attendant obligations to which it should, accordingly, be subjected. We therefore hold that, on the facts of this case, the FRBNY is a collecting bank for the purpose of subjecting it to such duties as are specified in U.C.C. §§ 4-202 and [§ 4-214].

II

Plaintiff contends that the FRBNY lost its right to "charge back" plaintiff's account under U.C.C. § 4-212 [§ 4-214] when it failed, "by its midnight deadline" after receiving the check from the FRBC on November 29, to return it or to send notification of having received it unpaid. We observe again that by November 29 any notification — by whatever means — would have been futile because the malefactor had completed his fraud on November 24. Accordingly, the question we are asked to decide is whether, in requiring "notification" or the "return" of the item, U.C.C. § 4-212(1) [§ 4-214(a)] establishes conditions precedent to the right of charge-back or whether it defines a duty of ordinary care relative to the right to charge-back. If it were the former, the non-occurrence of the condition would result in there being no right to charge-back — i.e., the collecting bank who failed to fulfill the conditions would be absolutely liable for the item. If it were the latter, the right to charge-back would be absolute, at least until settlement became "final," but a plaintiff could hold the collecting bank respon-

sible for such damages as were proximately caused by the collecting bank's failure timely to discharge its duty to notify or to return the item. In this case, no damages could be traced by the FRBNY's alleged failure to notify on or after November 29, because the damage could not then have been prevented.

We hold that U.C.C. § 4-212(1) [§ 4-214(a)] establishes a duty of care, not a condition to the right to charge-back. At oral argument plaintiff's counsel conceded, see Tr. 23–27, that the only reported case which specifically addresses the question before us is *Appliance Buyers Credit Corp. v. Prospect Nat. Bank*, 708 F.2d 290 (7th Cir. 1983) (Timbers, C.J., of the 2d Cir. in the majority panel). It holds, as do we, that U.C.C. § 4-212(1) [§ 4-214(a)] imposes a duty, not a condition and that plaintiff, therefore, has the burden of establishing the actual damages caused by the collecting bank's failures. Id. at 294–95. We could safely rest our holding on the persuasive statutory exegesis in *Appliance Buyers*. In addition, however, we observe that comment 1 to U.C.C. § 4-108 [§ 4-109] specifically refers to U.C.C. § 4-212 [§ 4-109(b)] as "prescrib[ing] ... time limits ... within which a bank, in fulfillment of its obligation to exercise ordinary care, must handle items entrusted to it for collection." (Emphasis added). Moreover, we would not impute to the drafters of the U.C.C. the intention of imposing a "duty" the performance of which would make no practical difference whatever. To be sure, the language of U.C.C. § 4-212(1) [§ 4-214(a)] is far from clear in this regard. Although clarity and consistency have never been the U.C.C.'s hallmark, see, e.g., D. Mellinkoff, *The Language of the Uniform Commercial Code*, 77 Yale L.J. 185 (1976), practicality is certainly one of its virtues. We would therefore require a clear indication of legislative intention before reading into U.C.C. § 4-212(1) [§ 4-214(a)] a collecting bank's obligation to perform an empty gesture. Plaintiff has called to our attention no such indication, nor has our own research uncovered any.

The clearest expression of the purpose to be served by the notification requirement in the charge-back statute is provided by comments 1 and 4 to U.C.C. § 4-207 (1950 Edition). Notification is intended, the comments tell us, promptly to advise an unsuspecting customer and to protect him from having checks (drawn on his account) returned unpaid. See, e.g., *First State Bank &*

---

[12] We have no occasion to consider whether a defendant ought to be considered a "collecting" bank with respect to an item it received truly by mistake — e.g., mislaid in a mail bag addressed to it. In this case the check was delivered to the FRBNY entirely by design. To the extent the *Martin case* can be read as holding that the FRBNY is not a collecting bank in this situation we disagree with its conclusion.

Trust Co. v. George, 16 U.C.C. Rep. 160 (Tex. Civ.App. 1974). *See also* U.C.C. § 4-212 [§ 4-214] comment 5. Even on the plausible assumption that the duty of prompt notification was also intended to allow the customer and a collecting bank to protect their rights against third parties, there is no logical reason to suppose that such intention implies that the violator of the duty be held liable, irrespective of the causal connection between the breach and the plaintiff's inability to collect on the item. Cf. U.C.C. §§ 4-202 (duty) and 4-103(5) [§ 4-103(e)] (measure of damages). Indeed, all decisions which we have been able to locate denying a defendant's right to charge-back under U.C.C. § 4-212 [§ 4-214] for failure to notify (or to forward the item), are cases in which "causation" is established because the defendant's failure led to a detrimental change in plaintiff's position, which change could have been avoided by prompt notification. * * *

Accordingly, we hold the cause of action under U.C.C. § 4-212 [§ 4-214] to be legally insufficient because plaintiff has pleaded no facts which establish that it is entitled to any damages, even if it prevailed on the issue of liability.

* * *

III

Plaintiff also charges the FRBNY with violating U.C.C. § 4-202(1)(e) [§ 4-202(a)(4)] because it did not send a notice of "delay in transit" after it received the check unpaid from Bankers Trust. Defendant FRBNY contends, on the other hand, that U.C.C. § 4-202(1)(e) [§ 4-202(a)(4)] was not meant to apply to a situation such as this one, but rather to cases in which the physical items are lost or destroyed when transported from one location to another. *See Citizens State Bank v. Martin,* supra, 227 Kan. at 588, 609 P.2d at 676 (dictum).

In our view defendant's position is the correct one. The history of U.C.C. § 4-202(1)(e) [§ 4-202(a)(4)] can be traced at least back to the Proposed Final Drafts Nos. 1 and 2 of Article III on commercial paper. The relevant section in Draft No. 1 was appropriately entitled "Lost Items," see § 715 (Draft No. 1, April 15, 1984) (emphasis added), and in Draft No. 2 it was called "Loss of Cash Items in Transit." See § 713 (Draft No. 2, July 30, 1948) (emphasis added). Their respective notes and comments leave no doubt that the "delays in transit" which the drafters contem-

plated were those occasioned by mishaps in the mails. See Notes and Comments to Draft No. 1 at 71 (April 15, 1948); Notes & Comments to Draft No. 2 at 17 (August 2, 1948). See also U.C.C. § 3-611(2) (1948 Edition). We have found nothing in the subsequent legislative history to persuade us that the several stylistic mutations which eventually led to U.C.C. § 4-202(1)(e) [§ 4-202(a)(4)] modified the above described legislative intent. See also N.Y. Law Revision Comm., Study of Unif. Com. Code - Article 4 at 97 (Leg. Doc. No. 65(E), 1955).

In this case the physical progress of the fraudulent check was never hindered by an accident, cf. *Girard Trust Bank v. Brinks, Inc.,* 422 Pa. 48, 220 A.2d 827 (1966), or by it being mislaid in the mail. Accordingly, we hold that the FRBNY was under no obligation to give such notice as is specified in U.C.C. § 4-202(1)(e) [§ 4-202(a)(4)].

IV

Plaintiff also contends that the FRBNY violated its duties under U.C.C. § 4-202(1)(a) [§ 4-202(a)(1)] because it failed to forward the check to the FRBC within the time limits specified in U.C.C. § 4-202(2) [§ 4-202(b)] after having received it unpaid from Bankers Trust. See Plaintiff's Memorandum at 12–13; Tr. at 8. This claim, for the time being at least, we must sustain.

In connection with a claim under U.C.C. § 4-202 there is no dispute that the appropriate rule for damages is the "but for" test of U.C.C. § 4-103(5) [§ 4-103(e)]. Moreover, this measure of damages for the violation of the duty of care in handling items for collection long antecedes the enactment of the U.C.C. *See American Nat'l Bank v. Bank of Bandon,*240 F. 624 (9th Cir. 1917); *Balsa Ecuador Lumber Corp. v. Securities Nat. Bank,* 141 F.Supp. 470, 476 (E.D.N.C. 1956); U.C.C. § 4-103 comment 6. With the foregoing in mind it is apparent that, even if it were able to establish that the FRBNY violated U.C.C. § 4-202(1)(a) [§ 4-202(a)(1)], plaintiff would be hard pressed to prove damages. It is equally clear, however, that in this procedural posture the claim may not be dismissed.

* * *

Accordingly, plaintiff will be allowed discovery for purposes of establishing the timing of the various stages by which the check progressed from New York to Chicago. Should the evidence prove that the FRBNY violated U.C.C. § 4-202(1)(a) [§ 4-202(a)(1)] by delaying the check's progress beyond the limits specified in U.C.C. § 4-202(2) [§ 4-202(b)], plaintiff will be allowed — indeed, required — further to establish that such delay caused it damage.

V

Finally, plaintiff charges that the FRBNY violated U.C.C. § 4-202(1)(b) [§ 4-202(a)(2)] by failing to send a notice of non-payment after it had received the check from Bankers Trust some time after November 13.[19] On the other hand, defendant contends, in substance, that U.C.C. § 4-202(1)(b) [§ 4-202(a)(2)] does not impose on it the duty to notify about Bankers Trust's non-payment because the drafters of the U.C.C. intended the "notice of dishonor or nonpayment" mentioned in U.C.C. § 4-202(1)(b) [§ 4-202(a)(2)] to originate with the payor bank; and that, accordingly, the FRBNY was not legally obligated to send the appropriate notice until it received it from Chicago.[20] See Defendant's Memorandum at 8-9; Defendant's Reply Memorandum at 7-9. We disagree.

The parties' submissions in this regard have amounted to no more than exchanges of unsupported conclusions. Such (necessarily incomplete) review of the U.C.C.'s sprawling legislative history as we were able to perform allows us to state that the drafters of the U.C.C. certainly expected that the "last" bank in the collection chain would be the wellhead of the notification stream "down" that chain, such expectation being part of generally shared institutional assumptions. A review of the mutations of U.C.C. § 4-202 — going back to § 712(1) and § 708(1), both entitled "Responsibility for Collection," of the 1948 Proposed Final Drafts Nos. 1 and 2 of Article III, respectively — shows, however, no evidence whatever of an affirmative legislative intention in this connection.[21] There is, in fact, no indication that any thought was given to the situation before us in this case. This is, of course, not at all surprising. The 1981 edition of a respected treatise on the law of check collections does not even mention "MICR fraud" — as this fraud has, appropriately, come to be known — in its sections dealing either with fraud or with the responsibility for losses due to improper encoding. See B. Clarke, *The Law of Bank Deposits, Collections & Credit Cards* chs. 6 and 10 (rev.ed. 1981). Indeed, the legal problems of loss due to improper encoding, let alone fraud, are of relatively recent vintage. * * * What we have, therefore, is a statute, U.C.C. § 4-202(1)(b) [§ 4-202(a)(2)], which — on the basis of the parties' submissions and our own research — cannot fairly be said to have been drafted in contemplation of the facts in this case. The question, then, is whether it should be interpreted to cover the situation at hand. We think it should.

Certain observations are in order concerning Article IV in general and U.C.C. § 4-202 in particular. The history of the U.C.C. makes it abundantly clear that, especially in the context of those provisions which impose a duty of care, the Code's watchword is "flexibility." It is well known that banks' early opposition to what is now Article IV could be traced in considerable measure to the fear that the possibility of any conduct not complying with procedures affirmatively approved could be found to constitute a violation of the obligation of care. See, generally, W. Malcolm, *Article 4 - A Battle with Complexity*, 1952 Wisc.L.Rev.265, 280-83 (1952). The Final Text

---

[19] We need not resolve the parties' disagreements on whether Bankers Trust's return of the check technically constituted its "dishonor." See U.C.C. § 3-507 [§ 3-502].

[20] It was observed at oral argument that in this case — the "Bank of Detroit" being a fictitious institution — there was no payor bank in the collection chain. As we have already pointed out, we do not regard the fact that the "Bank of Detroit" does not exist as determinative. See note 4, above. In any event, our ruling on the applicability of U.C.C. § 4-202(1)(b) [§ 4-202(a)(2)] does not turn on the existence (or non-existence) of a payor bank. We can, thus, take defendant's position in this case to be that the "notice of dishonor or non-payment" was intended to originate with the "last" bank in the collection chain and that the FRBNY was entitled to suppose that bank to be in the Chicago district.

[21] Defendant's only feeble attempt to "prove" his argument consists of a naked reference to U.C.C. § 4-301(1)(b) [§ 4-301(a)(2)] and the observation that it uses the same language as does U.C.C. § 4-202(1)(b) [§ 4-202(a)(2)] — "notice of dishonor or non-payment" — in describing what a payor bank must send "down" the collection chain in order to revoke a settlement. Such observation is entirely consistent with our view but falls well short of proving the assertion of legislative intent on which the FRBNY relies.

Edition of 1951 crystallized U.C.C. § 4-103(3) [§ 4-103(c)] and § 4-103(4) [§ 4-103(d)] which clearly established that approval of certain procedures did not constitute disapproval of other procedures found reasonable in light of sound banking practice. See also U.C.C. § 4-103 comment 5. This observation leads to two conclusions. First, there being no mechanical test for what constitutes "ordinary care" in a novel situation, the ultimate standard is dictated by the imperatives of sound banking practice, seasoned by the obligation of "good faith." See U.C.C. § 1-201(19).* Second, flexibility is a "two way street": just as a new task or procedure will certainly be acceptable if it reflects sound banking practice, so the lack of one — when such absence violates sound banking practice — should be actionable.

Concerning U.C.C. § 4-202 in particular, there are strong indications that the tasks described in U.C.C. § 4-202(1)(a) through (e) [§ 4-202(a)(1)-(4)] are not an exhaustive list of the actions to be taken by a collecting bank in order to satisfy its obligation of ordinary care. See U.C.C. § 4-202 comment 1 (the section described "basic" responsibilities); comment 3 (the section describes "types" of "basic" actions); comment 4 ("ordinary care" is used in its "normal tort meaning" and "[n]o attempt is made . . . to define in toto what constitutes ordinary care [or] lack of it"). This leads to the further conclusion that the enumeration in U.C.C. § 4-202(1)(a) through (e) [§ 4-202(a)(1)-(4)] should not be deemed — by negative implication — a bar to the reinterpretation (or expansion) of the duties owed by a bank in discharging its collection function with "ordinary care."

With the foregoing in mind the specific question before us is: "What should be considered good banking practice in a situation where it comes to a banker's attention that the routing codes on a check is inconsistent with the address on the face of the item?" If day-to-day banking experience should demonstrate that such inconsistencies are usually the result of simple error, there would be no reason to assume that a conscientious banker should become alarmed at learning of an inconsistency or deem it his duty

* [Editor: see U.C.C. § 3-103(a)(4), (7) (second sentence).]

to notify anyone.[23] On the other hand, if day-to-day banking experience should establish that such inconsistencies are usually an indication of fraud,[24] then it might well be argued that a collecting bank, in satisfying its obligation of ordinary care, should take steps promptly to notify a prospective victim in the collection chain.[25]

If there is a policy implicit in the U.C.C.'s rules for the allocation of losses due to fraud, it surely is that the loss be placed on the party in the best position to prevent it. See B. Clarke, *The Law of Bank Deposits, Collections & Credit Cards,* P6.1 (1981). At oral argument we suggested that plain-

---

[23] The existence of footnote 3 to 13 C.F.R. § 210.6(a) (1979), currently codified at 12 C.F.R. § 210.6(a)(2) (1983), may well be persuasive evidence that this is, in fact, the actual state of affairs. This provision absolves the Federal Reserve from liability for routing an item according to any addressing symbol that may appear on it. Although the parties have submitted nothing to clarify the background of this regulation, its very existence may indicate that inconsistencies in routing symbols are often to be found, without thereby suggesting the possibility of fraud. We observe, moreover, that footnote 3 has — in our view — no other direct bearing on the FRBNY's obligation to notify. On its face that footnote appears to deal only with the potential claims that may be raised under U.C.C. § 4-204 which prescribes due care in routing an item.

[24] This form of fraud is not nearly as uncommon as defendant seems to suggest. At oral argument it developed that there is an aggregate of some $2 million of such fraud in the early stages of litigation. Tr. at 45–46. In the last few months we have had before us a criminal case involving precisely this scheme.

[25] Defendant argues that if it were required to do so — in the absence of notification from a payor bank — it might be liable to an innocent drawer for misrepresentation or liable if the items later turned out to be properly payable. Defendant's Memorandum at 9. This argument is frivolous: all a collecting bank would be required to do is to tell the truth; namely, that there is an inconsistency in routing symbols and that the item, pursuant to 12 C.F.R. § 210.6(a)(2) is being forwarded elsewhere for further attempts at collection. It would be up to the depositary bank to draw its own inference in light of its experience with the customer involved. Moreover, the requirement of notification to would place no undue burden on the collecting bank. All that would be required would be routine instructions that such disparity be automatically referred to a given individual whose automatic duty it would be to notify the depositary bank.

tiff should be made to bear — on policy grounds — full responsibility for this loss. It is, after all, a bank's business to make certain that it doesn't deal with crooks.[27] On further reflection, however, we are not prepared to say that no share of the loss should be placed — on policy grounds — on a collecting bank which might be shown to have

known (or to be on notice) that fraud was afoot and did nothing to stop it, although it had the "last clear chance" to do so. However, on the record before us no facts are pleaded — let alone proved — which would shed any light on whether inconsistency between the routing code and the address on the face of the item could reasonably be regarded as a mere mistaken or should alert any knowledgeable banker to the probability of fraud.

---

[27] Plaintiff's counsel seemed at a loss to suggest what, precisely, his client could have done to prevent this scheme. * * * The question, however, is not what plaintiff could have done in this case but who (in the collection chain) is, generally, in the best position to prevent the fraud. He who deals with a malefactor must certainly be charged with the responsibility of discovering the fraud — nobody else in the collection chain can do better. As a matter of policy, moreover, the depositary bank is in the best position to distribute the risk over its client base through insurance. See, generally, E.A. Farnsworth, *Insurance Against Check Forgery*, 60 Colum. L. Rev. 284, 302–03 (1960).

CONCLUSION

The claims based on U.C.C. §§ 4-202(1)(a) [§ 4-202(a)(1)] and 4-202(1)(b) [§ 4-202(a)(2)] are, accordingly, held to be legally viable. The plaintiff may, if it be so advised, amend its complaint to allege facts suggesting that routing code inconsistency should be regarded as indicating the probability of fraud; and may conduct appropriate discovery on that issue. The remaining claims against the FRBNY are dismissed for failure to state a cause of action.

NOTE

1. The American Bankers' Association publishes a "Key to Routing Numbers" in software form. This will enable a bank to discover from the ABA Identifier in the MICR line the name of the bank on which the check has been drawn. The existence and use of this software would have prevented the check being routed to the FRBC and would have exposed the fraud at an earlier stage.

2. Note U.C.C. § 4-209. Would that section affect the outcome of this case? Who encoded the MICR symbols?

While a failure to act within the time limit indicated will give rise to an action for damages suffered, U.C.C. § 4–103(3)(e), the most serious effect of the delay is on a drawee who fails to act promptly in rejecting/dishonoring an item.[22] U.C.C Section 4-302 provides that the drawee will become accountable for the amount of the item if the drawee bank delays in acting on the item, i.e., it will not have accepted the item, but will nonetheless be liable to pay the amount of the item subject to any defenses it may be able to raise based on a breach of presentment warranties, U.C.C. § 4-208, or by showing that the person attempting to enforce this obligation of the bank is trying to defraud the drawee.

---

[22] *See also* Regulation CC, 12 C.F.R. § 229.33(a) as to notice of dishonor "by any reasonable means, including the returned check, a writing (including a copy of the check), telephone, Fedwire, telex, or other form of telegraph."

First Wyoming Bank, N.A. Sheridan v. Cabinet Craft Distributors, Inc.
624 P.2d 227 (Wyo. 1981)*

ROSE, Chief Justice.

The Uniform Commercial Code provides that except in certain circumstances a bank is liable for the amount of a check which it fails to timely dishonor. [U.C.C. § 4-302]. In this case, the appellee presented a check payable to itself to the appellant bank. The payor had insufficient funds on deposit with the bank to cover the check. The bank dishonored the check but failed to do so within the time mandated by the Uniform Commercial Code.

Appellee then sued in district court for the face amount of the check, interest and costs. The district court agreed with the appellee that the bank was liable under the Code and gave judgment accordingly. The bank has appealed and argues that its "excuse" for failing to timely dishonor the check is sufficient under the Code to enable it to escape liability. [U.C.C. § 4-109(b)].

We shall affirm the trial court.

The case was tried on stipulated facts. However, before presenting the stipulation, it is appropriate to reproduce the controlling Code provisions.

THE STATUTES

U.C.C. § 4-302 provides:

"[§ 4-302. Payor Bank's Responsibility for Late Return of Item.

(a) If an item is presented to and received by a payor bank, the bank is accountable for the amount of:

(1) a demand item, other than a documentary draft, whether properly payable or not, if the bank, in any case in which it is not also the depositary bank, retains the item beyond midnight of the banking day of receipt without settling for it or, whether or not it is also the depositary bank, does not pay or return the item or send notice of dishonor until after its midnight deadline; or

(2) any other properly payable item unless, within the time allowed for acceptance or payment of that item, the bank

either accepts or pays the item or returns it and accompanying documents.

(b) The liability of a payor bank to pay an item pursuant to subsection (a) is subject to defenses based on breach of a presentment warranty (Section 4-208) or proof that the persons seeking enforcement of the liability presented or transferred the item for the purpose of defrauding the payor bank.]**

The term "midnight deadline" is defined in U.C.C. [§ 4-104(a)(10)]:

"Midnight deadline" with respect to a bank is midnight on its next banking day following the banking day on which it receives the relevant item or notice or from which the time for taking action commences to run, whichever is later;

U.C.C. [§ 4-109(b)], provides:

[Delay by a collecting bank or payor bank beyond time limits prescribed or permitted by this [Act] or by instructions is excused if (i) the delay is caused by interruption of communication or computer facilities, suspension of payments by another bank, war, emergency conditions, failure of equipment, or other circumstances beyond the control of the bank, and (ii) the bank exercises such diligence as the circumstances require.]***

[§ 4-108 Time of Receipt of Items

(b) An item or deposit of money received on any day after a cutoff hour so fixed or after the close of the banking day may be treated as being received at the opening of the next banking day.]

In arguing that the delay in dishonoring the check was excusable, appellant bank also relies on 12 Code of Federal Regulations 210.14 which provides:

---

* [Editor: citations in [ ] refer to Revised U.C.C. Articles 3 and 4.]

** [Editor: we are setting out here the rephrased provisions of Revised U.C.C.-Article 4 since they do not reflect a change in substance.]

*** [Editor: Note Revised U.C.C. § 4-109(b) also includes interruption of computer facilities and failure of equipment. Situations previously not provided for.]

If, because of interruption of communication facilities, suspension of payments by another bank, war, emergency conditions or other circumstances beyond its control, any bank (including a Federal Reserve bank) shall be delayed beyond the time limits provided in this part or the operating letters of the Federal Reserve banks, or prescribed by the applicable law of any State in taking any action with respect to a cash item or a noncash item, including forwarding such item, presenting it or sending it for presentment and payment, paying or remitting for it, returning it or sending notice of dishonor or nonpayment or making or providing for any necessary protest, the time of such bank, as limited by this part or the operating letters of the Federal Reserve banks, or by the applicable law of any State, for taking or completing the action thereby delayed shall be extended for such time after the cause of the delay ceases to operate as shall be necessary to take or complete the action, provided the bank exercises such diligence as the circumstances require."****

The bank points out that under, U.C.C. Section 4-103 [§ 4-103(b)], if not under the supremacy clause of the Federal Constitution, the above regulation is controlling law in Wyoming. We agree that the regulation controls but fail to see how it adds anything to [U.C.C. § 4-109(b)], *supra*. In light of the stipulated facts to be presented immediately below, it appears that either under the statute or the regulation the bank must show that its delay in dishonoring the check was due to circumstances beyond its control and that the bank exercised such diligence as the circumstances required.

THE FACTS

* * * As we understand the facts, both parties to this suit have acted in good faith and the plain-

---

**** [Editor: Regulation J, 12 C.F.R. § 210.14 now provides: If because of interruption of communications facilities, suspension of payments by a bank or non-bank payor, war, emergency conditions, or other circumstances beyond its control, a bank (including a Reserve Bank) or non-bank payor is delayed in acting on an item beyond applicable time limits, its time for acting is extended for the time necessary to complete the action, if it exercises such diligence as the circumstances require.]

tiff-appellee has made no showing that it was prejudiced by the untimely dishonor of the check. The untimely dishonor of the check was due to delay in delivering checks from a computer center in Billings, Montana, to the bank in Sheridan. Normally, the same courier delivering the checks to the Montana computer center from Sheridan would have driven them back to Sheridan after the center had processed them. However, after the check in issue had been taken to Billings, the main road between Billings and Sheridan became flooded. Although the courier could have taken an alternate route back to Sheridan, the check was instead given to Western Airlines by the computer center to be placed on the next morning's flight to Sheridan. For unknown reasons Western Airlines failed to deliver the check to Sheridan although it made its usual flight. Western Airline's failure to deliver the check to Sheridan as planned caused the bank to miss its Uniform Commercial Code deadline for dishonoring the check. * * *

WYOMING CASE LAW

The only Wyoming case discussing [U.C.C. § 4-302], supra, is *American National Bank of Powell v. Foodbasket, Wyo.*, 493 P.2d 403 and 497 P.2d 546 (1972). (The earlier opinion was withdrawn on rehearing.) The case is not particularly relevant since the check payee in *Foodbasket* was not acting in good faith whereas the payee in the instant case is stipulated to have been acting in good faith.[2] * * *

Thus, a bad faith check payee may not demand enforcement of U.C.C. § 4-302, *supra*.

This analysis by the Montana Supreme Court is sound and consistent with our opinion in *Foodbasket, supra*.

CASE LAW FROM OTHER JURISDICTIONS
Liability under U.C.C. § 4-302

Courts generally interpret U.C.C. § 4-302, *supra,* as imposing strict liability upon a bank which fails to dishonor a check in time unless the bank meets its burden of proving a valid defense.

---

[2] The Montana Supreme Court has said that U.C.C. § 4-302, supra, is modified by U.C.C. § 1-203, which states:
> Every contract or duty within this act . . . imposes an obligation of good faith in its performance or enforcement.

In *Sun River Cattle Co., Inc. v. Miners Bank of Mont. N.A.*, 164 Mont. 237, 521 P.2d 679, 684 (1974), reh. den., the Montana Supreme Court spoke of U.C.C. § 4-302 as imposing a "standard of strict accountability" and cited the Official Code Comment for the proposition that the bank has the burden of proving an excuse under [U.C.C. § 4-109(b)], supra. *Sun River Cattle Co.*, *supra*, 521 P.2d at 685 and also citing 3 Anderson, Uniform Commercial Code 191. The United States Tenth Circuit Court of Appeals has said that if it is shown that a check has not been dishonored within the Code time limit, a prima facie case is established for imposing liability on the bank and the bank has the obligation of proving an excuse for untimely dishonor under [U.C.C. § 4-109(b)], supra. *Port City State Bank v. American National Bank, Lawton, Okl.*, 10 Cir., 486 F.2d 196, 198 (1973). The United States Fifth Circuit Court of Appeals recently said, "Failure . . . to perform these duties within the time limits prescribed [by U.C.C. § 4-302] mandates the imposition of strict liability for the face amount of any late instrument. * * *" *Union Bank of Benton v. First Nat. Bank*, 5 Cir., 621 F.2d 790, 795 (1980). The Supreme Court of New Mexico has said, "The liability created by [U.C.C. § 4-302, supra] is independent of negligence and is an absolute or strict liability for the full amount of the items which it fails to return, * * *" *Engine Parts v. Citizens Bank of Clovis*, 92 N.M. 37, 582 P.2d 809, 815 (1978).

Both the Illinois Supreme Court and the Kentucky Court of Appeals have rejected arguments that a bank which fails to timely dishonor a check under U.C.C. § 4-302, supra, is only liable if the delay in the dishonoring of the check injured the check's payee. *Rock Island Auction Sales v. Empire Packing Co.*, 32 Ill.2d 269, 204 N.E.2d 721, 723–724 (1965); and *Farmers Coop. Livestock Mkt. v. Second Nat. Bank, Ky.*, 427 S.W.2d 247, 250 (1968).

Other cases which have come to similar conclusions concerning the relevant Code provision include: *Pecos County State Bank v. El Paso Livestock, Tex. Civ. App.*, 586 S.W.2d 183, 187 (1979), reh. den:, and *Templeton v. First Nat. Bank of Nashville*, 47 Ill.App.3d 443, 5 Ill.Dec. 720, 362 N.E.2d 33, 37 (1977).

Thus, since there is no issue of bad faith, our examination of appellant bank's claim of a valid excuse under [U.C.C. § 4-109(b)], supra, does not entail a consideration of the equities involved. Rather our task is simply to determine whether the record demonstrates a sufficient excuse under the above statute.

CASE LAW FROM OTHER JURISDICTIONS
Excuses under [U.C.C. § 4-109(b)]

It is obvious that the flooded road between Billings and Sheridan which disrupted the normal procedure for delivery of the check was a "circumstance beyond the control of the bank" as contemplated by [U.C.C. § 4-109(b)], supra. Our inquiry is whether the bank used "such diligence as the circumstances required," in allowing the Montana computer center to give the check to Western Airlines for delivery and in not following up the failure of the airline to deliver the packet on schedule. In answering this question we must consider that the stipulated facts show that the bank had an alternative to using Western Airlines: its courier could have taken a different route. We are also somewhat handicapped by a lack of information. For example, although we know that the bank had previously used the airline's delivery service, we do not know what the airline's previous record for timely deliveries had been. We do not know if the computer center in turning the check over to the airline emphasized the need for a timely delivery. We do not know if the bank could have traced the checks which failed to arrive on the Western Airlines flight and gotten them sooner.

We have found no case involving a claimed [U.C.C. § 4-109(b)], supra, excuse identical to the one involved here and only a few cases involving somewhat similar excuses. Surveying the area in 1977 the Kentucky Court of Appeals found "only two cases involving the application of [U.C.C. § 4-109] to a payor bank's midnight deadline." *Blake v. Woodford Bank & Trust Co.*, Ky.App., 555 S.W.2d 589, 594 (1977). The two cases found by the Kentucky court are *Sun River Cattle Co.*, supra, and *Port City State Bank*, supra. We have not been able to discover any cases in addition to the Kentucky, Montana and Tenth Circuit decisions.

The Montana case is, perhaps, most in point. A bank in Butte, Montana, had its checks processed at a computer center in Great Falls, Montana. In the usual course of business the Butte bank's checks were sent by armored car to Great

Falls for processing. Ordinarily, the checks would leave Butte at 5:00 or 6:00 p.m. on the day of receipt, arrive at Great Falls about 10:30 p.m., be processed by 11:30 p.m., be loaded back onto the armored car headed for Butte at 4:00 a.m. and arrive back in Butte at 7:00 a.m. *Sun River Cattle Co.*, *supra,* 521 P.2d at 684.

Unfortunately for the Butte bank, it received some checks on May 11, 1970. That day the armored car broke down and did not reach Great Falls until 1:30 a.m., May 12. Moreover, the computer in Great Falls malfunctioned with the result that the checks were not returned to Butte until 2:30 p.m. on May 12, rather than at 7:00 a.m. on that date. The Butte bank's "midnight deadline" for dishonoring the checks was midnight of May 12. Id. and [U.C.C. § 4-104(a)(10)], supra. Thus, even though the armored car and computer breakdowns threw the bank off its normal schedule, it would have been physically possible for the bank to have dishonored the checks by midnight of May 12. The bank was unable to offer an explanation for failing to dishonor the checks by midnight of May 12.

The Montana court said:

Under the exception of section [4-109(b)] the bank must show: (1) A cause for the delay; (2) that the cause was beyond the control of the bank; and (3) that under the circumstances the bank exercised such diligence as required. In the absence of any one of these showings, the excuse for the delay will not apply, and the bank will be held liable under the provisions of section 4-302. * * * (Emphasis added.) 521 P.2d at 686.

Along these lines our appellee urges that we note that there is no evidence in the record that the appellant bank made any efforts to trace the checks when they did not arrive in Sheridan aboard the Western Airlines flight as scheduled. Perhaps a trace started on the missing checks that morning would have enabled the bank to obtain the checks that day and meet the midnight deadline for dishonoring the insufficient-funds check which is the focus of this appeal.

However, although the appellant does not discuss this case, there is a distinguishing feature about *Sun River Cattle* which favors the appellant's cause. In the Montana case the checks in question were drawn on a business greatly indebted to the Butte bank and in precarious

financial shape. The Montana court stated that it was holding the Butte bank to a stricter standard of proof under [U.C.C. § 4-109(b)], supra, than would ordinarily be required. *Sun River Cattle*, *supra,* 521 P.2d at 685.

Our appellant bank relies almost solely on the Tenth Circuit case. *Port City State Bank*, supra. In this case the defendant, American National Bank, failed to timely dishonor two checks submitted to it by Port City State Bank. It was stipulated that the midnight deadlines for the two checks were December 1 and December 3. On December 1, American National computerized its operations and the computer broke down on its inauguration day. Despite assurances from the manufacturer that it could be repaired quickly, the computer was not repaired until late at night. When it became apparent that the computer could not be rapidly repaired, American National decided to use an identical computer in a bank some two and a half hours away, under a previous backup arrangement. Processing of checks was begun at 11:30 p.m. on December 1 on the backup bank's computer. Work was proceeding nicely on the backup computer when American National was notified by the computer manufacturer that its own computer was ready. The American National employees returned to their own bank. American National's computer worked for awhile and then broke down on December 2 and was rendered inoperable until a replacement part was installed on December 4. Because of the second failure of its new computer, American National Bank was again forced to utilize its backup arrangement. However, because of the distance between the American National Bank and its backup computer, and the need of American to work around the schedule of the bank which owned the backup computer, American got behind in its processing.

The district court held that the cause of the delay in dishonoring the checks was the computer breakdowns, and the Tenth Circuit, applying its usual appellate rules, concluded that the holding was "not clearly erroneous." *Port City State Bank*, supra, 486 F.2d at 199. The Tenth Circuit also found that American reasonably relied on the assurance of the computer manufacturer that the initial malfunction could be repaired quickly; thus, the Tenth Circuit held that the bank was justified in not using the backup computer earlier. Id. at 200. Also, the Tenth Circuit accepted the argument that the bank's duty when the emergency became apparent was to remain open and serve its customers as best it could. "To abandon the orderly day by day process of bookkeeping to adopt radical emergency measures would have likely prolonged the delay in returning the bank to normal operations," the court said. Id. at 200.

As pointed out earlier, the Tenth Circuit stated in this case that it was the defendant bank's burden to prove an excuse under [U.C.C. § 4-109(b)], supra. We agree with our appellee in this case that the Tenth Circuit case is readily distinguishable from the case before us. The defendant bank in the Tenth Circuit case proved to the satisfaction of the trial court that it used the diligence required by the above statute and that its failure to timely dishonor the checks was due to circumstances beyond its control—computer breakdowns. The showing of diligence included proof of utilization of a backup system. In the case before us, there is no showing that defendant-appellant bank used any diligence when the packet of checks failed to arrive as scheduled on the flight from Montana.

The Kentucky case involved a failure to timely dishonor two checks. *Blake,* supra. The two checks in this case were presented for payment to the defendant bank on December 24, 1973, so that under the midnight-deadline rule the bank was responsible for dishonoring the checks by midnight of December 26, December 25, of course, being a bank holiday. Blake, *supra,* 555 S.W.2d at 591. Unfortunately for the bank, it did not send notice that it was dishonoring the checks until December 27. In the trial court the bank sought to justify the delay for several reasons. The bank presented evidence that while it normally processes only 4,200 to 4,600 checks a day, it had 6,995 to process on December 26. The bank had four posting machines but two broke down on December 26, one for two and a half hours and one for one and a half hours. Also, one of the four regular bookkeepers was absent on December 26 and had to be replaced by a less proficient substitute. The bank regularly employed a Purolator courier to pick up checks at 4:00 p.m. and take them to the Federal Reserve bank. Because of the above-described problems, the bank did not have the two checks in question processed on December 26 in time for the Purolator courier. Id. at 595–596.

The trial court found these excuses sufficient under [U.C.C. § 4-109(b)], *supra,* to relieve the bank of liability under U.C.C. § 4-302, *supra.*

The Kentucky appellate court reversed. The appellate court focused on additional facts. One of the bookkeepers had in fact discovered that there were insufficient funds to pay the two checks on December 26 after the Purolator courier left. However, because of "the lateness of the hour" there was no responsible bank official on the premises and the bookkeeper merely left the two checks on the desk of the bank official who was supposed to handle insufficient funds checks. Id. at 596. Thus, the bank did not send out notice that it was dishonoring the check until the next day.

The Kentucky appellate court concluded:

"Even though the bank missed returning the two checks by the Purolator courier, it was still possible for the bank to have returned the checks by its midnight deadline. Under U.C.C. § 4-301(d)(2) [footnote] an item is returned when it is 'sent' to the bank's transferor, in this case the Federal Reserve Bank. Under U.C.C. § 1-201(38) [footnote] an item is 'sent' when it is deposited in the mail. 1 R. Anderson, Uniform Commercial Code § 1-201 pp. 118–119 (2d ed. 1970). Thus, the bank could have returned the two checks before the midnight deadline by the simple procedure of depositing the two checks in the mail, properly addressed to the Cincinnati branch of the Federal Reserve Bank.

This court concludes that circumstances beyond the control of the bank did not prevent it from returning the two checks in question before its midnight deadline on December 26. The circumstances causing the delay in the bookkeeping department were foreseeable. On December 26, the bank actually discovered that the checks were 'bad,' but the responsible employees and officers had left the bank without leaving any instructions to the bookkeepers. The circuit court erred in holding that the bank was excused under § 4-108 [U.C.C. § 4-109] from meeting its midnight deadline. The facts found by the circuit court do not support its conclusion that the circumstances in the case were beyond the control of the bank." 555 S.W.2d 596–597.

The cases discussed above persuade us that the appellant bank has failed to prove an excuse sufficient under [U.C.C. § 4-109(b)], *supra,* to enable it to escape liability under [U.C.C. § 4-302], supra, for its failure to dishonor the check in question by the midnight deadline imposed by the

U.C.C.

The judgment of the district court is affirmed.

NOTE

The primary reason for the automatic or strict liability imposed by U.C.C. Section 4-302 has been expressed to be the need for finality and certainty in business transactions. The need for expeditious action on an item presented to a payor bank is clear when we look at the risk imposed on a depository bank. The depository bank is pressured by the depositor to allow access to these funds and by the Expedited Funds Availability Act which lays down a strict schedule when such funds must be made available to the depositor.

This raises the question whether U.C.C. Section 4-302 applies where the item had previously been dishonored by the payor bank and is now re-presented. Re-presentation of a check is not an unusual occurrence. The original dishonor may have been based on the existence of uncollected funds with the result that by the time the check is re-presented these funds may have been received by the drawee/payor bank to enable the check to be honored. It is, of course, also possible that at the time the check is re-presented the drawee will have received notice that due to dishonor these uncollected funds will not be available to meet the drawer's obligation on the check re-presented. In *Blake v. Woodford Bank & Trust Co.*, 555 S.W.2d 589 (Ky. 1977) the court stated:

> * * * In 1972, approximately 25 billion checks passed through the bank collection process. The Federal Reserve Banks handled 8 billion checks that year. *Community Bank v. Federal Reserve Bank of San Francisco*, 500 F.2d 282, (9th Cir. 1974) modified, 525 F.2d 690 (9th Cir. 1975), cert. denied 419 U.S. 1089, 95 S.Ct. 680, 42 L.Ed.2d 681.[11] An earlier study indicated that only one half of one percent of all checks were dishonored when first presented for payment. Of those initially dishonored, approximately one half were paid upon re-presentment. F. Leary, *Check Handling Under Article Four of the Uniform Commercial Code*, 49 MARQ.L.REV. 331, 333, n. 7 (1965). A significant number of previously dishonored checks are paid upon re-presentment in the regular course of the check collection process. Such checks are often presented through intermediate collecting banks, such as the Federal Reserve Bank in this case. Each collecting bank will have made a provisional settlement with its transferor, and, in turn, received a provisional settlement from the bank to which it forwarded the check. In this way, a series of provisional settlements are made as the check proceeds through the bank collection process.
>
> Under U.C.C. § 4-213(2) [§ 4-215(c)], final payment of a check "firms up" all of the provisional settlements made in the collection process. Under subsection (1)(d) of U.C.C. § 4-213 [§ 4-215(a)(3)], a payor bank makes final payment of a check when

---

[11] In this case, the United States Court of Appeals held that any bank, which utilized the check collection facilities of the Federal Reserve System by magnetic encoding its checks, becomes subject to Regulation J of the Board of Governors dealing with check collections. See also § 4-103(2) [§ 4-103(b)] of the U.C.C. and Comment 3 of the Official Code Comment. Although the parties have argued whether the bank has violated any of the provisions of Regulation J, this Court concludes that Regulation J imposed no additional duty on the bank relevant to this case.

it fails to revoke a provisional settlement "in the time and manner permitted by statute, clearing house rule or agreement." As to items not presented over the counter or by local clearing house, this means that a payor bank is deemed to have made final payment of a check when it fails to revoke a provisional settlement by its midnight deadline. See U.C.C. § 4-213, Official Code Comment 6 [§ 4-215 Comment 7]. In his article on check handling, Leary has described § 4-213 as the "zinger" section: "when provisional credit given by the payor bank becomes firm then—'zing'—all prior provisional credits are instantaneously made firm." Leary, op.cit., at 361. If a payor bank was not required to meet its midnight deadline with respect to previously dishonored items, then none of the other banks involved in the collection process could safely assume that the check had been paid. Consider the problems of the depository bank. It must permit its customer to withdraw the amount of the credit given for the check when provisional settlements have become final by payment and the bank has had "a reasonable time" to learn that the settlement is final. See U.C.C. § 4-213(4)(a) [§ 4-215(e)(1)]. The depository bank will rarely receive notice that an item has been paid. In actual practice, the depository bank will utilize availability schedules to compute when it should receive the check if it is to be returned unpaid. Leary, op.cit., at 345–346. If a payor bank is not bound by its midnight deadline as to previously dishonored items, then there is no way for the depository bank to know whether a previously dishonored item has been paid upon re-presentment except by direct communication with the payor bank. Such a procedure would impose an unnecessary burden upon the check collection process.

2. The Expedited Funds Availability Act[23]

The time lapse between the deposit of a check into an account with the depository bank and the depository bank receiving the amount due thereon or a notice that the check has been dishonored, made banks impose an arbitrary "hold on account." This prevented the customer from access to funds whether or not the check had been honored and the funds received. By imposing such unitary hold, it was often the case that the depository bank had received the amount due on the check from, or a credit to their account with, their transferee in the collection chain, while denying the customer the right to draw on his account. The Expedited Funds Availability Act is a response to this problem. The forward progress of the check leading to presentation had become an efficient process.[24] It was in the return process that delays occurred. Though the "zinger clause" effectively firmed up the provisional credit granted by a transferee,[25] banks in the collection chain, including the depository bank, were reluctant to allow a charge against the provisional credit entered in

---

[23] 12 U.S.C. §§ 4001 to 4010.

[24] Machine read MICR symbols speeded the sorting of checks and the overnight delivery service of checks to the appropriate Federal Reserve bank, and from there to the local clearing house meant that the average check would be presented to the drawee/payor bank within 24–72 hours from the time the check is deposited by the depositor into the depository bank.

[25] See F. Leary, *Check Handling Under Article Four of the Uniform Commercial Code*, 49 MARQ. L. REV. 331 (1965), discussed in *Blake v. Woodford Trust Co.*, 555 S.W.2d 589 (Ky. 1977), *see supra*.

favor of a customer until they received final settlement of the check. Banks had no way of discovering that a check had been dishonored until the check was returned to them, or they had received notice of its dishonor under the applicable provision of Regulation J of the Federal Reserve Bank.

"Settlement" means payment in cash, by clearing house block settlement, in a charge or credit or by remittance, or otherwise as agreed. A settlement may be either provisional or final. U.C.C. § 4-104(a)(ii).

Whether settlement has occurred will be governed by U.C.C. Section 4–213 subject to applicable Federal Reserve Regulations or circulars, clearing house rules and the like, or agreement. In some cases, however, a bank makes a direct presentment to a correspondent bank,[26] for example, where the depository bank and the drawee/payor bank have an agreement for electronic presentment.[27] Such an agreement would permit presentment by the transmission of an image of the item, or of information describing the item by an electronic data interchange between computers rather than by physical presentment of the item itself.[28] Presentment then will have occurred on receipt of such electronic presentment notice whether or not it is further agreed that the physical item will subsequently be sent to the payor bank.[29] U.C.C. Section 4-213 indicates that in such case

(1) the medium of settlement is cash or credit to an account in a Federal Reserve bank of or specified by the person to receive settlement; and

(2) the time of settlement is

(i) with respect to tender of settlement by cash, a cashier's check, or teller's check, when the cash or check is sent or delivered;

(ii) with respect to tender of settlement by credit in an account in a Federal Reserve Bank, when the credit is made;

(iii) with respect to tender of settlement by a credit or debit to an account in a bank, when the credit or debit is made or, in the case of tender of settlement by authority to charge an account, when the authority is sent or delivered; or

(iv) with respect to tender of settlement by a funds transfer, when payment is made pursuant to Section 4A-406(a) to the person receiving settlement.

---

[26] A correspondent bank is one which is in direct relationship with the bank. There may be corresponding balances held by each of these banks against which a charge may be made.

[27] U.C.C. § 4-110(a).

[28] Absent an agreement, U.C.C. § 3-501(b)(2) allows the drawee to demand that the instrument be physically presented.

[29] U.C.C. § 4-410(b). The agreement will have to provide for retention of the check or of an image, or for electronic storage of copies of checks, *see* U.C.C. § 4-110(a), so as to enable the drawee to comply with U.C.C. § 4-406(a), (b) which allows a customer to call for the item or a legible copy thereof. This illustrates "truncation." We have already noted the partial truncation that occurs when a drawee bank does not return checks to its customer but merely submits a statement of account. *See* U.C.C. § 4-406. Here the item may never be physically presented to the payor bank, i.e. "total truncation," has occurred. In some instances banks agree that the item after payment on an electronic presentment notice will be sent to the drawee for storage. *See* U.C.C. § 4-110(a).

(b) If the tender of settlement is not by a medium authorized by subsection (a) or the time of settlement is not fixed by subsection (a), no settlement occurs until the tender of settlement is accepted by the person receiving settlement.

(c) If settlement for an item is made by cashier's check or teller's check and the person receiving settlement, before its midnight deadline:

(1) presents or forwards the check for collection, settlement is final when the check is finally paid; or

(2) fails to present or forward the check for collection, settlement is final at the midnight deadline of the person receiving settlement.

(d) If settlement for an item is made by giving authority to charge the account of the bank giving settlement in the bank receiving settlement, settlement is final when the charge is made by the bank receiving settlement if there are funds available in the account for the amount of the item. [U.C.C. § 4-213].

The effect of this approach is to delay the availability of credit until settlement has occurred. The Expedited Funds Availability Act, however, requires funds to be made available to a depositor in accordance with a schedule that forces a faster response.[30] This schedule requires that cash deposits at a bank or at an automated teller machine,[31] and deposits made through Fedwire, CHIPS, NACHA or similar network between banks[32] be available for withdrawal not later than the next business day following the day such deposits were made.[33] Similarly a credit based on a check issued by the U.S. Government or any of its agencies, a state or local government check and a certified check, cashier's check or teller's check[34] that is endorsed only by the named payee must be allowed to be drawn on no later than the next business day following deposit.[35]

Other checks: these are divided into local checks and non-local checks. Local checks are drawn on a bank located in the same check processing region as the depository bank. All other banks are non-local banks and checks drawn on such banks are non-local checks. The funds due on a local check must be made available no later than the second business day following their deposit in the depository bank[36] while the funds drawn by a non-local check, are required to be available not later than the fourth business day following the

---

[30] Note the EFA Act is not confined to consumer accounts but applies to all checking accounts.

[31] EFA Act, 12 U.S.C. § 4002(e)(3). In those cases where the ATM is non-proprietary, i.e., is an ATM physically situated more than fifty feet from a bank or is not operated by a bank, these funds must be available no later than the second business day following the day of deposit. *Id.*, § 4002(e)(2), 12 C.F.R. § 229.2(aa). Note, more than one bank may operate the same ATM.

[32] 12 C.F.R. § 229.2(*ll*).

[33] EFA Act, 12 U.S.C. § 4002(a)(1).

[34] A special deposit slip may be needed to be able to demand the right to draw by the next business day on the amount represented by a check drawn other than by the U.S. Government. Such special deposit slip will indicate to the depository bank the need to expedite collection on the item even more speedily.

[35] EFA Act, 12 U.S.C. § 4002(a)(2).

[36] *Id.* § 4002(b)(1).

deposit of the non-local check.[37] There is nothing in the EFA Act which would prevent a bank from making funds available at an earlier time. Attempts to delay making these funds available, however, are circumscribed.

In all instances, the first $100 deposited by check or checks must be made available by the next business day.[38] Where a non-local check in excess of this amount is deposited into an account with the depository bank up to $100 per day can be drawn until the date on which the funds represented by such check become fully available. It is hoped by this provision to alleviate the problems a restriction on withdrawal has been found to create. But banks can impose restrictions on new accounts. A new account is one that has been established for less than thirty calendar days.[39] Such accounts can be restricted by allowing withdrawal only up to $5000. Such hold on one or a number of checks cannot exceed eight days.[40] There are other delays that are permitted to operate as safeguards to depository banks. Thus, a redeposited check, a check deposited into an account that has been overdrawn repeatedly during the last six months, or a check drawn by a drawer or on a drawee whose credit reputation gives the depository bank reasonable cause to believe that the check is uncollectible do not fall within the availability schedule.[41] The depository bank then can await payment by or accountability in the drawee. For example, a check once dishonored for insufficient funds would clearly fall within the category of checks that are outside the schedule both for the reason of being a redeposited check, and as an item giving a reasonable person a well-grounded belief that the check would not be honored when presented.

Further, an emergency such as disruption of communication facilities would allow a depository bank to delay the time before the customer is able to draw on the account.[42] Where such emergency arises, the depository bank must exercise such diligence as the circumstances require.[43]

The obligation to make funds available in accordance with the schedule prescribed by the EFA Act creates a risk in the depository bank that a depositor may withdraw funds before the depository bank has notice of a dishonor. The time that elapses as the check proceeds from the depository bank to the drawee bank, as outlined in this chapter as "the basic check collection system," clearly does not work to alleviate this risk. Should the check have to be returned by the same route, this risk is even increased. Since the EFA Act preempts state law and Regulation CC abolishes provisional credit being given by inter-mediary collecting banks,[44] there is little solace given a depository bank. Though the depository bank still has the power to charge back the item against its depositor, this is possible

[37] *Id.* § 4002(b)(2).

[38] *Id.* § 4002(a)(2)(D).

[39] *Id.* § 4003(a), 12 C.F.R. § 229.13(a)(2).

[40] *Id.* § 4003(a)(3).

[41] *Id.* § 4003(b)(c); 12 C.F.R. § 229.13(b), (c), (d), (e).

[42] *Id.* § 4003(d); 12 C.F.R. § 229.13(f).

[43] *Id.*

[44] 12 C.F.R. § 229.36(d).

only where the depositor has adequate funds on deposit. Thus, the depository bank primarily relies on the drawee/payor bank for timely notice of a dishonor of the check to be able to act on such notification.[45]

Regulation CC[46] imposes on the drawee/payor bank the duty to return the check in the most expeditious manner. Thus, a depository bank will require an endorsement not to be in a field on the back of the check which will obstruct the depository placing its MICR symbols on the back of the check. This will enable machine reading of the return route the check itself may have to take.[47] The duty is on the drawee/payor bank to return a local check so that it is received by the depository bank not later than 4 p.m. local time of the second business day following the banking day on which the check was received by the drawee/payor bank. In the case of a non-local check, the depository bank must receive the dishonored check not later than the fourth business day following the banking day on which the check was presented to the drawee/payor bank.[48]

Once more we note that this time table only reduces the risk somewhat. A further step is taken by Regulation CC by requiring a drawee/payor bank dishonoring a check in excess of $2,500 to provide a notice of dishonor to the depository bank by 4 p.m. local time on the second business day following the banking day on which the check was presented. "Notice may be provided by any reasonable means, including the returned check, a writing (including a copy of the check), telephone, Fedwire, telex, or other form of telegraph." 12 C.F.R. § 229.33(a). A failure to comply with these notice requirements may result in liability for failure to exercise ordinary care. The measure of damage is "the amount of loss incurred up to the amount of the check, reduced by the amount of loss that [the depository bank] would have incurred even if the [drawee/payor] bank had exercised ordinary care."[49] This would include a reduction of damages based on the comparative negligence of the depository bank.[50]

The effect of this time table is to stimulate truncation by means of which banks can agree to make electronic presentment. This will expedite the forward movement of the demand for payment.[51] Industrial pressure will also result in notice of dishonor being sent promptly by what is clearly the most expeditious means, namely electronic data interchange.

---

[45] Northpark National Bank v. Bankers Trust Co., 572 F. Supp. 524 (S.D.N.Y. 1983) (cash items are treated as available for distribution in accordance with an expectation under Regulation J); Blake v. Woodford Trust Co., 555 S.W.2d 589 (Ky. 1977) ("The depository bank will rarely receive notice that an item has been paid. In actual practice, the depository bank will utilize availability schedules to compute when it should receive the check if it is to be returned unpaid.")

[46] 12 C.F.R. § 229.30.

[47] If these numbers are illegible, the return route will be in accordance with the basic check collection system. Clearly a time consuming process increasing risk. If this method is used, each bank can charge back the original credit to recoup the settlement it has made. U.C.C. § 4-214.

[48] 12 C.F.R. §§ 229.30, 229.31.

[49] *Id.* § 229.38(a), (b). *Compare* U.C.C. § 4-103(e).

[50] *Id.* § 229.38(c).

[51] See U.C.C. §§ 3-501(b)(1), 4-110(a).

3. The Effect of Notice of Dishonor

Each of the banks in the collection chain retains the right to recoup a payment made or credit given should the drawee bank suspend payments or should the check be dishonored. Regulation CC, 12 C.F.R. § 229.36(d), does not intend that by stating that "settlements between banks for the forward collection of a check are final when made," this should imply that a final payment for the purpose of U.C.C. Section 4-215(a) has occurred which would preclude a bank from charging back the credit granted under U.C.C. Section 4-214.[52] Thus, on dishonor or suspension of payment by the drawee/payor bank, the depository bank will reverse entries, i.e., charge back, against the depositor the amount of the dishonored check. *See* U.C.C. § 4-214(a). The depository bank can charge back the credit or recover the amount of the item provided it gives notice of the suspension of payment or of the dishonor even if it is not able to return the item itself within the midnight deadline. U.C.C. § 4-104(a)(10).

---

[52] *See* 53 Fed. Reg. 19,486 (1988).

Appliance Buyers Credit Corporation
v.
Prospect National Bank of Peoria and Federal Reserve Bank of Chicago
708 F.2d 290 (7th Cir. 1983)*

COFFEY, Circuit Judge.

This is an appeal from the district court's dismissal of the plaintiff's claim under section 4-212 [§ 4-214] of the Uniform Commercial Code on the grounds that the plaintiff failed to establish its damages. Affirmed.

The Appliance Buyers Credit Corporation, a Delaware corporation with its principal place of business in Michigan, is a finance company that provides wholesale "floor-plan financing" to appliance dealers.[1] The corporation makes monthly inspections of participating dealers' inventory to determine whether the dealers are current in their finance payments to Appliance Buyers. During one of Appliance Buyers' monthly inspections of the Nevius Appliance & Furniture inventory it was determined that Nevius had failed

---

* [Editor: citations in [ ] refer to Revised U.C.C. Articles 3 and 4.]

[1] As a "floor-plan financier," Appliance Buyers finances the inventory of various appliance dealers and maintains a security interest in the merchandise so financed.

to report the sale of certain merchandise to Appliance Buyers and owed $65,736.78. Immediately following the inspection on October 17, 1979 Nevius gave a check to the Appliance Buyers Credit Corporation representative in the amount of $55,736.78 and delivered a $10,000 check to the corporation the next day, October 18, 1979; both checks were drawn on the Corn Belt Bank of Bloomington, Illinois. Appliance Buyers Credit Corporation deposited these two checks on October 18, 1979 with the Prospect National Bank, and Prospect National credited Appliance Buyers' account with a provisional credit. Prospect National processed these two checks through the Chicago Federal Reserve Bank who in turn forwarded the checks to the drawee bank, the Corn Belt Bank of Bloomington. On October 22, 1979, the Corn Belt Bank dishonored the checks due to insufficient funds (NSF) and notified the Federal Reserve Bank of the dishonor by telephone that day. On the day following, October 23, 1979, the Federal Reserve Bank of Chicago notified Prospect National Bank of the dishonor, by telephone, and returned the dishonored checks to the Prospect National Bank by mail. Prospect National, upon receipt of the NSF checks on October 29, 1979, immediately revoked the provisional credit given to the Appliance Buyers' account and notified Appliance Buyers of the dishonor that same day (October 29th). Appliance Buyers received the dishonored checks through the regular mail on the day following, October 30, 1979, and on the next day, October 31, Nevius Appliance & Furniture filed a voluntary petition for bankruptcy. Appliance Buyers then brought suit to recover the $65,736.78.

The district court dismissed the plaintiff's claim under section 4-202 of the Uniform Commercial Code initially finding that Prospect National Bank was negligent in failing to notify the Appliance Buyers Credit Corporation of the dishonor of Nevius' checks by the October 24th midnight deadline, the day it received a telephone notification of the checks' dishonor. However, notwithstanding the fact that Prospect National was negligent in notifying Appliance Buyers of the dishonor, in its order the district court also found that Appliance Buyers failed to establish its damages and therefore was not entitled to recover:

> Because the plaintiff has not demonstrated that it had a reasonable chance to collect all or part of the amount of the checks, the amount plaintiff was actually damaged, if any, as a result of the bank's failure to exercise ordinary care in notification is pure speculation. The court will not indulge in such speculation. [Appliance Buyers] has not produced any evidence that if it had known of the dishonor on October 24, 1979, it might have had a reasonable chance to collect any part of the money represented by the checks that it can't recover in the bankruptcy proceeding. Because the court is unable to determine what an appropriate award of damages would be in this case, if any, none can be awarded. (Footnote and citations omitted).

The district court denied the Appliance Buyers Credit Corporation's motion to modify the above quoted court order regarding the corporation's failure to prove its damages:

> The court is not convinced, however, that § 4-212 [§ 4-214] gives a depositor a complete and automatic windfall if the bank is late in notification of dishonor if deposited and provisionally-credited items, when it is not proved

that such lateness made any financial difference to the depositor, or, if so, within reasonable limits, how much difference it made. The court is not willing to adjudicate such an inconsistency of consequences between two sections of the Uniform Commercial Code dealing with the same subject, especially in a case where plaintiff took large checks it had substantial reason to suspect might "bounce," and now seeks thereby to saddle its bank with liability thereon after its debtor's bankruptcy.

The plaintiff (Appliance Buyers Credit Corp.) appealed.

Appliance Buyers does not "seek review . . . of the trial court's dismissal of [its] section 4-202 claim," recognizing that "the trier of fact's weighing of the evidence is not an appropriate subject for appellate review in this case." Because there is no challenge to the district court's application of section 4-202, the question in this case is one of first impression: is a bank strictly liable as the plaintiff contends for the face value of a check under section 4-212 [§ 4-214] of the Uniform Commercial Code if, after failing to give the depositor timely notice of the check's dishonor, the bank charges back the depositor's account?

Appliance Buyers Credit Corp. asserts that section 4-212 [§ 4-214] makes a bank liable for the face value of a check when the bank breaches its duty to give a depositor timely notice of the check's dishonor, as under section 4-212 [§ 4-214] timely notice of dishonor is a pre-condition to the bank's right to charge-back. While it is clear that the drafters of section 4-212 [§ 4-214] of the Uniform Commercial Code intended to condition a bank's right to charge-back upon the giving of timely notice of dishonor, section 4-212 [§ 4-214] fails to set forth language holding a bank "accountable" for the face value of a dishonored check if and when the bank fails to give timely notice of dishonor.

* * *

A reading of section 4-212 [§ 4-214] reveals that while the section conditions a bank's right to "charge-back" on a timely notice of dishonor, it is silent on the measure of damages a depositor can recover, if any, when the bank breaches its duty of giving a timely notice of dishonor and still charges back the provisionally credited check. In its brief, Appliance Buyers contends that the bank should be held strictly liable for the face value of the dishonored check and for any other damages arising out of the bank's improper charge-back. The plaintiff has failed to supply the court and we have been unable to find any legal support either in the Uniform Commercial Code or case law for Appliance Buyers' unique contention that banks should be held strictly liable for the face value of dishonored checks under section 4-212 [§ 4-214]. For example, certain sections of the Uniform Commercial Code such as [4-302(a)(1), 4-215(a)(3), and 4-215(d)] do impose liability on a bank for the face value of items in given situations, but we have found no similar obligation under section 4-212 [§ 4-214]. The specific language of sections 4-302(a), 4-213(1)(d) and 4-213(3) [4-302(a)(1), 4-215(a)(3) and 4-215(d)] holds the bank "accountable for the amount of" the item in question. Cases construing these sections hold that the term "accountable" is "the operative term . . . which imposes liability for the face amount of a check. . . ." *Colorado National Bank v. First National Bank & Trust Co.*, 459 F. Supp. 1366, 1372 (W.D. Mich. 1978). Section 4-212 [4-214] does not contain the "operative term" holding a bank "accountable" for the face value of a check if the bank improperly charges back the amount of a provisional credit against the depositor's account. It is obvious that if the drafters of the Uniform Commercial Code had intended to make a bank liable for the face value of a check under section 4-212 [§ 4-214], they would have held the bank "accountable" in specific language for the face amount of the check as they have under other Code sections. Because section 4-212 [§ 4-214] does not contain any language holding a bank "accountable" for the face value of a dishonored check, nor has our independent research uncovered any case law holding a bank "accountable" under section 4-212 [§ 4-214], we hold that the drafters of section 4-212 [§ 4-214] did not intend to impose absolute liability on a bank if the bank charged back a dishonored check against the depositor's account after failing to give the depositor timely notice of the check's dishonor.

Because section 4-212 [§ 4-214] is silent concerning a depositor's measure of damages arising out of an improper charge-back, we will examine the Code and case law to determine the proper standard to be applied when deciding what Appliance Buyers must establish in order to recover under section 4-212 [§ 4-214]. U.C.C. § 4-103(5) [§ 4-103(e)], the general damages section of the Uniform Commercial Code, provides:

> The measure of damages for failure to exercise ordinary care in handling an item is the amount of the item reduced by an amount [that] could not have been realized by the [exercise] of ordinary care. [If] there is [also] bad faith it includes [any] other damages the party [suffered] as a proximate consequence.

The official comment to section 4-103 states that "[w]hen it is established that some part or all of the item could not have been collected even by the use of ordinary care the recovery is reduced by the amount which would have been in any event uncollectible." In applying this standard to the instant dispute, the district court ruled that there was serious question as to whether Appliance Buyers could have recovered any of the disputed $65,736.78 even if it had received timely notice of the checks' dishonor, as Nevius Appliance was in severe financial difficulty during the period in question and filed for bankruptcy just nine days after the checks were dishonored. Indeed, the district court found that the "fact of bankruptcy within two weeks of issuance of the first check and other evidence concerning Nevius' [insolvency] during the relevant period . . . raise serious doubt that [Appliance Buyers] could have collected any part of the amount of the checks, even if notified of the checks' dishonor in timely fashion." When evidence at trial demonstrated that "some or all of the item could not have been collected" had Appliance Buyers received timely notice of dishonor, the district court found that under section 4-103 the burden was on Appliance Buyers to establish "that it had a reasonable chance of collecting something on the checks, before any award of damages caused by [Prospect National's] negligence could be made." We hold the district court was correct in placing the burden on Appliance Buyers to establish their damages and in dismissing the corporation's claim on the grounds that Appliance Buyers failed to prove to the court's satisfaction that they would have been able to recover any funds from Nevius had they in fact received timely notice from the bank.

A depositor bears the burden of establishing its actual damages under section 4-103 in order to recover damages arising out of the negligence of a bank for failing to give a timely notice under other sections of the Code. See generally *Marcoux v. Van Wyk*, 572 F.2d 651 (8th Cir. 1978); *Whalen & Sons Grain Co. v. Missouri Delta Bank*, 496 F. Supp. 211 (E.D. Mo. 1980); and *Bank of Wyandotte v. Woodrow*, 394 F. Supp. 550 (W.D. Mo. 1975). It is the Appliance Buyers' position that the bank's failure to give timely notice of dishonor has caused their difficulty in proving damages since Nevius' business records do not reveal whether Appliance Buyers could have recovered a measure of damages from Nevius Appliance by repossessing those items in which Appliance Buyers had a security interest. Thus, under the plaintiff's analysis, the bank must prove the amount Appliance Buyers could not have collected even had the bank given timely notice of dishonor and if it is unable to meet this burden, Prospect National should be held liable for the face value of the checks. However, Appliance Buyers has failed to cite any sections of the Code or case law that do in fact shift the burden of proof from the depositor to the bank to prove the extent of a depositor's loss.

In the absence of "accountability" under other Uniform Commercial Code sections such as section 4-202, courts have required depositors to prove the extent of their actual damages. For example, in *Marcoux v. Van Wyk* and the other cases cited herein dealing with untimely notice, courts clearly place the burden on a depositor seeking recovery to prove the amount "they would have had at least a reasonable chance to collect. . . . It is not enough to show that by a fortuitous combination of unlikely events there was a dim hope of collection." 572 F.2d at 655. Furthermore, the bank will not be held liable "unless there is a clear causal relationship between the bank's actions and the plaintiff's loss." *Whalen & Sons Grain Co.*, 496 F. Supp. at 215. . . . A fair reading of the Code and relevant case law reveals that since depositors must prove untimely notice and actual damages as conditions precedent to recovery under section 4-202, under section 4-212 [§ 4-215] depositors must also prove that they received untimely notice as well as the amount of actual damages suffered as a result of the untimely notice.[3]

---

[3] Contrary to the dissent's assertion, the language of section 4-103 does not place the burden on the bank to prove what "would have been uncollectible even if

* * *

The district court in its decision noted that when Appliance Buyers accepted Nevius' checks, Appliance Buyers "had substantial reason to suspect [the checks] might 'bounce'. . . . " Indeed, testimony was presented at trial that a representative of Appliance Buyers was told by Ken Nevius that he (Nevius) was unsure whether "we have enough money to cover this check." Moreover, one of Appliance Buyers' employees testified that although Nevius Appliance had agreed to make weekly payments on its account to Appliance Buyers, Nevius had not done so in the last month and a half prior to the time they issued the two NSF checks in question. Now, Appliance Buyers is attempting to shift the loss, caused by their own lax financial policy, to Prospect National Bank. Finance companies such as Appliance Buyers Credit Corporation have the obligation to actively police the floor plans of participating dealers and to ensure that dealers are current in their payments. When a finance company fails to develop a sound financial policy and allows dealers to fall behind in their payments, the finance company must bear the burden if the dealers fail to pay their bills when due. It is apparent from the record that having failed in its duty to protect its investments by keeping tighter reins on Nevius' account, absent proof that Prospect National Bank's untimely notice actually damaged the corporation, Appliance Buyers cannot now shift the responsibility for their own negligence to the bank.

We agree with and affirm the district court's decision and hold that in order for the plaintiff in this case to recover for damages arising out of Prospect National Bank's alleged failure to give timely notice of dishonor as required by section 4-212 [§ 4-214] of the Uniform Commercial Code, the burden is on the depositor (Appliance Buyers)

---

timely notice had been given." Rather, if the evidence at trial raises a question that some or all of the item was in any event uncollectible, under section 4-103 and the cases construing it, the burden remains on the plaintiff/depositor to prove their actual damages. This result is consistent with the time-honored principle of law that a party bringing a claim has the burden of proving their damages to a reasonable degree of certainty. The position advocated by the dissent is apparently based solely on policy considerations.

to establish that Prospect National failed to give timely notice, and the amount of damage Appli- ance Buyers actually suffered as a result of Prospect National's untimely notice.

NOTE

1. U.C.C. § 4-214(a) now provides:

> ... If the return or notice is delayed beyond the bank's midnight deadline or a longer reasonable time after it learns the facts, the bank may revoke the settlement, charge back the credit, or obtain refund from its customer, but it is liable for any loss resulting from the delay ...

2. Where the item is in a foreign currency and a dollar credit has been given by the depository bank, U.C.C. § 3-107, it is not that amount of dollars that has to be charged back against the account, but the dollar equivalent on the date the charge back can be made will govern the exchange value of the foreign currency item. U.C.C. § 4-214(f).

3. *See also* Regulation CC 12 C.F.R. § 229.33(d):

> *Notification to customer.* If the depositary bank receives a returned check or notice of nonpayment, it shall send notice to its customer of the facts by midnight of the banking day following the banking day on which it received the returned check or notice, or within a longer reasonable time.

What is the effect of a failure to notify the customer of a dishonor within the time indicated? *Northpark National Bank v. Bankers Trust Co.*, 572 F.Supp. 524 (S.D.N.Y. 1983), *supra* p. 330.

4. Encoding of Magnetic Ink Character Recognition Symbols

The need for prompt and expeditious presentment in the collection process led to the development of Magnetic Ink Character Recognition [MICR] symbols. Automated machine reading assists not only the depository and payor banks in recordkeeping, but also enables acceleration in the routing of items to the payor bank and facilitates a faster return of dishonored items. On deposit of a check the depository bank adds the dollar amount to the MICR routing line and adjusts its depositor's account by entering a provisional credit. An error can occur here by over-encoding or by under-encoding a credit. This error in the MICR symbols is not an alteration of the negotiable instrument to which U.C.C. Section 3-407 would apply. This encoding is merely for the purposes indicated. It does not effect "an unauthorized change in an instrument that purports to modify in any respect the obligation of a party."[53] Of course, if the encoding is fraudulently made, liability in fraud will have been incurred, but the obligation of the parties to the instrument will not be affected.

Once encoded, the item is only rarely examined. Unless the item results in an overdraft, is subject to a stop payment order, or is otherwise indicated by the computer to warrant a closer examination, all subsequent steps will be automated.[54] An over-encoding, such as,

---

[53] U.C.C. § 3-407(a)(i).

[54] *See* Rhode Island Hospital Trust National Bank v. Zapata Corp., 848 F.2d 291 (1st Cir. 1988), *supra* p. 235.

encoding an item for $1,900.00 as one for $190,000.00, will cause harm to the drawee bank which, paying $190,000.00, would only have authority to debit the drawer's account for the $1,900.00. Conversely, under-encoding does not relieve the issuer of the obligation due on the instrument. Nor would it relieve the depository bank from its liablity to the depositor under U.C.C. Section 4-202(a)(1) to "excercise ordinary care in presenting an item or sending it for presentment."

It could be argued that the payor bank's acceptance amounted to a dishonor by being an acceptance of only part of the check, i.e., the acceptance varies from the draft as presented. U.C.C. Section 3-410(a) gives the holder the power to treat such act as a dishonor, in which case the drawee can cancel the acceptance. Can it be asserted that the holder by acepting the lower amount, i.e., not rejecting this acceptance promptly, assented to such partial acceptance? A depositor into a bank would not be aware of the facts until receiving a statement of account, and cannot be deemed to have assented to such action by the depository or presenting bank. An alternative contention would be that, since there was no intention by such acceptance to vary from the terms of the draft as presented, or to dishonor the item, the draft has been accepted for the full amount stated in the draft.

Resolution of this conflict would affect not only the claim of the depositor against the drawer where there has been an under-encoding,[55] but also, holding the payor bank responsible for the full amount of the check as drawn, could give rise to a problem for the drawee/payor bank, should the drawer's account contain insufficient funds against which to charge the full amount of the check. *See* Official Comment 2 to U.C.C. § 4-209.

In the case of an over-encoding, an attempt to rectify the acceptance to recover payment of the excess from the presenter would be subject to the provisions of the law of mistake and restitution. U.C.C. § 3-418(b).

As between the depository bank and the drawee/payor bank, U.C.C. Section 4-209 places the responsibility for an error in encoding on the depository bank. The section provides that the depository bank warrants to any subsequent collecting bank and to the drawee/payor bank that the information is correctly encoded. U.C.C. § 4-209(a). Where the item is retained under a truncation agreement, a bank making an electronic presentment also gives such warranty whether or not it has itself encoded the item.[56] Breach of warranty resulting in damages can be recovered in "an amount equal to the loss suffered plus expenses and loss of interest incurred as a result of the breach." U.C.C. § 4-209(c). The official comment to that section states that where there has been an under-encoding "[t]here is no requirement that the payor bank pursue collection against the drawer beyond the amount in the drawer's account as a condition to the payor bank's action against the depository bank for breach of warranty." [Official Comment 2 to U.C.C. § 4-209.] Does this mean that the depositor has a cause of action against the drawee by asserting that there has been an acceptance of the item to the full amount thereof?

---

[55] U.C.C. § 3-414(b).

[56] Where the encoding is done by the depositor including a depositor who has an agreement with the depository bank to allow retention by the depositor of the item itself, i.e., total truncation U.C.C. § 4-110(a), the depository bank makes this warranty to all subsequent collecting banks and to the drawee that are parties with the depository bank to an agreement permitting the depository bank to make electronic presentment. U.C.C. §§ 4-110(a), 4-209(a), (b).

First National Bank of Boston v. Fidelity Bank, N.A.
724 F. Supp. 1168 (E.D. Pa. 1989)*

JOHN P. FULLAM, C.J.

This dispute between two banks over a mis-handled check transaction requires the court to explore some of the consequences which automation has visited upon the respective legal liabilities of banks under Article 4 of the Uniform Commercial Code, which was enacted before the advent of computerized check-processing.

The method of processing checks now in universal use in the United States, Magnetic Ink Character Recognition (MICR) was first adopted by the American Bankers Association in 1956, and has been in common use since the mid-1960s. See Note, *Computerized Check-Processing and the Bank's Duty to Use Ordinary Care*, 65 Tex.L.R. 1173–74 (1987). The form of each bank check is preprinted with magnetic characters, along the bottom of the check, toward the left-hand side.** These characters designate the bank upon which the check is drawn, and the account number of the maker. When a check is presented to another bank (the "depositary bank"), that bank adds additional magnetic encoding, at the lower right-hand side of the check, specifying the amount of the check. From that point on, the check works its way through the bank clearing system to the bank on which the check is drawn (the "payor" bank) and is charged against the maker's account—all without further human intervention. Thus, the role of the encoder at the depositary bank (which then assumes the role of "collecting" bank as well), is crucial, since all subsequent steps in the processing of the check for payment depend upon the accuracy of the encoded information; ordinarily, no other human being actually examines the check from that point on. The development of this method of processing checks, it is generally agreed, has enabled the banking system to meet the needs of our ever-expanding economy. A bank such as the defendant, for example, routinely

processes upwards of 300,000 checks daily.

The parties have stipulated the facts pertinent to their dispute. Plaintiff is the First National Bank of Boston (hereinafter "Boston"). The defendant is Fidelity Bank, National Association, successor to Industrial Valley Bank (hereinafter "Fidelity"). On or about September 22, 1986, one of defendant's customers, New York City Shoes ("NYC") issued a check in the amount of $100,000, to the Maxwell Shoe Company ("Maxwell"). The check was drawn on one of NYC's accounts at Fidelity in Philadelphia. Maxwell, a New England concern, deposited the check in its account at Boston, which credited Maxwell's account with the face amount of the check, and then proceeded to process the check through the Federal Reserve system. The check was properly encoded by Boston, and duly presented to Fidelity for payment. But NYC's account did not contain sufficient funds to cover the check, and Fidelity therefore returned the check to Boston for "non-sufficient funds."

Boston did not charge Maxwell's account because of the uncollectability of the check, but instead, at Maxwell's request, undertook to re-present the check to Fidelity. In order to re-process the check, Boston attached a "tape skirt" to the bottom of the check, and thereon re-encoded the check so that it could be processed through the Federal Reserve system. Unfortunately, however, Boston's encoder made an error, and encoded the amount of the check as $10,000, rather than $100,000. The computers which processed the check were, of course, unaware of the error and unable to appreciate it. When the check arrived at Fidelity, it was charged against NYC's account in the amount of $10,000, and that sum was duly forwarded to Boston. At that point, the error surfaced.

Boston made demand on Fidelity for the $90,000 difference between the face amount of the check and the amount which Fidelity had paid. The initial demands were made by telephone. On each occasion, Fidelity explained that it was unable to honor the request, because NYC's account continued to be insufficient to cover it. The first telephone demand was made by Boston on October 14, 1986. A second such demand was made

---

* [Editor: citations in [ ] refer to U.C.C. Articles 3 and 4.]

** [Editor: The encoding must be on a five-eighth inch band extending six inches in from the right edge of the check so that standardized machine reading is facilitated.]

on October 17, 1986. On both occasions, NYC's account lacked sufficient funds to honor the $90,000 request. * * *

After this final rejection of Boston's adjustment request, Boston attempted to collect the $90,000 from NYC. An agreement was reached for NYC to pay off the balance in installments. NYC paid a total of $40,000 on account, but then defaulted and, on July 7, 1987, filed for bankruptcy.

In this action, Boston seeks to recover from Fidelity the $50,000 remaining unpaid, and also requests a declaratory judgment which would require Fidelity to indemnify Boston in the event the Bankruptcy Court determines that all or any part of the $40,000 previously paid by NYC constitutes a voidable preference.

As the foregoing recital demonstrates, the court is presented with two separate but related sets of questions. The first is the liability of Fidelity as payor bank, for having paid only $10,000 when the check was in the amount of $100,000 and the effect of Boston's encoding error on that liability. The second area of inquiry centers upon Fidelity's handling of the adjustment request. * * *

I.

Under the provisions of the Uniform Commercial Code (U.C.C.), the liability of a bank is determined by the law of the jurisdiction in which the bank is located. [U.C.C. § 4-102(b).] Thus, Boston's liability is governed by Massachusetts law, Fidelity's by Pennsylvania law. Fortunately, the U.C.C. has been adopted in substantially the same form in both jurisdictions. Compare 13 Pa.Cons. Stat.Ann. § 4-213(a) (Purdon's 1984) with Mass.Gen.Laws Ann. Ch. 106, [§ 4-213(a)] (West 1958). * * *

Boston's argument is straightforward: * * * The fact that Fidelity listed the item in the wrong amount is irrelevant, since it is undisputed that Fidelity "completed the process of posting the item to the indicated account of the drawer" on October 3, 1986.[1]

The defendant, on the other hand, argues that,

for purposes of [§ 4-215(a)] the "amount of the item" for which the payor bank must account should be the encoded amount of the check, rather than its actual face amount. Alternatively, the defendant contends that equitable principles mandate rejection of plaintiff's claims.

Both parties find support for their respective positions in *Georgia R.R. Bank & Trust Co. v. First National Bank & Trust Co. of Augusta*, 139 Ga. App. 683, 229 S.E.2d 482 (1976), *aff'd per curiam*, 238 Ga. 693, 235 S.E.2d 1 (1977). The facts of that case are strikingly similar to the present case: plaintiff bank erroneously encoded a $25,000 check as a $2500 check. The defendant, the payor bank, charged the drawer's account in the lesser amount, and remitted that sum to plaintiff. The error was not discovered for several weeks, by which time the cancelled check had already been returned to the maker. When plaintiff made demand upon the defendant, the defendant brought the error to the maker's attention, but the latter refused to allow the defendant to charge his account with the additional $22,500. The Georgia court held, without extended discussion, that the defendant was liable to the plaintiff for the face amount of the check, pursuant to U.C.C. [§ 4-215(a)], and also pursuant to the "midnight deadline" provisions of § 4-302. The court reasoned that the defendant had made "final payment" by charging the maker's account, albeit it in the wrong amount, and that it was therefore liable as payor for the full amount of the check; and that, alternatively, it had retained the check beyond the midnight deadline without "completely settling for it".

Although the actual holding of the *Georgia R.R. Bank & Trust Co.* case plainly supports plaintiff's arguments, one part of the court's explanation for its decision suggests that the true rationale for the decision is one which vindicates defendant's position in the present case: the court made much of the fact that, at all times, the maker's account contained more than sufficient funds to honor the check in its full amount. The court stated:

"We are not here concerned with a situation wherein the drawee cannot recover from the drawer the amount of the deficiency. In such a situation, there would possibly exist a defense or counterclaim in favor of the drawee bank against the collecting bank which had under-encoded the check. See J. Clarke, *Mechanized Check Collec-*

---

[1] A payor bank can also become unconditionally accountable for the amount of a check by failing to return it or give written notice of dishonor by midnight of the banking day next following the day on which the item was received (i.e., by missing the so-called "midnight deadline"). That issue is not involved in this case.

tion, supra at 1004. The record in the present case shows that the drawer's account contained sufficient funds, as of the date payment was demanded by plaintiff, to cover the deficiency. 229 S.E.2d at p.484.[2]

It thus appears that, to the extent liability is sought to be imposed under the "final payment" rule of [§ 4-215(a)], the Georgia court might well sustain an equitable defense where plaintiff's encoding error caused the payor bank to suffer a loss which it could not avoid by charging its customer's account. Recognition of such equitable defenses is more problematical when liability is sought to be imposed under the "midnight deadline" provisions of § 4-302. With due deference to the views of the Georgia courts, however, I am not persuaded that § 4-302 has any application in these circumstances. The whole purpose of the "midnight deadline" rule is to promptly remove uncertainties concerning the collectability of a check, and to enable depositary and collecting banks to rely upon the payor's silence as an unconditional assurance of collectability. If the payor bank acts before the deadline, it seems to me, § 4-302 is no longer implicated.

Like the Georgia court, however, I reject the argument that the "amount of the item" for [§ 4-215(a)] purposes is the encoded amount, rather than the face amount, of the check. Stated that broadly, the argument is manifestly unacceptable, for if the encoded amount were greater than the face amount of the check, the error would produce a windfall for the collecting bank, and patently unjustifiable increases in the potential liability of the payor bank, the maker, or both. Any such rule would have chaotic repercussions, and would be totally inconsistent with the scheme of the U.C.C..

A more narrowly stated rule—that the "amount of the item" for purposes of § 4-215(a) is the face amount of the check or the encoded amount, whichever is less—is merely another way of stating what I conceive to be the true thrust of defendant's argument in this case, namely, that as between the encoding bank and all other banks in the collecting process, including the payor bank, the encoder is estopped from claiming more than the encoded amount of the check. Framing the argument in terms of estoppel is, I believe, preferable, in that it avoids the problems inherent in trying to ascribe different meanings to the same words in various parts of the U.C.C..

Section 1-103 of the U.C.C. preserves equitable principles and common-law tort law, except where inconsistent with specific U.C.C. provisions. Most of the decided cases have arisen under the "midnight deadline" provisions of § 4-302, which mandates automatic liability for missing the acceptance deadline "in the absence of a valid defense such as breach of a presentment warranty, settlement effected, or the like." In *Bank Leumi Trust Co. v. Bank of Mid-Jersey*, 499 F. Supp. 1022 (D.N.J.), *aff'd without opinion*, 659 F.2d 1065 (3d Cir. 1981), it was held that the quoted language precludes assertion of an equitable defense based upon mis-encoding, where the payor bank failed to act before the deadline. In *Chrysler Credit Corp. v. First National Bank & Trust Co.*, 746 F.2d 200 (3d Cir. 1984), however, the Court of Appeals expressly declined to consider whether the defense of equitable estoppel could be asserted in a "midnight deadline" case, because the evidence in that case did not adequately support the asserted defense. The court made clear that, at the very least, the facts giving rise to the claimed estoppel would have to be such as to have been a cause of the payor's failure to meet the "midnight deadline".

Whether or not equitable defenses are available in "midnight deadline" cases, I am satisfied that such defenses are not precluded under [§ 4-215]. That appears to be the view of most commentators. See, e.g., Clark, The Law of Bank Deposits, Collections and Credit Cards, para. 10.5 [3]; J. Clarke, *Mechanized Check-Collection*, 14 Bus.L. 989, 1004 (1959); Note, *Computerized Check-Processing and a Bank's Duty to use Ordinary Care*, 65 Tex.L.R. 1173 (1987). The proposed ALI/NCCUSL revisions to Article 4 (specifically, revised § 4-207 [§ 4-209]) would explicitly provide that an encoding bank warrants the accuracy of encoded amounts, and is liable for any resulting loss; this on the theory that the encoding bank is the party best able to avoid the loss. See Rubin, *Policies and Issues in the Proposed Revision of Articles 3 and 4 of the UCC*, 42 Bus. Law. 621, 653 (1988); NCCUSL, Amendments to Uniform

---

2 The per curiam affirmance by the Supreme Court of Georgia reflects a similar rationale, in noting that the maker's refusal to permit the defendant to charge his account was a nullity, since it was then too late for him to issue a stop-payment order.

Commercial Code, Article 4-Bank Deposits and Collections, § 4-207 (tentative draft October 19, 1988).

In my view, most, if not all, of the reported decisions can readily be harmonized with the existence of the right of the payor bank to hold the encoding bank liable for any under-encoding error, if this equitable right is considered in conjunction with the obligation to mitigate damages. That is, the payor bank has the corollary obligation of attempting to avoid loss altogether, by recourse to the account of the maker of the check. If the maker's account, when the check is correctly presented, is insufficient to cover the item, the payor bank has a claim against the encoding bank, which it can offset against any claim made by the encoding bank under [§ 4-215(a)].

I therefore conclude that Fidelity may not be held liable to plaintiff under [§ 4-215(a)] of the UCC, the "final payment" rule.

For all of the foregoing reasons, judgment will be entered in favor of the defendant.

NOTE

1. Under U.C.C. Section 4-209 the warranty that the information is correctly encoded is made by "a person who encodes" the information to any subsequent collecting bank and to the payor bank. This person usually is the depository bank, but could be the depositor itself. This warranty is not made by other banks in the collection chain. But where there is an electronic presentment and the presenting bank is to retain the item, i.e. truncation, U.C.C. § 4-110(a), it is the presenting bank that makes this warranty to the drawee bank. U.C.C. § 4-209(b).

2. Where damages have been sustained by an over-encoding, this warranty gives rise to a cause of action. What is the present approach to an under-encoding? What is the measure of damage, if any, recoverable? U.C.C. § 4-103(e). Should the doctrine of estoppel apply? U.C.C. § 1-103. Note U.C.C. Section 3-103(a)(7) holds a bank not to be in breach of the duty to exercise ordinary care where it uses automated means to process an item. *See* further Official Comment to U.C.C. § 4-209. Does a depositor have a cause of action where subsequent to an under-encoding and payment the drawer becomes bankrupt? U.C.C. §§ 4-202, 3-310.

3. Consider the fraudulent MICR encoding of the routing symbols leading to a non-existing bank. *Northpark National Bank v. Bankers Trust Co.*, 572 F.Supp. 524 (S.D.N.Y. 1983) *supra* page 330. Since a depository bank merely adds the amount of the check, would U.C.C. § 4–209(a) apply to hold the depository bank to have breached the warranty that the information is correctly encoded? *See* the last sentence of U.C.C. § 4-209(a), and note U.C.C. § 4-104(a)(5) and U.C.C. § 4-209(c).

5. Wrongful Dishonor

The dishonor of an item that is properly payable, including the dishonor of an item by reason that it would create an overdraft when there is an agreement to pay the overdraft is a wrongful dishonor. U.C.C. § 4-402(a). We have seen that banks need not hold back payment on post-dated checks "unless the customer has given notice to the bank of the post-dating describing the check with reasonable certainty." U.C.C. § 4-401 (c). Such notice has the effect of a stop payment order. U.C.C. § 4-403. The giving of a notice of postdating or the giving of a stop payment order may result in the drawer issuing further checks in the expectation that the amount in her account would be sufficient to enable the drawee/bank to honor these subsequent checks. A failure by the drawee to act on the notice of post-dating or on the stop payment order could result in a wrongful dishonor of these subsequently issued checks.[57]

A bank must act in good faith,[58] but is not under a duty to pay checks in any specific order, including the order of receipt.[59] Nor is there a duty on a drawee bank to pay as many checks as possible to reduce the number of checks that it will be dishonoring for "non-sufficient funds" (NSF) in the drawer's account or because the drawer has exhausted the credit granted by an overdraft agreement. In addition, automation prevents an allegation that there was a duty to exercise ordinary care breached by the drawee/bank in not seeking to minimize the harm suffered by the drawer as a result of the wrongful dishonor. U.C.C. § 3-103(a)(7). Thus the drawee/bank, having once determined the customer's account balance to be insufficient to cover payment of a check, need not make a further examination prior to acting within its midnight deadline, to ascertain whether the account has been augmented by a subsequent deposit that may have been credited by then. U.C.C. § 4-402(c). It would be inadvisable, however, for a bank to terminate a computer run just because a large check has been rejected for "non-sufficient funds" when a number of checks still await processing. The account may be adequate to cover some of these checks. As a result, a dishonor of such checks may be a wrongful dishonor.

Wrongful dishonor gives rise to a statutory cause of action for actual damages proximately caused to a customer by the wrongful dishonor.[60] U.C.C. Section 4-402(b) provides further that the customer has a cause of action for damages where he has been arrested and prosecuted under a state law making the issuance of a check on an account alleged not to have sufficient funds a crime.[61] Such arrest and prosecution is not a *novus actus interveniens* by the police and prosecutor to cut-off causation. Whether consequential damages are proximately caused by the wrongful dishonor is a question of fact.

Most cases involve the issue whether the complainant qualifies as a customer.

---

[57] U.C.C. §§ 4-401(c), 4-403(c).

[58] Knauf v. Bank of La Place, 567 So. 2d 182 (La. App. 1990) (bank cannot be selective when deciding which checks to honor).

[59] U.C.C. § 4-303(b).

[60] Compare the measure of damages for failure to exercise ordinary care, U.C.C. § 4-103(e).

[61] A dishonor due to "uncollected funds," i.e. there being insufficient funds presently in the account, but there having been deposited items into the account that have not yet settled or as to which there is still a "hold," is not likely to lead to a criminal prosecution. An example would be where the item previously deposited is still subject to the hold allowed by the Federal Expedited Funds Availability Act, 12 U.S.C. § 4002.

Loucks v. Albuquerque National Bank
76 N.M. 735, 418 P.2d 191 (1966)*

LA FEL E. OMAN, Judge.

The plaintiffs-appellants, Richard A. Loucks

---

* [Editor: citation in [ ] refer to Revised U.C.C. Articles 3 and 4.]

and Del Martinez, hereinafter referred to as plaintiffs, Mr. Loucks and Mr. Martinez, respectively, were partners engaged in a business at Albuquerque, New Mexico, under the partnership name of L & M Paint and Body Shop.

By their complaint they sought both compensatory and punitive damages on behalf of the partnership, on behalf of Mr. Loucks, and on behalf of Mr. Martinez against the defendants-appellees, Albuquerque National Bank and W. J. Kopp, hereinafter referred to as defendants, the bank, and Mr. Kopp, respectively.

Prior to March 15, 1962 Mr. Martinez had operated a business at Albuquerque, New Mexico, under the name of Del's Paint and Body Shop. He did his banking with defendant bank and he dealt with Mr. Kopp, a vice-president of the bank.

On February 8, 1962 Mr. Martinez borrowed $500 from the bank, which he deposited with the bank in the account of Del's Paint and Body Shop. He executed an installment note payable to the bank evidencing this indebtedness.

On March 15, 1962 the plaintiffs formed a partnership in the name of L & M Paint and Body Shop. On that date they opened a checking account with the bank in the name of L & M Paint and Body Shop and deposited $620 therein. The signatures of both Mr. Loucks and Mr. Martinez were required to draw money from this account. The balance in the account of Del's Paint and Body Shop as of this time was $2.67. This was drawn from this account by a cashier's check and deposited in the account of L & M Paint & Body Shop on April 18, 1962.

Two payments of $50.00 each were made on Mr. Martinez' note of February 8, 1962, or on notes given as a renewal thereof. These payments were made by checks drawn by plaintiffs on the account of L & M Paint and Body Shop. The checks were payable to the order of the bank and were dated June 29, 1962 and August 28, 1962. A subsequent installment note was executed by Mr. Martinez on October 17, 1962 in the principal amount of $462 payable to the order of the bank. This was given as a replacement or renewal of the prior notes which started with the note of February 8, 1962.

Mr. Martinez became delinquent in his payments on this note of October 17, 1962 and the bank sued him in a Justice of the Peace court to recover the delinquency.

As of March 14, 1963 Mr. Martinez was still indebted to the bank on this note in the amount of $402, and on that date, Mr. Kopp, on behalf of the bank, wrote L & M Paint and Body Shop advising that its account had been charged with $402 representing the balance due "on Del Martinez installment note," and the indebtedness was referred to in the letter as the "indebtedness of Mr. Del Martinez."

The charge of $402 against the account of L & M Paint and Body Shop was actually made on March 15, 1963, which was a Friday.

Although Mr. Martinez at one time testified he telephoned Mr. Kopp on either Friday or the following Monday about this charge, when he was questioned more closely he admitted he discussed the matter with Mr. Kopp by telephone on Friday. Mr. Loucks testified that as he recalled, it was on Monday. Both plaintiffs went to the bank on Monday, March 18, and talked with Mr. Kopp. They both told Mr. Kopp that the indebtedness represented by the note was the personal indebtedness of Mr. Martinez and was not a partnership obligation. Mr. Loucks explained that they had some outstanding checks against the partnership account. Mr. Kopp refused to return the money to the partnership account. There was evidence of some unpleasantness in the conversation. The partnership account, in which there was then a balance of only $3.66, was thereupon closed by the plaintiffs.

The bank refused to honor nine, and possibly ten, checks drawn on the account and dated between the dates of March 8 and 16, inclusive.

The checks dated prior to March 15 total $89.14, and those dated March 15 and 16 total $121.68. These figures do not include the tenth check to which some reference was made, but which was not offered into evidence and the amount of which does not appear in the record.

The case came on for trial before the court and a jury. The court submitted the case to the jury upon the question of whether or not the defendants wrongfully made the charge in the amount of $402 against the account of L & M Paint and Body Shop. The allegations of the complaint concerning punitive damages and compensatory damages, other than the amount of $402 allegedly wrongfully charged by the defendants against the partnership account, were dismissed by the court before the case was submitted to the jury. The jury returned a verdict for the plaintiffs in the amount of $402.

The plaintiffs have appealed and assert error on the part of the trial court in taking from the jury the questions of (1) punitive damages, (2) damages to business reputation and credit, (3) damages for personal injuries allegedly sustained by Mr. Loucks, and (4) in disallowing certain costs claimed by plaintiffs. * * *

The plaintiffs, as partners, sought recovery on behalf of the partnership of $402 allegedly wrongfully charged against the partnership account. This question was submitted to the jury, was decided in favor of the partnership, and against the defendants, and no appeal has been taken from the judgment entered on the verdict. They also sought recovery on behalf of the partnership of $5,000 for alleged damages to its credit, good reputation, and business standing in the community, $1,800 for its alleged loss of income, and $14,404 as punitive damages.

Each partner also sought recovery of $5,000 for alleged damages to his personal credit, good reputation and business standing. Mr. Martinez sought punitive damages individually in the amount of $10,000, and Mr. Loucks sought punitive damages individually in the amount of $60,000. Mr. Loucks also sought $25,000 by way of damages he allegedly sustained by reason of an ulcer which resulted from the wrongful acts of the defendants.

The parties have argued the case in their respective briefs and in their oral arguments upon the theory that the questions here involved, except for Point IV, which deals with the disallowance by the trial court of some claimed costs, are questions of the damages which can properly be claimed as a result of a wrongful dishonor by a bank of checks drawn by a customer or depositor on the bank, and of the sufficiency of the evidence offered by plaintiffs to support their claims for damages.

Both sides quote § 50A-4-402, * * *

It would appear that the first question to be resolved is that of the person, or persons, to whom a bank must respond in damages for a wrongful dishonor. Here, the account was a partnership account, and if there was in fact a wrongful dishonor of any checks, such were partnership checks.

We have adopted the Uniform Commercial Code in New Mexico. In § 4-402, it is clearly stated that a bank "is liable to its customer." In § [4-104(a)(5)], entitled "Definitions and index of definitions" it is stated that:

[a] In this article unless the context otherwise requires

(5) 'Customer' means any person having

an account with a bank or for whom a bank has agreed to collect items [including] a bank [that maintains] an account [at] another bank; * * *

This requires us to determine who is a "person" within the contemplation of this definition. Under part II, article I of the Uniform Commercial Code, entitled "General Definitions and Principles of Interpretation," we find the term "person" defined in § 1-201(30), as follows: "'Person' includes an individual or an organization * * *."

Subsection (28) of the same section expressly includes a "partnership" as one of the legal or commercial entities embraced by the term "organization."

It would seem that logically the "customer" in this case to whom the bank was required to respond in damages for any wrongful dishonor was the partnership. The Uniform Commercial Code expressly regards a partnership as a legal entity. This is consistent with the ordinary mercantile conception of a partnership. * * *

The relationship, in connection with which the wrongful conduct of the bank arose, was the relationship between the bank and the partnership. The partnership was the customer, and any damages arising from the dishonor belonged to the partnership and not to the partners individually.

The damages claimed by Mr. Loucks as a result of the ulcer, which allegedly resulted from the wrongful acts of the defendants, are not consequential damages proximately caused by the wrongful dishonor as contemplated by § 4-402. In support of his right to recover for such claimed damages he relies upon the cases of *Jones v. Citizens Bank of Clovis*, 58 N.M. 48, 265 P.2d 366 and *Weaver v. Bank of America Nat. Trust & Sav. Ass'n*, 59 Cal.2d 428, 30 Cal.Rptr. 4, 380 P.2d 644. The California and New Mexico courts construed identical statutes in these cases. The New Mexico statute appeared as § 48-10-5, N.M.S.A. 1953. This statute was repealed when the Uniform Commercial Code was adopted in 1961.

Assuming we were to hold that the decisions in those cases have not been affected by the repeal of the particular statutory provisions involved and the adoption of the Uniform Commercial Code, we are still compelled by our reasoning to reach the same result, because the plaintiffs in those cases were the depositor in the California case and the administratrix of the estate of the deceased depositor in the New Mexico case. In the present case, Mr. Loucks was not a depositor, as provided in the prior statute, nor a customer, as provided in our present statute. No duty was owed to him personally by reason of the debtor-creditor relationship between the bank and the partnership.

It is fundamental that compensatory damages are not recoverable unless they proximately result from some violation of a legally-recognized right of the person seeking the damages, whether such be a right in contract or tort. * * *

Insofar as the damage questions are concerned, we must still consider the claims for damages to the partnership. As above stated, the claim on behalf of the partnership for the recovery of the $402 was concluded by judgment for plaintiffs in this amount. This leaves (1) the claim of $5,000 for alleged damage to credit, reputation and business standing, (2) the claim of $1,800 for alleged loss of income, and (3) the claim of $14,404 as punitive damages.

The question with which we are first confronted is that of whether or not the customer, whose checks are wrongfully dishonored, may recover damages merely because of the wrongful dishonor. We understand the provisions of § 4-402, to limit the damages to those proximately caused by the wrongful dishonor, and such includes any consequential damages so proximately caused. If the dishonor occurs through mistake, the damages are limited to actual damages proved.

It is pointed out in the comments to this section of the Uniform Commercial Code that:

"* * *

"This section rejects decisions which have held that where the dishonored item has been drawn by a merchant, trader or fiduciary he is defamed in his business, trade or profession by a reflection on his credit and hence that substantial damages may be awarded on the basis of defamation 'per se' without proof that damage has occurred. * * *" Uniform Commercial Code, § 4-402, Comment 3.

If we can say as a matter of law that the dishonor here occurred through mistake, then the damages would be limited to the "actual damages proved." Even if we are able to agree, as contended by defendants in their answer brief, that the defendants acted under a mistake of fact in

"* * * that Mr. Kopp acting on behalf of the bank thought that the money was invested in the partnership and could be traced directly from Mr. Martinez to the L & M Paint and Body Shop," still defendants cannot rely on such mistake after both Mr. Martinez and Mr. Loucks informed them on March 15 and 18 that this was a personal obligation of Mr. Martinez and that the partnership had outstanding checks. At least it then became a question for the jury to decide whether or not defendants had wrongfully dishonored the checks through mistake.

The problem then resolves itself into whether or not the evidence offered and received, together with any evidence properly offered and improperly excluded, was sufficient to establish a question as to whether the partnership credit and reputation were proximately damaged by the wrongful dishonors. There was evidence that ten checks were dishonored, that one parts dealer thereafter refused to accept a partnership check and Mr. Loucks was required to go to the bank, cash the check, and then take the cash to the parts dealer in order to get the parts; that some persons who had previously accepted the partnership checks now refused to accept them; that other places of business denied the partnership credit after the dishonors; and that a salesman, who had sold the partnership a map and for which he was paid by one of the dishonored checks, came to the partnership's place of business, and ripped the map off the wall because he had been given "a bad check for it."

This evidence was sufficient to raise a question of fact to be determined by the jury as to whether or not the partnership's credit had been damaged as a proximate result of the dishonors. This question should have been submitted to the jury.

Damages recoverable for injuries to credit as a result of a wrongful dishonor are more than mere nominal damages and are referred to as "* * * compensatory, general, substantial, moderate, or temperate, damages as would be fair and reasonable compensation for the injury which he [the depositor] must have sustained, but not harsh or inordinate damages. * * *" 5A Michie, Banks and Banking, § 243 at 576.

What are reasonable and temperate damages varies according to the circumstances of each case and the general extent to which it may be presumed the credit of the depositor would be injured. *Valley National Bank v. Witter*, 58 Ariz.

491, 121 P.2d 414. The amount of such damages is to be determined by the sound discretion and dispassionate judgment of the jury. *Meinhart v. Farmers' State Bank*, 124 Kan. 333, 259 P. 698, 701.

The next item of damages claimed on behalf of the partnership, which was taken from the jury, was the claim for loss of income in the amount of $1,800 allegedly sustained by the partnership as a result of the illness and disability of Mr. Loucks by reason of his ulcer. We are of the opinion that the trial court properly dismissed this claim for the announced reason that no substantial evidence was offered to support the claim, and for the further reason that the partnership had no legally-enforceable right to recover for personal injuries inflicted upon a partner.

Even if we were to assume that a tortious act had been committed by defendants which proximately resulted in the ulcer and the consequent personal injuries and disabilities of Mr. Loucks, the right to recover for such would be in him. An action for damages resulting from a tort can only be sustained by the person directly injured thereby, and not by one claiming to have suffered collateral or resulting injuries. * * *

As was stated by Mr. Justice Holmes in *Robins Dry Dock & Repair Co. v. Flint*, 275 U.S. 303, 48 S.Ct. 134, 72 L.Ed. 290:

"* * * no authority need be cited to show that, as a general rule, at least, a tort to the person or property of one man does not make the tort-feasor liable to another merely because the injured person was under a contract with that other,

unknown to the doer of the wrong. * * * The law does not spread its protection so far."

The last question of damages concerns the claim for punitive damages. The trial court dismissed this claim for the reason that he was convinced there was no evidence of willful or wanton conduct on the part of defendants. Punitive or exemplary damages may be awarded only when the conduct of the wrongdoer may be said to be maliciously intentional, fraudulent, oppressive, or committed recklessly or with a wanton disregard of the plaintiffs' rights. * * *

Malice as a basis for punitive damages means the intentional doing of a wrongful act without just cause or excuse. This means that the defendant not only intended to do the act which is ascertained to be wrongful, but that he knew it was wrong when he did it. * * *

Although, as expressed above, we are of the opinion that there was a jury question as to whether defendants acted under a mistake of fact in dishonoring the checks, we do not feel that the unpleasant or intemperate remark or two claimed to have been made by Mr. Kopp, and his conduct, described by Mr. Martinez as having "run us out of the bank more or less," are sufficient upon which an award of punitive damages could properly have been made. Thus, the trial court was correct in taking this claim from the jury. * * *

It follows from what has been said that this cause must be reversed and remanded for a new trial solely upon the questions of whether or not the partnership credit was damaged as a proximate result of the dishonors, and, if so, the amount of such damages.

NOTE

1. U.C.C. Section 4-402 no longer contains a reference to liability where a mistake gave rise to a wrongful dishonor. The reference to "mistake" confused courts into believing that not only a different measure of damage would be applied, but also that the proof of damage would differ depending on the customer being a merchant or a consumer. In the case of a merchant the "Trader's Rule" indicated a *per se* doctrine, that the mere fact of dishonor of the check was a defamation of the trader's credit and, therefore, actionable. Although the Official Comment to prior Section 4-402 expressly rejected this *per se* rule, confusion persisted. This is now clarified by a rejection of any vestige of the Trader's Rule. Actual damage must be proved. Whether a bank would be liable for punitive damages or for "other non-compensatory damages," depends on an analysis of U.C.C. Sections 1-106 and 1-103. Although damages for emotional distress can be recovered as "other consequential damages," obviously a corporation or a partnership cannot allege to have suffered emotional

distress as actual damages. What must be shown is a nexus between the wrongful dishonor and the actual damage proven to have been caused thereby.

2. It would appear from a reading of the *Loucks* case that, where a corporation is the customer, only the corporation would have a cause of action under U.C.C. Section 4-402 and not the human at whose instigation the corporation is able to act. In *Kendall Yacht Corp. v. United California Bank*, 50 Cal. App. 3d 949, 123 Cal. Rptr. 848 (1975) the court in analyzing the facts, however, was prepared to "reverse pierce the corporate veil" and consider this corporation to be a mere sham, *i.e.*, the *alter ego* of the Kendalls. "It was, in effect, nothing but a transparent shell having no viability and separate and distinct legal entity." *Id.* 50 Cal. App. 3d 956, 123 Cal. Rptr. 853. *See Further* Crespi, *The Reverse Pierce Doctrine: Applying Appropriate Standards*, 16 J. of Corp. L. 33 (1990).

A majority of cases, however, apply U.C.C. Section 4-402 strictly and thus deny an officer standing to sue, even though such officer suffered the indignities of being arrested, arraigned, and held until bail was furnished prior to the charges being dismissed on the merit. In *Agostino v. Montecello Greenhouses, Inc.*, 166 A.D.2d 471, 560 N.Y.S.2d 690, 692–93 (N.Y. App. Div. 1990) the court recognized, however, that although exceptions to the *Louck*'s rule exist to permit

> 'a corporate officer to maintain such an action, individually, when there is a 'close intertwinement of [the corporate officer] and [the] company' or where 'the bank * * * treated [the officer] and the corporate depositor as one entity' (*Murdaugh Volkswagen v. First Nat. Bank of South Carolina*, 801 F.2d 719, 725) * * * there is no evidence in the record that such conditions existed in the case before us, we conclude that the plaintiff lacks standing to maintain an action pursuant to U.C.C. 4-402. * * *
>
> The plaintiff has properly pleaded a cause of action sounding in negligence against the bank, asserting that it owed him a duty to take reasonable care not to cause him loss and injury by what he claims is improper repudiation of the corporate check. (*cf. Becker v. Schwartz*, 46 N.Y.2d 401, 412-413, 413 N.Y.S.2d 895, 386 N.E.2d 807, *cert. denied* 488 U.S. 893, 109 S.Ct. 229, 102 L.Ed.2d 219). It would be incongruous to deny the plaintiff the right to bring a negligence action against the bank, considering that as a corporate officer he may be taken into custody and held criminally liable for allegedly issuing a bad check drawn on a corporate account (*see, Allen v. Dooley*, 156 A.D.2d 406, 407, 548 N.Y.S.2d 532; *People v. Dean*, 48 A.D.2d 223, 226, 368 N.Y.S.2d 349) while, at the same time, holding that he had no standing to bring a statutory cause of action to recover damages for wrongful dishonor under U.C.C. 4-402 because he is not a "customer" within the meaning of that provision. Moreover, the U.C.C. does not, either in language, spirit, or intent, proscribe such a cause of action sounding in negligence. Indeed, the Code impliedly permits it by providing that the principles of law and equity "shall supplement its provisions" (U.C.C. 1-103)."

Other causes of action may also be possible, besides negligence by the drawee bank. For example, an action against the payee based on defamation or malicious prosecution, may be possible where the payee has acted in bad faith in giving the information to the police to have the signer arrested, etc.

6. Payment and Discharge

The obligation embodied in a negotiable instrument is at an end by discharge or by payment of the instrument with "legal tender." If a check is given in payment, the tender of the check will result only in a conditional discharge unless the tender is by a certified check, a cashier's check or a teller's check. U.C.C. § 3-310. Neither discharge nor payment will release a party obligated on the instrument from claims by a holder in due course who took the instrument without notice that the instrument has been paid or that the obligation has been discharged.[62] The discharge can take the form of a simple contract,[63] the surrender of the instrument to the obligor, or any other indicia showing an intention by a person entitled to enforce an instrument to cancel the instrument.[64]

Tender of payment will terminate rights in the holder to demand interest on the sum due.[65] Payment must be to a person having the right to enforce the instrument, and will discharge the obligor, even if there is knowledge that there is a claimant to a proprietory right in the instrument,[66] including a right to rescind a negotiation of the instrument (U.C.C. § 3-202) so as to reclaim possession of it. Of course, knowingly paying a thief or a person known to be in wrongful possession of the instrument will not effectuate a discharge; especially in the case where there is knowledge that the presenter of the instrument has been enjoined from claiming these proceeds.[67] Where an obligor received an indemnity before paying on an instrument whose ownership is in dispute, e.g., where payment was demanded by a claimant asserting to be a person entitled to enforce the instrument, but alleging that the instrument was lost, stolen or destroyed, (U.C.C. § 3-309), there is no discharge should the payment have been made to the wrong person.[68]

As we have seen, in relation to banks we refer to settlement rather than payment. Thus on deposit a bank gives a provisional settlement even if it is an "on us" item. The bank retains the right to charge back the amount of the item should the drawer's account be insufficient to cover the item. Once the drawer's account is found to be sufficient, the drawee/payor will make final settlement. Not until this step has been taken will the drawee/payor have accepted. U.C.C. § 3-408. Similarly, unless a depository bank actually purchases the instrument, it will make a provisional settlement and await final payment by the drawee bank before making a final settlement of the item. U.C.C. § 4-215. If final payment by the drawee/payor bank does not occur, the depository bank will revoke the provisional

---

[62] U.C.C. § 3-601(b).

[63] U.C.C. § 3-601(a).

[64] U.C.C. § 3-604(a). Such intention can be shown by a written renunciation of rights which may relate to a specific party or parties. For example, after reacquiring an instrument a holder could strike out all intermediary endorsees since such would anyway have rights against him. U.C.C. § 3-415. In all other cases, by striking out an endorser's signature, the holder releases all subsequent endorsers from liability to him. This action, however, will not discharge these endorsers from liability to others, such as indorsees who took the instrument through them. U.C.C. § 3-604(b).

[65] U.C.C. § 3-603(c).

[66] U.C.C. §§ 3-602(a), 3-306.

[67] U.C.C. § 3-602(b)(i).

[68] U.C.C. § 3-602(b)(ii).

settlement and charge back the amount credited to its depositor's account, U.C.C. § 4-214. The drawee/payor must act within the midnight deadline (U.C.C. § 4-104(a)(10)) or be accountable for the item. U.C.C. § 4-302(a).[69] Once the provisional settlement becomes final[70] the obligation for which the instrument was given will no longer be suspended, but will be discharged to the amount of the instrument. U.C.C. § 3-310(b)(1).

Final payment by the drawee/payor bank occurs when the bank has first done any of the following:

(1) paid the item in cash

(2) settled for the item without having a right to revoke the settlement under statute, clearing-house rule, or agreement; or

(3) made a provisional settlement for the item and failed to revoke the settlement in the time and manner permitted by statute, clearing-house rule, or agreement. [U.C.C. § 4-215(a)].

In determining the means used and the time when final settlement occurs, Federal Reserve Regulations or circulars, clearing-house rules, and the like, or agreements between the parties govern.[71]

B. Collection of Documentary Drafts

In a sale of goods, tender of the goods and tender of payment are concurrent conditions. U.C.C. § 2-511(1). Unless the seller and the buyer are at the time of the sale located in the same place, the execution of the contract for the sale of goods will require a variation of this requirement. A provision for the extension of credit or an agreement for pre-payment would solve the legal question but would still leave the economic risk that the buyer would not pay once goods are in her possession, or that the seller, having been paid, would not perform. Thus, the seller does not wish to lose control over goods until payment is assured to him, while the buyer does not desire to pay for goods until assured of control over the goods. The solution to this problem is for the seller and the buyer to enter into a documentary sale, i.e., for the contract to be a sale of the documents symbolizing the goods in a negotiable document of title. Such documents of title would be issued by a warehouse or by a carrier.

The rights of the buyer on delivery of the goods to inspect the goods and to reject

---

[69] A failure by a payor bank to act within the "midnight deadline" will make such bank "accountable for the item." U.C.C. § 4-302(a). In connection with a documentary draft presented to a payor bank, U.C.C. § 4-104(a)(6), the midnight deadline does not apply. There is a requirement that prior to acceptance or payment of such draft, the payor bank examine the accompanying documents for compliance. The payor bank will have to act within the time agreed upon, for example, in accordance with the Uniform Rules for Collections, I.C.C. Publication No. 322, effective Jan. 1, 1979. Where no specific time has been agreed upon, a bank will have to act within a "reasonable time." U.C.C. § 1-204. In the case of a documentary draft drawn under a letter of credit, the issuer of the letter of credit, or a confirming bank, has three banking days in which to accept or to reject the presentation of the draft and its accompanying documents, U.C.C. § 5-112(1).

[70] U.C.C. §§ 4-213(a)(2), 4-302(a).

[71] U.C.C. § 4-213. In the absence of any such rules or agreements § 4-213 provides guidelines to determine the medium of settlement and the time of settlement.

them if non-conforming is not lost in a documentary sale,[72] albeit payment will have occurred following tender and inspection of the negotiable document of title. U.C.C. § 2-513(3)(b). The seller also runs a risk in that "[t]ender of payment is sufficient when made by any means or in any manner current in the ordinary course of business unless the seller demands payment in legal tender."[73] The current manner of payment is by check. We have seen that payment by personal check is a conditional payment[74] but the buyer may be in possession of the goods by the time the seller is informed that the check has been dishonored. An attempt to recover the goods[75] may be defeated by the existence of a bona fide purchaser of the goods,[76] or, where the buyer is a "merchant who deals in goods of that kind," by "a buyer in the ordinary course of business."[77] The documentary sale is clearly a risk reducer, but it does not eliminate all economic risk.

Where the parties to the contract are in distant places from each other, an exchange of documents for payment will require the use of agents. Banks, with their network of correspondent banks, are well suited to assist here. Further, unlike other business agents that are not financial institutions, banks will be prepared to advance funds secured by the negotiable document of title and the draft drawn on the buyer.[78]

On shipping the goods, the buyer would demand a negotiable bill of lading from the carrier. That bill of lading would name the seller as the consignor and also as the consignee to whose order the goods are to be delivered. It would further indicate that the carrier is to notify the buyer of the arrival of the goods. The buyer will be named as "the party to be notified," and not as the consignee to whose order the goods are to be delivered.

The seller, as drawer, then will draw on the buyer, as drawee, for the amount due under the contract of sale. This negotiable instrument—a draft—will name the seller as payee to whose order payment is to be made. Taking the draft and the bill of lading to a bank, the seller will endorse the bill of lading ordering delivery to the bank "or its order" and similarly endorse the draft making it payable to the bank "or its order." The draft and the bill of lading will then be sent by the bank to a correspondent bank after both have been endorsed by the bank. This will enable the correspondent bank to deal with the draft and the negotiable document of title. When tendering the document of title, a collecting bank only warrants its good faith and authority. The collecting bank does not warrant the genuineness or effectiveness of the documents, even though it may have made an advance to the seller collateralized by these documents, or even though it may have purchased the documents.

---

[72] U.C.C. §§ 2-601, 2-512(2).

[73] U.C.C. § 2-511(2).

[74] U.C.C. §§ 2-511(3), 3-310.

[75] U.C.C. §§ 2-507(2), 2-702(2).

[76] U.C.C. § 2-403(1).

[77] U.C.C. §§ 2-403(2), 1-201(9).

[78] Note, by taking the draft from the issuer/drawer the bank though being a holder, U.C.C. § 1-201(20), would not have taken by negotiation. U.C.C. § 3-201(a). But the bank, having made an advance to the seller, has a security interest in the draft and the accompanying document of title. Such security interest continues in the proceeds when the draft is paid on presentment, U.C.C. § 4-210.

U.C.C. § 7-508. The collecting bank need follow only those instructions which it receives from its transferor. U.C.C. § 4-203.

The correspondent bank will send a notice of presentment to the buyer calling on her to come to the bank to accept the draft, or, if the draft is payable on presentment, to pay the amount due on the draft, and to receive the bill of lading duly endorsed to the buyer. This will enable the buyer to obtain delivery of the goods. U.C.C. §§ 4-212(a), 7-404. The buyer has the right to examine the documents prior to acceptance. In such documentary sale the buyer does not have a right to inspect the goods before accepting the draft and obtaining the document of title. U.C.C. §§ 2-512, 2-513(3). Where the draft is an "on arrival" draft, i.e., it is to be presented to the buyer on arrival of the goods, presentment can be made after a reasonable time has elapsed after which arrival can be expected to have occurred. The buyer, however, will not have dishonored the draft by refusing to accept it until she has been notified by the carrier that the carrier wishes to make delivery of the goods.[79] The bank, however, must notify the seller that a late arrival of the goods is expected. Should the buyer dishonor the draft, the bank must promptly notify the seller of the dishonor[80] and request instructions what to do with the goods. If such instructions are not received within a reasonable time, the bank may store, sell or otherwise deal with the goods in a reasonable manner and recoup its expenses by foreclosing on the goods. The bank will have all the rights inherent in an unpaid seller.[81]

A carrier failing to comply with the order bill of lading by delivering the goods to the "party to be notified," where such party does not have the negotiable bill of lading endorsed to it, would be liable in conversion.[82]

---

[79] U.C.C. § 4-502.

[80] U.C.C. § 4-501.

[81] U.C.C. § 2-502(2).

[82] But note U.C.C. § 7-403(1) as to the defenses of a carrier who failed in his obligation to deliver to the consignee, especially where delivery occurred to a person whose receipt was rightful as against a claimant. U.C.C. § 7-403(1)(a).

Bank of California, N.A. v. International Mercantile Marine Co.
40 F.2d 78 (S.D.N.Y. 1929)

KNOX, D.J.

In this suit, libelant seeks to recover the value of forty-five tierces of salmon, which were shipped by Columbia Salmon Company, from Seattle, Wash., to Hamburg, Germany, on or about November 20, 1919. The goods were first delivered by the shipper to Oregon-Washington Railroad & Navigation Company, then being operated by the United States Railroad Administration, in exchange for an export bill of lading, calling for the carriage of the goods from Seattle, via New York, to Copenhagen. Sometime thereafter, and before the salmon reached Copenhagen, the shipment was diverted to Hamburg, Germany. A new export bill of lading, which was subject to the terms of the ocean bill, and providing for the delivery at Hamburg, was handed to the shipper in exchange for the one previously issued. The latter bill was indorsed by the shipper, and, for value, was delivered to libelant. When the salmon reached Hamburg, it was not delivered to the holder of the shipping documents but to parties who were to be notified of the arrival of the goods, and who, in the absence of possession of the bills of lading, were not entitled to receive them. As a result of such wrongful delivery, the libelant claims damage in the sum of $16,000.

The answer of respondents admits receipt of the goods, and does not contest libelant's allegation of wrongful delivery. It does, however, set forth that libelant failed to comply with a requirement of the bill of lading requiring notice of claim to be given to the delivering carrier within five days after the discharge of the steamer. Furthermore, a clause of the shipping document, limiting the valuation of the goods and liability thereon to $100 per package, is set up as a partial defense to the suit. . . .

Respondent takes the position that, since libelant has not shown compliance with the clause last quoted, there can be no recovery, and, in answer to the assertion that the time within which notice of claim should be given to the carrier was unreasonably short, says that such fact does not excuse the failure to give notice of claim for damages, but that the person asking damages should have given notice of such claim within a reasonable time. These matters would be entitled to consideration were it not that the proof is clear that respondent, through its unauthorized and affirmatively wrongful act, relieved the holder of the bill of lading from making a formal claim for damages. In other words, when a carrier deliberately, and without any semblance of right, converts goods intrusted to its care, it will not be permitted to take advantage of its tort by an insistence upon compliance by the wronged party of

such portions of the contract of carriage as would normally be binding upon him. While libelant, for some unexplained reason, did not approach respondent with respect to the goods until February 19, 1921, and, aside from the institution of suit, made no claim for damages against respondent, these circumstances, under the established facts, will not avail respondent. The carrier's wrong was complete and its liability became fixed as of the time of the wrong, and it cannot obtain exculpation through the apparent neglect of libelant in asserting its rights. Nor can the carrier take advantage of the limited valuation clause contained in the bill of lading. The wrongful delivery was nothing short of a conversion of the goods. It went to the essence of the contract of carriage, and vitiated the valuation clause. *The Sarnia* (C.C.A.) 278 F. 459.

Respondent further argues that, as the misdelivery took place in Germany, libelant's cause of action arose there, and that such damages as ensued should be calculated in German marks as of their value on the date on which this action was begun. This latter contention must also be rejected. Respondent was bound to an American corporation under an American contract, which respondent chose to breach in Germany. As previously said, the cause of action arose at the time of the breach, and the damages should be translated into dollars at the rate of exchange then prevailing.

Libelant may have a decree for its damages sustained as a result of the wrongful delivery of the merchandise.

NOTE

The duty imposed on the carrier by the negotiable bill of lading, is to hand the goods to someone in possession of the bill of lading through due negotiation.[83] This operates as a protection to the bank that the goods on which it relies as collateral will be available to it should the buyer default and the seller's account be unable to withstand an attempt under U.C.C. Section 4-214 to charge back the amount advanced. The carrier, having delivered the goods in violation of the contract of carriage, is liable to the holder of the bill of lading, namely the bank. This reduces the economic risk affecting a bank that has made an advance to the seller either by discounting the draft, or by allowing the seller to draw against the amount due on the draft before the drawee/buyer has accepted the draft and discharged her obligation on the draft by payment. It is only when there has been non-

---

[83] U.C.C. § 7-501(4).

acceptance of the draft and the seller's account is insufficient to repay any advance that the bank will have recourse to U.C.C. Section 4-504(b), by foreclosing on the goods.

A.B.F. Freight Systems, Inc. v. Austrian Import Service, Inc.
798 S.W.2d 606 (Tex. App. 1990)

ENOCH, Chief Justice.

The opinion of this court issued August 2, 1990 is withdrawn. This is the opinion of the court. This is a common carrier case. Appellee, Austrian Import Service, Inc. (Austrian), as consignee, brought suit against appellant, A.B.F. Freight Systems, Inc. (A.B.F.), seeking damages arising from a misdelivery of a shipment of clutches. Trial was before the court; judgment was rendered for Austrian in the amount of $24,693.05, including prejudgment interest, and against A.B.F., with a right of recovery for the judgment amount from third party defendant, Fritz Wilkinson d/b/a International Bolt & Automotive Company (International Bolt). The trial judge filed "Findings of Fact and Conclusions of Law" pursuant to a request filed by A.B.F. Thereafter, A.B.F. filed a "Motion for New Trial and Request for Additional and Amended Findings of Fact and Conclusions of Law," which the trial court denied. A.B.F. duly perfected its appeal. We reverse and remand.

FACTS

Wilkinson and Gunter Stromberger began doing business together in 1983. In 1984, Stromberger organized Austrian, a supplier of imported automobile parts for imported cars. Wilkinson, d/b/a International Bolt, continued purchasing auto parts from Stromberger at Austrian. In early 1986, International Bolt ordered a large number of clutches from Austrian. Austrian ordered the clutches from Daiken Clutch (Daiken) in two separate orders, resulting in two separate shipments.

The First Shipment

The first shipment of clutches was shipped from Daiken to Austrian by A.B.F. at the end of February 1986.[3] There is no dispute between the

parties as to the first shipment. When the first shipment arrived in Dallas, Stromberger's wife, who was an officer and employee at Austrian, authorized a drop shipment[4] of the clutches to International Bolt located on Switzer Avenue, even though the delivery receipt instructed A.B.F. to deliver the clutches to Austrian at its Manana address. Wilkinson also indicated in his deposition that he called A.B.F. and redirected the first shipment of clutches to International Bolt's address on Switzer Avenue, representing to A.B.F. that this was Austrian's new address.

The Second Shipment

The second shipment, which is the source of the parties' dispute, was shipped from Daiken to Austrian by A.B.F. on March 26, 1986. A.B.F. attempted to deliver the second shipment of clutches to Austrian at its Manana address on April 1, 1986, as authorized in the delivery receipt. However, because there was no one from Austrian at the address to accept the delivery, A.B.F.'s driver was unable to deliver the second shipment of clutches. The driver returned to A.B.F. with the clutches and unloaded them at the A.B.F. dock. He signed the delivery receipt and gave it to an A.B.F. dispatcher who was on duty at the time. The word "CALL" is written on the delivery receipt and Austrian's telephone number is noted in the upper left-hand corner of the delivery receipt, indicating that A.B.F. should call Austrian for further instructions regarding this ship-

[3] The first shipment, although a single order, involves two shipments of clutches since Daiken could not fill the complete order out of its Michigan warehouse. Daiken shipped the bulk of the order from its Michigan warehouse on February 27, 1986, having sub-

stituted the remaining clutches from its California warehouse, which had been shipped on February 18, 1986. Austrian received the delivery of California clutches, and then turned them over to International Bolt. Thereafter, Austrian authorized A.B.F. to deliver the Michigan shipment of clutches directly to International Bolt.

[4] A drop shipment delivery is defined as a shipment of goods directly from the manufacturer to a dealer or consumer rather than first to a wholesaler, though a wholesaler still earns profit because he took the order for the goods. BLACK'S LAW DICTIONARY 446 (5th ed. 1979).

ment. The word "CALL" on the delivery receipt, however, is scratched out. The next day, on April 2, 1986, A.B.F. loaded the clutches onto a truck and delivered them to International Bolt on Switzer Street. * * *

Stromberger testified that he did not authorize delivery of the second shipment to Wilkinson and that he did not instruct anyone else to do so, noting that Wilkinson was behind on his payments for the first shipment. Although Stromberger was in Europe when the second delivery arrived in Dallas, he said that he left instructions at Austrian to call up an additional warehouseman to unload the second shipment when it arrived. * * *

Stromberger returned from Europe sometime in May 1986 and called A.B.F. to inquire into the whereabouts of the second shipment of clutches. During this telephone conversation, Stromberger learned that A.B.F. delivered the second shipment of clutches to International Bolt. Austrian, however, failed to inform A.B.F. of the misdelivery at this time. Instead, Austrian notified A.B.F. of the misdelivery by letter dated December 1, 1986, some seven months after receiving notice of the misdelivery, but within nine months of the delivery date.

After the telephone call to A.B.F., Stromberger inquired at International Bolt about the second shipment. He said that he demanded a return of the shipment from Wilkinson, and that, when Wilkinson refused to return the clutches, Stromberger sought advice from his attorney. Stromberger stated that International Bolt had become delinquent in its payments for the clutches, and as a result, he was becoming delinquent in his payments to Daiken. Stromberger repossessed $22,605.25 worth of clutches from International Bolt on October 2, 1986, and sent them back to Daiken. Daiken then informed Austrian by letter dated November 5, 1986, that it was to receive a credit in an amount of $9,648.94 for the returned clutches. The terms of the credit included a forty percent (40%) restocking fee plus freight charges. Once Austrian learned the full extent of the loss, it informed A.B.F. that the second shipment had been misdelivered, and then filed this suit.

RATIFICATION/ESTOPPEL/WAIVER

In its fourth point of error, A.B.F. alleges that the trial court erred, as a matter of law, by failing to find that Austrian ratified the delivery of the second shipment of clutches to International Bolt. In its fifth point of error, A.B.F. alleges that the

trial court erred because, as a matter of law, Austrian was estopped from claiming that A.B.F. misdelivered the second shipment of clutches. In its sixth point of error, A.B.F. alleges that the trial court erred because, as a matter of law, Austrian waived its right to complain to A.B.F. or to sue A.B.F. about the misdelivery. A.B.F. bases its allegations on the fact that Austrian waited some seven months after it learned of the misdelivery to notify A.B.F.

A party may ratify a transaction by silence or acquiescence when there is a duty to speak. *Almar-York Co. v. Fort Worth Nat'l Bank*, 374 S.W.2d 940, 942 (Tex. Civ. App. 1964); *Continental Assurance Co. v. Supreme Constr. Corp.*, 375 F.2d 378, 383 (5th Cir. 1967). Where ratification is relied upon to establish a principal's liability for the unauthorized act of his agent, the burden of proof is on the party who asserts ratification. *BancTEXAS Allen Parkway v. Allied Am. Bank*, 694 S.W.2d 179, 181 (Tex. App. 1985).

Waiver is the "intentional relinquishment of a known right or intentional conduct inconsistent with claiming it." * * * Waiver can be implied where a party's clear and unequivocal acts infer an intent to relinquish a right and the opposing party has been misled to his prejudice. * * *

The principle of estoppel by silence is applied where a person, who by force of circumstances has a duty to speak, refrains from doing so thereby causing another party to believe in the existence of a state of facts, and that other party relies thereon to its prejudice. *A.R. Clark Inv. Co. v. Green*, 375 S.W.2d 425, 435 (Tex. 1964).

Interstate Commerce Act

State statutes regulating carriers are limited to matters affecting transportation within the state and do not apply to interstate traffic. *Nation v. San Antonio S. Ry.*, 115 Tex. 431, 437, 283 S.W. 157, 159 (Tex. Comm'n App. 1926). Under the power of the federal government to regulate interstate commerce, carriers engaged in interstate commerce are subject to regulation and control by Congress. *Houston, E. & W. Texas Ry. v. United States*, 234 U.S. 342, 351, 34 S.Ct. 833, 58 L.Ed. 1341 (1914). In this case, the second shipment of clutches involved interstate travel from Michigan to Texas. Therefore, the federal statutes control, and A.B.F. may be held liable for damages under provisions of the Interstate Commerce Act, which govern liability of common carriers providing interstate service or transportation. See *Walding v. Atlas Van Lines Int'l*, 632 F. Supp. 703, 705–06 (W.D. Tex. 1986).

Under the Interstate Commerce Act, a motor carrier moving cargo in interstate commerce is liable for the actual loss or injury that it causes to the cargo unless the carrier properly limits its liability. See 49 U.S.C.A. § 11707(a) and (c) (West Pamph. Supp. 1989) (recodifying, without substantive change, the Carmack Amendment to the Interstate Commerce Act, formerly 49 U.S.C. § 10730). The Interstate Commerce Act addresses limitation on actions by and against common carriers and provides that "[a] claim related to a shipment of property accrues under this section on delivery or tender of delivery by the carrier." 49 U.S.C.A. § 11706(g) (West Pamph. Supp. 1989). Moreover, the statute includes the following notice requirements:

> A carrier or freight forwarder may not provide by rule, contract, or otherwise, a period of less than 9 months for filing a claim against it under this section and a period of less than 2 years for bringing a civil action against it under this section. The period for bringing a civil action is computed from the date the carrier or freight forwarder gives a person written notice that the carrier or freight forwarder has disallowed any part of the claim specified in the notice.

49 U.S.C.A. § 11707(e) (West Pamph. Supp. 1989).

A.B.F. tendered delivery of the second shipment of clutches to International Bolt on April 2, 1986, and Austrian received notice of this delivery sometime in May 1986. Thereafter, by letter dated December 1, 1986, and within nine months from the date of the tendered delivery, Austrian filed its claim against A.B.F. for misdelivery.[5] We note that laws in force at the time and place of the making of a contract enter into and form a part of it as if they were expressly incorporated in its terms, and a bill of lading is a contract

---

[5] Since notice to A.B.F. by Austrian was within nine months of the date of misdelivery, we need not address whether the definition of "accrue" in subsection 11706(g) is subject to the equitable tolling doctrine. Aluminum Co. v. United States, 867 F.2d 1448, 1452 (D.C. Cir. 1989); Atchison, Topeka & Santa Fe Ry. v. Interstate Commerce Comm'n, 851 F.2d 1432, 1438–39 (D.C. Cir. 1988).

within this rule. *Northern Pac. Ry. v. Wall*, 241 U.S. 87, 91–92, 36 S.Ct. 493, 60 L.Ed. 905 (1916). Under the federal statute, Austrian clearly had a period of nine months in which to file a claim against A.B.F. for wrongful delivery. Since Austrian's legal duty to speak is defined by statute, Austrian's notice to A.B.F. was timely, and A.B.F.'s argument that it justifiably relied to its detriment upon Austrian's silence during this period is without merit. We hold that Austrian's claim against A.B.F. is not barred by the doctrines of ratification by silence, waiver, or estoppel as a matter of law. Points of error five and six are overruled.

Referring to its fourth point of error, A.B.F. further alleges that the trial court erred because, as a matter of law, Austrian ratified the misdelivery when it attempted to collect the value of the second shipment of clutches from International Bolt. A.B.F. alleges that ratification is established in Austrian's first amended petition by an admission that Austrian demanded payment from International Bolt for the misdelivered clutches. The petition alleges that "Wilkinson has refused to pay for the misdelivered merchandise." The petition further alleges:

> The amount due from Wilkinson on merchandise sold to him and merchandise misdelivered to him by A.B.F. Freight is $38,080.64. Plaintiff has previously made demand upon the Defendant Wilkinson for payment of said sums and no amount has been paid on the balance due.

A consignee may ratify a delivery of goods made to a third party. See *American Ry. Express v. Patterson Produce Co.*, 12 S.W.2d 158, 159 (Tex. Comm'n App. 1929). One factor in determining whether a consignee ratified delivery made to a third party includes attempts by the consignee to collect the value of the goods from the third party. See *Patterson*, 12 S.W.2d at 159.

In *Patterson*, the consignee, Patterson Produce Company, had contracted to sell one car of turkeys to Conron at twenty-nine cents per pound. Patterson intended to sell a second car of turkeys in New York, through DeWinter & Stewart, who was engaged in that business. The market price of turkeys in New York at that time was several cents above twenty-nine cents per pound. However, the carrier, American Railway Company, delivered both cars of turkeys to Conron. Upon being advised of the misdelivery, Patterson notified American and requested a delivery correction. American agreed to make the correction as requested, but failed to do so. Patterson initially drew a draft upon DeWinter & Stewart for the turkeys and forwarded it for collection through a bank. DeWinter & Stewart, having failed to receive the turkeys, dishonored the draft and suggested that Patterson present the draft to Conron. Patterson thereafter presented Conron with a draft for the second car of turkeys at the rate of twenty-nine cents per pound. Conron accepted the second car of turkeys and honored the draft which was accepted by Patterson. Patterson then attempted to recover from American the difference between what would have been realized by the sale of the turkeys at the market price and the amount received from Conron. Patterson testified, without dispute, that in dealing with Conron, his intention was to minimize the damages resulting from the unauthorized delivery and not to discharge American's liability for such damages. The court held that the facts conclusively established a ratification and that the legal effect of Patterson's acts could not be affected by his secret intention in doing them. *Patterson*, 12 S.W.2d at 159.

The facts in this case are distinguishable. The undisputed facts in *Patterson* show that Patterson received payment in full for the contract amount as negotiated between the buyer and seller after the misdelivery occurred. Stromberger, on the other hand, neither negotiated a new agreement with nor received any payment from International Bolt for the second shipment of clutches. We disagree with A.B.F.'s contention that Stromberger ratified the misdelivery merely by demanding payment from International Bolt for the second shipment of clutches. The burden of proof is on A.B.F. to prove ratification. *BancTEXAS*, 694 S.W.2d at 181. A.B.F. failed in that burden. A.B.F.'s fourth point of error is overruled.

NEGLIGENCE

In points of error one and two, A.B.F. alleges that the trial court erred, as a matter of law, because Austrian failed to establish negligence and prove the elements of its case. A.B.F. also alleges that the trial court erred, as a matter of law, by awarding Austrian damages in an amount of $18,640 because there is no evidence upon which to base such an award.

When reviewing a no evidence challenge, an appellate court must consider the evidence and reasonable inferences drawn therefrom which, when viewed in their most favorable light, support the jury verdict or court finding. The court must disregard all evidence and inferences to the contrary of the fact finding. *Stafford v. Stafford*, 726 S.W.2d 14, 16 (Tex. 1987); *Alm v. Aluminum Co. of America*, 717 S.W.2d 588, 593 (Tex. 1986). If there is more than a scintilla of evidence to support the finding, the challenge fails. *Stafford*, 726 S.W.2d at 16. The initial review of a matter of law point is the same as that required for a no evidence point. However, in addition to finding no probative evidence to support the jury finding, the court must also find that the contrary proposition to the finding is established as a matter of law. *Holley v. Watts*, 629 S.W.2d 694, 696 (Tex. 1982).

Duty/Breach

A.B.F. alleges that, under Texas law, Austrian was required to prove the elements of its negligence action. In this connection, it is well settled that Austrian has the burden of establishing each of the three elements of actionable negligence. The elements are a legal duty owed by one person to another, a breach of that duty, and damages proximately resulting from such breach. * * *

Proof of delivery of an interstate shipment to the initial carrier, and failure to deliver the same to the consignee, raises a presumption of negligence, giving rise to liability imposed by the Carmack amendment to the Interstate Commerce Act. *Galveston, Harrisburg, & San Antonio Ry. v. Wallace*, 223 U.S. 481, 492, 32 S.Ct. 205, 56 L.Ed. 516 (1912). The carrier then has the burden of proving that the loss resulted from some cause for which the carrier was not responsible in law or by contract. *Wallace*, 223 U.S. at 492, 32 S.Ct. at 207. In *Wallace*, the Court reasoned:

The plaintiffs were not obliged both to prove their case and to disprove the existence of a defense. The carrier and its agents, having received possession of the goods, were charged with the duty of delivering them, or explaining why that had not been done. This must be so, because carriers not only have better means, but often the only means of making such proof. If the failure to deliver was due to the act of God, the public enemy, or some cause against which it might lawfully contract, it was for the carrier to bring itself within such exception. In the absence of such proof, the plaintiffs were entitled to recover, and the judgment is affirmed.

Wallace, 223 U.S. at 492.

In this case, the record contains a freight bill for the second shipment of clutches, representing the bill of lading from Daiken to Austrian, which was shipped by A.B.F. However, A.B.F. delivered the second shipment of clutches to International Bolt and not Austrian, the named consignee on the freight bill. Both Stromberger and his wife, the individuals who were in charge at Austrian, said that they did not authorize delivery of the second shipment to International Bolt. We hold that based upon the evidence, viewed in the light most favorable to the judgment, A.B.F. failed to prove the absence of negligence in delivering the second shipment of clutches.

Proximate Cause

A.B.F. contends that Austrian failed to prove that it suffered damages, and, if so, whether the delivery of the second shipment of clutches to International Bolt proximately caused those damages. In applying the principles discussed above regarding a no evidence point, we review the record to determine whether there is any evidence of probative value to support the trial court's findings that Austrian suffered damages and whether A.B.F.'s misdelivery of the goods to International Bolt proximately caused Austrian's damages.

The trial court included in its findings of fact that "[t]he delivery of the said goods to International Bolt & Automotive Company resulted from the negligence of A.B.F. Freight Systems, Inc., and said negligence was the proximate cause of the loss and damages to Austrian Import Service, Inc." * * *

A.B.F. contends that Austrian offered no competent evidence to show that the misdelivery of the clutches to International Bolt proximately caused Austrian's damages. Stromberger admitted that he purchased the clutches from Daiken at the request of International Bolt and that, at the time of the purchase, Stromberger intended to sell the clutches to International Bolt. Stromberger, however, testified that he would not have sent the second shipment of clutches to International Bolt had A.B.F. delivered them to Austrian "[b]ecause the relationship started to smell after he did not pay on his first installment." Stromberger

explained that "the relationship was bad" and that "I didn't want to do business with him, I wanted out, I wanted my parts back and I wanted my money." Stromberger also said:

> And it ought to be my decision who I want to extend credit to and who I want to do business with if I pay for the parts. So even if he would have been able to pay, I would not have done business with him because I don't let my customers decide to be on open account or on credit at Austrian.

An invoice from Austrian to International Bolt for the first shipment of clutches, dated February 27, 1986, in an amount of $29,927.44, included the following payment terms: International Bolt was to pay one-half of the invoice amount within fifteen days, one-fourth within forty-five days, and the remaining one-fourth within sixty days. Stromberger testified that, in accordance with the invoice, International Bolt owed Austrian about $15,000 on March 15, 1986, and no payment was made.[7] On April 2, 1986, the date A.B.F. tendered delivery of the second shipment of clutches, International Bolt was already late in its payment to Austrian for the first shipment of clutches.

Stromberger then said that, had A.B.F. delivered the second shipment of clutches to Austrian rather than International Bolt, Austrian would have been able to sell the clutches to its other customers. "We would have sold them, we were in the auto parts business, Austrian Importers and auto parts distributors." Stromberger explained that Austrian had a salesman contacting an established customer base of about one hundred fifty auto stores. The salesman would call the customers periodically to see what they needed from the lines carried by Austrian.

Viewing the evidence in the light most favorable to the fact finding, we hold that there is some evidence of probative value to support the trial court's finding that A.B.F.'s misdelivery proximately caused Austrian damages. *Stafford*, 726 S.W.2d at 16. To the extent points of error one and two attack the findings on negligence and proximate cause, they are overruled.

In its third point of error, A.B.F. also attacks the finding of proximate cause and alleges that

---

[7] A partial payment on account was received several months later.

the trial court erred by failing to find that it was not responsible, as a matter of law, for the clutches once Austrian repossessed them from Wilkinson. To support its argument, A.B.F. relies upon *Vincent v. Rather*, 31 Tex. 77 (1868). *Vincent*, however, is distinguishable. The consignee in Vincent took control of cotton that the carrier had misdelivered by accepting a warehouse receipt from the third party to whom the cotton had been misdelivered. The consignee failed to remove the cotton and it was destroyed in a warehouse fire. The carrier was relieved of liability. *Vincent*, 31 Tex. at 79. In the present case, Austrian's losses were incurred while the goods were under the control of International Bolt, unlike *Vincent*, where the loss was incurred while the goods were under the consignee's control. We find no merit in this point of error.

Damages

Revisiting points of error one and two, we must now determine whether there is any evidence of probative value to support $18,640 in damages awarded to Austrian by the trial court. Although the uncertainty of damages is not fatal to recovery once the fact of damage is established, it is nevertheless a reasonable degree of certainty with which the extent of damages must be shown. *Southwest Battery Corp. v. Owen*, 131 Tex. 423, 426, 115 S.W.2d 1097, 1098 (1938); *State Nat'l Bank v. Farah Mfg. Co.*, 678 S.W.2d 661, 693 (Tex. App. 1984). There can be no recovery for damages which are speculative or conjectural. *Roberts v. U.S. Home Corp.*, 694 S.W.2d 129, 135 (Tex. App. 1985). The damages must be ascertainable in some manner other than by mere speculation or conjecture, and by reference to some fairly definite standard, established experience, or direct inference from known facts. *Berry Contracting, Inc. v. Coastal States Petrochemical Co.*, 635 S.W.2d 759, 761 (Tex. App. 1982).

The trial court's findings of fact include the following:

> The goods which were returned by International Bolt to Austrian Import Service were returned to Daiken Clutch USA. These returned goods were credited to the account of Austrian Import Service, Inc., in the amount of $9,648.94. Of the credit allowed, $6,985.00 was attributable to the March 26, 1986 shipment.
>
> As a result of the negligence of A.B.F. Freight

Systems, Inc., Austrian Import Service, Inc., suffered a loss of $18,640.00.

Austrian Import Service, Inc., is entitled to Pre-Judgment Interest in the amount of 10% compounded daily from October 3, 1986. Said interest is in the amount of $6,053.05.

In this case, Stromberger presented evidence showing that both shipments were valued at about $25,000 each, and that International Bolt eventually paid Austrian $12,000. In plaintiff's exhibit number eight, Stromberger lists a complete inventory of goods Austrian repossessed from International Bolt on October 2, 1986. Plaintiff's exhibit number nine is a ledger sheet from Daiken, which reflects the return of the inventory identified in plaintiff's exhibit eight. Daiken valued the purchase price of the inventory returned at $22,605.25. Exhibit number eight, however, includes items from both the first and second shipments. Stromberger said that some of the goods Austrian repossessed were exclusive to the first shipment only and not to the second shipment. The items exclusive to the first shipment, which are not prejudicial to A.B.F., total $2,765.11, and are listed in plaintiff's exhibit ten. Therefore, an amount of $19,840.25 for the clutches Austrian returned to Daiken are traced to both the first and second shipments without segregation.

Austrian must prove its damages to recover against A.B.F. for misdelivery of the second shipment of clutches. Damages must be calculated with a reasonable degree of certainty. *Berry*, 635 S.W.2d at 761. Austrian received a single credit against the amounts it owed Daiken for clutches in both the first and second shipments. Therefore, Austrian must identify the clutches it returned to Daiken from the second shipment in order to prove its damages.

Daiken credited Austrian $9,648.94 for the returned inventory after deducting a forty percent (40%) restocking fee and freight charges. Stromberger said that, in repossessing the clutches common to both shipments, he was unable to distinguish with absolute certainty which items came from the first and second shipments. Stromberger said that there was no definite way to determine the number of clutches from shipment two because "all the numbers are the same for the same (clutch) part on shipment one and two." Stromberger attempted to make an estimate using a last in, first out calculation, since he had witnessed International Bolt stock the clutches on top of each other. Stromberger explained that International Bolt had the clutches from the first and second shipments for a total of thirty-four weeks. Stromberger allowed International Bolt two weeks to stock and price the clutches from the first shipment until actual sale of the parts. This provided International Bolt two weeks in which to sell the clutches from the first shipment prior to the arrival of the second shipment. International Bolt then had thirty-two weeks in which to sell clutches from both the first and second shipments. Using the last in, first out calculation, the clutches from the second shipment would be sold first, and thereafter the clutches from the first shipment would be sold. Based upon the total return of clutches to Daiken, Stromberger suggested that $6,701.30 would come from shipment two, and the balance would come from shipment one. We note however, that Stromberger failed to provide any objective facts in determining the number of clutches sold at any time during the thirty-four-week period. Stromberger's estimate was based solely upon his experience in handling clutches. He testified that he was not a partner with Wilkinson nor was he involved in Wilkinson's business. He also failed to produce business records reflecting International Bolt's clutch sales during this time period to support his calcula-

tions. Moreover, Stromberger testified as a fact witness, and not as an expert on damages. Therefore, we hold that the evidence concerning Austrian's damages regarding the second shipment of clutches is legally insufficient to support the award. We sustain those portions of A.B.F.'s points of error one and two complaining of legal insufficiency of the evidence to support the damages award.

Having prevailed on its "no evidence" point as to damages, A.B.F. would ordinarily be entitled to rendition of judgment in its favor. *Vista Chevrolet, Inc. v. Lewis*, 709 S.W.2d 176, 176–77 (Tex. 1986). However, a court of appeals, having found error in the judgment of the trial court on the issue of damages, possesses the power to remand because such recourse "will subserve better the ends of justice." *Zion Missionary Baptist Church v. Pearson*, 695 S.W.2d 609, 613 (Tex. App. 1986) (quoting *Massachusetts Mut. Life Ins. Co. v. Steves*, 472 S.W.2d 332, 333 (Tex. Civ. App. 1971)). In this case, although Austrian did not prove its damages with reasonable certainty, there is evidence which shows damages generally in that Daiken applied a reduced credit to Austrian's account for the return of clutches in both the first and second shipments. Therefore, we hold that in the interests of justice, a remand is required in this cause for a determination of reasonably certain damages.

NOTE

The applicable state law provisions are set forth in U.C.C. Section 7-403.

§ 7-403. Obligation of Warehouseman or Carrier to Deliver; Excuse

(1) The bailee must deliver the goods to a person entitled under the document who complies with subsection (2) and (3), unless and to the extent that the bailee establishes any of the following:

(a) delivery of the goods to a person whose receipt was rightful as against the claimant;
(b) damage to or delay, loss or destruction of the goods for which the bailee is not liable, [but the burden of establishing negligence in such cases is on the person entitled under the document];

> **Note:** *the brackets in (1)(b) indicate that State enactments may differ on this point without serious damage to the principle of uniformity.*

(c) previous sale or other disposition of the goods in lawful enforcement of a lien or on warehouseman's lawful termination of storage;
(d) the exercise by a seller of his right to stop delivery pursuant to the provisions of the Article on Sales (Section 2-705);

(e) a diversion, reconsignment or other disposition pursuant to the provisions of this Article (Section 7-303) or tariff regulating such right;

(f) release, satisfaction or any other fact affording a personal defense against the claimant;

(g) any other lawful excuse.

(2) A person claiming goods covered by a document of title must satisfy the bailee's lien where the bailee so requests or where the bailee is prohibited by law from delivering the goods until the charges are paid.

(3) Unless the person claiming is one against whom the document confers no right under Sec. 7-503(1), he must surrender for cancellation or notation of partial deliveries any outstanding negotiable document covering the goods, and the bailee must cancel the document or conspicuously note the partial delivery thereon or be liable to any person to whom the document is duly negotiated.

(4) "Person entitled under the document" means holder in the case of a negotiable document, or the person to whom delivery is to be made by the terms of or pursuant to written instructions under a non-negotiable document.

C. Limitation Periods

Various periods of limitation are indicated in regard to specific activities. Thus, a customer must exercise reasonable promptness in examining a statement or items sent by the drawee bank to determine whether any payment was unauthorized. Such notification to the bank must be within thirty days of receipt of the statement, or the customer would be precluded from raising this defense against the drawee. Albeit, should the bank also have been negligent there will be an apportionment of the damages in accordance with comparative negligence standards. U.C.C. § 4-406.

There are other sections in U.C.C. Articles 3, 4 and 4A which impose a periodic requirement during which an action must be brought. The most important limitation periods are contained in U.C.C. Section 3-118. That section indicates not only the date deemed the "due date" from which the indicated period of limitation begins and thus during which time an action will have to be brought, but also it sets forth the limitation period applicable to specific instruments.

An action to enforce an obligation on a note must be commenced within six years of the due date indicated in the note. U.C.C. § 3-108. If the note contains an acceleration clause, the due date will be the date on which demand is made based on such acceleration. U.C.C. §§ 1-208, 3-118(a),(e). Should the note be one payable on demand, the due date is the date a demand for payment is made. In the absence of a demand having been made on the maker, an action on such note becomes statute barred after ten years from the date the note was issued. U.C.C. § 3-118(b).

Since a draft requires a presentment for acceptance so as to create a liability in the drawee, the due date is determined by the date on which the draft was presented. If the draft is dishonored, the action against the drawer or against an endorser must be commenced within three years of the dishonor. But if there has been a failure to present the draft for acceptance, no action can be brought on the draft after ten years have elapsed from the date it was issued; neither the drawer nor an endorser can be sued on the draft. U.C.C. § 3-118(c). In the case of a time draft accepted by the drawee, a further presentment for payment will be required. Such presentment for payment will have to be within six years of the due date. The due date may be indicated in the draft itself, for example, "pay sixty days after sight." If after presentment for acceptance the draft is payable on demand, however, the due date will be determined from the time of acceptance. U.C.C. § 3-118(f).

Although a teller's check, cashier's check, certified check and traveller's check require no prior presentment to make the financial institution that issued them liable thereon, the due date is the date the instrument is presented for payment. Should such instrument be dishonored, an action to enforce an obligation on these instruments has to be commenced within three years of the presentment for payment. This approach may be reasonable in the case of traveller's checks, U.C.C. § 3-104(i), which may be outstanding for a considerable time, but to create a distinction between ordinary checks and those issued by a bank does not appear to have a rational basis. Teller's checks, cashier's checks and certified checks are generally issued for a specific purpose that should be satisfied at the latest within a ten year period from their issuance.

Certificates of deposit, U.C.C. § 3-104(j), generally contain a due date or may be due on demand. Often such certificates of deposit also indicate that the redemption date can be accelerated before an indicated due date subject to the payment of a penalty for early redemption. This provision allows an acceleration by the holder which will affect the due date. An action to enforce a certificate of deposit must be commenced within six years from the due date. Should the certificate of deposit be payable on demand, the due date will be the date of issuance. A presentment of the certificate of deposit for payment made before the due date will not commence the period of limitation. The obligor on the certificate is not obligated to pay prior to the due date. U.C.C. § 3-118(e).

All other actions based on an instrument, such as an action for conversion, U.C.C. § 3-420, breach of warranty, U.C.C. §§ 3-416, 3-417, contribution among accommodation parties, or claims for reimbursement from a party accommodated, U.C.C. § 3-419(e),[84] will have to be commenced within three years of the cause of action accruing, U.C.C. § 3-118(g), regardless of the aggrieved party's lack of knowledge of a breach. U.C.C. § 4-111.

Under the U.N. Convention on International Bills of Exchange and International Promissory Notes, (CIBN), there is a general period of four years after which actions may no longer be brought on the instrument. The due dates for instruments to which the Convention applies is very similar to that applicable to such instruments under U.C.C. § 3-118. In one respect, however, the CIBN differs regarding the period during which an action will have to be commenced. Where a claim for contribution or reimbursement is possible, such claim will have to be commenced within one year of the claimant having satisfied her obligation to pay under the instrument. CIBN Art. 84.

---

[84] Note: Where the party accommodated has been discharged from the instrument, it will not be possible for the accommodation party to subrogate to the claimant on the instrument and recover. There will be no liability on the instrument remaining with which the party accommodated can be charged. U.C.C. §§ 3-604, 3-605(b). Thus, U.C.C. §§ 3-118(a)-(f) would be inapplicable. The recovery is purely a claim for reimbursement under U.C.C. §§ 3-419(e), 3-118(g).

X LETTERS OF CREDIT

The insecurity felt by a seller trading with foreign buyers was a powerful incentive to the development of the letter of credit. In essence, the letter of credit substituted the credit of a "bank or other person" believed to be more creditworthy for the obligation of the buyer under a contract of sale. Entering into a documentary sale enables the seller to keep control over goods while they are in transit to the buyer, but it does not assure the seller that the buyer will be able to pay for the goods when the documents are tendered. A failure to pay can cause not only inconvenience to the seller who will have to try to dispose of such goods while they are in the hands of a carrier or warehoused near the buyer's place of business, but also may cause economic loss due to the cost of warehousing while seeking a buyer who might be prepared to pay the contract price. A task that may not be easy.

The "traditional" letter of credit developed to minimize this risk.

Letters of credit evolved as a mercantile specialty entirely separate from common law contract concepts and they must still be viewed as entities unto themselves. Completely absorbed into the English common law by the 1700s along with the Law Merchant—of which it had become an integral part by the year 1200—2 W. Holdsworth, *A History of English Law* 570–72 (1922), letter of credit found its way into American jurisprudence where it flourishes today. Its origins may be traced even more deeply into history. There is evidence letters of credit were used by bankers in Renaissance Europe, Imperial Rome, ancient Greece, Phoenicia and even early Egypt. *See* Trimble, *The Law Merchant and The Letter of Credit*, 61 Harv.L.Rev. 981, 982–85 (1948). These simple instruments survived despite their nearly 3000-year-old lineage because of their inherent reliability, convenience, economy and flexibility. [*Voest-Alpine Intern Corp. v. Chase Manhattan Bank*, 707 F.2d 680, 682 (2d Cir. 1983).]

Under a traditional letter of credit the "issuer" engages itself to pay for goods or services by accepting a draft drawn on the issuer/drawee by the supplier of goods or services—the drawer, who is the "beneficiary" of the letter of credit. In order to clarify the applicable concepts, our discussion will concentrate on a documentary sales transaction. Since we are here dealing with a documentary sale, payment is due on tender of documents.[1] This obligation to pay, engaged in by the issuer of the letter of credit, makes the issuer neither a party to, nor will the issuer be affected by, the underlying contract of sale. This unique legal relationship develops directly from the engagement. Thus:

---

[1] U.C.C. § 2-513(3)(b).

A letter of credit is an idiosyncratic form of engagement that supports performance of an obligation incurred by a party other than the issuer of the engagement in a separate financial, mercantile, or other transaction or engagement.[2]

Other than having to be in writing and signed by the issuer, or by a confirming entity, the U.C.C. imposes no formal requirements. Primarily, an intent to issue a letter of credit must be shown.[3] Such intent can be illustrated by labelling the writing "letter of credit," or by the writing calling for presentment of a documentary draft which, in the case of a non-bank issuer, must be accompanied by a document of title. U.C.C. § 5-102(1).[4] Further, the writing must clearly show under what circumstances the obligation to pay will arise.[5] A call for presentment of a draft would satisfy this requirement.

We generally find that there are three transactions involved leading to the issuance of a traditional letter of credit:

(1) a basic transaction involving the seller and the buyer in a documentary sale whereby the buyer is obligated to pay on tender of documents. For example, in a cost, insurance, and freight (CIF) contract, the seller is required at his own expense and risk to

   (a) put the goods into the possession of a carrier at the port for shipment and obtain a negotiable bill or bills of lading covering the entire transportation to the named destination; and

   (b) load the goods and obtain a receipt from the carrier (which may be contained in the bill of lading) showing that the freight has been paid or provided for; and

   (c) obtain a policy or certificate of insurance, including any war risk insurance, of a kind and on terms then current at the port of shipment in the usual amount, in the currency of the contract, shown to cover the same goods covered by the bill of lading and providing for payment of loss to the order of the buyer or for the account of whom it may concern; but the seller may add to the price the amount of the premium for any such war risk insurance; and

---

[2] Proposed Official Comment to Proposed Draft § 5-101 (March 31, 1993). References to the Proposed Draft U.C.C. Article 5 are to the March 31, 1993 draft. *Note:* changes may occur before the draft is accepted by the ALI and NCCUSL.

[3] U.C.C. § 5-104(1). What legal rules are to be applied to letters of credit created by and satisfied by an electronic data interchange (EDI) is under consideration by a drafting committee of the National Conference of Commissioners on Uniform State Law (NCCUSL) that is reviewing developments in letter of credit law. That Committee is drafting amendments to U.C.C. Article 5 to incorporate such developments as well as other technical advances. The United Nations Commission on International Trade Law (UNCITRAL) also is considering a draft Convention applicable to "Independent Guarantees and Stand-By Letters of Credit". *See* UN DOC/CN.9/WG.11/ WP.76/Add.1 October 29, 1992. *See* also *Report of the Working Group on International Contract Practices*, UN Doc. A/CN.9/372, December 23, 1992. The International Chamber of Commerce (ICC), recognizing the important role letters of credit play in commercial activities, promulgated Uniform Customs and Practice Rules for Documentary Credits. (UCP # 500). These rules have been incorporated into the New York, Alabama and Missouri U.C.C. and will govern transactions governed by any one of these laws unless expressly excluded. In all other jurisdictions U.C.C. Article 5 will govern letters of credits unless the UCP is expressly made applicable to the transaction. *See* Guttman, *Bank Guarantees and Standby Letters of Credit: Moving Toward A Uniform Approach*, 56 BROOKLYN L. REV. 167(1990).

[4] NCCUSL Proposed Draft § 5-102(a)(9).

[5] Transparent Products Corp. v. Paysaver Credit Union, 864 F.2d 60 (7th Cir. 1988).

(d) prepare an invoice of the goods and procure any other documents required to effect shipment or to comply with the contract; and

(e) forward and tender with commercial promptness all the documents in due form and with any indorsement necessary to perfect the buyer's rights. [U.C.C. § 2-320(2)]

Additional documents may also be required such as an inspection certificate issued by an acceptable entity to assure that the goods when shipped conformed to the contractual description. In an international sale an export license may also be required.

(2) By requiring the buyer to obtain a letter of credit, the contract obligates the buyer to get a bank or other financially acceptable entity to engage itself, as issuer of the letter of credit, to pay against presentment of the document. The buyer will enter into a contractual relationship with such an issuer as an "account party"[6] against whom the issuer can proceed to recoup itself for any payments it has to make under the letter of credit, i.e., an indemnity agreement. Since in most instances the account party will not have to pay the amount due under the letter of credit until the issuer has to meet that obligation, this relationship will be based on the credit of the account party. The cost of issuing a letter of credit is minimal. Only a small fee, representing between $\frac{1}{4}\% - \frac{1}{2}\%$ of the amount due on the letter of credit, is usually charged by most issuers. Once the issuer has made payment, a debt to the issuer arises and not only the principal but also interest on this debt will become payable. The issuer is collateralized with regard to such debt by the document of title symbolizing the goods.

(3) The issuer of the letter of credit will communicate with the beneficiary and thereby establish its obligation under the letter of credit.[7] This communication will set out the engagement of the issuer to accept a draft drawn on itself requiring that the draft contain a reference to the letter of credit properly identified. In addition this letter of credit will indicate the specified documents that must be presented with the draft.[8] This engagement must be unconditional. It is not a contractual obligation but a legally binding engagement based on the "independence" of the letter of credit from the underlying transaction between the seller and the buyer.

To have a commercial value, the letter of credit must be an irrevocable letter of credit. *See Beathard v. Chicago Football Club, Inc.*, 419 F. Supp. 1133 (N.D. Ill. 1976). Peter Beathard and Lawrence Jameson had signed contracts with the Chicago Winds of the World Football League. To secure their pay should the league collapse and the club liquidate, the club obtained a letter of credit issued by the Mid-City National Bank. When the League disbanded and the club liquidated, Mid-City National Bank revoked the letter of credit.

---

[6] U.C.C. § 5-103(1)(g) refers to such person as a "customer." The proposed Draft § 5-102(a)(2) uses the term "applicant."

[7] U.C.C. § 5-106(1).

[8] These are the documents specified in the original documentary sale between the seller and the buyer.

The court held the letter of credit to be revocable and the beneficiaries were unable to recover.[9] U.C.C. Section 2–325 therefore provides

> [U]nless otherwise agreed the term "letter of credit" or "banker's credit" in a contract for sale means an irrevocable credit issued by a financing agency of good repute and, where the shipment is overseas, of good international repute. [U.C.C. § 2–325(3)].

A failure to provide an irrevocable letter of credit would be a breach of the sales contract. Should the issuer's letter of credit be revocable, the beneficiary could proceed against the buyer but not against the issuer, whatever liability the issuer may have against its customer/account party. The contract between those parties may have called for an irrevocable letter of credit to be issued entitling the customer/account party to sue for damages.

Unfortunately these issues arise only after a dispute has arisen, often after the issuer has attempted to revoke the letter of credit. U.C.C. Article 5 does not clarify whether a letter of credit governed by its provisions is an irrevocable letter of credit.[10] A revocable letter of credit has been categorized as "in reality, an illusory contract" that would impede the "purpose and function" of letters of credit.[11] A revocable letter of credit provides the beneficiary with little protection. Therefore, unless otherwise provided in the letter of credit itself, there should be a presumption in favor of irrevocability.[12]

The importance of categorizing a letter of credit as revocable or irrevocable is emphasized by U.C.C. Section 5–106(2) which provides that:

> Unless otherwise agreed once an irrevocable letter of credit is established as regards the customer [account party] it can be modified or revoked only with the consent of the customer and once it is established as regards the beneficiary it can be modified or revoked only with his consent.

No such restraint is imposed on the issuer of a revocable letter of credit. U.C.C. § 5–106(3).

When dealing with a foreign buyer, the issuer of the letter of credit is most likely a foreign bank which will be acting through a U.S. agent, a correspondent or advising bank. The advising bank will notify the beneficiary that a letter of credit has been established but would not itself be liable on the letter of credit nor on any draft drawn under such letter of credit. Its duty as an agent is to forward the documents and the draft to the overseas foreign bank, the issuer of the letter of credit, for acceptance and payment. Once more a risk may be incurred. There may be an insecurity relating to the economic viability

---

[9] The letter of credit was issued as governed by the Uniform Customs and Practice for Documentary Credits (UCP) rules promulgated by the International Chamber of Commerce (ICC). At that time, the UCP required that to be irrevocable, the letter of credit would have to be labeled "irrevocable". In 1992, the ICC changed this approach in UCP #500 Article 7 by providing that:

(b) The credit . . . should clearly indicate whether it is revocable or irrevocable.

(c) In the absence of such indication the credit shall be deemed to be irrevocable.

[10] *But see* Florida U.C.C. § 675.103 [§ 5–103] which specifically provides a presumption of irrevocability. Lewis State Bank v. Advance Mortgage Corp., 362 So.2d 406, 409 (Fla. Dist. Ct. App. 1978).

[11] West Virginia Housing Development Fund v. Sroka, 415 F. Supp. 1107, 1111–12 (W.D. Pa. 1976).

[12] The NCCUSL Proposed Draft § 5–106(a) provides:

A letter of credit that is silent as to its revocability is irrevocable.

of the foreign issuer bank and to the possible changes in law in the foreign country that may prevent the repatriation of funds from the foreign country.[13] But even in a domestic situation risks exist. The present economy, as it affects U.S. banks, has illustrated the possible weakness of domestic banks and their inability to meet obligations when they fall due. Furthermore, the U.S. Supreme Court has held in *Federal Deposit Insurance Corp. v. Philadelphia Gear Corp.*, 476 U.S. 426 (1986), that a letter of credit issued by a bank, although secured by an executory promissory note given by the account party to the bank, did not represent "an insured deposit." The relationship, account party-issuing bank, merely gave rise to a line of credit. There is no deposit to which the obligation of the FDIC would extend. There were, therefore, no funds on deposit with the insolvent bank which the FDIC had insured and thus no rights to which the beneficiary could subrogate.

To protect against these risks, the seller may require that the letter of credit be confirmed by a bank local to the seller, a bank in which the seller reposes confidence. By confirming the letter of credit, the confirming bank engages itself to honor a draft drawn on the confirming bank.[14] This is not an obligation that is assumed by a correspondent/advising bank, which merely undertakes to forward the draft and documents to the issuing bank.

Since forwarding the documents and a draft to the issuer of the letter of credit may delay receipt of funds, the issuer may designate the correspondent/advising bank as a "negotiating bank." The beneficiary will negotiate the documents to the negotiating bank and receive payment.[15] The negotiating bank, using the bank collection system, will be able to expedite payment by the issuer. The letter of credit permitting the use of a negotiating bank may also counter the power of an issuer to revoke a letter of credit. A provision in the letter of credit of a clause whereby the issuer engages to pay "drawers, endorsers, and bona fide holders" of drafts drawn under the credit will trigger U.C.C. Section 5-106(4). That section provides that where a negotiating bank pays the draft "under the terms of the original credit" it will be entitled to reimbursement from the issuer where the draft has been taken up by the negotiating bank "before receipt of notice of the modification or revocation and the issuer in turn is entitled to reimbursement from its customer." [U.C.C. § 5-106(4)]. Further, as an endorsee, the negotiating bank will be able to claim against the beneficiary/ drawer should the issuer/drawee dishonor the draft because of defects in the documents called for by the letter of credit. U.C.C. §§ 3-414, 5-111. This right is based on warranties. The drawer's denial of nonconformity of the documents does not affect the

---

[13] See also the possible hostility of a foreign court to a suit against its national. *Cf.* American Bell International, Inc. v. Islamic Republic of Iran, 474 F.Supp. 420 (S.D.N.Y. 1979).

[14] *See* U.C.C. § 2-325(2).
The term "confirmed credit" means that the credit must also carry the direct obligation of such an agency which does business in the seller's financial market.

[15] Proposed Draft § 5-102(a)(10) introduces the term "nominated person" to include not only a confirming bank, but also a person authorized by the issuer "to pay, accept, negotiate, or otherwise give value under a letter of credit." *See* further Proposed Draft § 5-107. "Transfer" of a letter of credit must be distinguished from "assignment of proceeds." In a transfer, a substitution of the beneficiary by the transferee occurs. In an assignment of proceeds, the right to the proceeds upon performance by the beneficiary is involved. *See* Proposed Draft § 5-112. Unless expressly permitted, a letter of credit is nontransferable.

rights of a negotiating bank. *Manufacturers Hanover International Banking Corp. v. Spring Tree Corp.*, 752 F.Supp. 522 (D. Mass. 1990).

The use of a letter of credit as a method of payment for goods to be manufactured or to be otherwise assembled for delivery to a buyer has a further advantage for a manufacturer/seller. By having an assurance of payment on completion of the contractual obligation between the seller and the buyer, the seller can use the letter of credit opened by the buyer, to obtain credit from its own bank or from a financial entity prepared to advance credit to the seller. In particular, the letter of credit could be used by the seller to collateralize a loan he is seeking. The seller would do this by assigning to his creditor the right to proceeds. An assignment of proceeds is possible even though the letter of credit provides that it is nontransferable or nonassignable by the beneficiary.[16] An assignment of proceeds is often found in connection with a letter of credit issued by the manufacturer's or seller's bank to secure the acquisition of raw materials or of goods to be sold to the buyer, i.e., when a back to back credit is created. Such credit, though dependent on the credit of the customer/account party/seller, is primarily based on the credit of the original buyer as affirmed by the original issuer of the first letter of credit. We can thus see how the letter of credit is a device that can provide the lubricant for the smooth working of a commercial transaction. It enables the infusion of other peoples money (OPM) as an assurance that payment will be received and thereby acts as a risk shifting device from the credit of a party to the transaction to that of a financial intermediary of good repute.

But just as the seller in the traditional "letter of credit" felt insecure about the buyer fulfilling her obligation to pay on presentment of documents, so the buyer may feel insecure that the goods on inspection may not conform, or that the seller or manufacturer may never fulfill his obligation under the contract. Until execution of a judgment in damages, the buyer would be put to inconvenience and to certain financial loss. Once more the letter of credit was the device used by banks to cover such risk. This led to the development of the "standby letter of credit."

The Independence Rule in Standby Letters of Credit

by

Michael Stern

52 U. Chi. L. Rev. 218 (1985)*

I. Analysis of the Standby Letter of Credit

Standby letters of credit and traditional letters of credit are both mechanisms for allocating risks among the parties in commercial transactions. By placing in the hands of

---

[16] U.C.C. § 5-116 [Proposed Draft § 5-114].

a neutral third party the responsibility for making payment when certain conditions are met, one party to a transaction is able to avoid the risk of nonpayment or nonperformance. The standby letter of credit differs from the traditional letter of credit, however, in the method by which it allocates the risks among the parties. The traditional letter of credit usually requires a third party to generate some of the documents that the beneficiary must present to the issuer (usually a bill of lading); under the standby letter of credit, the beneficiary usually generates all the necessary documents himself (usually a simple statement that the customer is in default).

The standby letter of credit thus involves a greater risk of improper demand than the traditional letter of credit, both for the customer and for the issuing bank.[25] Because the independence rule prohibits the bank from inquiring into the truth of the beneficiary's assertion,* the customer faces a risk that it will have to reimburse the bank for making a payment that was unjustifiably demanded. The bank's risk of loss is also increased because, unlike a bank issuing a traditional letter of credit, it receives no bill of lading. In a traditional letter of credit transaction involving the sale of goods, one of the documents that must be presented for payment is a bill of lading, which gives the bank title to the goods and allows the bank to claim the goods if the customer refuses to reimburse the bank. Without such a security interest, the bank's only recourse is against the customer himself.[30] Because of these increased risks, the standby letter of credit is analytically distinct from the traditional letter of credit.

The standby letter of credit can also be compared with another device that is commonly used to allocate risks among parties in commercial transactions—the performance bond. Both devices are used to protect a party against the risk of nonperformance of another party's contractual obligations. Nevertheless, standby letters of credit differ in several important respects from performance bonds. A performance bond is issued by a surety company, a private firm, or an individual, rather than by a bank, and guarantees a buyer of goods or services that the seller (the principal) will perform.[32] A surety's obligation is secondary to that of the principal, however, and the surety becomes liable only when the principal has in fact defaulted on its obligation. Thus, unlike the issuer of a standby letter of credit, the surety does not pay the buyer automatically upon the buyer's assertion that the seller has not performed: it may first investigate the truth of the assertion. If the surety determines that the seller has fulfilled the contract, then it may refuse to pay the buyer. The surety

---

[25] Although the bank is always entitled to reimbursement from the customer if it has honored a demand conforming to the terms of the letter of credit, *see* U.C.C. § 5-114(3), it assumes the risk of the customer's insolvency. Thus, any increased risk to the customer also increases the risk to the bank. The bank is free, however, to demand that the customer provide it with security to protect against that risk; when this is done, the customer effectively assumes the risk of an improper demand. . . .

* [Editor: the author explains the "independence principle" by stating "the issuer's obligation to pay upon a conforming demand is unaffected by any claims that the customer may have against the beneficiary on the underlying contract." *Id.* at 218.]

[30] The bank, however, may have protected itself with a security interest in assets belonging to the customer. *See supra* note 25.

[32] In a performance-bond transaction, the surety is analogous to the issuer of a standby letter of credit, the principal is analogous to the customer, and the party who benefits from the guarantee is analogous to the beneficiary.

may also assert any defenses against the buyer that would be available to the principal. Furthermore, the surety retains the option of actively intervening to ensure performance either by demanding that the seller remedy the defect in its performance or by completing the contract itself.

The standby letter of credit differs from the performance bond in the way in which it protects a buyer against the risk of nonperformance. The standby letter of credit allows the beneficiary to recover damages simply by asserting that the customer has defaulted on the contract; except where the fraud in the transaction exception applies. The issuer is not permitted to refuse payment based either on its belief that the beneficiary's assertion is false or on the existence of any defense that customer may have on the underlying contract. For a number of reasons, this basic difference between the standby letter of credit and the performance bond makes the standby letter of credit potentially more useful to the beneficiary than the performance bond. First, the beneficiary benefits from the greater "automaticity and brevity" of payment under the standby letter of credit: the bank may inspect only the tendered documents, and payment will not be delayed by the bank's investigation of the underlying contract. Second, the standby letter of credit is more flexible than the performance bond because it can be used in a wider variety of transactions. Third, the administrative expenses involved with a standby letter of credit may be lower than those involved with a performance bond, thus reducing the cost of a standby letter of credit; because the bank is only responsible for scrutinizing the documents presented upon demand, and because the bank will often already be very familiar with the customer's creditworthiness and with the underlying transaction, it will often be able to avoid incurring the additional or duplicative expenses of investigating and monitoring the underlying contract. Moreover, the standby letter of credit has the advantage that the bank incurs a much lower risk of becoming embroiled in litigation with the beneficiary than does a surety. Finally, the standby letter of credit allows parties to take advantage of the financial soundness of banking institutions; while banks are free to issue standby letters of credit, they are generally forbidden from issuing performance bonds.

While the standby letter of credit offers a number of potential advantages over a performance bond, it also increases the risks to the bank and customer. Unlike a performance bond, a standby letter of credit gives the issuing bank no control over the underlying contract and no right to refuse payment based on its opinion that the customer has properly performed.

* * *

NOTE

1. Since banks are subject to state and to federal regulations requiring conformity to "sound banking practices,"[17] an extension of a guarantee on a customer's obligation effective on the customer's default could scarcely be justified as sound banking practice. Banks, however, are permitted to issue standby letters of credit,[18] although in economic terms both

---

[17] *See* 12 U.S.C. § 1818 restricting U.S. banks to what is "the traditional business of banking." Similar restrictions appear to exist in other jurisdictions, e.g., Hong Kong, Singapore, etc.

[18] 12 C.F.R. § 7.7016.

bank guarantees and standby letters of credit are risk shifting devices. In both instances there is a serious risk of non-reimbursement by the account party/principal for whom the engagement was undertaken. Unless the financial institution has taken collateral outside the transaction in issue, its obligation is unsecured,[19] and thus entering into either obligation could not be justified as a sound banking practice.[20] The power to issue standby letters of credit is subject to the lending limits that are specified by law,[21] and such contingent liability must be disclosed even if default by the account party has not occurred.[22] This disclosure will affect the issuer's adherence to risk-based capital adequacy rules.[23] Thus it is not the often stated view that U.S. banks are prohibited by law from granting guarantees[24] that seems to have been the driving force behind the development of the standby letter of credit.[25] There have been many inroads in this prohibition both by the Comptroller of the Currency[26] and by state legislatures with regard to state-chartered banks.[27] The real motivation for the development of the standby letter of credit is the ease and certainty with which this form of banking activity can be carried out.

2. We must also note that the issuer of a letter of credit is not necessarily a bank. It can be an "other person." Although throughout we considered a letter of credit to be a tri-partite transaction, two of which are contract based,[28] recently transactions occurred in which a letter of credit was issued by the parent corporation of a buyer that is a party to the underlying contract giving rise to the demand for a letter of credit. The economic value of such letter of credit issued by what in essence is a party to the obligation is doubtful. There is no shifting of risk. Such letter of credit merely provides for a payment unaffected by the contractual obligation underlying the engagement. Payment has to occur against presentment of documents including a simple demand draft. A situation that can be achieved in a sale of goods under existing U.C.C. Section 2-513(3)(b). An irrevocable letter of credit

---

[19] As a result, the guarantor or issuer of the standby letter of credit will require protection. For example, the guarantor/issuer may insist that a compensating balance be maintained in funds of the account party/principal held by the guarantor/issuer with rights in the guarantor/issuer to offset expenditures against such compensating balance.

[20] *See* Treasury, Rules of the Comptroller of Currency 12 C.F.R. § 7.7016 (1977); Comptroller of the Currency, Interpretive Letter No. 376, Fed. Banking L. Rep. (CCH) ¶ 85,600 (Oct. 14, 1986); Lord, *The No-Guaranty Rule and the Standby Letter of Credit Controversy*, 96 BANKING L.J. 46 (1979).

[21] *See* Office of the Comptroller of the Currency. Risk-Based Capital Guidelines, 12 C.F.R. § Part 3, Appendix. A promulgated under the International Lending Supervision Act, 12 U.S.C. §§ 3901 et seq. and 12 C.F.R. § 567.6(2), promulgated under the Financial Institutions Reform, Recovery and Enforcement Act of 1989 (FIRREA), P.L. 101-73 § 3019(t). *See also* Sabel, *Risk-Based Capital Guidelines and Letters of Credit*, Letters of Credit Report 10 (July/August 1989).

[22] 12 U.S.C. § 84(a); 12 C.F.R. §§ 32.2(e), 32.3, 32.4(d), 32.5.

[23] *See* note 21, *supra*.

[24] *See* 12 U.S.C. § 24 (Seventh) (1988); H. HARFIELD, BANK CREDITS AND ACCEPTANCES, 154-67 (5th ed. 1974).

[25] *See New Jersey Bank v. Palladino*, 77 N.Y. 33, 386 A.2d 454 (1978).

[26] *See generally* Treasury, Comptroller of the Currency, 12 C.F.R. § 7.7000 et seq.

[27] *See, e.g.*, N.Y. Banking Law §§ 234(21), 383(12) (McKinney 1971).

[28] The contract between the account party and the beneficiary and that between the account party and the issuer of the letter of credit.

does create a liability in the drawee, however, who cannot avoid such liability by non-acceptance of the draft.

The letter of credit has developed further than being a mere appendage to the sale of goods domestically or in international markets. It is an everyday device used by government, the construction industry, courts, service industry and finance.[29]

A. The Independence Principle and Fraud in the Transaction

The purpose of the independence principle is to provide the beneficiary with an unfettered, immediate payment upon occurrence of the triggering event. The purpose is not to prevent any subsequent challenge to the validity of the beneficiary's claim against the account party, but to ensure that "contractual disputes wend their way toward resolution with money in the beneficiary's pocket rather than in the pocket of the" account party.[30] The issuer of the letter of credit will have to honor the letter of credit even if informed that there had been a breach of the transaction giving rise to the letter of credit.[31] The beneficiary merely warrants that "the necessary conditions of the credit have been complied with." U.C.C. § 5-111(1).[32] This does not involve a warranty that there has been no breach of the underlying transaction, it does mean, however, that the beneficiary warrants that the requirements of the letter of credit have been satisfied. The warranty is not affected by the independence principle.

---

[29] J.A. Byrne, *An Examination of U.C.C. Article 5 (Letters of Credit) A Report of the ABA Task Force on the Study of U.C.C. Article 5,* 45 Bus. Law 1521 (1990) estimates that approximately $200 billion in credit is now outstanding in the United States.

[30] *See Itek Corp. v. First National Bank of Boston,* 730 F.2d 19, 24 (1st Cir. 1984).

[31] *Maurice O'Meara Co. v. National Park Bank,* 239 N.Y. 386, 146 N.E. 635 (1925).

[32] Proposed Draft § 5-108(a) includes a warranty that there is no fraud.

Mellon Bank, N.A. v. General Electric Credit Corp.
724 F. Supp. 360 (WD Pa. 1989)

[The issuer refused to honor the letter of credit basing its defense on U.C.C. Section 5-111. The issuer/bank claimed that in order to be able to draw on the standby letter of credit, GECC would have to assert: (1) that there was a default on the underlying contract, *and* (2) that the amount of the draft was due and owing. The issuer argued that both of these assertions were false because, although there was a default in the performance of the underlying contract by non-payment of an installment, GECC had failed to give notice to the debtor so as to trigger the obligation under the letter of credit for the full amount due on the underlying contract. As a result the issuer argued that by not accelerating the debt, only the amount due on the unpaid installment became due. The court held:]

COHILL, Chief Judge. * * *

* * * Mellon argues under the terms of the Lease Agreement Woodings was *not* in default at the time of the draw even though it had failed to make a timely payment, and GECC therefore breached its § 5-111 warranty.

The sad part of all of this is that the issue of Woodings' default is utterly irrelevant to analysis of the § 5-111 warranties. Although GECC represented in its statement to Mellon that Woodings was in default at the time of the draw, and though the Letter of Credit Agreement between Woodings and GECC permits a draw only upon a default by Woodings, the Letter of Credit itself *does not require* such an assertion prior to a draw. The Letter of Credit states:

> We [Mellon] undertake to honor from time to time your draft or drafts at sight on us not exceeding in the aggregate U.S. $600,000.00 when accompanied by a signed typewritten statement by GECC stating *either* (i) *that the amount of the accompanying draft is due and owing by Customer to GECC, or* (ii) that a petition has been filed by or against Customer under Title XI of the United States Code or a similar or successor law. (Emphasis added.)

There simply is no requirement that GECC make any representation of Woodings' status under the contract. Default is irrelevant. The only representation necessary to a draw on the Letter of Credit, in the absence of Woodings' bankruptcy, is that the amount of the draft be due and owing. Thus GECC's assertion that Woodings was in default was merely gratuitous under the Letter of Credit. Though the issue of default may be relevant as between Woodings and GECC under their Letter of Credit Agreement, Mellon was not a party to that agreement, and neither the agreement nor its terms were incorporated in the Letter of Credit issued by Mellon. If no assertion of default is required by the Letter of Credit, no warranties attach to such an assertion. Therefore, even if GECC's statement that Woodings was in default was false, GECC would not be liable for breach of a § 5-111 warranty.

We return then to a consideration of what the Letter of Credit *does* require. As seen above, absent Woodings' bankruptcy, GECC was required to state that the amount of the draft "is due and owing by [Woodings] to GECC." In fact GECC submitted a draft for $600,000 and stated that this sum was due and owing at the time of the draw. Therefore § 5-111 is applicable, and GECC warranted to Mellon the truth of this assertion.

It is admitted that Woodings was late in making one monthly lease payment of $15,011.40. But GECC has asserted that $600,000 was due and owing, apparently on the basis of provisions of the Lease Agreement for acceleration of payments and stipulated loss.

The pertinent provisions of the Lease Agreement are found in Section XII:

> XII. DEFAULT: (a) If Lessee breaches its obligation to pay rent when due and fails to cure said breach within ten (10) days, or if Lessee breaches any of the terms hereof or any of terms or any Schedule here to . . . then in either such case, *Lessor may declare this Agreement in default*. Such declaration shall be by written notice to Lessee and shall apply to all Schedules hereunder except as specifically excepted by Lessor in such declaration. *Lessee hereby authorized Lessor at any time after such declaration* to enter, with or without legal process, any premises where any Equipment may be and take possession thereof. *Lessee shall, without further demand, forthwith pay to Lessor, as liquidated damages* for loss of a bargain and not as a penalty, *an amount equal to all rentals and other sums then due hereunder, together with the Stipulated Loss Value* of the Equipment, *calculated as of the date Lessor declared a default hereunder*, together with interest thereon at the highest rate allowed by law. . . . (Emphasis added.)

From these provisions it is clear that acceleration of payments and liquidated damages are invoked *only* after a declaration of default. Indeed accelerated payments and the Stipulated Loss Value are to be calculated "as of the date Lessor declared a default hereunder."

GECC admits that it did not declare a default prior to the draw on the Letter of Credit. Without such a formal declaration, the acceleration of payments and liquidated damages provisions are not applicable. Thus, on the date of GECC's draw on the Line of Credit, Woodings owed GECC the amount of one tardy rental payment. GECC's assertion that $600,000 was due and owing was erroneous, and constitutes a breach of its warranty under § 5-111.

II. Independence Principle

However, GECC objects to Mellon's reliance on the terms of the underlying Lease Agreement. GECC refers to this portion of the Letter of Credit:

> We agree that we shall have no duty or right to inquire as to the basis upon which GECC has determined to present to us any draft under this Letter of Credit.

GECC also invokes the doctrine known as the "independence principle," which prohibits reference to underlying contracts to determine the validity of a draft on a letter of credit. Under this principle the issuing bank may only determine whether the appropriate documents have been presented. It may not contest the truth of the assertions in those documents. *Intraworld Industries Inc. v. Girard Trust Bank*, 461 Pa. 343, 359, 336 A.2d 316, 324 (1975).

Although GECC states the principle accurately, it does not apply it correctly in this case. The independence principle, and the above-quoted portion of the Letter of Credit, speak only to the bank's obligation to honor the sight draft *in the first instance.* They do not preclude subsequent investigation and efforts at recovery. *Pubali Bank v. City National Bank*, 676 F.2d 1326 (9th Cir. 1982), appeal after remand, 777 F.2d 1340 (1985).

The purpose of the independence principle, and of the similar provision in Mellon's Letter of Credit, is to provide the beneficiary with an unfettered, immediate remedy upon occurrence of the triggering event on a standby letter of credit. The purpose is not to prevent any subsequent challenge to the validity of the beneficiary's claim, but to ensure that "contractual disputes wend their way towards resolution with money in the beneficiary's pocket rather than in the pocket of the contracting party." *Itek Corp. v. First National Bank of Boston,* 730 F.2d 19, 24 (1st Cir. 1984); *C.K.B. & Associates v. Moore McCormick Petroleum,* 734 S.W.2d 653, 655 (Tex. 1987).

Indeed, if interpreted in the manner GECC suggests, the independence principle would make a nullity of § 5-111. Little purpose would be served if § 5-111 created warranties as to the truth of the conditions necessary to a draw, while the independence principle precluded the bank from contesting the truth of those assertions.

For the reasons stated we conclude that the independence principle and the similar contract provision quoted above are inapplicable to an action for breach of § 5-111 warranties, and do not preclude reference to underlying contractual documents to determine the truth or falsity of the warrantied assertions.

Fundamental to the administration of justice is that courts should not allow themselves to be used to commit a fraud. There is a tension between U.C.C. Sections 5-114(1)[33] on one hand and U.C.C. Section 5-114(2)(b) on the other. The first reiterates the independence doctrine by calling on the issuer to honor a draw under the letter of credit "regardless of whether the goods or documents conform to the underlying contract for sale or other contract between the customer and the beneficiary." U.C.C. Section 5-114(2)(b) on the other hand provides that the issuer, if acting in good faith, may ignore notification from the account party "of fraud, forgery or other defect not apparent on the face of the documents *but a court of appropriate jurisdiction may enjoin such honor.*" (emphasis added). Thus, unless enjoined, the issuer can honor the letter of credit and demand reimbursement from the customer/account party.

To resolve this tension, the courts have been left the task of interpreting what would be the standard applicable for such an injunction to issue. In *Intraworld Industries, Inc. v. Girard Trust Bank*, 461 Pa. 343, 336 A.2d 316 (1975) the court stated:

---

[33] *See also* U.C.C. Section 5-114(2)(a) which provides:

(2) Unless otherwise agreed when documents appear on their face to comply with the terms of a credit but a required document does not in fact conform to the warranties made on negotiation or transfer of a document of title (Section 7-507) or of a certificated security (Section 8-306) or is forged or fraudulent or there is fraud in the transaction:

(a) the issuer must honor the draft or demand for payment if honor is demanded by a negotiating bank or other holder of the draft or demand which has taken the draft or demand under the credit and under circumstances which would make it a holder in due course (Section 3-302) and in an appropriate case would make it a person to whom a document of title has been duly negotiated (Section 7-502) or a bona fide purchaser of a certificated security (Section 8-302); and

In light of the basic rule of the independence of the issuer's engagement and the importance of this rule to the effectuation of the purposes of the letter of credit, we think that the circumstances which will justify an injunction against honor must be narrowly limited to situations of fraud in which the wrongdoing of the beneficiary has so vitiated the entire transaction that the legitimate purposes of the independence of the issuer's obligation would no longer be served. A court of equity has the limited duty of

> 'guaranteeing that [the beneficiary] not be allowed to take unconscientious advantage of the situation and run off with plaintiff's money on a *pro forma* declaration which has *absolutely no basis in fact.*'

Dynamics Corp. of America v. Citizens and Southern National Bank, 356 F.Supp. 991, 999 (N.D.Ga.1973) (emphasis supplied).
Id., 461 Pa., at 359, 336 A.2d, at 324–25.

Roman Ceramics Corporation v. Peoples National Bank

714 F.2d 1207 (3d Cir. 1983)

GARTH, Circuit Judge.

I.

The issue presented by this case is whether, under U.C.C. § 5-114(2)(b), a bank may refuse to honor a draft on a letter of credit, when a condition of the letter of credit is that invoices be submitted and certified as unpaid, and when the bank has been given notice that invoices submitted with the draft have in fact, contrary to the certification, been paid. We hold that, when a document required under the terms and conditions of a letter of credit is an invoice certified not to have been paid, submission of such a certified invoice, when the invoice is in fact known by the beneficiary to have been paid, is "fraud in the transaction" within the meaning of U.C.C. § 5-114(2), thus relieving the issuing bank, under § 5-114(2)(b), of the obligation to honor the draft.

II.

On February 28, 1979, appellee Peoples National Bank ("Bank") issued an irrevocable letter of credit in the amount of $65,000, in favor of the beneficiary, Roman Ceramics Corporation ("Roman"), and to the account of Michter's Distillery, Inc. The credit was made available to pay for Michter's orders of ceramic decanters from Roman, and was limited by its terms to invoices for ceramic decanters shipped to Michter's before September 1, 1979. The letter required that any draft on the credit be accompanied by the unpaid invoice and by a certification that the invoice had not been paid.[1]

On October 9, 1979, a meeting was held between Harold Roman, president of Roman, and T. D. Veru, president of Veru,[2] at which it was agreed that invoices dated on or before September 11, 1979, including the five in question here, and totalling $220,200, were due and owing to Roman. It was agreed that Veru would pay this amount forthwith and that Veru should receive a credit of some $3,000 to compensate for the cost of financing.

---

[1] Paragraph five of the letter provided:
Drafts, when presented for negotiation, must be accompanied by the following documents:
(a) Your invoice:
(b) Your signed statement certifying that Michter's Distillery, Inc., has not paid in full such invoice rendered on the above mentioned purchase order in accordance with your normal terms and policies, and the amount due and payable to you by reason of the nonpayment of such purchase order.

[2] On June 26, 1979 Michter's changed its name to Distillery Road, Inc. and sold its assets, including the right to use the name Michter's Distillery, to T.D. Veru, Inc. The Bank was assured by Veru that all obligations of Michter's incurred before July 26, 1979 would be paid by Veru.

Roman contended, and Veru denied, that this agreement and the credit were conditioned upon payment by Veru on the day following the meeting. In any event, on Monday, October 15, six days after the meeting, Veru wired $217,000 to Roman's account. Mr. Roman, claiming that the agreement reached at the October 9 meeting had lapsed because Veru had not paid by October 10, chose to allocate some of the wired funds to pay five invoices dated *after* September 11, 1979, and to pay one "pro forma" invoice drawn up by Roman for the occasion. As a result of this attempted allocation, Roman regarded five invoices, dated prior to September 11, 1979 as unpaid. It was these latter five invoices for which Roman attempted to collect payment by drawing on the letter of credit. Veru, having been notified by Roman of this intended allocation, instructed the Bank not to honor Roman's attempted draft, on the ground that the invoices had been paid.

On October 19, 1979, Roman presented to the Bank a draft for $64,020 on the letter of credit, attaching five invoices[3] totaling $64,020, and a certification by Roman's accountant that Michter's had not paid the invoices in accordance with normal terms and policies. On October 22 the Bank notified Roman that Veru had advised it that no invoices for shipments prior to September 1, 1979 remained unpaid, and that in consequence the letter of credit had expired.

III.

On April 15, 1980, Roman filed a complaint against the Bank in federal district court for the Middle District of Pennsylvania, claiming that the terms and conditions of the letter of credit had been satisfied by the documents submitted, and that Roman was therefore entitled to payment under the letter. The Bank's answer denied that the terms and conditions of the letter of credit had been met and raised, among others, the defense that all invoices for decanters dated before September 1, 1979 had been paid. The Bank also filed a counterclaim for attorney's fees. Roman moved for summary judgment, arguing on the basis of *Intraworld Industries, Inc. v. Girard Trust Bank*, 461 Pa. 343, 336 A.2d 316 (1975), that the Bank's defense was unavailing because the obli-

gations of the Bank on a letter of credit did not depend on performance of the underlying contract.

By order of August 27, 1980 the district court found, on the basis of the undisputed facts, that "the documents supplied by Roman with the draft comply, on their face, with the terms and conditions of the letter of credit[.]" Rejecting Roman's second contention, however, the district court held that, if the Bank correctly asserted that it had notice that the invoices had already been paid, then this would constitute fraud in the transaction within the meaning of § 5-114(2). The court held that a dispute of fact existed as to whether the invoices had been paid prior to the draft and whether the Bank had received notice of that fact. The court therefore denied Roman's summary judgment motion without prejudice and ordered the parties to provide further affidavits and documents.

On September 11, 1979, the parties filed cross motions for summary judgment and supplemental affidavits. In an opinion and order filed November 25, 1980, the court found that the Bank did have notice of Veru's claim that the invoices had been paid, and that Veru had intended that the wired funds be applied to the August invoices. The court held, however, that a dispute of fact existed as to whether Roman had agreed to apply the wired funds to the earlier invoices. Thus, the court denied the motions for summary judgment and ordered trial on the circumstances surrounding Veru's payment to Roman. Upon Roman's motion for reconsideration, the court amended the November 25, 1980 opinion to include the question of notice to the Bank as a disputed issue of fact.

After a non-jury trial, the court found, upon consideration of events at the October 9, 1979 meeting, and of Mr. Roman's conduct after the meeting, that payment by Veru within one day after the meeting was *not* a condition of the agreement reached at the meeting. The court found, upon further consideration of Mr. Roman's conduct, that Mr. Roman had knowingly and intentionally misallocated the wire payment, with the intention of drawing on the letter of credit so as to be paid twice for the invoices. Applying the test set out in *Intraworld Indus.*, *supra*, the court held that Roman's conduct in submitting the paid invoices was conduct befitting "an unscrupulous beneficiary" and that it "so vitiate[d] the entire transaction that the legitimate purposes of the

---

[3] One invoice dated August 8, 1979 and four invoices dated August 20, 1979.

independence of Roman's letter of credit with Peoples [Bank] are no longer served." App. 206a–07a (citing *Intraworld Indus.*, *supra*, and *W.Va. Housing Dev. Fund v. Sroka*, 415 F. Supp. 1107, 1108, 1114 (W.D.Pa.1976)).

The court therefore held that Roman's attempted draft constituted fraud in the transaction under § 5-114(2). The court also found that the Bank had had notice of Roman's fraud and held, therefore, that the Bank had acted within its rights under § 5-114(2)(b) in refusing to honor Roman's draft. Judgment was thereupon entered for defendant Bank.

Upon Roman's motion to alter or amend the judgment, the court agreed that, under Pennsylvania law, fraud must be established by clear, precise and convincing evidence, and that the burden is upon the party relying on fraud. The court found, however, that the Bank had met this burden. Roman's appeal followed.

IV.

Roman's letter of credit provides, and both parties agree, that it is to be governed by the Uniform Commercial Code of Pennsylvania. The district court read the Bank's seventh defense as raising a claim of fraudulent documents or fraud in the transaction under § 5-114(2). Thus, the court properly applied the standards for "fraud in the transaction" or "fraud in the documents" developed by the Pennsylvania Supreme Court in applications of Section 5-114(2)(b).

The definitive case setting forth the standards under Pennsylvania law for application of § 5-114(2)(b) is *Intraworld Industries, Inc. v. Girard Trust Bank*, 461 Pa. 343, 336 A.2d 316 (1975).[10]

---

[10] *Intraworld* involved a controversy that concerned whether, under the law of Switzerland, the lessor, Cymbalista, had terminated a lease of a Swiss hotel thus releasing the lessee, Intraworld, from payment of rent under the lease. Allegedly contingent on this question was the question whether the Swiss lessor could draw upon a letter of credit that the Girard Trust Bank had issued as security in connection with the lease. Because of the context in which the controversy arose (the denial of a preliminary injunction), the Pennsylvania Supreme Court was required to determine only if there was "an apparently reasonable ground" for the trial court's refusal of the injunction. The Pennsylvania Supreme Court held that because Intraworld, in this situation, had failed to show that Cymbalista lacked a bona fide claim to rent, there was "an apparently reasonable

Although in that case the Pennsylvania Supreme Court determined that "fraud . . . not apparent on the face of the documents" had not been demonstrated, the court announced the test under which the Section 5-114(2) exception to the issuer's duty to honor must be judged.

In its discussion of the appropriate standard, the Pennsylvania Supreme Court began by emphasizing that the basic policy of letter of credit law was to assure prompt payment of credit obligation from performance of the underlying contract. The court went on to emphasize that, in light of this basic policy, the exception to the duty to honor created by Section 5-114(2)(b) must be narrowly construed. After examination of the leading case of *Sztejn v. J. Henry Schroder Banking Corp.*, 177 Misc. 719, 31 N.Y.S.2d 631 (Sup.Ct. 1941),[13] the court announced its adherence to the *Sztejn* principle:

> We conclude that, if the documents presented by [the beneficiary of the letter of credit] are genuine in the sense of *having some basis in fact*, an injunction must be refused. An injunction is proper only if [the beneficiary], comparable to the beneficiary in *Sztejn*, *has no bona fide claim to payment* under the lease.

Intraworld Indus., *supra*, 461 Pa., at 361, 336

---

ground for refusing an injunction." *Intraworld*, *supra*, 461 Pa. at 363, 336 A.2d, at 327. Thus, despite the preliminary injunction context, the court did hold that the party relying on section 5-114(2) must show "no bona fide claim to payment" before the issuing bank may refuse to honor a draft on a letter of credit.

[13] *Sztejn*, on which great reliance was placed in *Intraworld*, involved a letter of credit issued to secure payment for a shipment of bristles. The complaint alleged that, although the documents accompanying the draft on their face conformed to the letter of credit, in fact, they were fraudulent because they represented not bristles, but boxes of worthless material fraudulently filled and shipped by the vendor of the alleged goods. The plaintiff buyer sought to enjoin payment to the seller on a draft drawn under the letter of credit; the bank moved to dismiss the plaintiff's action for failure to state a claim for relief. The *Sztejn* court denied the bank's motion to dismiss the plaintiff's complaint. It held that, where the seller was deemed to be fraudulent and the bank was deemed to have been given notice of the fraud in presentation of the draft, payment of the draft would properly be enjoined.

A.2d, at 325 (citation omitted) (emphasis added). The court then went on to conclude that honor of the *Intraworld* letter of credit ought not to be enjoined on the record then presented.

The district court in the present case was correct in concluding that, under Pennsylvania law, if the circumstances are such that the honor of the draft could be enjoined, then the bank was within its rights to determine on its own initiative that the draft should not be honored. Thus, if the documents submitted have "no basis in fact" and the beneficiary therefore, "has no bona fide claim to payment under the [underlying contract]," then the bank may properly be enjoined from honoring, and *a fortiori*, the bank may on its own initiative refuse to honor. * * * Thus, the district court here entered judgment for the bank which had refused to honor Roman's draft.

Roman's principal argument focuses on the Pennsylvania law applied by the district court. Roman contends that the district court, by inquiring at all into the basis for the documents submitted by Roman to the bank, "seriously erodes the policy reasons behind insuring the independence of the issuing bank's obligations."

The difficulty with Roman's argument, however, is that it is not advanced before the Pennsylvania state courts, but is rather urged in a federal forum, which is bound by the established state substantive law, in this case, the law of Pennsylvania. Thus, even if our judgment as to the proper interpretation of Section 5-114(2) fraud should differ from that established by the Supreme Court of Pennsylvania, and we do not intimate that it does, we would be required to accept the interpretation of that court as "the final arbiter of what is state law." . . . *Erie R. Co. v. Tompkins*, 304 U.S. 64, 78, 58 S.Ct. 817, 822, 82 L.Ed. 1188 (1938).

The Pennsylvania Supreme Court in *Intraworld* has already carefully weighed the competing strengths of the policies implicated by letters of credit. On the one hand, the highest court of Pennsylvania has recognized the need for unfettered commercial transactions, which a letter of credit serves. On the other hand, that court has also recognized the importance of the statutory exception to the general rule of independent obligations, when active fraud (as distinct from mere breach of warranty) is practiced by the beneficiary of the letter of credit. It is not our function to remake the difficult policy determinations leading

to the establishment of such substantive state law, when the necessary determinations have already been announced by a state's highest court.

The Pennsylvania Supreme Court has also made clear that:

> [a] party who relies on fraud or forgery has the burden in the first instance of proving the facts upon which the alleged fraud or forgery is based, and these facts must be established by evidence that is clear, direct, precise and convincing.

Carlson v. Sherwood, 416 Pa. 286, 206 A.2d 19, 20 (citation omitted). *See also Ratay v. Lincoln National Life Ins. Co.*, 378 F.2d 209, 212 (3d Cir. 1967). This evidentiary principle also applies to the use of fraud as a defense. *See Ratay, supra*, 378 F.2d, at 212. Thus, the district court was correct in holding that before the issuer of a letter of credit may be found to have been justified in refusing payment it must be shown by clear, direct, precise and convincing evidence that the claim of the party attempting to draw on the letter of credit "has no basis in fact," and thus that this party "has no bona fide claim to payment" at all. *Intraworld, supra*, 461 Pa., at 361; 336 A.2d, at 325. This very strong showing is consistent with the concern of the Pennsylvania Supreme Court in *Intraworld*, where the court sought to limit severely those situations where "the legitimate purposes of the independence of the issuer's obligation would no longer be served." *Intraworld, supra*, 461 Pa., at 359, 336 A.2d at 324–25. Thus, the Pennsylvania Supreme Court struck a balance between, on the one hand, the basic policy served by letters of credit and, on the other, the concern of courts of equity not to reward fraud, and in so doing established guidelines for those extreme situations where fraud vitiating the transaction was demonstrated.

The standard for Section 5-114(2) and the requirements of its proof having been established by the Pennsylvania Supreme Court, all that properly remains for a federal court sitting in diversity is to apply correctly that standard and those evidentiary requirements to the facts of the controversy before it. *Cf. Blair v. Manhattan Life Ins. Co.*, 629 F.2d 296, 304 n.1 (3d Cir.1982) (Garth, J., dissenting) (state standards of sufficiency of evidence to reach jury must be applied by federal court sitting in diversity). The district court so held, and we agree.

V.

Roman also contends, however, that the district court incorrectly applied the *Intraworld* standard. Roman argues, first, that in allocating Veru's wire payment to invoices other than those agreed upon, Roman made no misrepresentations, since it openly reported the invoice allocation being made. Roman argues, second, that the court's finding regarding the agreement reached at the October 9 meeting was based simply on a determination not to believe Mr. Roman's account of the meeting, and thus did not satisfy the clear, precise, direct and convincing evidentiary standard required by Pennsylvania to show fraud. Third, Roman argues that because Mr. Roman had a subjective belief that he had a right to payment under the underlying contract, dishonor was not justified.

1.

It is true that Mr. Roman notified Veru, by letter of October 18, 1979, of the allocation he intended to make of the wire payment. As the court noted, however, Mr. Roman on several other occasions took the inconsistent position that the wire payment had been used to pay all invoices dated on or before September 11, 1979.[15] It was,

indeed, largely because of the conflicting positions taken by Mr. Roman with respect to this and other issues that the court found that Mr. Roman had knowingly and intentionally allocated the wired funds in contravention of his agreement with Veru. By doing so, Roman thereby in effect misrepresented that the pre-September 11 invoices, which had in fact been paid by Veru's wire payment, still remained unpaid. That he openly acknowledged at the time that this was what he was doing, hardly excuses his conduct, since the gravamen of the charge is that he attempted, by drawing on the letter, to be paid twice. The district court specifically found both that the payment had been intentionally misallocated so that Roman could attempt to be paid twice for the pre-September 11 invoice,[16] and that this conduct "so vitiates the entire transaction that the legitimate purposes of the independence of Roman's letter of credit with People's [Bank] are no longer served." Thus, this fraudulent conduct was properly held to be sufficient to satisfy the exception under Section 5-114(2)(b).

2.

Roman argues that the court's findings are based only on a decision not to credit Mr. Roman's affidavit and therefore that they do not meet the clear and convincing evidence standard required by Pennsylvania for showing fraud. *See Easton v. Washington County Insurance Co.*, 391 Pa. 28, 137 A.2d 332 (1957). We do not agree.

* * *

3.

Finally, Roman's assertion that Mr. Roman was acting in subjective good faith when he submitted the draft documents to the Bank was simply rejected by the district court. As we have noted, the court found that Mr. Roman was aware at the

---

[15] The district court opinion characterizes the contradictions in Roman's position:

On one hand, Mr. Roman swears that the agreement reached at the meeting was for Veru to pay only for all invoices dated on or before September 11, 1979. This position is echoed by all parties in this proceeding and is supported by the available documents. (PX-2; PX-4.) We are firmly convinced that this was the agreement. On the other hand, Mr. Roman dispatched the October 18, 1979 letter in which he claimed that the agreement reached at the meeting was to pay for most, but not all, of the pre-September 11, 1979 [invoices], for all five invoices dated after September 11, 1979, and for some item of Mr. Roman's creation, a pro forma invoice.

When questioned about Veru's receipt of the October 18, 1979 letter and whether it led to any discussion, Mr. Bower responded:

A. Yes, we immediately recognized it was absolutely not what we agreed to.

Q. And —

A. We though it rather comical that Mr. Roman would find us paying invoices that had yet to even be billed, "pro formas," while at the same time leaving open invoices that are more than 30 days old. It is ridiculous on its face.

(Bower 38–39.) We agree with Mr. Bower's assessment of the alleged allocation.

App. 200a.

[16] The court stated:

Mr. Roman, however, intentionally misapplied the payment to all five post-September 11, 1979 invoices and the fictional pro forma invoice. He knew that Veru had satisfied its agreement with Roman and had paid for all pre-September 1, 1979 invoices, but he juggled Roman's record and the payment to show that five of those invoices remained unpaid. Having done so, he attempted to be paid twice for those invoices by drawing on the letter of credit.

time he submitted the draft that the pre-September 11 invoices had in fact been paid, and that he nevertheless submitted the draft, intending that he receive payment twice for the same invoices. We are satisfied that there was clear and convincing evidence from which the court could so conclude, and Roman brings forward no evidence that was not carefully reviewed by the district court.

4.

Thus, our independent review of the record satisfies us that the district court's finding, that fraud by Roman sufficient to invoke the exception of Section 5-114(2) had been shown by clear and convincing evidence, was not clearly erroneous. *See Krasnov v. Dinan*, 465 F.2d 1298 (3d Cir. 1972); *Hunt v. Pan American Energy, Inc.*, 540 F.2d 894, 901 (8th Cir. 1976) (clearly erroneous standard applied on context of "clear and convincing" state evidentiary burden). Because we must therefore accept those findings, we conclude, as did the district court, that Roman's attempt to draw on the letter of credit "had no basis in fact." Because Mr. Roman knew that the pre-September 11, 1979 invoices had already been paid, he could have had "no *bona fide* claim to payment." *See Intraworld, supra*, 461 Pa., at 361, 336 A.2d, at 325.

VI.

We conclude therefore that the district court correctly applied the proper standard for "fraud in the transaction" under § 5-114(2)(b), when that court determined that Roman, as an "unscrupulous beneficiary [seeking] to take advantage of the traditional independence of [the Bank's] obligations under the letter of credit," had no bona fide claim to payment. This conclusion, further, was supported by clear and convincing evidence more than sufficient to satisfy the Pennsylvania standard for showing fraud. The judgment of the district court will, accordingly, be affirmed.

ADAMS, Circuit Judge, dissenting . . .

I would reverse the judgment of the district court, inasmuch as I do not believe that the conduct complained of in this case amounts to "fraud in the transaction" as that term has been defined under Pennsylvania law. Moreover, I believe that the decision announced by the Court today will increase the pressure on financial institutions to dishonor letters of credit, thus making less certain

the underpinnings of many commercial transactions.

* * *

II

Because of the centrality of letters of credit to modern commercial transactions, the Pennsylvania Supreme Court has "narrowly limited" injunctions against the honoring of a letter of credit to those instances of wrongdoing that "so vitiate the entire transaction that the legitimate purposes of the independence of the issuer's obligation would no longer be served." *Intraworld Industries, Inc. v. Girard Trust Bank*, 461 Pa. 343, 359, 336 A.2d 316, 324–25 (1975). The majority today recognizes the *Intraworld* standard, but then holds that a seller, who submits certified but disputed invoices, commits a fraud that vitiates the entire transaction, thus justifying a bank in dishonoring a letter of credit. This conclusion, I believe, misreads *Intraworld* and threatens the stability of letter-of-credit transactions.

In *Intraworld*, the Pennsylvania Supreme Court affirmed a trial court's refusal to enjoin the honor of a draft under an international letter of credit. Intraworld sought an injunction on the basis of a "fraud . . . not apparent on the fact of the documents," alleging that the lease, for which the letter of credit stood as a guarantee of payment, had been terminated. 461 Pa. at 359, 336 A.2d at 324. The court refused to determine the beneficiary's entitlement to payment under the lease, explaining that this entitlement involved a collateral dispute between the parties to the lease that did not affect the agreement between the bank and the beneficiary under the letter of credit. The bank was obligated to scrutinize carefully all documents submitted by the beneficiary, "but once it determined that the documents conformed to the requirements of the credit, it bore no responsibility for the performance of the lease obligations or the genuineness of the documents." 461 Pa. at 364, 336 A.2d at 327. The parties to the lease naturally retain their full rights to have the contractual dispute settled in a court of law, but it would "place an issuer in an intolerable position if the law compelled it to serve at its peril as an arbitrator of contract disputes between customer and beneficiary." *Id.* In the case at hand, the majority's opinion, in my view, will put issuing banks in the intolerable position the Pennsylvania Supreme Court sought to avoid. The majority has, in addition, fallen victim to what the principal drafter of Article 5 of the Uniform Commercial Code has called the almost irresistible temptation to expand the notion of fraud. Such expansive interpretations are "disastrously inappropriate in a commercial letter of credit transaction." H. Harfield, Letters of Credit 5 (1979).

The leading case on fraud in the letter of credit context remains *Sztejn v. J. Henry Schroder Banking Corp.*, 177 Misc. 719, 31 N.Y.S.2d 631 (Sup.Ct.1941). In *Sztejn* the court enjoined the honor of a draft drawn on a letter of credit because the beneficiary had intentionally failed to ship any of the goods ordered by the buyer. It is this kind of egregious fraud that the court in *Intraworld* pointed to in concluding that an injunction is proper only if the beneficiary has no bona fide claim to payment. 461 Pa. at 359–60, 336 A.2d at 325.

In the case before us, the beneficiary had shipped merchandise of the type and quality ordered by the buyer. The sole dispute between seller and buyer concerns the terms of an oral agreement reached after the seller had fully performed its obligations under the sales contract. In holding that non-performance of the subsequent agreement constitutes fraud in the *Sztejn* sense, the majority's opinion will put pressure on financial institutions to go beyond the transactions they normally must monitor in discharging their obligations under letters of credit.

> The cardinal precept that a letter of credit is independent of, and to be construed without reference to, other contracts or arrangements, excludes adjudication of collateral controversies. A showing, however convincing, that there has been a breach of a collateral contract has no relevance to a dispute about the proper performance of a letter of credit contract. A transaction within the purview of Section 5-114 must, therefore, be so intimately related to the independent letter of credit contract as to be an implied term of that contract.

H. Harfield, Letters of Credit, 84–85.

To conclude that disputed oral agreements reached after one party has fully performed are so intimately related to the independent credit contract as to be an implied term would mean that issuing banks could never be sure of the terms of the agreement governing their obligations under letters of credit. Banks would constantly be drawn into litigation in which the primary dispute is between the beneficiary and the disappointed customer who already has an adequate remedy at law in a breach of warranty action. *See* § 5-111.

III.

Another facet of the Court's opinion causes concern. When an invoice, certified as unpaid according to the terms of a letter of credit, is in fact known to have been paid, the issuing bank, according to the majority, is relieved of its obligation to honor the accompanying draft.

Here, the record shows that the only notice of the beneficiary's alleged fraud received by the bank prior to dishonor was a telephone statement by an employee of the customer that the invoices in question had been paid and that the customer did not want the draft to be honored. This hardly amounts to the bank's knowing, in fact, that the invoices had been paid.

The district court was able to find fraud only after it had reviewed facts developed at an extensive trial and had answered some difficult questions of law. Although this kind of litigation is not appropriate, in my view, when the submitted documents conform on their face to the terms of a letter of credit and although the trial court defined "fraud in the transaction" too expansively, the court did have a fully developed record on which to base its judgment that the customer had committed fraud. The same is not true of the bank, and if the letter of credit is to have the desired effect, financial credit institutions should not be placed in the position of having to develop such a record.

The majority opinion appears to conflate the powers and responsibilities of credit institutions and those of trial courts. Declaring itself bound by Pennsylvania law, the majority correctly asserts that a court may enjoin honor of a draft drawn on a letter of credit when it discovers fraud going to the heart of the transaction. But then citing a comment appended to U.C.C. § 5-114(2), * * * the majority goes on to conclude that a bank may also refuse to honor a draft under such circumstances. I am wary of drawing such a conclusion. The comments to the Uniform Commercial Code are notoriously difficult to assess, and given the cautionary note sounded in *Intraworld*, I would await additional guidance from the Pennsylvania courts before relying on a comment to establish principles regulating commercial transactions of such obvious import to the Commonwealth.

IV.

In sum, I believe that the conduct of the seller here, however questionable, is not the kind of fraud that would justify the grant of an injunction against the honor of a letter of credit. In any event, because of the role letters of credit play in modern commerce, disappointed parties to the transactions underlying these letters should be compelled to resolve their disputes in a court of law. Equitable injunctions restraining banks from honoring letters of credit should be confined to narrowly limited circumstances so as to preserve the integrity and efficiency of this method of financing commercial transactions.

Accordingly, I respectfully dissent.

NOTE

1. The ALI and NCCUSL have not yet reached a conclusion whether to define "fraud" and if so how to define this term for the purpose of U.C.C. Article 5 Letters of Credit.

2. Proposed Draft, Sections 5-110(e)-(g), intended to revise U.C.C. Section 5-114(b) provides

(e) If a presentment is made that appears on its face strictly to comply with the terms of the letter of credit, but the beneficiary has presented documents that the beneficiary knows to be forged or materially fraudulent:

(1) if the honor is demanded by a nominated person that has honored in good faith without notice that the documents are forged or materially fraudulent, the issuer shall honor the draft or demand;

(2) if the conditions in paragraph (1) are not met, the issuer may honor or dishonor.

(f) If the applicant claims that the beneficiary has presented documents that the beneficiary knows to be forged or materially fraudulent, a court of competent jurisdiction may enjoin the issuer from honoring, or grant similar relief, only if the court finds that:

(1) the beneficiary, issuer, and any other person who may be adversely affected are adequately protected by bond or otherwise against loss that may be suffered by those persons if honor is enjoined or otherwise forestalled.

(2) all of the conditions to entitle one to an injunction under the law of the forum State have been met; and

(3) on the basis of information presented, the beneficiary is not entitled to honor under subsection (e)(1), the applicant will suffer irreparable harm if the draft or demand is honored, and the applicant is more likely than not to succeed under its claim of forgery or material fraud against the beneficiary.

(g) An issuer that has duly honored a letter of credit

(1) is entitled to be put in immediately available funds not later than the date of payment,

(2) is barred from the recovery that the issuer might otherwise have against the presenter or beneficiary under Sections [3-414] or [3-415], and

(3) except as otherwise provided in Section 5-108, is barred from recovery against the presenter or beneficiary on the ground of payment by mistake to the extent that any mistake concerns discrepancies in the documents or tender which could have been discovered on presentment.

This section omits the term "fraud in the transaction," now in § 5-114(2). To justify an injunction the fraud must appear in the form of a forged or fraudulent document and such fraud must be "material," i.e., significant to the underlying transaction. An injunction would not be justified by a "fraud" to which the beneficiary is not a party.

3. The issue of "fraud" as well as "abus de droit" has led to debate on the international level. *See* UNCITRAL Draft Report of the Working Group on International Contract Practices, Draft Uniform Law on International Guaranty Letters, Article 19, UN DOC. A/CN.9/361 (1962). The I.C.C. has not specifically dealt with the issue of fraud since it concentrates in U.C.P. # 500 on operational rules. The issue is left, therefore, to the court called upon to adjudicate disputes. *See*, however, U.C.P. # 500 Article 15 exculpating the issuer with regard to the genuiness, falsification or legal effect of any document.

B. Strict Compliance Versus Substantial Compliance of Documents

Issuers of letters of credit have consistently required the beneficiary to comply strictly with the letter of credit. The issuer is given a reasonable time to decide whether a draft accompanying the documents called for by the letter of credit will be honored. Under its contractual obligation to the customer/account party, the issuer must assure that the documents are in compliance with the letter of credit to be able to claim reimbursement from the customer/account party. The issuer satisfies this duty by acting in good faith and in observance of general banking usage when determining whether documents "on their face" appear to comply with the terms of the credit. Thus, even though a document submitted was not genuine, having been falsified, provided the document appeared to be regular on its face and an ordinary examination would not have disclosed the defect, the issuer will have satisfied that duty. U.C.C. § 5-109(2). In evaluating the performance of the issuer, the approach is whether the issuer acted in accordance with "ordinary care," i.e., in accordance with "reasonable commercial standards."[34] This does not require the issuer to act as a detective, but to act in a "reasonable manner. Thus, in determining whether there has been "strict compliance" of the documents to the letter of credit, the courts should apply a "reasonableness approach," based on actual banking practices.[35] To be overly strict in the literal sense would prevent any transaction being concluded.

Under the present provisions of the U.C.C. Article 5, Section 5-112(1), the issuer must honor the draft within three banking days or be liable for damages suffered by the presenter of the documents. U.C.C. § 5-115.[36] The presenter may consent to an extension of this

---

[34] *Compare* U.C.C. § 3-103(a)(7) and note U.C.P. # 500 ¶ 13a:
Documents which appear on their face to be inconsistent with one another will be considered as not appearing on their face to be in compliance with the terms and conditions of the credit.

[35] Kozolchyk, *Is Present Letters of Credit Law Up to Its Task*, 8 GEO. MASON U. L. REV. 285, 355 (1986).

[36] U.C.C. § 5-112(1) supplies the "time allowed for acceptance or payment" of a documentary draft under a letter of credit. *See* U.C.C. § 4-302(a)(2). Presentment of documents and of a draft should be made in time for the issuer to examine the documents well before the expiration of the letter of credit. The U.C.P. ¶ 14(d)(ii) requires the issuer to "state all discrepancies in respect of which the bank refuses the documents." Such provision does not presently exist in the U.C.C. which merely calls on the issuer to return the documents unless he is otherwise instructed. Proposed Draft § 5-109(b) adapts the U.C.C. to the U.C.P. # 500 by providing expressly that, in the notice of dishonor, the issuer "shall give notice to the presenter of all discrepancies in the documents or tender." Other than being able to assert that the beneficiary knew that the documents presented were forged or materially fraudulent or that the letter of credit had expired before presentment, the issuer is precluded from asserting as a basis for dishonor any discrepancy not stated in the notice. Should the issuer reject the demand for an indicated reason, the beneficiary may be able to cure the defect prior to the expiration date. Colorado National Bank of Denver v. Board of County Commissioners, 634 P.2d 32 (Colo. 1981) (presentment on last date indicated in the letter of credit, issuer rejected. No cure possible. Should issuer nonetheless have given a reason for rejecting?).

time. By making the letter of credit subject to U.C.P. # 500 an issuer would have to act within a "reasonable" time. Recognizing that a "reasonable document checker" may need more than three days to check complicated documents, the U.C.P. allows such reasonable time to the extent of up to seven banking/business days.[37]

Strict compliance can result in a draft being dishonored because the letter of credit may call for an invoice describing the goods in generic terms while the invoice submitted uses a proprietary name. A bank should not have to decide whether "coromandel ground nuts in bags" are the same things as "machine-shelled groundnut kernels" when rejecting the documents as non-compliant.[38] There is no liability "based on knowledge or lack of knowledge of any usage of any particular trade." U.C.C. § 5-109(1)(c).[39] On the other hand a customer should not be able to object where the issuer honored a draft although there were "minor defects." In *Bank of New York & Trust Co. v. Atterbury Bros.*, 226 A.D. 117, 234 N.Y.S. 442 (1st Dept. 1929) the draft was drawn by an "A. James Brown," though the letter of credit called for the draft to be drawn by "Arthur James Brown." There was no unauthorized signature on the draft, but the accompanying bill of lading called for by the letter of credit was a forgery. As a result, the customer refused to reimburse the issuer. The court, however, described the discrepancy as "trivial." The test appears to be whether the discrepancies are "so minute that no reasonable document checker worth his salt could possibly be misled by them."[40] The burden of proving this is on the beneficiary. Thus, although the issuer appears to have the power to reject a presentment that does not comply strictly with the letter of credit, in New York the issuer, when seeking reimbursement, can overcome objections by the customer on the ground that the defect was "minor" or "trivial." The rational for this approach is that it accords the bank flexibility in reacting to a crossfire of pressures from a beneficiary seeking payment and from a customer seeking "an out" when commodity prices have fallen.[41]

---

[37] U.C.P. # 500, Art. 13(b). Proposed draft § 5-109(a) seeks to conform the U.C.C. to the U.C.P. *See also* Proposed Draft § 5-113(b).

[38] *J.H. Rayner & Co., Ltd. v. Hambros Bank Ltd.*, [1943] K.B. 37 (England).

[39] The issuer, if a bank, is obligated to abide by general banking usages. This may give both the beneficiary and the issuer a defense to an allegation that the failure to abide strictly to the terms of the letter of credit results in loss of the right to be paid or to be indemnified. *Dixon, Irmaos & Cia., Ltd. v. Chase National Bank*, 144 F.2d 759 (2d Cir. 1944), *cert. denied*, 324 U.S. 850 (1948) (held, loss of bill of lading could be compensated by tender of an indemnity bond. An acceptable banking usage allows substitution of a bond for a missing document.)

[40] WHITE & SUMMERS, UNIFORM COMMERCIAL CODE, § 19-5, pp. 839–840 (3d ed. 1988, West).

[41] *See Bank of Cochin Ltd. v. Manufacturers Hanover Trust Co.*, 612 F. Supp. 1533, 1538 (S.D.N.Y. 1985).

Bank of Cochin, Ltd. v. Manufacturers Hanover Trust Co.

612 F. Supp. 1533, 1539–1540 (S.D.N.Y. 1985)

CANNELLA, D.J..

* * *

The bifurcated standard is designed to permit the bank to retain flexibility in dealing with simultaneous customer pressure to reject and beneficiary pressure to accept. This discretion ostensibly preserves the bank's ministerial function of dealing solely with documents and the insulation of the letter of credit from performance problems. The difficulty with applying a bifurcated substantial compliance standard to actions against a confirming bank is reflected in the realities of commercial transactions. An issuing Bank's good faith discretion is most required when its customer seeks to avoid payment by objecting to inconsequential defects. Although the bank should theoretically take comfort from a substantial compliance test if it honors the beneficiary's drafts over its customer's protests, the bank would usually not want to exercise its discretion in favor of the beneficiary for fear that its right to indemnity would be jeopardized or that its customer would break off existing banking relationships. Accordingly, the looser test of compliance does not in practice completely remove the issuer from its position between a rock and a hard place, but has a built-in safety valve against issuer misuse if the documents strictly comply with the letter.

A confirming bank, by contrast, is usually in relatively close geographical proximity with the beneficiary and typically chosen by the beneficiary because of past dealings. Although the confirming bank should not want to injure purposely its relationship with the issuing bank, the confirming bank would usually be somewhat biased in favor of the beneficiary. Additionally, the confirming bank is not in privity with the ultimate customer, who would be most likely to become dissatisfied if a conflict is resolved by the confirming bank. A biased issuing bank that in bad faith uncovers "microscopic discrepancies," N.Y. U.C.C. Study at 66, would still be forced to honor the letter if the documents are in strict compliance. A biased

confirming bank, however, can overlook certain larger variances in its discretion without concomitant liability. A safety mechanism against confirming bank misuse is therefore not present and it would be inequitable to let a confirming bank exercise such discretion under a protective umbrella of substantial compliance. Moreover, the facts of this case do not warrant the looser standard. MHT was not faced with a "cross-fire of pressures" or concern that a disgruntled "customer" would refuse reimbursement because Cochin had sufficient funds on deposit with MHT. The Court also notes that the bifurcated substantial compliance standard is only a suggested approach by courts and commentators and has not actually been followed by New York courts.[8] Finally, in *Voest-Alpine Int'l Corp. v. Chase Manhattan Bank, N.A.*, 707 F.2d 680 (2d Cir. 1983), the Court implied that confirming bank actions should be judged under a strict standard in wrongful dishonor as well as wrongful honor actions. It ruled that if the confirming bank waived material discrepancies in the drafts, the confirming bank would not be entitled to reimbursement from the issuing bank, which timely discovered the mistakes, because, "the issuing bank was entitled to strict compliance." 707 F.2d at 686. Accordingly, the Court finds that an issuing bank's action for wrongful honor against a confirming bank is governed by a strict compliance standard.

---

[8] In discussing New York's bifurcated standard, courts and commentators have mistakenly cited each other.... A closer reading suggests otherwise.

Voest-Alpine International Corporation
v.
The Chase Manhattan Bank, N.A.
707 F.2d 680 (2d Cir. 1983)*

CARDAMONE, Circuit Judge.

* * * * *

Since the great utility of letters of credit arises from the independent obligation of the issuing

---

* [Editor: citations in [ ] refer to Revised U.C.C. Articles 3 and 4.]

bank, attempts to avoid payment premised on extrinsic considerations—contrary to the instruments' formal documentary nature—tend to compromise their chief virtue of predictable reliability as a payment mechanism. *See Judicial Development of Letters of Credit Law at 160; Justice, Letters of Credit: Expectations and Frustrations—Part 2, 94 Banking L.J. 493, 505-06*

(1977). Viewed in this light it becomes clear that the doctrine of strict compliance with the terms of the letter of credit functions to protect the bank which carries the absolute obligation to pay the beneficiary. Adherence to this rule ensures that banks, dealing only in documents, will be able to act quickly, enhancing the letter of credit's fluidity. Literal compliance with the credit therefore is also essential so as not to impose an obligation upon the bank that it did not undertake and so as not to jeopardize the bank's right to indemnity from its customer. Documents nearly the same as those required are not good enough. *See* H. Harfield, *Letters of Credit* 51 (1979). See generally *Marino Industries v. Chase Manhattan Bank, N.A.*, 686 F.2d 112, 114-15 (2d Cir. 1982); *Venizelos, S.A. v. Chase Manhattan Bank*, 425 F.2d 461, 464-65 (2d Cir. 1970).

We note that there is a distinction between rights obtained and obligations assumed under letter of credit concepts. While a party may not unilaterally alter its obligations, nothing in the purpose or function of letters of credit forecloses the party from giving up its rights.

FACTS

Metal Scrap Trading Corporation (MSTC) is an agency of the Indian government that had contracted to buy 7000 tons of scrap steel from Voest-Alpine International Corporation (Voest), a trading subsidiary of an Austrian company. In late 1980 MSTC asked the Bank of Baroda to issue two letters of credit in the total amount of $1,415,550—one for $810,600 and the other $604,950—to Voest to assure payment for the sale. The credits were expressly made subject to the Uniform Customs and Practice for Documentary Credits.

The parties originally contemplated that Chase Manhattan Bank, N.A. (Chase or Bank) would serve as an advising bank in the transaction.** As

---

** [Editor: An advising bank has been described as "a person who, at the request of an issuer, confirmer, or other adviser, notifies the beneficiary that a letter of credit has been issued, amended, or transferred." Proposed Draft § 5-102(a)(1). An adviser is not a nominated person, i.e., it does not confirm, nor act as a negotiating bank by accepting, paying or otherwise giving value. To be a nominated person there must be an express authorization to act as described. Proposed Draft § 5-102(a)(10). *See* further Note, following U.S. Industries, Inc. v. Second New Haven Bank, 462 F. Supp. 662 (D.Conn. 1978) *infra*.

---

such, Chase was to review documents submitted by Voest in connection with its drafts for payment. Amendments to the letters of credit increased Chase's responsibilities and changed its status to that of a confirming bank, independently obligated on the credit to the extent of its confirmation.

The contract between MSTC and Voest provided that Voest, as seller, would ship the scrap metal no later than January 31, 1981. The terms and conditions of the credits required proof of shipment, evidenced by clean-on-board bills of lading; certificates of inspection indicating date of shipment; and weight certificates issued by an independent inspector. Sometime between February 2 and February 6 (beyond the January 31 deadline), the cargo was partially loaded aboard the M.V. ATRA at New Haven. Unfortunately, the ATRA never set sail for India. A mutiny by the ship's crew disabled the ship and rendered it unseaworthy. The scrap steel was later sold to another buyer for slightly over a half million dollars, nearly a million dollars less than the original contract price.

On February 13, two days before the expiration date of the credits, Voest presented three drafts with the required documentation to Chase. The documents contained what the district court termed "irreconcilable" inconsistencies. The bills of lading indicating receipt on board of the scrap metal were signed and dated January 31 by the captain of the ATRA. The weight and inspection certificates accompanying the drafts revealed, however, that the cargo was loaded aboard the ATRA sometime between February 2 and February 6.

Despite this glaring discrepancy Chase advised the Bank of Baroda on February 25 that the drafts and documents presented to it by Voest conformed to the terms and conditions set forth in the letters of credit. At Voest's request (Chase having provided Voest with an advance copy of the advice it planned to forward to the Bank of Baroda), Chase added the following language: "PAYMENT OF ABOVE-MENTIONED DRAFT ... WILL BE MADE AT MATURITY ON JULY 30, 1981, TO VOEST." The Bank of Baroda apparently looked at the documents with more care than Chase. It promptly advised Chase that the documents did not comply with the requirements of the letters of credit, that it would therefore not honor the drafts, and that it would hold the documents at Chase's disposal. When Voest presented the drafts for payment on July 30 Chase refused to honor them.

Voest thereupon instituted the present suit. It asserted that Chase waived the right to demand strict compliance with the terms of the credits and therefore wrongfully dishonored the drafts. Voest further alleged that regardless of whether the documents conformed to the letters of credit Chase was liable on the drafts because it accepted them. Chase, in turn, served a third-party complaint on the Bank of Baroda, alleging that were Chase to be held liable for wrongfully dishonoring the drafts, the Bank of Baroda should be liable to Chase in the same amount. In granting summary judgment against Voest the United States District Court for the Southern District of New York (Duffy, J.) found that Chase had not waived compliance with the terms and conditions of the letters of credit and that the drafts had not been wrongfully dishonored. The district court also rejected Chase's affirmative defense that Voest committed fraud in presenting documents which contained such obvious discrepancies. Voest has appealed from the order insofar as it granted summary judgment against it and Chase has cross-appealed from that part of the order which dismissed its third-party complaint against the Bank of Baroda.

DISCUSSION

I. Waiver

Voest urges that summary judgment was inappropriate because there were disputed factual issues as to whether Chase accepted any deficiencies in them. Chase contends that a waiver analysis is inappropriate because the defects in Voest's documentation were "incurable." In urging that such defects preclude any waiver on its part, Chase relies upon *Flagship Cruises Ltd. v. New England Merchants National Bank of Boston*, 569 F.2d 699 (1st Cir. 1978) and *American Employers Insurance Co. v. Pioneer Bank and Trust Co.*, 538 F. Supp. 1354 (N.D. Ill. 1981). These cases afford the Bank little comfort. In neither case was there any indication that the issuing or confirming bank accepted defective or untimely documents.

Two other cases including a decision of this Court have indicated that the terms and conditions of a letter of credit may be waived. In *Marino Industries Corp. v. Chase Manhattan Bank, N.A.*, 686 F.2d at 117, one of the questions raised was

whether an official of Chase, with apparent authority to act, had waived the expiration date of a letter of credit. Since that issue had not been resolved by the trial court the case was remanded for further consideration. By remanding on the waiver issue, the Marino court impliedly approved a waiver analysis even though it reaffirmed its adherence to the rule of strict compliance expressed in *Venizelos, S.A.*, 425 F.2d at 465. Moreover, the Court apparently recognized that a confirming bank may waive the requirements contained in the credit without approval of either the issuing bank or its customer who originally established the credit. *Id*. In the instant case Chase could have waived the right to demand strict compliance without approval from either the Bank of Baroda or MSTC.

In *Chase Manhattan Bank v. Equibank*, 550 F.2d 882 (3d Cir. 1977), Chase, as beneficiary of a letter of credit, contended that its untimely presentation of documents resulted from an agreement with the issuing bank (Equibank) to extend the time beyond that specified in the credit. The Third Circuit held that the possibility of a waiver of the time requirement by Equibank existed. The court stated that in such instances the "beneficiary bases his claim on the letter of credit as modified by the bank and acceptable to him." *Equibank*, 550 F.2d at 886. The court noted that such a waiver merely jeopardizes a bank's right to reimbursement from its customer, in the case of an issuing bank, see *Courtaulds North American, Inc. v. North Carolina National Bank*, 528 F.2d 802, 806 (4th Cir. 1975), or from the issuing bank, in the case of a confirming bank. *Id*. at 886–87 & n.6.

Chase argues that Equibank is distinguishable because in that case the defects were arguably curable while in the present case they are not. Chase contends that incurability of defect defeats any possibility of waiver. We reject this argument because it is totally at odds with the concept of waiver, which is defined as the intentional relinquishment of a known right. Whether or not a defect can be cured is irrelevant, for it is the right to demand an absence of defects that the party is deemed to have relinquished. Since a waiver by Chase of the inconsistencies in the documents is possible, we must determine whether Voest presented sufficient evidence which, if believed, could establish a waiver. As proof of waiver Voest relies most heavily on deposition testimony by the Chase official who inspected the documents that he "must have noticed" the discrepancy between the dates in the documents. Other evidence of waiver included: an initialed approval of the documents by a Chase official on the Voest letter which accompanied the presentation of the documents; a letter from Voest to Bank of Baroda, allegedly co-authored by a Chase official, stating that the documents had been accepted; the statement which appeared at the bottom of Chase's advice to Bank of Baroda that payment of the draft would occur on July 30; and a deposition by a Voest official in which he quotes an unknown Chase employee as stating that Chase had accepted the drafts and that payment would definitely be forthcoming.

All parties seem to agree that New York law governs. To establish waiver under New York law one must show that the party charged with waiver relinquished a right with both knowledge of the existence of the right and an intention to relinquish it. *See City of New York v. State of New York*, 40 N.Y.2d 659, 669 (1976); *Werking v. Amity Estates, Inc.*, 2 N.Y.2d 43, 52 (1956), *cert. denied*, 353 U.S. 933 (1957). There is little doubt that Voest sufficiently established Chase's knowledge of an existing right. Chase clearly had the right to demand strict compliance with the specifications required by the letters of credit, and since it is an established commercial bank we may assume that it had constructive, if not actual, knowledge of that right, see *Barry-Dorn, Inc. v. Texaco, Inc.*, No. 74 Civ. 5526 (S.D.N.Y. October 30, 1978) (constructive knowledge of right sufficient), *aff'd*, 607 F.2d 994 (2d Cir. 1979); *Zeldman v. Mutual Life Insurance Co. of New York*, 269 A.D. 53 (1st Dep't 1945) (same). The remaining question is whether that right had been intentionally relinquished.

The intention to relinquish a right may be established either as a matter of law or fact. Examples of the former include instances of express declarations by a party or situations where the party's undisputed acts or language are "so inconsistent with his purpose to stand upon his rights as to leave no opportunity for a reasonable inference to the contrary." *Alsens American Portland Cement Works v. Degnon Contracting Co.*, 222 N.Y. 34, 37 (1917). More commonly, intention is proved through declarations, acts and nonfeasance which permit different inferences to be drawn and "do not directly, unmistakably or unequivocally establish it." *Id*. In these instances

intent is properly left to the trier of fact. *See id.*; *Sillman v. Twentieth Century Fox*, 3 N.Y.2d 395, 403 (1957); *see, e.g., Barry-Dorn, Inc. v. Texaco, Inc., supra*.

Claims by a beneficiary of a letter of credit that a bank has waived strict compliance with the terms of the credit should generally be viewed with a somewhat wary eye. As noted earlier, if equitable waiver claims are treated too hospitably by courts, letters of credit may become less useful payment devices because of the increased risk of forfeiting the right to reimbursement from their customers which banks would soon face. Nonetheless, because Voest offered evidence which, if believed by the trier of fact, could establish the requisite intentional relinquishment of Chase's right to insist on strict compliance, summary judgment was inappropriately granted to Chase in this case.

II. Acceptance

Having discussed Voest's claim that Chase waived strict compliance, we turn to Voest's contention that Chase "accepted" the drafts drawn under the letters of credit. The issue is specifically addressed by Uniform Commercial Code (U.C.C.) § 3-410. This section states that acceptance is the drawee's signed engagement to honor the draft as presented and that it "must be written on the draft." The official comment acknowledges that § 3-410 [§ 3-409(a)] was intended to eliminate "virtual" acceptances by written promise to accept a draft still to be drawn and "collateral" acceptances proved by separate writing. By requiring written acceptance on the draft the U.C.C. impliedly eliminated oral acceptances as well. *Id*. The present record is silent as to whether Chase actually accepted the drafts by proper notation on them. Since this issue was not ruled on by the district court, it should be remanded for further consideration.

III. Fraud

Presentation of fraudulent documents to a bank by a beneficiary subverts not only the purposes which letters of credit are designed to serve in general, but also the entire transaction at hand in particular. Falsified documents are the same as no documents at all. *See Old Colony Trust Co. v. Lawyers' Title & Trust Co.*, 297 F. 152, 158 (2d Cir.), *cert. denied*, 265 U.S. 585 (1924); *Prutscher v. Fidelity International Bank*, 502 F. Supp. 535

(S.D.N.Y. 1980). We are not persuaded upon the present record, as was the trial court, that Voest did not intend to deceive Chase when it submitted deliberately backdated documents falsely indicating compliance with the terms of the credits in order to have the documents accepted. Since Chase has raised a sufficient question of fact regarding fraud, a trial of this issue is mandated. If it is found that fraud on the part of Voest caused Chase to act, then Voest would be estopped from claiming any benefit accruing to it from its misconduct.

IV. Chase's Cross-Appeal

Finally, we affirm the judgment in favor of the Bank of Baroda. All parties have acknowledged that the documents tendered Chase did not conform to the established terms and conditions of the letters of credit. The Bank of Baroda, as the issuing bank, was entitled to strict compliance and there is no claim that it waived that right. Further, Chase itself has acknowledged that its cross-appeal has been rendered academic in light of Voest's admission regarding the nonconformity of the documents.

CONCLUSION

This case must be remanded to determine the factual issues raised by the claims of waiver, acceptance and fraud. The order appealed from is thus affirmed in part, reversed in part and remanded for further proceedings in accordance with this opinion.

Is Present Letter of Credit Law Up to Its Task?

by
Boris Kozolchyk

8 Geo. Mason U. L. Rev. 285, 345–347 (1986)*

This writer has not advocated a dual standard, strict when judging beneficiary's tender in disputes between the issuing bank and the beneficiary, and flexible or reasonable in disputes between the issuing bank and the customer. Findings, first published in 1966,[143] have been misinterpreted as advocating a dual standard. What the findings showed was that, depending upon who was suing whom, the beneficiary suing the issuing bank after dishonor of his tender or the issuing bank suing or being sued by its customer upon honor of beneficiary's tender, courts were applying a different version of strict compliance.[144] The study also highlighted the centrality of the good or bad faith context in the adjudicator's mind. Reflecting the then prevailing presumption that paying bankers acted in good faith when rejecting beneficiary's documents, courts often as not supported the bankers' version of strict compliance. Conversely, reflecting the assumption that customers by and large were likely to shift the risk of bad bargain to the paying bank, courts rejected, in the majority

---

* Reprinted with permission from the author.

[143] *See* Kozolchyk, *Commercial Letters of Credit in the Americas*, (1966) at 264 ("The result of this is that courts ... are usually inclined to take more seriously a banker's objection of noncompliance raised against a beneficiary than a customer's objection raised against the issuing bank.").

[144] *Id.* Any attempt to apply different standards of examination to different relationships in the same transaction places the issuing or confirming bank in the untenable position of being liable to the beneficiary and to the customer despite compliance with the respective standards. For example, under the reasonable standard of compliance, the bank will be liable to the beneficiary unless the documents are examined "reasonably." Under the strict standard of compliance, however, the same bank will not be able to claim reimbursement from its customer unless it proves that the beneficiary's documents complied "strictly."

of instances, customers alleged discrepancies.[145] One need read only the scathing parallel between Dickensian and contemporary banking and letter of credit mores drawn by the court in *Crocker*[146] to appreciate how much courts are less willing now to impute good faith to the issuing or confirming banks. Yet, despite the obvious abuses and their institutionalization by practices that allow the customer to decide what is a curable discrepancy, courts continue to be criticized for doing the "heady stuff" of fairness. Not that these court critics dislike fairness per se. Their main argument is that adjudicating fairness entails a capricious and thus highly unpredictable outcome. It is respectfully submitted that they are seriously mistaken. Predictability, especially in commercial law, does not result from literal rigor any more than it does from one individual's morality. It results from the correspondence between the behavior implicit in a rule or principle of interpretation with the reasonable expectations of those who regularly participate in the transaction. To think that merchants who enter into a letter of credit transaction reasonably expect that the failure to supply an easily suppliable letter, word, statement, or formality is what determines their loss of veritable fortunes is to assume that they regard bank payment at best, as a form of lottery, and at worst, of clever larceny. If this is the result to which strict compliance must lead, letters of credit are not likely to live much longer.

If the history of commercial law offers one lesson for rulemaking, it is that as long as what is fair is determined not soley in camera or ivory tower but by paying close attention to what archetypal merchants do or are likely to do, the emerging rules ought to be observable and predictable. In this light, the mirror image-magnifying glass approach in present letter of credit law is merely the modern counterpart of the rigorous version of consideration prevalent in Lord Mansfield's days. According to this version, a banking promise issued for past consideration was unenforceable.[147] Mansfield, however, had observed that among merchants, and particularly bankers, consideration was essentially evidentiary in nature. Consideration helped to establish the seriousness of the merchants' intent, as did also their writings. Once merchants expressed their intent in a writing, "a nudum pactum," held Mansfield, "does not exist in the usage and law of merchants."[148] Significantly, to this day, despite the accidents of consideration law, no English court has invalidated a letter of credit promise because of the absence of present or past consideration. Lord Mansfield's version of enforceability of banking promises thus proved to be both the living and the predictable law.

Reliance on a reasonable banker approach in the above discussed representative decisions, therefore, deserves praise and encouragement as the one most consistent with the best tradition of commercial law decisionmaking. This approach, however, requires a mod-

---

[145] *Id.*

[146] *Crocker Commercial Services, Inc. v. Countryside Bank*, 538 F. Supp. 1360 at 1362 (N.D. Ill. 1981) (footnote omitted):

This time of year invariably brings forth a spate of dramas in which the hard-hearted banker is the villain, sometimes regenerate (Scrooge in Dicken's *Christmas Carol*), sometimes unregenerate (as in Frank Capra's *It's a Wonderful Life*). By chance this is the second occasion during the past two weeks in which the Court has had to deal with the unregenerate type.... "

[147] Pillans & Rose v. Van Mierop & Hopkins 3 Burr. 1663 (K.B. 1765).

[148] *Id.* at 1669.

ification of the U.C.C. and U.C.P.'s "facial appearance" test. A reasonable test of compliance must include the merchantability of documents and the paymaster's good faith or fiduciary fairness so as to be able to treat different discrepancies differently.

Accordingly, U.C.C. § 5-109 should be rewritten to require the issuing or confirming bank's reasonable care and fiduciary fairness toward its beneficiary and customer when ascertaining that the documents tendered are merchantable and when determining the type and curability of discrepancies.

* * *

NOTE

1. (a) Proposed Draft § 5-110(a)(b)(c) provides:

(a) Except as otherwise provided in subsections (e) and (f), an issuer shall honor a presentment that appears on its face strictly to comply; if a presentment does not appear so to comply, the issuer shall dishonor the presentment unless otherwise agreed with the applicant.

(b) An issuer shall perform its obligations to a beneficiary, an applicant, and a nominated person in good faith and with reasonable care. An issuer's rights and obligations are not affected by the performance or non-performance of any contract or arrangement out of which the letter of credit arises or to which it is linked. An issuer is not responsible for an act or omission of a person, other than itself or its agent, resulting in loss or destruction of a document in transit or in the possession of others. An issuer is not charged with knowledge of any usage of a particular trade. However, an issuer is charged with knowledge of any general letter of credit usage. The parties may not disclaim by agreement the duties of good faith and reasonable care, but may agree to standards to measure performance of those duties if the standards are not manifestly unreasonable.

(c) Unless other standards are expressly incorporated by reference, sufficiency of compliance of a presentment is measured by commercial banking standards and practices. The determination of the nature and scope of those standards and whether a presentment appears on its face strictly to comply with the terms of the letter of credit are questions of law.

(b). U.C.P. # 500 provides in Article 13a.

a. Banks must examine all documents stipulated in the Credit with reasonable care. Compliance of the stipulated documents on their face with the terms and conditions of the Credit shall be determined by international standard banking practice as reflected in these articles. Documents which appear on their face to be inconsistent with one another will be considered as not appearing on their face to be in compliance with the terms and conditions of the Credit. Documents not stipulated in the Credit will not be examined by banks. If they receive such documents they shall return them to the Beneficiary or pass them on to the Issuing Bank without responsibility.

(c). The I.C.C. Ad Hoc Study Group in proposing the adoption of a "standard banking practice" test in the examination of documents indicated that . . .

as any experienced banker knows, a word by word, letter by letter correspondence between documents and the credit terms is a practical impossibility. Thus, courts wedded to a "mirror image" version of strict compliance and reasonable care have failed to provide a functional standard of document verification. Conversely, courts that interpret strict compliance as allowing deviations that do not cause ostensible harm to the applicant, or that do not violate the courts' own version of "reasonableness," "equity," "good faith," or "boni mores" have equally failed to provide a standard, let alone a functional standard. These courts' decisions rely on a case by case analysis and such an analysis does not lend itself to generalization. * * *

Since letter of credit banking is both a highly competitive and cooperative endeavor, to succeed in it, banks must develop practices that encourage their customers' and correspondents' trust. Sharp, dishonest or negligent practices are invariably short lived and never attain the status of standard banking practices. Far from being arbitrary, negligent or dishonest, letter of credit standard banking practice contains the rules that embody the most honest, skilful and predictable practices. To elicit it, all a document checker needs to ask is, "what would an honest, knowledgeable banker do under the circumstances?"

2. In reaching a conclusion whether to honor a draw under a letter of credit, the issuer can ignore "non-documentary conditions." For an issuer to have to go outside the documents called for by a letter of credit would cause delay and may lead to "defensive" letter of credit banking. This would destroy the utility of the letter of credit. However, *conditions* should not be confused with *terms*. Future and uncertain events are "conditions" whereas events that are bound to take place can be categorized as "terms." Thus Proposed U.C.C. Section 5-110(d) provides:

(d) . . . an issuer shall disregard the non-documentary conditions and treat them as if they were not stated.

Compare U.C.P. # 500 Article 13c.

d. If a credit contains conditions without stating the document(s) to be presented in compliance therewith, banks shall deem such conditions as not stated and shall disregard them except where the Credit clearly stipulates that payment shall be made without presentation of a document or documents.

* * *

The decision to honor a draw under the letter of credit is that of the issuer. As U.C.P. # 500 Article 14c. provides:

If the issuing bank determines that the documents are not in compliance with the terms and conditions of the Credit it *may* in its sole judgment approach the applicant for a waiver of the discrepancies. This does not, however, extend the period mentioned in Article 13b. (emphasis added).

i.e., seven banking/business days.

Having to give notice to the beneficiary why a draw is denied, so that the presentment can be cured of the defect, indicates the duty of good faith calling for a speedy review of the documents. It also indicates that a delay will be actionable and may result in an estoppel should the beneficiary be induced thereby not to seek to cure a defect in the documents. Of course, an estoppel could also result from other acts of the issuer which lull the beneficiary into a belief of having complied with the letter of credit, even though the beneficiary may be aware of a discrepancy in the documents.

U.S. Industries, Inc. v. Second New Haven Bank
462 F. Supp. 662 (D. Conn. 1978)

MEMORANDUM OF DECISION

This is an action by the plaintiff, U.S. Industries, Inc., to recover damages from the defendant, Second New Haven Bank, for defendant's failure to honor an irrevocable letter of credit issued by the defendant in favor of the plaintiff. Jurisdiction is based on diversity of citizenship, 28 U.S.C. § 1332.

The material facts in this matter are largely undisputed. On June 6, 1975, on instruction from Railroad Salvage, Inc., defendant issued a letter of credit in plaintiff's favor for sums up to $80,000, covering certain goods to be shipped by plaintiff thereafter. The letter of credit required, *Inter alia*, that any drafts be accompanied by pertinent invoice and "drawn and negotiated not later than August 4, 1975," and further noted as "Special Instructions" that:

Drafts must be accompanied by your certified statement that the drawing represents payment of goods, which have been duly shipped to Railroad Salvage, and for which payment has been demanded and not received within seven (7) days of such shipment.

On Friday, July 25, 1975, plaintiff shipped goods contemplated by the letter of credit to Railroad Salvage. Accompanying this shipment were two invoices indicating a combined "Amount Due" of $28,044. Each invoice recited the words "Due 7 days Letter of Credit" in a "TERMS" box on the invoice.

On Saturday, August 2, 1975, plaintiff's controller, Mr. Clifford Boggs, found that Railroad Salvage had not yet made payment. Accordingly, he sent the defendant written demand for payment, enclosing drafts and attaching copies of the invoices. The demand letter expressly set forth the following:

We certify that the accompanying drafts represent drawings in payment for the merchandise duly shipped to Railroad Salvage and for which payment has not been received from Railroad Salvage within seven (7) days of such shipment.

The plaintiff's letter did not expressly certify that payment had been demanded of Railroad Salvage. The only references to demand for payment were in the invoices accompanying the demand letter.

On Monday, August 4, 1975, the expiration date of the letter of credit, the demand letter was received by the defendant. At some point during that morning, plaintiff's controller, Boggs, spoke with Mr. Richard Billings, an officer of the defendant who was in charge of letters of credit. After determining that Billings had received the demand letter and the accompanying documents, Boggs inquired whether the documents were in order. Boggs was told by Billings that "there did not appear to be any problems" with plaintiff's documents, and that if any problems arose, Billings would contact the plaintiff.

Later that same day, Billings determined that there were "minor discrepancies" in the documentation. He contacted Rubin W. Vine, President of Railroad Salvage, to see if Vine would approve payment despite the possible discrepancies. Vine indicated to Billings that Railroad Salvage did not want the drafts honored if indeed there were actual discrepancies in the demand letter.

On August 6, 1975, two days after the letter of credit had expired, plaintiff received a telex communication from Billings refusing payment because "(y)our certification lacks indication payment has been demanded from Railroad Salvage . . . as required . . . and our customer will not approve discrepancy."

I.

An issuer is obligated to honor a draft or demand for payment which complies with the terms of the letter of credit. C.G.S.A. § 42a-5-114. The first issue presented by the facts of this case is whether the documents tendered by the plaintiff to the defendant were in compliance with the terms of the letter of credit.

Plaintiff admits that its demand letter did not contain an express certification of demand for payment. However, the plaintiff argues that: (1) the invoices accompanying the demand letter clearly evidenced the demand for payment, and (2) "such a purely technical error cannot be said to constitute noncompliance." The defendant, on the other hand, contends that the general rule of strict compliance precludes such an interpretation.

Article 5 of the Uniform Commercial Code, which governs this transaction, does not specify what constitutes compliance with the terms of a letter of credit, nor does this Court find any guidance from the Connecticut courts. The Second Circuit has, however, enunciated the general rule that "the essential requirements of a letter of credit must be strictly complied with by the party entitled to draw against the letter of credit." *Venizelos, S. A. v. Chase Manhattan Bank*, 425 F.2d 461, 465 (2d Cir. 1970). See also *Parsons & Whittemore Overseas Co. v. Societe Generale de L'Industrie du Papier (RATKA)*, 508 F.2d 969, n.7 at 977 (2d Cir. 1974).

The Second Circuit's decision in *Venizelos* involved, in part, the problem of construing ambiguous terms in a letter of credit. The court, while establishing the standard of strict compliance in letter of credit transactions, did not state how that standard was to be applied in cases such as the one at bar. This Court, therefore, guided simply by the rule of strict compliance, carefully will review the facts in the present case to determine whether the plaintiff's demand letter complied with the terms of the letter of credit.

In the present case, although the plaintiff did not explicitly certify that a demand for payment had been made, the invoices attached to the demand letter indicated that such a demand had been made. Thus, on their face, the submitted documents put the defendant on notice that the plaintiff had made the required demand for pay-

ment. While a certified statement helps ensure a high degree of truthfulness and reliability in the representations so certified, inasmuch as the plaintiff in this case submitted copies of the original invoices we think that purpose has been served. Under the facts of the present case, this Court finds that the submission of the invoices in lieu of a certified statement of demand does not run afoul of the rule of strict compliance.

There is some support for this position in two cases decided by the First Circuit. In *Banco Espanol de Credito v. State Street Bank and Trust Company*, 385 F.2d 230 (1st Cir. 1967), a Spanish bank sued a domestic issuer bank because of the issuer's refusal to honor and pay two drafts drawn upon it under two irrevocable letters of credit. The letter of credit of the domestic bank called for the presentation of an inspection certificate by a named firm stipulating "that the goods (were) in conformity with the order." The issue was whether the domestic bank was justified in refusing to honor the drafts of the Spanish bank on the grounds that the inspection certificate did not meet the terms of the letter of credit. Some confusion occurred between the parties as to what was an "order" and what was a "stock sheet" resulting in the required inspection certificate stating that the "whole (order was) found conforming to the conditions stipulated (sic) on the Order-Stock-Sheets."

One of the questions which that court addressed was whether the "Order-Stock-Sheets" terminology was different from the "order" specifically called for by the letter of credit. The court recognized the necessity of strict construction of documents where financial transactions rest upon the accuracy of the documents rather than on the condition of goods they represent. However, the court stated:

(W)e note some leaven in the loaf of strict construction. Not only does Haec verba not control absolutely, see, e. g., *O'Meara v. National Park Bank*, 239 N.Y. 386, 146 N.E. 636, 39 A.L.R. 747 (1925), but some courts now cast their eyes on a wider scene than a single document. We are mindful, also, of the admonition of several legal scholars that the integrity of international transactions (i.e., rigid adherence to material matters) must somehow strike a balance with the requirement of their fluidity (i.e., a reasonable flexibility as to ancillary matters) if the objective of increased dealings to the mutual satisfaction of all interested parties is to be enhanced.

Banco Espanol de Credito v. State Street Bank and Trust Company, supra, at 234. The court then found that under the circumstances there was no meaningful variance from the terms of the letter of credit by the use of the term "Order-Stock-Sheets" in the inspection certificate rather than the term "order."

The First Circuit's decision in Banco Espanol was recently affirmed and expanded in *Flagship Cruises Ltd. v. New England Merchants' National Bank*, 569 F.2d 699 (1st Cir. 1978). In *Flagship Cruises*, the beneficiary of a letter of credit brought an action for wrongful dishonor against the issuer of the letter of credit and the bank which presented the letter of credit to the issuer. Among the issues that the court considered was whether the draft submitted by the beneficiary complied with the requirements of the letter of credit. The issuer argued that the draft did not comply because (1) the draft was drawn by the wrong party, (2) there was no statement linking the draft to the letter of agreement, and (3) the draft did not recite the precise legend described in the letter of credit. The court, in an opinion by Chief Judge Coffin, reversed the district court's finding that the discrepancies justified dishonor. In so doing, the court recognized that the rule of strict compliance ultimately must be viewed in terms of the policies and purposes underlying the use of letters of credit.

We do not see these rulings as retreats from rigorous insistence on compliance with letter of credit requirements. They merely recognize that a variance between documents specified and documents submitted is not fatal if there is *No possibility that the documents could mislead the paying bank to its detriment.*

Id. at 705. (emphasis in original). In similar fashion under the facts of the present case, it is not apparent to this Court how the demand letter and accompanying documents submitted by the plaintiff pursuant to the letter of credit possibly could have misled the defendant to its detriment. This Court finds, therefore, that the demand letter in this case met the standard of strict compliance.

II.

Although this Court holds that the plaintiff's documentary demand for payment was in strict compliance with the terms of the letter of credit, there is another legal basis on which the plaintiff is entitled to recover. As mentioned previously, plaintiff's controller, Boggs, on August 4, 1975, spoke with Billings, an officer of the defendant. Concerning the demand letter and accompanying documents, Billings told Boggs that "there did not appear to be any problems" with the documents and that if any problems arose, he (Billings) would contact the plaintiff. The defendant, however, did not notify plaintiff of the deficiency in the demand letter until after the expiration date of the letter of credit, effectively precluding the plaintiff from presenting a complying demand. In this regard, the Court finds persuasive the fact that the defendant admittedly knew of these discrepancies prior to the expiration of the letter of credit.

There are few reported cases dealing with the issue of estoppel in cases similar to the one at bar. In *Barclays Bank D. C. O. v. Mercantile National Bank*, 481 F.2d 1224 (5th Cir. 1973), the court dealt with the problem of whether the concept of waiver should be applied, in a proper factual setting, to letter of credit transactions.

There are no provisions in Article 5 which would indicate a belief on the part of the drafters that this doctrine of waiver should be inapplicable under the U.C.C. Absent a disavowal of the rule, a section providing to the contrary, or a section which conflicts with the purpose of this rule, § 5-102(3) provides an adequate source for the conclusion that this rule of waiver may be applied in appropriate cases. . . . Our decision that the rule should be applied to Mercantile is in accord with a court's duty to construe Article 5, as well as the other rules relating to letters of credit not codified in this Article, in such a manner as to conform the rules to an underlying sense of fair play so that the expectations of the parties to a business transaction will not be frustrated by the application of a rule which is not grounded in sound policy considerations.

Id. at 1237. This Court is of the opinion that this same reasoning is applicable to the doctrine of estoppel. In the present case, the plaintiff, based on the defendant's assurances, reasonably assumed that the defendant would honor its obligation under the letter of credit. Since the plaintiff acted in reliance and to its detriment, the defendant is estopped from asserting any defense it may have had concerning nonconformity of the documentary demand for payment without calling the discrepancy to the attention of the plaintiff prior to the expiration of the letter of credit. This situation, taken together with the fact that the goods concededly were sent and were received, leads this Court to the equitable conclusion that payment should be made pursuant to the letter of credit

and that the defendant be left to whatever remedies it may have against Railroad Salvage.

Under C.G.S.A. § 42a-5-115(1), the plaintiff is entitled to recover of the defendant the face amount of the two drafts in the combined amount of $28,044, together with interest at the rate of six percent from the date of dishonor, August 4, 1975, until paid. A judgment will be entered accordingly.

* * *

NOTE

Generally, the issuer of a letter of credit will not be at the beneficiaries' place of business. Thus to make presentment of the documents and of the draft called for by the letter of credit some intermediaries will be involved. Such intermediaries may qualify as a nominated person, i.e., a person whom the issuer has authorized to pay, accept, negotiate or otherwise give value under the letter of credit.[42] We have already noted the participation and liabilities of a confirming bank.[43] But prior to the letter of credit being acted upon, there will have to be an advice of the issuance of the letter of credit to the beneficiary.[44] An advisory bank[45] will often be nominated to communicate with the beneficiary; to instruct him of what is required to enable a drawing under the letter of credit.[46] Such advising bank does not, as such, assume any obligation to honor drafts drawn, or demands for payment made, under the credit.[47] Although the advisory bank warrants the accuracy of its statements,[48] an incorrect advice does not estop the issuer from asserting that its obligation is only in accordance with the original terms of the credit.[49] The converse, of course, is also valid and the letter of credit can be asserted against the issuer in accordance with its original terms.

A nominated person may be a negotiating bank. As such, the negotiating bank, having given value for the draft, will be able to assert rights of a holder in due course, provided

---

[42] *See* proposed U.C.C. § 5-102(a)(10).

[43] U.C.C. § 5-107(2).

[44] Although there is no need for any of the participants in this scenario to be banks, this is usually the case. As a result we will refer to the participants as banks.

[45] U.C.C. § 5-103(1)(e).

[46] *Chuidian v. Damir*, 1992 U.S. App. LEXIS 32318 (9th Cir. 1992) (an advising bank has no authority to pay, accept, negotiate or otherwise give value).

[47] U.C.C. § 5-107(1).

[48] *Id.*, *Integrated Measurement Systems, Inc. v. International Commercial Bank of China*, 757 F.Supp. 938 (ND Ill. 1991) (Advisory bank is not in a contractual relationship with beneficiary, but owes the beneficiary a statutory duty to relay information accurately and would be liable for damages caused by an inaccuracy in what is relayed to the beneficiary).

[49] *Banco di Roma v. Fidelity Union Trust Co.*, 464 F. Supp. 817 (DNY 1979) (Advising bank failed to indicate that goods be sent to "Beirut free zone in transit to Kuwait." Instead, goods were sent to Beirut Port and thus subject to duties. Held: issuer cannot be forced to honor letter of credit, though attempt to cure was made, this was too late. The credit had expired.)

all other elements of U.C.C. Section 3-302(a) have been satisfied. In addition, by being able to assert rights under the letter of credit, the issuer will be obligated to honor such draft when it is presented by a negotiating bank. U.C.C. § 5-114(2)(a).

Finally, we must note that under U.C.C. Section 5-111(2), all such intermediary banks, be they a confirming bank, a negotiating bank, or an advisory bank forwarding documents for presentment to the issuer, or an issuing bank presenting the documents and claiming payment from the customer/account party, merely give those warranties that are given by a collecting bank in respect to a draft, U.C.C. §§ 4-207, 4-208. As to the documents, the negotiating bank merely warrants its own good faith and authority. U.C.C. § 7-508. *See* further Chapter IX, *supra*. Any dispute that may arise will have to be resolved between the parties to the underlying transaction that gave rise to the letter of credit.

INDEX